Ancient Supplication

Ancient Supplication

F. S. Naiden

OXFORD
UNIVERSITY PRESS
2006

OXFORD
UNIVERSITY PRESS

Oxford University Press, Inc., publishes works that further
Oxford University's objective of excellence
in research, scholarship, and education.

Oxford   New York
Auckland   Bangkok   Bogotá   Buenos Aires   Cape Town   Chennai
Dar es Salaam   Delhi   Hong Kong   Istanbul   Karachi   Kolkata
Kuala Lumpur   Madrid   Melbourne   Mexico City   Mumbai   Nairobi
São Paulo   Shanghai   Singapore   Taipei   Tokyo   Toronto

Published by Oxford University Press, Inc.
198 Madison Avenue, New York, New York, 10016

www.oup.com

Oxford is a registered trademark of Oxford University Press

Library of Congress Cataloging-in-Publication Data
Naiden, F. S.
Ancient supplication / F. S. Naiden.
p. cm.
Includes bibliographical references and index.
ISBN-13 978-0-19-518341-2
ISBN 0-19-518341-X
1. Prayer—Greece.   2. Petitions—Greece.   3. Religion and law—Greece.
4. Rites and ceremonies—Greece.   5. Prayer—Rome.   6. Petitions—Rome
7. Religion and law—Rome.   8. Rites and ceremonies—Rome.   I. Title.
BL795.P6N35 2006
394—dc22   2005050879

2 4 6 8 9 7 5 3 1

Printed in the United States of America
on acid-free paper

For Elizabeth, who raised her father

Acknowledgments

Like a suppliant, the writer of a first book may hope to be found either worthy or pardonable. This writer has been fortunate in having many people who have helped him toward the first hope, though they are not responsible if he must settle for the second. Audiences at Tulane, the University of Texas at Austin, Harvard, Johns Hopkins, and the American Numismatic Society listened to parts of this book, as did panels at the 1998, 1999, and 2003 conventions of the American Philological Association. Some material fell by the wayside but appeared in articles listed under the author's name in the bibliography. Thanks go to the Duckworth Press for permitting the adaptation of one of these articles and to Tulane University and Tulane College, the latter acting on behalf of the Georges Lurcy fund, for defraying part of the cost of dealing with this and other copyrights.

Thanks also go to many individuals, beginning with Elissa Morris and Linda Donnelly at Oxford University Press, and Christopher Rodgman, my assistant at Tulane. Ernst Badian, Victor Bers, Wendell Clausen, Sebastian Heath, Sarah Morris, Gregory Nagy, Ariana Traill, and Raymond Westbrook gave bibliographical advice; Kenneth Harl, Christopher Jones, Dennis Kehoe, Nino Luraghi, John D. Morgan, Kent Rigsby, and Ian Rutherford read one or more chapters and communicated their suggestions. A friend, John Kirsch, was the first to read a complete draft, and Julith Jedamus brought a novelist's eye to the manuscript. When it came before them in the shape of a Harvard Ph.D. thesis, Gloria Ferrari-Pinney, the late Charles Segal, and Albert Henrichs, the adviser, checked the manuscript, and shortly afterward so did Christopher Carey, Robert Parker, and Sir Hugh Lloyd-Jones. As much as they improved it, the last reader, Edward Harris, left it clearer and shorter than he found it: *hoc illi praetulit auctor opus*.

CONTENTS

Spellings and Abbreviations

For convenience, some Greek and Roman names have been anglicized, some Greek names have been Latinized, and other Greek words have been spelled with Roman letters except in the instances when they are cited or refer to dictionary entries. In the footnotes, editors and commentators are listed by name, not by work, and authors of archaeological reports are listed by personal name and name of journal.

The names of journals are abbreviated as in *L'Année Philologique*. Except for "Demosthenes," rendered as "Dem.," and "Plutarch," rendered as "Plut.," the names of Greek authors and the titles of Greek literary and epigraphical works and collections are abbreviated as in *A Greek-English Lexicon*, ed. H. Liddell and R. Scott, rev. H. Stuart Jones (Oxford 1968) = *LSJ*; Latin names and titles are abbreviated as in the *Oxford Latin Dictionary*, ed. P. G. W. Glare (Oxford 1982) = *OLD*; and papyrological works and collections are abbreviated as in *Checklist of Editions of Greek and Latin Papyri, Ostraca, and Tablets* (Atlanta 1992), ed. J. F. Oates et al. Titles of books of the Bible are abbreviated as for the Septuagint in *LSJ*, and titles of Plutarch's essays are abbreviated in Latin. References to most objects are abbreviated as in the *Lexicon Iconographicum Mythologiae Classicae*, ed. H. Ackermann and J.-R. Gisler (Zurich 1981–97) = *LIMC*. If the object is not a coin or other item of a standard type, one or more dimensions are also given. Where possible, the notes for the illustrations refer to a standard work.

In some instances, newer editions of works and collections are also cited. These newer editions appear in the bibliography, where they are identified by editor. All commentaries are identified by commentator. Primary sources and collections not found in the works listed above and several reference works often cited in the notes are abbreviated as follows:

A/Ar   "A" scholia to Homer as at p. 41, *The Iliad: A Commentary, Volumes I and II*, ed. G. Kirk et al. (Cambridge 1985–93)

ABL   *Assyrian and Babylonian Letters Belonging to the Kouyunjik Collection of the British Museum*, ed. R. Harper (Chicago 1892–1914, reprinted New York 1977)

Alex. Rom.   *Die griechische Alexanderroman, recension gamma*, ed. U. von Lauenstein (Meisenheim am Glan 1962)

ARI	*Assyrian Royal Inscriptions*, ed. A. K. Grayson (Wiesbaden 1972–76)
Asb.	*Assurbanipal und die letzten assyrischen könige bis zum untergange Niniveh's*, ed. M. Streck (Leipzig 1916)
Babli Makkot	as in *Talmud of Babylonia*. tr. J. Neusner (Chico, Calif. 1984)
Bilgames	"Gilgameš und Huwawa A. I. Teil," ed. D. O. Edzard, *Zeitschrift für Assyriologie und vorderasiatische Archäologie* 80 (1990) 165–203
CGF	*Comicorum Graecorum fragmenta in papyris reperta*, ed. C. Austin (Berlin 1973)
CPG	*Corpus paroemiographorum Graecorum,* ed. E. Leutsch and F. Schneidewin (Göttingen 1839–51, reprinted Hildesheim 1958–61)
CPS	*Corpus der ptolemäischen Sklaventexte*, ed. R. Scholl (Stuttgart 1990)
Cr.	*Roman Republican Coinage*, ed. M. H. Crawford (London 1974)
CSEL	*Epistolae ex duobus codicibus nuper in lucem prolatae Sancti Aureli Augustini. Corpus scriptorum ecclesiasticorum Latinorum* 88, ed. J. Divjak (Vienna 1981)
D-S	*Dictionnaire des antiquités Grecques et Romaines*, ed. C. Daremberg and E. Saglio (Paris 1877–1919)
D-K	*Die Fragmente de Vorsokratiker*, ed. H. Diels and W. Kranz (Berlin 1952[6])
EGF	*Epicorum Graecorum fragmenta*, ed. M. Davies (Göttingen 1988)
Esar.	*Die Inschriften Asarhaddons Königs von Assyrien*, R. Borger. *Archiv für Orientforschung* 9 (Osnabrück 1967[2])
Eus.	*Histoire ecclésiastique. Eusèbe de Césarée*, ed. G. Bardy and E. Schwartz (Paris 1986–1994)
Eut.	*Breviarum ab urbe condita*, ed. F. L. Müller (Stuttgart 1995)
EV	*Enciclopedia virgiliana*, ed. U. Cozzoli (Rome 1984–1991)
FGrH	*Fragmente der griechischen Historiker*, ed. F. Jacoby (Berlin 1923–58). Fragments are identified by "fr."
Gerasa	*Gerasa, City of the Decapolis: The Inscriptions*, ed. C. B. Welles (New Haven 1938)
Geus	*Prosopographie der literarisch bezeugten Karthager. Orientalia Lovaniensia Analecta* 59, ed. K. Geus (Leuven 1994). Persons are identified by name and number.
Goldbacher	*S. Aureli Augustini Hipponiensis episcopi epistulae. Corpus scriptorum ecclesiasticorom Latinorum* 34, ed. A. Goldbacher (Vienna 1895–1921)
Gran. Ann.	*Grani Licinioni reliquiae*, ed. N. Criniti (Leipzig 1981)
Gratian	*Decretum Gratiani*, subdivided into causa [c.]; quaestio [q.]; and capitulus.

GrEW	*Griechisches etymologisches Wörterbuch*, ed. H. Frisk (Heidelberg 1955–72)
Hermeneumata	*Thesaurus glossarum emendatarum. Corpus Glossariorum Latinorum* 6–7, ed. G. Glotz (Leipzig 1899–1901)
Hist. Apoll.	*Historia Apollonii regis Tyri*, ed. G. A. A. Kortekaas (Groningen 1984)
Hist. F.	*Libri historiarum x*, ed. B. Krusch and W. Levison (Hanover, 1951)
IEG	*Iambi et elegi Graeci*, ed. M. L. West (Oxford 1989–92²)
IG i³	*Inscriptiones Graecae: inscriptiones Atticae Euclidis anno anteriores*, fasc. 1, ed. D. M. Lewis; fasc. 2, ed. same and L. Jeffery (Berlin 1981–)
Just.	*Epitoma historiarum Philippicarum Pompei Trogi*, ed. O. Seel (Stuttgart 1972)
Koerner	*Inschriftliche Gesetzestexte der frühen griechischen Polis*, ed. R. Koerner (Cologne 1993)
Lac.	*De mortibus persecutorum*, ed. J. L. Creed (Oxford 1984)
LSAM	*Lois sacrées de l'Asie Mineure*, ed. F. Sokolowski (Paris 1955)
LSCG	*Lois sacrées des cités grecques*, ed. F. Sokolowski (Paris 1969)
LSCG Supp.	*Lois sacrées des cités grecques. Supplément*, ed. F. Sokolowski (Paris 1962)
LT	*The So-Called Laudatio Turiae*, ed. E. Wistrand (Göteborg 1976)
Machsor Vitri	*Machsor Vitri*, ed. S. Hurwitz and H. Brody (Nurernburg 1923, reprinted Jerusalem 1988)
Malalas	*Chronographia Ioannis Malalae*, ed. J. Thurn (Berlin 2000)
M-L	*A Selection of Greek Historical Inscriptions to the End of the Fifth Century B.C.*, ed. R. Meiggs and D. M. Lewis (Oxford 1988²)
MME	*The Minnesota Messenia Expedition: Reconstructing a Bronze Age Environment*, ed. W. McDonald and G. Rapp (Minneapolis 1972)
MRR	*The Magistrates of the Roman Republic*, ed. T. R. S. Broughton (Chico, Calif. 1984–1986)
M-W	*Hesiodi fragmenta selecta*, ed. R. Merkelbach and M. L. West (Oxford 1990³)
Nil. Anc.	*Nili Ancyrani narratio*, ed. F. Conca (Leipzig 1983)
Nomima	*Nomima. Recueil d'inscriptions politiques et juridiques de l'archaïsme grec*, ed. H. van Effenterre and F. Ruzé (Rome 1994)
OCD	*Oxford Classical Dictionary*, ed. S. Hornblower and A. Spawforth (Oxford 1996³)
Olympische Forschungen	*Archaische Schildbänder. Ein Beitrag zur frühgriechischen Bildgeschichte und Sagenüberlieferung*, ed. E. Kunze (Berlin 1950)

Orosius	*Pavli Orisii historiarum aduersum paganos libri VII*, ed. C. Zangemeister (Vienna 1882, reprinted New York 1966)
PCG	*Poetae comici Graeci*, ed. R. Kassel and C. Austin (Oxford, 1983–)
PG	*Patrologiae cursus completus, series Graeca*, ed. J. Migne (Paris 1857–66)
PIR	*Prosopographia Imperii Romani Saeculi I, II, III*, ed. E. Groag and A. Stein (Berlin 1933–99²)
PLF	*Poetarum Lesbiorum fragmenta*, ed. E. Lobel and D. Page (Oxford 1955)
PMG	*Poetarum melicorum Graecorum fragmenta*, ed. M. Davies (Oxford 1991–)
RE	*Real-Encyclopädie der classischen Altertumswissenschaft*, ed. A. Pauly and G. Wissowa (Stuttgart 1894–1963, 1st ser.; 1914–72, 2nd ser.)
RIC	*Roman Imperial Coinage*, ed. H. Mattingly et al. (London 1923–94)
RLM	*Rhetores Latini minores*, ed. K. Halm (Leipzig 1863, reprinted Hildesheim 1964)
RSt.	*Römisches Staatsrecht*, T. Mommsen (Leipzig 1887–88)
RStr.	*Römisches Strafrecht*, T. Mommsen (Leipzig 1899)
SB	*The Babylonian Gilgamesh Epic: Introduction, Critical Edition and Cuneiform Texts,* ed. A. R. George (Oxford 2003)
Sg. 8	"Sargons Feldzug gegen Urartu, 714 v. Chr.," ed. W. Mayer, *MDOG* 115 (1983) 65–134
TGF	*Tragicorum Graecorum fragmenta*, ed. B. Snell et. al. (Göttingen 1971–)
Tod	*Selection of Greek Historical Inscriptions*, ed. M. Tod (Oxford 1951)
Trendall-Webster	*Illustrations of Greek Drama*, ed. A. D. Trendall and T. B. L. Webster (London 1971)
Vita Alex.	*Vita Alexandri magni*, ed. H. van Thiel (Darmstadt 1974)
Xiph.	Xiphilinus apud D.C. as in *LSJ*.

Ancient Supplication

1

Yes and No

After Odysseus returns home, he slays the suitors who have been eating his food and paying court to his wife. Phemius, a minstrel who has been entertaining the suitors, fears for his life and decides to supplicate. He has two choices: to take refuge at the altar of the household Zeus or to approach Odysseus. After hesitating, he runs up to Odysseus, clasps his knees, and asks to be spared. He adds that as a divinely inspired singer, he benefits any household where he plies his trade. And he has an excuse: the suitors forced him to come to the house and sing for them.[1] He did not entertain them willingly: "I came to your house to sing at feasts for the suitors *through no will or wish of my own*. They outnumbered me and were stronger, and brought me by force."[2] Telemachus, who is nearby, supports him, calling the minstrel "guiltless." Earlier, the narrator has supported him, too, saying that he sang "out of necessity."[3] To these arguments Phemius adds an appeal for pity.

The person whom Phemius supplicates, Odysseus (we will call him the supplicandus), decides to grant his request. Sparing him, he tells him to go sit at the altar, where he will be out of harm's way. The supplicandus and the suppliant have formed a tie. It extends beyond granting of the request and involves Zeus, who as god of the altar witnesses the arrangement between the two parties.[4] This episode in *Odyssey* 22 culminates in a solemn agreement.

Not all supplications succeed. Just before Phemius's successful request, one of the suitors, Leodes, also supplicates. He performs the same gesture, taking Odysseus by the knees, and he makes the same request, to be spared. He also makes similar arguments. Just as Phemius identifies himself as a singer, Leodes identifies himself as a performer of sacrifices, and just as Phemius says that he wronged Odysseus involuntarily, Leodes says that he has done no voluntary wrong and has even tried to prevent others from doing so. If Odysseus does not spare him, he will not be repaying the good turn that Leodes has done him, and will act unjustly. Like Phemius, he asks for pity.[5]

---

1. *Od.* 22.333–37.
2. *Od.* 22.351–53, especially οὔ τι ἑκὼν ... οὐδὲ χατίζων. Except where indicated, all translations are the author's, but the Loeb and Budé libraries have sometimes been consulted.
3. Telemachus's intercession: *Od.* 22.354–60. "Guiltless": ἀναίτιον (356). "Necessity": ἀνάγκῃ (331).
4. Odysseus's response: *Od.* 22.371–77. To the altar: 378–80.
5. *Od.* 22.310–19.

But the rest of the supplication differs considerably. No one defends Leodes, and Odysseus fastens on his performance of sacrifices, turning this argument against the suppliant. Leodes sacrificed on behalf of the suitors and against Odysseus, so he is guilty twice over:

> Since you claim to be in their company as a soothsayer, I suppose you must have often prayed in this house that the accomplishment of my longed-for return be far from me and that my wife follow you and bear you children.[6]

Leodes deserves not pity, but punishment, so Odysseus draws his sword and beheads him.[7] Neither the narrator nor any character condemns or punishes Odysseus for rejecting and killing Leodes. Killing the other suitors will cause a civil war, but rejecting and killing a suppliant leads to no adverse consequences.

Despite the different outcomes, these acts have four steps in common. The first step is an approach to an individual or a place. Phemius goes to Odysseus after considering whether to go to an altar, and Leodes goes to him immediately. Then comes the second step, the use of a distinctive gesture. Both Phemius and Leodes clasp the knees of the supplicandus, and to remove any confusion both also say that "I am grasping your knees."[8] The third step, the request for a boon, is wholly verbal. The two suppliants request the same thing, to be spared, and they make similar if not identical statements in support of the request. Leodes and Phemius identify themselves, defend themselves against suspicions of wrongdoing, and thus justify asking for pity. The fourth and last step is the response of the supplicandus, Odysseus. He evaluates the suppliants, decides whether to accept or reject each one, and carries out the decision that he has made. Odysseus evaluates Phemius with the help of a witness, Telemachus, and he evaluates Leodes without any witness. He then sends Phemius to the altar and Leodes to his death.[9]

All the steps matter. Without the first, the approach, the supplication cannot get under way, and without the second, the gesture, the suppliant cannot make his purpose known. Without the third step, the request, there is nothing to which the supplicandus can respond. Without the arguments that are part of this step, there is no way for the successful, such as Phemius, to distinguish themselves from the unsuccessful, such as Leodes. But the fourth and last step matters most. Odysseus finds that Phemius presents a strong case, and decides that he deserves help. He finds that Leodes makes a weak case, and decides that he does not deserve help. Odysseus judges each man, acquits the one whom he finds innocent, and condemns the one found guilty.

The same four steps and the same conclusion, a judgment founded on a standard of guilt or innocence, appear in another pair of supplications. These two acts

---

6. *Od.* 22.321–25.

7. *Od.* 22.326–29.

8. *Od.* 22.312, 22.344, using the same word, γουνοῦμαί.

9. A somewhat different view appears in Said, "Crimes des prétendants": Odysseus was not considering the punishment of the suppliants as distinct from the punishment of the suitors as a whole.

occurred in Rome in the first century BCE, and the suppliants and supplicandi were Roman politicians. In the first of these acts, a young Roman aristocrat, Quintus Caecilius Metellus, supplicated a tribune, perhaps Titus Calidius, in 98 BCE. No source says where the supplication occurred, but the likely place was the Roman forum. According to one source, Metellus approached the tribune and threw himself at his feet, a gesture somewhat different from clasping the knees.[10] He then made his request, which was for the tribune to introduce a bill allowing his father, Metellus Numidicus, to return from exile.[11] The sources do not say what argument the suppliant made, or even whether the tribune granted the request or made a pledge, but the tribune evidently did both, for he introduced and saw to the passage of the bill. This marked the fourth and last step of the act of supplication.

We can even reconstruct the omitted argument and response. Metellus Numidicus, a Roman senator, had refused to swear an oath to abide by a new law, and so he was vulnerable to prosecution.[12] The law at issue, one giving land to ex-soldiers, was popular, and so there was no doubt that he would be tried or that a jury would convict him. Other, less stubborn officials had sworn the oath. Not Numidicus: unlike the rest, he would not lend himself to what he regarded as a quid pro quo, a virtual bribe. He resisted, and so he went into exile to escape standing trial. But his son surely avoided this unwelcome topic. Instead he will have told the tribune that the law was invalid, a conclusion reached by other Romans as well.[13] Since it was invalid, the oath was superfluous, and so Numidicus ought to return to Rome without fear of prosecution. The effectiveness of this appeal made itself felt in the nickname given to the younger Metellus after the tribune granted his request. He became Metellus Pius—the dutiful Metellus, Metellus the best of sons—and the archetypal Roman suppliant. He and his father were in the right, and both the tribune and the community acknowledged as much.

In one respect, this act differs from the two in the *Odyssey*. There, the suppliants speak on their own behalf. Here, the suppliant speaks on behalf of another person. Rather than plead his own case, he intercedes. But this switch from a personal plea to an intercession does not prevent the same four steps from occurring. Nor does it prevent the supplicandus from considering the issue of wrongdoing. Just as Odysseus found that Phemius did no voluntary wrong, the tribune evidently found that Metellus Numidicus did no wrong regarding the oath. The two kinds of wrong are not identical, but each depends on some general standard. Phemius appeals to an implicit moral standard. The younger Metellus—Metellus Pius—appeals to an explicit legal standard.

---

10. Calidius: Cic. *Planc.* 69–70, *Red. Sen.* 37, and without supplicatory language at *Red. Pop.* 6, 9, 11. Furius, not Calidius: App. *BC* 1.4.33, giving the gesture; 99 BCE, not 98 *MRR* 3.23. The full names of Roman suppliants and supplicandi appear in appendices 1a and 1b, both described immediately below.

11. I.e., the "interdiction from fire and water" as in Cic. *Dom.* 82 with Greenidge, *Procedure*, 317.

12. Liv. *Per.* 69, Cic. *Red. Sen.* 37.

13. Or, if not invalid, immaterial; for the issue of validity, see Scullard, *Gracchi to Nero*, 401, with refs.

The chief source for this story, Cicero, tells it for a more pressing reason than to honor Metellus Pius. Like Pius's father, Cicero had been in exile, and like Pius's father he had hoped that others would intercede on his behalf. In particular, Cicero hoped that they would supplicate a tribune and request that the tribune use official powers to speed Cicero's return. The orator saw himself as a second Metellus Numidicus, vindicated after years in exile; he saw his intercessors as Metellus Pius; and he saw some helpful tribune as the T. Calidius of a new version of the story, this one occurring in 58 BCE, 40 years after the first one. And so one Gnaeus Oppius Cornicinus, a friend of Cicero's, approached the tribune P. Clodius Pulcher. The scene was likely the forum, as before, and the suppliant flung himself at the tribune's feet, also the same as before.[14] Only the request differed: rather than ask the tribune to introduce a bill, Oppius was asking the tribune not to object to a bill introduced by others. But the argument was the same: like Metellus Numidicus, Cicero had done no wrong. In particular, he had not broken the law against executing a Roman citizen without trial. Clodius, however, believed that Cicero had done just that five years before. Then consul, Cicero had executed citizens in order to suppress the conspiracy of Cataline. Clodius found no reason to help a suppliant guilty of such grave wrongdoing, and so he rejected the request of Oppius. Cicero would have to find his way home by some other means. Like Odysseus, tribunes could say both yes and no, and like Odysseus, they would look to some general standard. In the tribunes' cases, this standard involved lawbreaking, whereas in the Homeric cases this standard involved the breaking of norms.

Whether we choose Greek examples or Roman ones, supplication emerges as a practice with legal, moral, and religious elements. Thanks to the act of judgment in which it culminates, we may call it a quasilegal practice, and we may add, thanks to Cicero, that it may or may not involve a law. On the other hand, it is not a legal procedure like a trial, for it need not include anyone resembling a prosecutor or plaintiff. Instead it may include only the suppliant, who resembles a defendant, and the supplicandus, who resembles a judge. Even "unwritten law" is inappropriate. Greek phrases translatable as "unwritten law" are not ever used of supplication as opposed to some features of it, notably the final pledge.[15]

We must also reckon with several other features that are not essential to a legal procedure but form an indispensable part of supplication. The approach in the first step and the gestures in the second step are stereotyped to make recognizing them easy, and so supplication has the features of repetition and formality that characterize rituals, no matter what definition of ritual we subscribe to. Among the definitions that are especially relevant, Mary Douglas's describes repetition and formality as conventions that create order, whereas Jonathan Smith's describes these two qualities as conventions that create an impression of order, a fiction. In

---

14. Cic. *Red. Pop.* 12, *Sest.* 74.

15. For a collection of such phrases, see Hirzel, *Agraphos Nomos*; the pledge and other features are discussed in chaps. 3 and 4.

contrast to both Douglas and Smith, Maurice Bloch defines these two qualities as barriers to social change. Repetition and formality crop up in other definitions, too.[16]

But if the second step in supplication displays repetition and formality, it also displays variety. In the first step, the suppliant may approach a person or an altar, as shown in the *Odyssey*; and he may supplicate on his own behalf or on behalf of another, as shown in Cicero. In the second step, one suppliant clasps the knees, another falls at the feet; one describes his gesture, another does not. In the third, he may choose among requests and arguments, and turn his supplication into a political act, as the Roman suppliants do, or leave it a domestic act, as both suppliants do in Homer. In the fourth, the supplicandus may choose between "yes" and "no."

When compared to a ritual that it resembles, prayer, supplication differs with regard to the role of the gods. In prayer, the gods are the addressees. In supplication, a human being is the addressee, or, if the suppliant goes to an altar, and persons controlling the altar respond to him in a god's name, they and the god are joint addressees. Save in this situation, where a god is addressed, too, the gods are accessories. They may be invoked in the third step, when a suppliant makes his request and arguments, and they serve as guarantors of any offer of help made in the fourth and last step. Even so, they are less important than they are in prayer, meant for them alone.[17] Another feature also distinguishes supplication from prayer. The addressee in a prayer is absent. In supplication, the addressee is present. For this reason, supplication of a god is possible only if the god responds by an epiphany. In Latin literature, no such epiphany occurs. In Greek literature it occurs once. In the *Eumenides* of Aeschylus, Athena, supplicated by Orestes, a killer who has gone to her shrine, appears in her own person. She wishes to establish a new method of receiving suppliants of this kind. Having established this innovation, which is trial by jury, she does not need to appear in her own person in response to any other suppliant.[18] The upshot of these differences is that only one suppliant chooses the wrong practice and must then be told to pray instead of supplicating.[19]

Ancient usage respects this distinction between supplication and prayer. In Greek and Latin, which both have proper terms for supplication, words for supplication and words for prayer mostly differ.[20] Two important verbs, *hiketeuô* in Greek, and *supplico* in Latin, describe both practices, but in instances of supplication the person performing the acts called *hiketeia* or *supplicatio* often addresses

16. Douglas, *Natural Symbols*; Smith, *Theory in Ritual*; Bloch, "Symbols, Song, Dance" and "Property and Affinity." Other definitions: C. Bell, *Ritual*, chap. 1 with refs. A critique complaining of the neglect of historical and legal factors: Asad, *Genealogies*.

17. Different views of the distinction: Pulleyn, *Prayer*, chap. 4, and Aubriot-Sévin, *Prière*, 405–94.

18. A. *Eu.* 276–488. Orestes at her statue: 446. A foretold or ostensible epiphany: by any deceased person conceived as going to Persephone in the guise of a suppliant, or *hiketês*, as at A3.5, an Orphic gold leaf in Zuntz, *Persephone*, 304–5, with pl. 27.

19. Just. 20.2.11–12.

20. E.g., Greek *feugo*, *hizomai*, and *lissomai*, and Latin *obsecro*, seldom used in prayer.

himself to a person, not a god. If he addresses himself to an altar, those in charge of it respond, and once again the god does not. These differences persist even when a person or persons proceed to address a statue of the god.[21] In Greek sources save for Aeschylus, those making this kind of *hiketeia* are praying. In Roman sources, they are addressing the statue of a reigning emperor, and his magistrates respond to the supplication, so this time those making the approach are supplicating.[22] In contrast, any act of *hiketeia* addressed to a god or spirit of the underworld is the concern of the underworld alone, not of any human being. These acts are prayers, too, but prayers directed to a particular place, or, to be precise, in a particular direction—downward, toward Persephone or other denizens of the underworld.[23]

The sources we have just read, Homer and Cicero, reveal a practice that developed separately at either end of the Mediterranean. Metellus Pius no doubt knew his Homer, and he may have seen Greeks of his own time supplicate, but the place of his supplication, the forum, no less than the supplicandus, a magistrate of the Roman plebs, and the request, the introduction of a law in a Roman assembly, cannot be of Greek origin, any more than the *cognomen* "Pius" can be. Roman supplication is distinctive, the same as Greek, even as it is nonetheless an instance of the same steps in the same order. Along with Greek supplication, it forms an obvious topic of study, but, as we shall now see, no one has ever examined the whole of it—the four steps and their sources, the judgments of the king of Ithaca as well as the *plebiscita* of the Roman Republic.[24]

SCHOLARSHIP ON SUPPLICATION

As a scholarly topic, supplication is about 200 years old, but the view that has come to prevail appeared in John Gould's 1973 article, "*Hiketeia.*" Scholars as different as Simon Goldhill and Sir Hugh Lloyd-Jones have accepted his view, as have French, German, and Italian writers. According to Gould, supplication is a ritual that is not just repetitive and formal but also invariably successful, provided

---

21. Processions, noticed by Giordano, *Supplica*, 171–73: Th. 2.47.4, where the Athenians πρὸς ἱεροῖς ἱκέτευσαν; Pl. *Lg.* 9.854b, referring to temple visits and sacrifices; and Paus. 2.7.7–8, where a seer recommends *hiketeia* in order to appease the gods. *Il.* 6.297–311 is similar but lacks any word or gesture identifying it as supplication rather than prayer. Individuals: Jocasta at S. *OT* 919–21 (ἱκέτις ἀφῖγμαι) and *IG* i² 434, Πείσιδος ἱκεσία, a phrase written on an undated clay votive found on the Acropolis.

22. Liv. 23.10.11, Tac. *Ann.* 3.36.3–4, and Plin. *Ep.* 10.74, discussed at 252–53 below.

23. Examples of prayers of this unusual type: *Tab. Defix.* 100 (Athens, 360–30 BCE); *SEG* XLIII 434 (Macedonia, 380–50 BCE); Homolle, "Amorgos," 412–30 = *IG* xii 7 p. 1 from Amorgos, a second-century BCE lead tablet known only through a transcription. Noting the supplicatory aspect, Versnel, "Appeal to Justice," 63–66 calls *Tab. Defix.* 100 a "borderline" case; at 68–70 he calls the Amorgos tablet a "judicial prayer." The only long treatment of any of these texts, Voutiras, *Gamoi*, dealing with the Macedonian tablet, does not discuss supplication.

24. A comparably broad treatment of the subject of ancient treaties, but less cautious concerning origins, and omitting supplication: Knippschild, *Rechtssymbolische Acte*, especially chaps. 3–4. The only recent general treatment of ancient supplication: Auffarth, "Protecting Strangers." Greek and Hebrew supplication to the exclusion of Roman: Traulsen, *Das sakrale Asyl*.

that the requirements of the ritual are met.[25] In Gould's words, it is a "game" with "rules" characteristic of Archaic and classical Greece, the time and place from which he drew his evidence.[26] The purpose of the game is for the suppliant to obtain his request, and the rules state the conditions under which he may do so. Once the game is won, the suppliant receives his reward and forms a tie with the supplicandus.

This view centers on the first two steps, especially the second. In the first step, Gould takes notice of the difference between approaching a person and approaching an altar. In the second, he describes the gesture performed by a suppliant, including contact with the supplicandus or altar, and concentrates on the performance of this gesture. Performance and contact are the conditions under which the suppliant obtains his request. They compel the supplicandus to say "yes" or, if he fails to say "yes," to offend the gods:

> So long as contact was unbroken, there was no question but that any violence brought against the suppliant was a direct challenge, either to the power of the god whose sanctuary or altar was involved . . . , or more generally to the power of Zeus *Hikesios*.[27]

The "direct challenge" was one that the supplicandus would avoid. As a result, suppliants would persist. The supplicandus had only one recourse, to ignore them. This was difficult if the suppliants went to an altar and impossible if they approached a person.

In writing with what he called "the strict eye of a ritualist," Gould drew on a notion of gestures first expounded by Robertson Smith. This Old Testament scholar pointed to several gestures that guaranteed the safety of the suppliant, a phenomenon that German scholars termed *Kontaktmagie*.[28] For all these writers, gestures had magical power. The third edition of the *Encyclopaedia Britannica*, published in 1911, endorsed this view in its article titled "Ritual," a phenomenon described as possessing an "automatic and self-contained efficacy" inhering in

25. Goldhill, "Supplication and Authorial Comment"; Lloyd-Jones, "Ritual and Tragedy," 282. Among those elsewhere on the spectrum: Parker, *Miasma*, 181; Dreher, "Asyl von seinen Ursprüngen," 86, in regard to altars; and Gödde, "Hikesie," and Giordano, *Supplica*, in their dissertations. Partial dissent: Pedrick, "Supplication," and Mercier, rev. of Crotty, *Poetics*, in regard to literary factors; Pötscher, "Strukturen der Hikesis," in regard to psychological factors; Chaniotis, "Conflicting Authorities," in regard to legal factors. *OCD*, which contains no article on supplication, refers to Gould at the entry "Supplication, Greek."

26. Gould, "*Hiketeia*," 76.

27. Gould, "*Hiketeia*," 78 and 80. Similarly, Nilsson, *Griechische Religion*, 1.78, cited by Gould, as is Kopperschmidt, *Hikesie als dramatische Form*.

28. "Strict eye": Gould, "*Hiketeia*," 76, preceded by Robertson Smith, *Religion of the Semites*, 148–49. *Kontaktmagie*: Kopperschmidt, *Hikesie als dramatische Form*, 11–13, followed by Traulsen, *Das sakrale Asyl*, although at 177–78 the latter speaks of the suppliant as participating in a "taboo." Other versions of the concept: Nilsson, *Griechische Religion* and others discussed immediately below, and also Henssler, *Formen des Asylrechts*, confining himself to the early Germans. As it happens, the writer who most influenced Gould, Onians (in *Origins*), did not cite Robertson Smith.

gestures.[29] Through this article, among others, the magical power of gestures entered later scholarship.

Since supplicatory gestures are numerous, scholars needed some way to group them and make them eligible for *Kontaktmagie*. They especially needed to link clasping the knees, the gesture commonly used to address a person, and clasping an altar, the other common gesture. Robertson Smith had already made this link, but Onians stressed it, using a passage in Pliny the Elder that expressly compares reaching for the knees of a supplicandus and reaching for an altar.[30] A 1936 article of Gernet's strengthened the link by comparing the responses to the gestures. If a suppliant clasped knees, the supplicandus raised him to his feet, and if the suppliant clasped an altar, often while sitting at it, those in charge of the altar would do the same thing, raising him.[31] Gould cited Onians and agreed with (though he did not cite) Gernet.[32]

This same "efficacy" affected Gould's view in another way. Since it was "self-contained," it implied that ritual stood on its own, apart from the rest of religion, especially myth. As the third edition of *Britannica* says, "Ritual sustains and generates myth, and not the other way around." Just as this statement implies that ritual is superior to or independent of myth, another statement in the same article implies that ritual is superior to or independent of morality: "ritual is preserved because it preserves luck."[33] With regard to supplication, myths about its origin, beginning with Zeus's allowing the kin-killer Ixion to become the first suppliant, might be discounted, and so might acts of supplication that refer to moral standards. As a consequence, Onians did not discuss myth or morality, and passed down these omissions to Gould and later scholars. Instead he stressed the psychology of ritual, a topic that also entered into later scholarship, which sought to describe the emotions suitable for *Kontaktmagie*, notably *aidôs*, a sense of respect for the gods.[34]

Turning to the consequences of supplication, Gould held that the most common is *xenia*, the forming of a guest-host relation. Since this relation is symmetrical (unlike supplication, where the suppliant is in an inferior position), Gould held that the act of supplication improved the status of the suppliant. Once again, he argued from a gesture, but this time a gesture often performed by the supplicandus: raising the suppliant.[35] This gesture, the one noticed by Gernet, led Gould to begin with an Homeric example very different from those just cited: the supplication of

29. A similar view of the 1911 edition: Asad, *Genealogies*. A similar view of developments in the study of religion: Bremmer, "Sacred vs. Profane," and Naiden, "Supplication and the Law," 72–80, presenting the same criticism of Gould.

30. Plin. *NH* 11.103, cited by Gould, "*Hiketeia*," 77, and before him by Onians, *Origins*, 174–75, 180–82. These writers stressed the knee clasp, as did Deonna, "Le genou," whereas Robertson Smith stressed contact with holy ground.

31. Gernet, "Pénalité et la réligion," 333–37.

32. Gould, "*Hiketeia*," 77.

33. Quoting Lang, *Myth*, 251. For the difference between this view and those found earlier, down to the mid-nineteenth century, see Bremmer, "Sacred vs. Profane," and especially Asad, *Genealogies*.

34. E.g., Cairns, *Aidos*, and, on a single passage, Ferrari, "Figures of Speech."

35. Gould, "*Hiketeia*," 90–94, followed by Herman, *Ritualised Friendship*, 3.2.

Zeus by Thetis in *Iliad* 1, in which she asks him to vindicate the honor of her son Achilles. After approaching him, she clasps his knee and also touches his chin. Although he does not raise her, he nods, a comparably decisive response.[36] With *xenia* came a notion of social solidarity that Gould drew from a near contemporary of Robertson Smith, the anthropologist van Gennep. Van Gennep referred to supplication as a "unification ritual," in which "unification" accounted for the tie resulting from a successful act. For Gould, unification led to *xenia*.[37] Because *xenia* is prominent in his chosen period, early Greek history, Gould went so far as to hold that supplication existed only then, and not later, including Roman times. Here he followed other scholars, notably Gernet, who also divided ancient history in two.[38]

The chief weakness of this prevailing view of supplication is the "automatic efficacy," the *Kontaktmagie*, of the second step. First, it diminishes the importance of the third step. Requests, one part of this step, amount only to *xenia*; arguments, which are the other part, notably moral and legal arguments like those in the *Odyssey* and Cicero, become superfluous. Yet as both Homer and Cicero show, requests vary, and arguments are far from superfluous. Second, *Kontaktmagie* misrepresents the fourth step. It regards any failure as exceptional and liable to divine intervention, whereas the sources do not. When Odysseus rejects Leodes, the procedure is much the same as with Phemius, whom he does not reject: approach, clasp of knees, assertion of worth, with stress on the question of wrongdoing, then evaluation and the fateful choice: yes or no, life or death. Odysseus passes judgment, as do Cicero's tribunes, the difference being that the tribunes look to laws, not merely to a standard of judgment. Moreover, no god punishes Odysseus. Still less does any Roman god act against a tribune, a person regarded as sacrosanct during his term of office.[39]

In regard to the fourth step in a supplication, two more weaknesses arise. At the start of this step, the prevailing view fails to account for moral and legal standards considered by the supplicandus. In Homer, moral standards appear; in Cicero, legal standards do. But the prevailing view cannot acknowledge this similarity, any more than it can acknowledge the moral and legal standards themselves. At the end of this step, the prevailing view simplifies the ties that result from success. *Xenia* is one; another, implied by Cicero, is the passage of legislation to protect the innocent. Both change the status of the suppliant, but not in the same way. The former confers a new status and the latter restores an old status. Another weakness involves the entire procedure. If success is normal, as with the prevailing view, the supplicandus is an adjunct that is noteworthy only if he misbe-

36. *Il.* 1.495–530; Gould, *"Hiketeia,"* 76–77.

37. Van Gennep, *Les rites de passage*, 39, also pointing to the importance of physical contact, and thus of *Kontaktmagie*.

38. The distinction: Gernet, "Droit et prédroit," deriving from earlier historical schemes, especially Durkheim's.

39. A somewhat similar critique, but not limited to supplication: Remotti, "Essenzialità," 19–35, arguing that societies that absorb some strangers let other strangers remain unabsorbed; in effect, that they accept some suppliants and reject others.

haves. Attention centers on the suppliants—their gestures, their success, and their new ties. But in the *Odyssey* attention centers on both the suppliants and Odysseus, the supplicandus, and in Cicero it centers on both the suppliants and the tribunes. Supplication is two-sided, yet the prevailing view makes it one-sided, an error similar to the reduction of four steps to virtually two, the approach and the gesture.[40] Both errors lead to a loss of context—the social conditions implied by any request, the morals implicit in many arguments, the standards implicit in acts of judgment and in the making of a pledge. Whether or not supplication is deemed a "ritual," it does not resemble a "game" any more than any other course of events that may end in a beheading or in the introduction of a bill.

A response to some of these weaknesses came from Walter Burkert, who modified the prevailing view. Unlike Gould, who borrowed from anthropology, Burkert borrowed from sociobiology, which allowed him to describe supplication as a ritual occurring in both humans and other primates. Among creatures such as apes, supplication consists of a weaker male approaching a stronger one, groveling and exposing his neck to signify surrender, and then being either killed or welcomed into the group led by the other animal. In this sequence, most of supplication's four steps survive, including the approach; the gesture, which is groveling; the requests, but not the arguments; and the evaluation by the supplicandus, still followed by "yes" or "no," and, in the case of "yes," by a new tie between the participants. Among humans, the same scene may occur in situations that lead to incidental changes in Burkert's schema. Clasping the knees or other gestures may replace groveling, and the supplicandus may act on behalf of higher authorities.[41]

Two innovations allowed Burkert to respond to other writers' weaknesses. First, his supplicandus evaluates the request by asking whether admitting the suppliant to the pack or group will strengthen it. If so, he says "yes"; if not, "no." This choice allowed Burkert to restore the chief feature of the fourth step, even as he maintained his parallels between men and animals. Second, his supplicandus treats all suppliants alike, allowing Burkert to apply his view not only to any society, but also to any period and to several species. Both innovations sprang from the introduction of sociobiology.

Burkert also drew upon the Swiss scholar Karl Meuli, who thought that some rituals symbolized encounters with animals, especially prey. Meuli thought of these rituals, which he dated back to Stone Age hunters, as a "comedy of innocence" in which the hunters, guided by shamans, attempted to reconcile themselves with their prey. The hunters pitied them yet depended on them—an idea adaptable to the relation between supplicandus and suppliant.[42] Van Gennep's unification

40. Somewhat similar criticism of the concept of ritual as applied to Greek religion: Fowler, "Greek Magic." Morris, "Poetics of Power," takes a middle view, blending criticism with acceptance of the views of scholars like Gould.

41. Burkert, *Creation of the Sacred*, 85–90. An earlier version, *Mythology and Ritual*, 39–42, with illustrations, says more about human variations, but without reference to sociobiology. Schmitt, *Begriff des Politischen*, 26, anticipates Burkert's views by holding that primitive societies divide all strangers into friends or enemies and by implying that supplication might allow the one to become the other.

42. Parallel to Meuli, "Griechische Opferbräuche"; Propp, *Raíces historicas*, who also thought that many rituals dated from the Stone Age, but envisioned a background of primitive communism.

appears here, and so does magic, but Meuli has added violence and bad conscience, two elements that Burkert preserved. Writing a generation later, however, and thus after the Second World War, Burkert did not see fit to preserve the comedy of innocence, and substituted a "tragedy of guilt" in which the hunter felt not pity but fear of retribution.[43] As it happens, this "tragedy" supplied an interpretation of animal sacrifice, not supplication. Yet it anticipated later works in which supplication, not sacrifice, was the subject and the suppliants were regarded as a predator's victims, not because they were killed, but because they subordinated themselves to stronger males in a pack.[44] The substitution of a pack for a hunting party marked the shift from Meuli's paleontology to Burkert's sociobiology.

Burkert also may have drawn on Hegel's explanation of the origin of slavery, found in a passage that resembles a scene of supplication. Here a defeated warrior addresses himself to a victorious one and begs for mercy, only to become the victor's slave. The features of this passage that would appeal to Meuli and Burkert are these: weaker and stronger males, a surrender, and an evaluation that leads to either killing the suppliant or taking him into the group, which in this instance is the household.[45] Since the victor needs the services of the vanquished, Hegel even has Meuli's theme of the dependent supplicandus. Most of all, Hegel has Burkert's own interest in rank, in the position of the stronger male. But Burkert does not cite Hegel, and so this famous passage should be regarded as a guide to Burkert's and Meuli's orientation. It stands in contrast to (if it does not derive from) the Homeric passages explicated by classicists.

Although an influential historian of religion, Burkert has no followers among writers on supplication.[46] The reason may be that Burkert's ritual needs no gods, hence is ill adapted to sources in which the gods figure prominently. The same omission affects Burkert's reconfiguration of the fourth step. Restoring "no," he does not restore the range of reasons for it, especially the reasons found in Cicero. Burkert's rejected suppliants cannot be personal or political foes, and, by the same token, his accepted suppliants cannot be victims rather than assets. As with the prevailing view, the context falls away. A ritual based on sociobiology meets with the same objection as a ritual based on anthropology.

Ritualism, whether anthropological or sociobiological, did not prevent the development of its opposite: a point of view centering on supplication as a kind of discourse. Writers of this bent, all of them classical scholars, presented yet another version of the four steps. Approaches occurred, and so did gestures, and they mattered, but only as steps in an attempt to persuade the supplicandus. The third step, when suppliants presented their requests and arguments, was far more important, for it was then that they would have to do most of their persuading.

---

43. Burkert, *Homo Necans*, 19–22. Burkert's *hommage* to Meuli: 12–15. I owe the phrase "tragedy of guilt" to Albert Henrichs.

44. Burkert, *Creation of the Sacred*, 85–90.

45. *Phenomenology of Spirit*, IVa, 10–13.

46. A parallel development: Bloch, "Symbols, Song, Dance," who, like Burkert and Hegel, stresses the social inferiority manifest in rituals, though without discussing supplication.

Arguments were most important of all, and not just because of their substance. Skill mattered, too, especially rhetorical skill. In contrast, the fourth step declined in importance. Once persuaded, the supplicandus had no choice but to say "yes"; if not persuaded, he had no reason to fail to say "no." In either case, the act of judgment gave way. Legal and moral standards went with it, not because a suppliant might not refer to them, or because a supplicandus might or might not find them persuasive, but because such standards were incidental. A suppliant might succeed or fail without them.[47]

With this new view of supplication came a new view of the sources reporting it. Gould had thought that these sources, or at least the early ones, obeyed what he called "rules," and Burkert would not have disagreed. Not so: a source might make up its own rules, valid for it alone; or, with respect to Homer, valid only for a tradition. The rules found in a source might even change in the course of a story, or change in one story only to migrate to another. Kevin Crotty found just such a pattern in Homer. In the *Iliad*, the rules begin by favoring rejection. By the end of the poem, they change and favor acceptance, the norm in the *Odyssey*. Although the ritual no longer dictated the outcome of the act, the poem in which the act occurred fostered one outcome rather than another.[48]

This perspective was valuable for Homer, who introduces supplication at climatic moments such as *Odyssey* 22. It was no less valuable for Greek tragedy, which includes long statements by suppliants and supplicandi as well as acts that scholars regard as idiosyncratic.[49] The author best suited for this perspective, Aeschylus, devoted whole plays to acts of supplication that led either to disaster for the supplicandi or to innovations like the murder trial in the *Eumenides*.[50] According to some scholars, the supplicandus would be ill at ease during an idiosyncratic act, and so the suppliant would fail; according to other scholars, he would be overwhelmed, and so the suppliant would succeed.[51]

Like Burkert's and Gould's, this view reflected trends in the study of phenomena other than supplication. Most notably, it reflected the rise of narratology, and in particular it reflected the attack mounted by Pierre Bourdieu on the prevailing view of ritual. Bourdieu argued that no two performances of a ritual were or could be identical, and so there could be no fixed elements.[52] The reason that performances differed from one another was, he contended, that the participants were struggling for advantage. This struggle invalidated not only the notion of "automatic efficacy," but also J. L. Austin's theory of speech-acts. Austin's theory did

---

47. Lynn George, *Epos*, chap. 4, Goldhill, "Supplication and Authorial Comment," Crotty, *Poetics*.

48. A succinct statement of this view: Scodel, rev. of Giordano, *Supplica*, arguing against this follower of Gould.

49. See Burian, *Suppliant Drama* and "Hero Cult": Burnet, "Human Resistance"; Ferrari, "Figures in the Text"; and Henrichs, "The Tomb of Aias." All decribe supplication as a tool of characterization and dramaturgy.

50. Gödde, *Drama der Hikesie*, part of whose title, *"Ritual und Rhetorik,"* epitomizes scholarship of this type; see also her bibliography.

51. Idiosyncratic failure: Henrichs, "Choral Self-Referentiality," 64, though Henrichs also includes a general statement about wrongdoing. Success via transgression: Pötscher, "Strukturen der Hikesie," and Gödde, *Drama der Hikesie*.

52. Bourdieu, *Language and Symbolic Power*, 109.

not explain why some speech-acts fail, or, as Bourdieu might have put it, why the struggle for advantage sometimes ends with the defeat of some of those involved.[53] Bourdieu also struck at the notion of unification. Ritual, he said, was competitive, and one of the competitors might be the source that reported it and that wished to assign to it a different outcome.[54] Here Bourdieu ran parallel to Crotty in describing changes in Homeric supplication.

Burkert and the literary critics of supplication have contrasting weaknesses. Just as Burkert fixes on the second step, they fix on the third. Neither gives much attention to the fourth, and as a result neither regards supplication as a quasilegal practice. As concerns the evidence, Burkert fixes on examples of supplication that were inevitably wordless, and underestimates the importance of discourse, whereas the literary critics fix on examples affected by textual interpretation, and overestimate the importance of discourse. Burkert has ignored *Odyssey* 22, whereas Crotty has not, but both Burkert and Crotty have overlooked supplications addressed to tribunes, Burkert because the Roman forum is far removed from the milieu of sociobiology, Crotty because Cicero is far removed from Homer.

Unlike those mentioned so far, scholars of Roman law pay heed to the fourth step. It appears in several juristic texts that deal with supplication and also in historiographic reports that more or less illustrate these texts. Most of these texts and reports happen to deal with acts of supplication that took place at statues of the emperor. Since in these situations the supplicandus was often a magistrate acting on behalf of the emperor, the quasilegal character of the practice goes unquestioned, and scholarly interest centers on the grounds on which a suppliant may plead and on those by which the supplicandus may evaluate him.[55] As a consequence, the third step, in which the suppliant presents his arguments, receives no less attention from Roman legal scholars than the fourth. Yet the first two steps receive only perfunctory attention. Since only acts before statues and altars appear in the juristic texts, legal scholars have mostly ignored acts of other kinds, including those addressed to persons. The exception has been acts addressed to persons who grant the suppliant *deditio in fidem*, a quasilegal form of surrender.[56]

How old is this gap between legal and extralegal? In the seventeenth and eighteenth centuries, divines conversant with Hebrew as well as Greek and Latin regarded supplication in all these literatures as subject to regulation. Rather than distinguish between legal and extralegal, they distinguished between ap-

53. On the assumption that an act of supplication is a "perlocutionary" act, or one performed—and performed successfully—at the moment the words are spoken, as in Austin, *How to Do Things with Words*, 109. Recognizing this difficulty, Clark, "Chryses," 11–12, calls Chryses's supplication in *Iliad* 1 an "illocutionary act," defined by Austin, *How to Do Things with Words*, 107, as one in which failure is possible.

54. But unfair competition, since the powerful—in supplication, the supplicandi—benefit from norms that support their power, as argued by Bourdieu, *Language and Symbolic Power*, 50–51.

55. As in Gamauf, *Ad statuam licet confugere*, with bibliography on his topic, supplication at imperial statues, and Bauman, *Impietas*, chap. 4.3.

56. *Deditio*: Hölkeskamp, "Deditio in fidem," and Freyburger, "Supplication grecque," 521–22, both influenced by Gould. An example of a work on Roman social history where supplication goes unnoticed: Eilers, *Roman Patrons*, chap. 1.

proaches to temples or altars and approaches to persons. This split appears again in nineteenth-century dictionary articles about supplication or, rather, in articles titled "Asylum," meaning supplication at a temple or altar for the purpose of gaining refuge.[57] With this holistic view came an all-embracing historical scheme: supplication originated with the Hebrews, and then came westward to Greece and Rome through the Phoenicians.[58]

In nineteenth-century Germany, an alternative, secular history of asylum emerged with the legal scholar Bulmerincq. He credited the origin of supplication not to the Hebrews but to *Naturvölker*, including Africans and Australian aborigines as well as Europeans such as the Teutons. Next came Greece, which acted as a bridge leading to two peoples of the law, Israel and Rome. Last came Christianity and the broadening of the Christian heritage during the Enlightenment, notably by Kant. Like the divines who preceded him, Bulmerincq did not doubt that there were standards of judgment and that supplication culminated in "yes" and "no." This line of inquiry continued into the twentieth century, particularly in the study of Ptolematic papyri. In 1923, Woess made a study of these papyri that remains the only exhaustive treatment of acts of supplication in any time or place. This specialist reached conclusions that would have startled Robertson Smith or Gould: he said that any suppliant who arrived in a Greek shrine in Ptolemaic (or Roman) Egypt not only faced a legal procedure but even could find himself expelled on the grounds that he was a runaway or a criminal. Supplication was not an act of magic, of "automatic efficacy," and it did not always unify.[59] Woess cited parallels from the Roman juristic texts that provided for the expulsion of suppliants who committed *iniuria*, "wrongdoing," against others when supplicating at imperial statues.[60]

Other scholars, like the comparatist Hellwig, were not unfriendly to the innovations epitomized by 1911 *Britannica*, and combined them with Bulmerincq's work, arguing that primitive peoples turned supplication, which was magical or ritualistic, into a legal practice. This sequence of supplication and law had many followers, among them the English classicist Murray, who believed that trials began when murderers supplicated at heroes' tombs in pre-classical Greece. Murray did not describe the community's initial response to these acts, but eventually these wrongdoers came before juries.[61] The contemporary legal scholar H. J. Wolff has followed Hellwig and Murray. A scholar very different from Wolff and Murray, the French Marxist Gernet, followed Hellwig also.[62]

---

57. Perhaps the first: Caillemer, "Asylia," followed by Stengl, "*Asylon*," and others noted immediately below.

58. Carlholm, *Tractatus*, 6–7, cited by Bulmerincq, *Asylrecht*, 4. So also Osiander, *De asylis*.

59. Woess, *Asylwesen Ägyptens*, 170–79.

60. Woess, *Asylwesen Ägyptens*, 206–11, citing among other passages Call. *dig.* 48.19.28.7: "ad statuas confugere vel imagines principu in iniuriam altrius prohibitum est."

61. Murray apud J. Harrison, *Themis*, 361–62, with supplication as a *sacer ludus* that predates legal institutions; with regard to murder trials in Attica, Wallace, *Areopagus Council*, 9, agrees, as does Seaford, *Ritual and Reciprocity*, 96, and Crotty, *Law's Interior*, 6–9.

62. Wolff, "Origin of Litigation," 47, followed by Henssler, *Formen des Asylrechts*, and Crotty, *Law's Interior*, 7–8, and anticipated by Taubenschlag, *Law of Greco-Roman Egypt*, 421–22. Gernet, "Droit et prédroit," links legal to political and cultural developments.

This development proved crucial, for it divided supplication from law, and so it invited scholars to divide official acts, like introducing a bill, from unofficial acts, like sparing Phemius's life. It also led to a mistaken view of asylum. An "asylum" was, in fact, a place exempt from intrusion or from the seizure of persons or property. As such it differed from anything that a suppliant might do, even if he went to such a place. By the same token, the rights available in such a place differed from those accorded to an individual. Moreover, an individual could be exempt from seizure by means other than supplication. A community could grant him this privilege; it could also grant this privilege to all visitors from a given country or city.[63] Nevertheless, some scholars regarded an asylum as a place where written or unwritten law made rejecting a suppliant impermissible.[64] This view dovetailed with Gould's but confined itself to supplication at altars and shrines. Unlike Gould's view, it did not confine itself to early Greece.

A peculiar division of labor resulted. Woess and the legalists received the consolation prizes—inscriptions, Rome, and later antiquity.[65] Gould's school received Homer, thanks to *Kontaktmagie*, and tragedy, thanks to asylum.[66] Even forms of scholarly work were divided. Until very recently, legal scholars wrote all the encyclopedia articles, but scholars of ritual wrote most of the books.[67] Supplication split into a ritual found in poetry and an occasion for Hellenistic or Latin prose regulation.[68]

Forgotten in this division was the overlap between supplication and the law. In any act of supplication, the act of judgment is quasilegal. In some, it is regulated, and in others, the suppliant is a defendant pleading for pity from a judge or jury. How do supplication and the law affect one another, whether the act of supplication is regulated or not? This question has more than historical interest. Human rights articulated mainly in the twentieth century cover many occasions for supplication. Leodes, for example, would have the right to a trial. When and how have these rights come to replace supplication? Or, to ask the question from the view-

63. A summary view: Rigsby's introduction to *Asylia*, and, more briefly, Dreher, "Asyl von seinen Ursprüngen," 80–85. "Asylum" in the sense of protection for visitors and property: Bravo, "*Sulân.*"

64. Recently, Sinn, "Sakrale Schutzzone," and Traulsen, *Das sakrale Asyl*; earlier, Latte, *Heiliges Recht* 107–8, and Nilsson, *Griechische Religion*, 1.77–78.

65. Civic inscriptions: Chaniotis, "*Conflicting Authorities*," and Zelnick-Abramovitz, "Supplication and Request." Pilgrimage inscriptions: Dillon, *Pilgrims*, and Naiden, "*Hiketai.*"

66. Books and articles on ritual in Homer: Whitfield, *The Restored Relation*, Pedrick, "Supplication," Thornton, *Motif of Supplication*, S. Reece, *The Stranger's Welcome*, Giordano, *Supplica*. On Homer and tragedy: Gödde, *Drama der Hikesie*. Dissertations on ritual on tragedy: Kopperschmidt, *Hikesie als dramatische Form*, Zeitlin, *Ritual World*, chap. 4, Burian, *Suppliant Drama*. A book of this kind mostly on tragedy: Beaujon, *Dieu des suppliants*. Lateiner, *Sardonic Smile*, is compatible with Gould, but draws concepts from psychology as well as anthropology.

67. Legalists writing articles: Caillemer, "Asylia," Stengl, "*Asylon*," Wenger, "Asylrecht," and Fauth, "*Asylon.*" The first scholar of ritual: Gödde, "Hikesie." Largely legalist: Dreher, "Asyl von seinen Ursprüngen" and Chaniotis, "Conflicting Authorities." The only books by legalists: Woess, *Asylwesen Ägyptens*, followed by Gamauf, *Ad statuam licet confugere*, Derlien, *Asyl*, and Traulsen, *Das sakrale Asyl*. The only relevant article in *RE*, Jessen, "Hikesios," deals only with that word.

68. So, for example, Gould, "*Hiketeia*," scarcely mentions comedy (84 n. 51) and oratory (78 n. 24), whereas Hansen, *Apagoge, Endeixis, and Ephegesis*, and the legal historians Lipsius, *Attische Recht*, A. Harrison, *Procedure*, and MacDowell, *Law in Athens*, omit cases of possible expulsion in tragedy. Caillemer, "Asylia" predates the division of labor, and Schlesinger, *Griechische Asylie*, partially surmounts it. Only Derlien, *Asyl*, deals extensively with both Greek and Roman material, and even he omits discussion of all but a few instances of personal supplication; a brief general discussion at 45–50 omits some common Roman supplicatory gestures.

point of the supplicandus, when must he or they concede that they have no business refusing a request? When do "yes" and "no" give way to "yes," the quasilegal practice to the legal, perhaps universal, right? By the same token, the exercise of human rights has a ritualistic side that links it to supplication.[69] Just as supplication has more than one step, it has more than one tie to legal issues and systems.

SUPPLICATION AS A QUASILEGAL PRACTICE

The remainder of this book will seek to restore the four steps and to show the importance of each, especially the third and fourth. The gestures used in the second step matter less than in the prevailing view, standards of judgment matter in the third step, and the supplicandus matters in both steps. In the fourth step, results include more than *xenia*; above all, they include rejection. Each step is more varied than the concept of ritual may imply. As opposed to Burkert, the third and fourth steps involve legal, moral, and political factors, not just concern for individual or collective advantage. In reply to literary critics, especially those writing in the spirit of narratology, the task is a different one: not overrating the third step. Once again, legal, moral and political factors are important, but for a new reason: they provide criteria that the suppliant ignores at his peril. By the same token, the fourth step limits the freedom of action of both the suppliant and the supplicandus. No matter how persuasive the suppliant, rejection is final. At the same time, supplication is not a legal procedure, like a trial. It is not always a matter of record. Often it is only a matter of report, as in Homer.

This is not to deny that previous work has contributed much. By centering on Homer and tragedy, the prevailing view discovered a large and varied corpus of acts.[70] Burkert did not deal with many acts besides these, but made use of Greek prose, including epigraphy. Literary critics such as Crotty returned to Homer and tragedy but developed analyses that might be applied to other writers, including Latin ones. The legalists confirmed the potential of Roman sources.

The result of these labors appears in the appendices. Appendices 1a and 1b list acts of supplication in Greek and Latin literature, and appendix 1c lists acts in epigraphical and papyrological sources. Together, they contain more than a hundred acts of supplication at shrines. These acts come from nearly every major Greek and Latin author, led by Plutarch and Livy. As with altar supplication, so with personal supplication: these acts number some six hundred. Most common are acts featuring the three most common gestures, clasping the knees of the supplicandus, falling at his feet, and—a somewhat different gesture—prostrating oneself, as Themistocles does before the king of Persia.[71] With regard to per-

---

69. Or, to use the language of Donnelly, *Universal Rights*, 11–12, rights sometimes must be "asserted" in order to be "enjoyed," though he does not address the ritualistic side of any assertion of a right. Behind Donnelly's formulation lies the view that a right is a morally or legally valid claim, not a request such as is made in supplication.

70. Lists of acts in Homer: Gould, *"Hiketeia,"* 80 n. 39, Whitfield, *The Restored Relation*, 64–65. A list for tragedy: Zeitlin, *Ritual World*, chap. 4.

71. Plut. *Them.* 28.1–29.2, to Artaxerxes; to Xerxes according to Ephorus and others cited by Plut. *Them.* 27.1.

sonal supplication, Latin literature, which lacks reports of supplication at the altars of Roman gods, can compete with Greek.

These totals exclude near misses, doublets, and planned, supposititious, legendary, mythic, or fictional acts. Yet even by this cautious reckoning, the sum for both kinds of supplication would approach eight hundred. Only a hundred or so are sure to have occurred when and where and how the source reports, but some of these, found in Attic decrees and the *Res Gestae* of Augustus, are as detailed as any ancient public acts that we know. Another kind of public act, supplications made in Greek and Roman courts, is controversial. Many scholars consider them "figurative," and so all estimates so far have excluded them. If they were included, the total would rise again, for several dozen are attested, and many more may be assumed. If we also include a small number of acts that appear only in visual sources, mainly Greek vases and Roman coins, the total would rise still more.

A treatment that covers all this evidence has several advantages. First, more attention may go to Roman supplication. A search of the Bodleian and Widener libraries, and of the Library of Congress and the British Museum, reveals no book, monograph or even article expressly devoted to supplication as described by a Roman author other than Virgil—not even Livy, in which supplication features in diplomacy, or Tacitus, in which it features in the history of the imperial court.[72] Even supplication in the plays of Seneca has drawn no attention. Better known acts like that of Metellus Pius have figured in histories of Rome but not in treatments of the practice of supplication to magistrates or of supplication during the Republic.

Second, a comprehensive treatment removes a common shortfall in the study of ancient history, whether Greek or Roman—the absence of women, children, and slaves. All three groups supplicate in abundance. No other religious practice—no practice whatever—has so humble as well as diverse a cast of participants.[73] The record even includes a good deal of supplication by foreigners, reflecting a Greco-Roman assumption that supplication was universal, running from one extreme of their world, Britain, to the other, India, by way of Africa as well as Europe and Asia.[74] The very language of supplication reflects this assumption. Ancient

72. And for the Continent, the websites of the *Bibliothèque nationale de France*, the *Karlsruher Virtuelle Katalog*, and the *Biblioteche nazionali centrali* of Rome and Florence.

73. A gamut of Homeric suppliants: possible runaway slave (Philoetius, *Od.* 20.222–23), king (Priam, *Il.* 24.477–570), priest (Chryses, *Il.* 1.12–34), witch (Circe, *Od.* 10.323–47), all noticed by Whitfield, *The Restored Relation*, 64–65. A gamut in one novelist, Achilles Tatius: slave (7.13.3–8.19.2) and free man (8.2.2–19.1) to the same supplicanda, bandits (4.13.1–3), suitor (8.17.3–4). In one historian, Herodian: vestal virgin (1.11.4–5), staff of imperial household (1.16.5–17.1), emperor (2.12.5–6).

74. A sample of Europeans from west to east: Spaniards (App. *Hisp.* 61), Gauls (Caes. *Gal.* 7.47.5), Britons (Aug. *Anc.* 5.59), Etruscans (D.H. 4.27.4–6), Germans (*Hist. Aug. Prob.* 14.2), Illyrians (App. *Ill.* 28), Pelasgians (D.H. 1.20.1), steppe tribes (Lucianus *Tox.* 55). Asians from west to east: Phoenicians (Arr. *An.* 2.24.5), Arabs (Curt. 4.6.15–16), Armenians (Flor. *Epit.* 1.40), Assyrians (X. *Cyr.* 3.3.67), Medes (Hdt. 1.112), Persians (D.S. 17.35.5), Parthians ([Sen.] *Oct.* 627–8), Bactrians (*Hist. Aug. Had.* 21.14), Indians (D.S. 17.91.4). Africans from west to east: Numidians (*B. Afr.* 92.4), Carthaginians (D.S. 32.6.3–4), Egyptians (Hdt. 2.113). All these acts have a Greek, Roman, or Italian principal except Arr. *An.* 2.24.5, Hdt. 1.112, Lucianus *Tox.* 55, and X. *Cyr.* 3.3.67.

lexica, for example, readily translate Greek supplicatory terms into Latin.[75] The Septuagint has a Greek as well as Hebrew flavor when it says that Joab "fled" to an altar in *Kings* and that Esther humbled herself before Asahuerus, the Xerxes of the Greeks.[76]

A comprehensive treatment cannot always tell us what happened; often it cannot tell us what usually happened. But it can tell us what the Greeks and Romans found plausible or interesting, and it reveals much difference of opinion, not only about what happened in any given case, but about what should or could happen, about the reasons for "yes" and "no" in one time or place or in one community of discourse. It reveals cultural differences—a third advantage.

Fourth, a comprehensive treatment reveals generic and other differences. Some genres favor the suppliant, some the supplicandus. No two have the same motive for or manner of doing so, nor do any two have the same propensity to report supplication as opposed to some other way of making a request. Nor do any two handle the four steps in the same way. One problem is giving due weight, but not undue weight, to differences in gestures; another is generalizing from Homer, who is important for both gestures and requests. A third is giving due weight to the problems that arise when suppliants go to shrines, not persons, and to the idiosyncrasy of genres that describe these problems, such as tragedy, in which no suppliant is ever rejected and then expelled from an altar. Other problems do not concern any steps in the practice, but the difference between reports of acts and statements of rules. Homer, for example, reports acts, but unlike the Roman jurists does not state rules. By the same token, some genres or works make long reports and include every step (as in *Odyssey* 22 but not the rest of Homer), whereas others omit steps (as in Cicero, who does not report the tribunes' response to the suppliants). On the one hand, there are predictably biased writers, such as Thucydides, and unpredictably original ones, such as Virgil; on the other hand, contrasts between written and visual sources reveal differences between media as opposed to genres or works.[77] Greek vases provide an alternative view of supplications reported in myth and tragedy, and Roman coins provide an alternative view of supplications reported in historiography.[78] But comparison across genres and media provides a compensatory gain. Many well-known acts—and not just acts in tragedy

---

75. E.g., ἱκετεύω as *supplico, precor, obsecro, deprecor*; ἱκετήριον as *infulae*; and ἱκέτης as *precator, supplex Hermeneumata*: v. 7 ss. vv. The rendering of ἱκέτης as *supplex* also appears in Schlüsner, *Thesaurus* s.v. ἱκέτης, although he also translates it as *hostis*; in Pseudo-Cyril, s.v. same; and in *Cor. Gloss.*, ed Goetz s.v. same.

76. 3 *Ki.* 2.28, *Es.* 8.3–8. The Septuagint adheres so closely to the Hebrew text, reporting each act of supplication and adding none, that it does not appear in the appendices.

77. For a chapter-length treatment of supplicatory gestures, see Sittl, *Gebärden*, chaps. 9–10, followed by Neumann, *Gesten und Gebärden*, 68–73, and McNiven, *Gestures*, chap. 3. Briefer, but the only treatment of Roman gestures: Brilliant, *Gesture and Rank*, 4–7.

78. Roman sculpture provides the same alternative view as coins, but only for the Principate, as shown by Schneider, *Bunte Barbaren*, 22–31. Partly for this reason, and partly because of its scope, it will not figure in this book. Nor will Near Eastern sculpture depicting acts of submission or obeisance, practices differing from supplication; for obeisance, see 236–39 below.

and epic—prove to be atypical. To paraphrase the epigrapher Robert, to know even one act, one must know a thousand.[79]

At the same time, a comprehensive treatment does not cover Greece and Rome in any vague or general sense. Homer provides a *terminus post quem*, and the end of the Roman Principate provides a *terminus ante quem*. Before this second *terminus*, all genres and means of expression provide examples, whereas after it, only a few do. Literary change accounts for much of this shift—for example, there is little epic poetry after this period—and the rise of Christianity accounts for the rest. Christianity had two effects on supplication. First, by assigning every altar to the same personnel, an ordained priesthood, it introduced uniformity. Second, by establishing canon law for supplication, it introduced universality. By contrast, earlier supplication was diverse—four steps, but differing supplicandi and standards of judgment as well as differing gestures and venues.

A comprehensive treatment of Greek and Roman supplication cannot pretend to be a universal treatment of this practice. If supplication be described as having four steps ending in a divinely sanctioned pledge, it existed in the Near East long before Homer. In the *Epic of Gilgamesh*, Humbaba supplicates Gilgamesh, begging him to spare his life. Although the fragmentary standard version of the poem lacks most of the four steps, the second step seems to appear in later Mesopotamian illustrations in which Humbaba clasps Gilgamesh's knees (figures 1.1–3, a tripartite view of the scene, and figure 1.4).[80] Another early source, *Exodus*, describes supplication at altars by killers, a staple of Greek drama, and includes the same criterion of judgment as *Odyssey* 22, voluntary wrongdoing.[81] *Kings* provides an example of such an act; the suppliant is Joab, the altar is in the temple in Jerusalem, and the person who responds to the suppliant as Odysseus would have to Phemius, had he gone to the altar of Zeus, is King Solomon.[82] The rejection of Joab comes for the predictable reason that he has committed two voluntary wrongs, the murders of Abner and Amasa.[83] The acceptance of Esther is likewise predictable.

The reason for not putting these and other Near Eastern acts on a par with Greek and Roman acts, and thus putting this study on three bases, not two, is an historical accident: few reports of Near Eastern supplication survive. In spite of prominence of *Exodus*, Hebrew acts number less than a dozen; even during the

---

79. Robert, "Eulaios," 529: "Celui qui connaît un nom n'en connaît aucun. Il faut en avoir connu mille pour en connaître un."

80. *SB* 5.144–265, where Humbaba begs for his life, only to be rejected and slain by Gilgamesh. Fig. 1.1–3: a Luristan-type situla 16.1 cm. high from the early first millennium BCE, Staatl. Mus. Berlin XIc 4094 = Calmeyer, *Reliefbronzen*, 45. Fig. 1.4, a terra-cotta tablet 13 cm. wide from the time of the Larsa dynasty, Staatl. Mus. Berlin VA 7426, makes it hard to be sure that the gesture in 1.1–3 is supplicatory rather than defensive. An earlier version of the same act, but with the gesture performed after the suppliant's plea, an aberration: *Bilgames* 158–79.

81. *Ex.* 21.14. לְהָרְגוֹ: "deceptive malice," as in Schmid, "Miqlat." Otherwise: "malice aforethought." Cf. *Jd.* 9.2, where the same word appears.

82. 3 *Ki.* 2.28–32.

83. Abner: 2 *Ki.* 3.27. Amasa: 3.20.8–10. A survey: Barmash, *Homicide*, ch. 3.

FIGURES 1.1–1.3   A tripartite view of of Gilgamesh, Humbaba, and Enkidu.
Courtesy of Staatsliche Museen zu Berlin.

fall of Jerusalem to Nebuchadnezar, none are recorded.[84] The rest of the Near
East supplies even fewer examples. The place to begin looking for them would be
Mesopotamia, but although there is some supplicatory language in letters, there
are few records of acts.[85] Most appear in Assyrian royal inscriptions recording
surrenders. The defeated or the fearful surrender, approach, and "seize (the king's)
feet," or some similar gesture.[86] A request to be spared need not be made, and
except in three instances, the inscription does not even acknowledge that the
request is understood.[87] Nor need the suppliants make either of two obvious arguments: surrender saves the king the trouble of killing them and puts their wealth
and labor at his disposal. By imposing burdens such as tribute and the performance of corvée he signals his acceptance of these arguments and also imposes
surrender terms.[88] At the last step, the king can either accept, as by imposing

84. The closest to supplication: *Jer.* 21.9 = 38.2, where only a distinctively supplicatory term for "surrender"
is lacking. Another view: Gruber, *Nonverbal Communication*, 18–20, arguing that there is only a contextual distinction between supplication and obeisance, with evidence found in his chaps. 3–4. A sample of Near Eastern
acts appears in appendix 1d. References to supplication at altars in *Psalms* do not include references to any given
acts, as noted by Traulsen, *Das sakrale Asyl*, 43, with refs. at n. 145.

85. Letters of Assurbanipal: *upnī petû*, "open the fists," referring to supplication at *Asb.* 24, #11.16–17. Another
phrase, *qāta dekû*, "extend hands," appears in supplicatory letters (*ABL* 134, 281, 1089.5–r.6, 1431), and in one
instance the letter writer predicts an act of supplication (774.31–r.8). For these references and for related language for prayer, see Gruber, *Nonverbal Communication*, chap. 2.

86. *ARI* 2.467 (Tukulti-Ninurta II). Kissing feet: Sg. 8.72. Prostration: Sg. 8.55. Kneeling: Esar. 68.2.1.5.

87. Esar. 68.2.1.3-35, Sg. 8.55–61, 8.69–73, in the sample of acts included in appendix 1d.

88. Tribute and corvée *ARI* 2.546 (Ashur-nasir-apli ll). Tribute without corvée: 2.547, 2.558, 2.567. Same
but hostages taken: 2.601. Provincial governor imposed: Sg. 8.73.

FIGURE 1.4   Gilgamesh, Humbaba, and Enkidu, but a less supplicatory pose.
Courtesy of Preussischer Kulturbesitz.

burdens, or reject, the same as Odysseus with Leodes, and if he does reject he
may do so because of voluntary wrongdoing.[89] Missing only is some royal gesture
to show that the king has given a pledge. Sargon, however, makes a promise to
suppliants spared in his eighth campaign.[90]

Other surrenders differ from supplication because the king does not allow the
defeated to take any initiative. Rather than let them approach, he subdues them;
rather than let them fall at his feet, he compels them to lie there, and sometimes
places his own foot on their necks. Rather than let them make a request, let alone
justify it with an argument, he no sooner imposes some burden than he dismisses
them.[91] Still other surrenders may have included acts of supplication but the inscription describes these surrenders too briefly for us to be sure: the enemy surrenders and the kings shows mercy, followed by the imposition of some burden.[92]
These two kinds of surrenders explain why supplication by the defeated, which
surely occurred many times—perhaps as many as in Greece, given Assyrian successes—does not bulk large in the Assyrian records. Impressive as the king is when
receiving suppliants, he is more impressive when putting his foot on the necks of
his foes, or even when bestowing mercy and imposing burdens rather than granting requests. Supplication is not the most flattering outcome of a military campaign, and so the inscriptions understate it.

As for Phoenicia and Syria, we know almost nothing, save for acts at the
temple of Heracles Melkarth in Tyre.[93] With regard to Israel's other neighbor,

89. Esar. 68.2.1.3-35, 68.2.2.18-41, where it consists of disobeying orders.
90. Sg. 8.61.
91. ARI 1.715 (Tukulti-Ninurta I). Subduing and compelling only: 2.31 (Tiglath-pileser I).
92. ARI 2.27 (Tiglath-Pileser I).
93. Public regulation of this shrine: D.S. 17.41.7–8, D.C. 42.49.2–3. Other sources: Arr. An. 2.24.5, App.
BC 5.1.9, Just. 39.1.8. Other temples: Just. 27.1.4–7. The only act outside a temple: D.S. 33.5.1–4.

pre-Hellenistic Egypt, one important source, Herodotus, makes the mistake of reporting temple refuge where none existed. This author says that there was an asylum for suppliants in the Nile delta at the time of the Trojan War, but no Egyptian source confirms anything of the sort.[94] Other Greeks sources say that there was no asylum for suppliants in Egypt, or—a no less telling statement—that Egyptians did not understand the practices of the Greeks.[95] The Egypt of the Ptolemies does, of course, provide the evidence for supplication analyzed by Woess, but this evidence concerns only the shrines of several Greek gods and of Isis and Serapis. Similarly, the Greek novelists, two of whom set acts of supplication in Egypt and even in Ethiopia, acknowledge the difficulty of Greeks and Egyptians in communicating with one another during the procedure.[96] As for the considerable evidence for Ptolemaic and also Roman petitions, it is irrelevant, for a petition does not include the first step of the procedure, an approach by one party to another, and may not include supplicatory language.[97] Also irrelevant is any refuge provided by a Semitic temple in Mesopotamia. There is no evidence for supplication in these temples, which differ on this score from their Phoenician and Hebrew counterparts.[98]

The same objection, a lack of instances, applies to supplication among the tribes of ancient Europe, among whom evidence for pledges is entirely missing, as is evidence for supplication at altars. Most important, all evidence for supplication among these tribes comes from Greek and Latin authors who are no more reliable in this region of the world than they are in the Near East. Now dated notions of supplication among the early Germans prove unverifiable, not because reports have been lost, but because scarcely any reports ever existed other than those made by Caesar and Tacitus. These two sources suffer from both an obvious weakness, the bias of the authors, and a weakness that emerges in the appendices: Caesar and Tacitus seldom report how one German or Gaul supplicates another as opposed to supplicating a Roman. (Caesar does make one general statement about Gallic supplication, or about a practice of helping fugitives that resembles supplication, but it is cursory. On the one hand, he says, the Gauls help wayfarers; on the other hand, they deny *fides*, or pledges of protection, to deserters and traitors. Caesar may be right, but the Gauls must have refused to help some people other

94. Thus Woess, *Asylwesen Ägyptens*, 202–3. The only possible act in Philistia: 1 *Macc.* 10.83, where refugees at a statue may be suppplicating or only seeking safety in a likely spot.

95. Egyptian asylum: Hdt. 2.113. According to D. S., the law of Busiris forbade supplication by foreigners (1.67.9); Str. 17.1.6 agrees, but not 17.1.19. Uncomprehending Egyptians: A. *Supp.* 911–51. Hellenized Egyptian courts: Lucianus *Tox.* 35.

96. A bound Greek considers supplicating Egyptians who do not understand his language: Ach. Tat. 3.10.2–6. At Hld. 2.13.4–14.1, someone who speaks no Egyptian watches a supplication between two Egyptians and interferes, making a pledge to the suppliant without knowing what the suppliant wants or has said.

97. Which is not to say that supplication did influence the language and structure of these petitions or of other requests made in writing; see appendix 6.

98. At Curt. 10.9.21 Meleager flees to an unnamed temple in Babylon, but it is unclear whether he regarded it as a sanctuary from which he might not be removed, and thus as a place of supplication, rather than as a place in which he would not be slain; if he did regard it as a place of supplication, he was mistaken, for the Macedonians kill him on the spot with no objections from priests or others.

than these two kinds of wrongdoers.[99]) As for the larger world, beginning with India, here the objection is a lack of comparable instances—of the same four steps and the same culmination, a divinely guaranteed pledge. India, if not other lands, found its own way to meet the needs addressed by supplication.[100]

The Greeks and Romans were not the only important supplicandi in the ancient Mediterranean world. The Persians were important supplicandi, too. Yet the only Persian who receives Greek suppliants is Xerxes, approached by the Jewess Esther as well as by Themistocles. Along with some of her compatriots, Esther will figure from time to time in this study, but not as an example of Hebrew supplication. That is a separate topic. She and they will offer a reminder that supplication in one place overlaps with supplication in neighboring places. Otherwise Esther and Themistocles, the Jewess and the Athenian, could not have succeeded with the same supplicandus, Xerxes.[101]

TYPOLOGY AND DEVELOPMENT

The importance of the four steps dictates describing them in order. But two other ways of presenting the evidence also recommend themselves: first, according to genre, author, and medium, and second, according to the changing relation between supplication and the law. Chapters 2 and 3 describe the four steps, but in describing each step they divide the evidence according to genre and the like. Chapters 4 and 5 deal with the changing relation between supplication and the law.

Chapter 2 deals with the first three steps. The treatment of the first step, which is comparatively simple, is brief, but it shows the importance of the supplicandus and the need for the suppliant to choose among the options that supplication permits. Both points militate against the prevailing view, which slights the supplicandus and minimizes choice. The treatment of the second step, which is much less simple, is twice as long. The salient issue is whether all gestures make contact, as Gould and others have held. Also important is whether words are not sometimes an acceptable substitute for gestures. Additional problems arise from multiple gestures, and from gestures and words used by those who supplicate in groups or address groups rather than individuals. The last of these problems underscores the importance of the supplicandus.

Chapter 2 next describes the third step, on which literary critics have concentrated their attention. Here generic differences prove more important than they

---

99. The only instance of Gauls or Germans supplicating one another: Caes. *Gal.* 7.15.3–6, 7.26.3–4, 7.48.3. General statement: 6.23.9. Bibliography: Much ad Tac. *Ger.* 8.1. A different view: Wilutzky, *Vorgeschichte*, 106–10, citing medieval sources. A list of all acts reported by Greek and Latin sources but lacking Greek or Roman principals appears in appendix 1e.

100. A conclusion based on the Vedas, and in particular on the lack of gestures similar to the Greek and of pertinent cognate vocabulary.

101. A different view: Traulsen, *Das sakrale Asyl*, chap. 1, linking Hebrew and Greek supplication by confining Hebrew supplication to temple refuge; general treatments such as Löhr, *Asylwesen*, also confine Hebrew supplication in this way, as do studies of individual passages such as David, "Josua." Traulsen, 80 n. 349, notices 2 *Macc.* 4.33–34, but not Phoenician supplication.

do in the first two steps. Both requests and arguments, the two parts of this step, vary according to genre yet not according to culture. This finding shows that suppliants are less free than a rhetorical conception of supplication would imply. The same conclusion flows from the conventional nature of suppliants' arguments and from the predominance of moral and legal arguments. A suppliant may well be persuasive, as a rhetorical conception requires, but he must also be worthy.

Chapter 3 turns to the fourth and last step. As in the previous chapter, the chief target is the prevailing view, which linked successful supplication to *xenia*. Successful supplication involves much more, including instances of negotiation between suppliant and supplicandus. Success does sometimes lead to *xenia*, but it can lead to new ties that, unlike *xenia*, are asymmetrical. One such tie is the enslavement of the suppliant by the supplicandus, another illustration of how supplication adapts itself to the society around it. Most important, the new tie always includes a pledge given to the suppliant by the supplicandus and witnessed by the gods. It thus contributes to the quasilegal character of supplication, which resembles a divinely sanctioned contract.

No view has given much attention to unsuccessful supplication. Even Roman legalists have minimized it, assuming that the rejection of a suppliant results from his breaking a law. Not so: it can also result from his violating norms. Nor does the suppliant who meets with rejection after coming to an altar differ from the one who approaches a person. If rejected, the altar suppliant leaves voluntarily or, if he or she fails to leave, faces expulsion by those in charge of the altar. This result, anticipated by *Exodus*, befalls many Greek and Roman suppliants. As elsewhere, slaves hold a special place: they are easier to expel than free persons and are subject to a somewhat different procedure. And, as elsewhere, genre is intrinsic to the evidence. Although expulsion is unknown in tragedy, in comedy it is unremarkable, just as it is in both Roman and Hebrew legal sources.

Chapters 2 and 3, which combine an anatomy of supplication with generic factors, are typological. Chapters 4 and 5, which deal with the impact of the law on supplication, are developmental. Chapter 4 deals with the relation between supplication and written laws, especially in Classical Athens. Chapter 5, which deals with Republican and early imperial Rome, addresses the same relation between supplication and written laws but in a new situation, in which many suppliants address themselves to magistrates, and jurists comment on the results.

Classical Athens, the main subject of chapter 4, provides the first large body of evidence for the regulation of supplication. Supplication proves to be compatible with the written law of Athens and with the Athenian political system, every part of which affects the practice. For the most part, regulations formalize supplication, but sometimes regulations alter supplication in order to make it conform to the political system. Sometimes supplicatory norms and legal norms and concepts overlap; sometimes regulations mark a change in norms. The process of accommodation also occurs outside Athens. Supplication at Greek federal shrines conforms to the treaties or grants establishing the shrines. Supplication at shrines in the territory of the Spartan Alliance conforms to other legal and political arrangements.

Chapter 5 shows how the Romans devise new links between supplication and the law, notably in court. Here again, supplication molds itself both to the political system and to moral and legal norms, notably the concept of mercy, one almost entirely missing from Athenian supplication but crucial for Roman supplication in wartime. Mercy joins pity as a second ground for evaluation, making Roman supplication flexible. Meanwhile, magistrates and then emperors replace the courts and assemblies of Athens as the characteristic supplicandi. From the late Republic onward, the Romans regulate and restrict supplication at temples, effectively replacing it with supplication at the emperor's statue—in other words, supplication to the chief magistrate.

All this implies gains for the legal system at supplication's expense. So does the Roman innovation of providing rights that render supplication superfluous. Yet the Romans also move in the opposite direction, allowing supplication as a way of appealing mistaken verdicts and as a means of rectifying inadequate legislation. The give-and-take between supplication and the law assumes forms that continue in Medieval Europe, as shown by examples found in Gregory the Great and in modern times. A concluding chapter traces this give-and-take in a single example drawn from a 2001 newspaper story.

In using this example, I invite a comparison, not a contrast, with antiquity, and such an invitation may meet with scepticism from specialists if only because they fear lest it meet with credulity from laymen. And the specialists are right. The strangeness, the pastness of the past needs preservation. But the humanity of the past needs preservation, too. A story of suffering, like this one, should give pause. It should ask why supplication was or is necessary.

2

THE FIRST THREE STEPS IN SUPPLICATION

In the first three steps of supplication, the suppliant takes the initiative. He, not the supplicandus, approaches, gesticulates or speaks, and presents a request and perhaps arguments. At the fourth step, initiative passes to the supplicandus, who evaluates and responds. This chapter will confine itself to the first three steps, those belonging to the suppliant. If we compare supplication to a legal procedure, this chapter will deal with the parts of a trial or hearing that precede the decision made by the jury, judge, or magistrate.

At the first step, the suppliant must often choose between approaching a person and approaching an altar. Phemius faces this choice: shall he approach Odysseus or the altar of Zeus? He does not say why he chooses Odysseus, but do other acts show why he did, or show why other suppliants choose either person or altar? Do these reasons change if the suppliant avails himself of alternatives to the person and the altar, such as approaching with a bough?

The second step serves to announce the intent to supplicate. Phemius and Leodes convey this intent in two ways, using a distinctive gesture, clasping the knee, and also uttering a word meaning "I am at your knees." This combination raises several questions: were other gestures or words suitable, too, and if so, how many? Do options differ by genre or culture? Which is more common, a gesture, like the knee clasp, or a word? Is a gesture necessary, as many scholars have thought? If not, what does it add? When do suppliants follow Phemius's example and use a combination? Do combinations correlate with genres and cultures?

The third step in supplication falls into two parts, requests and arguments. Phemius and Leodes request to be spared, and support this request with moral, legal, and other arguments. What do suppliants ask for, and how important are requests that are less pressing than the request to be spared? As regards arguments, how important are legal and moral arguments as opposed to others? Phemius, for example, says not only that he has done no voluntary wrong, but that, if spared, he will bring benefits to the house of Odysseus—an argument that he will repay a kindness. What of an argument that neither suppliant makes, but others might, which is that they are members of the household or family? Related to arguments are appeals to pity, such as Leodes and Phemius also make. How do these consort with arguments?

These are pressing questions. Suppliants wish to choose the approach, gesture, and argument that make success likely. As Bourdieu argued in another connection, the first three steps mark a struggle for advantage.

APPROACHES

At first glance, the difference between approaching a person and approaching an altar seems great. A person or group is merely human, but since an altar belongs to a god, approaching it is tantamount to approaching a superior being. Only if this being were hostile to the suppliant would the approach to the altar seem less attractive. But a second glance reveals a different picture. When supplicandi come to altars, divinities almost never respond. One well-known exception, Athena responding to Orestes when he comes to her altar in the *Eumenides* of Aeschylus, proves misleading, for she refers him to an Athenian court. Another well-known exception, the altar of the Lord in *Exodus*, is merely symbolic. As a passage in *Joshua* shows, the elders of the town entertain the requests of those who come to the Lord's altar.[1] This is the true picture: no matter where a suppliant goes, human beings entertain his request.[2] Even if a suppliant goes to Delphi seeking an oracle from Apollo, the god does not decide whether to give him an oracle. The priests do. In one case, they even decide to let a group of suppliants obtain two oracles in response to the same question. The suppliants, Athenian delegates, will not accept the first oracle, which predicted that the Persians would defeat the Athenians. So the priests let the Athenians obtain the second oracle, which predicts the opposite. The role of the priests also emerges from a detail preserved by the source, Herodotus. Before receiving the second oracle, the Athenians take advice from a local man who knows the priests.[3]

Whom, then, does a suppliant choose to approach? A person or group that he or she can reach and that has the power to give help. The most powerful figures in the ancient world are kings, so suppliants often choose them. Alexander the Great, Lars Porsenna, who threatened (or conquered) Rome, Masinissa and Juba, African opponents of the Romans—all receive suppliants. So do kings as far away as Scythia.[4] Two Hebrew kings, David and Ahab, receive suppliants, and so of course does Xerxes.[5] Sometimes the suppliants are the king's subjects, like the Macedonian soldiers who have offended Alexander the Great and supplicate to regain his favor. Others come from abroad, and not just in Xerxes' case. Lars Porsenna receives an exile, Masinissa a captive. Many suppliants who approach kings in Homer are fugitives from justice. Achilles' friend and adviser, Patroclus,

---

1. *Jo.* 20.1–7. Another exception: fig. 3.6, discussed in chap. 3.
2. As surmised by Scodel, rev. of Giordano, *Supplica*, and stated by Diodorus (12.57.3).
3. Hdt. 7.141.
4. Alexander: Plut. *Alex*. 62.3, 71.4–5. Italy: Plut. *Pop*. 16.1 (Lars Porsenna). Africa: Liv. 30.12.11–18 (Masinissa), Luc. 8.287–88 (Juba). Scythia: Polyaen. 8.55.1.
5. David: 2 *Ki*. 14.4–24. Ahab: 3 *Ki*. 20.32–34.

is one; he killed a companion at dice.[6] The most famous of the suppliants from abroad is Themistocles, an alleged traitor driven from Athens to Molossia, where he supplicated the king of that country before going to Persia.[7] All these suppliants prove successful. The king has the power to forgive the wayward, protect the exile or captive, and shelter the fugitive, and he uses it.

But the most important royal *supplicandus* is the Roman emperor. Augustus receives supplications at every turn. When he goes to dinner, the host's slave supplicates him. When he receives foreign rulers, they supplicate him. When he travels and visits other cities, the processions staged during his entry allow his subjects to supplicate him.[8] Tiberius finds so much attention nerve-wracking, and he suspects one suppliant of trying to kill him. Since the source for this act is Tacitus, who dislikes Tiberius, the emperor is ludicrously wrong. The suppliant, a disgraced senator, is groveling before him. But the long face that Tiberius showed to at least one suppliant did him no good. Suppliants kept coming; on one occasion, the whole Senate supplicated him.[9] Later suppliants approach the emperors Caligula, Claudius, Nero, Vespasian, Domitian, Trajan, Hadrian, Marcus Aurelius, Commodus, Septimius Severus, and Caracalla.[10] Any emperor missing from this list surely received suppliants, too, a conclusion suggested by the range of those who are on it. Some, like Trajan, at least pretended to share power with the Senate, and others, like Caligula, did not, and so pro-senatorial writers such as Tacitus favor the one and detest the other. No matter: suppliants seek out the emperor—any emperor.

The royal *supplicandus* was prestigious enough to find his way into the New Testament, albeit under another name—the Christ, the king of the Jews. In two of the synoptic Gospels, the prominent Jew Jairus, father of a sick daughter, supplicates Christ on her behalf, and the *supplicandus* has the power to work a miracle. In the third, the same story is even more adulatory: the father supplicates even though the daughter has already died, and Jesus still complies with the request. No wonder no one in the Gospels supplicates any other person. In the New Testament, supplication is something to be rendered unto God's son, as prayer is to be rendered unto God, and not something to be rendered to Caesar, as it is in Roman sources.[11]

Often the royal *supplicandus* acts as commander in chief. When a concubine captured after the battle of Plataea seeks freedom, she goes to the commander of

6. Patroclus: *Il.* 23.85–90. Others: *Il.* 15.431–32, 16.570–74, *Od* 3.92–108, 4.322–50, 16.424–30; so also Hes. fr. 257 M-W. An analysis of the phenomenon, stressing the likelihood of other cases that Homer does not mention: Schlunk, "Theme of the Suppliant-Exile," 199.

7. Th. 1.136.2–37.1, Plut. *Them.* 24.1–3, Nep. *Them.* 8.5, D.S. 11.56.1–4, discussed at 38–39 below. Others: Hdt. 4.165–7.1 (a satrap), Paus. 10.19.7.

8. King: Aug. *Anc.* 5.54–6.38. Slave: D.C. 54.23.3. *Aduentio*: Hor. *Carm.* 4.14.35. This list includes one source for each act.

9. Attack: Tac. *Ann.* 1.13.7. *Immoto uultu*: 2.29.2. Senate: Toc. *Ann.* 1.11.1–13, Suet. *Tib.* 24.1.

10. Caligula: D.C. 59.19.5–6. Claudius: Tac. *Ann.* 11.30.1-2. Nero: Suet. *Nero* 13.2. Vespasian: D.C. 65.16.2. Domitian: D.C. 67.5.1. Trajan: Fro. *Parth.* 16. Hadrian: *Hist. Aug. Had.* 21.14. Marcus Aurelius: D.C. 72.16.1. Commodus: Hrd. 1.16.4–5. Septimius Severus: Hrd. 3.9.2. Caracalla: D.C. 78.19.3–4. Additional acts appear in chap. 5. This list excludes typical acts portrayed on coins.

11. *Ev. Marc.* 5.22–24, *Ev. Luc.* 8.41–42, *Ev. Matt.* 9.18–19. Similar: *Ev. Marc.* 7.25, *Ev. Luc.* 5.12–16, *Ev. Mat.* 8.2–4, 15.22–28.

the victorious Greeks, King Pausanias of Sparta, who grants her request.[12] Unsurprisingly, the sources assign more suppliants to the greatest conqueror, Alexander the Great, than to anyone else. The parade of petitioners begins in Miletus, on the coast of Asia Minor, and stretches to India, where some suppliants are Brahmins.[13] Also unsurprisingly, the sources put Julius Caesar in second place (the parade is not quite so long, extending from Gaul to Egypt).[14] Only a little less predictable is the third-place Trajan, depicted as being supplicated six times in the panels of the column commemorating his conquest of Dacia.[15] The reason for this ranking is not simply that these three rulers fight more, or even that they win more. Lucullus and Pompey were hardly less successful, but they receive far fewer suppliants in our sources.[16] Rather, Alexander and Caesar (and, to a lesser degree, Trajan) serve as paragons of success. They thus deserve the most suppliants. If more Near Eastern evidence survived, this conclusion would be all the stronger. The reason is that of all sources for supplication, none is so favorable to the conqueror as Near Eastern stelae commemorating military victories. These stelae contain long lists of the defeated, all candidates for acts of supplication. If more of them did supplicate, or if more such stelae survived, the leading Near-Eastern kings would boast more numerous suppliants than those of any Greek or Roman leader. But even Naramsin, the prototypical Babylonian conqueror, figures as a supplicandus on only one such stele.[17]

If the community is not a ruled by a monarch, deliberative bodies may replace the king. As we will shall shortly see, Greek suppliants prefer to approach a deliberative body by way of an altar, so Greek examples of this sequence are few; but Gylippus, a Spartan general in Syracusan service, refers Athenian suppliants to the Assembly of Syracuse.[18] In Rome, suppliants address themselves to the assemblies or Senate. In early Roman history, foreign emissaries approach the people; Livy's first 10 books, covering Roman history down to the early third century BCE, reports four instances, including one in which suppliants approach an assembly in another Italian city.[19] In later history, these emissaries (and some Romans) approach the Senate.[20]

---

12. Hdt. 9.76.2–3.

13. D.S. 17.22.4 (Miletus), 17.91.4, 17.96.5 (both Indians), 17.102.7 (Bhramins), 17.103.8 (Indians); Curt. 3.12.17 (Persian), 4.6.15–16 (Arab), 5.1.17–19, (Persian), 7.3.17, 7.5.33, 8.10.34–35 (all Indians), Arr. *An.* 5.1.4–2.4 (fictitious, Dionysiac Indians). Polyaen. 4.3.30 overlaps with these.

14. *Caes. Civ.* 2.11.4–13.3, *Gal.* 1.20.1–5, 1.27.1–28.2, 1.31.1–33.1, 2.13.2–15.1, 7.40.6, *B. Afr.* 89.4, 92.4, *B. Alex.* 32.3, 67.1–68, Luc. 4.337–64, Flor. *Epit.* 1.45.

15. Panels 39, 61, 75, 117, 123, 151 in Settis, *Colonna Traiana*.

16. Lucullus: App. *Hisp.* 52. Pompey: Plut. *Pomp.* 55.6, V. Max. 5.1.9, [Sal.] *Rep.* 1.4.1. So also Pyrrhus of Epirus: Just. 18.1.1. These lists include only one source for each act.

17. 2254–2218 BCE, first published by de Morgan, *Recherches*, 1.106, 1.144 with pl. 10. The inscription is missing, so even here a list of suppliants is lacking.

18. D.S. 13.19.2–33.1.

19. Liv. 2.49.12, 8.20.6, 8.37.9–10. Assembly at Gabii: 1.53.4–10. In a similar instance at D.H. 7.5.1–2, the suppliants use boughs, a detail that Hellenizes them.

20. Liv. 7.31.5–9, 9.20.1, 42.23.5–24.10, 43.2.2–3, 44.19.7–14, 45.20.9–25.4. Romans: 8.28.5–9, 22.60.1–61.3.

If the assembly is out of reach or cannot go into session, the suppliant approaches a magistrate who will, if he cooperates, introduce him to the assembly or bring his request to the assembly's attention. This sequence of magistrate and then assembly often occurs in Roman sources. The most famous example is the tribune Calidius, who helped Metellus Pius. A famous example of a magistrate receiving a suppliant who would or should later address another body, the Senate, is Titus Flamininus, who would have referred Aetolian suppliants to the Senate but found them obstreperous and put them in chains.[21] These contrasting examples stand at the forefront of others occurring throughout the Roman world. Some examples depicted on Roman coins do not even bother to include the magistrate or the deliberative body. He or it are taken for granted, and only the suppliant remains—the more exotic the better. On one late Republican denarius, an Eastern king who wishes to supplicate some magistrate, perhaps Pompey, then organizing the East, approaches on a camel. Having crossed some unseen and unidentified desert, he dismounts, takes the camel by the reins, and kneels (figure 2.1. As always, the suppliant is on the reverse, shown to the right in this and other pictures of coins).[22]

Finally, courts may replace the king insofar as he receives suppliants who, like Leodes, are accused of wrongdoing. Both Athens and Rome offer diverse examples. A prominent Athenian official, the archon Basileus, supplicated a court. So did another prominent Athenian of a different stripe, the courtesan Phryne.[23] Among the prominent Romans who supplicated in Cicero's time were an Italian notable accused of poisoning, a consul-designate accused of buying votes, and an elderly senator accused of committing an act of treason 40 years earlier.[24] Wherever courts

FIGURE 2.1   An Arab king supplicates, reins in hand.
Courtesy of American Numismatic Society.

21. Metellus Pius: as at chap. 1, n. 10. Flamininus: Liv. 36.27.5–8, a plan to go to the Senate, and 36.28.1–8, where the Aetolians prove obstreperous.

22. Fig. 2.1: a 58 BCE denarius of M. Aemilius Scaurus, ANS 2002.46.489 = Cr. 422.1a, discussed in Naiden, "Roman Coins." So also ANS 1987.26.112 = Cr. 431.1.

23. Archon: Dem. 59.81–83. Phryne: Ath. *Deip.* 13.590e-f, Posidipp. *PCG* 13.6–7. These are instances of supplication reported by these sources, not instances of supplicatory language in forensic speeches, and thus not instances falling short of supplication in the prevailing view.

24. Italian: Cic. *Clu.* 200. Consul-designate: *Mur.* 86–87. Senator: *Rab. Perd.* 37.

met, defendants must have supplicated them. So must have those who aided defendants, notably advocates. Cicero, for example, supplicated in his own person.[25]

These examples involve orderly, mostly peacetime settings. On a battlefield, a suppliant may discover that an individual soldier wields the power to spare or save him, and not any higher authority like a commander, let alone the king or assembly to which the commander is responsible (and to which, like Gylippus, he may defer). If the army is disorganized, the individual soldier may even wield this power in the absence of any orders from superiors. This possibility depends on culture and genre. Disorganized armies appear in epic and fiction, and organized armies appear mostly in Roman historiography.

Homer provides the most examples of the situation in which the individual soldier acts on his own. Achilles, Diomedes, and Odysseus all receive suppliants, the same as Agamemnon.[26] The reason is not that Agamemnon is weak; as one of four Greeks who receive suppliants, he is strong. But he has no control over the other three. Similarly, any pirate chief must reckon with sailors who will not obey his orders and who, if given the chance, will receive suppliants and collect ransom.[27] In Roman historiography, in contrast, not a single individual soldier receives suppliants on the battlefield. As we have noticed, this honor falls to commanders, especially the most powerful ones. In part, this phenomenon is misleading: surely in a thousand years of Roman military history, some individual on some battlefield spared an enemy. But in part, and perhaps in large part, it reflects the Roman commander's control over his men, illustrated by one act of supplication to Caesar by a soldier wishing to be pardoned for losing a shield, and by one in Livy in which soldiers supplicate on behalf of someone who has disobeyed orders.[28] The same conclusions hold good for Greek warfare in the classical period. From all reports, no individual spares another who surrenders to him. Surely some individuals did spare their enemies, but less often than in earlier times.

These examples all show that suppliants where public or military power lies. In a monarchy, they go to the monarch; in a Republic or a classical Greek polis, they go to a magistrate or public body. Where powers are divided and courts replace kings or assemblies, they turn to judges. Supplication is not un-Republican or undemocratic, and is not out of the question for citizens as opposed to subjects. On the battlefield, it may be the responsibility of either the commander or the warrior.

Just as suppliants know where public power lies, they also know where private power lies. Again and again, they address themselves to the head of the house-

25. Cic. *Lig.* 37, *Mil.* 100, 103, *Mur.* 86, *Planc.* 102, 104, *Rab. Perd.* 5, *Rab. Post.* 48, *Sest.* 147—some of which might be regarded as instances of supplicatory language, not supplication. Others supplicating in Cicero: appendix 1c, "Acts of Supplication in Cicero," particularly "Acts of Supplication by Defendants, Supporters, and Advocates in Cicero" and "Acts of Supplication by Plaintiffs in Cicero."

26. Agamemnon: *Il.* 11.130–47. Achilles: 20.463–69, 21.64–119, 22.337–60. Diomedes: 10.454–56. Odysseus: *Od.* 22.310–56, a quasimilitary situation.

27. Brigands: X. *Eph.* 3.8.4–5. Pirates: Hld. 5.25.1–2, X. *Eph.* 1.13.6–14.1.

28. Plut. *Caes.* 16.4, Liv. 8.35.3–8. Similar to Livy: Tac. *Ann.* 1.29.1–2.

hold. This figure can play any of several roles: receiver of strangers, master (and father) of slaves, husband and father of a family. All these persons may supplicate him. Here again, we begin with Phemius, who, when he says that he benefits any house to which he comes, acknowledges that he is a stranger and that Odysseus is his host. Elsewhere in Homer, Odysseus's son, Telemachus, visits and supplicates two household heads, Nestor and Menelaus. Odysseus himself does the same, visiting and supplicating another household head, Aeolus.[29] Slaves supplicate the household head because he is their owner and master, or they supplicate his wife. Examples are deceptively few, but run a gamut: Greek tragedy, Greek fiction, and Greek oratory, the last of these providing an indubitable example. In Lysias, a slave girl begs her master not to put her to work turning a millstone.[30]

The head of the house most often plays his two other roles, as husband and father. Husbands receive supplications from wives beginning with Meleager's wife, Cleopatra, who in Iliad 9 persuades him to fight those besieging his city.[31] The same pattern appears in later genres, including mythography, historiography, and fiction; the Old Testament parallel is Esther's supplication.[32] Some mothers (but no fathers) supplicate sons. One of them, Meleager's mother, fails where his wife succeeds.[33] These sons have the power to save a city, as Meleager and Hector do in the Iliad, or have some power to protect those of inferior status. The mother regards them as she would a husband, and, by extension, as a slave would a master, or a guest would a household head.

Children supplicate parents in no less diverse sources, beginning with Iphigenia in tragedy.[34] But they address themselves to the more powerful parent, the father. They supplicate mothers only in Euripides, and even in this author, the circumstances are abnormal. In Alcestis, the mother has chosen to die when she might have chosen otherwise. The children are the victims of her choice, and beg her not to leave them. In Medea, the mother plans to kill the children, and the chorus imagines them supplicating her. In Orestes, the child's parents are both dead, and the child is delirious, which explains why he can appeal to his mother.[35] Mothers, in short, receive appeals only if they are suicidal, murderous, or spectral. Given the ample evidence for supplication, this cannot be accidental. Nor can the frequency of supplication to fathers. As Plato says, the head of the household is a petty king.[36]

---

29. Od. 3.92–108, 4.322–50, 10.62–76.

30. E. Hipp. 325–35, X. Eph. 2.10.2, Lys. 1.19–20.

31. Il. 9.590–93, E. Tro. 1042–57.

32. Mythography by way of Ovid: Met. 5.514–32, 9.413–17, 14.372–85. Prose: D.H. 4.66.1–67.1, D.S. 37.19.5–20. A twist: Parth. 5.2, 17.5, where sons supplicate mothers for illicit sex.

33. Il. 9.451–53, E. El. 1206–15, Ph. 1567–69, Aeschin. 1.99.1, Is. 8.22, D.C. 47.8.5.

34. Iphigenia: A. Ag. 231–47. Other children: E. HF 986–95, S. OC 1267–1396, And. 1.19, Plut. Mul. Virt. 251a–c.

35. E. Alc. 400–3, Med. 856–65; Or. 255–58 is perhaps only a cry for help.

36. Pl. Leg. 3.680d–e.

Altars

Since the suppliant wishes to present himself or herself to some powerful person or group, why should he or she go to an altar? First, for convenience. If the supplicandi were a group that did not gather frequently or regularly, an approach to an altar put them on notice. They could hear the suppliant later, as shown by an Athenian case in which a suppliant comes to the altar of the Athenian Council during the Eleusinian Mysteries, when the Council was not in session, and deposits a bough to show that he has come. Another body of Athenian supplicandi, the assembly, heard suppliants once a month. If a suppliant came on another day, he, too, would have to go to an altar and leave a bough.[37] The suppliant did so not because he thought the altar was magical, as in the prevailing view, but to notify the body of his appeal.

Second, for visibility. This motive explains why suppliants tend to go to the most prominent altars in a community or region. In sources for Athens, marketplace altars and the temple of Athena are approached most often, followed by sites where the Council meets.[38] In sources for Sparta, another central shrine, the Brazen House, takes the lead.[39] In Achaea, the temple of Poseidon at the tribal center of Helice leads; at Tegea, all reported acts occur at Athena Alea, and in rural Arcadia all acts occur at the shrine of Zeus Lycaeus. In Messenia, all acts occur at Zeus *Ithometes*, and the only known regulations concern the shrine of Demeter at Andania, an important town.[40] The reason for this preference is the same. Going to the leading shrine will make the suppliant visible.

The tendency to choose the shrines of leading gods illustrates the same wish to seek out the powerful. The chief gods of supplication are Athena followed by Artemis, Zeus, and Poseidon. All entertain far more suppliants than those next in line, Apollo, Hera, Demeter, and (in Phoenicia) Herakles Melkarth.[41] Other gods

37. Council: And. 1.110–16, with other examples discussed at 174–75 below. Assembly: Arist. *Ath.* 43.6. Dramatic parallels: A. *Supp.* 506, where the king tells the suppliants to leave boughs on the altar while their case is being heard.

38. Athena: A. *Eu.* 276–488, Hdt. 5.71, 8.53.2, Paus. 1.20.7. Altars near marketplaces begin with Homer: Kolb, *Agora und Theater*, 13.

39. The only Spartan or Laconian supplications at altars other than at the Brazen House and at Taenarus: Plut. *Cleom.* 8.2, *Lyc.* 11.1.

40. Helice: Paus. 7.1.8, 7.24.6, Polyaen. 8.46.1. Athena *Alea*: Plut. *Lys.* 30.1, Paus. 3.5.6, 3.7.10. Zeus *Lykaios*: Th. 5.16.3. Zeus *Ithometes*: Th. 1.101.2–103. Andania: *IG* v.1 1390 = *SIG* 734.

41. The following list consists of one reference for each act addressed to a god whose shrines or altars are supplicated at least five times.

Athena (21, Brazen House asterisked, and Athena *Polias* double asterisked): A. *Eu.* 276–488**, Hdt. 5.71**, 8.53.2**, Paus. 1.20.7**, 3.5.6 bis, 3.7.10, 3.9.13, 6.9.6–8, 10.35.3, Plut. *Ages.* 19.1, *Agis* 11.5–12.1*, 16.3*, *Lyc.* 5.5, *Lys.* 30.1, *Amat. Narr.* 774f, *Unius in Rep.* 825b, Procl. *Chr.* 108 bis = *EGF* p. 62, Str. 6.1.14, Th. 1.134.1*, X. *HG* 4.3.20.

Artemis (17, Ephesus asterisked): Act. Tat. 7.13.3–8.19.2*, App. *BC* 5.1.4*, 5.1.9, *Mith.* 23*, Arr. *An.* 1.17.12*, Ath. *Deip.* 13.593a–b*, D.C. 48.24.2*, D.S. 19.63.5, Hdt. 3.48, Just. 27.1.4–7, Lys. 13.23–29, Paus. 7.2.7*, Plut. *Alex.* 42.1*, Suid. s.v. Ἔφορος, X. *An.* 1.6.7*, *HG* 6.5.9, 2 *Macc.* 4.33–38 (shared with Artemis).

Zeus (9): Apollod. *Epit.* 2.13, E. *HF* 1–327, Hdt. 5.46, 5.119.2, Paus. 3.17.9, 5.5.1, Procl. *Chr.* 107 = *EGF* p. 62, Th. 1.101.2–103, 5.16.3.

Poseidon (9, Helice asterisked, Taenarus double asterisked): Paus. 4.24.5–6**, 7.1.8*, 7.24.6*, Plut. *Agis* 16.3**, Polyaen. 8.46.1*, S. *OC* 1156–1205, Str. 8.6.14, Th. 1.128.1**, 1.133**.

receive no more than an act apiece. Dionysus receives notice only on a boundary stone that implies that supplication took place in the adjacent shrine.[42] For the most part, the gods of supplication are those of the community as a whole, as opposed either to Dionysus, a god of the *thiasos* or "cult," or to Ares, Hades, Hermes, Hephaestus, gods for individuals or other groups.[43] Most of the gods of supplication, moreover, are patrons or patronesses of cities. More than half of all acts performed to Artemis involve Artemis of Ephesus, where she is patroness. Almost half of all acts to Poseidon involve Poseidon at Helice, where he is patron of a federation. All acts performed to Heracles Melkarth involve his famous shrine at Tyre.

A third reason is access. A powerful person may not always be reachable. Instead he may be on the far side of a closed door, as described in *Odyssey* 4, in which Telemachus must wait at the door of Menelaus. A servant looks Telemachus over but refuses to admit him until the master of the house approves.[44] The same might happen in classical Greece. Complaining to Cimon as an Athenian army marched through the Isthmus, a Corinthian said that it was customary to knock on the door and to wait for an invitation. In Athens, the Corinthian might have added, only a decree of the Council and Assembly gave access against the householder's wishes.[45] A suppliant may find the way to the door or entry blocked by watchdogs, as happens to Odysseus when he tries to approach the hut of Eumaeus. He sits down, thus pacifying them.[46] In contrast, no suppliant ever finds the entrance to a shrine closed.[47] Nor were altars in marketplaces closed. And altars, even those in shrines, are accessible for another reason: they are numerous. When crossing a frontier, a suppliant who feared pursuers would duck into the first shrine

---

Apollo (7): A. *Eu.* 1–93, E. *Ion* 1255–1613, Hdt. 7.141, Ctes. 688 *FGrH* fr. 9, 2 *Macc.* 4.33–38 (shared with Artemis), Tz. ad Lyc. 307.

Heracles Melkarth (5) as in chap. 1, n. 93.

Demeter (5): Ar. *Thes.* 689–946, E. *Supp.* 1–361, Hdt. 6.91.2, Paus. 8.27.6, *P. Berol.* 11771.12–22 = *CGF* 239.12–22.

Hera (5): Apollod. 1.9.8, 1.9.28, Th. 3.81.2–4, X. *HG* 4.5.5–6, Tz. *H.* 1.456–92.

42. *LSAM* #75.

43. No acts to Hephaestus, Hades, and Iris. Two to Aphrodite: Pl. *Rud.* 559–680, 688–869. Among heroes and lesser gods: the Dioscuri (Th. 3.75.3–5, Plut. *Aem.* 23.11), Thetis (E. *And.* 1–412), and Proteus (E. *Hel.* 1–556). The one historical example: Schol. Dem. 1.41 (Amyntas). Proleptic supplication at a hero's shrine: S. *Aj.* 1171–1373.

44. *Od.* 4.20–36. A different view: Higbie, *Heroes' Names*, 155–56, and Gödde, *Drama der Hikesie*, 21 n. 52, both holding that Telemachus should have been admitted promptly. Also hostile: Meleager, who shuts the door against suppliants (*Il.* 9.581); Howald, "Meleager," 407, objects to this behavior as "burlesk." Admittedly comic: Anaxarete rejecting the liminal supplications of an *exclusus amator* (Ov. *Met.* 14.701–42). No trouble entering: Ov. *Met.* 7.298–300, but with disastrous results for those who admit Medea.

45. Plut. *Cim.* 17.1, Lys. 12.30 with remarks by Lacey, *Family*, 161–62, on one of the motives, the segregation of potential supplicandae. The legal background: E. Harris, *Aeschines*, appendix 9, Harrison, *Procedure*, 86. A Macedonian example of this kind of supplication: shunned by Alexander, his army supplicated his doorstep at Opis, in Mesopotamia (Arr. *An.* 7.11.4–7, Plut. *Alex.* 71.4–5.).

46. *Od.* 14.30–31, 511.

47. At. Hdt. 6.91.2, a temple is closed, but not the shrine in which it stands. I assume that suppliants in Phoenicia or even Carthage go to the shrine but not necessarily to a temple within it, but since the altar in a Phoenician or Carthaginian shrine would be inside a temple, not outside, suppliants wishing to reach the altar would need to go when the temple was open. Lézine, *Carthage*, does not discuss the issue.

that appeared. In Athens, Colonus and Marathon served this end.[48] Suppliants seeking to avoid pursuers by going overseas would stop at maritime shrines. In Athens, the temple of Artemis at the port of Munychia was available.[49] Sparta shows the same pattern. Those leaving it would cross over the border into Arcadia and head for the shrine of Athena Alea in Tegea. Or they would visit the shrine at Taenarus and leave by sea.[50]

Cultures other than Greece provided alternatives to the altar. A Hebrew alternative was the gate of the town of refuge. To this spot came suppliant killers seeking protection from avenging relatives as described in *Deuteronomy* and *Numbers*. This alternative had the advantages of convenience, since the elders would gather there for other reasons; of visibility, since it was a prominent place; and of access, since it was at the edge of town.[51] A Roman alternative, borrowed from Ptolemaic Egypt, was for the suppliant to go to a statue of the emperor. This had the same three advantages: convenience, because magistrates would respond; prominence, thanks to the emperor; and access, because statues were numerous.

The gate and statue gave suppliants access to public, political supplicandi such as judges and kings. Another place of appeal, the hearth, gave access to both public and private supplicandi. As hearths were the seat of a goddess, the Greek Hestia and the Roman Vesta, they were not less impressive than altars, and if the hearth was that of a king, it belonged to a powerful human supplicandus and his family.[52] Among the few suppliants able to reach a royal hearth, Themistocles leads, but this time because of his success in approaching the king of Molossia. When he arrived there, the king was away, so he presented himself to the queen, who welcomed him. When the king returned, he found Themistocles seated at the hearth holding the king's own infant son. The queen had given him the child to hold.[53] One source, Plutarch, presents two explanations for the collusion between the queen and the suppliant:

> Some say that the queen, Phthia, suggested to Themistocles this way of supplicating, and placed her young son with him before the hearth. Others say that king Admetus wished to be under a religious obligation not to deliver Themistocles to his pursuers and staged a sort of play for this purpose.[54]

Either way, the suppliant has combined an approach to the hearth, an approach to the king, and access to the king's family.

48. Marathon: E. *Heracl.* Colonus: S. *OC.*

49. Lys. 13.23–29, also Dem. 18.107 if the defaulting trierarchs described there ever fled Athens.

50. Athena *Alea*: as at n. 40 above. Poseidon at Taenarus: as at n. 41 above.

51. *Nu.* 35.9–25, *De.* 19.4–12. Elders at gate to judge suppliants: *Jo.* 20.1–7. At gate for other reasons: *Il.* 3.148–49.

52. Hearth as altar: schol. Aeschin. 2.45. Domestic hearth: Hdt. 1.35.1, perhaps 4.165.2; D.H. 8.1.5. Other suppliants in homes, hence probably at hearths: Paus. 10.19.7, when Ptolemy "the Thunderbolt" flees to Seleucus; and many foreign examples, including Plut. *Luc.* 14.7 and Cic. *Man.* 21, when Mithridates flees, or is expected to flee, to neighboring kings.

53. Th. 1.136.2–37.1.

54. Plut. *Them.* 24.2–3. Similar except for role of wife: Th. loc. cit. Supplication at *sacrarium* with child: Nep. *Them.* 8.4. At hearth without child: D.S. 11.56.1–4. Plutarch's "others" include Thucydides.

Plutarch calls this "the most sacred kind of supplication among the Molossians, and not to be refused," and Thucydides, the other important source for these events, even calls it τὸ μέγιστον ἱκέτευμα, or "the most powerful" of all.[55] Why these unparalleled statements? Not just because of the hearth, though it provides a venue for the suppliant.[56] Were the hearth the only factor, Plutarch and Thucydides would be saying something like what Plutarch says about the Persians, whose most powerful manner of supplication was for the suppliant to walk into a river carrying a sacred fire and threaten to drop it in the water if his request was not granted.[57] Or these authors would be saying something like what Greek sources report about the Scythians, another people with a "most powerful" form of supplication. Theirs was for the victim of wrongdoing to sit on a cowhide, hands behind his back, a posture that showed that the victim renounced vengeance.[58] The Persians esteemed an element, fire, and the Scythians esteemed a gesture, sitting on a hide. The Greeks, however, preferred an ensemble of elements: the hearth, the king, and access to the king's family.

An example from Homer shows that this sort of supplication was not suitable only for the semibarbarous Molossians. When Odysseus lands on Scheria, he solicits advice from Nausicaa, the king's teenage daughter, and when he arrives at her father's house, he sits at the hearth, as Themistocles did. Again like Themistocles, he speaks to the queen before he speaks to the king. The one difference is that he clasps the queen's knees before taking his place at the hearth. The two elements of hearth and royal supplicandus are otherwise the same. The third element, access to the royal family, changes more, but is still recognizable. Although Odysseus does not hold a child at the hearth as Themistocles does, he does have a cloak that Nausicaa has given him. The queen identifies the cloak, but she says nothing about it until her husband, the king, has accepted the suppliant.[59]

Scheria is an imaginary place, no more similar to classical Greece than Molossia is. But if we look for less far-fetched examples, only the Telephus of Euripides presents himself. This suppliant comes to the house of Agamemnon under a pseudonym. When Agamemnon discovers his identity and decides to attack him, Telephus

55. Plut. *Them.* 24.2 (ταύτην μεγίστην καὶ μόνην σχεδὸν ἀναντίρρητον ἡγουμένων ἱκεσίαν τῶν Μολοσσῶν) and Th. 1.137.1. A compatible view: Gomme ad Th. loc. cit., holding that the story is true and not derived from Euripides' *Telephus*. A third possibility: a Molossian source for Euripides, as implied by Hammond, *Epirus*, 492, when observing that Molossian society had many Homeric features. Whatever the skein of influences, the motif of suppliant and child was current.

56. Gould, *"Hiketeia"* 98–100 says that the hearth makes this kind of supplication distinctive. Other views: Newton, "Rebirth of Odysseus," 17, seeing an attempt by the suppliant to act as a son; Boegehold, *Gesture*, 14, assuming that Themistocles supplicated the queen by clasping her knees; and Bremmer, "Gelon's Wife," holding that in ancient Mediterranean societies the wife had the power to admit guests to the house, as in these cases and also at *Od.* 7.139–71, discussed immediately below, and *h. Cer.* 160–63.

57. Plut. *Primo Frigido* 950f. For the sacredness of fire, vital for ritual and associated with Ahura Mazda, see Widengren, *Religionen Irans*, 31–35. Some fires, like those from which temple fires were lit, were never allowed to go out, a custom that may inform this kind of supplication.

58. Suidas s.v. ἐπὶ βύρσης ἐκαθέζετο, citing a proverb also found in CPG 1.410, 2.416–17. In his description of a form of Scythian *hiketeia* used to ransom prisoners, Lucian stresses the same trait of self-abnegation on the part of Scythian suppliants (*Tox.* 40, 42).

59. *Od.* 7.238–39.

supplicates much as Themistocles and Odysseus do. According to Hyginus, "After [the king's wife] Clytemnestra warned him, he snatched the infant Orestes from the cradle and he went to King Agamemnon," words that may mean that the supplication occurred at an altar in the house.[60] Since Agamemnon, unlike the king of the Molossians, does not accommodate the suppliant, Telephus holds the child hostage.[61] Meanwhile the mother either keeps her distance or attempts to save the child.[62] In a parody in Aristophanes, the mother threatens to attack the hostage taker, Mnesilochus.[63]

At other times and places, no supplication includes the elements of hearth, king, and child, but these three examples form a bridge between supplication at a royal hearth in a monarchy—an event that must have occurred often, even without a child—and supplication at a comparable location, the common hearth of a community under an oligarchy or democracy. Though seldom reported, supplication at a common hearth must have occurred often.[64] Common hearths aside, the examples of Themistocles and company also form a bridge between supplication at a royal hearth and supplication at the hearth of a private home. Here, too, the hearth served as an altar. In Xenophon of Ephesus, where the suppliant is a slavemaster and the supplicanda is her slave, the owner uses the hearth in her own house to lend solemnity to an oath that she wishes the supplicanda to swear. This time the party controlling the hearth is—for the moment—a slave, not the head of the house, a reversal that confirms the norm.[65]

A problem that may arise with either altar or hearth is determining who controls it. This problem cannot have been frequent, but it does appear in Aeschylus and Euripides. As many scholars have observed, the suppliants in the *Suppliants* of Aeschylus do not know who controls the Argive altars to which they come out of fear of the pharaoh of Egypt. They think the king controls them. Yet the king says that he shares control of them with the Assembly.[66] The suppliants refuse to accept this explanation and threaten the king with punishment at the hands of Zeus. But he holds firm, insisting that the case go to the Assembly.[67] Not thinking that the suppliants are equal to the task of appearing there, he asks their father, Danaus, who has not made their mistake about control, to perform this task, and so Danaus goes there without them. The girls await the outcome of their father's appeal in a grove, often a place of refuge, here both a refuge and a waiting

---

60. Hyg. *Fab.* 101.2. *TGF* 699 may refer to Clytemnestra's helping Telephus, but the other fragments of the Euripidean play do not, nor do the rest of the sources canvassed by Handley and Rea, *Telephos*, 36–37.

61. Cf. Nep. *Them.* 8.4, "non prius egressus est (Themistocles), quam rex eum data dextra in fidem reciperet."

62. Mother to the rescue: Naples Mus. Naz. RC 141 (86.064) = *LCS* 340 n. 804, pls. 133, 34 = *LIMC* 12. s.v. *Agamemnon*, 18, an Attic red-figure vase.

63. Ar. *Thes.* 689–946. Ahl and Roisman, *Odyssey Reformed*, 296 n. 33, note the parallel with Odysseus and in particular with Arete.

64. Ar. 4.1759–61, Plut. *QG* 299d, Plb. 30.9.1–11; the altar of the Athenian council is also called a hearth (X. *HG* 2.3.52). Many instances of *hiketeuô* vel sim. may refer to public hearths without mentioning them.

65. X. Eph. 2.3.4–5.

66. A. *Supp.* 365–74, noticed by Garvie, *Aeschylus' Supplices*, 150–51.

67. Threat: A. *Supp.* 459–79 but with earlier hints at 154–61. Reference to the assembly: 481–85.

area.[68] Aeschylus contrasts both the king's and the father's understanding of supplication with the girls' ignorance.

Questions about control can also arise if the suppliants are Greek, as happens in the *Suppliants* of Euripides. This time, the women are Argives supplicating at Athenian altars, and their male chaperone is the erstwhile king of Argos, Adrastus. Rather than seek protection, the women ask for help in recovering the bodies of their husbands and sons, casualties in a war between Argos and Thebes. But these differences do not keep them from having the same problem: mistaking who has control. First they come to the altar, and, finding the queen mother there, supplicate both it and her, thinking that control belongs to her.[69]

At first the Argive women meet with failure. The queen cannot help them, and the king, who can, rejects them. Changing tactics, they leave both the altar and the queen and approach the king, who has been standing some way off.[70] And they are about to fail again when the king turns to his mother, still at the altar. She then talks her son into relenting and into helping the women with the Assembly, which shares power with the king, as in Aeschylus.[71] The greater complexity of the Euripidean scene rests on a double twist: two supplicandi, a queen as well as a king, and two supplications, one to her and the altar, and one to him. Meanwhile, the suppliants must eventually go to the Assembly and supplicate there, too, again as in Aeschylus. Euripides preserves old problems and introduces new ones, surpassing yet absorbing his predecessor.

Intercession

If a suppliant cannot appear in person or speaks poorly, he or she may send another person as a representative. Metellus Pius, for one, intercedes for a suppliants who cannot appear because he is in exile. Similar to him are the numerous suppliants who are diplomats. The largest groups of suppliants interceding on behalf of those who speak poorly are *sunegoroi*, supporters who may supplicate on behalf of defendants in Greek courts, and *patroni*, advocates who may supplicate on behalf of defendants in Rome.[72] Cicero often does so.[73]

Metellus Pius and Cicero aside, successful intercessors are often women.[74] The mythic model for these intercessors is Justice, sitting beside Zeus in Hesiod; the epic model is Thetis, crouching before the god on behalf of her son. Rome offers two models, one for the Principate and one for the late Republic. The model for the Principate is Livia, whom Tacitus describes as a *refugium* for those who

---

68. Girls to the grove: A. *Supp.* 509–12.

69. Altar: E. *Supp.* 1–361. Queen as well: 7–9.

70. Rejection: E. *Supp.* 249–50. Approach to king Theseus: 277–81.

71. The queen's advice to Theseus: E. *Supp.* 307–13, 320. The assembly: 349–51.

72. For Greek diplomatic acts directed toward Greeks, see 57 below. Diplomatic acts by or to Romans or Italians: D.H. 6.18.1–21.2, 7.5.1–2, 17/18.1.3–4, D.S. 32.6.3–4, Plb. 1.35.4, 15.8.12, Liv. 29.16.6–7, 45.20.9–25.4, Vell. 2.109.2, Zonar. 9.26. Greek but not diplomatic: Charito 5.10.4. Roman but not diplomatic: Liv. 3.58.1–6 (449 BCE), 22.60.1–61.3, Ov. *Pont.* 4.6.10–12, V. Fl. 4.60–79, D.C. 80.19.3 (222 CE). Hebraeo-Roman: J. *BJ* 1.566.

73. As in n. 213 below. Intercession by a supporter comparable to an advocate: V. Max. 2.7.8.

74. A similar formulation: Rehm, *Marriage to Death*, 98.

have offended Tiberius.[75] If Augustus's wife is an unsurprising model, her Republican counterpart is surprisingly like Metellus Pius. This woman was the wife of a well-placed but unknown Roman who, like many others, suffered during the proscriptions that marked the Roman civil wars. Seeking relief, she approached the triumvir Aemilius Lepidus, who was seeking to deny to her husband the help promised to him by Augustus. She was interceding, the same as Pius, she performed the same gesture, falling at the feet, and she made a similar argument: Augustus had issued a judgment in her husband's favor, so the law was on her side. Then, as if on cue, Lepidus's lictors beat her. To this indignity, she responded by displaying her wounds.[76] Lepidus, of course, found that he must accede to Augustus's judgment. The episode is so favorable to her (and Augustus) and so unfavorable to Lepidus that it is not only a record of an event that surely took place but also an exaggeration of this event so as to make a wife and mother no less dutiful than a son.

Successful imitators come in these genres and more, and failure is very rare.[77] The reason for these successes is not that the intercessors are female, for women sometimes fail at supplication.[78] Euripides, to be sure, tries to give the impression that supplication by women differs from supplication by men; some of his characters even say that men should not supplicate. But Euripides' own work belies him, and so do other sources from Homer onward.[79] (So, for that matter, do earlier Near Eastern sources. The first recorded act of supplication, in the *Epic of Gilgamesh*, features a male suppliant who asks another male to intercede for him. The suppliant, the monster Humbaba, turns to Enkidu because Enkidu can speak to Gilgamesh better than the monster can.)[80] Perhaps women are successful intercessors because they are less prepossessing. Metellus Pius must overcome being a consul's son and thus being superior to his supplicandus, a tribune. Justice, Thetis, and Livia have no such liability. Still less do other women suffer from it. Perhaps women are also more skillful. The most skillful is a nameless woman who

75. Hes. *Op.* 259, where καθεζομένη means "sitting" but evokes supplication. Thetis: as in n. 112 below. Livia: Tac. *Ann.* 5.3.

76. *LT* 10–15.

77. Successes by Romans: D.H. 1.79.2 (daughter to Amulius on behalf of Ilia); Polyaen. 8.25.3, Plut. *Cor.* 36.3–4, D.H. 8.40–43.2, 8.45.1–54.1 (Mother and others to Coriolanus on behalf of Romans); D.C. 47.8.5 (Julia to Antony on behalf of Lucius Caesar in 43 BCE). By or to Greeks, beginning with mythic and heroic examples, but excluding Thetis: Serv. *A.* 3.73 (Leto to Jupiter on behalf of Asterie), Plut. *Agis* 17.1–18.2 (daughter to father on behalf of husband), *Mul. Virt.* 262e (miners' wives to mine owner on behalf of husbands); perhaps Plut. *Sol.* 12.2 (Cylonians to wives of Athenian magistrates). Failures: Liv. 22.60.1–61.3, wives and mothers demanding a violation of *mos* in 216 BCE; X. *Eph.* 2.6.5, by a slave; perhaps Stat. *Ach.* 1.48–51, where Neptune rejects Thetis, an inversion of the norm, but where it is not clear that she interceding on Achilles' behalf rather than attempting to prevent him from achieving the fame that is his due; J. *BJ* 1.566, failure of Livia before Herod on behalf of Salome.

78. As shown by tables 3.1 and 3.2, listing the following rejected female suppliants: #11, 12, 17, 18, 21–23, 27, 47, 48, 54–56, 60, 65, or 15 of 70 in table 3.1; and #12, 14, or 2 of 34 in table 3.2. These tables appear at the end of chap. 3.

79. Supplication for women only: E. *Hel.* 947–51. For male suppliants in Euripides, see appendix 1a under this author.

80. *SB* 5.175–82. The forest-bred Enkidu might also sympathize with the monster. Two savages, they might collaborate in taming the anger of the civilized man.

intercedes on behalf of Joab when the latter wishes to ask King David to allow his exiled son, Absalom, to return. She makes two requests. The first, which David grants, mollifies him, making it easier for her to make the second request, for Absalom's return. David then grants this request, too.[81]

When suppliants enlist others to plead for them, they make the most dramatic choice occurring at the first step. But the most important choice is between person and altar (as with Phemius) and the most common is between one person or group and another, and between one altar or shrine and another. To make these choices, suppliants must see where power lies, and so they must understand politics. Their calculations vary by culture, and, as tragedy shows, they vary by genre and even by author. They do not suit either the ritual of contact posited by Gould or the ritual of submission posited by Burkert.

GESTURES AND WORDS

The second step of an act of supplication serves two purposes, one more common than the other. First, it always communicates the intent to supplicate. Both gestures and words may communicate this intent. Second, it sometimes expresses the suppliant's wish not only to be heard but also to be welcomed and accepted. On this score, gestures are more effective, including gestures in which the suppliant closes the distance between himself and the supplicandus and sometimes makes contact. But the superiority of gestures is not the whole story. Sometimes gestures are impossible or inappropriate, and then the suppliant resorts to words. Suppliants may use a gesture and words in combination, as Phemius and Leodes do when they clasp Odysseus's knees and also say that they are supplicating.

Words and gestures, then, are complementary means to the two ends of communication and expression. Both are "signals," a term derived from Aeschylus's *Suppliants*, in which the king of Argos calls the boughs that the Danaids place on the town altars a σημεῖον πόνου, or a "distress signal."[82] Such a signal is partly an SOS: it communicates. But it also expresses emotion. For instance, a drowning man extends his hands for both purposes. Drowning men happen to figure among ancient suppliants, and the gesture that they use is just this: to extend their hands.[83]

The difference between putting a bough on an altar and extending one's hands toward a passing ship points to another feature of the second step: variety. Though circumstances account for some of this variety, culture accounts for more of it. Greek gestures and words differ from Roman and Hebrew ones, which happen to resemble one another. Greek gestures begin with the knee clasp (prominent in Homer and tragedy) and include touching other parts of the body, extending hands

---

81. 2 *Ki.* 14.4–24, J. *AJ.* 7.182–84.

82. σημεῖον: A. *Supp.* 506. Similarly, Schlesinger, *Griechische Asylie*, 34–35 refers to "Abzeichen." A different view: Burkert, *Mythology and Ritual*, 43–45, linking the bough to the *stibas*, a ritualistic bolster or resting place made of branches.

83. Drowning and supplicating successfully: Ach. Tat. 5.9.3, Cic. *Inv.* 2.153. Supplicating from aboard ship, but not when drowning: Plut. *Cam.* 8.5.

to the supplicandus but not touching him, and depositing boughs on altars. Roman and Hebrew gestures begin with falling low, which also avoids contact with the supplicandus, and include donning mourning dress as well as extending hands.[84] The chief terms are Greek *hiketeuô* and its compounds and cognates; Greek *lissomai*, found in early sources; and Latin *supplico* and its cognates. Two other words may replace them, but only in certain circumstances. Greek *feugô* and its compounds may replace *hiketeuô* if a suppliant goes to the home of a supplicandus, but not otherwise. Latin *obsecro* and *deprecor* may replace *supplico* in acts of supplication in Cicero, an author prone to variation.[85]

None of these gestures or words suffice to establish that supplication is occurring. That requires all four steps.[86] But the number and variety of these gestures and words support two conclusions, first, that every gesture has its own merits, its own way of being expressive as well as communicative, and second, that whatever the merits of gestures of contact, these gestures are not indispensable. Rather than make all acts of supplication alike, gestures make many unique.

Gestures

The gestures that do make contact begin with clasping the knee and include touching the chin, hand, or feet. Most suppliants able to perform these gestures do so, and for obvious reasons: making contact is both expressive and arresting. Rich in content, gestures are signals of a distinct type, examples of what psychologists have termed "ideographic signs" that "diagram the structure of what is said."[87] They provide a second language to the suppliant, one that lets him commit his entire person and that obliges the supplicandus to respond in kind. In this respect, the knee clasp is especially effective. While letting the suppliant draw near, it also lets him raise his face in order to speak and emote. No less important, this gesture makes it impossible for the supplicandus to reject a suppliant without effort. More than any other gesture, and far more than any word, the knee clasp lends urgency to an appeal. In *Odyssey* 22, for example, the avenging Odysseus has worked without pause or distraction. When he finishes, he will have to fumigate the house—a task that he will carry out with the same single-mindedness. Unless he breaks his rhythm, he will give no more thought to killing the suppliants Phemius and Leodes than he has to killing a hundred others. So they must

84. The only comparably lengthy treatment: Sittl, *Gebärden*, chaps. 9–10, confined to gestures appearing in art. Treatments confined to the gestures achieving *Kontaktmagie* are brief and numerous; see 9–10 above. The only extant ancient treatment: Nil. Anc. 7, confined to gestures with the hands.

85. Especially when describing acts performed by defendants, supporters, and advocates. The appendix dealing with these acts shows that these two words mean the same as *supplico* vel sim, as at Cic. Mil. 100, 103; so also Caes. Civ. 1.22.3–6. A case where the suppliant asks the supplicandus to perform a gestures indicating acceptance, but does not perform a supplicatory gesture himself: V. Fl. 7.490–510.

86. No close study has dealt with the others, but for *lissomai* see Aubriot-Sévin, *Prière*, 455–65, preceded by Benveniste, *Vocabulaire*, 2.248. Both define it so that it may or may not accompany supplication, and R. Lattimore, *Iliad* concurs, translating it as "entreat" (*Il.* 1.282), "beg" (*Il.* 19.305), "supplicate" (*Od.* 2.68), and "implore" (*Od.* 4.328).

87. Richness of gestures: Birdwhistell, *Kinesics*, 85–91, followed by Poyatos, *Paralanguage*, who in his chaps. 9–11 gives examples of the manipulation of the meaning of gestures in modern European literature. "Ideographic" gestures: Kendon, "Current Issues in Nonverbal Communication," 31.

capture his attention no matter what the risk. Above all, they must draw close to him and make him see them as individuals, not targets. They should make him aware of their warmth and their breathing. That, too, may give him pause. Only the knee clasp meets these needs.

When Phemius and Leodes clasp Odysseus's knees, they follow the lead of about one-third of the suppliants in Homer.[88] Warriors use this gesture to avoid being slain. Circe uses it to bring Odysseus to bed, and one of Odysseus's soldiers, Eurylochus, uses it to avoid going into battle.[89] If every act of flight in Homer is thought to include this gesture (as is possible, since several suppliants enter homes, as fugitives do, and clasp knees) the proportion of those using it rises to one-half.[90] The proportion is high in other epic poets, too.[91] In tragedy, with its similar subject matter, the proportion is again about one-half, provided that we exclude acts performed at altars and that we assume that whenever a suppliant describes this gesture, or very nearly describes it, he is also performing it.[92] Nor is this proportion surprising. These suppliants, too, fear for their lives or for the loss of something scarcely less valuable, such as the loyalty of a family member.

In other genres, however, the proportion of suppliants clasping knees falls. In some instances in which a source says only that someone is a suppliant, *hiketês*, this gesture may be taken for granted. But this is far from the only reason that Herodotus, Thucydides, and Diodorus Siculus, three historians who survive in bulk, report clasping the knees in only one-quarter of all acts of personal supplication.[93] In Herodotus, for one, a shepherd's wife uses it when pleading with her husband not to follow the orders of the king of Persia and kill a foundling, and the Persian concubine uses it when pleading with her Greek captors after the battle of Plataea, but a diplomat does not use it when addressing the king of Sparta. Neither does Demaratus, a Spartan prince who approaches his mother to ask her to tell him the true identity of his father.[94] The latter situations are less urgent than the former. In Thucydides, no one uses it. Among those who do not are

---

88. Fourteen of 45 acts in all, including 6 in the *Iliad* (1.495–530, 6.45–65, 9.451–3, 20.463–9, 21.64–119, 24.477–570) and 8 in the *Odyssey* (7.139–71, 10.264–73, 10.323–47, 10.480–95, 14.276–80, 22.310–29, 22.330–56, 22.361–77). Twelve figurative knee clasps are excluded.

89. Battlefield: *Il.* 6.45–65, 20.463–69, 21.64–119, *Od.* 14.276–80. Eurylochus: *Od.* 10.264–73. Circe: *Od.* 10. 480–95. Others: *Il.* 1.495–530, 9.451–53.

90. The total rises by 9 to 23 out of 45 (adding *Il.* 2.653–57, 9.478–83, 13.694–97, 14.258–61, 15.431–32, 16.570–74, 23.85–90, *Od.* 16.424–30, 20.222–23).

91. A.R. 3.706, 4.82, 4.1011–12, or 3 acts of 6; Tryph. 263, 647, 2 acts of 3; but less in Latin writers: Sil. It. 8.74, 1 act out of 9, and V. A. 3.607, 10.523, 2 acts out of 13.

92. Seventeen acts performed on these assumptions, largely accepted by Kaimio, *Physical Contact*, chap. 5, with refs.: E. *And.* 537–40, 539–717, 894–984, *Hec.* 245–50, 342–45, 752–856, *Hel.* 894–1004, *IA* 900–936, 1214–75, *IT* 1068–78, *Med.* 324–51, 709–53, *Or.* 380–721, *Ph.* 923–59, *Tro.* 1042–57, *Phaethon* fr. 781.72–74 *TGF*, S. *OC* 1267–1396. Thirteen not performed: A. *Ag.* 231–47, *Ch.* 896–930, E. *Alc.* 400–403, *Cyc.* 285–327, *El.* 1206–15, *Hec.* 1127–28, *IA* 1153–56, *Or.* 1506–27, *Ph.* 1567–69, S. *Aj.* 587–90, *OT* 326–29, *Ph.* 468–529, 927–35. Four acts where knees are not clasped, but a chin or hand is clasped: E. *HF* 986–95, *Hec.* 286–305, *Hipp.* 325–35, 605–11.

93. Seven acts performed: Hdt. 1.112, 9.76.2–3, D.S. 17.35.5, 32.23, 34/35.28, 36.15.2–3, 36.16. Nineteen acts not performed: Hdt. 5.51, 6.68, Th. 1.136.2–37.1, 3.58.2–3, 4.38.1, D.S. 10.16.4, 11.56.1–4, 13.19.2–33.1, 17.22.4, 17.91.4, 17.96.5, 17.102.7, 17.108.3, 17.108.6–7, 24.10.2, 26.20.1–2, 31.5.3, 32.6.3–4, 33.5.1–4.

94. Hdt. 1.112 (wife), 9.76.2 (concubine) versus 5.51 (diplomat), 6.68 (prince).

Themistocles and two groups of soldiers. The latter are less vulnerable than Homer's individual warriors, and so once again the situation is less urgent.[95]

The absence of individual suppliants in Thucydides is revealing. Of the acts in which the three historians do report the knee clasp, all but two are performed by one person to another.[96] These two are serial acts in which a Roman politician supplicates each member of a Roman assembly.[97] Here the suppliant remains an individual, and the supplicandi are approached as individuals. In contrast, most of the acts in which the gesture does not occur are performed by or to a group.[98] The rest of the acts occur at or near a hearth.[99] Besides being urgent, the knee clasp is private.

Because it is both urgent and private, the knee clasp has its own social and literary profile. Socially, it is better suited to acts in which the supplicandus is a father or captor as opposed to a king or commander. In literary terms, it is better suited to acts that are described at some length, and so it gives the suppliant a chance to lay hold and speak rather than merely to present himself as an *hiketês*. These acts are tableaux suitable for recitation and especially for the stage, where action and words echo one another.[100] For both social and literary reasons, then, the knee clasp is better suited to epic and tragedy than to prose. And so it clusters in epic and tragedy.

This is not to say that authors cannot manipulate it. Fiction is a genre with many occasions for urgent, private, and dramatic gestures, and so it ought to include many knee clasps. Some acts of supplication in Greek fiction are described in Homeric terms, another reason to expect knee clasps.[101] And so two of the five extant Greek novelists, Chariton and Xenophon of Ephesus, include knee clasps in nearly every possible case.[102] But another, Longus, fails to include it in any case. He prefers that contact be erotic. The remaining novelist, Heliodorus, describes a siege, and here he omits the knee clasp because it does not suit a community addressing an army, but otherwise he includes it most of the time. When he does not, he may be taking it for granted. Unlike Longus, he does not stereotype physical contact.[103]

The handling of this gesture by the novelists points to a general conclusion: no one gesture can achieve every effect. This same conclusion explains why some suppliants do not rest content with the knee clasp and instead add two other gestures to it. They kiss the supplicandus's hand or clasp his chin. Several versions of Priam's supplication of Achilles in *Iliad* 24 show how the first of these two

95. Two groups: Th. 3.58.2–3, 4.38.1.

96. Including three such acts in Diodorus: D.S. 17.35.5, 32.23, 34/35.28.

97. D.S. 36.15.2–3, 36.16, both acts performed by Roman politicians to Roman assembly members.

98. Exceptions: Hdt. 6.68, perhaps D.S. 10.16.4.

99. Th. 1.136.2–37.1, Hdt. 1.35, 4.165.2–67.1, 5.51, perhaps DS 11.56.1–4.

100. As argued by Taplin, *Tragedy in Action*; see "Suppliancy" in his index.

101. Charito 2.7.2–3, X. Eph. 1.13.6–14.1.

102. Chariton: 5 times out of a total of 6 acts (2.7.2–3, 2.10.2–11.6, 3.2.1, 3.5.5–6, 4.3.9–4.2). Xenophon of Ephesus: 7 of a total of 11 acts (1.13.6–14.1, 2.5.6–6.1, 2.6.5, 2.9.4, 2.10.2, 3.5.5, 5.5.6).

103. Surrender: Hld. 9.6.1–2, 9.11.4–5. Included: 1.12.3, 4.18.1, 5.26.3, 7.23.7, 10.10.1, 10.38.1. Not mentioned, but perhaps taken for granted: 2.13.4, 5.25.1. Similar is Achilles Tatius, where the knees are mentioned only in connection with amatory requests (5.17.3–5, 8.17.3–4).

gestures, kissing the hand, affects the act in which it occurs. In Homer's version, Priam finds Achilles sitting in his chair (θρόνου, 515): "After slipping by the servants, great Priam entered. Standing beside Achilles, he took Achilles' knees in his hands and kissed the terrible, man-killing hands that had slain many of his sons."[104] Figure 2.2 shows how easy it is to perform these gestures in front of someone sitting.[105] But if Achilles is reclining, a number of painters reckoned that Priam could not reach both knees and hands, and must settle for the knees alone, as in figure 2.3.[106] Nor will Priam be eager to kiss a hand that, as in figure 2.3, holds a knife. This trio of versions shows that kissing the hand, like clasping the knee, requires suitable circumstances. As for the expressive effect of kissing the hand, the ancient commentator Eustathius remarks that the hand represents someone's capacity to act, τὸ πρακτικόν; similarly, it represents the power to make a pledge.[107] Priam, then, is expressing the wish that Achilles make a pledge; the kiss adds deference to this wish.[108] An example from Euripides follows this model. When the nurse takes hold of Phaedra by the knees but also by the hand, she is trying to extract a commitment from her. She does not kiss Phaedra's hand, and so she is not expressing deference; to the contrary, she must have often taken Phaedra's hand when Phaedra was a child, and so she is reminding the supplicanda of this tie between them.[109]

To explain the second gesture, taking the supplicandus by the chin, the commentator Eustathius says that the head represents decisiveness, τὸ ἡγεμονικόν, and so touching the latter would be a way of expressing a wish that the supplicandus make up his mind.[110] Hence another character in Euripides, Polyxena, regrets not being able to touch the chin of Odysseus.[111] Her failure makes it easier for him not to meet his responsibility as the supplicandus. On the other hand, Thetis is able to touch the chin of Zeus when she supplicates him in *Iliad* 1. Since she clasps his knees, too, she is expressing both urgency and a hint of just what his respon-

---

104. *Il.* 24.478–80.

105. Fig. 2.2: Copenhagen Nat. Mus. from Hoby = Trendall-Webster 57 III.1.22 = *LIMC* 1.2 s.v. *Achilles*, 687 (A. Kossatz-Deissman), a Roman silver goblet of the Augustan period.

106. Fig. 2.3: Fogg, Cambridge, Mass. 1972.40 = *Para.* 324 = *LIMC* 1.2 s.v. *Achilles*, 655, a hydria from ca. 510 BCE. A Priam who settles for nothing and instead extends his hands toward Achilles: Kassel T 674 = *Para.* 56.31 bis = *LIMC* 1.2 s.v. *Achilles*, 645. In Toledo Mus. of Art 72.54 = *CVA Toledo* 1 pl. 4.1, 5.1 = *LIMC* 1.2 s.v. *Achilles*, 649, he extends his hands toward Achilles' head, but he makes no gesture in Vienna Kunsthist. Mus. 3710 = *ARV*² 380, 171 = *LIMC* s.v. *Achilles*, 659. Or he can take a seat on the edge of the couch, again with no gesture: private coll. = *ARV*² 399, 1650 = *LIMC* s.v. *Achilles*, 661. These are black-figure vases.

107. Eustathius: ad *Il.* 1.427, where he explains these associations "according to the ancients" (τοῖς παλαιοῖς), among whom is Serv. A. 3.607. His association of the hand and τὸ πρακτικόν also appears in the *EM* 256.15–16. For the handclasp as a commitment to act, see Curt. 6.7.35, and Cic. *Ver.* 2.5.153, and dramatic examples at S. *Ph.* 813, Ar. *Thes.* 936.

108. So also [Quint.] *Decl.* 17.6, a source showing that the two gestures formed a familiar pair.

109. E. *Hipp.* 325–35, 267. Other views of the scene: Kaimio, *Physical Contact*, 50–51, Taplin, *Tragedy in Action*, 69–70, and Gould, "*Hiketeia*," 86–87, all centering on the oddity of a supplication in which the supplicanda, not the suppliant, is in danger.

110. Eust. ad *Il.* 1.427. Ath. *Deip.* 2.66c explains the sacredness of the head ἐκ τοῦ . . . κατ' αὐτῆς ὀμνύειν, relevant to supplication because of the guarantees of protection given to suppliants by means of an oath (e.g., E. *Med.* 749–53). A different view: Boegehold, *Gesture*, 18, holding that touching the chin expresses affection.

111. E. *Hec.* 342–45.

FIGURE 2.2   A Roman Priam and his Achilles. Courtesy of Copenhagen National Museum.

FIGURE 2.3   A Greek Priam with a reclining Achilles and a prostrate Hector. Courtesy of Fogg Museum, Cambridge, Massachusetts.

sibility is: to honor a woman who has helped him in the past but is too discreet to say so.[112] Zeus acknowledges his responsibility by nodding.[113]

All three gestures—knee clasp, kiss, and a hand on the chin—have the same disadvantage. The suppliant is committing himself to a single supplicandus or, if the suppliant deals with a group, to one supplicandus at a time. If the suppliant is not sure whom to supplicate, committing is unwise, and so the suppliant must hit on an alternative. This challenge befalls Cassandra, the priestess of Athena, in a vase painting (figure 2.4). Troy has fallen, and Ajax the Lesser is closing in, ready to drag Cassandra from the sanctuary and enslave her. Like Phemius, she must now decide whether to make an appeal to a person or to go to a holy spot, in this case, a statue instead of an altar. She chooses to go to (or remain at) the statue. She clasps the knees of the statue, committing herself. But then, unlike Phemius, she thinks better of her choice, and decides to approach Ajax, too. She extends a hand to him.[114] Once he draws close enough, perhaps she will clasp his knees as

FIGURE 2.4   Cassandra supplicating Ajax to one side and Athena to the other. Bartl 57.840, courtesy of the Deutsches Archäologisches Institut Rom.

112. Gestures: *Il.* 1.500–503. Services: 1.396–406.

113. Different views of the knee clasp: Kopperschmidt, *Hikesie als dramatische Form*, 51–52, from the perspective of *Kontaktmagie*, and Lynn George, *Epos*, 237–40, analyzing the relation between this gesture and the narrative context.

114. Fig. 2.4: Naples 81669 (H2422) = *ARV*[2] 189, 174 = *LIMC* 1.2 s.v. *Aias* II, 44 (L. Kahil), an Attic red-figure hydria of ca. 480 BCE. Battle of Athena and Ajax with Cassandra in the middle but making no appeal to either side: Berlin F1698 = *ABV* 136.54 = *LIMC* 1.2 s.v. *Aias* II, 18; New York MMA 41.162.43 = *ABV* 134.25 = *LIMC* 1.2 s.v. *Aias* II, 19; Wurzburg 249 = *ABV* 296.10 = *LIMC* 1.2 s.v. *Aias* II, 23. These three are Attic black-figure vases.

well. Rather than make one appeal, she is making two. In making the first appeal, she acts as a suppliant at an altar, but with a twist, which is that her gesture is suitable for a person as well as a god. In making her second appeal, she acts as a suppliant addressing a person, but with another twist: Ajax cannot help but notice where she is. If he wishes to remove her, he will be virtually attacking the goddess. Her improvisation puts him on the defensive.

In contrast to Greek sources, Roman ones seldom report the knee clasp or the associated gestures of kissing the hand or clasping the chin. Cicero lacks the knee clasp, and Livy, the source for more acts of supplication than any other Roman author, reports only one instance in which Romans performed it.[115] Only authors who Hellenize Roman supplication, Dionysius of Halicarnassus and Diodorus Siculus, report it frequently.[116] In compensation, Roman sources offer two other gestures, falling at the feet of the supplicandus and sometimes prostrating oneself as well. These gestures occur when a suppliant fears the displeasure of a king or emperor or of a magistrate who wields powers of life and death. In spirit as well as substance, these gestures resemble our own notion of "throwing oneself on the mercy of the court" or of an almighty god. They combine urgency with deference. The suppliant who performs them may be desperate, like his Greek counterpart, but remains circumspect.[117]

Like Metellus Pius, Romans often bend low and fall at the feet, even in Republican times. Pius did so in spite of being a consul's son. Other high-ranking Romans, including knights, performed the same gesture. Perhaps the most famous was Pius's rival in piety, the wife who interceded for her husband during the civil war. And the humble, including a Sicilian woman victimized by a Roman provincial administrator and aided by Cicero, performed this gesture.[118] The variety of Roman suppliants performing it shows that it reflects the character of political power in the society, and not the status of the suppliant. In contrast, only foreign suppliants kneel.[119] This familiar gesture thus differs from falling at the feet of the supplicandus. Unlike falling at the feet, it implies inferior status and links the act of supplication to worship.

The circumspect and worshipful suppliant need not be or approach a Roman, nor need he confine himself or herself to falling at the feet. In two Old Testament examples, women prostrate themselves when supplicating King David and the king

115. Liv. 8.35.3–8. Others do it five times (8.37.10, 25.7.1, 28.34.3, 30.12.11, 34.40.3) for a total of 6 out of 40 acts.

116. D.H. 4.67.1, 6.18.1, 8.43.2, D.S. 34/35.28, 36.15.2–3, 36.16; also V. Max. 5.3.3, 6.8.4. An exception: use of the gesture in the Roman imperial court or when supplicating the emperor elsewhere (J. *AJ* 19.234–36, Tac. *Hist.* 3.38, 4.81, *Ann.* 1.13.7, 11.30.1, 14.61.3).

117. The only two reports of both clasping the knees and groveling: *Il.* 24.478, 24.510 and Onos. 14.3.

118. Metellus Pius: App. *BC* 1.4.33. Knights: Cic. *Sest.* 26. Intercessor: *LT* 14. Humbler woman: Cic. *Verr.* 2.5.129. Others at feet: Apul. *Met.* 6.2, Caes. *Civ.* 3.98, *Gal.* 1.27.2, 1.31.2, Cic. *Att.* 1.14.5, *Q fr.* 2.6.2, *Fam.* 4.4.3, *Quinct.* 96, *Sest.* 54, *Phil.* 2.45, 2.86, *Red. Pop.* 12, Ov. *Met.* 10.415, Petr. 107.6, Sen. *Dial.* 3.40.3. Prostration to and by Romans in Greek sources: App. *BC* 3.8.51, D.C. 59.19.5, 77.9.3, D.S. 32.6.3, D.H. 8.54.1, Hrd. 7.5.4, Plut. *Aem.* 26.9, *Pomp.* 3.3, Plb. 1.35.4, Zonar. 9.24. In a Latin version of a lost Greek original: *Hist. Apoll.* 12. Freyburger, "Supplication grecque," 517–19, omits these gestures.

119. App. *Ill.* 9 (Pannonians) Liv. 43.2.2–3 (Spaniards), D.H. *Comp.* 12.18 (Persian), Hld. 9.11.4 (Egyptians). So, too, the suppliant king in the stele of Naramsin, as at n. 17 above, but he bends only one knee, not two.

of Persia, and one of them, Esther, kisses the king's feet.[120] In the New Testament, most suppliants prostrate themselves.[121] A similar but greater imbalance of power accompanies a similar but more abject gesture. Since prostration is more common in Hebrew sources than in Roman, gestures in the two cultures differ by degree.

All these gestures—clasping knees, hands, or chin, and falling low—assume that the supplicandus is nearby. But if the supplicandus is too far away to be clasped or even groveled to, the suppliant will simply extend his hands. Unlike the knee clasp or prostration, this gesture occurs in all cultures. Because it is highly visible, it lets suppliants communicate requests to a distant foe or friend. On the battlefield, it signifies surrender. Thebans use it to surrender during the Peloponnesian War, and some five hundred years later, Jews use it to surrender to Romans during the siege of Jerusalem.[122] Off the battlefield, it conveys appeals for help made not just by the shipwrecked but also by prisoners and the besieged, or anyone in a crowd.[123] If these suppliants have weapons, they drop them; pirates drop their oars.[124] Or if the suppliants are unlucky enough to have found their way into Ovid, with his taste for surprises, they extend their hands for as long as the course of the plot permits. Leucothoë extends hers toward the Sun, her lover, but only until she is buried alive.[125] In Ovid even more than in other sources, this gesture is pathetic.

Because extending hands is pathetic, it draws criticism never directed toward clasping knees or prostration. When Aeschylus's Prometheus refuses to beg for mercy, he condemns extending one's hands as contemptible and womanish: "Never think that Zeus's decision will make me panic and that I shall become womanish and address my much hated enemy with hands upturned in a woman's way. Ask him to release me from my bonds? I am far from it."[126] In one respect, Prometheus is wrong. Supplication is not womanish. But he is right about the gesture, which is not only womanish but childish.[127] It hardly differs from the gesture that chil-

120. 2 *Ki.* 14.4, *Es.* 8.3; so also 1 *Ki.* 25.23, to David before David is king; and J. *BJ* 1.353, 1.506, 1.621, 3.202. At J. *Vit.* 210, the suppliant throws himself on the ground. Two collective acts of prostration: J. *BJ* 2.171–74, 3.202–4. Persian acts: Plut. *Alex.* 30.5–7, *Art.* 29.6–7. The only Greek act: E. *Supp.* 22, by an Adrastus who succeeds in his supplication only with some difficulty. But Malalas 124 assumes that Priam threw himself at Achilles' feet (*Il.* 24.510).

121. *Ev. Luc.* 5.12, 8.41, *Ev. Matt.* 8.2, 9.18, 15.25.

122. Thebans: Th. 3.66.2 (427 BCE). Jews: J. *BJ* 4.77 (67 CE). The Romans used the gesture, too (Plut. *Ant.* 18.3, D.C. 64.14.4), but misunderstood a somewhat similar Macedonian gesture of surrender, raising spears, even though their commander, T. Flamininus, did understand it (Plb. 18.26.9–12). Other Greeks: D.S. 13.21.7.

123. Prisoners: App. *Mith.* 73, Plut. *Gen. Socrat.* 599c, J. *BJ* 1.58. Besieged: Plut. *Flam.* 15.5, Liv. 36.34.5, J. *BJ* 4.77, 5.318; similar are the surrounded Thebans at Hdt. 7.233. Crowd: *Liv.* 3.50.5. Endangered goddesses resembling suppliants: Sicily (Plut. *Dio* 22.1), Italy (*Pomp.* 66.4), Rome (Sil. It. 4.408–9). Similar is Cic. *Cat.* 4.18.

124. Hands extended after weapons thrown away: Th. 4.38.1, D.H. 8.17.6, 8.67.8. Weapons thrown away, hands not mentioned, but presumably extended: J. *Vit.* 328. Oars: Flor. *Epit.* 1.41.

125. Ov. *Met.* 4.238. Supplicating while buried is also a hazard for females in fiction: X. *Eph.* 3.8.4–5. The only article that deals with this gesture as opposed to knee clasps: Sullivan, "Tendere Manus."

126. A. *PV* 1002–6, as in Page.

127. A different view: Bremmer, "Walking, Standing, and Sitting," 22 with n. 21, who in analyzing the Aeschylus passage argues that the gesture is both womanish and passively homosexual. Sittl, *Gebärden*, chap. 10, reports the gesture, but in a broad context.

dren make when they are seeking out their parents or nurses, and so visual sources make it the gesture that children use when they supplicate in Greek tragedy.[128] An illustration of Euripides' *Iphigenia at Aulis*, presents Orestes as a toddler and the older Iphigenia (figure 2.5).[129] At the left, Orestes and his sister both reach out to Agamemnon, who has raised his right hand to his face in anguish. The little boy and the older girl use the same gesture, but the boy aims at the knees of the supplicandus and the girl at the chin. Iphigenia, who is unquestionably supplicating, mirrors her brother, who is so young as to be incapable of supplication as this book has defined it.[130] Elsewhere in figure 2.5, the children behave the same ambiguous way. On the right, Orestes reaches out to his mother, Clytemnestra, and uses the same gesture that Iphigenia uses is in the scene farthest to the right, where she is once again supplicating her father. Or perhaps I am underestimating the young Orestes. In figure 2.6, Telephus has kidnapped him and taken ref-

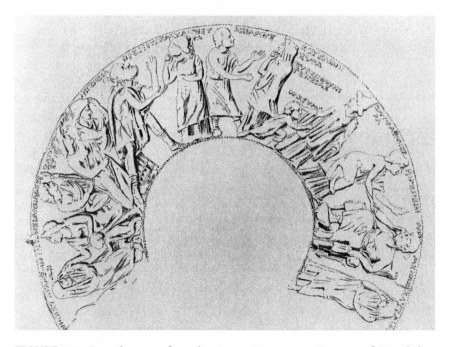

FIGURE 2.5   Several scenes of supplication to Agamemnon. Courtesy of Staatsliche Museen zu Berlin.

128. For this comparison, see Burkert, *Creation of the Sacred,* 85–90, seeing difference in size as characteristic of submissive gestures of all sorts, and tracing this submissiveness to the behavior of primates.

129. Fig. 2.5: a terra-cotta bowl of the first half of the second century BCE, Berlin Staatl. Mus. 3161 = Hausmann, *Reliefbecher,* 53 HB 10b pl. 21.1–2 = *LIMC* 3.2 s.v. *Iphigenia,* 9 (L. Kahil). In the last scene Orestes is absent, though at *IA* 1117–19 Euripides says he is present. Similar relief, also on a bowl: Athens Nat. Mus. 2114 = *LIMC* 3.2 s.v. *Iphigenia,* 8.

130. A similar gesture directed at a mother when she gives infants to a nurse: Vienna Kunsthist. Mus. IV 1773 = *ARV²* 972.2 = *LIMC* 1.2 s.v. *Akamas et Demophon,* 1 (U. Kron). Directed at a mother in fear: N.Y. 25.28 = *ARV²* 1110.41 = *LIMC* 1.2 s.v. *Alkmene,* 11 (A. Trendall), where Heracles' combat with the snakes frightens Iphicles. Both are Attic red-figure vases.

FIGURE 2.6   A captive Orestes supplicates from an altar.
Courtesy of Photo Archive, National Archaeology Museum,
Madrid.

uge at an altar, where he threatens to kill him.[131] Amid the confusion the child is
able to pick out his father and extend his hands in apparent supplication. In figure 2.7, an infant of Heracles conveys the same impression.[132]

In all these cases, the gestures either do not appear or differ from those in extant
plays. In *Iphigenia at Aulis*, for example, the daughter wraps herself around her
father's knees, a pose different from the one depicted on the bowl. But her words
offer a striking if unique confirmation of the resemblance between children who
reach out to parents and children who supplicate them:

> I was the first to call you father and you were the first to call me child. I was
> the first to put my body at your knees and give and receive caresses. And
> this was what you said, "Ah, my child, will I see you living happily in a

131. Fig. 2.6: a fourth-century Attic red-figure chalice crater, Staatl. Mus. Berlin V.I. 3974 = Trendall-Webster,
103 III.3.47 = *LIMC* 1.2 s.v. *Agamemnon*, 13.
132. Fig. 2.7: a red-figure calyx crater of 350–25 BCE: Madrid Mus. Arch. 11094 (L.369) = *RVP* 84.127 =
LIMC 3.2 s.v. *Heracles*, 1684 (J. Boardman).

FIGURE 2.7   A child of Heracles with his murderous father. Courtesy of Photo Archive, National Archaeology Museum, Madrid.

husband's house and flourishing in a way that is worthy of me?" I twisted your beard in my finger—I cling there now—and I said, "What about you?"[133]

"I cling there now": the suppliant is reliving infancy. It is prudent to notice that this appeal does not succeed, but it is also prudent to assume that Iphigenia cannot have been the only Greek suppliant who clung to the knees of a parent. Tragedy chose to preserve her memory—because she failed.

In other cases, only a moment or two separates the child's clinging to a parent and his supplicating another person. In Euripides' *Andromache*, Molossus leaves his mother's embrace to supplicate Menelaus, and Astyanax does the same in Seneca's *Trojan Women*.[134] The same also happens when an Indian queen successfully appeals to Alexander the Great, and it may happen when a supplicating mother sets her children before Vespasian in 79 CE. The source, Dio, does not say whether the children touch the emperor.[135] If they do, the emperor's decision to reject the mother will have been all the more pathetic.

All suppliants noticed so far extend both hands. But some that make their appeals at close range may extend just one, invariably the right, which betokens good faith.[136] In Silius Italicus, a minor Latin author whose handling of supplication plays off Virgil's, the only instance of a suppliant extending his right hand is blatantly ironic. The suppliant is Aeneas, and the person to whom he extends his hand is Dido, whom he is asking for protection on his arrival in Africa. When giving protection she will give herself into the bargain, and he will shortly abandon her, a story that Silius leaves mostly to the *Aeneid*.[137]

What if a suppliant cannot extend a hand? The sources answer this question in ways that show that they cannot conceive of a suppliant who lacks a means of communicating. Having lost his hand in battle, Cassius, the assassin of Caesar, extends a supplicatory stump to his captor. What bravery! says the Roman epitomator Valerius Maximus. But Valerius is not the only interested party. A god admires Cassius, too, and instantly reattaches the missing hand, allowing Cassius to extend it. The reward for making the extraordinary gesture is having the chance to make an ordinary one.[138] But the sequence of stump and hand is also appropriate for another reason. Both gestures are pathetic, and together they are doubly so. Like mother and child, they form a pair.

In another anecdote, a Greek extends a stump. When in one of his plays the poet Aeschylus reveals religious secrets, the Athenians put him on trial. Presumably he supplicates, but they sentence him to death. Then the poet's brother, who has lost a hand at Marathon, comes to his aid by throwing back his cloak and exposing his deformity. Since the pursuers know why he lost his hand, they are reminded of

133. Wrapped around the knees: E. *IT* 1215–16. The citation: 1220–27.
134. E. *And.* 537–40, Sen. *Tro.* 705–706.
135. Curt. 8.10.34–35, D.C. 65.16.2. Surely no touching by the children: Curt. 5.1.19, D.S. 37.19.5–6.
136. Right hand: S. *Med.* 28, *Tro.* 693, 709, V. *A.* 12.930. Unspecified: E. *HF* 987, *El.* 1215.
137. Sil. It. 2.412–13.
138. V. Max 6.8.4, expressing relief that the supplicandus, a *libertus* of Cassius, does not commit parricide.

Aeschylus's own war record, and so they spare the playwright.[139] This time extending the stump is not just a pathetic gesture. The brother can be proud of his stump. Unlike an extended hand, it has nothing womanish or childish about it.

Like extending one's hands, displaying boughs is a very visible gesture, and even better for communicating at a distance.[140] As Livy observes, Greeks often used boughs. So did Hebrews.[141] Heliodorus even attributes boughs to the Egyptians, who also used white flags, an alternative that we would think obvious but that appears nowhere but in this most exotic of novelists.[142] For clarity's sake, armed suppliants take up boughs after dropping their weapons. Josephus reports that he himself did this, and that other Jews did, too.[143] A bough also has the advantage of serving as a token. As we have seen, a suppliant will put a bough on an altar and leave it there. The father of the Danaids does so in Aeschylus, and many suppliants did so in Classical Athens.[144] Some of these suppliants represent others. The father of the Danaids, for example, represents his daughters. While he places the boughs they wait in their sylvan antechamber. Other suppliants also wait while spokesmen place boughs. Whole armies may wait, and even bivouac in a grove.[145] The bough is usually an olive branch, often twined with wool. Soft and woven by women, wool expresses pacificity.[146] Since priests wear woolen fillets, it also lends an air of sanctity. Association with altars has the same effect. So, unlike all the gestures discussed so far, displaying boughs conveys the character of the suppliant, who is both unthreatening and favored by the gods. These traits, in turn, explain the circumstances in which suppliants use this gesture. Those who are at a distance may be feared by the supplicandus, and so they display boughs to allay this fear. Those who fear being attacked display them to show that they have received protection from the gods.

Like the knee clasp, the bough combines with other gestures and tactics, but in these instances it achieves a new effect: a change in the suppliant's identity. The first suppliant in the *Iliad*, Chryses, a priest of Apollo, uses both bough and staff, combining a signal that is supplicatory with one that is not.[147] The supplicatory signal says, "I plead," but the other, the staff, or scepter, since this is Homer's

---

139. Ael. *VH* 5.19.

140. Ael. *VH* 3.26 and also Din. 1.18, D.S. 17.22.4 (334/3 BCE), Tac. *Hist.* 1.66, 3.31 (69 CE), J. *BJ* 2.497–98, 2.637, 4.553. A general contrast: Meleager supplicated at close range by household members without boughs (*Il.* 9.581–96), but at a distance by fellow citizens with boughs (Apollod. 1.8.3). Supplicatory boughs must be distinguished from others, as by Pley, *de lanae usu* 60–64, and from instances in which a common word for them, *hiketēriai*, may mean "entreaties" (J. *BJ* 4.573).

141. Liv. 29.16.6–7, J. *BJ* 2.637–41.

142. Hld. 9.11.4, 9.6.1.

143. J. *BJ* 4.553. Switch: D.S. 32.23, where Hasdrubal makes it. Trick: Ach. Tat. 4.13.1–3, where bandits use boughs.

144. A. *Supp.* 481–85; And. 1.110–16 with Arist. *Ath.* 43.6.

145. Hdt. 5.119; also 6.78–80, a force numbering five thousand according to Paus. 3.4.1.

146. A short treatment on what ancients called the *eiresiōnē*, which also had other uses: Blech, *Kranz*, 288, with n. 91. An ancient etiology at Plut. *Thes.* 18.1 does not, of course, address the psychological aspects. In the Near East, the palm replaces the olive; unlike the olive, it is never draped with fillets.

147. First suppliant in the *Iliad*: Pl. *R.* 3.393e with schol. ad E. *Or.* 383, as noted by Servais, "Στέμματ' ἔχων," 440.

word for it, says, "I speak authoritatively" and, if it is made of laurel, "I speak on behalf of Apollo."[148] Laurel boughs put to supplicatory use also appear in vase painting.[149] The reason for the twofold signal is that the suppliant does not know which way to deal with the supplicandus. So he combines ways, hoping that the Greeks will act both as supplicandi and as worshippers of his god, Apollo.[150]

A bough can also appear alongside symbols of sanctity that a suppliant improvises during a crisis as at Hellenistic Ephesus. To protect themselves from an invader, the citizenry put their entire city under the protection of Artemis by means of a half-mile cord connecting her shrine to the city walls. Then they took up boughs and approached the invader.[151] The longest account, in Aelian, is corrupt, but the Ephesians were probably seeking favorable surrender terms.[152] Or the community can use boughs and statues, carrying both of them out of the city when they approach the supplicandus. This combination achieves the same effect, sanctifying the supplication. Though it appears only once, in fiction, it would have recommended itself to any populace that feared violence on the part of the supplicandus.[153] When Theban refugees fleeing Alexander reach Arcadian forces at the Isthmus and seek aid, they wind olive branches around heralds' wands, using the same device of doubling and, since heralds were sacrosanct, achieving the same effect of sanctification. This time, though, the supplicandi are also supposed to act as a community that is receiving emissaries from another.[154] Other supplicating diplomats would wear fillets around their temples.[155] The effect is the same as carrying boughs.[156] Dionysius of Halicarnassus even gives the impression that some Italian tribes have all their diplomats supplicate. These tribes seem to have no knowledge of heralds.[157]

148. Chryses' bough laurel yet supplicatory: Doederlein ad *Il.* 1.14. Laurel and priestly: Crusius ad loc., following Eust. ad loc. Olive and supplicatory: Hermann ad S. *O.R.* 3. For bibliography, see Servais, "Στέμματ' ἔχων," 441–43, who opts for a scepter decorated with wool as opposed to any branch, and thus for compact ambiguity.

149. When Creusa supplicates at Pythian Apollo's altar in a vase painting based on Sophocles' *Creusa* (Attic red-figure vase, Basel, Gal. Palladion = Schaunberg 634 fig. 1.2 = *LIMC* 6.2 s.v. *Kreousa I*, 8), her bough resembles Apollo's laurel, held by the god as he sits overhead. She may thus be warning any pursuer against divine vengeance.

150. Same double appeal: Liv. 2.39.12, "sacerdotes . . . suis insignibus uelatos supplices."

151. Ael. *VH* 3.26 preceded by Hdt. 1.26 and Polyaen. 6.50, which both mention a cord but no boughs.

152. As opposed to a promise that the invaders would not enter. The mms. of Ael. *VH* 3.26 report that the Ephesians sought φυγήν or "sanctuary," something they could scarcely obtain from an enemy, so Toup apud N. Wilson ad loc. proposed ἀσφάλειαν or "safety" in the sense of "protection against pillaging." For comparison with the Cylonian conspirators, see Gould, "Hiketeia," 78.

153. Hld. 9.11.4–5, perhaps paralleled by fifth-century Messenians discussed at 210–12 below, and perhaps also by guards in the temple at Jerusalem, although Josephus does not say that they fled to the altar (*BJ* 4.311). The statue at Esar. 68.2.2.18–23 has a different purpose.

154. Din. 1.18–19. Cf. the use of heralds in *Il.* 9, where they accompany an implied supplication lacking both gestures and express words, but including a comparison between Achilles and the supplicandus Meleager (9.581–96).

155. App. *Hisp.* 52, where the attempt to impress L. Lucullus fails.

156. Cases like that of the Thebans: Hdt. 6.108.4 (Plataeans to Athenians), Dem. 50.5 (allies to Athens), *IG* ii² 404 (Ceans to Athens), all successful; Ephor. 70 *FGrH* fr. 186 (Greek *presbeis* to Gelon of Syracuse) is unsuccessful. Cases like that of Priam: Him. *Or.* 6.169–75 (Persians to Spartans), in which the supplicandi attack the suppliants. For the hazards faced by ambassadors, see Mosley, *Envoys*, chap. 15. Some cases may fall into either or both categories, like *Hist. Aug. Had.* 21.14, in which Bactrian legates approach Hadrian.

157. D.H. 1.20.1 (Pelasgians), 3.41.5 (Volscii), 6.18.1–3 (Latins), all without heralds. Aeneas and Latinus know better, and later the Romans are always the supplicandi in these episodes, never the untutored suppliants (1.58.4).

A suppliant trying to associate himself with heralds need not carry the herald's wand himself. In figure 2.8, an Archaic shield band, Priam supplicates Achilles by touching the chin, an Homeric gesture, but does not strike the pose familiar from *Iliad* 24.[158] Instead he identifies himself as an emissary by standing next to Hermes, the god of heralds, who takes the place of a merely human herald and carries the wand.[159] Like the Thebans, Priam is striving for diplomatic status, but he has an epic hero's advantage of converse with a god.

Another gesture, donning mourning clothes, resembles displaying a bough because it is visible at a distance. Unlike a bough, however, mourning clothes always portend a supplication addressed to a person or persons, not to an altar. Mourning clothes have two advantages over other gestures addressed to persons: they affect a group as much as they do any individual, and they allow the suppliant to go from place to place. In these respects, they differ most especially from

FIGURE 2.8   Hermes watching as Priam supplicates Achilles. Wagner 1 Olympia 2252, courtesy of the Deutsches Archäologisches Institut Rom.

158. Fig. 2.8: an Archaic bronze shield band, Inst. Olympia 2252 = *Olympische Forschungen*, 2.145–46 and pl. 19, identified as Priam because of the content of nearby bands.

159. Another view: Pötscher, "Hikesie," 12–15, unsure whether this gesture designates supplication but pointing out several differences between the shield band and *Iliad* 24.

prostration. The contrast with prostration is all the stronger because the use of mourning clothes, like prostration, occurs only in Rome and Israel.[160] In these two cultures, prostration and mourning clothes accomplish a division of labor. Like those who fall prostrate, those in mourning debase themselves, but they differ by expressing grief. Because they are mobile, these suppliants can broadcast their appeal to a crowd or mob as opposed to the ruler or magistrate. Mourning clothes thus lend supplication a horizontal, egalitarian element that balances prostration's vertical element. The alternation of these gestures is appropriate both for the forum with its magistrates and for the Hebrews under foreign rule.

Mourning clothes, in sum, provide publicity. Cassius Dio thought that Lepidus put on shabby clothes when passing among Octavian's army on the way to his fellow triumvir. Egyptian soldiers did the same when making their way to Caesar.[161] More numerous are Roman criminal defendants or their supporters, plus condemned persons hoping for mercy.[162] Also numerous are legates or plebeians who have come before the Senate.[163] These suppliants are all working Roman crowds. So are Senate leaders who change clothes.[164] Senators also remove senatorial insignia, as revealed by criticism of Publius Rutilius Rufus for failing to do so at his trial. Valerius Maximus, that arbiter of the obvious, says, "He did not don shabby clothes, remove his senatorial insignia, or beg and extend his hands to the knees of the judges."[165] Rufus may have especially offended the members of the court who were *equites*, or rich men below senatorial rank, for by retaining his insignia he reminded them of the difference between them and himself. But the first and chief complaint that Valerius Maximus reports is about the clothes.[166] Rufus accordingly fails to gain the sympathy of the judges, who convict him.

Unlike Roman sources, Hebrew ones refer to sackcloth, not mourning clothes, but this sartorial difference does not prevent Roman and Jewish practices from coinciding, the same as they do in regard to prostration. In the only Old Testament example, the servants of the Syrian King Ben-Hadad, just defeated by Ahab of Israel, don sackcloth and put rope on their heads and go among the Hebrews. Their dress protects them, spreading impressions of humility and peaceable intent. When they find Ahab, they supplicate, and he responds favorably, calling Ben-Hadad a brother. Emboldened by this response to his signals, Ben-Hadad ventures forth and

---

160. The only reported cases of Greek mourning dress: Just. 4.4.2, a latin text; and Polyaen. 6.7.1, where a defendant in Macedon, not Greece, dresses his wife and children in black. In other cases, Greek suppliants use some mourning gestures: Is. 8.22, a woman wailing and supplicating; AP 5.287.5–7 (Agathias Scholasticus), an amatory suppliant using mourning gestures.

161. D.C. 49.12.4, *B. Alex.* 32.3.

162. Defendants or supporters: D.S. 36.15.2–3, Liv. 3.58.1–6; and the numerous acts performed on behalf of Cicero, discussed at 270–72 below. Condemned: *B. Alex.* 67.1.

163. Legates: Liv. 29.16.6 (204 BCE), 44.19.7, 45.4.2, 45.20.10 (168–66 BCE). V. Max. 9.10.1; D.C. 68.10.1 (102 CE), dressed as captives. Plebeians: D.H. 6.51.2.

164. Senate leaders: Liv. 43.16.14.

165. V. Max. 6.4.4. Greek for "shabby clothes": ἐσθῆτα ... πιναρὰν (DS 36.15.2, 36.16, DH 4.10.6).

166. General statement confirming Valerius: Sen. *Con.* 10.1.7, calling *squalor* one of a suppliant's "necessaria ... instrumenta."

approaches Ahab, who spares him.[167] Examples in Josephus show that Jewish suppliants must have often used this method, which he says was customary.[168]

The politics of the forum perhaps accounts for the uniquely Roman custom of family and friends joining the suppliant in changing clothes.[169] Cicero even complained that although the public could see his brother's change of dress on his behalf, it could not see the same display by his wife and children.[170] His opponent, Antony, had been better served. When foes attempted to have Antony declared a public enemy, Antony's female relations had put on black and thrown themselves at the senators' feet. The gesture worked: Antony retained his civic and political rights.[171] Cicero, in contrast, went into exile.

Mourning clothes made such an impression that the jurist Venuleius reports that it was unlawful for anyone except relatives to wear mourning dress on behalf of an accused.[172] In the same spirit, the consuls forbade senators to wear mourning on behalf of the exiled Cicero.[173] (The Romans also thought that wearing sumptuous clothes inhibited supplication by discouraging the suppliant from bowing and scraping.[174]) No other supplicatory gesture or behavior undergoes such regulation. The reason is perhaps the crowd or mob to which the suppliant appeals. Changing clothes is not just visible, like extending a hand. It is theatrical, even demagogic. Rather than put on mourning dress, a few suppliants rend their clothes, another theatrical touch.[175] The usual terms for mourning clothes— *squalidus*, *sordidatus*, and related words—are a reminder that mourning clothes were shabby, unlike today, and thus all the more striking.[176] They were, of course, black, the same as today.[177]

Changing clothes also possesses another advantage. Because it is striking, it is easy to understand. This is important for any gesture, as shown by cautionary examples of gestures that are misunderstood to disastrous effect. Just before Esther supplicates the king of Persia, the king's minister, Haman, supplicates Esther.

167. 3 *Ki.* 20.32–34 revisited at J. *AJ* 8.385–87.

168. J. *BJ* 2.237–38, 2.322–25, 2.601–10. These suppliants are priests and magistrates, too. Customary: *AJ* 8.385.

169. As at Liv. 3.58.1, in which the *gens Claudia* changes dress for a member; Cic. *Planc.* 21, in which townsmen change clothes on behalf of the defendant; the public likewise for Cicero (*Red. Sen.* 12), the same as Cicero's brother (*Red. Sen.* 37). General statement: *B.Alex.* 32.3.

170. Cic. *Red. Pop.* 7, 8.

171. *App. BC* 3.8.51. Another view of mourning clothes: Arist. *Rh.* 2.1386b, linking them to other means of arousing pity.

172. Ven. *dig.* 47.10.37 pr. 2 (middle of the first century CE).

173. Cic. *Dom.* 113, *Red. Pop.* 13, *Sest.* 32.

174. Zeno *Stoic.* 1.14.6, surely an instance of a satirical commonplace.

175. Liv. 1.13.1, DC 48.31.6, 54.14.2–3. The only reported case of a Greek tearing his clothes: X. *Eph.* 2.5.6, perhaps a solecism in this imperfect archaizer.

176. *Sordidatus* and related words: Cic. *Red. Sen.* 12, Liv. 44.19.7, 45.20.10, Just. 4.4.2. *Squalidus* and related words: Asc. *Scr.* 18, Cic. *Red. Sen.* 37, [Quint.] *Decl.* 17.6, Tac. *Hist.* 1.54. V. Max. 9.10.1. Both: Cic. *Mur.* 86, *Sest.* 144, Liv. 29.16.6. *Mutata uestis* vel sim.: Liv. 8.37.9, 43.16.14; Cic. *Red. Pop.* 13, *Sest.* 26; Plut. *Cic.* 30.4; Tac. *Ann.* 2.29.1. Torn clothes: only D.C. 48.31.6, 54.14.2–3, 68.10.1, but this practice was surely widespread. D. C. also notices the resulting nakedness: 54.14.2–3.

177. *Atratus*: Suet. *Nero* 47.2. μελαίνη στολῆ: App. *BC* 3.8.51; J. *BJ* 1.506 before the cosmopolitan Herod. μέλαιναν ἐσθῆτα: D.H. 4.66.1. Mourning: D.H. 6.51.2, 8.45.1, D.S. 31.5.3.

Haman makes the mistake of sitting on her couch, a gesture that the king regards as seductive as well as supplicatory. He has Haman put to death.[178] A comic example appears in figure 2.9, a vase painting in which Odysseus performs the most delicate of all his supplications, addressed to Nausicaa, whom he meets after washing ashore on the island of Scheria. His gesture of choice is extending a bough, and it might seem commendably cautious, for he is naked and she is young. Is he supplicating her or uncovering his nakedness? His ambiguous gesture puts one of the servant girls to flight and causes the princess to hesitate, feet pointing one way, eyes the other. Athena admonishes him, but too late. He has done too much.[179]

As Odysseus learns, a gesture must be apt. Which inflection is right? Urgency? Modesty? Culture provides choices, but does not tell suppliants which choice to

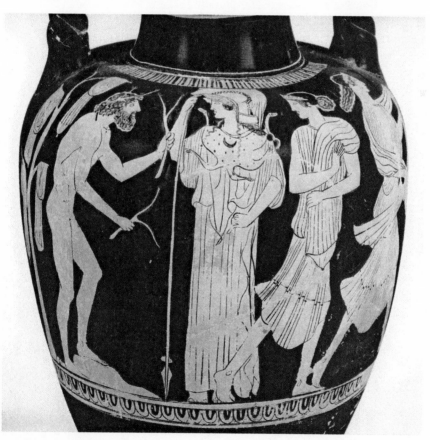

FIGURE 2.9   Odysseus supplicating Nausicaa, bough in hand. Courtesy of Staatsliche Antikensammlungen und Glyptothek München.

178. *Es.* 7.7–10.

179. Fig. 2.9: a red-figure amphora from Vulci of ca. 440 BCE: Munich Antikenslg. 2322 = *ARV*[2] 1107.2 = *LIMC* 6.2 s.v. *Nausicaa*, 2 (O. Touchefeu). Other painters followed Homer in giving Odysseus foliage to use as a coverlet, e.g., Boston MFA 04.18 = *ARV*[2] 1177.48 = *LIMC* 6.2 s.v. *Nausicaa*, 3, also a red-figure vase.

make. They must communicate an intent to supplicate, and they must do so clearly, but they must do more, even when they must seem to do less.

Words

All the suppliants described so far have been able to perform a gesture or handle an appurtenance like a bough. Many suppliants, however, do not perform a gesture and turn instead to words. For scholars who find gestures essential to supplication, words are a poor replacement. Words do not make contact, so they lack any magical effect, and they are also less expressive. Some scholars have even concluded that an act of supplication that lacks a gesture is not genuine or complete. They describe these acts as "figurative."[180] But the variousness of gestures suggests another approach to the topic. Suppliants who use words still meet the test of taking all four steps, and so they do indeed supplicate. But they discover that a gesture may be impossible or ill-advised, and so they use a word instead. They can still communicate their intent and can still achieve some expressive effect.

A gesture may be impossible because the suppliant is immobile, like the dying Hector. Since he cannot attempt to clasp Achilles' knees, he makes no gesture at all, and so Achilles mocks him by telling him μὴ γουνάζεο, "don't clasp my knee." Hector's helplessness is all the more pathetic because he is the only wounded man in Homer who supplicates in any way.[181] In the *Odyssey*, Odysseus is not tall enough to clasp the knees of the Cyclops, and in the *Iliad*, two suppliants riding a chariot are too high to clasp the knees of Agamemnon, who is on foot.[182] All three resort to words. Odysseus says that he is an *hiketês*, a suppliant, and the chariot riders use the word *gounazomai*, "to clasp the knees," but figuratively.

A gesture may be possible but ill-advised because the suppliant is out of bounds for erotic, social, or religious reasons, or for several of these at once. Erotic reasons come into play because suppliants do not forget the obligations of sexual modesty. Clytemnestra makes the point in *Iphigenia at Aulis*, saying to Achilles that her daughter, Iphigenia, may supplicate Agamemnon but may not supplicate an adult male from outside the household.[183] One of the heroines of Greek fiction, Chariclea, is reluctant to clasp male knees for the same reason, and rightly so. On another occasion, a male whom she supplicates takes pleasure in this gesture.[184] In contrast, a virtuous supplicandus will reject a seductive female suppliant, at least in pious authors, and so Octavian rejects Cleopatra.[185]

---

180. Figurative: Gould, "*Hiketeia*," 77, adapted from "formlos" in Kopperschmidt, *Hikesie als dramatische Form*, 20–22, who noticed the contrast in Arend, *Scenen*, between entreaties made with or without a knee clasp (105). Following Gould: Mercier, rev. of Crotty, *Poetics*; Pedrick, "Supplication," but with reservations at 129–32; and Clark, "Chryses," 15, with a telling reservation, which is that verbal acts often succeed.

181. Hector: *Il.* 22.345. Similarly, Ov. *Met.* 8.852–58 where the dying Procris cannot perform the gesture to Cephalus; and S. *Ph.* 485–86, where Philoctetes performs it with difficulty. Kaimio, *Physical Contact*, 54–55, notices the dramatic examples. Parody: Lucianus *Par.* 46, where Hector incongruously bows down.

182. *Od.* 9.250–80, *Il.* 11.130–47. At *Il.* 15.660–67, the suppliant is addressing numerous fleeing soldiers, and consequently cannot touch most of them.

183. E. *IA* 992–97.

184. Hld. 4.18.2, 5.26.3.

185. Flor. *Epit.* 2.21.

Nor do suppliants forget the privileges and obligations of social status. Although Homer's Thetis touches Zeus's knees and chin, she supplicates Hephaestus by saying γουνάζομαι without touching him. She is denying to the handyman, Hephaestus, the gesture that she gives to his employer, Zeus.[186] Prose reports the same precaution. In all the Greek writers listed in the appendices, freeborn persons use gestures to supplicate slaves on only three occasions, all in novels. In this genre, a recurring emergency justifies this slip: the master or mistress is in love and needs a slave's help.[187] In some circumstances, though, gestures confer an honor that the supplicandus may not want. So if the suppliant is sitting at dinner with the supplicandus, as happens to Telemachus when he visits Menelaus, the suppliant may not want to rise, interrupt the meal, and honor the supplicandus in one way while inconveniencing him in another.[188]

Both erotic and religious reasons to avoid contact appear in a pair of comic scenes, one in the *Odyssey* and the other in the Homeric *Hymn to Aphrodite*. In the *Odyssey* scene between the shipwrecked Odysseus and Nausicaa, we have already noticed that proffering a bough will not do. Neither will the obvious alternative, touching the girl: "If he clasped her knees, he feared that the girl would get angry." At the same time, Odysseus wishes to pay his supplicanda the honor of a display, knee clasp included. So he alludes to the gesture that he declines to perform, saying: "I clasp your knees, lady." To lend a touch of sanctity, he turns γουνοῦμαι into an implicit verb of prayer, asking: "Are you some goddess or a mortal?"[189] With this touch, he introduces his second, religious reason, which is to honor a presumed goddess.[190] Conduct that was pathetic for Hector is now politic.[191]

The same two reasons—one erotic, one religious—figure in the second scene, found in the Homeric *Hymn to Aphrodite*. This time, though, genders switch. The suppliant is female, and the supplicandus is male. The female is not an ostensible goddess, as Nausicaa is, but instead is a true goddess, Aphrodite, who at first appears in disguise. The man she approaches, the shepherd Anchises, does not know what to make of her. She seems to be a Phrygian girl, and she makes her request discretely, using the word γουνάζομαι in a figurative sense. This is the Odyssean standard of good conduct, found not only in the Nausicaa episode but also in several others.[192] But the request—that he marry her—makes him

186. *Il.* 1.500 vs. 18.457. In Virgil, the smith god fares better, but when supplicated by his wife (8.382). Other views: Giordano, *Supplica*, 94–95, regarding this as an instance of *xenia*, and van Wees, *Status Warriors*, 229, reasoning that Thetis behaves submissively because she is not an Olympian.

187. The three cases: X. Eph. 2.3.4–5, 2.9.4, Charito 2.10.2–11.6.

188. *Od.* 3.92–108, another instance of figurative language. At *Od.* 4.332–50, the suppliant is in bed, the supplicandus standing over him.

189. *Od.* 6.142–46. "I clasp your knees": γουνοῦμαί σε, . . . (149). Clark, "Chryses," 16, notices the skillfulness of this supplication.

190. Cf. also Ar. *Pax* 1113–21, where the priest supplicates by saying πρὸς τῶν γονάτων but does not bend down, as shown by his readiness to snatch meat at 1118. Here the explanation for not performing the gesture is that it would inconvenience the suppliant.

191. A similar view of this scene: Pedrick, "Supplication," 138. A different view: Gödde, *Drama der Hikesie*, 59–60, envisioning figurative contact.

192. γουνάζομαι: *h. Ven.* 187. In a similar situation, Odysseus evidently touches Circe, but Circe is not an Olympian (*Od.* 10.481). He avoids touching Athena (13.226–49, 13.324–51), and cannot touch a river god while he founders at sea (5.444–550).

suspicious. It occurs to him that she may be a goddess. If so, granting her request is risky, for many unions between mortal men and goddesses end poorly. But questioning her is fruitless, for she refuses to answer truthfully. And so Anchises has the problem that Odysseus only pretends to have: how to respond. Only after he grants her request does she reveal herself. For caution's sake, Anchises now supplicates her, and he says γουνάζομαι rather than touch her. What she did out of modesty, he does out of fear. Then comes the ironic climax: he begs for protection. He wants to avoid any adverse consequences of saying yes to his erstwhile suppliant.

The parody of the scene in the *Odyssey* is elaborate. The man must now supplicate sincerely, and the woman has the task of supplicating insincerely. He holds back fearfully, she coolly. He is in distress and she is in command. And so the meaning of γουνάζομαι changes. Rather than mean "In these circumstances, I prefer not to touch you," as it does in the *Odyssey*, γουνάζομαι now means either "I might touch you" or "I dare not touch you."[193] Similar religious and erotic material yields two dissimilar supplications.

Taken together, these reasons to speak rather than touch affect numerous acts. In the *Iliad*, only 5 of 22 acts lack gestures, but in the *Odyssey*, 13 of 23 acts lack gestures.[194] Among Greek historians, Herodotus and Thucydides both include acts in which the suppliant uses only words to identify himself. In Herodotus, the suppliant, the Spartan prince who is trying to learn the identity of his father, sacrifices animals to the gods for help and at the same begs his mother to reveal his parentage. When he speaks to her, he holds the entrails of the animals in his hands, and thus cannot make a gesture. In Thucydides, a large group of suppliants, all battlefield captives, stand trial before their captors, and can no more touch the supplicandi than the king can.[195]

To dismiss all these acts as "figurative" overlooks the resourcefulness of the suppliants. When he met Nausicaa, what was Odysseus to do? Not ask for help? The hero and the story must go on. Odysseus speaks, and he succeeds.

Combinations

Words do not always appear in lieu of gestures. A suppliant may want help from coadjutors, and so he or she will use a word and leave gestures to others who supplicate as well. These persons may act before the suppliant does, and they may continue their efforts during and after the suppliant's own appeal. A defendant, for example, may supplicate his judges before trial, using gestures. Both before and during the trial, others may supplicate on his (or less often, on her) behalf, and they, too, may use gestures. Then, when the defendant speaks *in propria persona*, he uses supplicatory words. The reason for the shift to words is the size and character of ancient courts. The judges are too numerous and too far away for the defendant to

---

193. *H. Ven.* 130–54 vs. 181–95.

194. As in the appendices. Unless Homer says otherwise, I have assumed that all fugitive murderers use a gesture; *Il.* 16.574, where *hiketeuô* is used of one murderer, Epigeus, shows that they all supplicate.

195. Hdt. 6.68. Th. 3.58.2–3.

use any gesture that makes contact. Among other gestures, prostration is inappropriate, and boughs would encumber the defendant's speechmaking. On the other hand, court offers an ideal opportunity to perform multiple acts. The defendant usually has family and friends at hand, and since the stakes are often high, he has every reason to ask for help, and they have every reason to give it. And time is ample. The defendant and his circle can orchestrate their efforts.

Defendants, in short, do not perform a single act of supplication. They and their supporters perform—and orchestrate—verbal and gestural acts that coalesce into a scenario. To understand such scenarios, we need to trace them from start to finish and include any verbal act. In isolation, such an act might seem "figurative," like other verbal acts. In context, such an act amplifies a collective effort.

Before a trial, Aristophanes reports, a typical defendant would supplicate in person, and the Old Oligarch supports him, saying that even defendants from allied states had to do so.[196] A third piece of evidence comes from Posidippus, who says that Phryne, the famous courtesan accused of impiety, took each judge by the hand, and thus accomplished the same thing. Although this report may be fictitious, the examples from Aristophanes and the Old Oligarch make it plausible.[197] In Rome, friends and family, including women, would circulate outside the court, as in Antony's case.[198] These multiple acts, some by the defendant, some by others, all occur before the defendant utters even a word in the course of the trial.

Supplication continues during the trial. Here we lack Greek sources, but not Roman ones. In the late Republican period, when judges numbered 75, relatives of the defendant, especially notables, would share the responsibility of supplicating, and in one case a commentator on Cicero makes it clear that they reached all or almost all the judges.[199] The defendant was Marcus Aemilius Scaurus, a prominent Roman and the son of an even more prominent father, on trial for bribery in 54 BCE:

> Those who were at the judges' knees making entreaties divided into two groups: on the one side, Scaurus [the defendant]; Manius Glabrio, the son of his sister; Lucius Paulus; Publius Lentulus, a son of the flamen Lucius Cornelius Lentulus Niger; another son, Lucius Aemilius Buca; and Gaius Memmius, Fausta's son [and the defendant's in-law].[200]

Other than the defendant, this list includes the consul of 67 BCE, a curule aedile of 56, just two years before the trial; and the praetor of 58, four years before the trial.[201] On the other side, the suppliants were

---

196. Ar. *V.* 555–59; X. *Ath. Pol.* 1.18.
197. Posidipp. *PCG* 13.6–7.
198. The earliest reported example: Liv. 3.58.1 (446 BCE).
199. Asc. *Sc.* 25. Large numbers in the early Republic: Liv. 3.58.1.
200. Asc. *Sc.* 25, reading L. Paulus rather than P. Paulus.
201. As in *MRR* except for Lucius Aemilius Lepidus Paulus as cur. aed. as in *OCD* s.v. *Aemilius Paullus*, 3.

Faustus Sulla, Scaurus's brother; Titus Annius Milo, whom Fausta had married a few months before, once she was divorced from Memmius; Gaius Peducaeus; Gaius Cato; and Marcus Laenas Curtianus.[202]

This coterie includes the quaestor of 54, the year of the trial, the praetor of 55, a future legate, and a tribune of the plebs in 56.[203] But impressive as these lists are, they nonetheless exclude the nine consulars who testify for Scaurus and also his six advocates. Suppliants are high-ranking family members. By contrast, witnesses are higher ranking friends, and advocates are ranking orators.[204]

Granted that some of these offices lack Attic counterparts, the scheme should hold good: a suppliant's coadjutors comprise his family and friends, his *philoi*, as Hyperides calls them, the more prestigious the better.[205] They take on distinct tasks. A scenario can rise to the scale of opera.

Now comes the climax of the scenario, the aria—the defendant's own speech or that of his advocate. A Greek defendant would often use a tricolon crescendo, saying ἱκετεύω and also δέομαι καὶ ἀντιβολῶ.[206] Usually, ἱκετεύω comes last: "Gentlemen, I beg, I beseech—no, it is my God-given right to ask—. . ." Such language tends to occur either at the start of the speech, when the speaker is asking the audience to listen, or at the end, when he is asking them to render the proper verdict.[207] Latin again offers parallels, *obsecro* serving to invoke the gods, and *obtestor* serving to summon them as witnesses.[208]

The use of strong language at these critical moments is self-evident, but two motives for it may escape notice. The first, to discourage the interruptions common in court,[209] explains why the tricolon crescendo is more common in forensic oratory than in Assembly and Senate speeches.[210] The second, which is exclu-

---

202. Asc. *Sc.* 25, ctd.

203. As in *MRR*, excerpt for M. Laenas Curtianus, about whose career nothing is known. The identification of Peducaeus as legate of 43 is tentative.

204. For the lists of the six *patroni* and nine witnesses, all of the latter being consulars, see Asc. *Sc.* 20, 28. A different interpretation of these lists: Marshall p. 150–56, seeing political factors at work; D.C. 39.63.5 says that in 54 BCE Pompey supplicated on behalf of the defendant Aulus Gabinius, cos. 58.

205. Hyp. *Eux.* 41. According to Dem. 23.206, judges related to the defendant would entreat those who were not. At Lys. 14.21, 15.1, the defendants are glad to have generals speak on their behalf, but we do not know whether they are supplicating.

206. Dem. 43.84, 45.1, 45.85 (prosecutors); 27.68, 57.1 (defendants or appellants); Lys. 4.20, 18.27, 21.21 (all defendants); Is. 2.2, 2.44 (defendant).

207. Begging to be heard, including tricola: Dem. 21.7, 45.1, 57.1, Is. 2.2. To be acquitted, or some similar outcome, also including tricola: Aeschin. 2.180.1; Dem. 27.68, 28.20, 57.70 with suicide threat; Is. 2.44; Lys. 4.20, 18.27, 21.21; And. 1.149 καταφεύγω in same sense. Similarly, Quint. *Inst.* 4.1.28 recommends confining appeals to pity to the peroration. Parody: Lucianus *Phal.* 1.14, *Bis Acc.* 21.

208. As in Remmius Palaemo apud. Suet. p 312 ed. Roth, who distinguishes both from the weaker *oro*, which resembles *deomai*: "Inter obsecrat obtestatur et orat: obsecrat qui per opes sacras rogat; obtestatur qui fide aliqua interposita rogat, quasi testem habiturus aliquem precum suarum; orat qui sic rogat ut moueat affectu animum."

209. For disruption, see the catalogue compiled by Bers, "Thorubos," 3–8, who does not cite any instance in which the judges interrupted someone using the language of supplication. Discouraging interruptions as a standard part of *proemia*: Arist. *Rh.* 3.1415a. As elsewhere, supplications should be distinguished from prayers, also uttered at critical moments; examples in the orators appear in Kuettler, *Precationes*, 11–12.

210. A Roman symbouleutic case: D.C. 53.9.1, where Augustus supplicates the Senate. A possible Greek case: Dem. 24.49–52, asserting supplication by Timarchus. In Cicero, there are seven symbouleutic cases, including four in deliberative bodies (*Att.* 1.14.5, *Red. Pop.* 13, *Red. Sen.* 31, 37, *Brut.* 90) and three in other public

sively Greek, is to contrast the speaker's requests with the requests of his opponent, which may be described by the weaker word *deomai*.[211] This distinction
between *hiketeuô* and *deomai* passes to later writers, who use it to distinguish
between those they wish to describe as suppliants and those who have not earned
this status.[212] But these factors of timing and style matter less than the contribu-
tion that the speaker makes to the ensemble of efforts on his behalf. He and others
have clasped knees and hands. Now he uses charged language that alludes to these
gestures and reminds the judges that every gesture and word has but one aim—
making his request for acquittal a supplication. Roman practice adds to all these
elements a new one, the role of the advocate. Cicero will say that both he and the
defendant supplicate the judges. If the defendant cannot supplicate plausibly, the
advocate supplicates for him.[213] Cicero likes fantasy, too: whole social groups
supplicate, as in the *Pro Sulla*, and in the orator's most momentous speeches,
against Catiline, the Fatherland itself supplicates.[214] These vignettes build on
examples like that of Scaurus.

Cicero also makes use of other appeals that fall short of supplication to the
judges. According to the *Pro Sulla*, the defendant supplicated Cicero to defend
him, but a supporter of the defendant, the great Messala, did not go quite so far.
He addressed "entreaties" to Cicero to the same effect. During the trial some other
supporters, the Marcelli, father and son, weep for the defendant. At the end of
Cicero's speech, the advocate claims that the defendant's little son is somehow
speaking on his behalf and that Sulla is supplicating, too, but figuratively, by fleeing to the altar of the law.[215] Pathos pours from many voices, both individual and
in chorus. Cicero does not neglect the fundamentals: knee clasps before the trial,
words during it, reiteration, and variation. But no other supplications attain the
same thoroughness, vigor, and invention. With Cicero, opera rises to grand opera.

Is Cicero—and his army of coadjutors—too vigorous for their own good?
Quintilian, for one, attacks speakers who say they have supplicated but in truth
have not.[216] But prosecutors found supplication by defendants so powerful that
they sometimes imitate them, and beg that the beggars be convicted. We do not
know much about what Roman prosecutors say, because Cicero, our main source,

---

gatherings (*Pis.* 80, *Planc.* 24, *Sest.* 107); in contrast, there are 17 forensic speeches in which one or more acts
occur, as indicated in the appendix on acts of supplication in Cicero. The only reference to a forensic case in any
other Roman author: V. Max. 8.1.6.

211. Pejorative *deomai*: Antipho fr. 77. For a similar study of rhetorical tactics, but concentrating on legal and not
behavorial issues, see Konstan, *Pity Transformed*, 37–42, on Lys. 21.21. The same distinction in historiography: Th.
5.60.6 describes an Argive general who supplicates successfully at an altar in 418 BCE, whereas D.S. 12.78.5 describes
the same general and others as making use only of δεήσεως. Diodorus's bias against the Argives: 12.78.2.

212. Including writers who, like Polybius and Isocrates avoid *hiketeuô* as emotional; only gestures, especially
the placement of boughs, designate supplication.

213. Advocate and defendant: *Mur.* 86–87, *Rab. Perd.* 5, 37. Advocate alone. *Mil.* 100, 103. Advocate and
family: *Lig.* 36–37, *Planc.* 102, 104.

214. *Patria*: Cic. *Cat.* 4.18. *Res publica*: Charisius apud Rut. Lup. 2.6. The biggest cast: *Red. Sen.*, where the
crowd, Pompey, and Cicero's brother Quintus all appeal on behalf of the exiled Cicero (12, 31, 37).

215. Cic. *Sul.* 20, 88, 89.

216. Quint. *Inst.* 6.1.43. A hint of parody: Luc. 7.70–71.

hardly ever prosecutes, but one Roman prosecutor does use supplicatory words.[217] Of the Greek prosecutors who use supplicatory words, in particular ἱκετεύω, three warn judges that the defendants will use such words.[218] Other prosecutors use the words themselves, and thus compete with the defendants.[219] In *Against Midias*, Demosthenes even claims that he, like a defendant, is being wrongfully attacked. One prosecutor even uses the tricolon crescendo, though defendants must have used it far more often.[220] They use it most in private as opposed to public cases.[221] In private cases, the prosecutor did not represent the community, and found it harder to compete with the defendant.

Since Quintilian is not writing about courtroom oratory only, he prompts the observation that collective supplication occurs in several genres. Tragedy is one, but the Greek term for defendants, *feugontes* or "fleeing ones," points to the citizens of besieged or captured cities. Like Danaus and his daughters or the defendant and his supporters, these suppliants might parcel out words and gestures to sundry groups: hair-rending to women, speechmaking to elderly men.[222] A king who supplicated amid a thousand retainers, as described in Josephus, no doubt outperformed either a Greek chorus or Aemilius Scaurus.[223] Supplication by groups, then, does not appear only in court. Since this kind of supplication is common in court, it does have an institutional cast; it may even seem perfunctory, like the Sunday best worn by the defendant's relatives when they sit behind him in court today. But group supplication in antiquity is more energetic than this comparison implies. Each of the king's 1,000 retainers supplicated individually.

From gestures we have come to words, and then to combinations of words and gestures, to scenarios. But suppliants have not ceased to try to make advantageous choices. Contact suits the paternal supplicandus, whereas a slight distance, as observed in prostration, suits the supplicandus who is godlike. A striking gesture from a great distance, the extended pair of hands, suits the hostile supplicandus. A bough suits the supplicandus who is at some physical but temporary remove. Mourning clothes suit the supplicandus passed in the street or market, the curious or friendly crowd. Words suit the supplicandus who remains distant not for any extrinsic reason, but because of traits such as gender or status. Scenarios suit the most complex supplicandus of all, the court, accessible at one stage of a proceeding, inaccessible at another, first a congeries of individuals, later a group operating under written rules.

By the same token, gestures and words must suit the culture in which the supplicandus appears. Contact is mostly Greek, mourning clothes entirely Hebrew and

217. Cic. *Quinct.* 99. The sources listed in Alexander, *Trials,* contain no others.

218. Warnings: Lys. 6.55, 22.21, Lycurg. *in Leocr.* 143.

219. Dem. 43.84, 45.85, 46.28; Is. 6.57, 8.45, 9.37.

220. Dem. 21.7.

221. Preponderance of defendants: Johnstone, *Disputes and Democracy*, 118. Public cases: Dem. 21.7, Aeschin. 2.180.1, Lys. 21.21.

222. E.g., Luc. 7.369–84, where Roman groups are supposed to be supplicating Pompeians. Speeches by men, tears from women and children: Liv. 6.3.4. Children added along with much else: Hld. 9.11.4–5. Elderly men on behalf of females in tragedy: A. *Supp.* 480–85, E. *Supp.* 113–262.

223. J. *AJ* 20.54–59.

Roman. Scenarios link Greece and Rome, but a tendency to self-abasement, toward prostration as well as mourning, links Jerusalem and Rome. Even the difference between Greek and Roman legal sources affects the portrayal of supplication. Greek legal sources, almost all speeches, report that defendants use supplicatory language. They do not mention supplication by family and friends. Cicero, the Roman source, reports what he and other advocates say and what friends and family do. The Greek context seems smaller—a misleading impression, even if Phryne did not kiss the hands of every member of the Areopagus, the court in which she stood trial. The Areopagus included all former high-ranking magistrates, like the Roman Senate. Perhaps these men's hands were too many, even for her.

But differences aside, all words and gestures must accomplish the aim of communicating the suppliant's intent. Hence an oddity found in numerous acts, beginning with those performed by Phemius and Leodes in *Odyssey* 22. Both men describe the gesture that they are performing. So do suppliants in Greek tragedy.[224] These suppliants do make contact, but they also make announcements. They do not put their trust in contact alone. The hand on the knee, the personal touch, or humble air—supplication is not a time for intimacy or ruth. Too much is at stake.

REQUESTS AND ARGUMENTS

The third step consists of the suppliant's request and the arguments made to justify it—the "what" and the "why" of an act of supplication. The link between this step and the previous two is variety. Just as approaches and gestures vary according to the character of the supplicandus, requests vary according to the needs (and character) of the suppliant. The link between this step and the fourth, when the supplicandus responds to the suppliant, is the justification of the request by some argument that the supplicandus can accept. Within the third step, the need for justification is of a piece with two other traits: most requests are serious, and some are legal. For this reason, they lead to some tie between the suppliant and the supplicandus. This tie is often lasting and always significant.

In contrast, the prevailing view holds that requests are mostly for some sort of inclusion in a group, especially inclusion in a family or community, but also inclusion in a smaller group, a pair of persons joined by a tie of mutual hospitality, *xenia*. Similarly, Burkert holds that requests for inclusion mirror an animal's request to join a pack or herd. Arguments matter little in either view. In the prevailing view, the suppliant can attain success without them, thanks to the use of proper gestures, and thus does not need them. The same holds true for Burkert, who believes that the suppliant succeeds or fails depending on whether the pack will be stronger if the suppliant joins it. The suppliant must step forward and undergo evaluation, but he or she need not argue. Literary critics have

---

224. A Euripidean locution: E. *Heracl.* 227 (beard), *IA* 909 (beard and hand), *Med.* 709 (beard and knees), *Hipp.* 605–607 (right hand and knees). I assume, with Taplin, *Tragedy in Action*, 30, that any supplicatory act that is described is also being performed. A different, more cautious view: Kaimio, *Physical Contact*, 6–7.

disagreed with these conclusions, but they have not thought of arguments as justifying requests. They regard appeals to emotion as more important than arguments.[225]

How varied are requests? A suppliant can ask for rags, as Telephus does in tragedy, or a golden fleece, as Jason does in epic; a special bow, as Neoptolemus does in mythography, or special armor, as Thetis and Venus do in epic.[226] He or she may want to have a spouse's mistress killed, as Phoenix's mother does in Homer, or to learn how to arouse a teenage girl, as the shepherd Daphnis does in the pastoral novel of Longus. Many requests are pathetic. Let the suppliant drink just once from the enemy's stream, as happens during the siege of Jerusalem by the Romans, or live forever on an island at the mouth of Danube, as Achilles will thanks to his mother. Let Cleopatra have a moment to dress and be at her best when she confronts the hostile Octavian. Let Medea have enough time to gather her children and possessions and move to another city—nothing more.[227] Jewish priests beg on behalf of sacred objects, Greek priests beg for meat.[228] Other requests are not unusual, but still reflect the idiosyncrasy of the suppliant. If the suppliant wants to join a group, he may ask to become a curule magistrate, as was done at Rome, as opposed to a mere citizen, as at Athens. If he wants legal help, he may ask to have a fine reduced as opposed to having some financial burden remitted.[229] These last examples come from prose sources, and the suppliants are men, and so they show that the diversity of requests does not derive solely from poetry or from women.

But even if we gather the most checkered requests that we can, most are serious, and this trait of seriousness furnishes the standard by which to classify requests. The most serious request of all, the request to be spared in battle, should come first, followed by requests for protection. Less serious are requests for some benefit, be it an improvement in or restoration of status or some other kind of help. Other less serious requests are for vengeance and pardon; some of these are legal.[230] Requests cluster by genre, but as our checkered examples suggest, they do not cluster by culture.

The request to be spared by an enemy comprises about one-third of all requests in the *Iliad*.[231] Hector requests to be spared; so does his half-brother Lycaon; so does the spy and turncoat Dolon. Requests to be spared also bulk large in Caesar,

225. As in chap. 1, but see especially Burkert, *Creation of the Sacred*, 85–90, and Crotty, *Poetics*.

226. Ar. *Ach.* 414–34; A.R. 3.967–1014; *Il.* 18.421–67, V. A. 8.382.

227. *Il.* 9.451–53, Longus 3.18.1; J. *BJ* 6.319–21, Philostr. *Her.* 746; Xiph. 77.8, E. *Med.* 324–51.

228. Jewish priests: J. *BJ* 2.322–25; other Jews do likewise at 2.192–201, 2.233. Greek priest: Ar. *Pax* 1113–21.

229. Sal. *Jug.* 85.1 versus *IG* ii² 336; Th. 3.70.5–6 versus Serv. *G.* 2.161.

230. Other views: R. Parker, *Miasma*, 181, divides requests into "spare me" and "help me," as does Cairns, *Aidos*, 1.3.5; Traulsen, *Das sakrale Asyl*, 96–114, distinguishes "die flehendliche Bitte" and requests by "die Fremde." Gould, "*Hiketeia*," 81, holds that battlefield supplication is atypical but otherwise does not distinguish among requests.

231. *Il.* 6.45–65, 10.454–56, 11.130–47, 20.463–9, 21.64–119, 22.337–60. So also for the second, Iliadic half of Virgil's *Aeneid*, where they constitute three out of seven (10.522–36, 10.594–601, 12.930–52).

who deals in groups, including the Helvetii and four other tribes.[232] The writer who records more acts of supplication than any other, Josephus, does not lack requests to be spared.[233] But not all requests to be spared come from suppliants on the battlefield. Travelers ask pirates to spare them.[234] Children ask parents to spare them—a request that cannot have occurred only in myths like that of Iphigenia and Agamemnon. Are these requests for inclusion? Sometimes. To be spared and taken prisoner is to be included in the camp of the victor. But travelers who are spared are asking to be released, not included. So is Iphigenia.

In all these cases the suppliant faces an immediate threat. In other cases, the threat appears at some remove, but remains lethal. Then the suppliant will ask not to be spared but to be protected, the next category. Here the paradigmatic cases come not just from Homer, who provides several examples, but also from the Old Testament, in which the suppliant who comes to an altar evidently does so in order to escape the relatives of the man that he has killed. Usually he remains in a town of refuge, an instance of inclusion in a group. But under one circumstance he may leave, obviating inclusion.[235] The same two outcomes appear in Homer. Suppliants like Patroclus, who flees after the fatal dice game, remain with the supplicandus, who may make him a family member—another instance of inclusion. But sometimes the fleeing man stays only temporarily, as is true of the father of Antinous in the *Odyssey*. He comes to Odysseus when the people of Ithaca wish to kill him for the offense of making war on friendly neighbors, and Odysseus protects him until the people give way.[236] In such cases, inclusion is missing. In general, inclusion is frequent but not universal.

The suppliant may also be escaping those who wish to capture him but not necessarily kill him. In *Oedipus at Colonus*, the pursuer, Creon, wants only to ensure that Oedipus dies and is buried in Theban territory. In the *Suppliants* of Aeschylus, the pursuer wants only to compel the suppliants to marry his sons.[237] In historiography and fiction, pursuers want to imprison suppliants, sell them into slavery, or put them on trial; Herodotus reports all three, and so does Livy.[238] Other pursuers want to convict; they are prosecutors at trials. The career of Cicero alone shows how many suppliants faced this threat. In all these instances, inclusion is

232. Caes. *Gal.* 1.27.1–28.2 (Helvetii), 2.13.2–15.1 (Bellovaci), 2.28.2–3 (Nervii), 7.15.3–6 (Bituriges).

233. J. *BJ* 2.497–98, 2.601–10, 4.311, 4.360, 4.553, 6.271, 6.356–57, 6.378–79, 7.202–6, *Vit.* 328–29, or 10 acts out of 57.

234. Hld. 5.25.1–2.

235. The death of the high priest (*Nu.* 35.13, *Jos.* 20.6). How this circumstance affects the evaluation of the killer by elders is disputed; Rofé, "*Joshua* 20," 136, holds that this circumstance is incompatible with the rest of the procedure. Other Hebrew examples of requests for protection: J. *BJ* 2.314, 5.548–52.

236. Patroclus: *Il.* 23.85–90. Father of Antinous: *Od.* 16.424–30. Other Homeric examples: *Il.* 2.653–57, 9.478–83, 16.570–74, *Od.* 15.256–84.

237. S. *OC* 44–641, A. *Supp.* 1–519; also *Eu.* 276–488, E. *And.* 1–412, *HF* 1–327, *Hel.* 1–566, *Ion* 1255–1613, *Alexander*, *Dictys*, S. *Tyro*.

238. Hdt. 1.157–59 (imprisonment), 3.48 (enslavement), 5.71 (trial); Liv. 3.50.5 (intercession against domestic confinement), 8.28.5–9 (same), 45.5.1–6.10 (trial by the local authorities). So also Longus 2.20.3 (enslavement). A similar case in lyric poetry: Alc. *PLF* 130.31–35, assuming that the poet took refuge when threatened by political enemies who wished to imprison him.

once again incidental. Oedipus finds inclusion in Athens, but suppliants who fear imprisonment or are standing trial want freedom, not inclusion.

If the suppliant need not escape a pursuer but remains fearful, he asks for safety. Much peaceable surrender to the Romans falls into this category. This kind of supplication differs somewhat from surrender during a battle or siege. During a battle or siege the suppliants may be slain, ransomed, or sold into slavery, but peaceable surrender to the Romans seldom leads to these dire results. Instead the suppliants become dependents of Rome and perhaps of the general who accepts their surrender. Also somewhat different, but no less vital, are women's requests to be protected against rape. They appear in several genres, too, but surely are less often reported than are requests to surrender to great powers.[239] Less grave than the request to be spared, and perhaps less noticed, the request to be protected appears in more sources and genres.

A request for another kind of protection comes from suppliants who go to a healing shrine and ask for a cure for their ill health. They would travel to shrines of Asclepius, often over great distances, perform ablutions or other rituals when they arrived, and then enter the *abaton*, or "sanctuary," and spend the night. If the god responded favorably to their supplication, he would cure them in a dream, or dispatch dogs or snakes to lick the sleeping suppliant and accomplish the same end. Since no human being performed the cure, these pilgrims would seem to be worshippers, not suppliants.[240] They nonetheless take all four steps found in the practice. The approach is a long and arduous one, but the shrine that receives them regards them as (and they surely thought of themselves as) suppliants, *hiketai*, a word used in many of the *iamata*, or records of cures.[241] Next comes a request made to Asclepius, and the god's response. If the god accepts the supplication, he treats the suppliant and performs a cure. If the god rejects the supplication, the suppliant leaves untreated.[242] Aside from the four steps, the trip to an Asclepieum is often a last resort, and so these suppliants are scarcely less serious than other suppliants seeking protection.[243]

Following requests for protection come requests for a benefit. They fall into two groups, requests to help the suppliant improve or regain his status—in short,

239. Avoid rape: Ach. Tat. 5.17.3–5, Paus. 7.2.7, Plut *Th.* 8.1, Plut. *Mul. Virt.* 251a–c, to which can be added every instance of collective supplication during the plunder of a capture city—a list that, if complete, would number hundreds. Avoid enslavement and sexual exploitation: Hdt. 9.76, a plea by a prisoner of war that must have had many counterparts not reported in the historical record. A woman fearing rape as well as seeking to avenge her father: Plut. *Amat. Narr.* 774f.

240. Hence Gould, *"Hiketeia,"* and others have omitted pilgrims of this kind. An early recognition of these pilgrims as visitors to an asylum if not as suppliants: Segre, "Asclepieio di Pergamo."

241. *Hiketês* vel sim.: *IG* iv² 1.121.4, 121.15, 121.20, 121.23, 121.34, 121.72, 121.90, in each of which this word precedes the phrase ποὶ τὸν θεόν, all cited by Nehrbass, *Sprache und Stil* 55. *Hiketês* vel sim. elsewhere: 1.125 (Epidaurus, third century BCE), 1.126 (Epidaurus, ca. 160 CE), 1.516 (Epidaurus, Roman period CE), 1.537 (Epidaurus, first to fourth centuries CE); *IC* 1.xvii 9 (Lebena, second century BCE) 17–18 (Lebena, first century BCE). All these sources appear in Edelstein, *Asclepius.*

242. Acceptance: Philostr. *VA* 4.11. Rejection: *VA* 1.10.

243. Last resort: examples at Weinreich, *Antike Heilungswunder,* 195–97, in which repeated failures by physicians precede wondrous cures obtained at healing shrines. In one of the *iamata,* a man about to undergo surgery avoided it by going to Epidaurus instead (*IG* iv² 1.121 #4). But some shrines drew mainly local persons: Aleshire, *Asclepieion,* 66–67.

requests involving honor—and requests to help him in some other way. The former are usually more serious, just as a request to be spared is more serious than one to be protected. Inclusion forms part of only some of these requests.

A suppliant seeking to improve or regain his status may ask for *xenia*, the status of a guest-friend, for purification, for elevation to citizenship or even election to office or ascension to a throne. The first of these, requesting *xenia*, does lead to the inclusion of the suppliant in a pair: himself and the supplicandus. But requests for *xenia* have two traits that affect this act of inclusion. First, suppliants making this request do not make it in so many words. Like Telemachus in the *Odyssey*, they prefer to let the host discern their request.[244] In all of ancient literature, only the Odysseus of the *Odyssey* expressly requests to become a *xenos*, and even he makes this request only once, to the Cyclops.[245] Second, the implied request for *xenia* (or Odysseus's express request) may accompany other requests. Telemachus wants information about his father, and Odysseus wants gifts from the Cyclops. Classical suppliants who request honors from a city such as Athens ask for "just deserts," a phrase that entails tax breaks and other advantages and not just hospitality in the form of meals at public expense.[246]

Requests for purification appear in inscriptions from Cyrene and Lindus, not to mention literary examples beginning with the *Argonautica*, in which Jason and Medea request purification from Circe.[247] Here the suppliant seeks restoration of status, but not inclusion. Also common are requests for political boons ranging from citizenship to royal power. Greek requests for just deserts, which include citizenship, and Roman requests for votes reflect differences in political values and organization, but have more in common with each other than the requests to gain or regain a crown, the Near Eastern counterpart.[248] Here inclusion occurs if the suppliant joins a group such as a citizen body or a board of magistrates, but not if he (or she) ascends a throne.[249] Nor does inclusion occur if the suppliant requests not to win an office but instead to keep one, as Antony did once Octavian attacked him.[250] And inclusion hardly occurs if the suppliant asks a monarch or tyrant to abdicate or, on the other hand, asks someone else to seize a throne.[251]

Requests for other kinds of help vary in solemnity. The most solemn such request, for help in burying the dead, appears not just in epic or tragedy, but also in the orator Isaeus. In verse, the dead are warriors, and so the suppliant must

244. Telemachus: *Od.* 3.92–108, 4.332–50. Grants of *xenia* in the form of the right to dine in a public hall, a right not sought by the suppliant: A. *Supp.* 1010–11, *IG* ii² 218.20–21, 276.11–12.
245. *Od.* 9.267–71.
246. "Just deserts": *IG* ii² 211.4–6, 218.14–16, the second by supplement. Other honors: as at 177 below.
247. *SEG* XXXIX 729 (Lindos, third century BCE) and Servais "Suppliants" (Cyrene, 331–23 BCE), both discussed at 186–90 below.
248. Citizenship: *IG* ii² 336. Votes: [Cic.] *Commentar. Petitionis* 8 and examples discussed at 231–33 below. Senate membership as opposed to election to office: D.C. 54.14.2–3, under the empire. Thrones: J. *AJ* 20.54–59, *BJ* 1.281–84, Plut. *Pop.* 16.1, Polyaen. 8.47.1 bis, 8.55.1, Str. 14.2.17, Val. Max. 5.1.9; and S. *OC* 1267–1396, 1156–1205 being preparatory.
249. Inclusion also occurs if the suppliant asks to join a retinue or army, as at X. *An.* 7.1.21–22.
250. Plut. *Ant.* 59.1, where Antony acts through intercessors.
251. Abdication: Plut. *Timol.* 4.5–6. Ascension of another: D.C. 45.32.3–4.

approach an enemy, as Priam does in *Iliad* 24, or ask someone else to do the same, as the Argive women do in Euripides, when they ask Theseus to approach the enemies who are withholding the bodies of their men. But in Isaeus the dead person is a head of household whom a male heir wants to lay out for burial in one place, and the widow wants to lay out for burial in another, and so she, like Priam or the women in Euripides, must supplicate the stronger party. These suppliants are not necessarily seeking inclusion, either. Priam and the Argive women are, insofar as they wish to reclaim the body, but the widow in Isaeus is not. The deceased happens to be in the house where she lives, and she wishes to retain him.[252]

Some that seek help are trying to obtain information. The information sought may be religious, personal, or political, and in one case, the suppliant wants to impart rather than receive it.[253] The motives for this request vary no less than the information itself. In Sophocles, the people of Thebes ask Tiresias for information that will help them put an end to a plague, and so they want to be spared. Many suppliants wish to impart information in exchange for immunity from prosecution.[254] In Tacitus, the brother of the emperor Vitellius wants to make himself useful, and so he begs for a chance to impart information rather than to receive any. The information is false, another unique feature of this act, but suited to this author.[255]

Slaves' requests for better treatment appear only in prose, including epigraphical sources. Most striking is that only two slaves ask for less onerous work. Lysias's slave, facing the prospect of turning a millstone, like a mule, begs to be allowed to remain in domestic service. She succeeds, but a Hebrew slave who asks not to work in the mines meets with rejection.[256] Other slaves ask for a new master, a common practice leading to legal difficulties reserved for chapter 5. None ask for freedom. Modest as they are, slaves' requests rank ironically low.[257]

Requests for help overlap with legal requests. Among these, the most serious is a request to be acquitted, one nearly as common as courtroom supplication, which, as we have seen, comes mostly from defendants.[258] Next come requests for vengeance. Any attempt to recover a throne likely involves vengeance.[259] Women seek vengeance, too—Greek, Roman, and other women—and they seek it for political as well as personal reasons. Hecuba wants vengeance on Helen, who caused the war that led to the deaths of her children. At the other extreme, Lucretia wants her

---

252. *Il.* 24.477–570, *Od.* 11.66–80, E. *Supp* 1–361, Is. 8.22.

253. Political and personal: Hdt. 6.68. Religious: E. *Ph.* 923–59, Hdt. 7.141, V. Fl. 4.535–49, V.A. 6.42–115. Personal: Ov. *Met.* 10.414–30, Sen. *Con.* 10.2.10.

254. S. *OT* 326–29; Plut. *Per.* 31.2–3, *Timol.* 16.5–8.

255. Tac. *Hist.* 3.38.

256. Lys. 1.19–20, J. *BJ* 6.433–34.

257. See also appendix 2. A modest (or comparatively modest) request by a goddess: *Il.* 5.357–63, where the request does not lead to a tie.

258. If the charge against the defendant is capital, this request is one to be spared, as at Cic. *Clu.* 200, *Mil.* 100, and *Rab. Perd.* 5, 36–37. The lack of comparable Greek cases must be accidental. A cross between judicial and military requests to be spared: D.C. 77.9.3, taking place in a tribal camp. Another mixed case: Lys. 1.25–27, where the supplicandus is the head of the household, the same as Odysseus in *Odyssey* 22; see 198–200 below.

259. Other than thrones: X. *An.* 7.2.33, *Cyr.* 4.6.1–10, Paus. 2.6.2.

father to take vengeance on the prince who raped her.[260] But a woman can also seek vengeance on those who removed her family from power, as in Herodotus.[261] At the other extreme are requests for a trial or hearing. These crop up in conditions in which a wanted man cannot find or gain access to a court by any means other than supplication. The oldest example is the Old Testament murder regulations that give the suppliant access to the elders. Greek examples occur, too, whether in Athens or in out-of-the-way places like the Ethiopia of Heliodorus's novel.[262]

Other requests are for pardon. They come from slaves and soldiers, and must have been far more numerous than the few instances that survive.[263] This category differs somewhat from requests to be spared. There, the suppliant sometimes claims to be a member of a group eligible for mercy, like surrendering soldiers. Here, he or she claims to be an innocent of wrongdoing, or, failing that, claims to be worthy enough to make his or her particular request: one suppliant who has offended Josephus asks to have one hand cut off, not two, and gains his wish.[264] Unlike modern counterparts, the suppliant does not ever admit wrongdoing and plead for clemency. Asserting innocence, he or she pleads for pity.[265]

All the requests so far have been express, but sometimes suppliants follow the example of Telemachus and suppress a request. The reason is that the supplicandus may grant one thing only after he has granted another. When unpopular generals go to the nearest altar, they ask to be spared; only later will they ask for a chance to speak to, and win over, their pursuers.[266] Many diplomats find themselves in the reverse situation. They request a hearing, but they may also be afraid, and so they may be suppressing a request to be spared.[267] Another recourse is to make a request without supplication and then to make a request with supplication, as when some women taken captive by Scipio Africanus make a request for food. They do not use supplicatory language, so the request strikes him as trivial. Although responding favorably to it, he fails to give a pledge. Then, emboldened, the captives ask for protection against Roman lust, and they do use supplicatory language. Now he adds a pledge to his favorable response.[268] This, he knows, is supplication, but until the women tested him they did not dare try it.

260. Hecuba: E. Tro. 1042–57. Lucretia: D.H. 4.66.1–67.1.

261. Pheretima to Satrap (Hdt. 4.1652–67.1). Others: Mandana to Darius (D.S. 11.57.3), a Thracian princess to Seleucus I (Paus. 1.10.4).

262. Athens: schol. Aeschin. 2.14, referring to requests for justice; And. 1.44. Ethiopia: Hld. 10.10.1–2. Others: E. And. 358–60, Hrd. 1.11.4–5, Lucianus Pisc. 1–10.

263. Slave: Petr. 17.9–18.4, 30.7–11. Soldier: Plut. Caes. 16.4.

264. J. BJ 2.643–44.

265. Exceptions to this rule: some Roman suppliants who commit lesser wrongs and deserve clemency, discussed at 240–46 below.

266. Generals: Th. 5.60.6, 8.84.3, perhaps a problem arising in this author for autobiographical reasons. It does not arise elsewhere. Explicit request for protection, implicit request for revenge: J. BJ 1.32.

267. Diplomats supplicating to ensure their safety: D.S. 16.45.2–3, App. Hisp. 52. No reason given, but perhaps safety: Ephor. 70 FGrH fr. 186, Liv. 34.40.2–4, Sal. Jug. 47.3–4, Paus. 1.12.1, Him. Or. 6.169–75; Front. Parth. 16, by a ruler.

268. Plb. 10.18, with supplication at 18.7. Liv. 26.49.11–15 makes the first request one for all manner of help, justifying supplication to obtain it. The second request is then added.

Requests do not include begging for food or money. In Homer, for example, Odysseus says that beggars should be fed, if not paid, and the wickedness of those who refuse shows that Homer agrees, but Odysseus does not, strictly speaking, supplicate for food. No one in Homer does.[269] No one in tragedy does—not even Oedipus in *Oedipus at Colonus*, a situation in which there would not seem to be any other way for him to survive.[270] In classical Athenian prose, there is once again not a single report of supplication for either food or money. Instead, pensions for the poor suggest that the state did not want citizens to beg.[271] Even refugees coming from abroad do not supplicate for food. The Plataean refugees described by Isocrates complain of being beggars, but they do not say that they supplicate when they beg, and when they address the Athenian Assembly, they ask for much greater boons, mainly military action against their enemies.[272] Supplicating for food is also missing from Latin sources. Rather than make this request, Drusus starves to death.[273] The exception is begging attributed to provinces that receive, and presumably request, food from emperors.[274] The reason for the exception is that there is an enduring tie between suppliants and supplicandi. Most begging for food lacks this aspect of the fourth step.[275]

Supplicating for money is rare for the same reasons.[276] Closest to it is the practice of supplicating for loans, reported by Basil, the fourth-century Cappadocian bishop. This time the suppliant received help, like a beggar, but also contracted a debt that formed an enduring tie between the parties. These supplications included the familiar figures of the pitiless supplicandus and the pitiable suppliant: "Seeing a man bending down on his knees out of necessity, supplicating, . . . the creditor does not pity him who is suffering undeservedly; . . . He remains unbending and heartless."[277] But the creditor then changes his mind and considers the suppliant's request for a loan: "But when the man that is seeking the loan speaks of interest and names his securities, then . . . the creditor lowers his brow, smiles, and re-

---

269. Odysseus begging with a supplicatory gesture: *Od.* 17.365–66. But he calls himself an *epistatēs* (17.455), not a suppliant. Wanderers who beg but are not said to supplicate: 14.124–32. A different view: Segal, *Singers, Heroes, and Gods*, chap. 7, linking the beggar with the bard, a prestigious figure, though not with suppliants. A somewhat similar view: van Wees, *Status Warriors*, chap. 5, showing the limits of monetary exchange in Homeric supplication.

270. Nor does Odysseus supplicate when begging in Troy at E. *Rh.* 503–7, 710–16, passages anticipated by *Od.* 4.244–56, where again he does not supplicate.

271. Pensions: Loomis, *Wages*, chaps. 13–14. There is one report of supplication to have a pension restored (Aeschin. 1.104).

272. Begging: Isoc. 14.46.

273. Tac. *Ann.* 6.23.

274. Reverse of an aureus of Trajan's, ANS 1958.214.18, where Italy supplicates him and the legend identifies him as ALIM IT, "feeder of Italy." Also J. *BJ* 5.438, but here the beggars ask not to be deprived of food of their own.

275. Other begging customs fall short of supplication for another reason: the supplicandus has less occasion to pass judgment. Herodotus 4.35.2 thus does not call customary begging on Delos supplication. Plut. *QG* 299c, about a festival commemorating the suppliant beggar Charila, allows for supplication during a legendary event that inspires a custom.

276. Pl. *Ps.* 507, *As.* 245–48; Quint. *Decl.* 260.10, and also the spurious [Quint.] *Decl.* 6.23–24, 9.1; Lucianus *Nigr.* 21. At Philostr. *VA* 4.10 begging and supplicating do not occur at the same moment, but do occur in the same place. The same conclusion: Hands, *Charities*, 14, but while saying that the poor seldom evoke pity.

277. *PG* 29.265b–68a, part of an exegetic homily on Psalm 14.

members some family tie." A "family tie" was a long-standing reason to accept a suppliant, and so was a money payment. In contrast, the payment of interest and the provision of securities were not. They show that the supplication is in fact a transaction. Basil thus denounces it. The enduring tie is of the wrong kind.[278]

A third kind of request, for sexual favors, may or may not lead to an enduring tie. Perhaps the earliest example comes from the inside of a fourth-century pyxis or lekanis lid: "A handsome (jar . . .) and a handsome writer . . . I beg you (ἱκετεύω). . . . Eudicus . . . after summoning . . ."[279] Who are the principals in this act of supplication? The "writer" is probably not the painter of the lid. Instead he is probably the person who has recorded these words, and he is also likely to be the suppliant. The supplicandus is likely to be his love interest, and the jar is likely to be a gift that he is presenting to the supplicandus. If these guesses are right, the suppliant is saying, "Love me. I am as handsome as my jar and besides, I have made you a gift." Whatever the suppliant's argument, the supplicandus will have many chances to consider it. Every time he opens the jar and looks at the lid he will read the inscription, and so the argument—and the request—will be reiterated. When presenting the gift, the suppliant has no doubt made this very point.[280] What we cannot say is whether this act of supplication ends in an enduring tie. We can only say that it includes a reiterated request.

Another problem is lighthearted bad faith, the concern in a passage of Achilles Tatius in which one young man takes another in hand and begins by explaining: "Prepare her and make her easy to lead; approach her pleasantly; keep quiet, mostly, as though you were at an initiation; get close and kiss her gently."[281] As the young adviser goes on to show, the girl in question is not being seduced. She is reluctant, and so she must be supplicated. As he says, "Giving a lover's kiss to a beloved who is willing, is a demand, but giving one to a beloved who is unwilling, is a supplication."[282] And so, Ovid would add, is a request for better kisses than those given a rival.[283] But the usual outcome of amatory supplication, rejection, differs from the rejection of other supplicatory requests. Amatory rejection is sometimes welcome.[284] In Ovid, the more violent the rejection, the better. More

---

278. For the first of these two motives, see Holman, *The Hungry are Dying*, who discusses the same homily at 120–23.

279. *SEG* XLIV 524, from Chalastra, 400–350 BCE:

Καλὸν [λεκάνιον---|---]δος, καλὸς δὲ ὁ γράψας πρ[---|---]λησον
ἱκετεύω σε κ[---|---]ει Εὔδικος Μενεστ[---||---]ω δὲ κελεύσας
Εὔ[δικον---|---]ας

On the outside of the lid: a picture of two seated women with a bird in between. In his *editio princeps*, Tiverios, *Egnatia* 3, provides no supplements.

280. For a summary of debate on the social setting for *kalos* inscriptions, many of which appear on vessels used in symposia, see Slater, "The Vase as Ventriloquist," 161–63, who warns against paying too much attention to the seducer and target and too little to others who would read or listen to the inscription.

281. Ach. Tat. 1.10.5.

282. "Supplication": ἱκετηρία.

283. Ov. *Am.* 2.5.49–52.

284. Rejection of supplicating lovers taken for granted: Pl. *Ps.* 311. Ovidian examples: *Met.* 13.854–56, 14.372–85, 14.701–42.

violence, the amatory suppliant explains, means more contact.[285] But how can failure be success?[286]

If a request leads to a genuine tie, it is obviously serious. But this trait of seriousness has two sides: for the supplicandus it means that the request is risky or difficult to grant, but for the suppliant it means that the request is vital. The suppliant seeking better health evidently feels this, but so does the threatened suppliant or the suppliant seeking justice.[287] In contrast, a request need not encompass inclusion in a group. Many suppliants want to be spared, released, or vindicated, not included.

The more serious a request, the more reason to argue in favor of it. In the remainder of this section we shall learn what suppliants say in defense of their requests.

Arguments

Of all parts of an act of supplication, arguments best rebut the view that supplication is a ritual of contact. According to this view, the suppliant need not justify himself. Instead his gesture justifies him. But suppliants do not expect their gestures to perform this task, any more than they expect the manner of approach to perform it. The suppliant must perform it himself, by arguing. Arguments also rebut the view that supplication is an act of persuasion, including persuasion by way of an appeal to the emotions. Arguments are, of course, more or less persuasive, but they are not persuasive in a vacuum. They appeal to shared values and often appeal to fairness, a moral if not legal value. Suppliants who seek acquittal or pardon are not the only ones to make these arguments about fairness. So do suppliants such as Phemius and Leodes, who say that it would be unfair to put them to death.

Some arguments about fairness are so common that they appear in ancient rhetorical handbooks advising defendants how to plead. Most detailed is the chapter on pity in Aristotle's *Rhetoric*, which contains an arsenal of arguments suitable for suppliants as well as for defendants. Central to these arguments is Aristotle's observation that judges favor those who are deserving. For this is the most common argument of all: the suppliant deserves to obtain what he requests, and so denying it to him would be unjust. Greek suppliants of the classical period make this argument by asking for just deserts.[288] Other suppliants promise to be worthy in

---

285. Ov. *Am.* 1.7.61–68.

286. Besides the passages noted immediately above, amatory requests appear at Longus 2.37.1, 3.18.1, 4.16.1–17.1, Lucianus *D deor.* 9.2, Parth. 5.2, 17.5, X. *Eph.* 3.2.3. Apul. *Met.* 6.2, the only amatory request in this novelist, does not concern human beings. Epic precedent: V. *A.* 1.666. Dramatic parallel: Sen. *Phaed.* 622–24, 667–706.

287. Metaphysical concepts of the character of requests: Gernet, "Pénalité et la réligion," 331–37, followed by Beaujon, *Dieu des suppliants*. Social concepts: Gould, "Hiketeia," followed by Herman, *Ritualised Friendship*, 3.2. Social concepts but with stress on affective and not political or economic aspects: Crotty, *Poetics*. Aristotle's list of misfortunes causing pity exceeds any notion of being made whole (*Rh.* 2.1386a).

288. "Worth" in Athens: n. 246 above. So also *BGU* 4.1053.2.6 (Ptolemaic Egypt), Michel #371 = *LSCG* #123 (Samos), and Suid. s.v. Ἀξίωμα ἡ ἱκετεία. Zelnick-Abramowitz, "Supplication and Request," 554, notices the resemblance to language when honors are granted but the recipient has not supplicated. A later example: App. *Pun.* 84. Latin *celebris* in same sense: Curt. 5.1.18.

the future, as in *Kings*, where Solomon says that a suppliant must prove himself "worthy" by being a loyal subject.[289] Most of the time, though, the suppliant does not pause to make this claim in so many words and instead lets it emerge from three other arguments: the first about reciprocity, the second about family ties, and the third about fairness.[290] The argument about reciprocity says that the suppliant has done or will do the supplicandus a service; the argument about family ties says that he is a loved one or friend; and the argument about fairness says that he is in the right or at least is not irredeemably in the wrong.[291]

Arguments do not exclude appeals to the emotions of the supplicandus, especially appeals to pity. Aristotle explains these appeals: pity is due to those who are legally innocent and morally worthy, and so it results from the suppliant's making successful arguments on these two scores.[292] Because of this link between emotions and arguments, this section will begin with the three main arguments—reciprocity, family, and fairness—and then turn to pity, the reward for the deserving.[293]

Reciprocity

Just as the most serious request is to be spared, the most compelling argument is reciprocity, a statement that the supplicandus owes the suppliant a favor. It takes two forms: claims that the suppliant has aided the supplicandus in the past, and claims that the suppliant will aid him in the future once his request is granted.[294] The argument may also be divided into claims addressed to individuals and those addressed to communities—into personal claims and political ones.

Several scholars have denied suppliants this argument, saying that the suppliant's inferior position makes it untenable.[295] But not all suppliants are in an inferior position in every respect. Many advert to whatever they are owed or can provide. Because it addresses both past and future, the argument about reciprocity is far-ranging, and touches on everything from mother's milk to gold bullion.

Claims of past services to the supplicandus begin with services done to him in his infancy. Mothers expose their breasts and say to the supplicandus, "I nursed you," and nurses expose theirs and say, "I nursed your king." In Euripides' *Phoenician Women*, Jocasta makes this argument offstage when addressing her quarreling

---

289. 3 *Ki.* 1.52, "a son of power" contrasted with one in whom "a wrong is found."

290. My source for the three arguments: X. *Mem.* 4.2.18–24, worshipping gods, honoring parents, and returning favors to those who do them. Virtually identical formulation: A. *Eu.* 269–72. Similar: E. *Hipp.* 996–1001, honoring gods and *philoi*, and E. fr. 853 *TGF*, honoring gods, parents, and common laws of the Greeks. A Roman version: Cic. *Inv.* 2.161, just before he goes on to say that these norms can be part of a procedure, *consuetudine ius* (2.162).

291. By Aristotle's standards, these arguments fall under two headings, *logos* or "argument," and *êthos* or "character" (*Rh.* 1.1356a); the reason not to follow Aristotle's distinction between these two categories is that the argument to family and friendship falls into both.

292. Arist. *Rh.* 2.1385b; similarly, *Po.* 1453a.

293. Arguments have received little attention, but see Gödde, *Drama der Hikesie*, 135, remarking on what she calls the "instumentarium" of supplicatory arguments.

294. *Rhet. Her.* 2.25. Donlan, "Reciprocities in Homer," calls the former "compensatory" and the latter "compactual" reciprocity.

295. Gould, "*Hiketeia*," 90, Gauthier, *Symbola*, 22, Pulleyn, *Prayer*, chap. 4, all holding that *xenia*, the much-noted result of supplication, is an occasion for reciprocity, but that supplication is not.

sons, Eteocles and Polynices. The source, a messenger, says that she supplicated them, but she does not report her exact words or provide any other information except that she failed.[296] In some other sources, supplicatory language is missing, but otherwise the act is the same. In Homer, Hecuba makes Jocasta's argument when she exposes her breast to Hector in *Iliad* 22 and unsuccessfully begs him not to fight: "Hector, my child, if I ever gave you a breast that relieved your wants, respect this gesture and pity me! Remember it, and take your stand within the city walls."[297] Hecuba is standing on one of these walls, and Hector on the ground, far away, but Aeschylus's Clytemnestra makes the argument when face to face with Orestes: "Stop, my child. Respect this breast. You used to drowse and suck it with your gums as you drew the milk that nourished you well."[298] As if to acknowledge the argument, Orestes wavers in his resolve, asking "Pylades, what am I to do? Should I be ashamed to kill my mother?"[299] But he does not waver for long. Apollo's command, of which Pylades reminds him, trumps the imitation of Priam's wife, and does so in spite of the horrendous result, which is not just rejection but matricide.[300] Such supplications—such failures?—were common in drama.[301]

Jocasta, Hecuba, and Clytemnestra all do fail. Since Jocasta and Hecuba are giving military advice, they may fail because they seem impertinent, whereas Clytemnestra, who is in effect asking her son to ignore his duty to his father, may fail because she seems hypocritical. But later suppliants who use the same argument and gesture fail, too, suggesting that there may be another reason for these maternal failures.[302] This reason emerges from two more Homeric examples, both involving Thetis. Not only is she too discreet to mention a favor that she has done for Zeus, she is too discreet to mention a favor done for her other supplicandus, Hephaestus. Aristotle praises her, saying that supplicandi do not like to be reminded of services done to them.[303] These reminders may seem impertinent.[304]

296. E. *Ph.* 1567–69, where Jocasta is called ἱκέτις.

297. *Il.* 22.82–85.

298. A.*Ch.* 896–98. Tenderness: παῖ followed by τέκνον and the dative with πρός, more delicate than the genitive of the source. Clytemnestra points to her breast, according to Taplin, *Tragedy in Action*, 61, or bares it, according to Sommerstein, "Notes," 71 with n. 32. In other plays, breast-baring takes place offstage: E. *El.* 1208, *Ph.* 1568. S. *El.* 1409–12 suppresses the gesture, and sympathy for Clytemnestra along with it, as noted by Segal, *Interpreting Greek Tragedy*, 351–56, in his comparison of the three dramatic versions of her death.

299. A. *Ch.* 899.

300. Hecuba's supplication is missing from lists of Homeric supplications in Gould, "*Hiketeia*," 80 n. 39, and Whitfield, *The Restored Relation*, 63–65, though noted by Pedrick, "Supplication," 139.

301. Common in drama: E. *Or.* 566–71, noted by Segal, *Interpreting Greek Tragedy*, 351 n. 6. Vases may establish that Eriphyle was one such mother: two Attic red-figure vases, Malibu Getty Mus. 80.AE = *RVP* 183–84 = *LIMC* 3.2 s.v. *Klytemnestra*, 31, and Nauplios Mus. 11.609 = *ARV*² 1061.154 = *LIMC* 3.2 s.v. *Klytemnestra*, 36, show either Eriphyle or Clytemnestra baring a breast to an approaching killer.

302. Plb. 15.31.12–13, where a nurse of the minor king of Egypt exposes her breast to a hostile crowed while her nearby brother, the regent, extends his arms; and Charito 3.5.5–6, a mother's supplication to a son but accompanied by the quotation of Hecuba's words to Hector.

303. Thetis's favor to Hephaestus: *Il.* 18.395–409. Aristotle: *EN* 4.1124b. Past services not mentioned in fiction: Charito 2.7.2–3.

304. But the gesture of baring maternal breasts does not seem to be unsuccessful among the Germans, where women perform in order to encourage warriors to defend them (Caes. *Gal.* 1.51, Tac. *Ger.* 8 noticed by Halm, *Germania des Tacitus*, 22, and Much ad loc.). Here, however, there is no occasion for a pledge, so the gesture cannot be said to be part of an act of supplication.

Examples involving male suppliants confirm this conclusion. In Homer, Leodes reminds Odysseus of his attempt to curb the mischief of the suitors, and Odysseus takes offense.[305] In Euripides, Orestes makes the same claim, telling his supplicandus, Menelaus, that Orestes' father, Agamemnon, fought the Trojans for Menelaus's sake and that this service redounds to the credit of Orestes.[306] Orestes is right about Agamemnon, of course, and the argument that this service redounds to the credit of a son is of a piece with the Greek (and Roman) belief that a son would inherit the social ties made by his father. Yet Menelaus does not respond to the argument, and shortly afterward he abandons Orestes.

If the suppliant appeals to a collective body, reminders are not unwelcome. So, when Attic suppliants who want just deserts say that they have earned them by their services, the supplicandi, the Athenian Assembly, respond by acknowledging their duty to repay these services. One suppliant, a metic or freedman named Asclepiodorus, says that he served in a trireme, and the Assembly responds by saying that it wants all to know that it honors wartime service.[307] Another metic, Archippus, says that he provided unspecified military services and a third, Antiphas, a public slave, says that he kept his post in battle. The Assembly acknowledges them, too.[308] Greek suppliants make similar arguments when supplicating the Romans: we helped you in a war against our common enemy, Macedon, and now you should have mercy on us.[309] Romans also make the argument to each other. The model for this type of supplication is a Roman soldier who supplicates and refers to his past service. This suppliant adds a gesture: he displays his battle scars. These scars must, of course, be on his chest and face and not his back.[310]

Claims that the suppliant will do services in the near or distant future tend to be even more blatant. Many suppliants offer gifts or payments. Homeric offers, all made to ransom captives, run from Chryses in *Iliad* 1 to Priam in *Iliad* 24. Some of these suppliants bring their gifts. Other suppliants, such as Adrastus, who has been captured on the battlefield by Menelaus, have no gifts handy, and so they explain how they will raise the money.[311] Suppliants in historical sources make these offers, too.[312] What prevents such offers from always succeeding, and thus turning supplication into a transaction that would be less onerous for the suppliant than the transaction to which Basil objected? Many such offers follow a request that the suppliant be spared. The supplicandus who entertains the request is hostile, and so success is uncertain. For this reason, suppliants take care when

305. *Od.* 22.314–19.

306. E. *Or.* 448–55, especially 453; so also E. *Hec.* 829–30, where a mother takes credit for a daughter's services to the supplicandus.

307. *IG* ii² 276.7–10, 276.15–18.

308. *IG* ii² 336.14–6, 502.16–20.

309. Liv. 36.27.5. An argument to past services made by one Roman to others: D.H. 4.11.5. The same argument attributed to Etruscan: D.H. 5.3.2.

310. D.C. 54.14.2–3, Cic. *Rab. Perd.* 36–37. A different view of displaying scars: Harding and Ireland, *Punishment*, 193, saying that it is humiliating.

311. Chryses: *Il.* 1.13. Priam: 24. 275–76. Adrastus: 6.46–50. Others: 11.131–34, using the same words as Adrastus.

312. Tac. *Hist.* 3.48.

describing their offers. In Homer, they use the term ἄποινα, meaning "ransom," literally "payoff."[313] This word contains two elements, the prefix ἀπό, meaning "removal," and ποινόν, based on the Indo-European root *$k^w ei$, meaning "payment."[314] In contrast, suppliants avoid a related word, ποινή, which Rütte's handbook defines as *Entschädigung* or "compensation."[315] Just as a ransom is money offered, compensation is money due. "Compensation" implies debt or guilt, and so it would invite the supplicandus to condemn the suppliant.[316]

Outside of epic, though, few suppliants offer money or gifts. Knowing that they could surrender and survive, classical Greek warriors do not make such offers, which is not to say that their families or cities did not later pay ransom. In Herodotus, supplicandi may regard a money offer as a bribe and accordingly reject it. One supplicandus described by this author rejects a bribe, and another accepts a bribe and then rues his error.[317] In other sources, to be sure, supplicandi are sometimes less fastidious. In instances described by Josephus and the novelist Apoleius, some bribes succeed and others fail.[318] Athenian law allowed killers to supplicate and ask for pardon from the relatives of the dead, and one source says that these suppliants should pay money to the relatives. A Demosthenic scholiast describes their supplications in his definition of *Aidesis*: "to make the relatives of the murdered man feel ashamed by means of supplication and payments of money."[319] Demosthenes himself says that homicides had to be *akousioi*, or "involuntary" killers, like the suppliants of *Exodus*. In the light of Homeric ransom, they are also suppliants who offer something like ἄποινα—a parallel that makes it easier to understand the scholiast's account.[320]

Alternatives to money or gifts are diverse. The Numidian Bocchus, who appears on the reverse of the Roman Republican coin shown in figure 2.10, offers a captive. As he extends an olive branch to his supplicandus, Sulla, he presents the bound and helpless Jugurtha, Rome's leading enemy. "Do not seize me," Bocchus

313. ἄποινα as ransom in a plainly supplicatory context: *Il.* 1.13, 1.20, 1.23, 1.95, 1.99, 1.372, 1.377 (for Chryseis), 6.46, 6.49 (Adrastus), 10.380 (Dolon), 11.131, 11.134 (Hippolochus and Pisander), 21.99 (Lycaon), 22.349, 24.137, 24.266, 24.502, 24.555, 24.579 (Hector), 24.686 (Priam if captured by the Greeks). In an apparently supplicatory context: 2.230, 6.427.

314. Formation: *GrEW* s.v. ἄποινα; similarly, Chantraine, *Dictionnaire*, s.v. ποινή.

315. As Rütte notes, Homeric ποινή means "retribution" for the loss of a loved one (*Il.* 13.659, 14.483, 17.207) and for the loss of a comrade in arms (16.398 and *Od.* 23.312) as well as "compensation" for murder (*Il.* 9.632–33, 18.498) or rape (5.265–66).

316. Rütte also cites two well-known cases where ἄποινα seems to mean not "ransom" but ποινή or "compensation" (*Il.* 9.120, 19.138.). In Book 9, Agamemnon offers ἄποινα to Achilles to induce him to return to battle; in Book 19, Agamemnon repeats the offer. Each time, he performs an incomplete supplication. The first case lacks an approach to Achilles by Agamemnon, who instead uses emissaries; both cases lack an introductory word or gesture. Hence some ancient commentators avoid calling the mission to Achilles a "supplication," or ἱκεσία, the word used by Porph. ad *Il.* 9.167, and instead call it an "embassy" or Πρεσβεία (i.e., Ἐξεσίη), as at Eust. ad *Il.* 9.1 citing ἡρωϊκὴ ἐπιγραφή; or an "entreaty," or Λιτανεία or Λιταί, as at schol. and Eust. ad *Il.* 9.1, Pl. *Hp. Mi.* 364e.

317. Hdt. 5.51, 1.159.

318. Fail: J. *BJ* 1.663. Succeed: Apul. *Met.* 9.18–19.

319. Schol. ad Dem. 23.72.

320. A contrary view of Dem. 23.72: Gagarin, *Drakon*, 50–51, holding that intentional murderers were eligible. Cairns, *Aidos*, 224 n. 28, provides bibliography. A parallel from outside Athens: Paus. 2.20.2, where a maiden kills a man responsible for her being ravished, then supplicates successfully, although the friends of the dead man raise an army of a thousand to avenge his death.

FIGURE 2.10   Bocchus supplicating the young Sulla.
Courtesy of American Numismatic Society.

seems to say; "seize Jugurtha instead. Take him and release me."[321] Another flesh-and-blood offer comes from a Roman emperor, Sardanapalus, who faces soldiers who wish to kill his favorite. When supplicating them, he offers his own life instead.[322] By contrast, only a few suppliants make vague or implausible offers, and those who do make such offers compensate by making them large. Among them are conspirators or royal exiles who offer a share of the gains from the conspiracy or from the attempt to regain a throne.[323] Women make their own offers. When begging Nero to spare her, Poppaea promises to bear him a child. Medea promises Aegeus, to whom she will flee at the end of Euripides' play, a cure for his childlessness.[324] The Sabine women of Dio Cassius improve on Poppaea's or Medea's offers. They have already borne children and hold them forth to both their husbands and their fathers when asking both groups of men to make peace. Their argument: think of your heirs.[325]

The Sabine women bridge the gap between offers made to individuals and offers made to communities. Some of the latter offers are military. After his victory at Cannae in the second Punic War, Hannibal releases some of his Roman captives, and they return home and beg the Senate to pay ransom for them and their comrades. When this is accomplished, they say, they will return to arms. The Senate rejects their request, finding them unworthy despite their offer. The second case occurs nearly two hundred years later. Veterans of Pompey's army come to Caesar and supplicate, promising not to take up arms against him.[326] Caesar accepts their vow. He finds them worthy, perhaps because no foreign power has defeated them. A few suppliants offer not military services but information leading to the

321. Fig. 2.10: a 56 BCE denarius of Faustus Sulla's, ANS 1944.100.2609 = Cr. 446.1. Literary sources report supplication by Jugurtha, not Bocchus, and omit Sulla: Sal. *Jug.* 38.1, 47.3. The larger reality of Jugurtha as supplicandus: D.S. 34/35.31.

322. D.C. 80.19.3.

323. S. *OC* 1342–43, Curt. 6.7.11.

324. Tac. *Ann.* 14.61.5, E. *Med.* 717–18. Medea also makes promises to Jason (A.R. 4.87–88).

325. Sabine women: D.C. 1.5.5–7, Plut. *Rom.* 19.1–6 as well as Liv. 1.13.1–5.

326. Liv. 22.60.1–61.3; Luc. 4.356–58, led by Afranius.

conviction of criminals. Wanted men themselves, they are the suppliants who request immunity.[327]

All these claims and offers turn on the relation between the suppliant and the supplicandus, not the suppliant and other persons. The suppliant never says, in effect, "Help me, and the world will help you." He or she says, "We shall help each other."[328] The suppliant is looking forward to the fourth step, in which the answer to the request comes not from an all-knowing god, but from a blinkered mortal, a supplicandus.

Threats

More desperate than the suppliants who pledge future services are those who make threats. These suppliants make an argument about reciprocity but invert it, saying: "If you do not grant my request, I shall do you an ill turn." Or they may say that the gods will punish the supplicandus for rejecting them. Several scholars have recognized the problem presented by this inverted argument: why would someone who has prostrated himself or stooped low to clasp a pair of knees speak so boldly? Walter Pötscher has answered that these gestures have been misunderstood.[329] Although submissive, they might sometimes be aggressive. Suppliants might thrust themselves upon supplicandi, and so threats might be appropriate. On this view, the Danaids of Aeschylus, who threaten to kill themselves and thus pollute the shrine where they are staying, are exemplary. A broad view, however, shows that threats are rare and almost always fail. In contrast, invoking a god when asking for help is common and unexceptionable. It provides an alternative to threats.

The best threat would seem to be to kill a member of the family of the supplicandus. As we have noticed, two suppliants, Telephus and his comic imitator, Mnesilochus, threaten to kill infants whom they have kidnapped. In the event, an oracle justifies Telephus, and Mnesilochus is punished. These two cases, however, are the only ones in which suppliants threaten to kill others. Next would come a threat to kill oneself and pollute a shrine that the supplicandus controls— the threat made by the Danaids. Here we find a total of four cases. Aside from the Danaids, Menelaus makes this threat in Euripides' *Helen*, the Athenian oracle seekers make it in Herodotus, and so do some Jews who beg to have to Caesar's image kept out of Jerusalem.[330] All these suppliants succeed, and they do so only after making their threats.[331] Threats would seem to account for their success.

But the Danaids do not succeed because of their threat. They make the threat, and then the king turns to their father, Danaus, and asks him to make an appeal

---

327. As at n. 254 above.

328. In the language of Donlan, "Reciprocities in Homer," the suppliant appeals to "balanced" and not "generalized" reciprocity.

329. The thesis of Pötscher, "Strukturen der Hikesie," 74, followed by Gödde, *Drama der Hikesie*, 198–210, on the Danaids. Other views of threats: R. Parker, *Miasma*, 185; Sinn, "Sakrale Schutzzone," 93–94.

330. J. *BJ* 2.171–4. The same tactic and same request, but a different supplicandus: 2.192–201.

331. E. *Hel.* 980–87; A. *Supp.* 457–67; Hdt. 7.141.2. Threats should be distinguished from suicide as a response to rejection (Th. 3.81.3, where the suicide is carried out, and S. *Ph.* 1001–2, where it is not). Parth. 5.2 is an instance of a threat that leads to the unintended and not the intended death of the suppliant.

to the assembly. To say that the threat succeeds would be to say that without it the king would not have turned to Danaus and asked him to undertake this errand. But the king had every reason to prefer him to them. The Danaids have trouble with several matters, not just with the issue of control of the shrine. They need instruction about what to do and about the extent of the shrine. Danaus makes no such mistakes, and he also warns them to behave properly.[332] Not only is he the better choice, but the errand of going to the Assembly is unavoidable. As the king says, he and the Assembly share control of the altar.[333] If this threat is unimpressive, what of Menelaus's? This suppliant refuses to use supplicatory words or gestures.[334] His wife, Helen, who is in Egypt with him, and who addresses the same person, the priestess Theonoe, does use appropriate gestures, but she makes no threats.[335] The pattern is the same as Aeschylus, but with a reversal of sex roles. Whether male or female, the ill-mannered make threats, but the mannerly make successful supplications.

In the remaining two examples of suicide threats, those making the threats do supplicate, and they can claim responsibility for their own success, but they enjoy the benefit of mitigating circumstances. In the first example, the Athenians have obtained the first, unsatisfactory oracle and decide to seek another—not an unprecedented choice. After receiving advice from their local helper, they remain in the sanctuary and refuse to eat. They use no violence, and as long as the staff removes them before they die, they will cause no pollution. The oracle therefore accommodates them.[336] In the second example, the Jews are trying to keep their god from being dishonored. Yes, these two threats succeed, but they are mannerly threats. They express patriotism and piety, not the alienation and despair felt by the Danaids and Menelaus.[337]

Rather than threaten to kill a child or himself, a suppliant might threaten to ask a god to harm a recalcitrant supplicandus. Yet only one suppliant, Clytemnestra, makes a statement resembling such a threat. She predicts, though she does not request, that the Furies will harm her son.[338] She goes to this extreme because her son is going not only to reject her but also to slay her. Also rare is the milder threat that the gods may be displeased if the suppliant is rejected. This threat

---

332. Danaids. Ordered to sit: A. *Supp.* 188–90. To leave boughs: 506. Informed that grove is part of sanctuary: 508–10. Warned by father: 197–201. Similarly, Winnington-Ingram, *Aeschylus*, 57; Burian, *Suppliant Drama*, 62–63; Naiden, "Supplication and the Law," 86. Approving of the Danaids: W. Harris, *Rage*, 161.

333. Similar views of the Danaids, but without describing the procedure: Burian, *Suppliant Drama*, 51–52; Turner, "Perverted Supplication," 27, 33.

334. Menelaus's refusal: E. *Hel.* 947–48.

335. E. *Hel.* 894–1004.

336. Double response: Hdt. 7.141. A parallel, but involving a prophet, not an oracle: Stat. *Theb.* 10.589–96, where the Thebans approach Tiresias and he denies their request, only to yield a moment later. But in this instance there is no threat.

337. A parody of a threat: X. Eph. 2.3.4–5, where a mistress supplicates her own slave in order to obtain help in winning a lover and does not scruple at threatening her.

338. A. *Ch.* 924. No such threat when she supplicates in E. *El.* 1206–15; Sophocles declines to report a supplication. Similar is a threat to curse the supplicandus (S. *Aj.* 1175–79). This threat protects a child who has taken the unusual course of supplicating beside a dead body.

occurs only when the suppliant asks for proper burial of a relative.[339] In both cases the suppliant obtains his request.

This last outcome points to a general conclusion: rather than threaten to use his own power or threaten to ask the gods to use theirs, successful suppliants present themselves as pious individuals. They may accomplish this by making a pious request such as proper burial, one that placates the spirits of the dead and that Zeus endorses in *Iliad* 24. If they do not make a pious request, they may ask the supplicandus to help them in the gods' name. In Homer, Odysseus mentions Zeus *Hikesios* when addressing the Cyclops, and so does one suppliant in the *Iliad*, Lycaon, when addressing Achilles; in tragedy, Philoctetes imitates these two. A group of suppliants at an altar, the Danaids of Aeschylus, mention Zeus. One suppliant, the Chryses of *Iliad* 1, mentions Apollo.[340] A few suppliants from later antiquity join them.[341]

Why do more suppliants not make such serviceable, inoffensive statements? These statements mark a response to initial rejection. Rather than kill others or themselves, or bring down curses on the supplicandus, the suppliants who have met with this disappointment respond with one more reason that the supplicandus should lend a friendly ear. Then they proceed with their arguments, the next of which is family or friendship.

Family or Friendship

Like the argument to reciprocity, the argument to family ties or friendship looks to both past and future. "We have been close," says the suppliant, and "we should continue to be." Although less common than reciprocity, this argument has a bearing on the issue of the importance of inclusion in a group, be it a household or a community or Burkert's pack. Whatever the group, suppliants are supposed to wish to join it. But the argument about family or friendship is for suppliants who already belong to a group. These suppliants fear lest their tie to the group weaken, a possibility that scholars have overlooked.[342]

A son or daughter may make the argument when appealing to a father, a son when appealing to a mother, one sibling or cousin when appealing to another.[343] As before, the suppliant may be discreet and refrain from making the argument. In Homer, the father, mother, sisters, and wife of Meleager all supplicate him, begging him to defend them and their city, yet none of them put this argument

---

339. *Il.* 22.358, *Od.* 11.73. Idle, trivial threat: Pl. *Rud.* 629–32.

340. Odysseus: *Od.* 9.270. Lycaon: *Il.* 20.74–75, but implicitly. Philoctetes: S. *Ph.* 484. A. *Supp.* 345–47, 381–86, 402–6, 418–37, leads to king's turning to their father, Danaus. Apollo:*Il.* 1.21. Omitted: perfunctory appeals "in the gods' name," as at E. *Hec.* 1127–28.

341. *Variatio*: D.H. 4.11.5. Homeric coloring: Lucianus *Pisc.* 3, Ov. *Met.* 7.853. Spurious appeal: Longus 4.16.4.

342. The link between family and friendship: the two senses of *philos*, one objective, one subjective, as at Hamp "Φίλος" with refs. The former appears at *Il.* 24.371, the latter at 24.373.

343. Appeal by son to father: S. *OC* 1267–1396. By daughter to father: E. *IA* 1214–75; implicit at A. *Ag.* 231–47. By son to mother: Charito 5.10.4, Plut. *Art.* 2.2. By one sibling to another: E. *And.* 894–984, A.R. 3.701–39. By distant cousins to a cousin: A. *Supp.* 531–37, E. *Heracl.* 207–11. Appeal of mistress to her master, but in name of their son: S. *Aj.* 587–90.

into words. Nor do Meleager's ἑταῖροι, or "companions."[344] If the suppliant does put this argument into words, unusual circumstances have induced him to forgo his discretion. In *Oedipus at Colonus*, Polynices supplicates his father, Oedipus, who is embittered because Polynices allowed him to go into exile. Polynices makes the argument in hopes of mollifying his father.

Among friends, however, the suppliant will put the argument into words more often.[345] In tragedy, friendship can even be established at the start of a scene and appealed to at the end of the same scene, as described in *Philoctetes*.[346] Besides linking one person to another, friendship, or *philia*, can link (or supposedly link) the supplicandus to a city that is begging for better treatment from a conqueror.[347] Similar to *philia* is *xenia* between suppliant and supplicandus; it, too, may or may not be put into words.[348] This argument, needless to say, differs from a request to become a *xenos*, which is rare; it is the common claim that the suppliant is a *xenos* already. Also similar is the camaraderie among those who accompanied Xenophon on his retreat through the Persian Empire. Like family ties, such a bond may or may not be put into words. In this case, the soldiers supplicate Xenophon by making an argument to reciprocity. Their link to him goes unspoken.[349]

In all these cases the suppliant, whether one person or several, addresses an individual. But collective supplicandi, most of them Greek victors, also entertain this argument. Defeated Greeks supplicate them, asking to be spared, and make this argument by saying that both parties are Greek. Thucydides calls this argument a *nomos*—in others words, an irrefragable argument that leaves the supplicandus no choice but to accede or face accusations of flouting the norms of warfare.[350] Other sources agree with him, and instances in which the argument meets with rejection are few and notorious. Such is the force of this argument that it might be regarded as an appeal to international military law.[351] Among Jews, however, the same argument is rare and is never called a law.[352] In any event, this argument shows how the appeal to family ties survived into the classical and Hellenistic periods, when, as we have noticed, soldiers tend to supplicate in groups rather than as individuals.[353]

344. Yet only the mother is evidently unsuited to making it (*Il.* 9.581–89). Speculation on the order in which the suppliants appear: Kakridis, *Homeric Researches*, 19–21.

345. App. *BC* 4.9.67–70. Hld. 2.13.4.

346. Sophocles' Philoctetes uses phil- words four times in 18 lines between 224–42, as noted by Rose, "Sophocles' Philoctetes," 65, and proves his friendship by expressing grief at death of supplicandus's father (336–38). Having created the bond, he appeals to it at 468–529. ·

347. App. *BC* 4.9.67–70; D.H. 4.10.6–12.3, including an argument to reciprocity.

348. J. *BJ* 1.281–84.

349. X. *An.* 7.1.21–22.

350. Th. 3.58.3; also D.S. 13.23.5, 13.26.3, Sopat. Rh. *RG* 8.241.

351. Thus Sheets, "Conceptualizing Law," arguing that the enforcement of such law can depend on public opinion rather than on sanctions, a view that places him on the side of Barkun, *Law without Sanctions*, in the controversy about whether sanctions are indispensable for the existence of laws as opposed to norms; on the other side stands Hart, *The Concept of Law*, 20–25, followed by MacDowell, "Law, Athenian."

352. J. *BJ* 4.311 goes no further than to imply cusomary mercy for those who surrender.

353. Missing from the sources are examples of appeals to groups larger than a family but smaller than a community or nation. To a community but with an intimate touch: Th. 1.24.6–7 (by colonists to mother city) and Liv. 2.6.2–4 (an exile to citizens of city where he was born), D.S. 33.5.1–4 (by citizens of one city to a neighboring city).

The link between the argument about family and international military law reveals a tendency common to this argument and the argument about reciprocity. The surrendering soldier may say that rejecting him is wrong. The suppliant who has rendered services to the supplicandus may say the same thing. Both assertions segue into arguments about fairness, the largest category of all.

Fairness

When invoking fairness, suppliants may say that they have done no wrong or they may say that others have wronged them and that they need help. Alternatively, they may direct their arguments to the supplicandus and say that the supplicandus has a duty toward them. When suppliants are on trial, or come before a hearing comparable to a trial, they usually make the first of these three arguments, saying that they have done no wrong according to the law that they stand accused of breaking. If they are outside court, they usually make the second and third arguments, saying that they have been wronged or that the supplicandus is duty-bound to give aid.

Amid this panoply of arguments, the similarity between arguments made at trials and hearings and arguments made elsewhere is the chief aspect that the prevailing view of supplication has overlooked. According to the prevailing view, supplication at a trial is "figurative," a matter of verbal ornament.[354] It has no bearing on the question of guilt or innocence. But both Greek and Roman law court speeches show that defendants who supplicate do assert their innocence—and that they often assert their innocence at the very moment when they supplicate. By the same token, those prosecutors who supplicate assert that the defendant is guilty under the law and beg the judges to consider the law when they render their verdict. Far from being extrinsic to guilt and innocence, supplication is intrinsic to it. The innocent—or allegedly innocent—are those who may ask for help.

As with trials and hearings, so with other venues. In the prevailing view, supplication in other venues is a ritual of contact, and as such has no room for arguments about fairness. But supplication in these circumstances abounds in arguments that the suppliants have done no wrong or have been wronged themselves, including the argument that the suppliants have committed an involuntary wrong that the supplicandus should overlook. The difference between these arguments and those made in court is that the usual argument heard in court, that the suppliants have done no wrong, is specific. To make this argument, suppliants refer to a law. The usual argument heard elsewhere, that the suppliants are the victims of wrongdoing, is general. To make this argument, suppliants appeal to some principle of fairness. But the prevailing view is not the only one that has undervalued arguments about fairness. Legal historians implicitly agree with the view that supplication at trials is ornamental, and they have ignored the similarity between

---

354. The view of Gould, "*Hiketeia*," and others, given at n. 180 above.

arguments made at trials and arguments made elsewhere. The reason that the prevailing view and the view of legal historians coincide with one another is that neither view regards supplication as a quasilegal practice, and so neither expects suppliants to speak like lawyers. But some suppliants do, and in this section we will listen to them.[355]

Thanks to the mention of suppliant murderers in *Exodus*, Israel, and not Greece or Rome, might seem to be the place to begin. A Hebrew murderer such as *Exodus* has in mind would go first to an altar and then to some place where a panel of judges would hear his case. This sequence also occurs in Greek drama, suggesting some link between Semitic and Greek practices, perhaps by way of the Phoenicians. But no murderer in the Old Testament performs this sequence, or even goes to the altar mentioned in *Exodus*. One suppliant, Joab, does goes to an altar, but it is a different one, the altar in the temple in Jerusalem, and once again no trial occurs.[356] Nor does any book of the Old Testament say whether there should or could have been a trial of this suppliant.[357] This want of trials, in turn, makes it impossible to bring to bear passages that try to distinguish among mitigating factors like involuntary wrongdoing. *Numbers*, for example, asks whether the killer struck the victim, but without any ill will, or threw something at him unawares. *Exodus* asks fewer questions, leading to a question of preference: at a trial, which would be followed? Or—more cautiously—what forensic traditions did the two passages belong to?[358]

In contrast, suppliant murderers and other suppliant defendants are Greek and Roman commonplaces. This consideration alone would prompt the conclusion that supplicating defendants would behave like other defendants, and in particular would take pains to assert that they are innocent of the charges against them. And suppliants do just this. The charge may be embezzlement, bribe-taking, wounding with intent to kill, or treason; aside from other punishments, the stakes may be loss of an inheritance or of citizenship.[359] The suppliant may plead not guilty or, less often, appeal an unfavorable decision by a lower court or defend a decision by an arbitrator.[360] The suppliant may speak on his or her own behalf, or an advocate may in his or her place, as Cicero does so often.

Let us begin with a case where a suppliant known to us as the son of Eucrates defends himself against an attempt to confiscate his property. The grounds for this attempt are that his father embezzled public money, for under Athenian law, the property of such a miscreant was liable to confiscation. The suppliant needs

---

355. Though one legal historian, Woess, *Asylwesen Ägyptens*, proves a considerable exception. Habicht, "Samische Volksbeschlüsse" and "Hellenistische Inschriften," also notices the legal element in supplication outside of court, but deals with only one venue, the Heraeum on Samos.

356. J. *AJ* 8.14 has Solomon offer a trial to Joab, a detail that *Kings* lacks, but no trial occurs, because Joab rejects the offer. Only the medieval *Machsor Vitri* 341–42 reports that a trial took place.

357. Talmudic disputes on this point: *Babli Makkot* 12a, dating from the seventh to eighth centuries CE.

358. *Nu.* 35.22–23, *Ex.* 21.12–13. Levine, *Numbers*, 565–69, assumes that the only proceeding was the evaluation of the suppliant.

359. Confiscation: Lys. 18. Bribe-taking: Lys. 21. Wounding: Lys. 4. Treason: Aeschin. 2. Inheritance: Dem. 27, 28, Is. 2. Citizenship: Dem. 57.

360. Appeal: Dem. 57. Defense: Dem. 27.

to show that his father was not an embezzler, and so, when he supplicates at the end of his speech, he tries to establish that his father (and his father's brother) were paragons who "took the lead in running risks for the sake of freedom" for Athens. And the suppliant is right: the father's brother was Nicias, leader of the Athenian expedition to Syracuse, and rich enough to make his and his family's property well worth defending. So the suppliant "begs and beseeches—no, it is his God-given right to ask—" for what he has a right to expect.[361] The anonymous suppliant defending himself against charges of bribery in Lysias 21 ends his speech with the same argument. His accusers say that he took bribes while in public office, so he must show that he would never take money to the city's detriment. When he supplicates, he tries to establish just this. Far from taking any money, he has spent much of his own wealth on public benefactions. So he, too, "begs and beseeches" and asserts his God-given right to ask for acquittal.[362]

These are property cases, but the same pairing of supplication and innocence appears in trials of crimes of violence and political crimes. The anonymous suppliant on trial for wounding someone in Lysias 4 must show that he did not do so deliberately, a part of the charge against him, and so he must show that he is not a malefactor. Since he and the alleged victim quarreled over the favors of a slave girl, he also needs to show that he has been fair towards the victim. He tries to achieve both these aims when supplicating near the end of his speech. To achieve the first, he asks "What citizen did I ever wrong in any way?" To achieve the second, he asserts that he never wronged the victim.[363] In this case the punishment was banishment and loss of property, but if we raise the stakes to the alternative punishments of banishment and death, and change the charge to treason, and also make the suppliant the famed orator Aeschines, the technique remains the same. The gravamen of the treason charge against the orator was accepting gifts to the detriment of Athens while serving as ambassador to Philip of Macedon in 346 BCE. Aeschines dealt with this matter of the gifts at several points, including one point at which he supplicates. Immediately after begging and beseeching, and, since he speaks at far greater length than the suppliants just mentioned, begging the gods, the older judges, and then all the judges—three groups, one after another—he pauses and says, "A few words more, and I shall step down." The judges must have wondered how this tripartite supplication would end with only "a few words more," but Aeschines duly explains: "a few words" suffice to make the argument that will clear the suppliant of the charge of taking gifts: "The only power I had [as ambassador] was this—to do you no wrong." Other suppliants would end here, but Aeschines, not content with the "few words" that he promised, goes on and makes the same point a second time. This time, though, he speaks figuratively.

361. Lys. 18.27: τῶν ὑπὲρ τῆς ἐλευθερίας προκεκινδυνευκότων, . . . δέομαι καὶ ἀντιβολῶ καὶ ἱκετεύω.

362. Lys. 21.21–22. Similar case: Is. 2.44–46, where supplication (2.44) precedes summary of legal arguments (45–46).

363. Lys. 4.19–20, especially τί κακὸν πώποτε τὴν πόλιν ἢ αὐτὸν τοῦτον εἰργασμένος, ἢ εἰς τίνα τῶν πολιτῶν ὁτιοῦν ἐξαμαρτών;

Instead of supplicating, he entrusts himself to the judges, and instead of saying that he is innocent, he puts "the law" in their keeping.[364]

All these suppliants are defendants, but prosecutors use the technique, too. They, however, make the second of the three arguments. Rather than say that they have done no wrong, and in particular, that they have not broken the law, they say that they are the victims of the defendant's wrongdoing. In one speech the prosecutor, Apollodorus, is bringing a charge of false witness, and so the harm that he claims that the defendant has done is indirect. Rather than arise from false witness, itself this harm arises from the results of false witness, which include the prosecutor's losing a lawsuit to a freedman—and a rich freedman at that, a banker. The argument that the suppliant was wronged fades into bias against freedmen and envy of nouveaux riches.[365]

Cicero's speeches differ from Attic speeches by adding assertions of innocence made by Cicero as advocate. More of his defendants are prominent, like their advocate, and thanks to other sources, especially Cicero's letters, they are better known to us. But the practice remains the same. Cicero asserts that his client is innocent of the charge against him, be it failure to register as a citizen, bribery, extortion, political violence, poisoning, parricide, or treason.[366] In the same breath, he and his client beg for acquittal.

Here again we may begin with a case in which the charge is not grave. Archias, a Greek poet in the service of the great noble Lucullus, found his claim to Roman citizenship impugned. The case turned on whether Archias was a citizen of an Italian town, Heraclea, as citizenship there would make him a Roman citizen as well. A delegation from Heraclea vouched for Archias, and so did Lucullus. In his peroration Cicero adverts to the "authority of the town, and the testimony of Lucullus," and in the next sentence "implores" the court "to place him under your protection." This is not the plain speaking of Aeschines, but it still links an argument about a law, in this case, a law about citizenship, to a supplication.[367]

Sometimes Cicero speaks of himself. In his defense of Sestius, who was accused of bribing voters, he reasons that the attack on Sestius is an attack on Cicero, a greater figure, and that the motive for the attack is the help that Sestius gave him at several points. Well, Cicero reasons aloud, a man who has helped me cannot be the sort of man to commit bribery! Instead Sestius is a defender of the state and the courts.[368] In most cases, though, Cicero makes no mention of himself and says only that the suppliant has done no wrong. Fonteius, a minor political figure accused of extortion, is "innocent," and so his sister, a vestal virgin, may

364. Aeschin. 2.183, 2.184, especially Ἐγὼ γάρ, ὦ ἄνδρες ᾿Αθηναῖοι, τοῦ μὲν μηδὲν ἀδικεῖν ὑμᾶς κύριος ἦν, . . .

365. Dem. 45.85–86.

366. Failure to register: Cic. Arch. Bribery: Mur., Planc., Sest. Extortion: Flac., Font. Political violence: Sul. Poisoning: Clu. Parricide: Mil., S. Rosc. Treason: Rab. Perd. For the pertinent supplications, see appendix 1b, "Acts of Supplication in Cicero."

367. Cic. Arch. 31, especially "petimus . . . in uestram accipiatis fidem."

368. Cic. Sest. 144. Similar characterization of defendant as a friend of the advocate: Planc. 102–3. Similar use of the general character of the defendant: Mur. 87.

supplicate on his behalf.[369] Even Milo, a political gangster accused of acts of public violence—a man Cicero cannot claim will supplicate himself, for Milo is obdurate—faces "a punishment that he does not deserve." This prospect drives Cicero to tears, and to the Roman version of "beg and beseech."[370] Innocence, supplication, and Milo: this trio is bold, perhaps too bold, for it reveals how easy it was to link innocence, supplication, and a defendant.[371]

As at trials, so at hearings before magistrates or kings. When Orestes appears before Athena in the *Eumenides*, and she acts as a magistrate, he says that he has done no wrong.[372] In Josephus, hearings before kings take the place of trials, but the same arguments appear. When Antipater comes before his father, Herod the Great, he asks for a chance to establish his innocence. When the attempt fails, he says that God is a witness to his blamelessness. Pheroras, Herod's brother, comes before the king with an argument about involuntary wrongdoing: yes, he says, he was guilty of disloyalty, the same as Antipater, but his love for his scheming wife drove him to it. She had deranged him.[373]

In short, a suppliant who is a defendant or who finds himself in similar circumstances asserts his innocence. Far from ignoring the charges against him, he rebuts them and begs for acquittal. But as shown by the examples with which we began, those of Phemius and Leodes, other suppliants use arguments about fairness, too. These arguments include involuntary wrongdoing, which we have so far found only in the supplication of Pheroras.

Fairness Outside of Court

Outside of court as well as inside it, suppliants appeal to moral and legal standards. Many are wanted men; some are slaves and women. These suppliants are more likely than their courtroom counterparts to appeal to principles of fairness, not laws.

Free persons who approach a shrine want to establish their own innocence, and thus deprive the supplicandi of a reason to turn them over to those pursuing them. At the start of the *Suppliants* of Aeschylus, the Danaids announce that they are not killers who have come to Argos to escape pursuit by relatives of the dead man. Instead, they are refugees who seek to avoid unwanted marriages to their own cousins. In Euripides' *Madness of Heracles*, the suppliants, mostly children, make the same point, but speak through their guardian, Iolaus. We are children, they say, innocents incapable of harming those who pursue us.[374]

369. Cic. *Font.* 49, especially "innocentem."

370. Cic. *Mil.* 104–5, esp. "poenas . . . non debitas . . . oro obtestorque." Quint. *Inst.* 6.1.25 observes that Milo dare not supplicate himself.

371. Other instances: Cic. *Clu.* 202, where the defendant is "innocentissimum" (202) and relies on "ueritas" when being interceded for (200); *Rab. Perd.* 5, where Cicero supplicates on behalf of a man innocent of the crime with which he is charged (18–19), an argument that does not appear in the lacunose peroration.

372. A. *Eu.* 85.

373. Antipater: J. *BJ* 1.621, 1.639. Pheroras: 1.506.

374. A. *Supp.* 15–18; E. *HF* 207, with comic parallel at Pl. *Rud.* 642, and prose parallels at Hdt. 3.48 and Hld. 9.12.1, the second of which is a military scene; E. *And.* 570–71.

Slaves arriving at a shrine establish their innocence in a different way, by show-ing that they have not wronged their masters. In a Greek epigraphical source, this argument is implicit. Regulations governing the treatment of runaway slaves who come to the shrine of Hera on Samos require that they "justify themselves" to the staff of the temple. Although they do not say how the runaways justify themselves, showing that they have not wronged their masters is surely a part, if not the whole, of this task.[375] Achilles Tatius's account of slaves taking refuge at the Artemisum in Ephesus confirms this interpretation. In this case, a slave had to show that he "had done no wrong" to his master.[376] In Roman legal sources, a slave who runs away to a statue of the emperor—the same kind of supplication, but in a different sort of place—must not do *iniuria*, or wrong, to his master. Here the argument is explicit.[377]

If the runaway slave is female, justifying oneself is harder. Besides doing no wrong to the master, it may also include meeting another standard, one that ap-plies to women only: virginity. In Achilles Tatius, at least, it includes a test for this attribute. The authorities confine the female runaway in a grotto belonging to Pan and let the god vet her. If she passes the test, she will emerge from the grotto unscathed; if not, the god will remove her to parts unknown. We do not need to ask whether there ever was such a test to grasp the link to the children of Heracles and the Danaids: the suppliant must show that she is innocent.[378]

A few statements of innocence come from suppliants who have not gone to temples and need not fear pursuers. These are dubious (if famous) characters attractive to historians and satirists. Poppaea Sabina, the alienated wife of Nero, knows that fertility is not grounds enough to save her, and so she proclaims her-self untainted by disloyalty. Throwing herself at Nero's knees, she asks: "What crime have I committed against anyone? What offense have I given to anyone?"[379] In spite of her status, she resembles a slave who must show loyalty. And, like a slave, she cannot ever succeed in removing all doubts. She is too helpless, too desperate, to be trusted not to lie.[380] Yet a group of suppliants in Livy turn the suspicions of the supplicandus to their own advantage. Children in tow, Livy's Sabine women enter the battle between their Roman husbands and Sabine fa-thers. If they were like Dio's Sabines, they would say that they and the children are innocent, and beg the two sides to stop fighting. When they run out between the two sides and hold their children aloft, this argument and request would seem to be in the offing. But the women do not say that they and the children are inno-cent, nor do they ask for a truce. Instead they argue that they themselves, the mothers, are to blame for the war, which would not, in fact, have started had the

375. Habicht, "Samische Volksbeschlüsse," #59.4–5, from the late third century BCE. "Justification": ὅταν ἐπὶ τῶν νεωποιῶν δικαιολογ[η-]/[θέντες φανεροὶ ὦσ]ιν, supplemented by Habicht. The rest of the sentence deals with the repossession of slaves by their masters, a topic discussed in appendix 2.

376. οὐδὲν .... ἀδικῶν (Ach. Tat. 7.13.3).

377. Labeo *dig.* 47.10.7.8 (before 22 CE), with later sources discussed at 254–55 below.

378. Ach. Tat. 8.6.

379. Tac. *Ann.* 14.61.5: "quod alioquin suum delictum, quam cuiusquam offensionem?"

380. Similar indignant protests: Petr. 107.5–7.

Romans not abducted them. "Turn your weapons on us, the guilty party," they say, "and kill us." Yet this argument and request shame the men into a truce. The innocent have succeeded in their supplication, but by pretending to be guilty.[381] The contrast with Dio Cassius is between Dio's condescension and Livy's irony. Dio's Sabines are valuable because fertile, Livy's guilty because loved.

More common is the argument of Phemius and Leodes: I am innocent because I have an excuse. In court, this argument does not appear, perhaps only because of a gap in the sources, but it does appear elsewhere in many sources other than Homer. A suppliant may say that some other person or circumstance compelled him to do wrong, or that something in his own mind compelled him to do so. The first sort of compulsion is external; the second is internal.

The argument about external compulsion is precisely that of Phemius and Leodes.[382] It also appears in *Oedipus at Colonus*, where it undergirds Oedipus's plea to be admitted to the shrine of the Furies. Those who first evaluate him, the local elders, ask about his crimes, and he replies, "I have justice on my side." When they ask why, he explains (following one of two likely emendations), "I killed and committed murder because I was a victim of mischief," mischief sent by the gods, *Atê*.[383] This argument is dubious: Oedipus acted rashly when he killed his father, so he deserved to suffer. But for the suppliant's own notion of his case, the crucial term is "justice," or *dikê*: Oedipus is in the right. Later, Oedipus explains why. He killed "against his will," or *akôn*.[384] He did not deserve his fate.

The argument about external compulsion passed into prose, where Thucydides presents it in the form of a general statement. In Book 4, some Athenian soldiers have captured the temple of Apollo at Delium in Boeotia and taken refuge in it. When the Boeotians order them to leave, the Athenians reply that they are suppliants even as they admit to wrongdoing. As they explain to the sceptical Boeotians, their wrongs are "involuntary," a qualification to emphasize: "It is reasonable for all measures made necessary by war . . . to be forgiven, even by the god. If misdeeds are *involuntary*, altars provide a refuge." Aside from the god's approval, a standard of fairness exonerates these suppliants: "Those who do evil of their own free will are said to break laws, not those who are a little bold in times of distress."[385] Hobbes, whose translation I have adapted, writes "break laws" for the Greek word παρανομία. Since these "laws" are not statutory, one might also translate this word as "violate norms."[386] The standard of fairness comprehends both.

---

381. Liv. 1.13.1–5.

382. And also Tlepolemus (*Il.* 2.653–57, with inadvertent killing established at Apollod. 2.8.2), noticed by Cantarella, *Norma e sanzione*, 273–76.

383. S. *OC* 545–47. Lloyd-Jones 547: ἄτᾳ ἁλοὺς. Porson: καὶ γὰρ ἄνους. Codd.: καὶ γὰρ ἄλλους.

384. S. *OC* 962–68; similarly Antigone, 238–40. A reason for the switch: Oedipus is now arguing with Creon, who has said that the Areopagus would not approve of Oedipus entering Attica. By claiming that he killed *akôn*, Oedipus has removed the killing from the jurisdiction of the Areopagus, which did not deal with murder cases of this type.

385. Th. 4.98.6. "Involuntary": τῶν ἀκουσίων ἁμαρτημάτων.

386. Cf. S. Lattimore, *Peloponnesian War*: "transgressor."

Other authors supply particulars. When Aeneas supplicates native Italian leaders, he does not need to use this argument when speaking to those whom he has not attacked. He does need it when speaking to those whom he has, and so, in the passage in Dionysius of Halicarnassus in which Aeneas attacks Latinus and then supplicates him the Trojan leader resorts to this argument, saying that circumstances compelled him to fight. This episode is fictional, but there is nothing fictional about the argument: Herodotus and Josephus report it, too.[387] Roman tax collectors who could not pay monies due and supplicated for relief used the argument in this way: they maintained that a flood had wiped out the crops that would yield the taxes. Julius Caesar accepted the argument.[388]

In contrast to this argument about external compulsion, the argument about internal compulsion appears only in literary sources. Each time, the suppliant blames his own cast of mind. Homer gives the example of Patroclus, who supplicates after killing in a rage.[389] Livy's Rhodians blame their own "stupidity," and so does another suppliant described by this author, a barbarian king. And, if we follow the other emendation of Sophocles, Oedipus killed because he was "unreasoning." But no other cases survive, even from a handbook. The reason may be that a suppliant who blamed his cast of mind defied the supplicandus to verify the story, but the suppliant who blamed circumstances did not.[390]

All these arguments—innocence and external or internal compulsion—are less common than an argument that in court belongs only to prosecutors: "I have been wronged." Those making this argument are seeking to justify a request for vengeance or help. The most voluble of them is Hecuba in Euripides' play of the same name. She takes Agamemnon by the knees and chin and asks him to help her avenge herself on a Thracian prince responsible for the death of one of her children—and she does so despite the irony that Agamemnon is responsible for the deaths of many of her other children and that he keeps her daughter Cassandra as a concubine. Undaunted, she asks for her due under "the law," or *nomos*, even as she wonders whether the law will help her.[391] But suppliants described by Plutarch, Livy, and Josephus do not express doubts when they assert that their cause is just. They say that they have been wronged—Livy's term is *scelus*, for the "crime" committed against them—and plead for help in avenging the wrong.[392] Most different from Hecuba is Plutarch's Coriolanus, who leaves Rome to supplicate a neighboring king, saying that he seeks vengeance against the Romans. This suppliant is anything but doubtful. Nor need the suppliant be a princess or a patrician. A runaway slave described in an Egyptian papyrus makes the same

387. D.H. 1.58.3; Hdt. 7.233, where surrendering Thebans obtain mercy by telling the Persians that they are involuntary wrongdoers in 480 BCE; Hdt. 9.76, where a concubine says she had no choice; J. *BJ* 1.506.

388. Serv. *G.* 2.161.

389. *Il.* 23.85–90, noticed by Cantarella, *Norma e sanzione*, 273–76.

390. "Stultitia": Liv. 45.23.11–12 (the Rhodians), 44.31.13. The only general statement: Stat. *Theb.* 12.506–11, referring to "errore nocentes."

391. E. *Hec.* 798–805. Other tragic or fictional requests for just revenge: E. *Tro.* 1044–45, Longus 2.19.1.

392. Plut. *Cor.* 23.3, Liv. 2.6.4, 3.50.5, J. *BJ* 2.230.

argument: her master wronged her, and so she fled him and supplicated in a temple.[393]

Suppliants who say that they are victims and ask for help are so common as to appear in a rhetorical handbook attributed to Quintilian. Here the rhetorical experts, always in search of new conundrums, imagine a situation that would make effective arguments difficult. Suppose, they say, that a son accused of attempting to poison his father tells the court that he tried to placate his father by supplicating him. Can he plausibly say that he supplicated the victim of his alleged crime? Yes, the experts answer. But he must be willing to rebut the charges.[394] Polyaenus, an author on sabotage, likes trying situations, too. In his example, the suppliant and the suppliant's employer, Philip of Macedon, arrange for the suppliant to be beaten in public by the king's men. The suppliant then flees to Rhodes and begs the Rhodians for help. The trick works so well that even the Macedonians who happened to be in Rhodes think that the suppliant had been treated unjustly.[395]

These arguments concern the suppliant's past. If the suppliant argues about his future, he will say not that he or she has been wronged, but that he or she will be—thus justifying a request for protection. Any suppliant who comes to an altar when fleeing from pursuers might make this argument. In the *Suppliants* of Aeschylus, the Danaids do. Unless they receive protection, they will be forced to make the incestuous marriages that they regard as wrongful. Livy and Tacitus also report the argument.[396]

All the arguments so far, whether in court or elsewhere, involve suppliants who speak about themselves—as innocent persons, involuntary wrongdoers, and actual or potential victims. But some suppliants choose to speak about the supplicandus instead. In this case, the argument about fairness becomes an argument about the supplicandus's duty. In court, the suppliant points out that the supplicandus has sworn an oath to acquit the innocent. This is the ploy of supplicating prosecutors.[397] But the suppliant may also refer to his rights (*iura*), as Massilliote suppliants do when addressing the besieging Romans. The rights to which they refer must have been granted to Massilia under its treaty with Rome, so some solemn ceremony, including an oath, lay behind them.[398] Such rights derive from written laws or legal instruments. Yet unwritten laws or mere norms could serve the suppliant, too. In Roman comedy, a suppliant will serve up the cliché *ius fasque* ("right and proper") to justify his request for money, even if the request is much more impudent than it is supplicatory. In Homer, Odysseus refers to a similar notion, *themis*, when asking supplicandi to grant him hospitality.[399] Like showing

393. *PCair. Zenon* 4.59474.19.
394. [Quint.] *Decl.* 17.6.
395. Polyaen. 5.17.2. Similar are Liv. 8.28.5–9, Just. 11.10.6–9.
396. Liv. 1.53.4–10, Tac. *Ann.* 14.61.5.
397. Dem. 27.68, 43.84, Is. 2.47. But other suppliants also cite oaths by supplicandi: App. *BC* 4.9.68, *Pun.* 85, Th. 6.19.1.
398. Luc. 3.301–3; so also D.H. 5.3.
399. Plin. *Bac.* 1025; *Od.* 9.270–71, reprised at E. *Cyc.* 299–301.

discretion, giving hospitality is a norm that the suppliant will endow with every possible force.

Like requests for acquittal and pardon, arguments about fairness introduce a legal element into supplication. These arguments show how legal arguments and moral factors overlap, and they confirm the similarity between supplication inside court and outside court. By the same token, they unify the act of supplication up to this point. Approaches, gestures, and requests vary—especially the last of these—but arguments coalesce. Not even differences in speaking skills blunt this effect. Cicero speaks more and better, but he does not display originality. He does not dare. The stakes are high, and as the last step approaches, they may seem to increase.

Appeals to Pity

Describing supplication as quasilegal would seem to ignore a common feature of suppliants' appeals to supplicandi—a feature as common as any argument, including arguments about fairness. Suppliants often ask for pity. Several literary critics have fastened on this feature of supplicatory appeals and held that whether a supplicandus feels pity is crucial to the outcome of any act of supplication. In their view, those who feel pity say "yes" and those who do not say "no."[400] Opinion depends on emotion. But the sources do not support these ideas about pity and about opinion and emotion. As for pity, some suppliants do not ask for it; Roman suppliants ask for it less often than Greek ones. The appeal to pity is optional, and it is not always successful. As for opinion and emotion, the sources do not show that opinion depends on emotion. Instead they show that pity goes to those who are found deserving. Emotion depends on opinion.

Pity appears several times in Homer. "Pity me," Leodes and Phemius say to Odysseus; three other Homeric suppliants say the same.[401] But most Homeric suppliants do not ask for pity. Nor do those who ask for pity fare better than those who do not. Of Homer's five, three succeed, and two fail, Leodes and Lycaon, a suppliant in *Iliad* 21. If both Homeric poems let an appeal to pity fail, so do a few of the other sources in which suppliants ask for pity and the source reports the results. In four cases outside of fiction, three suppliants succeed. The fourth, a Jewish rebel, Castor, asks for pity from Titus, his Roman foe, but does so under false colors; then the act of supplication is interrupted.[402] The remaining examples, five in all, occur in Greek novels or Apollonius of Rhodes. All the suppliants succeed, but one of them is in disguise, and two of the others address a statue of a goddess, and the goddess, not a human being, grants the requests. Three of these four suppliants are women or husbands and wives,

---

400. The thesis of Crotty, *Poetics*, and implicit, though not explicit, in MacLeod, *Iliad XXIV*, who, like Crotty, traces the humanization of Achilles in *Iliad* 24. The prevailing view does not stress pity; Burkert's view omits it.
401. Leodes: *Od.* 22.312. Phemius: 22.344. Others: Lycaon (*Il* 21.74), Hecuba (22.82), Priam (24.503).
402. Philoctetes: S. *Ph.* 501, 967. Sabine women: D.C. 1.5.5. Perisan women: Just. 11.9.14 Castor: J. *BJ* 5.318.

suggesting why more suppliants do not make the appeal for pity: unlike supplication, this appeal is humiliating and womanish, like the gestures scorned by Prometheus in Aeschylus.[403]

Roman literature contains even fewer examples of suppliants who appeal for pity and are known either to fail or succeed. In Caesar, a pitiful tribe of suppliants succeeds, but in Ovid an ugly lover, Polyphemus, appeals for pity from his nymph, Galatea, and fails.[404] In Cicero, Murena, Sulla, and Flaccus appeal for pity or let Cicero appeal for them, and all succeed in obtaining an acquittal.[405] This list is, of course, misleadingly short. Roman literature abounds in unanswered or interrupted appeals, and so does Greek.[406] But the occasional failure should also be normal for the many appeals of this kind. Even if an appeal is successful, it often accompanies the impression that the suppliant has something to offer the supplicandus, some claim to be a relative or friend, or some claim to be innocent or to have been victimized.[407] Perhaps the last two of these, which are about fairness, are the most important. This conclusion rests on the cardinal form that appeals to pity take, especially in Greek sources. Rather than ask for pity for himself, the suppliant asks for pity for his wife and especially for his children—pity for those whose innocence is unquestionable. This argument varies by genre and period, but it persists from early Greece to the Roman courtroom.

In Greek mythography and epic poetry, the suppliant refers to the children of the supplicandus. Like Themistocles, a few suppliants even lay hold of a child. Either way, the suppliant may seem to be appealing to family feeling. But the suppliant is not claiming to be someone's relative or friend. Instead the suppliant is grasping a symbol of innocence and associating himself or herself with it. The suppliant may also grasp the supplicandus's parents, another symbol. The reasoning is the same: like one's own child, one's parents are sacrosanct, if not innocent. If the suppliant is not laying hold of any children or parents, but only referring to them, the reason may not be only that the children or parents are out of reach. The suppliant may be trying to make several appeals instead of one. When Priam goes to Achilles, for example, Hermes advises him to beg in the name of Achilles' father, mother, and son. When Elpenor speaks to Odysseus, he seems to know that Odysseus's mother is dead, so he begs in the name of Odysseus's father, wife, and son.[408] Sophocles' Philoctetes, in contrast, lacks information about his sup-

---

403. Fiction: Leucippe as Lacaena (Ach. Tat. 5.17.3), Anthia (X. Eph. 5.4.10, a prayer), besieged Synaeans (Hld. 9.11.4), husband and wife (Lucianus *Lex.* 12, a prayer). Apollonius: A.R. 2.1121–36, where the supplicandus responds favorably because of the fulfillment of a prophecy, not because of a feeling of pity.

404. Caes. *Gal.* 2.28.3, Ov. *Met.* 13.855–6.

405. Cic. *Mur.* 86, *Sull.* 88, *Flac.* 106. Omitted from Roman acts: Sen. *Her. F.* 1192, *Med.* passim, *Phaed.* 622.

406. Note especially the general statements at Cic. *Inv.* 1.109, *Mur.* 62, Quint. *Inst.* 6.1.42. Greek: Antipho fr. 1. Similar prosecutorial fear of such an appeal: Lycurg. *in Leocr.* 143, Lys. 6.55, 22.21.

407. Arist. *Rh.* 2.1385b, Cic. *Tusc.* 4.18. E. Stevens, "Commonplaces," 10, speculates that Thrasymachus's lost *Eleoi* anticipated Aristotle; Konstan, *Pity Transformed*, 51, holds that Aristotle's was the general Greco-Roman view, as shown by examples from Homer and tragedy described in his chap. 2. A different view: Havelock, *Liberal Temper*, 144, on pity as a social cement rather than a reward for innocence.

408. *Il.* 24.466, *Od.* 11.67. When speaking to Athena, who has no parent but Zeus, Odysseus remembers to mention only her father (*Od.* 13.324).

plicandus, so he appeals to "father, mother, and any other family members."[409] But this sort of appeal does not rest solely on information or guesswork. Some suppliants mention only the family member who suits their purpose. Since Priam is a father, he speaks to Achilles about Achilles' own father, Peleus, but not about the others whom Hermes has recommended. Since Clytemnestra is a mother, she speaks to Achilles about his mother, Thetis.[410] The suppliant aims to associate himself with some symbol of innocence, but he gives more weight to himself and hence to those who resemble him.

So much for references to the children or parents of the supplicandus. No matter how effective, these references were sure to be few. It was much easier for the suppliant to refer to, and even present, his own children—and many do. This time, the suppliant says, "I am as innocent as my own child." Several biographers report supplications of this type, including one involving Molossian refugees who use an infant who would someday be famous as Pyrrhus of Epirus. They set the child before their host, the king of Illyria. Even as a newborn, Pyrrhus was preternaturally bold, creeping across the floor and taking the king by the knees. Like little Orestes, Pyrrhus was "practically supplicating." The source just quoted, Plutarch, adds that the king's wife was present.[411] Inevitably, the Illyrian king protects the refugees.

Had the Molossians taken the same scenario to early Rome, they might have found it similarly efficacious, for the Sabine women use it when displaying their own children.[412] And the Molossians might have met with the same result in Athens, for here, too, suppliants stage scenarios with children, but in an Athenian venue: a courtroom. These suppliants, however, differ from the refugees who brought Pyrrhus to Illyria in that they present the entire family, wives included.[413] Along with this social difference comes a structural one. In Epirus, the scenario of sharing the child "practically" includes an act of supplication. In an Attic court, however, there is no act of supplication at the moment the children appear. As we have seen, multiple suppliants beset the supplicandi. Then, if they all fail, the suppliant turns Molossian and uses his wife and children. As a judge in Aristophanes explains: "If we don't give in to all that, he drags up his children, girls and boys, by the hand. I listen as they cringe and bleat."[414] If the father is unable to speak well, his sons may speak for him.[415]

409. S. *Ph.* 468.

410. *Il.* 24.486–506, E.*IA* 909; so also S. *Aj.* 587–88.

411. Plut. *Pyrr.* 3.1–2. "Practically supplicating": ὥσπερ τις ἱκέτης ἐχόμενος. In another version that Plutarch reports, the child grabs an altar. The same technique in the same place, Molossia: E. *And.* 537–40, where it fails in spite of coaching by the mother.

412. Liv. 1.13.2, although Livy does not say that the women presented the children to the supplicandi, a gesture added by the painter David. The same ploy: D.H. 8.46.1, the supplication by mother, wife, and children to Coriolanus. An imperial example: D.C. 65.16.2.

413. For the advantages of introducing one's family and friends, see Lavency, *Logographie judiciaire*, 81. Forced supplication when besiegers make use of children as hostages: D.S. 37.19.5–20. Voluntary supplication by children occurs only in a fictional siege: Hld. 9.11.4.

414. Ar. *V.* 568–71. The most prominent example of the appeal: Aeschin. 2.179.

415. Lys. 30.35.

Perhaps this kind of supplication became a cliché. This conclusion springs from the parody in Aristophanes' *Wealth*, in which a character confuses a suppliant going to an altar with one going to a courtroom, and thus imagines the children as being seated (the usual pose at an altar) and not as standing (the usual pose in court).[416] But this type of appeal remained popular. About one-fifth of all known Athenian prosecutors say that the defendant will beg and weep.[417] The proportion of defendants who put children on stage was at least that high, and in Roman courts the proportion may have been comparable. The Romans seem to have made just one change in the appeal: allowing the *patronus*, or advocate, to present the children.[418] This Roman adaptation shows that the use of children was not exclusively or essentially democratic.[419] Molossian examples show the same, and point to the conclusion that this kind of appeal for pity—like the arguments to reciprocity, family, and fairness—appears throughout Greco-Roman antiquity. The Old Testament, in contrast, does not report any appeal using children. Even the supplication of David by the nameless woman, one who is obviously a mother, does not include this appeal. Yet this supplication does not lack for children once it undergoes elaboration by Josephus, who writes in Greek. In his *Jewish Antiquities*, the same woman comes to David and asks him to prevent a threat to harm to her only son. When he agrees, she thanks him for taking pity on her old age and her dependence on an only child.[420]

The appeal to pity, then, is an appeal to innocence, but not a straightforward appeal. Through children, suppliants say that they are innocent by association. They are arguing symbolically and vicariously, but without losing sight of the request to be given one's deserts. First request, then arguments: first an impression of the suppliant's needs and then an impression of his or her character. But it must be a good impression. Only then will it be fair to grant the request.

Pièces de Resistance

When Menelaus recovered Helen in Troy, he wanted to kill her, and so she supplicated him. As Euripides tells the story, she clasped his knees and made an argument about fairness: like Oedipus, she was a victim of *Atê*, mischief sent by the gods, and so she was innocent of wrongdoing by virtue of an excuse. No, Menelaus answered: she was guilty, for she had done wrong willingly.[421] He regarded her as Odysseus did Leodes, not as Odysseus did Phemius, and so he rejected her. At the end of the scene, he drags her offstage, vowing to put her to death.[422] But Euripides'

---

416. Ar. *Pl.* 382–85. A less demanding parody: a defendant's pet puppies brought to the *bêma*, V. 975–78. The most famous: *Th.* 689–724, based on E. *Telephus*.

417. Johnstone, *Disputes and Democracy*, 115–17. Similar: Lacey, *Family*, 175–76.

418. E.g., Servius Galba at Cic. *de Orat.* 1.228, a display that Cicero calls "tragoedias." The same advocate manipulating children on his own behalf: *Brut.* 90. General statement: Quint. *Inst.* 6.1.42.

419. A different view, affirming the democratic character of the practice: Johnstone, *Disputes and Democracy*, 123–25.

420. J. *AJ* 7.182–84.

421. Her gesture and excuse: E. *Tro.* 1042–43. His evaluation: 1037–39.

422. E. *Tro.* 1047–48. This rejection occurs just before he leads her to the ships, as in the *Iliou Persis* (Procl. *Chr.* 107 = *EGF* p. 62)

was not, and could not have been, the only version of the story. Helen survived, so her supplication must have eventually been successful, and she must have made a persuasive argument. But what argument was there for this famously wicked woman? None. Vase paintings (and some lost poetry) provide her another expedient. She exposes her breasts, and Menelaus decides to spare her.[423]

This gesture may seem to resemble Priam's mother's, but it is erotic, not maternal, and it is not merely retrospective. In figure 2.11 it is the unseen factor that haunts the pursuing Menelaus. In this version of the story, Helen must have an altar to run to, and he has not yet overtaken her. But he is remembering or anticipating something vivid enough to make him drop his sword.[424] When he reaches her, he will spare her. The two other figures in the scene, Aphrodite and *Peitho*, or "persuasion," confirm this result.

What sort of supplication is this? The approach is to undress, the gesture to entice. The request is both obvious and ambiguous. Nonetheless, Helen is supplicating,

FIGURE 2.11   Menelaus pursuing Helen. Courtesy of Réunion des Musées nationaux.

423. For Helen's exposed breast see *LIMC* 4.1.498–501 s.v. *Hélène*, where Kahil traces the motif in her commentary. The oldest known source: Lesches (schol. Ar. *Lys.* 155 = *EGF* p. 58).

424. Fig. 2.11: an Egnatian bell crater of ca. 450 BCE = *ARV*² 1077.5 = *LIMC* 4.2 s.v. *Hélène*, 268. For the interplay between *aidôs* as sexual modesty, a quality found in this scene, and *aidôs* as the quality evinced by a suppliant, see Ferrari, "Figures in the Text," 5–8, dealing with Iphigenia in Aeschylus. The altar of Aphrodite: Ibycus *PMG* 296.

and doing so successfully. Nor should we suppose that Euripides, at least, objected to this irregular act. Nothing in his scene prevents Helen from making this appeal offstage. Even in Euripides—even in a play where another suppliant, Hecuba, begs Menelaus to reject Helen, the only case where any suppliant begs for another's rejection—Helen prevails. Nor is Helen alone. What a demigoddess may do, so may a courtesan. Phryne, the best-known woman of her profession in fourth-century Athens, followed Helen's example. She was on trial on charges of impiety. We do not know the particulars, but we do know that one of her lovers, the orator Hyperides, was suspected of the same crime.[425] Their love affair and the suspicions against him were two reasons for him to defend her. The court was the Areopagus, famous for its probity—and for its prudery.[426]

Like Helen, Phryne tried behaving conventionally. If we discount Posiddipus's claims about her taking judges by the hand, we can still reckon that she followed the example of Pericles' mistress, Aspasia, who stood trial on the same charge, impiety, and made no statement on her own behalf. Instead she let someone else, perhaps the orator Hyperides, speak for her.[427] But convention failed her. As Athenaeus reports, "Hyperides was accomplishing nothing by his speech in defense of Phryne and the judges seemed likely to find her guilty." As a last resort, Phryne performs Helen's gesture: "Hyperides brought her into view, removed her clothes, and exposed her breasts. In his peroration he evoked grief at the sight of her." When the woman who was supposed to be the model for the Cnidian Venus was exposed to the judges, the effect should have been erotic; since Hyperides may have been her lover, it may have been pathetic, too. But Athenaeus reports another effect: "He made the judges dread this servant and devotee of Aphrodite. Gracious towards her thanks to a feeling of pity, they spared her."[428] The words "servant and devotee," which may come from Hyperides' speech, may refer to Phryne's participation in the Aphrodisia on Aegina. If so, these words show the supplicandi that the suppliant is favored by a goddess, hence deserving of pity. But the chief effect is "dread." And this effect is humorously ironic: although charged with impiety, the suppliant is honored as though she were a goddess. Some sources did not care for this irony, and so they reported that Phryne exposed her breast while tearing her clothes in mourning.[429] But even in these sources, the act of exposure remains the same. So does the result: success.

Few suppliants were demigoddesses, and few inspired dread. Only two others in Greek and Latin literature are said to be attractive or to be successful because of their charms.[430] But there may have been many who, like Helen and Phryne, did not need to make an argument.

425. Ath. *Deip.* 13.590d.
426. Prudery: Aeschin. 1.82.
427. Plut. *Per.* 32.2–3.
428. Ath. *Deip.* 13.590e–f. "Dread": δεισιδαιμονῆσαι as at Arist. *Pol.* 5.1315a. A briefer account without "dread": Plut. *X Or. Vit.* 849e. Perhaps her lover: C. Cooper, "Hyperides," 307–12, questioning Athenaeus's statement that he was.
429. Anon. *Rh.* 7.335, the explanation preferred by C. Cooper, "Hyperides," 315–16.
430. Ach. Tat. 5.17.4. Curt. 8.10.34–35.

SEQUENCE VERSUS LENGTH

Any review of the first three steps should present them in order: approach, gesture or word, request, and argument. That is how suppliants performed them, and what supplicandi (and ancient readers and listeners) expected. But this way of presenting them is nonetheless misleading. The three steps are not of the same length and the same complexity, and modern students have not treated them as such. The prevailing view has concentrated on the second step, especially gestures, and some literary critics have concentrated on the third, especially on appeals to pity. The victim of this disparity has been the first step. At this point suppliants have more choices than the obvious one between addressing an altar and addressing an individual. To choose well, they must know the politics of the community in which they find themselves. Or if they find themselves in a home or on a battlefield, they must know where power lies. Yet because they must make a choice as soon as the act of supplication begins, this choice may escape notice.

If the first step, occurring at the moment a supplication starts, seems so short that it might vanish, the second step, occurring immediately afterward, seems long. One reason is that it can indeed be very long. Waving boughs during a siege, for example, can take hours. Even gestures that are brief, like clasping and holding the knees, do not seem so, for they make up in intensity what they lack in length. We find it easier to assess them, and to appreciate the choices that suppliants must once again make. The chief concern is no longer politics, however, but instead is the personality and identity of the supplicandus. The right choice for Odysseus to make with Nausicaa is not the right choice for him to make with Circe, so he prays to the virgin and clutches the witch. Contact may be either appropriate or inappropriate, and gestures themselves may be either appropriate or inappropriate. Sometimes gestures and the alternative to gestures, words, are both inadequate. Then the suppliant resorts to combinations, as in court. These combinations can make the second step long, too.

The third step can be even longer. In Greek tragedy, suppliants devote hundreds of lines to their requests and arguments, and so any mere list of them may give a misleading impression of brevity. In addition, a list does not acknowledge that a suppliant may make more than one request and that many suppliants make more than one argument. The first act of supplication in the *Iliad*, by Chryses, includes appeals to the gods and to reciprocity.[431] Phemius and Leodes make arguments about reciprocity and involuntary wrongdoing. Tragedy features combinations, too: in the *Children of Heracles*, the suppliant argues about kinship, reciprocity, and fairness; in *Oedipus at Colonus*, about fairness, kinship, solidarity among *xenoi*, and reciprocity.[432] We do not know the arguments used by the paradigmatic Roman suppliant, Metellus Pius, but he surely said that to ask for

431. *Il.* 1.20–21.
432. E. *Heracl.*: kinship, 207–11; reciprocity, 215–22; and justice, 250–52. S. *OC*: just cause, 1305–7; family ties, 1333–35; solidarity among *xenoi*, 1333–34; and reciprocity in the form of a promise to end Oedipus's exile, 1342–43.
433. J. *BJ* 1.281–84.

help in bringing his father back to Rome was only fair, since his father did not deserve exile, and he surely asked that the supplicandus respect the wishes of a dutiful son. Josephus rounds out this list: when Herod supplicates Marc Antony, he cites his personal merits, ties of *xenia*, and undeserved misfortune.[433]

Multiple arguments bespeak resourcefulness, another quality that any list will miss. Instead of clasping a pair of knees, a suppliant may, through a claque, clasp up to 75 pairs of knees at a time, as Aemilius Scaurus does. Or he may keep his distance, as the naked Odysseus does. Or he may besmirch himself, as both Hebrews and Romans do. He may well say god loves him, but he will more likely say that he has ready money or dare the supplicandus to reject his wife and children, as Attic defendants do. He may say nothing, and remove some of his (or her) clothes. He may seem to do anything and everything except make threats, and in Euripides, he will do even that. But length and variety do no make supplication disorderly. The first two steps lead to the third, and the third often features either a request like acquittal or pardon, an argument from fairness, or an appeal to pity that only an innocent can make. And so the first two steps, which are not in any way legal, lead to one that often is in some way legal. The fourth step, in turn, resembles the third. As a supplication proceeds, the legal elements come to the fore, and the ceremony of approach and gesture recedes.

Once they have finished the first three steps, do suppliants feel hopeful or despairing, abused or disabused? Do they look through some window of privacy and see themselves from the outside? No source says so. The stakes are high. All eyes fall on the supplicandus.

3

The Fourth and Last Step

The immediate consequence of an act of supplication is that the person addressed must respond. First he evaluates the suppliant, and then he decides whether to grant or deny the suppliant's request. This choice to grant or not is no less momentous for him than it is for the suppliant. If he grants the request, he gives a pledge to the suppliant, and the two of them enter into a lasting tie. Since breaking this pledge is an act of betrayal, it is virtually binding. If he does not grant the request, he rejects the suppliant, and sometimes he even goes so far as to expel the suppliant from the altar. The evaluation and decision resemble a verdict, and the pledge, though not punitive, resembles a legal judgment. All three tasks echo the legal character of some suppliants' requests and the quasilegal character of many suppliants' arguments.

In recent scholarship, none of these tasks has received as much attention as earlier steps. Because the prevailing view assumes that acceptance is automatic, given the proper gestures, the prevailing view misses the first two tasks: the evaluation and the decision to say "yes" nor "no." Because it considers these gestures binding, it misses the third task, giving a pledge. It acknowledges rejection and expulsion but only as aberrations. The prevailing view does, in contrast, stress the new tie formed by suppliant and supplicandus but holds that this tie takes the form of admitting the suppliant into a group, as in the anthropology of van Gennep and Durkheim.[1]

Other views have missed most of these tasks, too. Burkert acknowledges the evaluation and decision, and he also acknowledges rejection, but he does not acknowledge moral or legal grounds for them. Like the prevailing view, his view misses the pledge and regards the new tie only as an occasion for joining a group.[2] The parallels between the fourth step and legal proceedings go unremarked, as they do in the works of literary critics studying supplication in Homer and tragedy. Legal historians make room for evaluation, decision, and both acceptance and rejection, but only if the suppliant is appealing to a supplicandus who is a

---

1. The prevailing view adapted to concentrate on the last step: Herman, *Ritualised Friendship*, 3.2. An anticipation of the prevailing view: Gernet, "Pénalité et la réligion," 332–37. The prevailing view restricted to temple refuge by a member of the community in which the temple was located: Traulsen, *Das sakrale Asyl*, 179, "interne hikesie."

2. Burkert, *Creation of the Sacred*, 85–90.

priest or magistrate subject to regulation.[3] They do not notice legal principles in extralegal settings.

All of these views neglect the most important figure in the fourth step, the supplicandus. "Yes" and "no" are his responsibility, one made vivid on a Roman coin that unlike other images of supplication does not show what the supplicandus will say. To the left, the Roman emperor Magnentius rides across a battlefield. To the right, a defeated German extends his hands (figure 3.1, reverse). He has put aside his shield and his broken spear, another sign of supplication. Now the emperor must respond. Will he kill the suppliant or spare him? Precedents favor sparing him, but we have come to this spot too early to be sure. The image conveys the emperor's power to decide, but not his decision.[4]

ACCEPTANCE

From the viewpoint of the supplicandus, "yes" and "no" are not only different outcomes but also different tasks. Both include an evaluation and a decision, but "yes" leads to a pledge and a tie, and "no" does not. Instead "no" imposes two other burdens: that the supplicandus explain his decision and that he deal with any rejected suppliant who refuses to leave the altar. "Yes" requires a dutiful supplicandus, "no" a forceful one.

Evaluation, the unavoidable starting point, begins with acknowledging the suppliant, a courtesy that very few supplicandi neglect. One way to commit this oversight is to mistake the suppliant for an assailant, as a demogogue supposedly

FIGURE 3.1   A German supplicating the emperor. Courtesy of American Numismatic Society.

3. Antecedents for my own view among scholars of Greek religion: Welcker, *Götterlehre*, 2.198–201, and Lloyd-Jones, *Justice of Zeus*, 5–7, on Zeus's role in watching over promises; Hirzel, *Der Eid*, 121–23, adds a comparison between Zeus and Yahweh. Another development of the idea of sacred promises, but further removed from supplication: Knippschild, *Rechtssymbolische Acte*, chap. 1. Antecedents for my own view among scholars of Greek law: Schlesinger, *Griechische Asylie*, 55–57, and Chaniotis, *"Conflicting Authorities,"* both acknowledging that suppliants might be rejected, but on narrower grounds than those described below.
4. Fig. 3.1: a nummus of Magnentius, ANS 1984.146.2162 = *RIC* VIII p. 185, #115. Similar is *RIC* V.2 p. 104, #808 (Probus).

would.[5] Another is to walk away, something the suppliant will condemn. In Euripides' *Orestes*, Menelaus listens for a time to his nephew's request for protection from a court that is going to convict him of murdering his mother. Then Menelaus walks away, and Orestes calls him a villain.[6]

Listening is the other part of evaluating. When considering how Achilles will react to Priam in *Iliad* 24, Zeus expatiates on this task, saying that Achilles should "not be witless or heedless or deaf to entreaties."[7] Another character in Homer, Penelope, rebukes an evil man, Antinous, for not "paying attention" to a suppliant.[8] Prose reports only three instances of this kind of mistreatment, by a barbarian, a tyrant, and a Roman official. The barbarian, a Persian king, slaughters suppliants seeking to surrender, and does so even though the leader of the suppliants assures him that they will not only surrender but do so unconditionally. Diodorus calls the king's "rage" "beyond the reach of argument." The tyrant shoots arrows at the suppliants but fails to harm them, a twist that makes the tyrant both malicious and ridiculous.[9] The Roman official, L. Quinctius Flamininus, brother of the general who "liberated" the Greeks, did not follow any example of his brother's when he received a Spanish suppliant at dinner. He suspended a sword over the suppliant's head, listened to the man's request, and killed him as a joke. Livy calls this act a "serious crime," and Cato the Censor expelled Flamininus from the Senate.[10]

Besides listening, a supplicandus may take advice, as Menelaus does when dealing with Adrastus.[11] But most supplicandi who take advice are off the battlefield, and so, unlike Menelaus, they are free to consult an expert such as an oracle. Sparta consulted oracles several times.[12] Twice, the suppliants were rebels. One group were Helot laborers who rebelled in the fifth century and sought protection. The other were the offspring of slaves and the Spartan women who took slaves as partners when the Spartan army was absent during a long war. These *partheniae*, "born out of wedlock," attempted to rebel a century or so earlier than the Helots. Pardoning either group would have upset social equilibrium. On the other hand, condemning them would have required the Spartans to kill many community members. The oracle found an answer: let them leave and found a colony. Another occasion for consultation was a hard case in which the supplicandi, residents of a small city, were unsure whether to offend a great power. This instance also shows that consultations were frequent. Disgruntled at the supplicandi, the

---

5. D.S. 34/35.28a.

6. E. *Or.* 717–21.

7. *Il.* 24.157. "Not deaf to entreaties": οὔτ' ἀλιτήμων, a term derived from *lit-*, as argued by Kearney, "*Alitemon.*"

8. "Pay attention": *Od.* 16.422, ἐμπάζεαι.

9. Barbarian: D.S. 16.45.2–3, with ὀργὴν ἀπαραίτητον. Tyrant: Plut. *Sul.* 13.3.

10. Liv. 39.42.10–12, with the *facinus* denounced at 39.43.4; Cato acts at 39.42.5. An example in myth and art: the slaughter of Dryas, the supplicating son of Lycurgus, by his father in an Attic red-figure hydria, Rome Villa Giulia = *ARV*² 1343a = *LIMC* 6.2 s.v. *Lykourgos I*, 12 (A. Farnoux); and in another Attic red-figure hydria, Cracow Mus. Nat. XI.1225 = *ARV*² 1121.17 = *LIMC* 6.2 s.v. same, 26. Literary sources do not report Dryas's supplication.

11. *Il.* 6.53–62; so also E. *Supp.* 286–339. But nowhere before *Aeneid* 12 does a supplicandus change his mind after considering his own feelings, as discussed at 275–76 below.

oracle says that it will give no more answers, a threat implying that it has already given many.[13]

Sometimes a supplicandus asks questions having to do with supplication, as opposed to other questions that he asks because a suppliant is a visitor or stranger. The king of Argos in Aeschylus's *Suppliants* asks numerous questions about the arguments of the Danaids. When they say that they are kin, he questions them at length and stops only when told the story of Io, a common ancestor who migrated to Egypt. When they say that they will be enslaved unless he helps them, he is no less sceptical, asking who will act unlawfully against them.[14] In the *Suppliants* of Euripides, the king of Athens asks questions about the request made by the widows of Argive soldiers through their leader, Adrastus. He starts by asking about their request, which is to obtain help burying the dead, and then, when he learns that these dead need burying because Adrastus has unsuccessfully attacked Thebes, asks Adrastus to justify this attack. He is as sceptical about this attack as his counterpart is about the migration of Io.[15] In the *Eumenides*, the supplicanda, Athena, is crisper and more professional. The suppliant, Orestes, stands accused of murder, so the goddess asks him the questions a magistrate might: who are you and how do you answer the charges against you?[16]

At this point the supplicandus must decide whether or not to grant the request. If he decides in favor, he uses a gesture or word meaning "yes" but also meaning that he is making a pledge, his remaining task. Because his gesture does this double work, it needs to be clear and vivid, like the gestures used by suppliants, and it achieves these qualities by imitating suppliants' gestures yet inverting them. If the suppliant clasps the knees or sits by the hearth, two common gestures, the supplicandus extends a hand and raises him, Greek *anistêmi*.[17] The *Iliad* includes only one such act of raising, but this act is the very last one in the poem—Priam's supplication of Achilles, who responds by raising him, ἀνίστη. The *Odyssey* includes two such acts, one of which features raising someone and seating him in a chariot. Here the raiser is the pharaoh, who has just defeated a pirate raid led by Odysseus.[18] Although fantastic, this scene confirms the ubiquitousness of the gesture, which appears in the Old Testament, where the situation is the same: the Israelite King Ahab, in a chariot, raises his Syrian counterpart, the defeated Ben-Hadad, who is on the ground.[19] A range of later authors report similar acts.

---

12. Str. 6.3.2, Th. 1.103.2, Isoc. 6.23. Non-Spartan: Plut. *QG* 299d.

13. Hdt. 1.159.4. A possible case of supplication leading to consultation of an oracle: *IG* v.2 262, according to which murderers may have entered a sanctuary to supplicate, as discussed by Chaniotis, "*Conflicting Authorities*," 75–78, with refs.

14. Kin: A. *Supp.* 292–324. Unlawful act: 336. Help: 340.

15. Request: E. *Supp.* 115, 125. Attack: 131–61. Questions that would be asked regardless of whether the visitor supplicated: S. *OC* 143–224, E. *Heracl.* 80–96.

16. A. *Eu.* 436–38; cf. Is. 6.12–13.

17. Esther rises without being raised (*Es.* 8.5), perhaps because of Persian court ceremonial, also evident at Plut. *Them.* 28.1–29.2; Hdt 1.35 may be similar.

18. *Il.* 24.515; *Od.* 7.168–69, also a prestigious venue, and with chariot at 14.276–80.

19. 3 *Ki.* 20.32–34.

In Thucydides, the Athenians raise suppliants who have gone to altars at Mytilene after the Athenians capture this rebellious city. Other historians and biographers from Herodotus to Dio Cassius, some six hundred years later, also report it.[20] So do two novelists, Xenophon of Ephesus and Heliodorus. Some of these acts occur at altars, too, or in shrines.[21] The only difference that an altar makes is that any bough left by the suppliant is removed.[22]

If the source describes the supplicandus's gesture from the viewpoint of the suppliant, the same verb appears in the middle voice or in the intransitive, two forms denoting reciprocal, complementary action. Here again a range of sources report, from the orator Aeschines to Plutarch and the novelist Achilles Tatius.[23] A few sources report variations: in Euripides, the compound *exanistêmi* means "to raise by hook or crook," while in prose the phrase *peithô anastênai* has a similar meaning of "to raise while making persuasive promises."[24]

In Rome, raising occurs less often, but a common, even standard term for it appears on coins, where the most prestigious of supplicandi, the emperor, appears as RESTITVTOR, meaning both "raiser" and "restorer" in scenes such as the reverse of figure 3.2. Here Hadrian, *restitutor Achaiae*, "raiser of Greece," extends his right hand to a personified Achaea.[25] Hadrian's use of his right hand does not merely show that he is saying "yes," the obvious sense of a gesture of raising and restoring. As Eustathius says, and as other sources confirm, taking someone by the right hand symbolizes giving a pledge.[26] A few sources go so far as to say that

FIGURE 3.2   Achaea on one knee before Hadrian. Courtesy of American Numismatic Society.

20. Mytilene: Th. 3.28.2. Elsewhere in Th.: 1.126.11, 3.75.5 (shrine). Others: Hdt. 5.71 (statue), App. *Ill.* 9, D.H. 4.66.2, Plut. *Aem.* 27.1, *Cor.* 36.4, Liv. 39.13.3 (*attollere*), D.C. 36.52.4.

21. X. Eph. 2.10.2, Hld. 2.14.1, 5.26.4; so also *Hist. Apoll.* 12.

22. S. *OT* 143, E. *Supp.* 359–61.

23. Aeschin. 1.61, Plut. *Lyc.* 5.5; Ach. Tat. 5.17.4 is a command to a slave.

24. *Exanistêmi* as "raise by hook or crook": E. *And.* 435–36; at Plut. *Cor.* 36.4 and D.C. 36.52.4 it means merely "raise." At Aeschin. 1.61, πείθουσιν ἀνιστάναι means "persuade to leave a sanctuary after an offer of protection."

25. Fig. 3.2: an aureus, ANS 1994.100.4557 = *RIC* III p. 377, #321, with *restitutor* in the dative.

26. Plin. *NH* 11.251, Liv. 29.24.3.

the Latin goddess *Fides*, "Trust," resides in the right hand.[27] One type of Roman pledge, a *pignus*, is also a matter for the right hand.[28]

Coins like the aureus of Hadrian are perhaps the most numerous illustrations of supplication in the ancient world.[29] Two other emperors, Aurelian and Valens, issued them, and two other provinces, Bithynia and Hispania, appear on them. So do larger entities, the Roman East and the entire Roman Empire.[30] These images establish that the practice of raising with the right hand is normal, but not just because these images are numerous. The emperor is the most powerful and desirable of supplicandi, and his opposite number, a province or region, is the largest if not worthiest of suppliants. The relation between the emperor and the province is also an allegory of countless relations between the emperor and his officials on the one side and provincial notables as well as the provincial populace on the other. Some of these relations involved acts of supplication, and so the image on the coin invites the viewer to assume that other acts resemble this one.

Literature points to the same conclusion. Among the Greek prose authors who report raising with the right hand are Dionysius of Halicarnassus, the historian of early Italy; the biographer Plutarch; and Polybius, the historian of the middle Roman Republic.[31] So do the Latin prose authors Curtius Rufus, whose subject is Alexander, and Livy, whose subject is Rome, and the poets Ovid, whose subject is myth, and Silius Italicus, whose subject is Rome.[32] Still more authors report raising but mention a hand without saying that it is the right hand.[33] And many authors report raising without mentioning a hand. But we should notice that no supplicandus ever raises a suppliant using his left hand or using both hands.[34] All others use the right, including the Greek novelist Achilles Tatius and the Syrian Greek novelist Heliodorus; two Greek historians, Herodotus and Diodorus Siculus; two Roman historians, Suetonius, and Tacitus; the Greek playwright Euripides and a Roman one, Plautus; and a medley of minor authors including Apollodorus, Valerius Maximus, and Velleius Paterculus.[35] And these are only cases where the source says that the supplicandus raised the suppliant. The supplicandus may have done so in any case where the suppliant bent

---

27. S. A. 3.07, Val. Max. 6.6. pr., and other passages discussed by W. Otto, *RE* 6.2.2281–86, s.v. *Fides*, here 82–83. A different view: Freyburger, "Supplication grecque," 521–22, linking *fides* not to pledges but to *aidôs*.

28. The king: *Es.* 8.3–8. Pignus: Curt. 6.7.4, 6.7.35, Ov. *Met.* 6.506.

29. Other aurei of Hadrian's: ANS 0000.999.20159 = *RIC* III p. 464, #947 (Bithynia); ANS 1001.1.11994 = *RIC* III p. 377, #326 (Hispania). These are reverses.

30. An aureus of Aurelian's, in which the female suppliant represents the whole Roman East: ANS 1990.64.1 = *RIC* I p. 304, #351. Of Valerian's, in which the woman represents the Roman empire: ANS 1944.100.27158 = *RIC* I p. 42, #50. These also are reverses.

31. D.H. 4.66.2, Plut. *Cor.* 23.5, Plb. 10.18.14.

32. Curt. 6.7.35, Liv. 30.12.18, Ov. *Met.* 6.506, Sil. It. 8.59–60.

33. *H. Ven.* 155, J. *BJ* 3.335, Caes. *Gal.* 1.20.5, Vell. 2.80.4. Hands of collective supplicandi: E. *IT* 1068. Curt. 3.12.12, 3.12.17 show Greek influence.

34. Only one, the king of Persia, raises a suppliant without touching; see n. 17 above.

35. Ach. Tat. 5.17.4, Hld. 2.14.1, 4.18.3, 5.26.4, with Homeric coloring; Hdt. 5.71.1, D.S. 19.63.5 "violently raise," i.e., without saying yes or pledging; Suet. *Nero* 13.2, Tac. *Ann.* 12.19.1; E. *IA* 915–16, Pl. *Rud.* 280; Apollod. 1.9.28, V. Max. 5.1.8, Vell. 2.80.4; Sil. It. 14.177.

low, sat, or prostrated himself, and the source may have omitted this common response, just as Homer usually does.[36]

If all supplicandi use the right hand, why do only some sources say so? They mention the right hand when they wishes to stress the pledge and omit it when they wish to stress acceptance instead. If the source wishes to stress both, it includes the right hand as a flourish. When describing the request for protection that Medea addresses to her lover, Jason, Apollonius of Rhodes does so:

> She spoke in distress. But Jason's mind was glad. After she fell at his knees he raised her and embraced and encouraged her: "As Olympian Zeus himself is my witness, along with Hera, his mate and the goddess of marriage, I will make you, lady, my lawful wife in my home—once we return and reach Greece." He said this and immediately put his right hand in hers.[37]

To say "yes" and mean it: that is what Medea wants from her supplicandus. By putting the right hand last, and interposing an oath, Apollonius has let Jason grant her wish.[38] Like other features of supplication in Apollonius, this one has no Homeric precedent.[39]

A choice few supplicandi use another gesture, a nod. When Thetis asks Zeus to bring honor to her son Achilles in *Iliad* 1, a request that we have noticed because of her discretion, Zeus replies with his own small if not discreet gesture, a nod that the god says makes heaven and earth tremble. Augustus imitates him, nodding to Cleopatra.[40] An emperor's son and a few gods also presume to imitate him.[41] These weighty supplicandi inversely correspond to the gesture that they make. The value of their pledges also inversely corresponds to the gesture, for the most valuable divine pledge is Zeus's, and the most valuable human pledge is the Roman emperor's. Just as raising is the norm, nodding is the variation, a gesture meant to put distance between not only the supplicandus and the suppliant but also between the greatest supplicandi and all others. Similar to the nod is the hand that the Roman emperor extends in pardon. Trajan extends his hand this way in several panels of the column commemorating his conquest of Dacia.[42] In such a situation, the supplicandus is too far away for a nod to be visible.

36. Homeric success without report of raising or any other gesture, but with report of clasping of knees by the suppliant: *Il.* 9.451–53, *Od.* 10.264–73, 10.323–47. Without report of raising or preceding knee clasp: *Il.* 2.653–57, 9.581–96, 13.694–97, 15.431–32, 16.570–74. 18.421–67, *Od.* 3.92–108, 4.322–50, 6.141–94, 11.66–80, 13.226–49, 13.324–51, 14.29–54, 15.256–84, 16.424–30. *Od.* 10.480–95 is ambiguous.

37. A.R. 4.82–100. Same effect, but achieved by several acts of supplication leading to an oath: V. Fl. 7.410–60, 7.475–87, 7.490–510.

38. A contrary view of the right hand: Gödde, *Drama der Hikesie*, 52 n. 144.

39. A.R. 4.82, 4.93, where the supplicating Medea reduces three supplicandi to one; and 4.1106–9, where the supplicandus, Alcinous, changes his mind. Both innovations reflect the character of Medea and the practice of Euripides.

40. Zeus: *Il.* 1.524–27; so also Ov. *Met.* 13.600. Augustus: Xiph. 77.8.

41. Other supplicatory nods: Titus (J. *BJ* 6.378–79), Venus (V. Fl. 6.461), Artemis (Lucianus *Lex.* 12). Lucianus *Symp.* 22, a nod given by a mortal, is another instance of parody in this author. The nod sought at S. *Ph.* 484 is not given, nor is that at V. Fl. 7.497. An implicitly different view: Knippschild, *Rechtssymbolische Acte*, 94–99, saying that nods are common ways of sealing treaties.

42. Panels 39, 123, 151 in Settis, *Colonna Traiana*.

Most suppliants who are at a distance must have received a verbal reply. Esther and Themistocles are examples. But even when the parties touch one another, some "compacts" may be entirely verbal.[43] The same is true of some *pisteis*, or "undertakings."[44] Unless the suppliant is a foreigner, reports of Roman supplication seldom refer to a pledge accompanied by a gesture, so some of these pledges must be verbal, too.[45] When suppliants wear mourning clothes, and once again are often at a distance, the response is at least partly verbal, and in one case the supplicandus tells the suppliant to change his clothes.[46] In contrast, words and gestures occur together wherever the supplicandus swears an oath, as Jason does.[47] A vow is similar.[48] Or the language may imply a gesture but not guarantee one, referring to a pledge of faith, or *fides*.[49]

Against these examples of gesture, word, and pledge stands one exception: the response of the supplicandus who has been asked to heal the suppliant. In this situation the supplicandus touches the suppliant but does not raise him. Instead the suppliant rises under his own power. Jesus touches the sick, including lepers, and up they come, raised by the supplicandus's miracle rather than by the supplicandus himself.[50] Asclepius anticipates Jesus. He or a familiar of his touches suppliants when they are in the place of incubation, curing them. Because the supplicandus has restored the suppliant, he does not need to make a pledge, but the beneficiary of the miracle—at least the beneficiary of the miracle of Asclepius—makes a thank offering to the benefactor.[51] On this score, Jesus is less demanding.

Once the supplicandus gives his pledge, or even while he is in the midst of doing so, he may pause to explain why he has decided to grant the request. In the *Children of Heracles*, the king rehearses the arguments made by the suppliants, which are about family ties and past services, and adds an argument about the wishes of Zeus. In the *Suppliants* of Aeschylus, the Danaids are the one who make

43. As at Parth. 9.3 and D.C. 72.16.1, where Zanticus and Marcus Aurelius ἐς ὁμολογίαν ἦλθον in 175 CE. So also X. *An.* 7.4.24, App. *BC* 5.3.19, *Hisp.* 61, X. *Eph.* 3.2.3, D.C. 64.14.4; and Petr. 18.4, where no gesture is mentioned. At J. *BJ* 2.281, where the language is δοὺς ἔμφασιν, no gesture is possible.

44. Th. 1.133.2, without a gesture; similarly, X. *An.* 1.6.7, Lys. 1.20, Plut. *Thes.* 8.1; and D.S. 13.26.2, where a πίστις is said to be given to surrendering soldiers; App. *Hisp.* 61; J. *AJ* 14.15–16. Sophocles omitting the gesture as a signal of coming betrayal: *Ph.* 813, referring to Neoptolemus's failure to nod to Philoctetes at 484. Hellenistic *pisteis* in written form, also called *logoi asylias*: Woess, *Asylwesen Ägyptens*, 184–92.

45. Foreigners may be raised, a gesture discussed immediately below. The verb for this gesture is *attollo* in Silius Italicus (8.74–75, 14.176–77) and *adleuo* (Tac. *Ann.* 12.19.1, Suet. *Nero* 13.2) or *erigo* (Cic. *Sest.* 58) in prose.

46. Partly verbal: 3 *Ki.* 20.33–34, where the suppliant is raised into a chariot and given a compact. Change clothes: Sen. *Thy.* 524–25.

47. Other oaths: Paus. 4.23.9, 6.18.3; Plut. *Lyc.* 5.5; Polyaen. 8.55.1; Tz. *H.* 1.462; X. *Eph.* 2.9.4, 3.5.5; Hld. 7.24.1, made to the suppliant's son; D.H. 1.59.1, where Aeneas supplicates and receives them; Sil. It. 15.317–19, where Philip does and receives them from Rome, and 16.274, where Scipio Africanus does and receives them from Syphax. Oath and no gesture: V. Fl. 7.500.

48. Vow: *Il.* 18.464–67. A compact accompanied by a gesture: Hld. 5.25.2.

49. Sometimes *deditio in fidem*, discussed at 264–67 below. *Fides* pledged but no *deditio* by the suppliant: Sen. *Med.* 247–48 anticipated by 224, Tac. *Hist.* 3.48, Ter. *Hec.* 402.

50. As in all the cases listed in appendix 1a.

51. The norm of thank offering: *IG* iv² 1.121 #5. Comparable to an offering: the erection of tablets describing the cure that the god effected, as in *IG* iv² 1.121–23 and other evidence discussed in Naiden, "*Hiketai.*"

the argument about Zeus, saying that the gods will punish Argos for rejecting them, and the king repeats the argument, as does the assembly to which he refers the case.[52] Roman magistrates repeat suppliants' arguments, too. In one instance, Caesar repeats arguments evidently made by Deiotarus, an Eastern ruler who supplicated him after supporting Pompey in the civil war. The source, a military history written by someone in Caesar's circle, says only that Caesar accepted Deiotarus on grounds of *xenia*, friendship, and past services to Caesar as opposed to Pompey, but even though it does not say that Deiotarus made these arguments, Caesar will have repeated them, not thought them up.[53]

Supplicandi give only one reason for acceptance that suppliants do not. Some late sources call this reason *philanthropia*, "charity."[54] We might modernize it by calling it "human kindness" or even "humanity." But "humanity" is a term to be used charily. When Menelaus welcomes Telemachus to his house in *Odyssey* 4, he says that he has received hospitality from many, and thus will offer it to many, but he is speaking of hospitality, not of humanity, and of many, not all. In Sophocles, Theseus goes further, accepting Oedipus partly because "I realize that I am a man and that I have no bigger share of tomorrow than you do."[55] The next step would have been to generalize this idea and let the suppliant use it as an argument. Some Stoics did generalize it and even applied it to pleas for mercy on the battlefield.[56] Yet no ancient suppliant goes so far as to put this idea into words. It remains the privilege of the supplicandus. And well it should: it does not rest on human rights possessed by the suppliant or on compassion for fellow men.[57] Instead it rests on a perception by the supplicandus. When evaluating the suppliant, he remembers himself and finds himself comparable to the suppliant. A supplicandus of this kind confirms Aristotle's contention that one man will pity another who resembles him.[58] But most supplicandi are not of this kind. As the rhetoricians say, it is "irksome to supplicate outsiders," in other words, to supplicate by appealing to a sense of humanity rather than to friendship, reciprocity, and the like.[59]

Far more common are occasions when the supplicandus speaks in order to allay fear or mistrust felt by the suppliant. That most talkative of supplicandi, the king in the *Suppliants* of Aeschylus, is once again an illustration. He has offered to put the Danaids in the grove attached to the shrine, but they hesitate, and so he says, "You have caused auspicious things to be said, so let my statement to you be auspicious." Like other supplicandi, he is giving a pledge to the suppliants, but he is

52. E. *Heracl.*: family tie (207–11), services (215–18), and the same plus Zeus (236–41). A. *Supp.*: Danaids (381–84), king (478–79), and assembly (616–18).

53. *B. Alex.* 68.2.

54. As at D.S. 13.29.5. General statement: *Rhet. Her.* 4.65.

55. *Od.* 4.33–35; S. *OC* 566–68.

56. Cic. *Off.* 1.35. The argument appears at J. *AJ* 20.61 and D.S. 13.23.3.

57. Similar is Rhodes, "Graeco-Roman Perspective," holding that antiquity lacked the concept of human rights. Auffarth, "Protecting Strangers" rightly adds that supplication itself provides a right of access as opposed to a right to a benefit.

58. Arist. *Rh.* 2.1386a.

59. Sen. *Con.* 1.1.12. A somewhat different view: Konstan, *Pity Transformed*, 91, holding that antiquity lacked any human rights but without commenting on Theseus's speech.

also reassuring the Danaids by reciprocating, a response that builds trust.[60] The king also reveals why some supplicandi say nothing and instead tacitly accept the arguments made by the suppliant. Tacit acceptance is an auspicious reply. It is not, however, the voluble reply that would suit this supplicandus or satisfy these suppliants.

Another possibility is that the supplicandus, not the suppliant, will feel some fear or mistrust or wish to state reservations. Then the supplicandus will wish to negotiate with the suppliant and say, "yes, but." Greek examples begin with the myth of Demeter and Persephone as recounted by Ovid. When Demeter begs Zeus to let her daughter return to her, Zeus agrees, but with a reservation, a *lex certa* restricting the times at which Persephone may return.[61] In Homer, Odysseus imposes a condition on the supplicating Circe and exacts an oath that she will fulfill it. In Apollonius, Circe is the supplicanda, and negotiates in a different way, answering Jason and Medea's request for purification but denying another request of theirs, for refuge.[62] In another instance in this author, the supplicandi ask that the suppliant swear an oath that helping him will not offend the gods. Or the supplicandus may grant part of a request.[63] In comedy, suppliant slaves flee to altars and negotiate for better treatment.[64] This may have happened offstage, too, but we cannot be sure. Ancient writers like slaves to be just barely defiant enough to be ridiculous. (We can be sure that Euripides knew of the practice. His Telephus not only kidnaps Orestes and takes him to the altar, but dickers with Agamemnon afterwards. Telephus wants protection for himself, and Agamemnon wants it for the child.[65])

In historiography, many capitulating cities supplicate and then negotiate surrender terms. The Byzantines supplicated and negotiated with the Athenians in 409 BCE, and won the right to a trial in Athens; the Selgians supplicated and negotiated with the Seleucid general Achaeus some two hundred years later and raised a siege by agreeing to pay an indemnity; some two hundred years after that, the Massilians supplicated and negotiated with the troops of Caesar.[66] Armies do likewise.[67] So do small groups or individuals.[68] In *Kings*, Solomon negotiates with

60. A. *Supp.* 512: εὔφημον εἴη τοῦπος εὐφημουμένη. Wecklein ad loc. noticed the parallel with *Il.* 1.18, where the assembly is unable to make a pledge without the support of Agamemnon, even though their way of expressing their approval of the suppliant, ἐπηυφήμησαν (22), has a religious air.

61. Ov. *Met.* 5.531. Another early but not Homeric negotiation: Tz. *H.* 1.456–62.

62. *Od.* 10.342–48; A.R. 4.700–17 followed by 4.739–48.

63. A.R. 2.251–62. In the cycle, the Greeks spare Ajax the Lesser after making him swear an oath (Paus. 10.26.3). Part of a request: Liv. 42.24.6–10, Sen. *Med.* 282–95, St. *Theb.* 11.748–50.

64. Pl. *Most.* 1094–1181. Slaves, negotiations, but no altar: Pl. *Cist.* 566–84.

65. Slaves: D.S. 11.89.6–8, but Bradley, *Slavery*, 54, doubts Roman parallels. Euripides: as at chap. 2, n. 61 above. Aristophanic parodies of the parody: *Ach.* 425–34, *Thes.* 689–765. Cf. London BM E382 (36.2.11–28)-*ARV²* 632: *LIMC* 1.2 s.v. *Agamemnon*, 11, an Attic red-figure vase.

66. D.S. 13.67.7; Plb. 5.76.9–10, in 218 BCE; Caes. *Civ.* 2.11.4–13.3, in 49 BCE, though the Massilians betray him. Negotiations between diplomats and the Roman Senate: see 229–30 below. Negotiations are rejected at Sidon in 351–50 BCE (D.S. 16.45.2–3).

67. Th. 4.38.1; other reported truces may include negotiations that are not described.

68. Group: *Chr.W.* 330, where farmers abandon their tasks and flee to a temple, evidently to negotiate better conditions. Individual: X. *Cyr.* 4.6.1–10, V. Max. 5.5.1.

the Adonijah, the suppliant who had to prove himself worthy in the future. If he did not, Solomon told him, Solomon would punish him.[69] In Herodotus, negotiation combines with intercession to save the life of Cyrus the Great, the future ruler of Asia. Endangered as an infant, Cyrus survives because of the supplication of a shepherd by his wife. The shepherd has received orders from the king of the Medes to kill the newborn Cyrus, but before he can carry them out, his wife supplicates him, clasping his knees and interceding on the child's behalf. He asks her how he is to escape detection if he spares the child, they form a plan, and he spares him.[70] If this Near Eastern scene is fictional, such fiction does not come only from Greek authors. Curtius Rufus says that Persian captives negotiated with Alexander the Great's deputy Leonnatus while on their knees. Since this gesture is Roman, Curtius likely added it.

In all these cases, the supplicandus negotiates at the same time as he says "yes" and makes his pledge.[71] In one case in Homer, the supplicandus says yes, lets some time elapse, tests the suppliant, and only then commits himself. This supplicandus is Telemachus and the suppliant is Theoclymenus, a wanted man. The two meet on Pylos. As Telemachus is about set sail, Theoclymenus appears by surprise and stands beside Telemachus's ship. Presumably he does not touch Telemachus. He does supplicate him, though, but cautiously, begging—the Greek term is ἱκέτευσα—to learn who he is. Then, after Telemachus replies, Theoclymenus asks to be taken aboard, and Telemachus complies. The two sail to Ithaca.[72] Meanwhile, Telemachus gives no pledge to Theoclymenus. In particular, he does not promise to act as his host and protector when they arrive.

Now the two make port. At first, Telemachus ignores Theoclymenus and turns to his crew, telling them to go to town and wait for him. Anxious about his fate, Theoclymenus asks whether he should go to someone else's house or that of Telemachus. Telemachus apologizes for not being able to take him home and suggests that he go to the house of Eurymachus, one of Penelope's suitors. Will Theoclymenus accept this suggestion and lodge with the would-be step-father of his supplicandus? Before letting Theoclymenus answer, Telemachus drops a hint, saying that Eurymachus's chances of marrying Penelope depend on whether Zeus will allow Eurymachus to live that long. Then Zeus drops another hint, sending an omen. Theoclymenus grasps the two hints, praising Telemachus and condemning the suitors. For his part, Telemachus realizes that he has gained a friend. Gratified, he reverses himself, telling Theoclymenus to go to another, better house.[73] The negotiations between suppliant and supplicandus have ended in

---

69. 3 *Ki.* 1.50–53. Other Hebrew negotiations: J. *BJ* 2.643–44 and probably 1.139, a diplomatic scene.

70. Hdt. 1.112.

71. Two exceptions: J. *BJ* 2.336–41, Charito 2.10.2–11.6, where the negotiations or adjustments occur immediately after the pledge. Similar: Tac. *Hist.* 3.38, where the supplicandus need only acknowledge information given to him by the suppliant and respond later.

72. *Od.* 15.257–81. ἱκέτευσα: 277.

73. *Od.* 15.503–43, a passage brought to my attention by William Race.

establishing a relation of *xenia*, as elsewhere, but only after a tardy exchange without parallel either in the *Odyssey* or later.

As we have noticed, Homer is often atypical. So are negotiations. They occur because the two sides are not sure what one can do for the other, an uncommon problem. But the mere existence of this problem tells against the view of supplication as a ritual of contact. In such a ritual, the outcome is known in advance, and so there is no reason for negotiation. There is also less reason for listening to the suppliant and tacitly accepting the suppliant's arguments. Yet these responses are indispensable. If a supplicandus does not listen to the suppliant, he does not know what he may be agreeing to, and if he does not accept the suppliant's arguments, he does not know why he is agreeing. Either way, he is less able to make the commitments that form the next phase of that complicated word "yes."

A Conspectus of Pledges

So far, we have described how supplicandi say "yes" and make pledges. Now we turn to the things that they pledge to do. Since no common request—from asking to spared or protected to asking for help or honor—fails to gain approval from some supplicandus or other, responses vary as much as requests. But making a pledge lends a distinctive character to the supplicandus's response. The supplicandus forms a tie with the suppliant, and often this tie is enduring or permanent. It entails a relation between two parties, not just the granting of a request.

In the prevailing view, these ties all provide for the incorporation of the suppliant, who becomes either a party to a guest-host tie, *xenia*, or a member of a group or household. One reason for this view is that *xenoi* and new household members somewhat resemble initiates, a group of interest to Vernant and others.[74] Another, given by Gould, was that the gesture of raising creates parity, a characteristic of *xenia*.[75] In the background lies the influence of van Gennep, who in calling supplication "a unification ritual" suggested the topic of ties among strangers and thus of *xenia*.[76]

Some new ties fit the prevailing view. They include *xenia*, or some similar outcome; they sometimes lead to membership in a group, and they sometimes create parity. Best known is when the supplicandus raises a suppliant and provides *xenia* to him. The two then form a symmetrical pair. But this sequence should not be simplified. Some suppliants request help, not *xenia*; one of them is Telemachus, who receives *xenia* from Nestor and Menelaus in the *Odyssey*.[77] Other suppliants may have requested either *xenia* or protection. One of these is Telemachus's father, Odysseus. When he goes to the Cyclops, he asks for *xenia*, making a pointed reference to Zeus *Xenios*. Had he received it, the Cyclops would also have pro-

74. Vernant, *Mythe et pensée*, 130, Gould, "*Hiketeia*," 97–100, Bremmer, "Gelon's Wife." The same view without initiation: Schlesinger, *Griechische Asylie*, 38–39, anticipated by Eust. *Od.* 1.341.

75. Gould, "*Hiketeia*," 90–94, followed by Pulleyn, *Prayer*, chap. 4.

76. As in. n. 74 above.

77. *Od.* 3.92–108, 4.322–50. Similar: 14.29–54. For a different view, see S. Reece, *Stranger's Welcome*, 15–16, holding that Telemachus does not supplicate; for a similar view, see Giordano, *Supplica*, 3.4.

tected him against the dangers of an unknown country. When he goes to the pharaoh after defeat in battle, he asks for protection, but he gets the boons of both protection and *xenia*.[78] *Xenia* comes with protection if the suppliant fears for his safety.[79]

If these examples all come from the *Odyssey*, the reason is that in other sources, the suppliant asks for protection, the supplicandus raises him, and the new tie is not *xenia* but *philia*, meaning friendship or membership in a household. This time, the suppliant joins a group but may not obtain parity with all members. A remark of Odysseus's hints at the difference. When speaking to Eumaeus, his host in *Odyssey* 14, Odysseus speaks of suppliants and *xenia*, as with the Cyclops, but, since Eumaeus is a slave of his, he also links suppliants to *philia*.[80] Many Homeric fugitives are suppliants who go to a hearth, request protection, are raised, and become *philoi* and household retainers as opposed to slaves.[81] But the Old Testament furnishes an example, too: Ben-Hadad, a surrendering king who becomes the "kin" of the captor who entertains his supplication.[82] And later Greek literature does as well, including examples of suppliants who become *philoi* but remain inferiors.[83]

In all these instances, the suppliants are male. But brides, regarded as suppliants by two philosophers, Iamblichus and Aristotle, undergo a similar process. They go to a hearth, rise, and become inferior members of a group. The process is the same as for yet another group, one including both sexes: slaves being introduced into the household. Here again the new arrival goes to the hearth, rises, and takes an inferior place. Clinching the similarity is the use of the same ritual at the hearth, *katachusmata*, "anointing."[84] The parallel between brides and slaves shows that not all inferiors are equally inferior, and so it marks a further departure from the suppliant as the peer of the supplicandus.

In one respect, the parallel is questionable. Slaves entering the household may not have received a pledge. Brides, in contrast, did receive a pledge. One of our two philosophers, the Pythagorean Iamblichus, insists on this feature:

> Let the husband also consider that he has led his wife from the hearth after giving a pledge; she has been brought to him in the gods' sight, just like a

78. Request to Cyclops: 9.267–8. Pharaoh: 14. 276–77. Similar: 7.151–52. A list of acts of supplication ending in *xenia* in the *Odyssey*: Arend, *Scenen*, 68–76, listing eight, nearly all of which include supplication of the host by the guest.

79. Other views: Herman, *Ritualised Friendship*, 3.3, on *xenia* and supplication in general; Gödde, *Drama der Hikesie*, 62, on the two practices in Aeschylus.

80. *Od.* 14.322.

81. Patroclus: *Il.* 23.85–83. Phoenix: 9.478–83. Other Homeric fugitives turned retainers: Schlunk, "Theme of the Suppliant-Exile," 201–4, but without reference to *philia* or *xenia* as consequences of pledges. Outside Homer: Triph. 262–87.

82. 3 *Ki.* 20.32–34, where the suppliant becomes a "brother," אָח.

83. *Philos* and inferior: Sinon (Tryph. 286–87). *Philia* for Oedipus at Colonus, one aspect of a complex case: Blundell, *Helping Friends*, 231–32.

84. The ritual: Ar. *Pl.* 768 with schol., Dem. 45.74, Theopomp. Com. *PCG* 15. The view that the suppliant wife is a domestic initiate: Vernant, *Mythe et pensée*, 101–3, and also Gould, "Hiketeia," 97–98; Bremmer, "Gelon's Wife"; and Seaford, "Tragic Wedding," 112.

suppliant. Let his prudent and orderly life be an example to all in the house where he lives and to his fellow citizens.[85]

The reason for demanding good behavior may be that what Pythagoreans regarded as misconduct was common. On this view, the bride's status as a suppliant had not protected her against such misconduct, and so the Pythagoreans decided to reinterpret the act of supplication, saying that the pledge was one of good behavior.[86] Before, the supplicandus agreed to take the bride into his house; now he agreed not to mistreat her.

We do not know how common bridal supplication was, nor can we even guess at how many (or how few) husbands followed the Pythagoreans' admonition and gave a pledge of good behavior. We can say that this and the preceding examples show that *philia* ranks alongside *xenia* as an outcome, just as the argument to family ties ranks alongside the argument to reciprocity.[87] If we add dubious cases in which communities and not just individuals supplicate and become *philoi*, it may rank higher. The word *philos* does not appear in these passages, but in one case Pausanias says that the suppliants "mixed" with the supplicandi, meaning that they married them.[88]

Next come cases in which the supplicandus raises a suppliant and gives a pledge as a result of which the suppliant becomes not a *xenos* or *philos* but a citizen or free subject, in other words, a member of a large and not a small group. The few examples run a gamut of times and places. In a legendary case, the Minyans of wealthy and troubled Orchomenus make the long trip to Sparta, settle for a time, and depart. In an historical case, the Plataeans come en masse to nearby Athens after the fall of their city to their neighbor and enemy, Thebes. But the suppliant need not come in a group from far or near. An individual resident alien at Athens supplicated for honors and received citizenship.[89] The value of these examples lies partly in the status of the suppliants. At the time that they supplicate they are free, and they remain free after gaining membership in a group. They offer a reminder that suppliants of this kind need not be inferiors like slaves or even brides. Status is a variable, not a constant.

Other suppliants join a large group but without becoming citizens or the like. Slaves address themselves to a shrine, and when the officials at the shrine accept them they become temple attendants, *hierodouloi*. As it happens, Greek examples

---

85. Iamb. *VP* 48 [= 58 D-K C 5]. "Just like a suppliant": καθάπερ ἱκέτιν. "To him," i.e., αὐτὸν Nauck. αὐτὴν codd.

86. Similarly, Seaford, "Tragic Wedding," 112 n. 68, sees the bridal suppliant as vulnerable to a violent husband.

87. *Philia* replacing *xenia* as the outcome of supplication: Benveniste, *Vocabulaire*, 2.252–54.

88. Paus. 4.34.10, 8.23.3; 9.5.1, with ἀναμιχθῆναι. "Mixing" also occurs at V. Max. 4.6 ext. 3, about the Minyans, who do not mix with Spartans at Hdt. 4.145.4–47.1.

89. Minyans at Sparta at Hdt. 4.145.4–47.1, where the language is vague, but Val. Max. 4.6 ext. 3, confirms the supplication, and A.R. 4.1759–61 offers a parallel; the Plataeans at Hdt. 6.108.4. Citizen: *IG* ii² 336. The status of Oedipus in S. *OC* is controversial, especially at line 637; a partially legal treatment is J. Wilson, *Hero and City*.

confine themselves to the temple of Artemis at Ephesus and to legendary sources, and West Semitic examples are lacking.[90] Egyptian examples are indubitable, but are too few to show how commonly *hierodouleia* resulted from supplication.[91] But slaves are not the only such suppliants. The Dryopes became dependent on the Spartans after supplicating.[92] In Rome, the same dynamic applied to both individuals and groups. The Roman institution of clientage, *clientela*, could begin with an act of supplication by the client to his future patron. Some clients were foreign communities, and others were individuals.[93] One kind of *clientela*, however, was more or less nominal. The patron was an advocate, like Cicero, the client was the party whom the advocate represented in court, and the advocate would claim that the client supplicated him. Some clients may have supplicated in this way, but most did not. One such client was P. Cornelius Sulla, Patrician kinsman of the dictator. Cicero's claim to the contrary, Sulla did not beg Cicero to represent him. Sulla was of higher social rank than Cicero, who reported this act in order to make Sulla a more likeable defendant.[94]

Other pledges lead not to *xenia* or membership in a small or large group but to some other tie. Truces establish a temporary tie; treaties, a permanent tie.[95] The chief distinction is between those ties that include the trait of parity and those that do not. Truces include this trait, and so do treaties between peers. In Silius Italicus, Scipio Africanus supplicates the African chief Syphax, but they sit together *pari sub honore*, "with equal status."[96] Treaties between unequals do not include this trait of parity. Here again, Silius furnishes an example. Like Syphax, Philip V of Macedon makes a treaty with the Romans, and like Scipio, he supplicates, but unlike Syphax and Scipio, he does not enjoy equal status.[97] As before, the status of the participants is the chief point of Silius's example, but the relation between the two parties has changed. Status remains a variable.[98]

Numerous as these cases are, they are not as frequent as those that do not lead to *xenia*, membership in a group, or an equal or unequal tie. Instead these cases lead to a transaction with lasting, often profound results. In a word, these cases

90. Paus. 7.2.7, Ach. Tat. 7.13.3. A different view: Sokolowski, "Sacral Manumission," on lines 40–49 of the *Lex Sacra* of Cyrene, for which see Servais, "Suppliants," 117. Debord's more recent account, in "Esclavage sacré," does not deal with supplication. The distinction between *hierodouleia* and chattel slavery: Westermann, *Slave Systems*, 49–57.

91. The only extant example: UPZ 1.3, 1.4 = CPS #83.

92. Paus. 4.8.3. So also perhaps the Thracian Penestae who "surrender themselves" at Archemachus 424 *FGrH* fr. 1. There is no evidence that the Helots became such through supplication.

93. V. Max. 4.1.7, and many cases where *clientela* vel sim. does not appear, like V. Max. 3.2.16, where Spaniards approach Cato the Censor, or 5.1.9, where Tigranes II approaches Pompey. The first two examples, where the suppliants form a community, are early, as argued by Eilers, *Roman Patrons*, chap. 2. In the last example, the new client is an individual.

94. Cic. *Sul.* 20. A more plausible request for legal services: *Sul.* 81, by Catiline to L. Manlius Torquatus.

95. Truce, i.e., *spondai*: Th. 1.103.1, 4.38.1, Paus. 7.1.8, Ael. *VH* 6.7, Polyaen. 2.36, Plb. 5.76.9–10, Zon. 9.26. *Indutiae*: Liv 34.40.3. Truce sought but not granted: Hrd. 3.9.2. Treaty: D.H. 1.20.1, 1.58.3, 3.41.5, 9.17.2, 9.36.2, 17/18.1.3–4, Lucianus *VH* 1.19–20, *Tox.* 55 (φιλίαν ποιεῖσθαι), Paus. 1.36.6, Plb. 15.8.12, Zon. 9.24 bis, Sil. It. 15.319, 16.274. Treaty sought but not granted: Liv. 9.20.3. Treaty confirmed after outbreak of hostilities: Orosius 4.12.3.

96. Sil. It. 16.244. Treaty: 16.274.

97. Syphax's treaty: Sil. It. 16.274. Philip V: 15.317–19.

98. Surely equal: *IG* ii² 404.4–8, with Cean suppliants discussed at 181 below.

are economic, and so they veer away from the anthropological emphasis of the prevailing view. One such transaction is ransom. Here the supplicandus raises the suppliant, sparing him, and pledges to accept ransom. On payment of the ransom, the suppliant returns to his own community. This occurs often in the *Iliad*, albeit not in the foreground, where we see Achilles and Agamemnon killing those offering ransom. Only in the background, where the ransom-paying Priam observes that Achilles sometimes does accept ransom, do we glimpse this outcome. The mother of Andromache, Hector's wife, is the most prominent of those whom Priam and other wealthy Trojans ransom from Achilles.[99] Those in the foreground who offer ransom and die have chosen the wrong, heroic part of Homer's canvass. Those who remain in the background, like Andromache's mother, have chosen the right, commercial part.

Also commercial are transactions in which the supplicandus raises the suppliant, spares him, but sells him into slavery. In the *Iliad*, this sequence of events accounts for the supply of slaves that enables the Greeks to trade for wine. Priam says that even Achilles sells suppliants, and Homer does not fail to include an example recounted at some length.[100] After capturing Lycaon, Achilles sells him to a man on Lemnos, a nearby island, for a hundred oxen. Since Priam buys back Lycaon for three times that many oxen, the hero might have held out for a higher price.[101] Later captors who sold suppliants into slavery surely were more astute, if only because they were pirates.[102] Heroes or pirates, these supplicandi were slave traffickers. They and their transactions stand apart from the traits of *xenia*, group membership, and parity.

Was this supplicatory slave trade uncommon? Achilles, after all, also operates in the Homeric background where suppliants are ransomed, not sold into slavery. In later antiquity, moreover, piracy was a crime that the Romans suppressed. Pompey took the lead, and even made some pirates, the erstwhile supplicandi, beg him for mercy.[103] But the enslavement of suppliants often occurred when a city fell. It was rare, to be sure, when the fallen city was Greek. Between them, Herodotus and Thucydides report only one instance—Persian enslavement of the Thebans, who have betrayed the rest of the Greeks and therefore deserve their fate, including disfigurement.[104] But other instances crop up in Diodorus Siculus. Greeks, Macedonians, Romans, and Carthaginians, the enslavers of Greeks are diverse and numerous enough to suggest how many other enslavers have gone

99. Killed by Achilles: Lycaon (*Il.* 21.114–19). By Agamemnon: Adrastus (6.63–65), Peisander, and Hippolochus (11.143–47). Ransomed by Achilles but not listed as suppliants in the appendices because supplication is not stated to have occurred: Andromache's mother (6.425–27), Isus and Antiphus (11.104–6).

100. Trade: *Il.* 7.470–75. Priam: 21.45.

101. Lycaon: *Il.* 21.37–48, before he was caught by Achilles again, and supplicated unsuccessfully. Price: 21.75–82. Minimizing slavery in the *Iliad*: Wickert-Micknat, *Kriegsgefangenschaft*, 51–55, with refs.

102. Besides the many examples that might be cited from tragedy and historiography, two from incidents on the high seas: X. Eph. 1.13.6–14.1 and Plut. *Cam.* 8.5.

103 Plut. *Pomp.* 24.7, 29.2.

104. Hdt. 7.233.

unreported.[105] Yet only when Greeks do the enslaving does Diodorus pause to supply details. His Argives raze temples, and the tyrant Dionysius of Syracuse levels an entire city.[106]

As for the enslavement of other peoples, we might begin, as the sources do, with the enslavement of Romans, but their military record made this experience rare. Just one source, Appian, reports even the capture of numerous Roman suppliants.[107] The enslavement of suppliants who were neither Greek nor Roman should have been more frequent, but to what degree? This, too, is an event that Greek and Roman historians and biographers report only once: Tusculans surrender to Rome after one of the city's early wars and are enslaved.[108] Yet similar events must have occurred many times. And so Lycaon's fate—a suppliant of some worth, perhaps three hundred oxen, but still no better than a chattel—stands as a rebuke to the prevailing view. Supplication could end in the most inhuman of transactions.[109] If we glance back at the scruples of Basil, he seems to be less a humanitarian and more a man of his time, objecting to suppliants being charged interest but not objecting to suppliants being enslaved.

Other pledges depart from the prevailing view by sometimes allowing suppliants to depart rather than remain on the scene as they would when joining a group. These pledges grant some kind of relief. Slaves supplicate and request either a new master or, as Diodorus says, better treatment from an old one. Either way, they continue to be slaves, and so they return to some place of servitude.[110] Here we have come as far from the prevailing view as we did with regard to the enslavement of suppliants—but not in the same direction. Instead of giving way to the greed of the supplicandus, group membership gives way to the suppliant's desire for justice as opposed to inclusion. Similar are suppliants defeated by a supplicandus who grants them not justice but mercy. These suppliants come to the supplicandus, make their case and depart, sure of better treatment than they had the right to expect. On the reverse of figure 3.3, a Parthian who supplicates the Romans, and particularly Augustus, offers them the standards captured from Rome at the battle of Carrhae.[111] Augustus surely pledged to spare him rather than kill him.

---

105. Alexander at Thebes in 335–34 BCE (D.S. 17.13.6, 17.14.3–4); Marcellus at Syracuse in 212 BCE (26.20.1–2); Carthaginians at Selinus, Himera, Acragas, and Dionysius at Motya in the fifth and early fourth centuries (13.57.3–4 with 13.58.2; 13.62.4; 13.90.1–2; 14.53.1–4).

106. D.S. 11.65.4–5, where the Argives raze Mycenae, evidently including temples, and enslave the inhabitants in 468 BCE, and D.S. 14.15.2, where Dionysius razes the "walls and houses" (τείχη καὶ οἰκίας) of Naxos in 403 BCE.

107. At Ephesus following the Roman Vespers of 88 BCE (App. Mith. 23, saying ἐξέλκοντες ἔκτεινον) but with the mention of enslavement. Cic. Phil. 2.86 implies that Caesar enslaved the supplicating Mark Antony—but adds that Antony was not obliged to be enslaved and instead wished to be enslaved. Like other variations, this one gains pungency from the norm to which it alludes.

108. V. Max. 9.10.1.

109. A list of plundered Greek cities suggesting how often these results might have occurred: Ducrey, Prisonniers de guerre, 295–300.

110. D.S. 11.89.6–8. Athens: as in appendix 2.

111. Fig. 3.3: a denarius of Augustus, ANS 1944.100.38324 = RIC I p. 72, #127.

FIGURE 3.3   A Parthian on one knee before Rome—or
Augustus. Courtesy of American Numismatic Society.

If the prevailing view cannot account for many pledges, what of other views?
Burkert's notion of the suppliant as a recruit into a pack or herd would account
for instances in which the supplicandus, like the pack, looked to his or her own
survival. Just as the new recruit can help the pack survive, the new member of a
community can help it prosper. The serf or slave is such a new member. In some
respects, so is the bride. But a bride's entry into her new home has sentimental
and legal sides that Burkert does not address. Nor can Burkert account for the
suppliant who obtains honor or recovers his freedom. Burkert does not allow for
a disinterested supplicandus, yet supplicandi such as juries sometimes were disinterested. In contrast, literary scholars have overlooked pledges, the canny Telemachus notwithstanding. So, surprisingly, have legal scholars.

Every suppliant wants some benefit, but these benefits take many forms. *Xenia*,
membership, parity: these are optional. So are other, overlooked categories. Some
acts end in transactions that resemble commercial dealings. Others end in a change
in legal status, as when the suppliant becomes a wife or a citizen, signs a truce or
treaty, or goes free. All end in pledges, quasilegal responses that are not inappropriate for some of these legal outcomes. But the pledge is not quasilegal just because it provides what legal procedures might. As we shall now see, the pledge
binds the one making it.

Betrayers of Pledges

The supplicandus is free to accept or reject. Once he chooses to accept, however,
he is not free to break his promise. The prudent supplicandus accordingly keeps
his promise. The supplicandus who fails to keep his promise stamps himself a
betrayer and finds himself punished either by gods or by mortals acting at the behest of or in the spirit of the gods. Keeping promises is a norm, whereas acceptance and rejection are options.

The punishment of supplicandi who betray suppliants is a commonplace of
Greek literature. A passage is Plato's *Laws* is the longest example:

Among offenses against either foreigners or fellow countrymen, those that concern suppliants are always the most serious. When a suppliant has supplicated and a god has witnessed the supplication, and the suppliant is then deprived of his compact, that god becomes the special guardian of the victim. As a result, the suffering of the victim could never go unavenged.[112]

Several passages in Homer substantiate Plato's claims about divine witnesses. In the *Odyssey*, Zeus is said to be a witness to a supplication presumably occurring at a domestic hearth; in the *Iliad*, Zeus himself gives a pledge to Thetis, who has clasped his knees.[113] Legal sources substantiate Plato, too. In court, where suppliants use the word ἱκετεύω, the gods witness the subsequent court ballot.[114] In the same spirit, Solon instructed the Athenians to swear by Zeus *Hikesios*.[115] The god of supplication would accordingly witness a "compact"—in this case, a compact in the form of an oath. Diverse gods also witness supplication at altars, including Yahweh. Numerous passages also substantiate Plato's claim that divine witnesses punish breaches of faith. These passages, assembled by Dover in *Greek Popular Morality*, say that the gods punish perjury.[116] As Dover shows, the phrase used in passages about the gods and perjury is usually "the gods," a collective and indefinite plural appropriate to supplication.[117]

Nor does Plato exaggerate when he says that the violation of supplicatory compacts is among "the most serious" of offenses. In Hesiod, wronging a suppliant is one of several heinous acts that Zeus will punish:

> The same for a man that wrongs a suppliant or a guest, or gets into bed with his brother's wife, a perverse act, or foolishly sins against orphan children, or quarrels with his old father at the evil threshold of old age.[118]

112. Pl. *Leg.* 5.730a. "Compact": ὁμολογιῶν. "Is deprived": ἀπέτυχεν, Badham, Schanz apud England ad loc. Mss: ἔτυχεν, "and obtained his compact," but without changing the thought that if there are "wrongs" done to the suppliant, there will be "vengeance."

113. Hearth: *Od.* 16.421–23, where Penelope says that Zeus is a witness to the supplication of Antinous's father, presumably occurring at Odysseus's house. Knee: *Il.* 1.500–501, 523–27. The lexical range of *homologia* in Plato: compacts in connection with oaths (*R.* 4.443a); with contracts (*Cr.* 52e); and with harmonious movement (*Ep.* 991e).

114. Divine witness to votes: Antipho 6.6, holding that the gods will be offended by the wrong verdict; similarly, Lycurg. *in Leocr.* 146.

115. Poll. 8.142. For the *axones* that made this injunction prominent, see Cook, *Zeus*, 1093–95. Pherecyd. 3 FGrH fr. 175, discussed by Usener, *Götternamen*, 159–60, refers to ζεὺς δὲ Ἱκέσιος καὶ Ἀλάστορος.

116. Perjury injures the gods: Dem. 48.52. Divine hostility to perjurers: X. *Symp.* 4.49. So also Lycurg. *in Leocr.* 127, but conceiving an oath as a hostage given to the gods. Dover, *Greek Popular Morality*, 257–61, discusses most of these passages and also others, as does de Jong, *Iure iurando* 2.1. A different view of oaths: Hirzel, *Der Eid*, 103, arguing that they were fundamentally secular, with a "religiöse Hülle."

117. West ad Hes. *Op.* 248–50, also noting a few cases in which the gods overlook perjury, but none of these is supplicatory.

118. Hes. *Op.* 327–32; 329 sec. West. For the standard of supplicatory justice implied by this passage, see Lloyd-Jones, *Justice of Zeus*, 17–18, and West ad 259, both comparing it to Phoenix's allegory at *Il.* 9.501–12, though Phoenix does not imply that the suppliant is innocent.

Though Hesiod does not mention betrayal as opposed to other wrongs, Menander does mention betrayal in a similar passage: "Do not betray a suppliant, an old man, or a poor man."[119] The comparison of betrayal with the worst crimes is another commonplace, this one studied by M. L. West in *East Face of Helicon*, where he gathered evidence for divine displeasure at perjury, moral lapses, and a third offense, challenges to the gods, which enters into supplication when betrayal occurs at an altar.[120]

Because betrayal is punished and condemned, the prudent supplicandus eschews it, even if keeping one's word is costly. In *Oedipus at Colonus*, Theseus receives a suppliant who is trebly undesirable—a murderer, a party to incest, and an occasion for a diplomatic dispute and threats of war. Oedipus himself points out the dispute and also the threat. But Theseus is so far from flinching from the consequences of accepting Oedipus that he encourages his suppliant to speak: "Have confidence in the man before you. I will not betray you." When Oedipus replies, "I wouldn't bind you by an oath as though you were a villain," Theseus takes offense at the idea that an oath would be necessary: "Well, you would get nothing more than you would by relying on my word." When Oedipus explains the situation, and again expresses doubts, Theseus declares, "Don't teach me what I must do."[121] Theseus then does his duty, protecting Oedipus even at the cost of a sortie against the Thebans.

Theseus is a paragon, but other supplicandi in tragedy do not trail far behind. The king in Aeschylus's *Suppliants* worries that accepting the Danaids will cause a war. After he and the Argives accept them, war does result. But when a herald from the pharaoh of Egypt warns him, he does not flinch: "Our decision has been driven home like a nail."[122] The king goes on to say that it does not matter that the decision has not been reduced to writing. He is referring to a "compact" as opposed to a document.[123] Prose offers briefer examples.[124]

In contrast, the treacherous supplicandus meets with some sort of catastrophic punishment. Sometimes the gods impose the punishment; sometimes their agents do; and sometimes the supplicandi are punished by persons related to those whom they betrayed. Culture and genre make no difference. Zeus and Yahweh, the gods of Homer, and the gods of late authors like Pausanias—all chastise the betrayers of suppliants.

In six cases of betrayal, the gods intervene. In a case reported by the mythographer Apollodorus, the supplicandi are the people of Corinth and the suppliants are the children of Medea. Medea had used the children to send poisoned gifts to the family of the king of Corinth, causing the death of the king's daughter, and in

---

119. Men. *Mon.* 605. Similar lists: Sen. *Ben.* 7.27.1, Cic. *Inv.* 1.103.

120. West, *East Face*, 124–27.

121. S. *OC* 649–51, 654; S. *Ph.* 927–30 alludes to the same norm of trustworthiness. A different view: Gödde, *Drama der Hikesie*, 113, seeing Oedipus and Theseus as "Teilnehmer eines einstudierten Rollenspiels."

122. A. *Supp.* 944–45.

123. A. *Supp.* 946–47. Similar: E. *Supp.* 572–82.

124. Hdt. 1.157–60. discussed at 159 below.

this version of Medea's story she put them in the temple of Hera in order to protect them when she fled to Athens. The angry supplicandi forswear violence, as well they might: the children have committed only involuntary wrongs. But after raising the children, they change front and kill them. In response, Hera sends a plague.[125] Thucydides, a very different author, reports that some Helots fled their villages and their labors for the Spartans and took refuge at Taenarus, at the shrine of Poseidon. Perhaps they wanted exile or better treatment. Thucydides says that the Spartans raised the Helots and then betrayed them by killing them. Like Hera, Poseidon responds to the violation of a pledge by causing a cataclysm: this time, an earthquake.[126]

In two more cases, the supplicandi give pledges in some way besides raising, but otherwise the particulars are similar. Two cases occur in Herodotus. In around 625 BCE the Olympic victor Cylon attempted to raise a revolt in Athens. He failed and escaped, but his coconspirators, who were left behind, retreated to the Acropolis. Acting on behalf of the public, some magistrates promise not to put them to death; other sources report similar promises. They then break their promise and kill the suppliants. Pollution, *miasma*, descends on the magistrates.[127] In Herodotus's other case, an Argive army defeated by the Spartans at Sepia in 494 BCE, a turning point in the Spartan-Argive rivalry, takes refuge in the shrine of a hero. The leader of the Spartans, King Cleomenes, promises to ransom the Argives. He then beaks his word and kills them. The hero, Argus, now proves he can punish betrayal as well as any god. He drives Cleomenes mad.[128]

All these betrayals offend Greek gods, but the remaining two cases offend barbarian, Roman, and Hebrew gods. The first involves Romans who receive surrendering Spanish suppliants, set terms for the surrender, and then violate these terms. The astounded Spaniards invoke the gods who watch over "pledges" and oaths—gods evidently shared by them and the Romans. Unmoved, the Romans continue to violate the terms, killing many Spaniards.[129] The gods then manifest themselves: when the Romans attack more Spaniards, they find themselves visited by "terrors" at night, and later, when they retreat, they fall into a reservoir in large numbers and drown. They escape their troubles only when a new commander makes a treaty with the Spaniards and takes pains to observe it.[130]

No less ecumenical is a betrayal that offends both Greek gods and the Lord of the Hebrews in *Second Maccabees*. When the High Priest Menelaus decides to have his predecessor Onias murdered, Onias does what some Greeks in Syria do: he flees to the shrine of Apollo and Artemis near Aleppo.[131] Once Onias enters the sanctuary, the priest Menelaus, the villain in the tale, summons a subaltern, Andronicus:

---

125. Apollod. 1.9.28 with plague at Paus. 2.3.6.
126. Th. 1.118.1; so also Ael *VH* 6.7.
127. Hdt. 5.71. Th. 1.126.11: a promise to do no harm. Plut. *Sol.* 12.1: a promise of a trial.
128. Hdt. 6.78–80. This is the only punishment that has two explanations (Hdt. 6.84).
129. App. *Hisp.* 52. Pledges: πίστεις.
130. App. *Hisp.* 53. Terrors: φόβοι.
131. Greeks: Just. 27.1.4–9, Str. 16.2.6.

Taking Andronicus aside, Menelaus urged him to kill Onias. Andronicus approached Onias, and, relying on treachery, gave him his right hand along with an oath. In spite of being suspected, he persuaded Onias to come out from the place of refuge. Showing no respect for justice, he immediately dispatched Onias.[132]

This story—fear, flight, an altar, a right hand, and then betrayal—belongs in Thucydides or Herodotus. The difference is the binational setting:

When the king returned from the region of Cilicia, the Jews in the city appealed to him concerning the senseless murder of Onias, and the Greeks shared their hatred of the crime.

No doubt acting in the name of Artemis and Apollo, the king, the Seleucid Antiochus, put Andronicus to death. But the source adds, "The Lord repaid him with the punishment he deserved."[133] Yahweh and Leto's twins do not differ: betrayal deserves punishment. The Greek and Roman insistence on this point reaches out to enfold neighboring societies, a contrast with the Greek and Roman awareness that gestures vary.

In four other cases the gods act not on their own but through agents. In these instances the supplicandus dies soon after betraying a suppliant, but by human hands. In Diodorus, the tyrant Polycrates of Samos is assassinated soon after betraying some Lydians who have come to him for protection.[134] In Curtius Rufus, the betrayal involves intrigue. A retainer of Alexander the Great's, Dymnus, hears of a conspiracy against the king and tells it to his lover Nicomachus, who, unbeknown to Dymnus, is one of the conspirators. He begs Nicomachus not to put this information in the wrong hands, and Nicomachus gives Dymnus a pledge, *pignus*. Then Nicomachus violates the pledge. Learning of Nicomachus's disloyalty and treachery, Alexander executes him.[135] Here the supplicandus offends *Fides* by violating a solemn agreement.

Two other accounts are longer and come from more skillful hands. They show how the agency of the gods is doubly indirect, first because there is a human agent and second because of the substitution of some law or laws for the gods themselves. These laws are partly norms of supplication described in legal terms and partly other norms or laws of the community. These should be reverenced, not traduced, and when betrayal traduces them, the betrayer is punished. In both stories the suppliants come to altars, and the supplicandi raise them, as in cases where the gods act directly.

In Aeschines, the circumstances are more involved than in Curtius Rufus. Aeschines' enemy, Timarchus, had an affair with a freedman, Pittalicus, while

---

132. 2 *Macc.* 4.34, followed by 4.36 immediately below.
133. 2 *Macc.* 4.38: τοῦ κυρίου τὴν ἀξίαν αὐτῷ κόλασιν ἀποδόντος.
134. D.S. 10.16.4. The form of pledge: ὁ δὲ τὸ μὲν πρῶτον αὐτοὺς φιλοφρόνως ὑπεδέξατο, . . .
135. Curt. 6.7.3–15. *Pignora*: 6.7.4.

Timarchus's lover was out of town. When the lover returned, he and Timarchus recruited a gang of bullies, broke into Pittalicus's house, and vandalized it. Encountering Pittalicus, they assaulted and whipped him. Outraged, Pittalicus went to the Altar of the Twelve Gods and supplicated. But Timarchus's abuse of the freedman did not end there. He approached the freedman at the altar and raised him, promising to make amends, and then broke his promise.[136] This is the past of the defendant Timarchus, Aeschines now tells the court: the judges should find Timarchus guilty of conduct unbecoming a citizen and deprive him of his civic rights. In this case, the human agent is the court, and the supplicandus has violated the norms of supplication and a law of Athens. [137]

Thucydides is even more involved than Aeschines. His case occurs amid political disputes on Corcyra, where suppliants have gone to a shrine to protect themselves. The supplicandi promise them a trial, then betray the promise more cleverly than their counterparts in other authors: they convict everyone who leaves the altar and goes to court.[138] This piece of treachery sparks a civil war between the associates of the suppliants, who are oligarchs, and the associates of the supplicandi, who are the popular party. The war is a catastrophe, like Hera's plague, but human error rather than divine retribution causes it: "And as for the universal laws for such cases, laws that give hope to all that suffer, . . . men did not wish to leave them intact." These "laws," or *nomoi*, are the norms of supplication and other norms of good conduct. Because Thucydides conceives these *nomoi* as "established," I have called them "laws," as Hobbes does.[139] These are not, however, written laws like that which Timarchus violated. They are norms, the most important of which is the violation of oaths.[140] This violation heightens the theme of betrayal and also deepens the resulting punishment. The difference between this story and the previous one is the identity of the avenging party. What Aeschines would have the court do, Thucydides would have the guilty do. Thucydidean punishment of betrayal is ironic and perverse.

In just two instances, the supplicandus for some reason fails to carry out his betrayal—a last-minute switch that suits drama and occurs nowhere else. One possibility is for an unrepentant supplicandus to find himself checked by a higher authority who halts the act of betrayal just in time. This turn of events benefits the title character of Euripides' *Andromache*. First she flees to an altar out of fear of Hermione, the jealous wife of her captor and owner. Then Hermione enlists the aid of her brother Menelaus, who promises to spare Andromache's life if she leaves the altar. Trusting Menelaus, Andromache steps down. Menelaus is about to break his promise and kill her in spite of her protests when Peleus, the head of

---

136. The attack: Aeschin. 1.58–59. The supplication: 1.60.

137. Aeschin. 1.62–64.

138. Th. 3.81.2–3.

139. Th. 3.84.3: ἀξιοῦσί τε τοὺς κοινοὺς περὶ τῶν τοιούτων οἱ ἄνθρωποι νόμους, ἀφ᾽ ὧν ἅπασιν ἐλπὶς ὑπόκειται σφαλεῖσι . . . καὶ μὴ ὑπολείπεσθαι. Hobbes's translation is adapted also by S. Lattimore, *Peloponnesian War*, whose version I follow closely. In similar contexts, Ostwald, *Nomos* 82–83, prefers "precepts." Similar to Th. but sentimental: D.S. 13.23.5.

140. Betrayal: Th. 3.81.2. Oaths: 3.82.7.

the house where the altar stands, heeds her protests and rescues her.[141] The interest in this case is rhetorical and psychological. Suppose, Euripides suggests, that the suppliant speaks up. Will it make a difference? Yes, but the reason is not the protest alone. Menelaus, for one, does not heed it. He must be forestalled. Punishment gives way to rescue.

The other possibility is for the supplicandus to repent, as Neoptolemus does in Sophocles' *Philoctetes*. At first Neoptolemus betrays Philoctetes by not keeping a promise to take him back to Greece. Philoctetes protests at some length, and the decision by Neoptolemus to change his mind comes hundreds of lines later and forms the climax of the play. This time the interest is psychological and ethical. Suppose, Sophocles suggests, that the suppliant protests and the supplicandus does what Menelaus does not, and pays heed. Will it make a difference? Yes, but once again, protests are not the only reason. Philoctetes curses Neoptolemus, giving him pause. Punishment gives way not to rescue but to second thoughts.[142]

Protests that take place offstage, however, do not matter. One case in which punishment does not follow betrayal omits the punishment precisely to accentuate the haplessness of the protest. In Plutarch, the betrayal of Hagesistrata, a queen, horrifies both her and the Spartans, but the betrayers go unpunished.[143] The anomaly prompts the question of why the community is incapable of doing what Alexander or Aeschines' court did or should do, and the answer is that, like the Corcyra of Thucydides, it is suffering from the evils of civil war. Tacitus reports an anomaly, too, but his attitude is cynical rather than regretful. Why, Tacitus supposes his readers may ask, did the king of the Sedochezi betray Anicetus, an enemy of Rome who came to him for protection? Because the Romans bribed the king.[144] The Romans accordingly do not punish the king, and no other group or person is strong enough to.

These two anomalies—and two cases where we lack information—do not offset six divine punishments, four human ones, and two dramatic twists.[145] With few exceptions, betrayal is punished. This total of 16 cases—for there are no others—also establishes that betrayal is rare. Plato is right: pledges given to suppliants are serious and are usually honored. And Plato explains why: pledges are "compacts," solemn agreements. Within the bounds of these agreements, suppliants and supplicandi become partners. The agreement may be either limited or far-reaching, but it is practically indissoluble.[146]

---

141. Betrayal at E. *And.* 435–36. Protest by Andromache, who threatens divine vengeance: 439.

142. Betrayal: S. *Ph.* 923, reversed at 1287–89. Philoctetes threatens to curse Neoptolemus at 1181–82.

143. Plut. *Agis* 20.2–4.

144. Tac. *Hist.* 3.48. Pledge: "tutum sub auxilio" followed by "proditionis."

145. Just. 27.1.4–7, with a promise of protection implied by "dolo circumuenta" but with no information about the consequences; and schol. *Dem* 1.41, a dubious account of betrayal by Philip II. In addition, one betrayal is temporary (Plut. *Mar.* 37.2–4, 37.5–6), and another is condign punishment (Polyaen. 7.48.1).

146. An introduction to scholars holding other views: Kullmann, "Gods and Men," 14–20, holding that moralizing gods are characteristic of the *Odyssey* rather than the *Iliad*.

Keeping his word is only the last of the supplicandus's duties. Tradition says that he must take the task of evaluating seriously, and many examples show that he must form a tie with the suppliant. He acts somewhat like a judge or magistrate, and in one respect may do more than they, for the tie can impose diverse obligations of which *xenia* is only one. But these duties come with a countervailing freedom to choose a gesture and negotiate an understanding. Nor does the acme of this freedom lie in uttering even a negotiable "yes." It lies in an unequivocal "no." To this, the supplicandus's other choice, we now turn.

REJECTION

If the fourth step in an act of supplication is "no," it is simpler than if it is "yes." First, the supplicandus who says "no" must communicate his decision by making a gesture. Next, he must give reasons for his decision; if he does not, the source conveys these reasons by somehow impugning the character or request of the suppliant. Last come the consequences of rejection. On the battlefield, the supplicandus may kill the suppliant. More often the suppliant is free to go and leaves. If the supplicandus has come to an altar, the suppliant is still free to go. If he refuses to go (for there is no record of a woman refusing), he is ignored unless he is a wanted man. Then the supplicandi sometimes expel him. None of this is extraordinary or sacrilegious. Rejection occurs in every genre and culture, and it occurs regardless of the suppliant's choice of gesture, his choice of argument, or his request. Nor does it offend the gods, who do not punish it—in contrast to their punishment of betrayal.

Ordinary though rejection is, scholars seldom acknowledge it. For those holding the prevailing view, the reason for this neglect is that rejection is aberrant. Because a supplicandus has a duty to accept a suppliant who performs properly, rejection occurs only when a suppliant does not perform properly—for example, when a suppliant fails to make and keep contact with an altar. The prevailing view also simplifies the consequences of rejection. Instead of being free to go and leaving, the suppliant is obliged to stay and maintain contact.[147] In Burkert's view, rejection is not aberrant, for suppliants face it whenever they try to join a herd or pack that does not want them, but Burkert holds that the reason for rejection is always collective advantage, never any moral, legal, or personal motive. In contrast, legal historians do envision one of these motives, the legal one, but they believe that it is relevant only to acts of supplication regulated by law or occurring in court. Their analysis needs to be enriched with moral and political reasons for rejection and to be extended to other acts of supplication.[148]

---

147. As in Gould's interpretation of the supplication of Lycaon in *Iliad* 21, discussed immediately below.

148. "Does not": the assumption of Woess, *Asylwesen Ägyptens*. "Should not" but sometimes may: the assumption of Gamauf, *Ad statuam licet confugere*. Burkert as at 12–13 above. The only general statement about rejection in literary criticism: Henrichs, "Choral Self-Referentiality," 64, where he observes that persons in tragedy who perform rituals for a wrongful purpose meet with rejection.

Rejection often begins with a gesture that negates a gesture made by the suppliant. If the suppliant is not touching the supplicandus yet has drawn near to him, the supplicandus withdraws. If the suppliant is standing beside him, as the crippled Philoctetes does beside Neoptolemus, the supplicandus averts his body. If the supplicandus is Roman, as when defeated Greeks supplicate their "liberator" Flamininus, he confines himself to averting his hand.[149] If the supplicandus is interrupted in his own act of supplication by persons who take him by the chin, he can turn away. The freedman Pittalicus did just this when supplicating for help at the Altar of the Twelve Gods. When Timarchus approached Pittalicus there and asked him to stop supplicating, Pittalicus turned his back on him.[150]

If the suppliant clasps the supplicandus's knees, the supplicandus cannot turn his back and instead pushes the suppliant, as Menelaus does Adrastus in the *Iliad*. If the suppliant clasps the supplicandus's hand, the supplicandus withdraws the hand, as Hippolytus does when supplicated by the nurse in Euripides.[151] (As a precaution, the supplicandus may hide his hand, as Odysseus does in *The Trojan Women*.) If the suppliant touches his chin, the supplicandus will jerk his head, another responses of Odysseus's: "Odysseus," Polyxena says to him, "you are hiding your right hand under your cloak and you're turning your face away." She adds, "I won't touch your beard. It's all right. You've escaped my Zeus *Hikesios*."[152] Other suppliants look askance, as Odysseus does when responding to Leodes.[153] Far from being mild, this gesture sometimes precedes an attack on the suppliant.[154] Or the supplicandus may remain expressionless and walk away.[155] An unusual gesture is covering one's head, used when the supplicandus cannot bring himself to withdraw.[156] Pompey does the opposite to a suppliant who tries to make him late for dinner: he strides on as though the suppliant had not laid hold of him.[157]

All these gestures, from that of Menelaus to that of Pompey, come in response to suppliants who have made contact with the supplicandus. According to the prevailing view, these gestures ought to be rare. Yet of 70 cases of rejection in Greek sources (setting aside cases in which a suppliant is both rejected and expelled from an altar), 17 include either contact or intimacy where contact would have been possible. In Homer, Achilles' rejecting Tros echoes Odysseus's reject-

149. S. *Ph.* 934–35, and also *OC* 1272; Liv. 36.34.6.

150. Aeschin. 1.61. Other examples: App. *BC* 4.67–70; perhaps Paus. 8.11.11, where the suppliant is repelled, ἀπωσθείς.

151. Menelaus: *Il.* 6.62–3. Hands: *Hipp.* 606; App. *BC* 4.69.

152. E. *Hec.* 342–45.

153. *Od.* 22.320, *Il.* 10.446; S. *Ph.* 934–35, where the supplicandus is also silent. Gould, "*Hiketeia*," 85 n. 55, notices looking askance, which Holoka, "Looking Darkly," 3–4, describes as a response to a violation of propriety.

154. *Od.* 22.320; *Il.* 10.446.

155. Tac. *Ann.* 2.29.2, "immotu . . . uultu."

156. V. Max. 3.8, ext. 4, where suppliant and supplicandus are lovers.

157. Plut. *Pomp.* 55.6.

ing Leodes.[158] More pointedly, the Agamemnon of Aeschylus and also of Euripides rejects his own daughter, who at least in Euripides has clasped his knees.[159] If the phrase "by your knees" is taken literally, supplicandi reject suppliants who have touched their knees in the *Phoenician Women*, *Hippolytus*, and *Trojan Women*; if *prospitnêmi* means "fall (and touch) the knees," rejection of this kind occurs twice in the *Phoenician Women*.[160] But even if these words are not taken literally, the suppliants in these passages have drawn close to their supplicandi and achieved intimacy. Anthia, the heroine of Xenophon of Ephesus, falls and perhaps touches her supplicandus three times in the same way.[161]

Suppliants depicted in historiography and oratory do not clasp knees and meet with rejection, but many of them meet with rejection after coming to an altar and touching it or leaving a bough there. In Polybius, a Greek refugee from Roman pursuers is rejected this way.[162] So is King Perseus of Macedon when he comes to Samothrace in Diodorus.[163] These suppliants presumably touched an altar with their hands. Others described in the orators left boughs, including all three rejected suppliants in Andocides and Demosthenes.[164]

As he does elsewhere, Homer includes a surprise: a suppliant who ceases to perform a gesture and leaves the supplicandus with nothing to do. After being captured by Achilles for the second time, Lycaon concludes that Zeus has forsaken him and says so to Achilles. Then he lets go of Achilles' knees.[165] In another expression of despair, he lets go of Achilles' spear.[166] This suppliant is not deciding to substitute one gesture for another. A suppliant might make that choice: in Homer, Odysseus does, first clasping Arete's knees, then sitting at the hearth, a switch that evidently requires him to let go of her. Lycaon is giving up, as shown

158. Tros to Achilles, *Il.* 20.463–69 (also listed in table 3.1 as #1), with the arguably conative imperfect ἥπτετο . . . γούνων, 468. Leodes to Odysseus, *Od.* 22.310–29 (#10) with the aorist λάβε γούνων, 310, acknowledged by Gould, "*Hiketeia*," 81. Mercier, Review of Crotty, *Poetics*, notes these two Homeric cases, but not two others, *Il.* 10.454–56 with intimacy (#5) and 6.45 with contact (#7).

159. E. *I.A.*: 1216–17 followed by 1258.

160. "By your knees": S. *Ph.* 923–24, E. *Hipp.* 607 (table 3.1 #17), E. *Tro.* 1042 (#18). *Prospiptō*: *Ph.* 924. Kaimio, *Physical Contact*, 56–61, classifies these doubtful cases as either gestural or verbal. A passage in Livy provides a salutary warning: at 39.13.1 a suppliant falls at the supplicanda's feet, but at 39.14.1 she repeats the gesture, "aduoluta rursus genibus," a phrase showing that the first gesture, which achieves intimacy, is the same as the second, which achieves contact.

161. X. *Eph.* 2.6.5 (Table 3.1, #54), 3.8.4 (#55), 5.5.6 (#56). Except at 3.8.4, the phrase is a form of *prospiptō gonasi* vel sim.

162. Plb. 30.9.12–13 (table 3.1, #42).

163. D.S. 29.25.1 (table 3.1, #44).

164. And. 1.44 (table 3.1, #29), 1.110 (#30), Dem. 24.12 (#31).

165. The sequence: clasp of knees and spear (*Il.* 21.71–72), hateful to Zeus (83), consequent despair (84, saying he will be "short-lived"), reinforced by Achilles' speech at 106–13 after a change in heart (95), and, last of all, the release of knees and spear (115–16).

166. Other views: Gould, "*Hiketeia*," 81, holding that as a warrior, Lycaon is not truly a suppliant, and citing Lycaon's statement that he appeals "in the place of (ἀντὶ) a suppliant" (21.75). Similarly, Cairns, *Aidos*, 117 n. 208, holds that this phrase recognizes that Lycaon has been an enemy of Achilles and hence cannot supplicate, and Traulsen, *Das sakrale Asyl*, 121 with refs., holds that this phrase recognizes that Lycaon has been a prisoner of war and hence cannot supplicate. In my view, assuming that warriors, enemies, and prisoners cannot supplicate requires setting aside numerous instances in Homer as well as other sources. Leaf ad loc. thought that the phrase meant that Lycaon thought of himself not as a suppliant, but a *philos*, thanks to his having been spared when captured before. This view encounters a different difficulty: Achilles sells a *philos* into slavery.

by his spreading his hands wide. Left at liberty, Achilles can respond in any way he likes, and he chooses to kill Lycaon, who accepts his fate. If most suppliants are active—and require an active, gestural response—Lycaon is passive and requires only a coup de grâce.[167] But this exception does more than illustrate Homer's inventiveness. Like other Homeric passages, it confirms the norm from which it departs. This norm is for the suppliant to make expressive gestures, not for him to persist. If persistence were the norm, Odysseus would not let go of Arete and sit at the hearth.

Other suppliants have not made contact or drawn near; they receive a verbal response. When this response occurs in court, the judges vote to convict and let the vote be announced. In an assembly, they vote to refuse other requests and once again let the vote be announced.[168]

Whether the supplicandus uses a gesture or a word or neither, the suppliant is usually free to go. At the start of the *Iliad*, Chryses leaves the Greek army after unsuccessfully pleading for the release of his captive daughter; an angry Agamemnon even reminds him to go. Aeolus does likewise when rejecting Odysseus after Odysseus comes to his palace looking for help. Prose is the same: after rejecting Carthaginian legates, two Roman consuls tell them to "go back."[169] If the supplicandus is a god, the reminder to go may be given indirectly, as it is in the *Life of Apollonius of Tyana*. So, when Asclepius finds out that a suppliant has committed incest, he uses a dream to tell a priest to "Let him go." The suppliant no doubt goes.[170]

Other supplicandi feel no need to issue reminders. At the start of the Peloponnesian War, Epidamnian emissaries sit at altars in Corcyra, meet with an unstated verbal rejection, and then leave with their mission unfulfilled. Corcyrans who sit in shrines in order to reduce fines meet with rejection in the form of an unfavorable vote in the Corcyran Council and then depart, bent on vengeance. Several servants of Emperor Commodus approach him, meet with an angry rejection, and depart peaceably.[171] Like much in Greek prose, these withdrawals also offer an incidental rebuke to Homer—this time, to Homer's Lycaon. The man of affairs or the imperial servant may give up, but unlike Lycaon he does not martyr himself. He keeps his aplomb and leaves.

What about leaving holy ground, especially an altar? In Euripides' *Suppliants*, Adrastus and the Argive women approach the king's mother, who happens to be at the altar at the time. Depositing boughs, they clasp the altar and make their request for help in persuading the Thebans to return the bodies of the Argive dead. As we have noticed, Theseus rejects the request at some length. Then, like the suppliants

---

167. *Il.* 21.115–18.

168. A rare example from other genres: Ar. *Thes.* 208, where Agathon says "no" to the supplicating Euripides and goes back to his writing.

169. *Il.* 1.32–34, *Od.* 10.76, App. *Pun.* 90.

170. *VA* 1.10: ἀπίτω.

171. Epidamnians at shrines in Corcyra: ἰκέται καθεζόμενοι (Th. 1.24.7). Corcyrans at shrines in their home town: ἰκέτων καθεζομένων (3.70.5–6). Commodus, who is supplicated in person: Hrd. 1.16.4–5. Voluntary departure elsewhere: Hdt. 5.119, X. *HG* 4.5.5–6, Plut. *Aem.* 23.11.

of Thucydides, they choose to depart. First Adrastus says, "If you do not want to accept us, I must respect your decision. What am I to do? Come on, old women, go your way." This is the response of many rejected suppliants. He then adds:

> Leave behind the gray-green boughs as a covering. Let the gods, the light of the sun, and Demeter, the goddess who carries a torch, be witnesses of how our prayers to the gods failed.[172]

After this last touch of pathos, he and the women start to leave, only to be stopped by Theseus, who has changed his mind.[173]

The "how" of rejection thus proves easy. Whatever gesture the suppliant has used, the supplicandus who is saying "no" can negate it; whatever the situation, the supplicandus who is saying "no" can respond aptly. Yet the "why" of rejection is not as easy. Save for those who ignore suppliants, supplicandi give reasons for their decisions. At this stage, the supplicandus proves not just adept but voluble.

Reasons for Rejection

Rejection is not an arbitrary decision. Many supplicandi state reasons for denying a request or act on reasons that the source has made clear, and some supplicandi or sources go so far as to rebut the argument made by suppliants. Instead of being friends, say, suppliants may be enemies. Instead of having some argument from reciprocity, they may be hypocrites, asking for what they do not value. Instead of being innocent by association, thanks to children, they may be guilty by association, thanks to a relative or companion who has harmed the supplicandus. Instead of being in the right, they may be in the wrong. Rather than be worthy, they may be worthless, or *nequam*, as Cicero says of one suppliant.[174]

Numerous though they are, the reasons for rejection have received little attention. In the prevailing view, there can be only one reason for a response that any pious supplicandus will avoid—fear of war, the pervasive threat in tragedy.[175] Otherwise the supplicandus will respect the "rules" of the "game" of contact. Gould and others thought that the Greek term for this respect was *aidôs*, a term found in Homeric and tragic supplication scenes.[176] Burkert did not disagree with this

---

172. E. *Supp.* 256–62. "Go your way": ἄγ᾽, ὦ γεραιαί, στείχετε. Unlike the others, Adrastus has clasped Theseus's knees (164–65). A different view: Mastronarde, "Optimistic Rationalist," 203, calling Theseus's rejection "shocking," as it is within the context of extant tragedy as opposed to supplication as a whole. Similar are Burian, *Suppliant Drama*, 137–38, and Kopperschmidt, *Hikesie als dramatische Form*, 133–35; Cairns, *Aidos*, 285–87, does not describe the passage as shocking, but does not concede that rejection is permissible.

173. Theseus's change: 334–57. A different view of the change: Zuntz, *Political Plays*, 10, placing as much weight on the Argive mothers' gestures of supplication at 271–79 as on Aethra's speech.

174. Cic. *Q.f.* 2.6.2. For some of these categories, see Schlesinger, *Griechische Asylie*, 55–57, but the other authors who take an interest in the moral aspects of supplication, Welcker, *Götterlehre*, Caillemer, "Asylia," and recently Lloyd-Jones, *Justice of Zeus*, do not delve into them.

175. Gould, "*Hiketeia*," and those following, as at 8 above; also Burian, *Suppliant Drama*, 250, and Mastronarde, "Optimistic Rationalist," 203, two commentators on tragedy; and Konstan, *Pity Transformed*, 79, in a book on pity. At Seaford, *Ritual and Reciprocity*, 72, 174, acceptance is normal. One form of rejection, the expulsion of suppliants from temples, has elicited statements that would apply to rejection generally; for these, see n. 249 below.

176. Gould, "*Hiketeia*," 85–90, Cairns, *Aidos*, 1.3. 5, Ferrari, "Figures of Speech."

notion of *aidôs*, though he implied that supplicandi would ignore it if they found suppliants unsuitable for membership in the pack or herd. Legal specialists did not disagree with this notion, either. They expressed a different reservation, which was that a supplicandus might ignore *aidôs* or any other religious feeling when regulations provided grounds for rejection.[177] *Aidôs*, however, means more than "respect." It also means a sense of responsibility. For a supplicandus, one responsibility is to allow the suppliant to present himself and make his request. Several passages in Greek literature refer to this responsibility.[178] The supplicandus also has the responsibility to do justice to suppliants. Several passages refer to this, too, notably a statement by the oracle at Dodona, second only to Delphi, that suppliants are "sacred" and "should not be wronged."[179] Yet another responsibility is to feel anger at those who have offended the gods. This anger, called *nemesis*, permits the supplicandus to reject some suppliants. It even permits him to reject suppliants who complicate his task by referring to *aidôs*, as Leodes does.[180] In this regard, the prevailing view has erred by not placing *aidôs* in context. *Aidôs* and *nemesis*, respect and anger, form a pair, as they do in both Hesiod and Aristotle.[181]

Nemesis, anger at those offensive or even hateful to the gods, dooms several kinds of suppliants. Concerning one kind of offensive suppliant, those who despoil a god's temple, Diodorus lays down a rule: these persons may not supplicate in any temple whatever.[182] If these reprobates avoid temples and address themselves to persons, they may still be rejected, as happens to the people of Didyma. To please Xerxes, they once violated the famous shrine of Apollo in their community. After that, they were removed to the east, where Alexander the Great discovered their descendants a century and a half later. Like others in Alexander's path, they supplicate, hoping to be spared. Citing the offense to the gods (and also relying on the notion of inherited guilt), Alexander rejects them.[183]

Demonic possession also renders a suppliant hateful to the gods. An example appears in the *Life of Apollonius of Tyana*, where the gods' wishes manifest themselves not only in dreams but in flashes of insight on the part of the sainted Apollonius. Encountering a beggar, Apollonius called upon a crowd to stone him. When the crowd objected, seeing that the man was supplicating, Apollonius insisted, and rightly so: the man was a demon who promptly metamorphosed into a Molossian hound. As soon as the crowd put him to death, a plague in the community ceased.[184]

177. Burkert, *Creation of the Sacred*, 85–90. Rejection via regulation: Gamauf, *Ad statuam licet confugere*.

178. Responsibility: Williams, *Shame and Necessity*, chap. 4. *Aidôs* evinced by use of boughs: E. *Heracl.* 101–4. By exposure of mother's breast: *Il.* 22.82–84. By a suppliant's words: A. *Supp.* 194.

179. Paus. 7.25.1. So also Isoc. *Plat.* 52, a normative statement. Statements about individual suppliants: *IG* ii² 218.20; *IG* iii Ap. 98, a supplicatory prayer.

180. Leodes: *Od.* 22.312. Others: *Il.* 1.22–25, 21.74, 22.123–24, A. *Ch.* 896, E. *Hec.* 286. Rejection of suppliants referring to Latin *pudor*: Sen. *Phaed.* 250, Pl. *Rud.* 620. Similar rejection but without use of the word *aidôs* vel sim. and after words spoken by an intercessor rather than a suppliant: D.S. 13.21.4–5.

181. A comparable contrast: pity for the accuser as opposed to the accused (*Rhet. Her* 2.31, Quint. *Inst.* 6.1.8.)

182. D.S. 16.58.6.

183. Didyma: Curt. 7.5.28, 7.5.33. The same tale without supplication: Plut. *Ser. Num. Vind.* 557b.

184. *VA* 4.10. Rejection of a likely suppliant on the grounds that accepting her will offend a god: Paus. 7.21.3–4.

Other suppliants are hateful for unstated reasons, as is Odysseus, who is found "hateful to the gods" when he revisits Aeolus. This encounter counts as a supplication because Odysseus makes an approach, performs an introductory gesture, sitting at the supplicandus's doorway, and presents a request.[185] Odysseus then uses supplication's "soft words" to explain the reason for his return. Aeolus not only sends him away but says why:

> Go from my island and quickly, too, most contemptible of living things: *no duty compels me to entertain a man that is hateful to the gods* or to help him on his way. Since you have come here even though hateful to the gods, I say, go.[186]

Since Aeolus is feasting, this rejection would seem to violate the norm of Homeric suppliants' success in obtaining hospitality. Not so: elsewhere in Homer the suppliants are not "hateful to the gods" and thus are not rejected. They have not committed any offense comparable to the one that he has, abuse of a gift—in Odysseus's case, Aeolus's gift of the bag of winds.[187]

Sometimes a suppliant makes a request that gives offense because the supplicandus is being asked to violate a family tie or a bond of friendship. When Medea asks Creon for permission to remain in Corinth, he says that he owes it to his family to reject her request.[188] When Thucydides' Epidamnian envoys meet with rejection on Corcyra the reason is that the Corcyrans are friends with the Epidamnians' enemies.[189] Jews hear the argument during the siege of Jerusalem by the Romans. When the Zealots seize Niger, a prominent moderate, and he responds by supplicating, the reason the Zealots reject him is that he threatens the solidarity that they wish to foster among the people of the city.[190]

More often, a suppliant makes a request to be spared on the battlefield and encounters the enmity of his foes. The frequent rejection of suppliants of this kind, especially in Homer, has presented difficulties both for the prevailing view and for other views. In the prevailing view, rejection is rare, and so the rejection of battlefield suppliants, which is common and obvious, is anomalous, leading to the notion that battlefield suppliants are not truly suppliants or that they are suppliants of a distinct type. For literary critics, battlefield suppliants are victims of

---

185. The schol. *Od.* 10.70 calls this scene *hiketeia* (οὐ καθάπτεται γὰρ αὐτὸν ἀλλ᾽ ἱκετεύει), but Whitfield, *Restored Relation* 61–63, and Gould, "*Hiketeia*," 80, do not include it in their lists, nor do Pedrick, "Supplication" or other critics mention it. Other doorways: Plut. *Alex.* 62.3, 71.4–5.

186. *Od.* 10.73–75, especially "No duty compels me, etc.":

> οὐ γάρ μοι θέμις ἐστὶ κομιζέμεν οὐδ᾽ ἀποπέμπειν
> ἄνδρα τόν, ὅς κε θεοῖσιν ἀπέχθηται μακάρεσσιν.

187. If Odysseus said that the crew was to blame for this insult, Aeolus could find him guilty by association. Other suppliants are found guilty for this reason [*APl.* 16.114 (Cosmas), Curt. 7.5.28, 7.5.33], but the outstanding if atypical instance is the Greek attitude toward Trojan suppliants, discussed at 142–44 below.

188. E. *Med.* 327, 329.

189. Th. 1.26.3.

190. J. *BJ* 4.360.

vengeance, perhaps of vengeance by an Achilles who has not yet turned to mercy, as he will in the last book of the *Iliad*.[191] Supplicandi, however, do not describe battlefield suppliants as belonging to a different type, nor do they always describe these suppliants as the objects of vengeance. Sometimes they describe them as enemies. Diomedes responds to the supplication of Dolon, a Trojan caught spying, by describing Dolon in just this way. He also rules out accepting Dolon and either taking ransom from him or releasing him: "If we ransomed you or let you go, you might turn up later by the ships of the Achaeans as either a spy or a soldier at the front. If you die now while in our hands, you will never again cause trouble for the Argives."[192] The reason for describing a battlefield suppliant as an enemy is that this argument does not allow the suppliant to reply that he is innocent. Several battlefield suppliants make such replies; Lycaon even tells Achilles that he is innocent because he is Hector's half-brother rather than his full brother.[193] Lycaon and other suppliants also offer *apoina*, the term for ransom that implies that the suppliant has done no wrong. These claims might deter a supplicandus seeking vengeance. They cannot deter a supplicandus who wishes to reduce the number of enemy effectives.

No other supplicandus states the same reason for rejecting an enemy as Diomedes. But Achilles says that he rejects Lycaon partly because the Trojans have slain Achaeans and thus have proved themselves enemies.[194] A piece of Greek armor evinces the same thought. Figure 3.4 shows an Archaic greave with a *gorgoneion* at the knee, and figure 3.5 shows a pair of such greaves.[195] The purpose of these *gorgoneia* was to ward off the enemy, the same as *gorgoneia* on shields, but since these *gorgoneia* covered a warrior's knees, they would be most noticeable when someone supplicated him. The enemy would be on the ground, helpless, extending his hands, but he would see no less hostile a face than when he had been standing and fighting.

Peacetime supplicandi do not admit that they reject on the basis of enmity. As we shall see, they speak of wrongdoing, just as many Homeric captors speak of vengeance. But a bon mot against Cicero suggests that enmity was sometimes a motive. An anonymous invective condemned Cicero as *supplex inimicis, amicis contumeliosus*, meaning that Cicero had forgotten that a suppliant should address himself to friends and associates and not to enemies.[196]

---

191. Not truly suppliants: Gould, "*Hiketeia*," 81. Distinct type: R. Parker, *Miasma*, 181–83. Victims of vengeance: Pedrick, "Supplication," 139. Untimely victims: Crotty, *Poetics*, 133–34, saying that the Iliadic victims might have survived in the *Odyssey*. Similar to Pedrick is Aubriot-Sévin, *Prière*, 405–94, holding that supplication is a "démarche piaculaire," and thus an attempt to forestall vengeance.

192. *Il.* 10.449–53.

193. *Il.* 21.95–96.

194. *Il.* 21.133–35.

195. Fig. 3.4: sixth-century bronze greave from Ruvo, 41 cm. high , London BM 249 = *LIMC* 4.2 s.v. *Gorgo, Gorgones*, 253 (I. Krauskopf). Similar greaves were well-known in the classical period, as shown by fig. 3.5, a drawing of a scene on a fifth-century Attic red-figure crater, Paris Louvre 406g = D-S 4.1.5372 s.v. *Ocrea* (G. Karo).

196. [Sal.] *In M. Tullium Ciceronem* 5. A similar view of the Homeric cases just described: Cairns, *Aidos*, 117.

FIGURE 3.4   Greaves inscribed with Gorgons. Courtesy of the
Trustees of the British Museum.

Hypocrisy

Supplicandi expect suppliants to be sincere. The test of sincerity is usually the
suppliant's conduct during previous acts of supplication. If the suppliant has acted
improperly during these acts, the supplicandus reasons that the suppliant does
not deserve to obtain his request. There shall be no rewards for hypocrisy—a maxim
applied by a model supplicandus, King Agesilaus of Sparta. Far from being in-
clined to reject suppliants, he made a show of sparing them. Following the battle
of Coronea, for example, he spared soldiers who took refuge in the temple of
Athena.[197] But his compassion did not prevent him from rejecting suppliants who
had acted improperly and counted as hypocrites. Two years after Coronea, in
392 BCE, he encountered such hypocrites in Corinth. Oligarchs in the city had
battled unsuccessfully against democrats and taken refuge in the Heraeum, where
Medea put her endangered children. The democrats had burst in on the suppliants and killed them at the altar, a gross impropriety.[198] Now, as the struggle con-

197. X. *HG* 4.3.20, Nep. *Ag.* 4.6–8.
198. X. *HG* 4.4.3–5.

FIGURE 3.5   Thetis admiring her son's greaves.

tinues, Agesilaus arrives with a Spartan force that reinforces the oligarchs, and so the democrats find that they must take refuge in the same temple.

Agesilaus does not merely reject them. He rejects their hypocrisy, too. First he decides not to kill them on the spot and thus imitate the crime that the suppliants themselves committed in the same temple. Next he declines to give them any sort of pledge. As they wait, unsure of what he will do, he proceeds to seize their cattle and property. Thanks to the seizures, they feel mounting pressure to leave the sanctuary. When they do leave, they still lack any pledge, and so they are vulnerable to attack by their oligarchic enemies. As Agesilaus and the Spartans stand aside, the oligarchs fall upon the hypocrites and slay them.[199]

Other *supplicandi* reject suppliants on the mere ground that these suppliants have rejected others in the past. Witness Eurystheus, who pursues the children of Heracles to Athens and then, when they supplicate in Athens, asks the Athenians to surrender them. After the Athenians refuse, Eurystheus makes war on Athens, is captured, and must supplicate the Athenians himself, just as the children did. He meets with the opposite result: the Athenians reject him, condemn-

---

199. Slaughter of suppliants: X. *HG* 4.4.3–5. Slaughter of the slaughterers: 4.5.5–6. Among those who left sanctuary were some innocent persons, all of whom Agesilaus sold into slavery.

ing his previous conduct.[200] The same grounds for rejection appear in statements by prosecutors in court, who tell the judges that no one should feel pity for the pitiless.[201]

One supplicandus rejects a suppliant on the grounds of hypocrisy that the supplicandus witnesses himself. When Odysseus and his men arrive on the island of the Cyclops, they find his cave unguarded and help themselves to food and drink. The men want to steal what they can and return to the ships, but Odysseus insists on staying: he wishes to see whether Polyphemus will act as host to the Greeks once he returns from the pasture where he is tending his herds. Odysseus also hopes to receive gifts from him.[202] Yet when Polyphemus does return, Odysseus and his men flee to the back of the cave, and the Cyclops discovers them only after lighting a fire. Given no choice but to present themselves, the intruders supplicate.[203] The rest is folklore: failing the test that Odysseus has set him, the monster sets about eating his suppliants one by one. To save themselves, Odysseus and his men must blind the Cyclops and escape from the cave by clinging to the bellies of sheep being sent to pasture.

Folklore aside, Odysseus has conducted himself poorly. Save when a god gives aid, a suppliant should stop at the entrance of a house, as Odysseus does when he stops at Aeolus's doorway.[204] He should ask for food and drink, not take it, and he should not supplicate out of curiosity or in order to obtain gifts.[205] Often among the most skillful of suppliants, here Odysseus is among the least, committing errors at the first step, by trespassing, and at the third, by taking instead of asking. He traduces the practice, proving himself a hypocrite. Nor does Odysseus apologize for his conduct. When recounting the episode, he says only that he should have taken his crew's advice and left the cave, stolen goods in hand.[206] Zeus, however, is not deceived. When Odysseus sacrificed one of the stolen animals to Zeus, the god "did not heed my offering, but planned the destruction of all my well-benched ships and my faithful companions."[207] Zeus had no use for such a sacrifice or for those who made it.[208]

---

200. Isoc. 4.59–60, 12.194–95.

201. Dem. 21.100. One supplicandus goes so far as to prevent such a hypocrite from even attempting to supplicate (Antipho 1.26). General statement: Sen. *Dial.* 4.34.4, except that this author disapproves of rejection for this reason.

202. Food and drink: *Od.* 9.231–32. Pleas of the crew: 9.224–27. Test: 9.172–76. Gifts: 9.229.

203. Hide: *Od.* 9.236. Supplicate: 9.266–70.

204. Divine help: *Od.* 7.139–40 and *Il.* 24.452–9. The norm: *Od.* 4.20–22. An exception: D.C. 3.12.10, condemning false promises.

205. Impropriety of the request for gifts: Burkert, *Mitleidsbegriff*, 109. The impropriety of the test has gone unnoticed.

206. *Od.* 9.228. A parallel insight: Higbie, *Heroes' Names*, 164, notes that the Cyclops episode is the only one in which Odysseus denies that he has a name, different from his usual trick of inventing a name, and indicative of a loss of narrative authority.

207. *Od.* 9.553–55.

208. The punishment of Polyphemus usurps Zeus's place: Reinhardt, *Von Werken und Formen*, 85–86. Other views: Fenik, *Odyssey*, 222–23, saying that the rejection of the sacrifice is irrational, and Heubeck ad 9.550–55, saying that it does not result from Odysseus's misconduct. Odysseus himself avoids the issue, saying that he punished Polyphemus for murdering his men, *Od.* 23.12. For Gould, "Hiketeia," 81, this supplication is merely figurative.

Zeus, to be sure, had other motives. He wished to acknowledge the grievance of Poseidon, Polyphemus's father, and he was also enforcing the familiar moral of not abusing *xenia*, another practice that Odysseus traduced. But among these motives, disapproval of hypocrisy stands out as the only one that pertains to supplication, and in particular as the only one that links supplication to a principle important to suppliants, supplicandi, and the chief god of the practice. This principle is reciprocity. It would seem a likely principle for supplicandi to invoke when rejecting suppliants. But unless a want of reciprocity takes the form of hypocrisy, supplicandi do not mention it.[209] Supplicandi do not care about reciprocity in general. They care about reciprocity as a norm of the practice in which they are participating.

Like rejection of a hateful person or of an enemy, rejection of a hypocrite reflects Cicero's judgment that the suppliant is *nequam*, worthless.[210] But rejection of hypocrites also overlaps with the next reason supplicandi give for rejection: wrongdoing.

Wrongdoing

The most frequent reason given for rejection is that the suppliant has done some wrong. Some supplicandi who give this reason are judges who object to crimes committed by the suppliant, but many others are not judges and object to wrongdoing of other kinds. This balance between legal and moral reasons for rejection confirms the quasilegal character of supplication.

Rejection on grounds of wrongdoing falls under several headings. We have already noticed one heading, wrongdoing that figures among several offenses against the gods.[211] Three other headings concern wrongdoing and mortals. One, murder, is legal wrongdoing. Two others, violations of *xenia* and unjust war, are moral and political. If we include not only acts of rejection, but also acts of expulsion of suppliants from altars, we might add another category, wrongdoing by slaves, but on the understanding that expulsion (and slaves) stand apart, we will examine only these three, which do not lack for variety.[212] Murder appears in Greek texts of every genre and period; violation of *xenia* appears in Homer and Herodotus; and unjust war in classical Greek and Roman texts.

In Homer, murderers who supplicate all succeed, thanks to two advantages. One is practical: they have already gone into exile and placed themselves beyond the reach of the victim's relatives. The other is legal: they are not expressly said to have committed deliberate homicide. Closest comes Patroclus, who killed in a fit of anger during a dice game.[213] But Homer should not distract us. In other sources,

---

209. Hypocrites in Josephus: *BJ* 1.58, 4.77, 5.109–19, 6.319–21.

210. As at n. 174 above.

211. Though only one case of offenses against the gods expressly refers to wrongdoing, Tiresias's rejection of Creon's supplication in the *Phoenissae*. When Creon asks Tiresias to suppress news of a prophecy, Tiresias replies, ἀδικεῖν κελεύεις μ' (E. *Ph.* 926).

212. Also omitted: a case where the wrongdoing is contested (D.C. 49.12.1 on Lepidus's supplication to Octavian).

213. Patroclus: *Il.* 23.85–90. But there is no evidence of extenuating circumstances in the case of Theoclymenus, who is said only to "kill," κατακτὰς (*Od.* 15.272).

some murderers lack the second advantage and do not succeed. After Heracles slays his guest Iphitus, a deliberate killing, he flees to Neleus and meets with rejection.[214] The same apparently happens to Poemander, who kills one of his own sons in unstated circumstances and is unable to find refuge. Another of his sons has to supplicate for help.[215] The same also happens to King Philip V of Macedon. When he took refuge in the Shrine of the Great Gods at Samothrace, his supplication was "invalid" because he had murdered his brother.[216] In a famous case in Aeschylus, circumstances differ, for the murderer, Clytemnestra, does not go abroad. But Orestes rejects her supplication on the same grounds as Neleus and the rest.[217]

If rejection on these grounds runs parallel to the condemnation of murderers in the Pentateuch, rejection on a similar ground, conspiracy to commit murder, is distinctively Greek. When Pisander and Hippolochus supplicate and offer ransom to Agamemnon in *Iliad* 11, he rejects them on the grounds that their father urged the Trojans to kill Menelaus and Ulysses when the two Greeks were visiting Troy on a diplomatic mission. As diplomats, these two men traveled with a herald and thus enjoyed immunity. For this reason they escaped harm, but even so there remains a kind of wrongdoing serious enough to merit rejection. To this wrongdoing Agamemnon adds the familiar feature of guilt by association.[218]

None of these murderers sought purification, but another case shows that the purification of a murderer does not prevent rejection. In the *Argonautica* of Apollonius, the poem in which Medea finds Jason to be an accommodating supplicandus, she finds that other supplicandi are not accommodating. As we have noticed, Circe purifies Medea but does not grant her refuge. Now we can state the reason: Medea led her half-brother, Apsyrtus, into a fatal trap, murdering him.[219] Circe's scruples anticipate an historical case, that of the Spartan regent Pausanias. While campaigning in the Hellespont, Pausanias had seized a Byzantine girl, Cleoniche, and tried to make her his concubine. She died resisting him, another crime of murder. Like Medea, Pausanias found he must supplicate: "Finding that he could not escape this pollution, he underwent all sorts of purifications and became a suppliant of Zeus *Phyxios*, the God of Flight." And, like Medea, Pausanias met with rejection. Years later he supplicates again in Sparta's Brazen House, a much-recounted incident that has no bearing on the murder and instead results from suspicions that he had taken bribes from foreign powers. A mob blockades the shrine and starves Pausanias to death. But never mind this incident, says Byzantine tradition: "Pausanias paid a fitting

---

214. Apollod. 2.6.2. Language of supplication is missing from this case, but we may supply it in light of the similarity between this case and those cited immediately below.

215. Plut. *QG* 299d, *POxy.* 2463.6–20.

216. D.S. 29.25. "Invalid": ἄκυρον.

217. A. *Ch.* 904–29.

218. Supplication: *Il.* 11.130–47. Grounds for rejection: 138–42.

219. A.R. 4.698–99, Apollod. 1.9.24. A case in which the relation between arguable purification and implied supplication is unclear: *Il* 24.480 with bibliography provided by Richardson ad loc.

penalty to Cleonice and to the god."[220] In the Byzantine view, neither purification nor lapse of time would make a murderer a successful suppliant. The belief about lapse of time runs parallel to Athenian if not other Greek law. Murder admitted of no statute of limitations. By the same token, the rejection of a murderer could never be gainsaid.[221]

In contrast, killers who fall short of murder supplicate successfully after being purified. Heracles killed his children, but in his madness did not comprehend his actions. When he went into exile, he received purification from those to whom he came and then supplicated them successfully.[222] Heroes who resemble Heracles in this regard are Peleus and Tydeus. They killed men in hunting accidents, received purification, and supplicated successfully.[223]

Supplicandi sometimes show their grasp of the distinction between the two degrees of homicide by discriminating among suppliants. When Marc Antony comes to Ephesus after the defeat of the Republicans at Pharsalus, he pardons all those who have taken refuge in the Artemisium, including Republicans, with two exceptions—a man guilty of murdering Caesar and a centurion guilty of betraying an ally of Antony's. When other Republicans hear of the pardon given at Ephesus, they approach Antony in person, and he responds in the same way, sparing all but those guilty of murdering Caesar. Although sparing most of his foes, Antony rejects those who double as murderers and the like.[224]

Unlike rejection of murders, rejection of those who abuse *xenia* appears only in early Greek literature. This kind of rejection lies embedded in the plot and themes of Homer and Herodotus, and so it contrasts with rejection of murderers in numerous less artful sources. In Homer, the rejection of abusers of *xenia* is the last of several events beginning with the *causa belli* of the Trojan War, the abduction of Helen. As Agamemnon would have it, this abduction wronged Menelaus, Paris's host (although Agamemnon overlooks whether Helen as well as Paris committed this wrong—that would be for Menelaus to decide when he received his wife's supplication, sword still in hand). The next event in the story was that the Trojans received Paris and his prize and refused to surrender her, even after Menelaus defeated Paris in a duel meant to settle the dispute between husband

220. Paus. 3.17.9. "Became a suppliant": ἱκεσίας δεξαμένῳ Διὸς Φυξίου. "Paid a fitting penalty": δικὴν δὲ ἦν εἰκὸς ἦν Κλεονίκη τε ἀπέδωκε καὶ τῷ θεῷ. A version of the story without supplication: Plut. *Cim.* 6.4–6.

221. Lys. 13.83 with Lipsius, *Attische Recht*, 2.853 n. 24.

222. After the murder of his children, purification is obtained from Thespius (Apollod. 2.4.12), Sicalus (schol. Pi. *I.* 4.104g) or Nausithous (A.R. 4.539–41), who all accept Heracles; similarly, after the murder of Oeneus's cupbearer, justifiable because accidental, purification is obtained from Ceyx, who also accepts him (Apollod. 2.7.6–7, Paus. 1.32.6, D.S. 4.36.5). Though these are not sure to be acts of supplication, supplicatory language appears at Apollod 2.7.7.

223. Peleus to Eurytion (Alcmaeon fr. 1, D.S. 4.72.6), Peleus to Acastus (Apollod. 3.13.2, Pi. fr. 48), Tydeus to Adrastus (Apollod. 1.8.5). Others who are purified and successful: Carnabas (schol. ad *Il.* 4.88), Hyettus (Hes. 257 M-W = Paus. 9.36.6–7). Supplicatory language appears at Apollod 3.13.2, 1.8.5.

224. App. *BC* 5.1.4, 5.1.7. At D.H. 10.24.6–8, Cincinnatus observes a similar distinction when accepting the surrender of Aequi; at Just. 11.10.6–9, Alexander does when accepting the surrender of Syrians. Some cases of killing are controverted, like that of Orestes in Aeschylus; for the interplay of alleged murder and purification in his situation, see Sidwell, "Purification," 45–47, with refs. So far as supplication is concerned, the vital point is that his case goes to trial.

and abducter.[225] The Trojans thus become accessories after the fact to the crime of violating of *xenia*.[226] Now the third event, an act of supplication. Menelaus has just captured a Trojan warrior, Adrastus, who makes the usual offer of ransom, *apoina*. Menelaus intends to accept the offer, the usual practice in the Homeric background. Agamemnon, who is nearby, intervenes. As Menelaus stands over Adrastus, who has clasped his knees, and beckons to his servant to take Adrastus in hand, Agamemnon exclaims, "What, Menelaus! Do you care about these people? Did your household get the best of treatment from the Trojans?"[227] This is not Diomedes' argument that enemies must die. It is an argument that accessories after the fact must die—an argument for capital punishment for a city full of accessories to an offense committed by one man.

Who would endorse this sort of justice other than Agamemnon and Menelaus? One endorser is the narrator of the *Iliad*. In his only comment about the outcome of any act of supplication, he says, "So the hero spoke, and influenced the heart of his brother, for he gave fit advice."[228] The Greek for "fit advice," αἴσιμα παρειπών, has several senses. One is "proper" or "appropriate," as shown by the rejection of other battlefield suppliants. Another is (as Simon Goldhill urged) "fateful advice," the meaning of the same two words in Book 5, where Agamemnon tells Menelaus not to fight Hector and thus saves his life.[229] A third sense emerges from a passage in the *Odyssey*, where the phrase is used of "correct' advice about a ritual.[230] All these senses apply to the rejection of Adrastus, which is "proper" in light of the battlefield parallels, "fateful" as part of the fall of Troy, and thus "correct" as a supplicandus's response. Taken together, these three senses integrate the rejection of a single suppliant into a conception of both the subject matter of the Trojan cycle and the norms of the practice.

Why, though, does the narrator comment on this act and no other? One answer lies outside the confines of the *Iliad* but not of the *Iliad* and the *Odyssey* taken together. The suitors are wicked guests just as Paris is, and those who help them, like Leodes, are accessories just as Adrastus is. To endorse the killing of Adrastus is to endorse the climax of the plot of the *Odyssey*—to use supplication to unify the corpus of Homeric poetry.[231] To endorse the killing of Adrastus is also to endorse the climax of the Trojan cycle, the rejection and killing of Priam at the

---

225. Judgment of Paris: Procl. *Chrest.* 102 = *EGF* p. 31. Purpose of duel: *Il.* 3.86–100.

226. As Nestor implies (*Il.* 2.353–65).

227. *Il.* 6.54–55.

228. *Il.* 6.60–61:

Ὣς εἰπὼν ἔτρεψεν ἀδελφειοῦ φρένας ἥρως
αἴσιμα παρειπών·

229. Goldhill, "Supplication and Authorial Comment," 375, offering a translation that downplays the moral aspects of supplication and thus supports Gould. My translation draws on Fenik, *Homer and Nibelungenlied*, 24–25, and on the Iliadic scholiast who says that Agamemnon is being praised.

230. Menelaus's death: *Il.* 7.104–8, 121. Ritual: *Od.* 14.433. Similarly, *LSJ* s.v. αἴσιμος II, citing αἴσιμα πίνειν or "to drink in decent measure" and φρένας αἰσίμη or "right-minded."

231. A different view: Crotty, *Poetics*.

altar of Zeus—and to use supplication as a structural device to unify the corpus of epic poetry that coalesced around the *Iliad* and the *Odyssey*.

Violation of *xenia* can also prompt rejection without superadded guilt by association. Aristagoras, an Ionian diplomat sent to recruit Spartan aid in the Ionian struggle against the Persians, has no small mission: if the Ionians do not receive this aid, halting the Persian advance in or near Asia Minor will be impossible and the Greeks will have to halt it in Greece. Yet Aristagoras sabotages his mission by his misconduct in the house of the Spartan king Cleomenes. First he barges into the house without any formalities, no doubt discomfiting the slaves at the door. Next he presents a bough that identifies him as a suppliant but is inappropriate for use in a home.[232] Then Aristagoras tries to bribe Cleomenes. Unsuccessful at first, Aristagoras persists: "After Cleomenes rejected the bribe, Aristagoras kept increasing the offer until he promised 50 talents." Enter the king's eight-year-old daughter, Gorgo:

> The child said, "Father, unless you go away the stranger will corrupt you." Pleased at his daughter's advice, Cleomenes withdrew into another room and Aristagoras straightaway quit Sparta.[233]

Rejection takes the form of the withdrawal of the supplicandus plus an explanation issued by an adviser—in this case, an eight-year-old.

The daughter's name, translatable as "Gorgon," refers to her apotropaic quality (also the quality of the *gorgoneia* on the greaves of figures 3.4 and 3.5). Thanks to this quality, she not only sees what the adults do not—the threat overlooked by her father and the offense unacknowledged by Aristagoras—but also protects the adults from the consequences of what they are about to do. They are venal or weak but she is strong, a contrast that is all the greater because they are leaders. This contrast aside, Herodotus's scene alludes to other scenes in which suppliants manipulate children. Here, though, the child prevents the suppliant from manipulating the supplicandus. The historian has upended the norm, but unlike his character Aristagoras, he has done so without impiety.

The rejection of those who make unjust war flows from both Homer and Herodotus. Like the Trojans, aggressors are guilty, and, like Aristagoras, they are defamed. Unlike either the Trojans or Aristagoras, however, aggressors form a large, well-attested group about which there is a correspondingly long statement: the speech of the Spartan general Gylippus urging the Syracusans to reject Athenian invaders who supplicated after their attack on Syracuse failed in 413 BCE. On this speech Diodorus Siculus lavishes every rhetorical effort, and so scholars have been suspicious of it as evidence for the thinking of supplicandi.[234] But Gylippus's rheto-

---

232. Only two other suppliants use a clearly superfluous bough, the terrified Rhodians who go before the Roman Senate at Liv. 45.25.1, and the melodramatic Latins who go before it at D.H. 6.18.3.

233. Hdt. 5.51.

234. E.g., R. Parker, *Miasma*, 183; for Gould and others, Gylippus is a late and thus untrustworthy source.

ric does not fail to contain a characterization of the suppliants as aggressors. First, the Athenians lacked good cause for attacking Syracuse:

> How are we to regard the prisoners? As unfortunates? Well, what misfortune forced men who had not been wronged to make war on Syracuse?

Lacking good cause, the Athenians count as wrongdoers to be punished:

> Those who chose an unjust war should freely submit to the terrible consequences of their choice. The humanity due to a suppliant should not prevent the punishment of men who would have been unsparingly cruel towards you had they won.[235]

Into the allegation of aggression Gylippus has woven two other strands: accusations of bad character ("unsparingly cruel") and hypocrisy. These multiple grounds for rejection embolden him to deny that the Athenians have a right to supplicate:

> If the fact is that they suffered these defeats because of cowardice and greed, . . . let them not appeal in the name of supplication.

That appeal, he continues, is only for those who are worthy of it: "It is reserved for those who have pure hearts but hard luck."[236]

Even more than the designation of Roman tyrannicides as murderers, this designation of a hostile power as a voluntary but collective wrongdoer confirms the political as well as legal character of some grounds for rejection. But this mixed character does not make Gylippus's claims abnormal. Other statements about unjust wars work with the same tools of ethical categorization and slander.[237] These statements include two speeches in Josephus in which supplicandi reject aggressors.[238]

The three headings of murder (a crime against one), *xenia* (a crime against a household), and aggression (a crime against a community) show the breadth of reasons for rejection on grounds of wrongdoing. They also show overlap among reasons. The murder of Caesar is objectionable on both legal and political grounds, and so it is an assassination. The gifts of Aristagoras are objectionable on both moral and political grounds, and so they constitute bribery. The attack on Syracuse is objectionable on both moral and political grounds also, and so it constitutes a

---

235. D.S. 13.29.5–7, translated in three parts. Diodorus's source may be Ephorus, as suggested by Collmann, *Diodori fontibus*, 21–22, or Timaeus or Philistus. Too little is known of their work to know which of them is most likely to moralize about supplication.

236. D.S. 13.29.7: . . . τὸ τῆς ἱκεσίας ὄνομα. τοῦτο γὰρ παρ' ἀνθρώποις φυλάττεται τοῖς καθαρὰν μὲν τὴν ψυχὴν ἀγνώμονα δὲ τὴν τύχην ἐσχηκόσιν.

237. The same criterion of aggression, i.e., wars not fought for the sake of self-defense or vengeance: Isoc. 12.177 and other sources discussed at Chaniotis, "Territorial Claims," 4.1.

238. Somewhat shorter: J *BJ* 6.345–51. Very brief: πάνυ γοῦν ἐστὲ δίκαιοι ἱκέται καὶ χερσὶ καθαραῖς τὸν βοηθὸν ὑμῶν παρακαλεῖτε, a sarcastic expression at J. *BJ* 5.403.

war crime, an offense so grave that supplication by those responsible is purportedly inconceivable. Add the moral flavor of rejection on grounds of offense to the gods and of hypocrisy, and wrongdoing supplies the supplicandus with his reply to the refrain that the suppliant should not be wronged: the suppliant should not wrong others.

Rejection and the Supplicandus

Unlike rejected suppliants, who sometimes are killed, the supplicandi who reject them almost never face adverse consequences at the hands of gods or mortals. Of the seventy rejecting supplicandi in Greek sources, only one, Aeschylus's Agamemnon, faces punishment by the gods, and even in this case the gods enlist a human helper, Clytemnestra, who puts him to death to avenge Agamemnon's killing Iphigenia.[239] Meanwhile, the god of the Hebrews, ready to punish a high priest for betraying a suppliant, punishes no one for rejecting a suppliant. No less striking is that only four supplicandi suffer punishment at the hands of mortals: three Greek supplicandi—Timoleon's brother, the Cyclops, and Euripides' Menelaus—and a Hebrew supplicandus in Josephus.[240] Of the total of five, all but Menelaus are punished for multiple crimes, leaving only one supplicandus punished for rejection alone.[241] The gods, then, do not punish mortals for rejecting suppliants, and mortals follow the gods' lead. This conclusion emerges especially from the rejection of those requesting burial and of those requesting that the supplicandus spare places of worship.[242] Supplicandi rejecting these unimpeachable requests meet with no punishment.

In later historians and in novelists, the author might be expected to be the party to express disapproval, not gods or other mortals, but among these authors, Polyaenus has no interest in supplication, and so he says nothing, whereas Herodotus, Thucydides, and Diodorus, who do have an interest in it, do not express sympathy for rejected suppliants. Among the five extant Greek novelists, the paucity of rejection contrasts with earlier authors, and the contrast is all the greater because the novelists set their stories in the classical period. One exception, Xenophon of Ephesus, limits rejection to slaves and captives, and to three requests: (1) not to be enslaved, (2) not to be punished by a master, and (3) not to be sold.[243] Another prose writer, the biographer Philostratus, reports the rejection of a demon and of those who have offended the heroes Asclepius and Achilles.[244] This author is accommodating rejection to a religious theme. But neither Xenophon of Ephesus nor Philostratus includes any criticism of rejection.

239. A. *Ag.* 231–47, also listed as #11 in table 3.1.

240. Timoleon's brother: table 3.1, #45 (Plut. *Timol.* 4.5–6). Cyclops: #9 (*Od.* 9.250–80.). Menelaus: #19 (E. *And.* 537–40). The punishment of the Cyclops is clearer in Euripides, where Odysseus could escape without blinding him (*Cyc.* 590–607), than in Homer, where he has no choice but to blind him. Zealots: table 3.1, #67 (J. *BJ* 4.360), #68 (*BJ* 6.118–21).

241. Berenice's rejection is avenged (Polyaen. 8.50.1), but not by punishing those whom she supplicated.

242. Burial: table 3.1, #3 (*Il.* 22.337–60), #27 (Aeschin. 1.99.1). Protection of synagogue: #64 (J. *BJ* 2.292), #66 (*BJ* 4.311).

243. Table 3.1, #54 (X. Eph. 2.6.5), #55 (3.8.4–5), #56 (5.5.6).

244. Table 3.1, #51 (Philostr. *VA* 1.10), #52 (4.10), #53 (4.16).

Since Roman suppliants seldom make contact with the supplicandus, the prevailing view would suggest that rejection in Latin writers might somehow differ from rejection in Greek writers, yet it does not. Aside from love poetry, Ovid's *Metamorphoses*, Greek sources, and drama—aside, in other words, from works under strong Greek influence—acts of rejection number 34, a figure comparable to 70 given the smaller number of acts of supplication.[245] Epic poetry has only 4 acts, but there is less such poetry in Latin than in Greek.[246] The two historians who report the most supplication, Livy and Tacitus, also report the most rejection.[247] Nor does any Latin writer report that the gods punish those who reject suppliants. The Latin epigraphical source containing the funeral oration for the woman who suffered at the hands of the lictors of Aemilius Lepidus does not fail to say that Lepidus suffered for his brutality, but no god punishes Lepidus. Instead Augustus does, and the punishment is for beating her and for ignoring Augustus's wshes, not for rejecting her.[248]

Since rejection may end fatally, it underscores the cardinal feature of the fourth step: the power of the supplicandus. He makes a gesture of rejection without fear of impediment, cites reasons without fear of contradiction, and usually decides without fear of punishment. The restraints under which he labors are two: he must listen and consider as *aidôs* requires, and he must find reasons that fall into categories characteristic of supplication as a whole, notably wrongdoing. Rejection is not arbitrary, an impression strengthened by how leading sources handle it. Homer makes it the occasion for a rare narrative comment, Herodotus makes it the occasion for a negative example, and Diodorus, important for his numerous reports of supplication, makes it the occasion for a long speech.

These and other sources convey the cardinal feature of rejection: it is one of two choices. Homer conveys this feature by matching the rejected Leodes with the accepted Phemius. In the same spirit, Attic oratory contrasts the accepted children of Heracles with the rejected Eurystheus, who pursued the children before turning suppliant and coming to Athens for help, as the children had. Since the children and Eurystheus both came to altars, they introduce the next phase of this overlooked topic: rejection of suppliants who come to holy ground.

EXPULSION

A suppliant may appeal to either a person or a collective body. If he prefers a collective body, he often—and in Greece almost always—goes to an altar or shrine. Like any other supplicandus, the collective body passes judgment and, like any other supplicandus, it may reject the suppliant. If it does reject him, the suppli-

---

245. Eight acts with knee clasps or intimacy: table 3.2, #1 (V.A. 10.522–36), #6 (Cic. *Sest.* 26), #9 (*Red. Pop.* 12), #11 (*Att.* 1.14.5), #25 (Tac. *Hist.* 2.46–47), #26 (*Hist.* 3.10), #30 (Val. Max. 5.3.3), #32 (9.5.3).

246. Table 3.2, #1 (V. A. 10.522–36), #2 (10.594–601), #3 (12. 930–52), #4 (Luc. 3.303–72).

247. Livy, table 3.2, #16 (2.39.12), #17 (22.60.1–61.3), #18 (36.34.5), #19 (39.42.10–12), #20 (44.42.4), #21 (45.4.2). Tacitus, #25 (*Hist.* 2.46–47), #26 (3.10), #27 (*Ann.* 1.29.1–2), #28 (2.29.1), #29 (2.29.2).

248. *LT* 18 with D.C. 49.12.4, where Lepidus supplicates Augustus to avoid punishment.

ant may leave, as Adrastus and the Argive women do when they leave behind their boughs as a reminder of their unsuccessful prayers. But the suppliant may also stay. Then rejection entails either ignoring the suppliant—something never reported, though not necessarily rare—or expelling the suppliant. And expulsion is risky. The suppliant is often a wanted man, so the decision to expel often leads to his capture and death. If the decision is mistaken, it leads to criticism or even punishment at the hands of the gods.

Criticism or punishment, in turn, depend on control over the altar to which the suppliant has gone. In chapter 2, we saw that most suppliants did not let the issue of control affect them. They approached and waited for a priest, a king, or the community to come. One of these parties would evaluate the suppliant. If they rejected him and he did not depart, they had to see to his expulsion. If a foreign army captured their city, they yielded the altar to the conquerors, and so the conquerors performed these tasks and bore the consequences—a second, different situation. In both situations, however, control is clear. At other times the community or conqueror would not come to the altar, and a third party, those pursuing the suppliant, arrive instead. Now control is no longer clear. If the pursuers restrain themselves and do not expel the suppliant, and instead pressure the suppliant by means of a blockade or arson, all is well, so far as the consequences go: the pursuers have not laid claim to the shrine and do not merit reproof. But if the pursuers do not restrain themselves and expel the suppliants, the reverse is true: they have interfered, and they meet with either rebuff from tardily arriving supplicandi or punishment meted by the gods. In these two situations, expulsion differs from the previous ones by involving a third party.

In the prevailing view, expelling suppliants from altars or shrines is both rare and sacrilegious.[249] In fact, it is nearly as common as other kinds of rejection, and it is not usually criticized or punished. It embodies a decision to reject, or, in the case of a captured city, a recognition of the rights of the conqueror.[250] It does, however, feature the distinctive issue that we have just noticed: control of the altar. It also has a distinctive cast of characters and a distinctive generic stamp, for it is more common in Greek tragedy than elsewhere.

Supplicandi expel suppliants from shrines in Greek Asia Minor, in Athens, in Boeotia, and in Greek Sicily. Save for one mythic example, the earliest occurs around 546 BCE, the latest in 88 BCE. Two occur at a great shrine, the Ephesian

---

249. Ostwald, *Popular Sovereignty*, 144, saying that there are almost no examples of expulsion; Hall, *Inventing the Barbarian*, 187–88, calling it un-Greek, and 203, calling it "outrageous"; similarly Lane Fox, *Pagans and Christians*, 127; Cohen, "Prosecution of Impiety," 696; Sinn, "Greek Sanctuaries," 90–91; Schumacher, "Sanctuaries of Poseidon," 69, following Sinn; Mikalson, *Honor Thy Gods*, 73–76; and Giordano, *Supplica* 190–91. The same view finds its way into the commentary of Owen ad E. *Ion* 1312–19, and into the reference articles of Mannzmann, "Asylia," Fauth, "Asylon," and Chaniotis, "Asylon." Cf. Schlesinger, *Griechische Asylie*, 54–55, and Chaniotis, "*Conflicting Authorities*," 72–75, both recognizing legal criteria but not discussing cases of expulsion. Older articles, like Caillemer, "Asylia," draw distinctions among types of shrines.

250. Other statements about permissible expulsion: Woess, *Asylwesen Ägyptens*, who reached his conclusion because of *agôgimos* clauses in contracts (172) and because of evidence for the expulsion of slaves in UPZ 1.121 = CPS #1.81 (176–78); Rigsby, *Asylia*, 540–43, citing *BGU* 8.1797, an instance of possible proper expulsion not discussed by Woess.

Artemisium, but most at unspecified locations that probably were altars in the marketplace.[251] Linking this diversity is a political and moral strand: tacit approval of supplicandi who expel a tyrant or criminal, criticism of supplicandi who expel worthy suppliants, and divine punishment of supplicandi who expel a herald or (in Herodotus) take bribes. At Ephesus, for example, the community drags the tyrant Syrphax from the altar with the tacit approval of the source, Arrian. Arrian says that Alexander the Great, who is nearby, prevents further removals, but the Macedonian king does not prevent this one, and with reason: his own policy is to depose tyrants and replace them with democracies.[252] In another venue, the Athenian Council, the councilors expel Andocides from the Council altar in 415 BCE with the tacit approval of Andocides himself. In a speech in which he describes this episode, he admits that he was considered a criminal and tells how a citizen spotted and denounced him and how the councilors expelled him from the altar after he leapt atop it in a vain attempt to escape arrest. After expelling him, the Council put him in prison.[253]

The supplicandus who justifiably expels a suppliant also appears in texts that provide not examples but rules. These texts are Greek (and also Hebrew) regulations for the expulsion of suppliants. Unlike the texts that provide examples, they deal not with politics and diplomacy but with murder and runaway slaves. As it happens, the only regulation dealing with murder is *Exodus*: if a suppliant commits deliberate homicide, Yahweh commands the Hebrews to "remove him from my altar, that he may die." *Exodus* does not say who removes the suppliant, but when suppliants came to the cities of refuge supposedly established by Moses, the elders at the town gate were those responsible for rejecting a suppliant and turning him over to pursuers who were presumably relatives of the victim.[254] Had any Greek regulation survived, it might be similar. Magistrates would replace the elders and the community would have the power to impose the death penalty, as it did on Syrphax.

Several extant Greek regulations deal with runaway slaves. A suppliant of this sort will arrive at the shrine and explain himself to those in charge. If they find him unworthy, they rule in favor of the master and let him repossess his property. In the Ephesus of Achilles Tatius, the master who convinces the temple that he would treat his slave well may repossess the slave.[255] Other sources provide for somewhat different procedures. The most detailed, an inscription containing regulations for the Mysteries at Andania in Messenia and dated to 91 BCE, deals with the expulsion of slaves at this festival site. Since the inscription concerns only the

251. Asia Minor other than Ephesus: table 3.3, #2 (Plb. 30.9.1–11), #6 (Hdt. 1.160, 545 BCE). Ephesus: #1 (Arr. *An.* 1.17.12), #5 (App. *Mith.* 23, 88 BCE). Athens: #3 (And. 2.15), #4 (X. *HG* 2.3.52–55). Boeotia: #8 (D.S. 19.63.5). Sicily: #7 (Polyaen. 5.5.1–2). Marketplace: #2, 6. Omitted from table 3.3: Lys. 13.23–29, Lycurg. *in Leocr.* 93, Paus 7.24.6, all with legal complications discussed in chap. 4; and the sketchy App. *BC* 5.1.9.

252. Table 3.3, #1. Similar: #2, where the suppliant, Polyaratus, is regarded as a traitor to Greek interests by Polybius.

253. Table 3.3, #3. For the legal procedure used, *endeixis*, see 184 below.

254. Altars: *Ex.* 21.14, *De.* 19.11–12. Elders: *Jos.* 20.1–7.

255. Repossess: αὖθις τὴν θεράπαιναν ἐλάμβανεν (Ach. Tat. 7.13.3).

period when the festival takes place, the procedure for dealing with runaways may have been different at other times, but the difference may have been that at the time the Mysteries of Demeter were celebrated the place of refuge was larger.[256] Other doubtful points abound, but the priest of Demeter is clearly the person whom the suppliants address:

> Let the shrine be a place of refuge for slaves. . . . Let the priest judge (ἐπικρίνειν) the cases of the runaways who come from our city and sit [at the altar] and let him return those whom he rejects to their masters. If he does not return them, the master may depart with his slave(s) in his possession.[257]

Since the slaves "sit" in a shrine, this act is surely supplication, but two terms distinguish it from supplication by a murderer, as in *Exodus*. The word "slaves" replaces the word "suppliants," and the word "judge" alludes to the resolution of disputes arising from sacral manumission.[258] These lines do not say which slaves were repossessed by their masters, but they may have been the same sort as described in Achilles Tatius.

Evidence for the expulsion of slaves elsewhere in Greece is scanty.[259] Nonetheless, Ephesus and Andania show that expulsion of slaves was licit in a range of times and places, the same as expulsion of free persons. Ephesus and Andania also show that expulsion must have been common. If it were not, slaves would have run away in such great numbers that supplication would have threatened their masters' hold on their property. The prospect of frequent expulsion, in turn, makes it more likely that Andania and other places used the Ephesian standard for deciding how many slaves to expel.

But supplicandi do not expel only such unprepossessing persons as slaves. Athens' Thirty Tyrants expel Theramenes, a member of their clique who leaps atop the Council altar as Andocides does. Far from being of the same ilk as the rest of the Thirty, Theramenes has favored a less oppressive policy. Xenophon, the source, assigns Theramenes a long speech of protest against the Thirty's abuses. After the Thirty ignore the speech and expel him, they compound their offense

---

256. The view of *LF* 2.256, saying that it was easier for slaves to reach the refuge during the festival, necessitating a larger place of asylum.

257. *IG* v 1.1390.81–84 (= *LSCG* #65.81–84):

τοῖς δούλοις φύγιμον ἔστω τὸ ἱερόν. . . . ὁ δὲ ἱερεὺς ἐπικρινέτω περὶ τῶν δραπετικῶν ὅσοι κα ἦνται ἐκ τᾶς ἁμετέρας πόλεος, καὶ ὅσους κα κατακρίνει, παραδότω τοῖς κυρίοις· ἂν δὲ μὴ παραδιδῶι, ἐξέστω τῶι κυρίωι ἀποτρέχειν ἔχοντι.

"Judge" as in *SGDI* 1971.14 (150–40 BCE, Delphi), where a court decides cases arising from a manumitted slave's not fulfilling his obligations during a transitional period or *paramonê*.

258. A different view; Christensen, "Theseion," 26–27, who follows Latte, *Heiliges Recht*, 107, in arguing that ἀποτρέχειν, which I translate as "depart," means "run away," and that the last sentence means, "If the priest does not return him, the slave shall be allowed to run away from him (i.e., shall be emancipated from) the master who owns him." My own translation follows the lead of Barth, *Asylis*, 75–76; Woess, *Asylwesen Ägyptens*, 175 n. 3; and Thür and Taueber, "Prozessrechtlicher Kommentar," 220 n. 55. "Depart" in a legal context: Plb. 3.24.1, quoting a treaty.

259. See appendix 2.

by killing Theramenes. Just as it is right to expel a tyrant or a murderer, it is wrong for tyrants to expel and murder a comparatively worthy suppliant.[260]

Most emphatic are sources that disapprove of supplicandi who expel a herald or take bribes. For heralds, the evidence is negative, but strong. However provoked by a bullying herald, the Athenians never attack one and compel him to supplicate for his own safety.[261] For bribery, the evidence is as positive as Herodotus can make it. In this author, the people of Chios expel Pactyes, a fugitive rebel against Persia, for a reason Herodotus finds improper—a Persian bribe.[262] The gods respond by sending a plague to Chios. The reason for divine intervention in this case is obvious, even blatant: the supplicandi have violated a norm.[263]

In the second of the situations in which expulsion occurs, cities fall, and the conquerors take on the responsibility of being supplicandi. The range of results remains the same: tacit approval, authorial disapproval, or divine punishment. But the cast of characters differs somewhat. Instead of finding tyrants or rulers in shrines, conquerors find potential slaves whom they regard as the spoils of victory.[264] On the other hand, they still find heralds and other special persons, the same as before, and are punished by the gods if they expel them. And once again the cases are diverse. Cities fall on three continents: Troy in Asia, Alexandria in Egypt, and Thebes and Athens in Europe, not to mention four cities in Sicily. Suppliants turn to Athena, Demeter, and the nymphs.[265]

The strongest expression of tacit approval for the expulsion of suppliants by conquerors is a display of indifference to the suppliants by the god of the shrine to which they have come. According to the tradition in Heraclea, a Doric city, Ionians who were longtime enemies besieged the city and conquered it. Some inhabitants fled to the shrine of the patron goddess, Athena, and gathered within sight of her statue. The goddess responded to this invasion of her shrine, but not by defending the suppliants or attacking the Ionians. Instead the statue in the shrine blinked, expressing Athena's indifference. The Ionians seized the temple and those inside it. Athena had to decide whether to object to this act of expulsion, and she chose not to. (The source, the rationalistic Strabo, does not doubt this tradition.)[266]

Nymphs in the pastoral novel of Longus do the same. First the heroine, Chloe, comes to their shrine and is expelled by those pursuing her. Then her lover,

---

260. Table 3.3, #4 (X. *HG* 2.3.52–55). Similar: #5, where Appian expresses disapproval of Ephesian rebels against Roman rule by reporting that they, like the Thirty, kill the suppliants whom they expel (*Mith.* 23).

261. Dramatic heralds acting as bullies: A. *Supp.* 911–51, E. *Supp.* 464–584, as well as E. *Heracl.* 51–287.

262. Table 3.3, #6 (Hdt. 1.160).

263. Insufficient information about the attitude of the source toward the supplicandus: table 3.3, #8 (D.S. 19.63.5). Same, and also insufficient information about the expulsion, P. *Athens* 8.

264. Th. 4.98.2 on control of sanctuaries; X. *Cyr.* 7.5.73 on control of persons and property in captured cities. Garlan, "War, Piracy, and Slavery," 10–11, gives additional passages. Chaniotis, "Territorial Claims," 4.1. establishes an exception for conquerors who fight unprovoked wars.

265. Athena at Troy: table 3.3, #18 (Procl. *Chr.* 108 bis = *EGF* p. 62). Athens: #17 (Paus. 1.20.7). Alexandria: #10 (Plb. 15.33.8). Sicily: #13–16 (D.S. 14.53.1–4, 13.57.3–4, 13.62.4, 13.90.1. Nymphs: #11 (Longus 2.20.3).

266. Table 3.3, #9 (*Str.* 6.1.4). Strabo does doubt another tradition, which is that the statue is still blinking in his own day.

Daphnis, comes to the shrine and complains to the nymphs that Chloe not only has been denied protection but also will be enslaved. They answer that Chloe will be rescued and spared enslavement, but they do not admit that Chloe's being expelled was wrong. Nor do they promise to punish those who performed the expulsion.[267] Daphnis leaves with only one of his two complaints assuaged. The same distinction between enslavement and expulsion appears in Diodorus. Of all his passages about the enslavement of Greeks, the most indignant concerns the capture of Thebes in 335 BCE by Alexander the Great. Alexander's expelling the Thebans from shrines and then enslaving them ranks as an "outrage."[268] But several other acts of expulsion in this author do not rank as outrages.[269]

The similarity between supplicandi who expel and conquerors who do the same is most striking with respect to the punishment of those who remove privileged persons such as heralds and priests.[270] In figure 2.4 one such suppliant, Cassandra, reaches out to both the conqueror, Ajax the Lesser, and to a statue of the goddess Athena. Since she is priestess of Athena's cult, her claim on Athena is strong. Ajax nonetheless seizes her and takes her away as his captive. He will not be able to keep her, but not because he or the Greeks let her go. Instead the Greeks hand her to Agamemnon. Why, then, does Athena hunt down Ajax and causes his death at sea?[271] As a priestess, Cassandra belonged to her, not to the conqueror. To make amends for Ajax's crime, his supposed descendants in Locris performed an annual ritual.[272]

This case has its complications. Some sources say Ajax dragged away not only Cassandra but also the goddess's statue, despoiling the shrine. He would then be no less hateful to Athena than any despoiler of a shrine is to the outraged god.[273] Other sources do not report despoilment but suggest that Ajax raped Cassandra.[274] Or perhaps he did no wrong in removing Cassandra. This is the view of Philostratus, who does not flinch from the consequences: the Greeks should not have taken her from him or given her to Agamemnon. Athena killed Ajax, but for other reasons.[275] The view that Cassandra is not a suppliant but a possession of the goddess thus competes with other views. The reason for the

---

267. Expulsion: table 3.3, #11 (Longus 2.20.3). Complaint: 2.22: Reply by nymphs: 2.23.2–5. Chloe rescued: 2.26.5–29.

268. Table 3.3, #12 (D.S. 17.13.6, 17.14.3–4). "Outrage": expulsion μετὰ τῆς ἐσχάτης ὕβρεως (17.13.6).

269. Table 3.3, #12–16, an inconsistency on Diodorus's part, since these suppliants are enslaved, too. A similarly inconsistent view emerges from Arist. *Pol.* 1.1255a, reporting diverse opinions on the justice of enslaving captives.

270. Herald: table 3.3, #17 (Paus. 1.20.7), where the god responds to the expulsion and killing of a herald with a plague.

271. Table 3.3, #18 (*Procl. Chr.* 108 = *EGF* p. 62) and Philostr. *Her.* 706–7.

272. Chiefly Lyc. *Alex.* 1141–73 with schol. A third-century inscription describing the ritual: *IG* ix² 706. Disputes about the ritual's origins do not affect this purpose, nor do disputes about links between this ritual and the city of Troy, as in Fontenrose, *Delphic Oracle*, 134–35, with refs.

273. Despoilment by dragging away Athena's statue: *Iliou Persis* (Procl. *Chr.* 107 = *EGF* p. 62).

274. No despoilment: E. *Tro.* 70, Alc. fr. 298 *PLF.* Rape: Triph. 647–48, saying that Ajax "shamed her," ἤσχυνεν; so also Alc. fr. 298.8 *PLF* as tentatively supplemented by Lloyd-Jones with ἠΐσχυν'. Other supplements either do not mean "violate" or are ambiguous; see Lloyd-Jones, "Cologne Fragment," ad loc.

275. Philostr. *Her.* 706–7, conceding that Agamemnon had a claim to Cassandra, but not that Cassandra had a right to be exempt from seizure.

competition is that the custom that the conqueror may seize and enslave suppliants is colliding with the custom of respect for shrines. The more crimes Ajax has committed, the easier it is to prevent this collision by showing that he is disqualified from playing the conqueror's part. He is, tradition says, in the wrong. This response does not prevent tradition in one locality, Heraclea, from holding that the same goddess with the same cult title, Athena *Ilias*, ignored the expulsion of less favored suppliants.

Blockade and Arson

In the third and fourth of our four situations, the suppliant faces a new concern: a confrontation with those who are pursuing him. These pursuers arrive, take charge of the shrine—the protests of the supplicandi notwithstanding—and pressure the suppliant to leave by means of a blockade or an act of arson or go so far as to try to expel him. Pressure often succeeds; where it fails, a god or hero intervenes on behalf of the worthy or innocent. Attempts to expel often fail and also meet with rebuff or punishment. These attempts challenge the assumption that the supplicandus controls the altar.[276] Blockade and arson do not challenge this assumption.

In instances of blockade or arson, the supplicandi are divided or distracted, giving the pursuer the chance to close in and besiege the shrine. If the pursuers choose to mount a blockade, they seek to starve the suppliant. When he capitulates and chooses to leave the shrine or temple, they seize him. If he refuses to leave, they wait until the suppliant is near death and expel him on the ground that by dying in the shrine he will cause pollution. Since no shrine is known to have fed suppliants as a matter of course, still less as a matter of public policy, this way of pressuring the suppliant sometimes succeeds.[277] But it requires not only a divided community but also manpower and time. Absent any of these elements, the blockade fails.

The best-known blockade meets all the requirements. Unlike the Byzantines, the Spartans found themselves divided about how to respond to the misdeeds of the regent Pausanias. The division even affected the officials who tried to arrest him. According to Thucydides, some ephors, or leading magistrates, were going to make the arrest, but another ephor warned Pausanias, giving him a chance to escape and reach safety. According to Diodorus, the division in the community continued to affect the response to Pausanias after he reached the temple. Diodorus says that once Pausanias arrived, no magistrates took part in the succeeding events.[278] The assembly failed to act, too.[279] Thanks to these divisions,

---

276. Other views, all holding that alternatives to expulsion are needed because expulsion is sacrilegious: Gomme and Sandbach ad Men. *Per.* 1; P. Stevens ad E. *And.* 43; Gould, "*Hiketeia*," 84 on Pactyes.

277. Varr. *Vit. Pop.* fr. 4 says that anyone that fled to Ceres obtained bread, but surely because this practice was exceptional. A suppliant in Egypt in the third century BCE fed by friends outside: *PCair. Zenon* 4.59620.14–15 = *CPS* #79.

278. Table 3.3 #19 (Th. 1.134.1). One ephor in Thucydides helps Pausanias; so also Nep. *Paus* 5.2, Amp. 14.7.

279. ἀπορούντων δὲ τῶν Λακεδαιμονίων εἰ τιμωρήσονται τὸν ἱκέτην (D.S. 11.45.6). No information on the assembly or ephors: Lycur. *in Leocr.* 128, Aristodem. 104 *FGrH* fr 1.8.3–4, Chrysermus 287 *FGrH* fr. 4, Tz. *H.* 12.472–82, Polyaen. 8.51.

the way now lies open for the blockaders to approach the shrine, besiege it, and begin to starve Pausanias. To make it harder for him to get help, they wall him in, placing bricks at the door of the temple. Diodorus adds that the suppliant's own mother or father places the first brick.[280] However implausible, this detail shows that the mob includes prominent Spartans, hence is likely to be numerous. Since no one interferes, the mob has the time it needs. Pausanias now starves nearly to death, only to be taken from the shrine to prevent pollution.[281] The Spartans consider giving him a criminal's burial, but change their minds—a last instance of the divisions among them—and erect a statue in his honor at the behest of the Delphic oracle.[282]

In Herodotus, blockaders have time and manpower, but the community rallies against them, and so they fail. The blockaders are Corinthians, who come to Samos bringing youths who are to be castrated and sold into slavery. When the youths escape to the shrine of Artemis, those in charge of the temple—perhaps magistrates, perhaps priests—do nothing to prevent the Corinthians from establishing a blockade and attempting to starve the suppliants. Nor do the authorities do anything to meet the crisis. The Corinthians have enough time and men to persist, and seem sure to prevail. But public opinion turns against them, and persons entering the shrine begin to smuggle food to the suppliants. The reason for the change in opinion is that these suppliants have not divided the community. As innocent potential victims, they unify it. The blockade fails, and the Corinthians leave Samos without their captives.[283]

In two other cases, some particulars are missing.[284] But the difference between the divisive regent Pausanias and the Corinthian boys points to a unifying contrast. The factors needed for success tend to appear when the suppliant seems unworthy, as Pausanias does, and they tend to be wanting when the suppliant is worthy, as the boys are. This contrast resembles two others: first, the contrast between expelling tyrants and expelling heralds and priests, and second, the contrast between saying "no" to a suppliant and saying "yes."

The other possible tactic, arson, is an accelerated blockade: the same siege, but greater pressure. It also reveals the same distinction between the unworthy and the worthy. If the suppliant is unworthy—and especially if he or she is guilty of a crime—magistrates arrive, prevent the act of arson, and arrest the suppliant. If the suppliant is dubious, some other legal process supervenes, prevents the act

---

280. Mother: D.S. 11.45.6. Father: Chrysermus 287 *FGrH* fr. 4. Interpretations centering not on the mob and its psychology, but on holy ground: Gould, "*Hiketeia*," 82 n. 45, following Diodorus and the Delphic oracle (D.S. 11.45.9, Th. 1.134.4), who both disapproved of the killing.

281. Other successes: table 3.3, #20, where the mob does not need to wait since the suppliant, King Agis of Sparta, makes the mistake of leaving the shrine and exposing himself to capture by the mob (Plut. *Agis* 11.3–12.1, 16.3); and #21, where the suppliants make the mistake of going to a hypaethral temple and so the mob pelts them with tiles thrown through the open roof rather than brick them up (X. *HG* 6.5.9).

282. As at n. 280 above.

283. Table 3.3, #22, (Hdt. 3.48).

284. Table 3.3, #23 (Batto of Sinope 268 *FGrH* fr. 3) and #24 (Th. 1.101.2–103).

of arson, and the suppliant and the pursuers negotiate.[285] If the suppliant is worthy, gods or heroes rescue him.

The *Women of the Thesmophoria* of Aristophanes shows a magistrate at work in response to the discovery of an unworthy suppliant. An intruder at a woman's festival spies on the women, committing impiety. He compounds his offense by being a kidnapper. This is the luckless Mnesilochus (if that is his name). Outraged on both counts, a chorus of festivalgoers proposes to set fire to the altar to which he has fled. In response, the magistrate arrives to prevent the act of arson and arrests the suppliant.[286] In Plautus's *Casket*, a slave owner is the one who proposes to set fire to the altar to which the suppliant, a slave of his, has fled. No authorities respond, but a friend appears on the scene to act as a *disceptator*, "arbitrator," and prevent the catastrophe.[287] Here the suppliant is dubious but not evidently unworthy, and negotiations ensue. A switch from comedy to tragedy brings forward worthy suppliants, and also several other changes—from magistrates to heroes and from arson to rescue. In Euripides' *Andromache*, for example, Peleus rescues the suppliant, Andromache, from her arson-bent pursuer, Hermione, and from Menelaus, the villain who betrays her.[288] Just as comedy favors the suppliant's departure, tragedy opposes it. Not coincidentally, the comic suppliants are vicious, whereas the tragic suppliants are virtuous: Andromache declares herself innocent of the crime of poisoning of which Hermione accuses her and even asks for a hearing.

If the results of blockade and arson are often positive—the undeserving starved or arrested, the deserving fed or rescued—the results of pursuers' attempts to expel suppliants are often negative. If the pursuer is a foreign ruler who claims suzerainty over the supplicandi, he is regarded as though he were a conqueror. Like conquerors, he may face criticism for expelling the innocent, but he will not face punishment. If the pursuer cannot claim suzerainty, he is thought to have usurped the place of the supplicandi. Sometimes the supplicandi rebuff him, and sometimes the gods punish him. In either event, the pursuer does not suffer merely because expulsion is impermissible. He suffers for his own misdeed, be it unmerited expulsion or unauthorized expulsion.

Two pursuing foreign rulers are Antipater, ruler of Macedon, and Marc Antony, ruler of Rome's eastern possessions. According to Polybius and other sources, Antipater expels numerous Greek patriots from shrines to which they have fled after an unsuccessful war against Macedon. Polybius sympathizes with the patriots

285. The exception to these more or less legal responses: arson by conquering armies, which resembles the seizure of spoils by these armies, as at Hdt. 6.79–80 (Spartans at Argos), 8.53 (Persians at Athens). Paus. 10.35.3 (Thebans at shrine of Athena at Abae, exculpated at D.S. 16.58), App. *Mith.* 53 (Ilians at shrine of Athena).

286. Table 3.3, #25 (Ar. *Thes.* 726–27, 929–46); the name "Mnesilochus" is not spoken in the play. Worthlessness of this suppliant: Halliwell, "Uses of Laughter," 284–86.

287. Table 3.3, #27 (Pl. *Most.* 1114, 1137).

288. Table 3.3, #28 (E. *And.* 257, 59). Number 30 (Sen. *Her. F.* 506–8) follows the pattern, but #29, from E. *HF* 240–46, includes a variation: the community objects to the use of arson (252–67) but then despairs (268–69) because, as Wilamowitz says ad 251, the tyrant's men have bullied them.

but does not say that Antipater was punished.[289] Antony expels suppliants at the behest of Cleopatra. Although we cannot tell exactly whom she asks him to expel, we can say that the suppliant was a sibling of Cleopatra's and that Antony was not punished.[290] The impunity given to these two unadmired rulers underscores the strong position of the suzerain.

A pursuer who is far from a suzerain, the Theban Creon, meets with rebuff when he attempts to expel a suppliant from Athenian territory. Arriving in Attica in order to bring Oedipus back to Thebes, Creon at first presents himself as Oedipus's friend. But the villainy of the pursuer becomes clear: when Oedipus refuses to go, Creon resorts to kidnapping Oedipus's children.[291] The supplicandus, Theseus, rides after Creon, rescues the children, and after capturing Creon upbraids him:

> Nor would Thebes praise you if it learned that you are despoiling my possessions and the gods' by violently driving away wretched people, suppliants.

This bit of moralizing is of a piece with Theseus's remarks to Oedipus. But the topic has changed from good conduct by supplicandi to misconduct by pursuers. Just as Theseus will not betray Oedipus, Creon should not expel him:

> If I entered your country I wouldn't drag or drive away anybody, not even if I had justice entirely on my side—*at least not without the approval of the authorities.* No, as a guest among townsmen I would know how to act.[292]

What is true of Creon, a ruler of a neighboring state, is also true of heralds who represent foreign rulers. When in several tragedies heralds attempt to expel suppliants, the supplicandi rebuff them. It does not matter whether the herald has (or thinks he has) right on his side. The Argive herald who comes to expel the children of Heracles tells the king of Athens that he is in the right, and when the king refuses to permit the expulsion, the herald remonstrates with him: "Not even if I have justice on my side and I prevail in our discussion?" Yet the king says, "How is it just to drive away suppliants by force?"[293] Nor does it matter when the heralds interfere. Creon interferes after Theseus has given a pledge to Oedipus, and in another play a herald tries to remove the children of Heracles even before Theseus appears on stage. Either way, interference meets with rebuff.[294]

---

289. Table 3.3, #31 (Plb. 9.29.4). Paus. 2.33.3 refers to these events but without specifying supplication.

290. Table 3.3, #32 (D.C. 48.24.2).

291. Table 3.3, #33 (S. *OC* 728–803).

292. S. *OC* 921–28, especially "at least not without the approval of the authorities": ἄνευ γε τοῦ κραίνοντος.

293. Table 3.3, #34 (E. *Heracl.* 55–74). Citation: E. *Heracl.* 254–55, especially the herald's seemingly reasonable question: οὐκ ἦν δίκαιον ἤι τι καὶ νικῶ λόγωι;

294. Also table 3.3, #35 (A. *Supp.* 824–953). Two possible cases excluded from this appendix: E. *Dictys*, provided that Polydectes, the likely pursuer in this play, is pressuring the suppliants or is about to expel them; and S. *Chryses*, provided that Iphigenia and Orestes take refuge with Chryses, who then refuses to allow pursuers to expel them.

In comedy, pursuers who try to "drive away" suppliants meet with punishment. In *The Rope*, the pimp Labrax barges into a shrine and expels suppliants who he claims are his slaves. The Andania inscription shows the procedure that he should have followed: he should have addressed himself to the authorities, especially the temple staff, and made his case. Instead he attacks the priestess of Venus. Following the demands of the genre, a citizen who wishes to marry one of the suppliants arrives and beats him into submission before hauling him to court.[295] Rebuff and punishment are so much the norm that the sources report only two instances in which the pursuers persisted, overcame the supplicandi, and expelled the suppliants. In these instances, punishment comes later.[296]

So far, we have said nothing about pursuers who kill suppliants at altars rather than expelling them and killing them afterward. In the prevailing view, these killers have violated a *nomos*, and so they meet with divine punishment or authorial criticism.[297] The prevailing view about these killers is correct.[298] But we should notice two exceptions that show the importance of the suppliant's worth. When Greek tyrants are killed at altars—not expelled as Syrphax was, but killed on the spot—the sources express tacit approval. And when Solomon has Joab killed at the altar, the source again expresses tacit approval. Even when human bloodshed pollutes shrines, a condemnation of the unworthy excuses the desecration.[299]

This gallery of some two dozen harried, burned, or starved suppliants does not lack for monotony: amid the disasters, the sources tend to simplify. Passing judgment may be difficult, errors and criticism may cause embarrassment, and a few errors may lead to punishment, but the sources other than Sophocles ignore these flaws in favor of apportioning praise or blame. The reason is the pursuer's intrusion on the commerce between supplicandus and suppliant. At this intrusion the sources express unanimous shock. So did the ancient audiences that saw many of these scenes enacted on stage. In no aspect of supplication do dramatic sources bulk so large. These sources include dramatically inspired vase painting like figure 3.6, where Heracles' mother, chased to an altar by a jealous husband, watches as he sets the altar afire. Zeus sends vases full of water to put out the flames. First fire, then flood: this is expulsion as audiences preferred it.[300]

295. Table 3.3, #36 (Pl. *Rud.* 559–680). Appendix 3 discusses legal complications.
296. Table 3.3, #37 (Polyaen. 8.46.1) and #38 (Paus. 4.24.5–6).
297. An additional *nomos* against killing a suppliant carrying a bough: D.S. 34/35.31.
298. Slain on the spot, but avenged: Priam (Procl. *Chr.* 107 = *EGF* p. 62), Cleopatra's sister (J. *AJ* 15.89–90, *App.* BC 5.1.9). Slain on the spot to author's dismay, a widespread occurrence: Samians (Hdt. 3.147), Messenians (Paus. 4.5.9), Athenians (Hdt. 8.53.2), Corinthians (X. *HG* 4.4.4–5). Syracusans (D.S. 19.7.2–4). Others: Sidero (Apollod. 1.9.8), sons of Thyestes (Apollod. *Epit.* 2.13), Meda and Clisithyra (*Epit.* 6.10), Ptolemy "the Son" (Ath. *Deip.* 13.593a–b), friends of Orsilaus (Plut. *Unius in. Rep.* 825b), Meleager (*Curt.* 10.9.21). Tz. ad Lyc. 307 is but one version of Troilus's death; others, such as Eust. *Il.* 24.251, lack supplication.
299. Tyrants: Hdt. 5.46, Plut. *Timol.* 4.5–6. Joab as at 89 above.
300. Fig. 3.6: Paestan Red-figure bell crater of 350–25 BCE, London F149 = *CVA*² vol. IVEa pl. 1 (81) = *LIMC* 1.2 s.v. *Amphitryon*, 2 (A. Trendall). Fragments from Euripides' play on this theme do not refer to any action by the community (fr. 91, 92, 94 *TGF*).

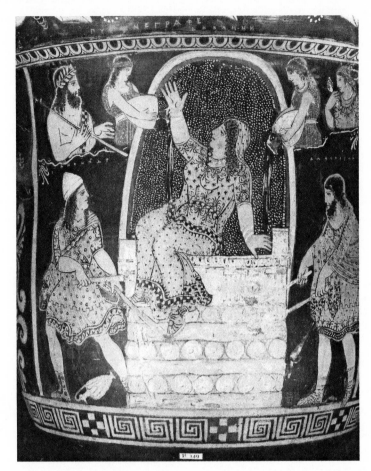

FIGURE 3.6   Rainfall from Zeus rescues Alcmene. Courtesy of the
Trustees of the British Museum.

Dismissal

Describing the fourth step as a decision by supplicandi raises an obvious question: what if the supplicandi cannot make up their minds? The question is most urgent when a suppliant has come to an altar. Rejection now means expulsion, and so we may ask the question this way: What if there are pursuers, but the supplicandi do not decide to stand aside and allow the pursuers to mount a blockade or set a fire? What if the supplicandi refuse to take responsibility? These are not idle questions. The pursuers will be closing in, and they often will be armed.

In this situation, the supplicandi may choose to dismiss the suppliant: not to accept or reject him, but to let him go elsewhere. Some suppliants go elsewhere to supplicate and find refuge in another community. Then the refusal to take responsibility has no adverse consequences. Some, though, cannot find refuge elsewhere, and so the pursuers overtake them. Then the refusal to take responsibility leads to the suppliant's death. Dismissal is a matter of stark alternatives.

Tragedy once again provides examples. Before the children of Heracles reach Athens, they have supplicated elsewhere, but supplicandi pressured by the pursuing Eurystheus have dismissed them. In one of Euripides' versions of these events, the suppliants pointedly ask whether Athens will be the last place where they seek refuge.[301] But we should not leap to the conclusion that dismissing suppliants occurs only or mainly in tragedy. When a fugitive from Alexander's court, Harpalus, reached Athens, he supplicated, asking that the Athenians give him refuge. He presumably went to a prominent altar, but the sources skip this detail in favor of recounting the bribes he may have paid to Athenian leaders who might intercede on his behalf. Meanwhile the Macedonians loomed in the background. Caught between Harpalus's money and Macedonian spears, the Athenians refused to take responsibility and dismissed Harpalus.[302] Other dismissed suppliants come not to altars but to hearths. Themistocles, interesting to scholars because his supplication at the hearth of the king of Molossia illustrated "the most powerful kind of supplication," did not gain the measure of success that the most powerful of supplications ought to have provided. The king declined to protect him. Themistocles' Greek enemies were closing in, so the king dismissed him. Themistocles joined Esther among the Persians.[303]

In these examples, the suppliants have all found shelter elsewhere, so the refusal to take responsibility has proved harmless. A case where the suppliant fails to find refuge occurs in Herodotus, who describes at some length how Pactyes, an enemy of Cyrus the Great, flees to the Ionian city of Cyme, an episode occurring before Pactyes comes to Chios. When an oracle says to surrender him to Cyrus, the Cymaeans temporize. As an enemy of a ruler who threatens the Cymaeans, Pactyes arouses sympathy; perhaps his rebellion against Cyrus seemed just. But those very considerations make Pactyes risky. So, instead of surrendering him on the one hand or protecting him on the other, the Cymaeans send him to Mytilene. Now they discover that refusing to take responsibility can have adverse consequences: Mytilene is willing to surrender Pactyes in return for a bribe. No doubt shamed by this news, the Cymaeans take him away from Mytilene and send him to Chios. The Chians accept him, the Cymaeans sail away, and the happy ending crumbles when the Chians do what the Mytileneans would have done and take the Persian bribe to expel Pactyes.[304] By dismissing Pactyes, the Cymaeans cause his death.

Another long account reveals another danger: failure to provide an escort. In 168 BCE, the notorious Evander, guilty of an assault on King Eumenes II of Pergamum, took refuge in the chief shrine on the island of Samothrace. The Assembly

---

301. Table 3.3, #39 (E. *Heracl.* 389–473, especially 440–41). So also #40 (A. *Eu.* 90–93).

302. Table 3.3, #41 (D.S.. 17.108.6–7). The term of supplication: ἱκέτης (17.108.6). Dismissal but without language of supplication: Curt. 10.2.3, a version denying Harpalus the dignity of becoming a suppliant. Plut. *Dem.* 25.1 is ambiguous. A similar case: table 3.3, #42 (D.S. 11.92.1–4). A possible case in an official notice: *IG* iv 492, discussed in appendix 4a.

303. Table 3.3, #43 (Th. 1.137.1. So also Aristodem. 104 *FGrH* fr. 1.10.2). Persia: Plut. *Them.* 24.3. Dismissed under guard: table 3.3, #44 (D.S. 18.66).

304. Table 3.3, #45 (Hdt. 1.157–59). Mytilene and Chios: 1.160.

at Samothrace ordered their chief magistrate to tell Evander to leave the temple and stand trial. As the magistrate said to Evander, "If he dared not stand trial, he should free the shrine of pollution and provide for himself."[305] The Assembly, however, provided no escort to help Evander evade Roman pursuers who were manning a flotilla offshore. Realizing that he could not escape the Romans, Evander declined to leave the temple, only to be killed there by confederates.

Dismissing a suppliant means not only finding someone who will give him refuge but also deploying ships and men as escorts. Unlike the Scottish verdict of "not proven," dismissal does not bring the case to a conclusion. At best it accomplishes a change in venue.

PATTERNS OF REJECTION

Rejection and expulsion reveal much about a better known topic: acceptance. Because they show that supplicandi make choices, they also show that a supplicandus need not say "yes" and that he need not always say "yes" in the same way. *Xenia* and joining a group are only two responses; the others range from grants of citizenship to enslavement, and they include negotiations between the parties. At the same time the prospect of rejection lends weight to acceptance and to the pledge with which acceptance concludes. Rejection and expulsion also correct any notion that acceptance is arbitrary. Many of the rejected are enemies and wrongdoers, and many of the expelled are wanted men. The accepted, in contrast, include only a few enemies: Greek soldiers surrendering to Greeks, and others paying a ransom conceived as having no taint of guilt. The accepted also include only two large groups of wrongdoers: those who have committed an involuntary wrong, like Phemius, and those who have fled the household or community in which they committed the wrong and have come to another.

Rejection and expulsion are also large topics in their own right. Rejection can come at the hands of either a person or a collective body in charge of an altar; it can lead to a suppliant's either being killed or departing; if the suppliant is a wanted man and refuses to leave, it can lead to expulsion. Expulsion likewise takes several forms. Supplicandi can expel, or conquerors and pursuers can, but only pursuers meet with rebuff. Even if the supplicandi are divided and distracted, outcomes vary: blockade, arson prior to legal action, and arson prior to rescue. If supplicandi refuse to say either "yes" or "no," they can dismiss a suppliant, only to compel him to supplicate elsewhere with more or less hope of success.

These outcomes are common and widespread. Of the hundred-odd acts of rejection without expulsion, 56 occur in Greek sources other than Josephus, and 34 in Latin sources without Greek subject matter; Josephus adds 14 more. Nor is the number for any genre small. At least 10 acts occur in Homer, in drama, and in historiography; almost 10 occur in both oratory and fiction. Even differences among authors are not great. The *Iliad* contains more acts of rejection than the *Odyssey*

---

305. Table 3.3, #46 (Liv. 45.5.6–12). The citation: 45.5.8.

(#1–7 vs. #8–10 in table 3.1) and Euripides more than Aeschylus and Sophocles (#16–24 vs. #11–15), but no major author lacks instances. Herodotus, Thucydides, Polybius, Diodorus, Plutarch—all report rejection. Among the four Greek novelists, three lack rejection, but Xenophon of Ephesus reports three cases (#54–56). Among Latin authors, four acts of rejection occur in epic, about the same number in proportion to the total (#1–4 in table 3.2). No major narrative author lacks rejection. Livy, the most voluminous author, leads with six acts (#16–21).

One reason for the differences among authors is subject matter. Rejection is more common in the *Iliad* than in the *Odyssey* because battles are more frequent, and it is more common in historiography than in fiction for the same reason. But one author may differ from another for reasons having nothing to do with subject matter. Thucydides (#38–40 in table 3.1) reports more rejection than Herodotus (#37) thanks to his Corcyran showpiece of the collapse of law and order. Euripides reports more than Aeschylus and Sophocles because of the rejections attributable to Menelaus in *Orestes, The Trojan Women*, and *Andromache* (#18–20) and to Odysseus in *Hecuba* (#21–22). Latin authors have their own penchants. In Livy, Coriolanus is the only supplicandus who rejects Roman rather than foreign suppliants. In Cicero's speeches, half of those rejected are supplicating on Cicero's behalf.[306]

As with the sources for rejection, so with the rejected requests. Many rejected suppliants ask that someone be spared, including nine in Homer and Virgil, seven in tragedy, two in Lysias, eight in historiography, and one in Xenophon of Ephesus.[307] Six ask for protection: one in Sophocles and five in Greek or Roman historians.[308] Three make the most solemn of requests, for help in burying the dead.[309] Others make less solemn requests. A suppliant in Josephus asks for an arranged marriage, and the Polynices of Sophocles asks for a blessing. Sophocles' Oedipus asks for information. The Greek priest who asks for food turns up on the list, and so do some merchants from a Greek city in Egypt who want to recover their capture property from the Athenians.[310] In Cicero, suppliants fail to persuade one supplicandus to endorse a bill, and fail to persuade another to withdraw a bill. They also fail to persuade a supplicandus to change his vote in the Senate.[311]

As with rejection, so with expulsion: outside of Rome, it is widespread. Not only does it occur everywhere from Sicily to Jerusalem, it occurs in many places in each of its three types: expulsion by supplicandi (#1–8 in table 3.3), by conquerors (#9–18), and by others (#31–38). Expulsion also mirrors the generic features of rejection. Like rejection, it occurs in most genres, but differences in subject matter prevent it from occurring in some authors. It is missing from Homer because he sets few scenes in temples, but it occurs in epic poetry that describes the fall

306. Livy: Table 3.2, #16. Cicero: #6, 9, 10.
307. Homer: table 3.1, #1, 2, 4, 5, 7, 10. Virgil: table 3.2, #1–3. Tragedy: table 3.1, #11, 12, 16, 18, 19, 21, 22. Lysias: table 3.1, #34, 35. Historiography: table 3.1, #43, 48 and table 3.2, #23, 24, 26, 27, 30, 33. Xenophon of Ephesus: table 3.1, #54 (punishment only).
308. Sophocles: table 3.1, #13. Historians: table 3.1, #42, 57, 58, and table 3.2, #14, 19.
309. Homer: table 3.1, #3. Aeschines: #27. Josephus: #67.
310. Josephus: table 3.1, # 59. Sophocles: #14, 15. Aristophanes: #26. Demosthenes: #31.
311. Endorse: table 3.2, #6. Withdraw: #9, 10. Change: #11.

of cities. It is missing from tragedy but occurs in comedy for a different reason: as Aristotle would lead us to expect, tragedy's suppliants are worthy and do not deserve expulsion, whereas comedy's are unworthy and do deserve this fate.[312] Not coincidentally, tragedy's worthy suppliants often are children (#33–35 in table 3.3), whereas comedy's occasionally are kidnappers (an aspect of #36). Pollution caused by the violence of the pursuer in tragedy contrasts with pollution caused by the presence of a criminal on holy ground in comedy.[313]

The reason for this contrast is not that tragedy alters the nature of the fourth step. This step may still end in rejection, and, since pursuers arrive, demanding the return of the suppliant, it may end in expulsion. In Aeschylus's *Suppliants*, the Assembly could have voted not to accept but to expel or, to be precise, to let the herald representing the pursuers repossess what he calls "his property." In the *Suppliants* of Euripides, the Assembly could have met the pursuers' demand that the suppliant Adrastus and his company be driven from Athens. In the *Children of Heracles*, no assembly convenes, but it might have convened had the pursuers demanded it, and it, too, could have voted to convict and let the pursuers seize the suppliants, who consist of the children of the title, their mother, and their uncle Iolaus.[314] No expulsion occurs because of the character of the suppliants and—no less important—the willingness of the supplicandi to risk the displeasure of the pursuers. Unsurprisingly, the supplicandi are mostly the Athenian people, and the pursuers mostly come from Boeotia or the Peloponnesus.

Rejection and expulsion also illustrate the quasilegal character of supplication. Just as those who are accepted are often innocent, those who are rejected are often guilty, and those who are expelled are often wanted. The few who are killed at an altar and not expelled first—and who are killed with the tacit approval of the sources—are tyrants, alleged enemies of legal institutions. Also quasilegal is the tradition that betrayal of a supplicandus's pledge prompts punishment by a god or hero or those knowingly or unknowingly acting in a god's name. This and other traditions concerning punishment—for example, the punishment of those who expel heralds and priests from shrines—are not scattershot or thoughtless. They all address the same problem: the independence of the supplicandus. Unlike magistrates, he is not answerable to a higher authority. Traditions of punishment restrain him without depriving him of his power.

Because the supplicandus was powerful, he provided irrevocable justice. Because he charged no fees, he provided cheap justice. He provided simple justice, too, without arcana or technicalities. At the same time, he relied on principles familiar from law codes. As the legal institutions of Greece and Rome developed, they influenced and sometimes controlled supplicandi, but these institutions did not replace them. Instead, institutions and supplicandi entered into a centuries-long dialogue about legal and quasilegal methods of righting wrongs and resolving disputes.

---

312. Arist. *Po.* 1448b.

313. Cf. Seaford's view, found in *Ritual and Reciprocity*, chaps. 5–6, that tragedy presents a democratic viewpoint hostile to tyrants and monarchs; comedy, I would suggest, presents a populist viewpoint hostile to criminals and undesirables. The citizen is thus watchful on two fronts.

314. A. *Supp.*: 918. Adrastus to be driven from Athens: E. *Supp.* 469–71.

TABLE 3.1 Acts of Rejection in Greek Sources

Supplicandus/ Rejected Suppliant/Citation	Contact or Intimacy	Request
Homer (10 cases)		
Iliad (7)		
1. Achilles/Tros (20.463–69)	yes	spare life
2. Achilles/Lycaon (21.64–119)	yes	spare life
3. Achilles/Hector (22.337–60)		provide burial
4. Agamemnon/Pisander and Hippolochus (11.130–44)		spare life
5. Diomedes/Dolon (10.454–56)	yes	spare life
6. Hector/Hecuba (22.79–91)		leave battle
7. Menelaus/Adrastus (6.45–65)	yes	spare life
Odyssey (3)		
8. Aeolus/Odysseus (10.62–76)		*xenia*
9. Cyclops/Odysseus (9.250–80)		*xenia*[a]
10. Odysseus/Leodes (22.310–29)	yes	spare life
Drama (16)		
Aeschylus (2)		
11. Agamemnon/Iphigenia (*Ag.* 231–47)	yes	spare life[b]
12. Orestes/Clytemnestra (*Ch.* 896–930)		spare life
Sophocles (3)		
13. Ajax/Tecmessa (*Aj.* 587–90)		give protection
14. Oedipus/Polynices (*OC* 1267–1396)	yes	give blessing
15. Tiresias/Oedipus (*OT* 326–29)		supply information
Euripides (10)		
16. Heracles/children (*HF* 986–95)	yes	spare life
17. Hippolytus/nurse (*Hipp.* 605–11)	yes	give aid
18. Menelaus/Helen (*Tro.* 1042–57)		spare life
19. Menelaus/Molossus (*And.* 537–40)	yes	spare life
20. Menelaus/Orestes (*Or.* 380–721)		give aid
21. Odysseus/Hecuba (*Hec.* 286–305)	yes	spare two lives
22. Odysseus/Polyxena (*Hec.* 342–45)	yes	spare life
23. Polynices and Eteocles/Jocasta (*Ph.* 1567–69)		leave battle
24. Tiresias/Creon (*Ph.* 923–59)	yes	supply information
Aristophanes (2)		
25. Agathon/Euripides (*Thes.* 179–208)		give aid
26. Trygaeus/priest (*Pax* 1113–21)		share food
Oratory (9)		
Aeschines (2)		
27. Timarchus/mother (1.99.1)		provide burial
28. Council/pauper (1.104)		give aid
Andocides (2)		
29. Council/councilors (1.44)		avoid prosecution
30. Council/unknown (1.110)		unstated
Demosthenes (1)		
31. Assembly/shipowners (24.12)		recover property
Dinarchus (1)		
32. Arcadian authorities/Thebans (1.18–19)		form alliance
Isocrates (1)		
33. Athenians/Plataeans (14)		give aid
Lysias (2)		
34. Euphiletus/Eratosthenes (1.25–27)		spare life
35. Athenians/Eurystheus (2.15)		spare life[c]

(*continued*)

TABLE 3.1 (Continued)

SUPPLICANDUS/ REJECTED SUPPLIANT/CITATION	CONTACT OR INTIMACY	REQUEST
Mythography and Historiography (14)		
Apollodorus (1)		
36. Meleager/Calydonians (1.8.3)		give aid[d]
Herodotus (1)		
37. Cleomenes/Aristagoras (5.51)		give aid
Thucydides (3)		
38. Corcyrans/Epidamnians (1.24.6–7)		form alliance
39. Corcyrans/fine-payers (3.70.5–6)		appeal decisions
40. Spartans/Plataeans (3.59.4)		acquit
Ephorus (1)		
41. Gelon/Greeks (70 *FGrH* 186)		give aid
Polybius (1)		
42. Caunians/Polyaratus (30.9.12–13)		give protection
Diodorus Siculus (2)		
43. Syracusans/Athenians (13.19.2–33.1)		spare life
44. Samothrace/Perseus (29.25)		give refuge[e]
Plutarch (2)		
45. Timoleon's brother/Timoleon (*Timol.* 4.5–6)		abdicate tyranny
46. Tanagrans/Poemander (*QG* 299d)		give refuge
Polyaenus (2)		
47. King of Cyprus/Pheritima (8.47.1)		vengeance
48. Mob/Berenice (8.50.1)		spare life
Himerius (1)		
49. Spartans/Persian legates (*Or.* 6.169–75)		forfeit sovereignty
Fiction and Fictitious Biography (7)		
Parthenius (1)		
50. Mother/Periander (17.5)		give improper aid
Philostratus (3)		
51. Asclepius/rich Cilician (*VA* 1.10)		heal eye
52. Townspeople/demon (*VA* 4.10)		spare life
53. Heroized Achilles/Trojans (*VA* 4.16)		make peace
Xenophon of Ephesus (3)		
54. Apsyrtus/Anthia (2.6.5)	yes	avoid punishment
55. Brigands/Anthia (3.8.4–5)	yes	avoid enslavement
56. Clytus/Anthia (5.5.6)	yes	avoid being sold
Josephus (14)		
57. Herod the Great/brother of Malichus (BJ 1.238)		give protection
58. Antony/Alexas (BJ 1.393–94)		give protection
59. Herod the Great/Antipater (BJ 1.561–65)		arrange marriage
60. Herod the Great/Livia (BJ 1.566)		spare Salome
61. Herod the Great/Antipater (BJ 1.621–40)	yes	grant pardon
62. Jailers/Antipater (BJ 1.663)		grant release
63. Cumanus/Galilaeans (BJ 2.233)		restore peace
64. Florus/Jews (BJ 2.292)		protect synagogue
65. Florus/Berenice (BJ 2.314)		halt pillage
66. Idumaeans/temple guards (BJ 4.311)		protect synagogue

TABLE 3.1 (Continued)

Supplicandus/ Rejected Suppliant/Citation	Contact or Intimacy	Request
67. Zealots/Niger (*BJ* 4.360)		provide burial
68. Zealots/Jews (*BJ* 6.118–21)		surrender to Romans
69. Romans/Jews (*BJ* 6.271)		spare life
70. Romans/John of Gischala (*BJ* 6.433–34)	yes	grant pardon

[a]Also E. *Cyc.* 285–327. In this and other instances, later sources appear in footnotes. Gould, "Hiketeia," and others giving lists of acts of supplication in Homer do not give lists of rejections. Excluded: rejections in Lucian, for which see appendix 1a.

[b]E. *IA* 1214–75.

[c]Isoc. 4.59–60.

[d]At. *Il.* 9.581–96, one Calydonian, Meleager's wife, succeeds.

[e]Liv. 45.5.1–6.

TABLE 3.2 Acts of Rejection in Latin Sources

SUPPLICANDUS/ REJECTED SUPPLIANT/CITATION	CONTACT OR INTIMACY	REQUEST
Epic (4 cases)		
Virgil (3)		
1. Aeneas/Magus (10.522–36)	yes	spare life
2. Aeneas/Liger (10.594–601)		spare life
3. Aeneas/Turnus (12.930–52)		spare life
Lucan (1)		
4. Caesar/Massilians (3.303–72)		negotiate
Oratory of Cicero (6)		
5. Verres/Senate of Panormus (*Verr.* 2.5.21)		end oppression
6. L. Gabinius/knights on behalf of Cicero (*Sest.* 26) and crowd on behalf of same (*Red. Sen.* 12)	yes	endorse bill
7. Piso consul/C. Piso on behalf of Cicero (*Sest.* 54)	yes	oppose bill
8. Atilius Glavianus/father-in-law (*Sest.* 74)		hold proceedings
9. Clodius/Cn. Oppius on behalf of Cicero (*Red. Pop.* 12)	yes	withdraw bill
10. Clodius/several on behalf of Cicero (*Red. Sen.* 12)		withdraw bill
Letters of Cicero & Pliny (2)		
11. Senators/Clodius (Cic. *Att.* 1.14.5)	yes	change votes
12. Pliny/mother-in-law (Plin. *Ep.* 1.18.3)		abandon prosecution
Historiography (22)		
Caesar		
13. Caesar/Mandubii (*Gal.* 7.78.3–5)		make peace
Florus (1)		
14. Octavian/Cleopatra (*Epit.* 2.21)		give protection
Fronto (1)		
15. Trajan/Parthamasiris (*Parth.* 16)		negotiate
Livy (6)		
16. Coriolanus/priests (2.39.12)		make peace
17. Senate/captives (22.60.1–61.3)		pay ransom
18. T. Flamininus/Naupactians (36.34.5)		negotiate
19. L. Flamininus/fugitive (39.42.10–12)		give protection
20. Roman sailors/Macedonians (44.42.4)		rescue
21. Aemilius Paullus/Macedonians (45.4.2–6)		pay ransom
Sallust (1)		
22. Metellus Numidicus/Jugurtha (*Jug.* 47.3)		negotiate
Attributed to Sallust (1)		
23. Pompey/Domitius Ahenobarbus, Cn. Papirius Carbo, and M. Junius Brutus (*Rep.* 1.4.1)		spare life
Scriptores Historiae Augustae (1)		
24. Troops/Balbinus (*Max.* 9.3)		spare life
Tacitus (5)		
25. Otho/Troops (*Hist.* 2.46–47)	yes	fight war
26. Troops/Tampius Flavianus (*Hist.* 3.10)	yes	spare life

TABLE 3.2 (Continued)

Supplicandus/ Rejected Suppliant/Citation	Contact or Intimacy	Request
27. Drusus/troops (*Ann.* 1.29.1–2)		spare lives
28. Libo/wife's relatives (*Ann.* 2.29.1)		give aid
29. Tiberius/Libo (*Ann.* 2.29.2)		same
Valerius Maximus (3)		
30. Sextilius/Caesar (5.3.3)	yes	give protection
31. Senate/Hannibal (9.2 ext. 2)		give aid
32. Pompey/Hypsaeus (9.5.3)	yes	give aid
Velleius Paterculus (2)		
33. Antony/Sextus Pompey (2.79.5)		spare life
34. Caesars/legates of Maroboduus (2.109.2)		negotiate

For Virgil, see Horsfall, *A Companion to Virgil*, 192–216, with Homeric parallels. No list for any other Latin author has been compiled.

TABLE 3.3 Acts of Expulsion

Expelled/Location/Citation	Additional Results
Expulsion by Supplicandi (8 cases)	
1. Syrphax & sons/Artemis of Ephesus (Arr. *An.* 1.17.12)	slain
2. Polyaratus/common hearth at Phaselis (Plb. 30.9.1–11)	
3. Andocides/Athenian Council altar (And. 2.15)	
4. Theramenes/Athenian Council altar (X. *HG* 2.3.52–55)	slain
5. Romans/Artemis of Ephesus (App. *Mith.* 23)	slain
6. Pactyes/unnamed at Chios (Hdt. 1.160)	
7. Megarans/unnamed at Leontini (Polyaen. 5.5.1–2)	
8. Friends of Alexander, son of Polyperchon/ Artemis of Orchomenus (D.S. 19.63.5)	slain
Expulsion by others (10)	
9. Heracleans/Athena of Heraclea (Str. 6.1.4)	
10. Oneanthe/Demeter of Alexandria (Plb. 15.29.7–33.8)	slain
11. Chloe/shrine of the nymphs (Longus 2.20.3)	enslaved
12. Thebans/altars (D.S. 17.13.6, 14.3–4)	enslaved
13. Motyans/shrines (D.S. 14.53.1–4)	enslaved
14. Selinuntians/temples (D.S. 13.57.3–4)	
15. Himerans/temples (D.S. 13.62.4)	
16. Acragantines/temples (D.S. 13.90.1)	
17. Aristion/Athena *Polias* (Paus. 1.20.7)	
18. Cassandra/Athena *Ilias* (Procl. *Chr.* 108 = *EGF* p. 62)	enslaved
Blockade (6)	
19. Regent Pausanias/Athena of the Brazen House (Th. 1.134.1)	starved
20. Agis/same (Plut. *Agis* 11.5–12.1, 16.3)	slain
21. Tegean minority/Artemis of Pallanteum (X. *HG* 6.5.9)	slain
22. Corcyran youths/Artemis of Samos (Hdt. 3.48)	
23. Unnamed/Artemis of Ephesus (Batto of Sinope 268 *FGrH* fr. 3)	
24. Messenians/Zeus of Ithome (Th. 1.101.2–103)	
Arson[a] (6)	
25. Mnesilochus/unnamed altar (Ar. *Thes.* 726–27, 929–46)	arrested
26. Labrax/Venus of Cyrene (Pl. *Rud.* 761–68, 1281–87)	tried
27. Tranio/unnamed altar (Pl. *Most.* 1114, 1137)	
28. Andromache/Thetis (E. *And.* 257, 259)	rescued
29. Heraclidae/Zeus (E. *HF* 240–46)	rescued
30. Same (Sen. *Her. F.* 506–8)	rescued
Expulsion by Foreign Sovereigns and Others (8)	
31. Patriots/various (Plb. 9.29.4)	slain
32. Cleopatra's brothers/Artemis of Ephesus (D.C. 48.24.2)	slain
33. Children of Oedipus/Furies of Colonus (S. *OC* 728–803)	rescued
34. Children of Heracles/Zeus *Agoraios* (E. *Heracl.* 55–74)	rescued
35. Children of Danaus/unnamed at Argos (A. *Supp.* 824–953)	rescued
36. Palaestra and Ampelisca/Venus of Cyrene (Pl. *Rud.* 559–680)	rescued
37. Themisto/Poseidon of Helice (Polyaen. 8.46.1)	slain
38. Convicts/Poseidon of Taenarus (Paus. 4.24.5–6)	slain
Dismissal (9)	
39. Heraclidae/various (E. *Heracl.* 389–473)	
40. Orestes/Apollo of Delphi (A. *Eu.*90–93)	
41. Harpalus/unnamed at Athens (D.S. 17.108.6–7)	
42. Ducetius/unnamed at Syracuse (D.S. 11.92.1–4)	
43. Themistocles/King of Molossia (Th. 1.137.1)	

TABLE 3.3 (Continued)

EXPELLED/LOCATION/CITATION	ADDITIONAL RESULTS
44. Phocion/Alexander, son of Polyperchon (D.S. 18.66)	tried
45. Pactyes/unnamed at Cyme (Hdt. 1.157–59)	
46. Evander/Great Gods of Samothrace (Liv. 45.5.6–12)	
47. Corcyrans/altars (D.S. 12.57.3–4)	

Similar but not identical lists: Caillemer, "Asylia" and Barth, *Asylis*; Rigsby, *Asylia* passim lists most of these cases. The encyclopedia articles of Stengl, "Asylon"; Wenger, "Asylrecht", Mannzman, "Asylia"; Fauth, "Asylon"; and Chaniotis, "Asylon" do not include exhaustive lists. If an act appears in more than one source, only the oldest source is given.

[a]In Men. *Per.* it is impossible to tell what will happen to the slave threatened with burning.

4

SUPPLICATION AND GREEK LAW

Supplication depended on moral and religious standards, but long before Metellus Pius it also depended on standards set by law. These two kinds of standards sometimes coincided. In Greece, for example, moral and religious standards coincided with the numerous laws and legal and political institutions affecting supplication in the classical poleis. If moral and religious standards are conceived as divine laws, these laws did not clash with communal laws that might be described as human instead, or that might be described as written rather than unwritten. The Greek term *nomos* refers to laws of both kinds.

Students of Greek supplication have discussed the relation between these divine and human *nomoi* for more than a century. Among the leading contemporary scholars, Walter Burkert does not consider these two kinds of laws, but literary scholars mention them when supplication and the laws of the polis cross paths in some scenes in Greek comedy.[1] Legal historians have said more, but only with respect to Ptolemaic Egypt and Rome, where they have observed that the community regulates supplication at public altars and even allows for expulsion by magistrates and others.[2] The prevailing view has said most. On this view, unwritten norms (or as Gould called them, "rules") of supposedly divine origin differ from written laws or codes of merely human origin.[3] The distinction between the two often dovetails with some historical scheme: unwritten law or *thesmos* falls into disuse while written law or *nomos* comes into being and protolegal ritual gives way to legal regulation. In *Nomos and the Beginnings of Athenian Democracy*, Martin Ostwald writes,

> The change from *thesmos* to *nomos* came about at a time when the Athenians were disenchanted with living under laws imposed on them from above and decided instead to consider as laws only norms that they themselves had ratified and acknowledged to be valid and binding.

---

1. Discussed in appendix 2.

2. Egypt: Woess, *Asylwesen Ägyptens*, 19–20, on *PBerlin* 11311.15–20, a decree that he thought provided for the expulsion of the tax-evading suppliants; for the contrary view, see Taubenschlag, *Law of Greco-Roman Egypt*, 421–22. Expulsion from imperial statues: 254–56 below.

3. As at 9 above.

Ostwald identifies this period as the middle of the fifth century. Before that, laws came "from above"; afterward, they came from fellow citizens. Similar formulations appear in other authors, notably Louis Gernet, who differs from Ostwald in stressing cultural and political reasons for the change.[4]

Although this distinction is both current and widely accepted, it is not altogether new. For it was in 1896 that Prott divided laws into two kinds, sacred and profane, not in order to distinguish the divine from the human, or the pre-classical from the classical, as later scholars would, but to extend ancient classifications of *hieroi nomoi*. These laws regulated sacrifices and purifications and protected temple property, but Prott regarded the Greek cult calendars as sacred laws, too, and his collaborator Ziehen added more laws about rituals.[5] However, few of Ziehen's laws concern supplication, a practice that came within the ambit of sacred laws a generation later, in Latte's *Heiliges Recht*. Latte did not say much about supplication, but he did regard it as subject to a divine law, one of Ostwald's laws from above.[6]

This distinction between the divine and the human—the sacred and the secular—does not apply to supplication. Supplication incorporates divine sanctions against perjury and against the expulsion of the innocent from altars and divine injunctions to allow a suppliant to approach and have his request heard. Yet as we shall now see, it also incorporates numerous regulations passed by the assembly of any given community, notably Athens. For their part, the gods endorse sanctions, injunctions, and regulations. For its part, the assembly addresses every aspect of the practice. Besides regulating how citizens deal with one another and with the community, it regulates how the community deals with the gods.[7]

By the same token, supplication incorporates early, widespread elements like the use of altars, found in Israel, Phoenicia, and Greece, and later elements peculiar to a given community, like the Athenian practice of a suppliant's going before the Council first and the Assembly second. The latter elements do not correct or improve the former. Instead they show how supplication adapts itself to a given political system. Meanwhile the essentials of the practice remain unchanged. No regulation proposes a new step in the procedure or a new standard of judgment at the crucial fourth step. Instead, regulations formalize the practice.[8] In Athens, all the chief elements of the political system—the Assembly and the Council, the magistrates, and the courts—contribute to this formalization.[9] The Assembly writes

4. Ostwald, *Nomos*, 55, Gagarin, *Early Greek Law*, 140. Ostwald, *Popular Sovereignty*, 130, say that *nomoi* were not enforced before Cleisthenes. Criticism of Gernet, "Droit et prédroit," and of Gagarin from the standpoint of legal anthropology: Burchfiel, "Prelaw" following Pospisil, *Anthropology of Law*, the latter of whom does not deal with Greek law.

5. *Hieroi nomoi*: *I. Pergamum* 1.246.61–2, 248.3, 60; *LSCG* #154 a.6.

6. Latte, *Heiliges Recht*, 107–8.

7. So also R. Parker, "Sacred Laws," 66–67, but not in reference to supplication.

8. Coherence of divine and human elements in Athenian laws: Harris, "Antigone the Lawyer," 21–31, and especially 27, pointing out that Demosthenes (25.16) requires that laws conform to the will of the gods as well as the wishes of community.

9. These three elements: Arist. *Pol.* 4.1298a, pointing out that they are not exclusively democratic, and anticipated with respect to a tripartite division by Th. 2.37.1.

laws and passes resolutions, magistrates enforce these laws and exercise incidental judicial authority, and courts consult laws when rendering verdicts.

The same formalization of supplication also appears in relations among poleis. Greek federal bodies like the Delphic Amphictyony evolved rules that enabled communities to cooperate in dealing with suppliants. In the Peloponnesus, Sparta enjoyed extraterritorial rights affecting some shrines in states belonging to the Spartan Alliance and also affecting shrines in communities dependent on Sparta. Common to these developments was need to establish jurisdiction over shrines that—unlike shrines in Attica—were subject to several authorities. For federal shrines and shrines in states in the Spartan Alliance, treaties and grants assigned jurisdiction. Where such agreements were missing, Sparta prevailed over dependent communities or turned to mediation. A shrine in Messenia occasioned a dispute that led to mediation by the Delphic oracle.

Treaties and grants—like oracular pronouncements—did not always prove easy to interpret. For this reason, a familiar feature of supplication, the dubious rejection of a suppliant, does not fail to appear in these intercommunal cases. One of Thucydides' set pieces, the Plataean debate, centers on such an act of rejection.

SUPPLICATION IN CLASSICAL ATHENS

In Athens, supplication at public altars—a practice found not only in Greece but in *Exodus* and throughout the Eastern Mediterranean—became a regulated procedure. Yet it did not lose any of its four steps: the approach to the altar, the use of a bough or of contact with the altar, the presentation of a request to the community, and a decision by a king or by the community. Regulation effected two changes. First, the Assembly became the chief supplicandus. Second, the Assembly wrote the rules and issued the instructions that formalized supplication.

According to the Aristotelian *Constitution of the Athenians*, the Athenian Assembly set aside frequent, regular meetings to deal with supplications addressed to it.[10] Several inscriptions along with passages in the orators show how these supplications proceeded. We will trace one of them, a supplication by a metic named Dioscurides who approached the Assembly in 364–63 BCE. Like many others, he began by approaching the altar of the Athenian Council. This attempt to interest the gods in the supplication echoes in the language of the Attic decree that is the only source for his appeal. The superscript of the decree lists some of the gods who might respond to Dioscurides when he approached: "The Gods— (The Hero) Abderos—Athena—Dioscurides, the son of Dionysodorus."[11] Abderos is a hero of Abdera, Dioscurides' home city and once part of the Athenian empire, and Athena is the goddess of the city in which he resides. These references to Athens and its institutions balance the reference to the gods as a whole.

10. Arist. *Ath*. 43.6.
11. *IG* ii² 218, translated in five parts.

Next Dioscurides placed a bough on the Council altar. The inscription does not mention this gesture, but we may take it for granted thanks not only to passages in the orators but also to a third-century Samian inscription that describes a supplication made by a Samian priest of Isis. Like Dioscurides, he addressed himself to the Assembly of his city after appearing before the city's Council:

> Good fortune. During the term of office of Marsias and Mnesimbrotus, the Council and Assembly passed a decree. Phocylus proposed, "In regard to the matters about which the priest of Isis placed a suppliant branch in the Council, he has been judged to be legitimate in regard to his request to take collections on the goddess's behalf the same as before."[12]

Unlike Dioscurides and the priest, some suppliants gain the attention of the Council by placing a bough elsewhere, notably at the altar of the Twelve Gods. Pittalicus went there, as did informers and some diplomats and others arriving from abroad. Trierarchs seeking relief from financial obligations went to the altar of Artemis in the port of Munychia.[13]

The next lines in the inscription say when the supplication occurred and, in particular, when it led to the passage of a resolution. Even more than the superscript, they locate Dioscurides in the Athenian political system:

> When Archias was archon in the prytany of Acamantis and Cephisodorus, the son of Athenophanes, a Phlyan, was secretary, Euboulides the son of Antiphilus, a Halimousian, made the following proposal, . . .

Because these lines refer to a proposal that will lead to a decree, they show that Dioscurides will eventually succeed, and so they also show that the Assembly as well as the Council responded favorably to him. From this response we can deduce that Dioscurides not only approached and placed a bough but also performed the rest of the procedure, beginning with the third step, the presentation of requests and arguments.

As it happens, the inscription does not immediately describe this step. Instead it passes on to the fourth step and explains how the Council evaluated him:

> In the opinion of the Council Dioscurides of Abdera has been found to make a legitimate supplication [ἔδοξεν ἔννομα ἱκετεύειν ἐν τῆι βουλῆι], and so the Council has resolved that the *prytaneis* who are in office should introduce him to the Assembly at the first meeting and dispose of his business, and should present to the Assembly the Council's recommendation.

---

12. *LSCG* #123 = Michel #371. Orators: And. 1.110, Dem. 24.12.

13. Informers: Plut. *Per.* 31.2. Diplomats: Hdt. 6.108.4. Others: Lycurg. *in Leocr.* 93, though it is not clear that this suppliant went before the assembly. Trierarchs: Dem. 18.107, though again it is not clear that any of these suppliants went before the assembly. Instead they might negotiate with those persons to whom they owed debts, since as Rhodes, *Boule*, explains at 157–58, these debts were not collected by the authorities.

The phrase ἔδοξεν ἔννομα ἱκετεύειν ἐν τῆι βουλῆι, is notable, especially the word ἔννομα. The Samian decree contains a form of this word, too: ἔννομος translated as "legitimate" in the phrase, "has been judged to be legitimate." So do several other Attic decrees concerning suppliants.[14] We will return to this word, but for now we will notice that it supplies some information about the third step. Whatever request and whatever arguments Dioscurides made, the Council found the request and arguments "legitimate," in short, morally and legally acceptable.[15] This definition accords with the two meanings of *nomos* noticed at the start of this chapter.

When the Council turned from Dioscurides' supplication to the help that it believes that Athens should give him, it finally described the third step:

> Since Dioscurides and his brothers Charmes and Anaxipolis, sons of Dionysodorus of Abdera, ask the people for their just deserts, the Council and the generals and the magistrates in the cities of the Athenians should see to it that they are not wronged.

The suppliant asks for "just deserts": here is the request, but couched in a form that also conveys the argument. The term for "just deserts," ἄξια, is the same as the term used of "worthy" suppliants in other inscriptions. "Worthiness" is, as we have seen, the most common reason to grant a request. In literary sources, this quality takes many forms. Thetis, for example, says that her son deserves honor.[16] Here we cannot be sure what the "deserts" are, but since Dioscurides will shortly receive honors from Athens, he may have said that he deserved them. If so, this portion of the inscription conforms to the pattern described in chapter 3: a request and an assertion of worth by the suppliant, the acceptance of this assertion by the supplicandus, and then the granting of the request. Along with the new reason (the suppliant's legitimacy) comes the old reason (his worth).

After citing these two reasons, the Council sent Dioscurides to the Assembly with its approval. Like any supplicandus, it was not obliged to give him such help. Instead it might have sent him to the Assembly without its approval.[17] Then Disocurides would present himself on less advantageous terms.[18] Or the Council might have refused to send him to the Assembly. In that case his supplication

---

14. Found in four grants of honors, three Attic from the fourth century BCE (*IG* ii² 218, 276, 337), and one Samian from the third century BCE (*LSCG* #123 = Michel #371); restored in three other grants on the basis of the extant or partially preserved words ἔννομα or ἱκετεύειν (*IG* ii² 336, 404, 502); and supplied by Wilhelm in two others (*IG* ii² 192, 211). Analysis of the Attic grants: Rhodes, *Boule*, 55–57, and Zelnick-Abramovitz, "Supplication and Request."

15. Similar double conception of *ennomos* as both moral and legal: Ostwald, *Nomos*, 24–26, where Ostwald does not discuss supplication.

16. *Il.* 1.505–10.

17. I.e., "open *probouleuma*," as in Rhodes with Lewis, *Decrees*, 486–91.

18. Council approval followed by Assembly approval, as in 218: *IG* ii² 276.5–6. Open *probouleuma* followed by Assembly approval: *IG* ii² 336.5–8; 337.6–7, 30–31. No information about the Council, but approval by the Assembly: *IG* ii² 404, 502. Sometimes the suppliant may have bypassed the Council and gone to the Assembly straightaway, as argued by Rhodes, *Boule*, 55; for the contrary view, see Wilamowitz, *Aristoteles*, 252–53.

would have been "illegitimate" or *paranomos*, a term that is not attested in inscriptions because unsuccessful supplication did not lead to the passage of a decree.[19]

Dioscurides was now through with the Council and proceeds to the Assembly, which performed a second act of evaluation. This pair of evaluations, one by the Council, one by the Assembly, forms a distinctive feature of supplication before Athenian deliberative bodies. For our purposes, the vital point is that the Assembly evaluates the suppliant in the same way as the Council. In particular, it finds that he has "made a legitimate supplication":

> Diopithes the son of Diopithes, from Sphettos, made the following proposal, "In the opinion of the Assembly, Dioscurides has been found to make a legitimate supplication. In order that the Athenian people may honor benefactors and care for the city's friends whenever they are in need, let the Assembly pass a resolution exactly as the Council recommends."

Now comes the help that the Assembly will give Dioscurides and also his family:

> "But let the Assembly further resolve that Dioscurides and Charmes and Anaxipolis, the sons of Dionysodorus of Abdera, and their descendants may live in Athens until they return to their own city. They may pay property tax and serve in the army as Athenians do [or: with Athenians]."

Passage of a resolution to grant honors brings the supplication to its fourth and last step, the pledge made by the supplicandus, that is, the Assembly. A stele gives this pledge a permanent, public form.[20]

Among the four steps of this type of supplication, the distinctive feature is dual evaluation by the Council and Assembly. Since the laws of Athens required the Council to vet legislative business, this feature shows supplication adapting itself to the political system. The Athenians, however, thought that there had always been dual evaluation of suppliants in their city, even under the monarchy. They thought the same of early Argos, a city that was their ally, as shown by the *Suppliants* of Aeschylus. As we noticed, the king shares control of the altar with the Assembly, but this sharing occurs by way of a dual evaluation: the king evaluates the Danaids at the start of the play, and the Assembly does afterward. The same happens or is about to happen in two other plays that we have noticed. In the *Suppliants* of Euripides, the king of Athens, Theseus, rules in favor of the suppliants after initial doubts and then advocates their cause in the Assembly. In the *Children of Heracles*, another king of Athens, Demophon, allows the suppliants

---

19. *Paranomos* of supplication elsewhere: Th. 4.98.6, discussed at 94 above. References to law-breaking: E. *Med.* 1121 (murder); Th. 6.28.2, Lys. 14.42 (sacrilege); And. 4.10 (adultery); Lys. 3.10 (assault). References to violation of norms: Th. 1.132.2, 6.15.4; And. 4.10, 30, 33; E. *Tr.* 283; P. *R.* 7.537e. Both meanings are given by *LSJ* s.v. παράνομος.

20. The suppliant might also make his own copy, as at *IG* ii² 337, a revised copy of a grant of honors. The reason, of course, was to make sure that the honors granted were not ignored.

to stay at the altar and promises an Assembly meeting to the herald who wants to repossess the suppliants. *The Eumenides* offers a variant: first Orestes is evaluated by Athena, and then, after Athena establishes the court of the Areopagus, he is evaluated by the Areopagus.[21] In contrast, monarchs alone evaluate the suppliants who go to altars in Thebes in the *Madness of Heracles* and *Oedipus Rex*. To judge from these plays, dual evaluation is a tradition inherited from Athenian heroes and not a democratic innovation.[22]

Supplication to the Assembly also points to other salient features of Athenian democracy. As the *Constitution of the Athenians* says, slaves and the resident aliens known as metics could both supplicate, and they and foreigners comprise the great majority of suppliants in the 10 extant cases of supplication of this kind.[23] Three metics supplicate: Dioscurides; Asclepiodorus, given honors in return for naval service; and Archippus, who is about to become a citizen.[24] The suppliant Pittalicus is a freedman, and another suppliant, Antiphates, is a public slave who has served in the Athenian navy.[25] Diverse diplomats and foreigners also supplicate: Cean legates seeking an alliance with Athens, Plataeans seeking Athens's aid, Egyptian merchants seeking to recover lost cargo, and the fugitive treasurer of Alexander the Great, Harpalus, who is the most famous of all those who present themselves to the Athenians as *hiketai*.[26] Also diverse are the results, which range from dining privileges to the right to own land and citizenship.[27] Metics gained income and prestige through honors, and metics and public slaves could gain status thorough a grant of citizenship.[28] Diplomats obtained treaties and alliances, and fugitives and informers gained protection.

No matter what the suppliant's station and request, the supplication that he or she makes must be *ennoma*, or the suppliant must be *ennomos*—the Samian formulation. The moral side of these terms appears in the assertion that Dioscurides is worthy. But the legal side is larger and more complex. In regard to the first two steps, *ennoma* or *ennomos* means that suppliant is eligible to supplicate and has done so at the right time. *Ennomos* in the Samian inscription supplies the first meaning, "eligible to supplicate," and *ennoma* in the Attic inscriptions sup-

---

21. Assembly: A. *Supp.* 600–5; E. *Supp.* 349–58; E. *Heracl.* 250–2, superseded by war.

22. E. *HF* 1–327, S. *OT* 1–77. But if Diodorus's likely source, Ephorus, is to be believed, dual evaluation also existed at Sybaris in the late sixth century BCE (D.S. 12.9.4). Euripides avoids it in his *Orestes*, as noted by de Romilly, "Assemblée du peuple," 237–40.

23. The only citizen: And. 1.110–16, where the supplication is alleged. The 10 cases: Aeschin. 1.60, 1.104, Dem. 24.12, D.S. 17.108.6–7, *IG* ii² 218, 276, 336, 337, 404, 502. A likely case: Isoc. 14, discussed immediately below. Likely but fragmentary: *IG* i³ 14, ii² 192, 211.

24. Metics: *IG* ii² 276, 336. Metics or *xenoi*: *IG* ii² 337. Some scholars prefer other terms for these residents, such as *xenoi* or *perepidemountes*; see Whitehead, *Athenian Metic*, chap. 1.

25. Freedman: Aeschin. 1.60. Public slave: *IG* ii² 502. These two examples are incompatible with the view of Gauthier, *Cités grecques*, 181–90, which is that supplication is for foreigners as opposed to citizens; so is And. 1.110–16.

26. Diplomats: *IG* ii² 404. Merchants: Dem. 24.12. Harpalus *hiketês*: D.S. 17.108.6–7, where he approaches the Athenians but perhaps not the Council. The same may be true of the Plataeans in Isoc. 14.

27. Dining: *IG* ii² 218.21–22, 276.11–12. Crowns: 276.10–11, 336.13–14. Ownership: *IG* ii² 337.36–38. Same tax status as citizens: 276.13–14.

28. Citizenship confirmed (though not obtained): *IG* ii² 336. Perhaps sought by a slave: 502.

plies the second meaning, which is presenting oneself at the right time. In regard to the last two steps, *ennoma* complements *hiketeuein* as a verb of speaking and means that the suppliant has made a lawful request. Finally, since the lawful request has led to the passage of a decree granting honors, *ennoma* also means that the supplication has proved "valid," a sense of *ennoma* in other legislative contexts.[29]

With regard to the first step, the law of Athens established that some persons were eligible to supplicate at the Council altar and others were not. The latter could not supplicate because they were forbidden to approach any public altar. Murderers were one such group.[30] In addition, other felons caught red-handed were liable to arrest, and nothing in the sources says that going to a public altar would protect them.[31] The example of Mnesilochus argues the contrary: this felon finds himself expelled from an altar by a magistrate in Aristophanes.[32] A broad category, felons included kidnappers, thieves, robbers, burglars, and assailants.[33] The Athenians also banned another group, the *atimoi* or "disenfranchised," from going to public altars. This category included male prostitutes, cowards, deserters, draft dodgers, and impious persons.[34] It may have also included unsuccessful prosecutors of public cases and others.[35]

With regard the second step, Andocides reports that the Assembly passed a law regarding the use of boughs. This law forbade placing a bough on the Council altar during the Eleusinian Mysteries. In the course of denying that he has broken this law, Andocides not only quotes it but also points out that it is inscribed on a stele found standing in the Council chamber. His reason for going to such trouble is to remove any doubt as to the penalty, which is moderate. He is addressing the man who has accused him: "Callias, . . . the stele by which you are standing orders a fine of a thousand drachmas if anyone deposits a bough in the Eleusinium."[36] Callias, in contrast, claims that the penalty is death. He is evidently

---

29. ἔννομοι or "valid" assembly votes: Delph. III.2 19.2, 20.2. Assemblies: *IG* ix.1 3.3–4 (Antikyra), 330.7 (Chaleion), ix.2 11.11 (Hypata), 259.5–6 (Kierion), xii.3 325.21, 326.15 (Thera). A similar view of fifth-century legal usage: Ostwald, *Popular Sovereignty*, 97–99.

30. Murderers: Dem. 23.80, discussed by MacDowell, *Law in Athens*, 121–22, and Hansen, *Apagoge, Endeixis, and Ephegesis*, 99–108, who point out that there is no way to know how strictly the ban was enforced. A myth about the ban: Phanodemus 325 *FGrH* fr. 13, in which an early Athenian king does not want Orestes to be admitted to shrines until he has been found innocent.

31. "Felons" or *kakourgoi* liable to arrest by a magistrate using the procedures called *ephêgêsis* and *apagôgê*: Dem. 22.26, Democ. fr. 3, cited by Hansen, *Apagoge, Endeixis, and Ephegesis*, 25, for *ephêgêsis*, and Antipho 5.9, Isoc. 15.90, Lys. 13.78, Dem. 22.26–28, 24.113, 35.47, Aeschin. 1.90–91, cited by Hansen, 39–40, for *apagôgê*.

32. Ar. *Thes.* 929–46. Perhaps similar is the fragmentary *PBerol.* 11771.12–22 = Austin #239.12–22, where a similarly contemptible felon conducts himself in a way that invites expulsion.

33. I give the list of Lipsius, *Attische Recht*, 1.78–79. Hansen, *Apagoge, Endeixis, and Ephegesis*, 36–48, includes others, and discusses the need to distinguish between legal and moral meanings of *kakourgos*.

34. Male prostitutes: Dem. 24.181. Deserters, draft dodgers, and cowards: Aeschin. 3.176.1 and schol. Guilty of impiety: And. 1.8, Lys. 6.9, 24 (decree of Isotomides). Other sources mention lesser penalties, as noted by Hansen, *Apagoge, Endeixis, and Ephegesis*, 63–65.

35. Unsuccessful prosecutors: Hyp. *Eux.* 34. Others: three-time convicts for idleness (Lys. fr. 10), and those who refused to divorce an adulteress (Dem. 59.87). Ruschenbusch, *Untersuchungen*, 19, 29, thought that public debtors and male prostitutes had the right to enter temples in the fourth century, though not before; for criticism, see Hansen, *Apagoge, Endeixis, and Ephegesis*, 65–66.

36. And. 1.116. Other views of the requirement: Aubriot-Sévin, *Prière*, 426; Blech, *Kranz*, 291; R. Parker, *Miasma*, 157 n. 72; and Sinn, "Sakrale Schutzzone," 83. All compare it to requirements in other rituals.

wrong, and perhaps the law was never as he says. What is sure is that in the late fifth century the Athenian Assembly regulated the use of boughs in supplication.

Who may supplicate the Council and when are matters of procedure. But the Assembly also regulated the third and fourth steps in an act of supplication of this kind and thus dealt with matters of substance. One such matter was punishment, relevant to the third step; another was adherence to other laws, relevant to the fourth step. At the third step, the Assembly forbade suppliants from asking that the Assembly reverse convictions or even reduce punishments such as fines. This time, evidence comes from Demosthenes, who objects to what he describes as a supplication by his enemy Timocrates. Timocrates had been fined, and Demosthenes contends that he used supplication to obtain relief. Demosthenes attributes the law forbidding supplicandi from reversing convictions and the like to Solon:

> It is hard, judges, to go through all the laws that this man has undermined, but if any law must be mentioned, let it be the one I have just read. The author of this law, . . . knew that you are humane and kindly and he had seen how much you had already suffered because of these qualities. To make sure that the community would not be harmed, he decided that *those who have been convicted of wrongdoing by due process and in a court of law should not enjoy the fruit of your good intentions—that is, the right to plead and supplicate in times of misfortune.*[37]

The law's aim, Demosthenes continues, was to preserve the principle of *res iudicata*:

> He utterly forbade either the culprit or anyone else to supplicate or speak about such cases. He ordered everyone to do what the law required without protest.

Since Demosthenes is referring to a response to a supplication made to obtain relief from a fine, we might wonder whether the same principle affected a more serious request, such as a supplication made to escape the consequences of a conviction for murder. We might also wonder whether this principle applied not only to the Assembly but to those who acted in the name of the Assembly, including priests at public shrines. A passage in a novel that makes only ironic reference to *res iudicata* nonetheless shows that the principle applies to convicted murderers who supplicate priests rather than the Assembly. At the novel's climax, the hero, Clitophon, has been found guilty of murder and condemned to death, and he is then given a brief stay of execution that he uses to go to the Artemisium to visit his beloved, who is supplicating there. She is the virgin who

---

37. Dem. 24.51–52, especially the words italicized for emphasis: βουλόμενος δὴ μηδεμίαν πρόφασιν τοῦ τὰ κοινὰ κακῶς ἔχειν ὑπολιπεῖν, τοὺς μετὰ τῶν νόμων κρίσει καὶ δικαστηρίῳ μὴ δίκαια ποιεῖν ἐγνωσμένους οὐκ ᾤετο δεῖν τῆς εὐηθείας τῆς ὑμετέρας ἀπολαύειν, τὸ δεῖσθαι καὶ μετὰ συμφορᾶς ἱκετεύειν. A different view: Traulsen, *Das sakrale Asyl*, 200, holding that the aim of the law was to uphold public authorities, not to distinguish between the deserving and the undeserving.

will pass the test of the Pan pipes.[38] Out of both fear and sympathy, he supplicates along with her.

When the stay of execution is over, the prosecutor goes to court demanding that Clitophon be executed. He points out that it does not matter that Clitophon is in the temple and is supplicating there. He even assails the priest of the temple:

> What temple regulations say that the Council and its officers shall find people guilty and sentence them to death and that you will then snatch them away from justice and undo their bonds—that you shall make yourself more powerful than the judges and the courts?[39]

He now declares:

> The goddess has never released anyone that is in bonds or freed anyone sentenced to death. Her altars are for the unlucky, not for wrongdoers.

He speaks before a statue of Artemis that underscores his words.[40]

The priest of Artemis does not challenge the principle on which this argument rests: convicted murderers should not have their sentences reversed by supplicating in the Artemisium.[41] Instead the priest presents another defense: Clitophon is innocent of the charge against him. For this reason, Clitophon goes free. Had Clitophon committed the murder, *res iudicata* would have prevailed. Even in a capital case, the most famous sanctuary in Greek Asia Minor adheres to this principle.

At the fourth step, the Assembly consulted other laws when evaluating requests. The only example of this among the 10 cases also happens to be the only example of a rejection of a supplication in which the sources preserve the reason for this decision.[42] In 355 BCE, eight years after Dioscurides won his honors, Athenian naval vessels seized the goods of merchants from the Egyptian town of Naucratis. These vessels were sailing either to or from Mausolus, the ruler of Caria, when they chanced upon an Egyptian ship and captured it. When the merchants supplicated the Council and the Assembly, their request reached the Assembly, and it evaluated the request according to law. First, a law provided that that "goods obtained in this way become public property."[43] The Athenians were thus entitled to keep the property. Second—and no less important—no law prevented the Athenians from granting a request from a suppliant, including a request to have such property returned to him. The suppliant would need to induce the Assembly to evaluate him favorably. This the Naucratites failed to do. The reason for the fail-

---

38. Clitophon condemned: Ach. Tat. 7.12.1. Brief reprieve: 7.12.3, 7.16. 2. His supplication: 8.2.2.

39. Ach. Tat. 8.8.6.

40. Ach. Tat. 8.8.9. Statue of Artemis in court: 8.9.1, παρὰ τὴν θεόν.

41. As another speaker says at Ach. Tat. 8.10.3. Habicht, "Samische Volksbeschlüsse," 229, notices laws similar to those at Ephesus.

42. Rejection by the Athenian Council on unstated grounds: Aeschin. 1.104.

43. τοὺς νόμους [ἀνέγνω] καθ᾽ οὓς τοῦτον τὸν τρόπον πραχθέντων τῆς πόλεως γίγνεται τὰ χρήματα (Dem. 24.12).

ure revealed the military and diplomatic factors that impinged on supplication before a public body. At the time of the supplication, Egypt was rebelling against its master, Persia. If the Athenians wished to remain friendly to Persia, they would regard the Naucratites as the citizens of a hostile power and thus as enemies. If the Athenians felt unfriendly toward Persia, they would regard the Naucratites as subjects of Persia, rebellion or no, and might again regard them as enemies.[44] We do not know which view prevailed, but the Assembly decided that the Naucratites were indeed enemies, and cited this reason for rejecting their supplication.[45]

This reason was not original. Diomedes called Dolon an enemy and rejected his supplication.[46] But the Assembly acted somewhat differently than an Homeric supplicandus. Under the law it had a right to the property (and it would assert this same right against the individuals who captured the ship and delayed in surrendering the property to the community).[47] Only if a suppliant met a standard of worth would it surrender this right. The law and the standard formed a whole. The supplication did not stand at some remove from the law. Nor did it stand at some remove from political concerns.[48]

The Assembly gave a similar response to another supplication by foreigners, this time a successful supplication by Ceans who asked Athens to abide by a treaty between Cean towns and Chabrias, an Athenian admiral. The date of this supplication is unsure, and so are the difficulties between Ceos and Athens that led the Ceans to supplicate, but the Ceans were appealing on the basis of a treaty and of a familiar standard, the sacredness of the oaths sworn by their towns and Chabrias.[49] The Assembly accepted the legal obligation to honor the treaty and the religious obligation to honor the oaths, and it surely considered the international situation.

Treaties and oaths, but especially treaties, are also the arguments adduced by the suppliants who come before the Assembly according the longest record of any act of ancient supplication, Isocrates' *Plataean Oration*. These suppliants are the Plataean refugees who came before the Athenian Assembly in 373 BCE. The highlights of recent relations among Plataea, Athens, and Thebes all contribute to this encounter: the *Koinê Eirênê* or "Common Peace" of 386 guaranteeing the integrity of Plataea; the success of the Thebans in compelling the Plataeans to join the Boeotian Federation in 377–76 BCE; and the Plataean rejection of the Boeotians in 373 BCE. That year, the Plataeans quit the federation, and in response the

---

44. As suggested by Badian, "Road to Prominence," 23, preceded by Sealey, *Demosthenes*, 104.

45. ὡς ἔθεσαν τὴν ἱκετηρίαν ὧν ἦν τὰ χρήματα ἄνθρωποι, ὡς ἀπεχειροτονήσαθ' ὑμεῖς μὴ φίλια εἶναι, the vital word being μὴ (Dem. 24.12).

46. *Il.* 10.446–53.

47. Leading to a successful lawsuit against these persons (Dem. 24.11–15) with remarks by Rhodes, *Boule*, 158. Timarchus's attempt to circumvent *res iudicata* occurred after he was fined in accordance with the penalty provided by this suit.

48. Other views of *ennomos* and *ennoma*: Zelnick-Abramowitz, "Supplication and Request," 565, as referring to "ceremonial rules," and Gauthier, *Cités grecques*, 189, as referring to the resolution by which the Assembly responded to the suppliant.

49. *IG* ii² 404.10–15. Possible date: 360s BCE according to Dreher, "*IG* ii² 404," with refs.

Thebans destroyed Plataea and annexed Plataea's territory. The Plataeans fled to Athens, where they supplicated.[50]

We do not know how much their speech differed from that of Isocrates, which may be either a speech that they commissioned but did not give, a revision of a speech that they did give, or a work of propaganda.[51] But it doubtless contained the arguments that Isocrates believed an Assembly listening to suppliants would expect. These arguments prove to be both legal and moral.

The legal arguments depend on several treaties or *synthêkai*. First comes Common Peace, violated by the Thebans' destruction and annexation of Plataea. Athens was a signatory to this treaty. Second come agreements providing independence for the communities of Boeotia. The Thebans violated these treaties in 377–76 BCE when they compelled the Plataeans to join the federation and again in 373 BCE when they invaded. Athens was not a signatory to these agreements, so in this case the Plataeans are asking the Athenians to vindicate treaties between the suppliant and a third party.[52] In making these arguments about treaties, the Plataeans go so far as to insist that treaty obligations should prevail over other considerations such as alliances, military necessity, or friendship.[53] Supplicandi should fight wars to vindicate suppliants who fall victim to broken treaties.

From treaties and their enforcement through war, the Plataeans turn to intercommunal federations founded on treaties. They take pains not to object to the Boeotian Federation that, under Thebes' leadership, has recently destroyed their city. On the contrary: in destroying Plataea, the Thebans have violated the treaties on which the federation rests. They compelled Plataea to join, a violation of the principle of independence that is integral to the treaties. Worse still, they deprived Plataea of its territory—in effect, annihilated Plataea—the most severe violation of independence.[54] Rather than attack Plataea, the Thebans should have brought their grievances against Plataea before another federation, the Athenian Alliance established in 377 BCE. This federation, say the Plataeans, provides freedom for its members, whereas the Boeotian Federation, now that the Thebans have perverted it, forces its members into slavery.[55]

The moral arguments stem from the character of these and other Greek treaties: the participants did not so much sign these treaties as swear to them. Treaty breakers are perjurers, offenders in the eyes of the gods. Arguments about laws and morals coalesce with religious feeling and form a whole—an international supplicatory appeal running parallel to appeals made in a single polis. Like other skillful suppliants, the Plateaeans (or rather, Isocrates) work up a juggernaut, but a lawyer's or diplomat's juggernaut rather than a poet's.

50. D.S. 15.46.4–6, X. *HG* 6.3.1.
51. Propaganda: Mathieu and Brémond, *Isocrate II*, with refs.
52. Isoc. 14.63.
53. Ally: Isoc. 14.39. Necessity: 14.11. *Philia* on part of Athens toward Thebes implicitly discounted: 14.33.
54. Isoc. 14.8–9.
55. Isoc. 14.18–19.

Just as many suppliants who appealed to Athenian laws and norms were metics or slaves, these suppliants were stateless persons, outsiders making use of supplication to gain the Assembly's attention. As the *Constitution of the Athenians* says, supplication was not merely for citizens or other privileged persons such as diplomats. It served those who lacked credentials or who might be afraid to come forward, like the Ceans.[56] It gave these persons access. For this reason, it counteracted a weakness in the Athenian system—the small number of citizens compared to slaves, metics, allies, and others with business in Athens. Outsiders outnumbered insiders, creating imbalance. Supplication redressed this imbalance.[57]

Supplication did not, however, provide an alternative to this system. It did not pit the gods against the community, tradition against innovation, or unwritten norms against written rules. It operated under an umbrella that included Athenian laws, Assembly decrees, and treaties but also included Homeric maxims about enemies and Greek commonplaces about oaths. Suppliants like Dioscurides and the Plataeans would need to argue accordingly. For its part, the Assembly retained the freedom of action of any other supplicandus. It passed a decree on behalf of Disocurides but chose to reject the supplication made by the Plataeans. Perhaps some in the Assembly made counterarguments about the treaties cited by the Plataeans. Just as Athenian law brought new factors to bear on the rest of the practice, both Athenian law and international agreements brought new factors to bear on the climax—the decision to say "yes" or "no."

Supplication and Magistrates

The Assembly often gave the responsibility for enforcing laws about supplication to magistrates and priests. They enforced laws forbidding certain persons from supplicating, an issue arising at the first step in supplication. They also enforced laws that dictated the manner in which suppliants should act, especially suppliants seeking purification, an issue arising at the first and second steps in supplication. But they did not confine themselves to issues of procedure. The Areopagus, a council of former magistrates that wielded jurisdiction over minor offenses and entertained suppliants who sought this boon, heard requests and arguments and passed judgment, issues arising at the third and fourth steps. Magistrates also performed the task of arresting suppliants who were wanted men, a task occurring after a trial. Besides enforcing the laws and making arrests, magistrates and staff were subject to penalties for misconduct.

Magistrates and priests, surely, enforced laws like those preventing murderers and others from entering shrines and supplicating there. Perhaps the most numerous

---

56. Instead of supplicating, the Ceans might have presented credentials (Poll. 8.95); for this and other standard practices, see Mosley, *Envoys*, chap. 15.

57. De Romilly, *Loi dans la pensée grecque*, 27, draws a somewhat different general conclusion: practices based on unwritten law filled gaps in the written law. Minimizing any help given to metics: scholars reviewed by Whitehead, *Athenian Metic*, 1–4. Arguing from considerations other than supplication, these scholars believed the status of metics to be low. Minimizing help for metics on a procedural ground, the use of *procheirotonia*, or voting without debate: Hansen, "*Procheirotonia*."

persons subject to these laws were runaway slaves. Suppose that a slave woman in Athens went to the Theseum, where slave refuge was customary. Once she arrived, a priest would receive her. But now suppose that she went instead to the shrine of Athena *Polias*. A human law, a *nomos* passed by the Assembly, would prevent her from even entering the shrine, let alone taking refuge.[58] This time the priests or magistrates would not receive but expel her.

Suppliants were also subject to the legal procedure of *endeixis*, which allowed citizens to point out trespassers to officials. At the start of *Oedipus at Colonus* the situation is this: Oedipus arrives in the Attic township of Colonus and stations himself in the grove of the Furies. He is supplicating, the traditional practice. But he has chosen a place that the community regards as off-limits, a matter of local if not written law. A passerby notices Oedipus, realizes that Oedipus is breaking the law, and considers expelling him. Oedipus says that he is supplicating, and the man stops short, telling Oedipus, "Well, until I report what you are doing, it is not my business to expel you without the community's say-so."[59] The word for "report," ἐνδείξω, is a legal term for a request to a board of magistrates, the Eleven, to authorize an arrest. When the orator Andocides returned to Athens, leapt atop the Council altar, and was expelled, a citizen used the very same word when he caught sight of Andocides in the Council chamber. Like the local man at Colonus, he appealed to the authorities, in this case, to the councilors. "I report this man to you," said the citizen, τοῦτον ἐνδεικνύω. Andocides responded by jumping on the Council altar but to no avail. The Council expelled him and put him in prison.[60]

As it happens, Andocides, who is the source for this event, does not expressly acknowledge the power of the citizen and magistrates to act against him. Instead, he says that he was taken into custody rather than executed. But Sophocles feels no compunction about expressly acknowledging the magistrates' power. His local man uses the word ἐξανιστάναι, "expel," which leaves no doubt.[61] Nor is there any doubt about the identity of the Sophoclean magistrates. They are the elders of Colonus and King Theseus, figures of an earlier era but nonetheless given the same power as the Eleven. A suppliant who acted improperly during the first step of a supplication and chose the wrong place found himself liable to a legal procedure. The citizen started the procedure, and the magistrates or their counterparts completed it.[62]

---

58. *IG* i³ 45.5–7, from 434–31 BCE, providing for a wall to keep slaves out, as noted by Chaniotis, "*Conflicting Authorities*," 72.

59. S. *OC* 47–48. Of the emendations reported in Kamerbeek and Jebb, all preserve ἐνδείξω in the sense of "report" except Schneidewin's ἐνδείξῃ τί δρῶ, "until (the city) shows me what to do."

60. And. 2.15, a case of *endeixis* missing from the list of Hansen, *Apagoge, Endeixis, and Ephegesis*, 11. The same response by the Council, but under the Thirty Tyrants and thus without *endeixis*: X. *HG* 2.3.52, noticed by Zelnick-Abramowitz, "Supplication and Request," 564.

61. For ἐξανιστάναι as a synonym of *apospaô*, see E. *And.* 263, 267, Arr. *An.* 5.1.4. Lloyd-Jones, *Sophocles*, translates it as "turn you out." For the procedure of *endeixis*, see Hansen, *Apagoge, Endeixis, and Ephegesis*, 9–24, arguing against the view of Lipsius, *Attische Recht*, 1.331, which was that the magistrate made the arrest.

62. Other eligible authorities: the priestly guild of the Eumolpidae, able to ban polluted suppliants from shrines according to R. Parker, *Athenian Religion*, 296.

Many more magistrates enforced other laws involving the first two steps in supplication. The surviving examples are laws for suppliants seeking purification and other temple regulations. As it happens, none of these laws come from Athens, but Athenian laws may have been similar.[63] The participating magistrates are shrine administrators with two responsibilities, one of which reflects the traditional practice and the other of which reflects the needs of the community. The first responsibility is a matter of the first two steps in any supplication at a shrine: the suppliants must know where to go and what to do. Magistrates (and once again priests) assist them. The second responsibility is a matter of public law and policy: officials must control the suppliants for the community's benefit. Suppliants must deal with authorized persons, pay fees, and refrain from conducting unauthorized business within marketplaces in shrines. For their part, magistrates and staff face penalties for improper conduct of their own.

Fourth- and third-century inscriptions from Cyrene and Lindos provide for suppliants seeking to be purified. The Cyrene inscription stresses the need to control the suppliants and the Lindos inscription stresses the need both to control them and to extract revenue. Both inscriptions incidentally show magistrates and others assisting suppliants and the Lindos inscription imposes penalties on misconduct by temple staff.

At Cyrene, the Assembly is regulating the reception of suppliant murderers. First the suppliant obtains an escort who helps purify him. The suppliant then proceeds to some unknown place and eventually presents himself to a local committee.[64] The relevant lines of the fourth-century law instruct the escort in his duties:

> The third type of suppliant is a murderer.[65] Escort him on his way to the [municipal] . . . and to the magistrates of the three tribes. When he announces that he has come, seat him on the threshold on a white fleece and

---

63. At Athens, we know only of priests who performed the purification of suppliants according to instructions in a book that one source calls the *Customs of the Eupatridae* (Ath. *Deip.* 9.410b).

64. 50–59 of side B [=132–41 of the entire law] as in Servais, "Suppliants," 117–18:

ἱκέσιος τρίτος, αὐτοφόνος· ἀφικετεύεν ἐς [ca. 4]
πολίαν καὶ τριφυλίαν. ὡς δέ κα καταγγήλε[ι ἱκέ-]
σθαι, ἵσταντα ἐπὶ τῷ ὠδῷ ἐπὶ νάκει, λευκ[ῶι νί-]
ζεν καὶ χρῖσαι, καὶ ἐξίμεν ἐς τὰν δαμοσί[αν]
ὁδὸν καὶ σιγῆν πάντας, ἦ κα ἔξοι ἔωντι, [εὐθὺ-]
[ς] ὑποδεκομένος τὸν προαγγελτε[ῖρα, καὶ. . .]
[. . .]ν παρίμεν τὸν ἀφικετευ[ό]μενο[ν. . . .]
[. . .]εων καὶ τος ἑπομένος [--------------------]
[..θ]υσεῖ θύη καὶ ἀλλ [----------------------]
[-------------] δὲ μὴ [--------------------------]

λευκ[ῶι νί]ζεν: Maas apud Servais, who reads λευκ[ιμονί]ζεν. Other supplements: Servais, 118–19, and *LSCG Supp.* #115.

65. αὐτοφόνος, which could also mean "kin-killer," but as R. Parker, *Miasma*, notes at 351, this meaning is rare in prose. "Killer with his own hand" differentiates a murderer from those who conspire to commit this crime but leave the performance of the deed to others. "Killer," a third possibility, would erase this distinction.

wash and anoint him. Let him go out on to the public road and let everyone keep silent while you and he are outside and let them obey the herald. . . . Let the man being escorted proceed . . . [rest fragmentary].[66]

In this tangle of events, purification must precede presentation to the committee, but how much else must precede it is unclear, as is the location of the threshold where the purification takes place.[67] Also unclear is the nature of the presentation. The committee might evaluate the suppliant, or it might certify the performance of the ritual of purification. If it evaluated the suppliant, it would either accept him and allow him to stay, or reject him and compel him to leave.[68] If the committee only certified the ritual, the result was less dramatic. Perhaps the suppliant proceeded to the Assembly and made some request. Then the supplication described in this paragraph would resemble the procedure in the Athenian Council. The difference between this procedure and the Council procedure would be that the Council heard the request that the suppliant later brought to the Assembly: dual evaluation. Here the committee would not hear the request and instead would certify the ritual. Whatever the procedure, the escort must still shepherd the suppliant through the first two steps. In this respect, the escort resembles the king of Argos in Aeschylus or Athenian councilors who present suppliants to the Assembly.[69] The complexities of the procedure do not eliminate these tasks.

On Lindos, the Assembly regulates the same kind of supplication. Once again the suppliant deals with an "escort" and heralds and obtains purification. The third-century decree on the subject differs from the Cyrenean law in providing for fines levied on "escorts" and on δεκόμενοι or "receivers" who presumably differ from escorts. There is no "committee," but the citizenry can bring charges against lawbreakers:

> If anyone breaks the law while escorting or receiving suppliants, let him pay a thousand drachmas to the goddess. If the priests or heralds give any instructions contrary to what has been decreed or do not purify suppliants according to regulations, let them be subject to the penalties of the law. . . . Let anyone that wishes to file a charge against them do so according to law."[70]

---

66. "Magistrates" of the three tribes: Servais, "Suppliants," ad loc., "on a white fleece": Wilamowitz, "Heilige Gesetze," ad loc. "You and he," i.e., the person obtaining the release and the suppliant: R. Parker, *Miasma*, 350.

67. Meeting place of the magistrates: Servais, "Suppliants," ad loc. Home of escort: Wilamowitz, "Heilige Gesetze," ad loc. Latte, "Sakrales Gesetz," 49, thought that a separate supplication was addressed to each of the three tribes.

68. Certification: Latte, "Sakrales Gesetz," loc cit., followed by R. Parker, *Miasma*, 350, and Traulsen, *Das sakrale Asyl*, 199. Ambiguous: Wilamowitz, "Heilige Gesetze," ad loc., defining ἀφικετεύεν, which I have translated as "escort," as "durch *hiketeia* losmachen." The Cyrene law also deals with two other kinds of "new arrivals," or ἱκέσιοι, one perhaps a ghost, and the other an initiate, as at R. Parker, *Miasma*, appendix 2, with refs. and Servais, "Suppliants," 113–16. For other possible "receivers," see appendix 5.

69. *IG* ii² 218.10–11, 337.14–17.

70. *SEG* XXXIX 729.

The provision for lawsuits by citizens against temple staff confirms that the source for laws like this is the Assembly, which expects that those who serve in it will take notice of any violation of regulations. The law under which the citizens will file charges is unstated; perhaps it was a law against *hierosulia*, the crime of despoiling temples. Similar provisions may have existed at Cyrene, too, and in any of the numerous cities that had purification regulations and likely had regulations for those suppliants who sought purification.[71]

Other shrines receiving suppliants also raised revenue, but from fees. At two healing shrines, Pergamum and Oropus, the temple charged an entry fee for every suppliant, and the priests at Epidaurus may have done the same.[72] All these healing shrines also imposed other charges on the suppliant.[73] Hence the orator Libanius called Asclepius "a lover of profit."[74] Why the interest in revenue, never a factor in acts of supplication not subject to municipal regulation? One answer is financial. Supplication at shrines could help defray the cost of running the shrine. Another answer flows from the character of the acts of supplication performed under these rules. At Cyrene, the escorts and even the local committee may not have evaluated suppliants. At Lindos, the temple staff may not have evaluated them, either. The personnel mentioned in these inscriptions may be confining themselves to the first two steps. If so, their stake in the procedure was small. Fines would ensure that they obeyed the law. Fees would have the same effect on suppliants.

Just as there is no Athenian evidence for the regulation of purification, there is none for the regulation of any marketplaces in shrines frequented by suppliants. Nor do any regulations of this sort antedate the Hellenistic period. They appear then as a result of the tendency for supplication to become a transaction. On the one hand, the attempt to raise revenue from supplication made it more likely that suppliants would lack the resources to provide for themselves and would attempt to earn money while in shrines. On the other hand, the absence of the evaluators would encourage suppliants to break any rules that forbade them to earn money.

The first change, raising revenue, did not prevent a shrine from providing for a suppliant paying only a brief visit, as at a temple of Aesculapius.[75] If the suppliant became a *hierodoulos*, as might have happened to the heroine in Achilles Tatius, the shrine would surely provide for him or her; if the suppliant was a notable, like

---

71. Given the popularity of purification regulations. Chaniotis, *"Conflicting Authorities,"* 74 n. 36, refers to the biggest collection of these regulations, Wächter, *Reinheitsvorschriften*, 118–23.

72. Cyrene: *LSCG Supp.* #115.b.41–44, money that Wilamowitz, "Heilige Gesetze," 170, thought was an entrance fee, as at healing shrines. Lindos: *SEG* XXXIX 729.4–7. Samos: Thür and Taeuber, "Prozessrechtlicher Kommentar," 209–12.14–15. Pergamum: Habicht, *Asclepieion* #161.8. Oropus: *LSCG Supp.* #35.4–6. Other charges: buying grain, wreaths, and wood, all sold at regulated prices (*LSCG Supp.* #22).

73. Not to mention the thank offering as at chap. 3 n. 51 above.

74. *Lib. Or.* 34.49. "Lover of profit": φιλοκερδῆ, with mythic parallel at Pl. *R.* 3.408b–c. The contrary view: *Lib. Or.* 34.24.

75. Paus. 2.27.6, 10.32.12.

Aelius Aristides, the shrine would once again provide.[76] The poet Alcaeus was no doubt such a person, although the only thing a fragment of his verse tells us about his reception in a shrine on Lesbos was that a beauty contest in honor of Hera enlivened his stay.[77] And, of course, the assembly might provide for a suppliant who went before it and won approval of some request.[78] Otherwise, though, the supplicandi would not provide for the suppliant, even in tragedy.[79] The reason was that the duty of the supplicandus was to evaluate. Hospitality did not precede acceptance. It followed acceptance. Until given this hospitality, suppliants must usually fend for themselves. The greater the cost of being a suppliant, thanks to fees, the more likely that they would need to earn money while in shrines.

The second change, the absence of the evaluators, gave the suppliants a head start. They would be dealing with priests, receivers, and the like. Unless the assembly promulgated regulations allowing these officials to control suppliants or control those who gave suppliants work, the suppliants would be at liberty. Even if the assembly did promulgate regulations, it might be reluctant to punish suppliants as opposed to other persons doing business in marketplaces. The reason for this reluctance was the same as before: the duty of the supplicandus was to evaluate. So the supplicandus would punish those who hired, helped, or even hid the suppliants, as the assemblies in Cyrene and Lindos did.

In a small shrine, these two changes might not matter. But in a big shrine like the Samian Heraeum, the needy suppliants were numerous, and so were the rules that they broke. When the Assembly responded with punitive regulations, it placed burdens on the temple staff who had to enforce these rules. By sometime in the second half of the third century BCE, the staff felt obliged to ask the Samian Assembly to revise them. The Assembly responded with a decree sometimes called "The Samian Shopkeepers' Law."[80] For the first time a supplicatory regulation shows some awareness of how suppliants in shrines lived: who they are, whom they see and why, how they survive. And for the first time a regulation gives the impression that some of its provisions may be dead letters.

The first topic in the law is how suppliants earn an income while staying in the shrine. Some suppliants are working for shops there, including unauthorized shops that are competing with authorized ones belonging to "the renters":

> Let no one rent more than one shop and let the shopkeepers reside there throughout the year. *No slave, soldier, jobless man or suppliant shall help the shopkeepers do business nor shall any shopkeepers except the renters do busi-*

---

76. Aristides spent two years at the Pergamine temple of Asclepius, where he relied on a social network including friends and ranking temple staff, as explored by Remus, "Voluntary Association."

77. *PLF* 130.31–33.

78. *IG* ii² 218, 276.

79. E. *HF* 51–53.

80. Habicht, "Hellenistische Inschriften" #9, Thür and Taeuber, "Prozessrechtlicher Kommentar."

ness in any form or fashion. The keeper of an unauthorized shop shall pay a fine of . . . drachmas to the renters.[81]

The rule of conduct that applies to suppliants appears in italics. The fine mentioned in the next sentence seems inadequate to the purpose of making suppliants obey this rule. The reason is that the fine falls on the unauthorized shopkeepers but not on the two other parties, "the renters" and the suppliants. "The renters" may apparently hire suppliants without being penalized.

Besides holding jobs, suppliants were leasing some of the authorized shops belonging to "the renters":

> *The renters shall not assign their shops to any jobless man or suppliant in any form or fashion.* (The renter) who makes an assignment to any of these persons shall pay a fine of . . . drachmas to the goddess. The temple officers and the treasurer of the temple moneys will levy the fine.[82]

Once again the rule of conduct precedes the fine, and the fine is likely to be inadequate. This time the reason is that the fine falls on the renters and not the suppliants.

The next issue addressed by the Assembly—suppliants in business for themselves—was the most serious of all, but the Assembly meets this issue with the usual remedy, a rule of conduct:

> *The renters shall not receive anything from a slave or suppliant or soldier or jobless man* nor sell any grain coming from the countryside[83] nor anything else on any pretext except when a landowner or a licensed grain dealer sells crops.[84]

In this instance, the rule of conduct once again falls upon the renters, not the suppliants, but no fine accompanies the rule. The suppliants go scot-free even as

---

81. Emphasis added to the translation of Thür and Taeuber, "Prozessrechtlicher Kommentar" l. 6–12, especially 9–11:

[οὔτε δοῦλος οὔτε σ]τρατιώτης οὔτε ἄπεργος οὔτε ἱκέτης ο[ὔτε ἀλ-]
[λος κάπηλος οὐδεὶ]ς τρόπωι οὐδὲ παρευρέσει οὐδεμιᾶι πλὴ[ν τῶν μι-]
[σθωσαμένων·

Other supplements: Thür and Taeuber loc. cit., with refs. at 206–9.

82. Thür and Taeuber, "Prozessrechtlicher Kommentar" l. 12–17, especially 12–14, which are emphasized:

οἱ δὲ μισθωσάμενοι οὐ παραδώσου[σιν τὰ κα-]
[πηλεῖα οὔτε ἀπέρ]γωι οὔτε ἱκέτηι τρόπωι οὐδὲ παρευρέσε[ι οὐδεμί-]
[αι.

83. Or "from the local people": Habicht, "Hellenistische Inschriften" ad loc.
84. Thür and Taeuber, "Prozessrechtlicher Kommentar" l. 17–21, especially 17–18, which are emphasized:
οἱ δὲ μισθωσάμε]νοι οὐχ ὑποδέξονται παρὰ δούλου οὐθὲν [οὐδὲ παρὰ]
[ἱκέτου οὐδὲ παρὰ σ]τρατιώτου οὐδὲ παρὰ ἀπέργου.

they play a role comparable to that of licensed grain dealers and of landowners who evidently have the right to sell crops to the shrine. The suppliants have accomplished a further social and economic ascent.

All the provisions so far point to the same question: why have the staff not expelled the suppliants who have helped cause these difficulties? The next and last proviso of the law reveals part of the answer. The shrine cannot locate some of the suppliants because these suppliants have gone into hiding in the shops of the renters. They are runaway slaves:

> The renters shall not receive into their shops any slaves who have taken refuge in the shrine nor shall they accept anything from them in any form or fashion. If any of the magistrates in office catch anyone doing anything forbidden by law, the party responsible will be liable to prosecution by the temple officers.[85]

As the law acknowledges, the slaves who have gone into hiding are paying or otherwise compensating the renters. This abuse—and no other—prompts the Assembly to break with its reliance on rules and fines and to introduce the alternative of prosecuting offenders.

The other part of the answer to this question lies in the purpose of the law. It seeks to control the shrine, and so the target is unauthorized shopkeepers, and sometimes also authorized ones. By the same token, the effect of the law is to levy fines and raise revenue, and sometimes to provide for prosecutions. Suppliants and their jobless companions are incidental. Yet the suppliants and their companions are indispensable to the abuses that the Assembly is combating. They provide the labor, some of the goods, and some of the management.

This oversight on the Assembly's part focuses attention on the temple staff. The Assembly has presented them the task of controlling shopkeepers while overlooking another group, employees and lessees. One tool given to the staff, levying fines, must have been more useful than the other tool, enforcing rules of conduct. These rules may have been dead letters. At best they were broken often enough to inspire the fines.

Perhaps the Samian Assembly required suppliants to register; some sanctuaries required all who entered to do so.[86] But even in isolation, this law shows the Assembly at work imposing rules, establishing fines, and providing for prosecutions. At the same time, it shows the Assembly deferring to the long-standing practice that made suppliants eligible for evaluation as opposed to either charity or punishment. Yet the Samian Assembly cannot help changing what it preserves. Just as Athens turns supplication into an occasion for dual evaluation, Samos turns

---

85. Thür and Taeuber, "Prozessrechtlicher Kommentar," l. 22–26.
86. E.g., the Amphiaraeum at Oropus (*IG* vii 235.39–44), noted by Sinn, "Sakrale Schutzzone," 91.

it into an occasion for commercial regulation.[87] Otherwise supplication would become not just a transaction, but a black market.

The Areopagus and the King Archon

Magistrates and other officials did not confine themselves to procedural business arising at the first two steps of supplication. In Athens, the former magistrates who comprised the Areopagus could impose fines for minor offenses.[88] If a person that they intended to fine appeared before them and supplicated, they would have to evaluate his plea and either accept it or reject it, and they would have to have their reasons. They would act as supplicandi, not as escorts, receivers, or the like. The Athenian Areopagus played this role in the pseudo-Demosthenic *Against Neaera*, in which Theogenes, the king archon, a leading magistrate, violated Athenian law by marrying a woman who was not an Athenian and a virgin. When the Areopagus learned of this act and proposed to fine him, he supplicated them, arguing that he had done this wrong in ignorance. He was, he said, "inexperienced." As an appeal to mitigating circumstances, this argument resembled the common excuse of involuntary wrongdoing.[89]

But supplication was not the only source for such an argument. The Athenian legal system supplied such arguments, too. Aristotle calls them arguments from *epieikeia*, "fairness." In the following passage from the *Rhetoric*, he describes *epieikeia* through several contrasts. In each of these contrasts, *epieikeia* differs from the text of the published laws or what Aristotle calls "the law as such" or "the lawgiver's wording":

> Fairness looks not to the law as such, but to the lawgiver, not to the lawgiver's wording but to his purpose, not to the deed but to the intention, not to the part but to the whole, not to what someone is now, but to what he has always or mostly been. And it remembers good turns rather than bad, and good turns done for oneself rather than good turns done for others.[90]

Epieikeia is a set of distinctions allowing for better interpretation of the law.[91] It prevents rigidity and narrowness. Although Aristotle says nothing about supplication, the similarity between *epieikeia* and supplicatory arguments is striking. My intentions are good, says Phemius. Recently I have sung for the suitors, he admits, but before that I sang elsewhere. Remember my good turns, Leodes says,

---

87. Another view of how shrines met the needs of suppliants: Sinn, "Sakrale Schutzzone," especially 83–97, holding that many suppliants made long sojourns in shrines but not giving legal particulars.

88. Arist. *Ath.* 8.4 with Wallace, *Areopagus Council*, 112.

89. Dem. 59.81–83. "Inexperience": ἀκακίαν.

90. Arist. *Rh.* 1.1374b.

91. A somewhat different view: Harris, "*Epieikeia*," stressing extenuating circumstances. Other views: Meyer-Laurin, *Gesetz und Billigkeit*, minimizing the role of *epieikeia* in Athenians courts, and Todd, *Athenian Law*, 54–55, in rebuttal.

and not my doing services for the suitors. Be fair to me. It is a suppliant's refrain, put under the rubric of *epieikeia*. A defendant who wishes to supplicate, as the king archon did, can make two arguments in one.[92]

Against Neaera reports that the Areopagus accepted the king archon's claim that he married in ignorance, took note of his "inexperience," and rescinded the fine. In effect, they looked "not to the deed" of the defendant but "to the intention"; by considering his "inexperience," they also looked "to what he had always or mostly been." In doing so, they did not depart from the practice in other courts. In *Against Midias*, Demosthenes says that defendants expect to benefit from *epieikeia*, while in the *Areopagiticus*, Isocrates says that defendants are receiving more *epieikeia* than they deserve.[93] The Areopagus was following precedent.[94]

Magistrates expelling suppliants from altars acted not only in conformity with other judges but at their behest. Because they did so, they were able not only to expel such suppliants but also to arrest them. This twofold action distinguishes legal expulsion from other expulsion. Other parties merely expelled suppliants. The Chians expelled Pactyes; the heralds of several tragedies try to expel those whom they pursue. Mnesilochus shows how much more Athenian magistrates did: besides being expelled, he is arrested and left in the custody of one of the Scythian archers serving as Athens's police force. With the twofold action come two distinct motives. Expelled because he is unworthy, the suppliant is also arrested because he is wanted for some crime. Mnesilochus is unworthy because he is spying on a women's festival and wanted for a crime that is truly just bad luck—his stealing a wineskin that a mother mistakes for her child.

In Lysias 13, magistrates expel and arrest another suppliant, a public slave named Agoratus who has been charged with treason. The expulsion and arrest occur at the shrine of Artemis in the Athenian port of Munychia. Unlike the expulsion and arrest of Mnesilochus, the action taken against Agoratus is a sham. The Thirty Tyrants have not yet seized power but are maturing their plans and have decided to use Agoratus as an informer who will ferret out opponents to their pro-Spartan foreign policy. They plan for the Council to issue a warrant for the arrest of Agoratus. After Agoratus takes sanctuary and calls on his friends for help, the magistrates will expel and arrest him. Once in custody, Agoratus will denounce those who answered his call for help. He and they will both go to jail but later, when the Thirty seize power, Agoratus will be freed, and his friends will not. On the one hand, Agoratus will take part in a legal proceeding. On the other, he will take part in an intrigue.

Now for action: the Council issues the warrant, Agoratus flees to the shrine in Munychia, calls for help, and his friends gather around him. Far from thinking that

---

92. A different view: Carey, *Nomos*, describing differences between courtroom *epieikeia* and Aristotle's conception.

93. Dem. 21.90, Isoc. 7.33–34.

94. Another example of petty jurisdiction ceded to others by the Assembly: Aeschin. 1.104, where the Council rules on a supplication by an indigent citizen seeking to be restored to the public dole.

the business is a sham, the friends urge Agoratus to leave the shrine. Some of them have just posted bail for him, so the source refers to these men as "sureties":

> They sat and argued about what should be done. The sureties and everyone else thought that they should send Agoratus away as soon as possible and after sending for two vessels they asked him to quit Athens, no matter how.[95]

If Agoratus remains at the shrine, expulsion and arrest are certain. Agoratus's friends make this point in a practical way: "The sureties argued they that if he were brought up before the Council he would be tortured."[96] When the magistrates arrive, Agoratus either is arrested and goes willingly or is arrested and expelled.[97] Since he has no choice, there is no practical difference. For there is no doubt about his fate: he must go. No one, even his friends, says that he cannot or should not.[98] Nor do we need to wonder whether this portrait of Agoratus, which comes from a prosecutor, is fair. Like Isocrates' portrait of the supplicating Plataeans, it need only be what a skillful orator—this time Lysias—believed the audience wished to hear. Like Mnesilochus, Agoratus is both wicked and guilty—wicked because he is an informer and guilty according to the warrant. Like Mnesilochus, he offends both the norms of supplication and the law. He deserves both expulsion and arrest.

If a magistrate were not available, a citizen might perform the same two tasks of expulsion and arrest. Here an example comes from Cyrene by way of Plautus's *The Rope*, in which the pimp Labrax finds himself headed for court after a citizen, Plesidippus, prevents him from performing an improper expulsion. The citizen pauses to explain his action: *Lex est apud nos*, "we have a law for such a situation."[99] Magistrates whom Plautus calls *recuperatores* then settle the dispute. *Recuperatores* defies translation, for the legal particulars are unknown, but the phases are clear: the suppliant is expelled, arrested, and brought before the authorities, the same as in Lysias 13 or Aristophanes. The difference between Greek and Roman legal procedures also informs this scene, but it does not obscure these phases, nor does the adaptation of a Greek original by Plautus obscure the usual combination of wickedness and guilt. The pimp's wickedness is proverbial, and his guilt has emerged from events taking place just before Plesidippus arrests him.[100]

95. Lys. 13.24.
96. Lys. 13.25.
97. "Went willingly" (Lys. 13.29): ἑκὼν ἀνέστη. "Expelled by force," Agoratus's claim: βίᾳ ἀποσπαθῆναι. "Went willingly" implies that Agoratus believed that he would receive protection from the magistrates. A similar view: Volonaki ad loc., not choosing between the alternatives. A different view: Bearzot ad loc. regarding the alleged expulsion of Agoratus as a "violazione sacrale."
98. Procedure: *apagôgê phonou*, as described in Dem. 23.80, according to MacDowell, *Law in Athens*, 120–21, or *apagôgê kakourgou*, according to Hansen, *Apagoge, Endeixis, and Ephegesis*, 101–2.
99. Expulsion performed: Pl. *Rud.* 664–76. Suppliants to the altar: 688. Offer of arbitration: 712–16. "Lex est apud nos": 724, a translation of the Greek of Diphilus, νόμιμον τοῦτ' ἐστι, βέλτιστε, ἐνθάδε (Diphilus PCG 31.1), but the passage in Diphilus does not concern supplication. For the *recuperatores*, see appendix 2.
100. The only possible evidence for another action that magistrates might take, dismissing a suppliant: appendix 4a.

Unlike Plesidippus, magistrates do not always act lawfully toward suppliants. Suborned as it is by the Thirty, the Council in Lysias 13 arguably does not act lawfully, and some magistrates in Plutarch plainly do not. These magistrates meet with condemnation—far more severe condemnation than the fines imposed on heralds and receivers in purification regulations.

Plutarch's magistrates appear in a version of the deaths of the Cylonian conspirators that differs from the better-known versions of Thucydides and Herodotus. These two authors present the conspirators' deaths as the result of a betrayal later punished by the infliction of pollution. But Herodotus, who says that the Cylonians were promised "liability" short of capital punishment, hints at some proceeding that they would undergo, and Plutarch guesses what the proceeding was.[101] The Megacles of this passage in Plutarch is Athens' chief magistrate: "Megacles the Archon persuaded the conspirators who took refuge in Athena's temple to come down and stand trial."[102] The evaluation of the suppliants now belongs to a court. Megacles' task, like that of Plesidippus or of the "receivers" in the inscriptions, is to escort the suppliants to an appointed place. But Megacles does not perform this task:

> The conspirators had tied a rope to the statue of the goddess and had gone down towards the tribunal while holding on to it. Then, when they came to the altar of the Furies, the rope broke of its own accord. Megacles and the other magistrates rushed to seize the conspirators.

Instead of giving escort, Megacles arrests the suppliants. Since some of them now go to the altar of the Furies, and he removes them from there, he also expels some of them. These acts lie outside his charge, which was to provide the suppliants access to a court.

Because this version adds a trial to the issue of betrayal, it ends with a trial as well as pollution. Some 50 years after the incident, Solon persuades the community to try the descendants of the archon before a select court of three hundred. Inherited guilt thus complicates the tardy punishment of the offending magistrate.[103] But this guilt does not obscure Plutarch's assumption about the role of magistrates: they are subordinate to the court. And Plutarch is right. In banning some persons from shrines, magistrates serve the Assembly; in collecting fees, levying fines, and controlling suppliants, they again serve the Assembly; in arresting wanted men, they serve the courts. If they or temple staff serve poorly at the first

---

101. "Liable": ὑπεγγύους (Hdt. 5.71). Trial: ἐπὶ δίκῃ (Plut. *Sol.* 12.1). Trial before the Areopagus: schol. Ar. *Eq.* 445.

102. An adaptation of Dryden's trans. of Plut. *Sol.* 12.1. The bibliography provided by R. Thomas, *Oral Tradition*, 272 n. 104, does not include treatment of supplicatory aspects. Three versions without the rope: Hdt. 5.71, Th. 1.126.3–127, Paus. 7.25.3. One with a rope: Aristodem. 104 *FGrH* fr. 1.197–99.

103. Plut. *Sol.* 12.2. We do not know whether the charge was *asebeia*; as it happens, no known case of supplication other than Phryne's involves this charge, nor do analyses of this charge in Rudhardt, "Délit d'impiété," or Cohen, "Prosecution of Impiety," include any discussion of violation of the rights of suppliants.

two steps, they pay fines. If they serve poorly in regard to arrests or expulsions, matters of the fourth step, they might well be put on trial.

If we look back to the Assembly and its dealings with suppliants, we will find another reason why Plutarch made the guess that he did. Megacles attacked the suppliants "on the grounds that the goddess had rejected the supplication."[104] The archon thus contrasted the goddess's judgment, which he thought decisive, with that of the court, which he thought superfluous. This contrast was erroneous. The Assembly does not put the gods at the head of the grant of honors to Dioscurides because the Athenians' opinion of the suppliant differs from the gods' opinion. Instead the gods endorse the Assembly's opinion. Nor do the assemblies of Cyrene and Lindos offer purifications to which the gods object. Instead they provide for the orderly and thrifty conduct of purifications of which the gods approve. Nor does the Samian Assembly expel those who have sought Hera's protection. Instead it fines and punishes other persons. Nor does any magistrate or citizen performing an expulsion arrest a man who is wanted for a crime yet who is pleasing to the god of the altar. Instead the informer or pimp is as hateful to the gods as to the city.

To return to the perspective of Ostwald and other scholars, the gods and the city do not hold differing views of proper conduct toward suppliants. Religious laws about supplication do not differ from other laws. If they did differ, Megacles might have prospered in his assumption that Athena's view of the Cylonians should prevail over the court's view. Instead, a curse descended on him, them, and their city. Through this curse, the goddess vindicated both the suppliants' right not to be betrayed and the court's duty to pass judgment. As we know from the *Eumenides*, Athena favored the courts. She created the Areopagus—a myth that encapsulates the Athenian attitude limned in this section.

Supplication and the Courts

As Chapters 2 and 3 have showed, suppliants both in and out of court argued for their own innocence. Common as it was, this argument was one of the chief reasons to call supplication quasilegal. But in an Athenian court, a suppliant did more than insist on his innocence, and the judges did more than evaluate him by this standard. For their part, suppliants might follow the example of the king archon and argue from *epieikeia*. This method of argument kept them from having to express remorse.[105] As for the judges, they looked to their oath, part of which enjoined them to consider only "the subject of the prosecution."[106] The effect of this instruction must have been to reinforce the avoidance of any expression of remorse. The one exception may have been a trial's second phase, when the court

---

104. ὡς τῆς θεοῦ τὴν ἱκεσίαν ἀπολεγομένης (Plut. *Sol.* 12.1).

105. Cairns, "Remorse and Reparation," 177–78, when noting that remorse or *suggnômê* is seldom mentioned in Attic courts; similar is Konstan, *Pity Transformed*, 43.

106. περὶ αὐτοῦ οὗ ἂν ἡ δίωξις ᾖ (Dem 24.151); so also 45.50 and Arist. *Ath.* 67 for private if not all suits. For the value of the oath, see Rhodes, "Keeping to the Point," rebutting any notion that it was a formality. The opposing view, deprecating the oath: Lipsius, *Attische Recht*, 3.918–19, and later scholars noticed by Rhodes.

considered what punishments to impose on those found guilty, and even here, we lack evidence that any suppliant failed to say that he was innocent.[107]

No less important was a part of the oath that enjoined the judges to render their verdict according to "the established laws."[108] These would evidently include the law under which the suppliant was charged, but they would also include the rest of the Athenian law code and also the wishes of the gods. The Athenians associated all these with supplication, and so suppliants being judged according to "the established laws" would meet with no approval if they attempted to contrast the one with the other. Least of all would they meet with approval if they asked the judges to acquit them because of some aspect of their supplications that did not conform to "established laws."

Aristotle, as it happens, did not accept this conflation of supplication and the "established laws." In one passage in the *Rhetoric*, he refers to supplication by describing appeals to pity and condemns such appeals as one of several distractions that defendants or prosecutors used to mislead judges: "Verbal attack and pity and anger and such emotions of the soul do not concern the facts but appeal to the judge." "It is unacceptable," he continues, "to warp the court by leading them into anger or envy or pity. That is the same as if someone made a ruler crooked before using it."[109] But this condemnation does not square with the organization of the *Rhetoric*, which contains a chapter telling defendants how to use this "crooked ruler." Anaximenes includes a similar chapter.[110] Nor does this condemnation address the relevant issue: supplication as a whole and its relation to the "established laws."

Another fourth-century source does address this issue, but to the opposite effect: supplication and the dictates of the law are mutually compatible. In *Against Leocrates* the speaker, Lycurgus, describes the expulsion and arrest of a suppliant, and he takes pains to say that this action has a rationale in Attic law and also the support of a god, Apollo:

> What old man does not remember and what young man has not heard of the fate of Callistratus, whom the community condemned to death? He fled and after learning from the god at Delphi that he would be treated according to the *nomoi* if he came back to Athens, returned and took refuge at the altar of the Twelve Gods. The community executed him nonetheless. And they were right.[111]

---

107. We do not know, for Socrates is the only defendant whose speech at this phase survives.

108. κατὰ τοὺς κειμένους νόμους (And 1.91; similar is Antipho 5.96).

109. Arist. *Rh.* 1.1354a.

110. Pleas for pity: Arist. *Rh.* 1.385b–6b, *Rh. Al.* 1445a, an inconsistency discussed by Barnes, *Companion to Aristotle*, 25–62. A defense of Aristotle: J. Cooper, *Reason and Emotion*, 392, implying that Aristotle, who objects only to "irrelevant" emotions, might regard pity as "relevant." Aristotle would thus be less modern than he seems—less similar, for example, to J. Moore, *Manual*, 4.04, explaining that appeals to pity must be divorced from considerations of guilt and innocence according to #403 of the Federal Rules of Evidence.

111. Lycurg. *in Leocr.* 93.

Since we are not told what happened, it is possible that Callistratus left the altar willingly, like the Cylonians. Perhaps he asked for a trial, though if he did, the Assembly may have cited the principle of *res iudicata* and rejected his request. Whatever he did, he had no choice but to leave the altar. The *nomoi*, the man-made laws, dictated his departure, and Apollo seconded this result.

Lycurgus makes the same point at the end of his speech, but allows an exception. As he asks the judges to envision supplication and the laws as cooperating with one another, his language is figurative, not to say fanciful:

> Athenian men, I want you to imagine that your country and its trees are begging you to help them, and its harbors and dockyards and city walls, too, and that the temples and shrines think that it is your duty to give this help. Remember the charges brought against Leocrates.[112]

But hearing the trees call for conviction does not suffice. The orator foresees that Leocrates will beg for help, too, and that he may persuade the judges to acquit him. Supplication and the law may not cooperate, and the consequences may be grievous. The orator describes these consequences by way of a warning to the judges:

> Make Leocrates an example to others: you do not value pity and tears more than the preservation of the laws and the people.

When Leocrates was acquitted, the begging trees notwithstanding, the orator would be ready to explain this verdict.[113] The judges had given too much weight to supplication. Their verdict formed an exception to the norm of cooperation.

Of the other prosecutors who supplicate, Dinarchus says little, but in undelivered his speech against Midias, Demosthenes says more.[114] Like Lycurgus, he worried that the defendant, whom he would accuse of committing outrages against the dignity of a religious festival, would supplicate successfully. He even predicted that Midias would present his children to the court and ask the court to acquit him for their sake. In response, Demosthenes sides with the law as opposed to the children:

> When Midias embraces his children and says that it is right for you to cast your vote on their behalf, you must realize that I am standing close by, embracing the laws and the oath that you swore and saying that it is right— pleading that it is right—for each of you to vote for them instead.[115]

---

112. Lycurg. *in Leocr.* 150.
113. Aeschin. 3.252.
114. Din. 1.17 without language of supplication; Demosthenes returns to the theme at 21.211. Johnstone, *Disputes and Democracy*, 61, notices these passages but regards them as undermining the judicial oath.
115. Dem. 21.188.

Demosthenes surely misrepresents what Midias would have done. Like other users of children, Midias would have said that he was innocent and pitiable.[116] But Demosthenes does not wish to allow Midias to make both an assertion of innocence and an appeal to pity. He wishes to deprive Midias of the assertion, and then, by turning the laws into children of a different sort, to make his own appeal to pity. He again resembles Lycurgus, who appeals for pity, too, but he invokes laws and not trees. He also differs by keeping pity and the laws together. That is his way of effecting the norm of cooperation.

Personifying "the laws" is not unusual, but personifying them by comparing them to children was perhaps inept. Elsewhere, the laws are compared to adults; Socrates calls them "parents."[117] By comparing them to children, not parents, Demosthenes may seem to demean them. Especially demeaning is any impression that the laws may weep rather than speak solemnly as they do to Socrates. But Demosthenes did not err in commingling supplication and the laws.[118] Nor did he err in bringing this overlap to the attention of the judges that were soon to render a verdict. Their oath bade them consider the law relevant to the charge and the laws as a whole. These "established laws" did not exclude supplication. Even prosecutors insisted that these laws included supplication.

Supplication and Self-Help

In a few instances, Athenian law allowed a citizen to receive suppliants who had been or might be convicted of a criminal offense. The most common instance was supplication addressed by some murderers to the relatives of the deceased. The person found guilty could approach them and supplicate, asking to remain in Attica, and the relatives could either say yes or let the law the law take its course. Then the guilty person had to leave Attica.[119] We lack examples of this situation, however, and in contrast we do have one example of another situation, the supplication of an adulterer caught in the act. The injured husband, Euphiletus, catches his wife *in flagrante delicto* with her lover, Eratosthenes, and deals with this seducer as harshly as the law allows, even though Eratosthenes supplicates.

After Euphiletus learns from one of his slaves of the affair between Eratosthenes and his wife, he interrogates the slave, who has served as a messenger for the adulterous couple. At first the slave denies everything.[120] When Euphiletus threatens to send her to work at the mill, she persists in her denials.[121] Then, when he reveals that he has full information, she panics, falling at his feet. As she confesses, she no doubt envisions the millstone that she will have to turn. But the

---

116. As at 99–100 above.

117. Pl. Cr. 51c. Other complementary personifications: *LSJ* s.v. νόμος, I.2.

118. A contrary view: Cohen, *Violence and Community*, chaps. 4–5, emphasizing social factors rather than ethical and legal ones and thus seeing no link between written law and supplication.

119. Schol. Dem. 23.72 discussed at 82 above.

120. Lys. 1.15–18.

121. Turning the millstone: Lys. 1.18. Somewhat different views: Carey ad 1.19, calling her resistance "a plausible detail," and Hunter, *Policing Athens*, 72, arguing that the information that she possesses makes her valuable to her master.

person reporting this incident, Euphiletus, envisions a contrast with the forthcoming supplication by Eratosthenes. The slave is asking to be spared after proving her loyalty to Euphiletus, but Eratosthenes will ask to be spared after proving his contempt for Euphiletus.

With the slave's help, Euphiletus lures Eratosthenes into his home and overpowers him. Eratosthenes tries to escape and reach a hearth, but Euphiletus ties his hands and restrains him, forestalling any supplication at this spot.[122] Eratosthenes responds by supplicating Euphiletus with the word *hiketeuô*.[123] Euphiletus now has three choices: arrest the suppliant and prosecute him later; kill or abuse him; or accept ransom.[124] By offering ransom, Eratosthenes shows which choice he wishes Euphiletus to make. Along with death, ransom happens to be an Homeric choice found in the *Iliad*.[125] In Athens, however, this choice and all the others come with the law's imprimatur. When Euphiletus chooses to kill Eratosthenes, he can say to him, "I will not put you to death. No, the law of the community shall put you to death—the law that you valued less than your own pleasure."[126] This response marks the lawful rejection of a suppliant.

This case does, however, present a complication. Eratosthenes' relatives charge that Euphiletus entrapped his victim, making Euphiletus's revenge a criminal act.[127] Supplication enters into this complication because Euphiletus needs to give the impression that he is incapable of entrapment, and his conduct as supplicandus does not give this impression. Rather than be accessible, attentive, and open to the possibility of either acceptance or rejection—the Greek and especially the Homeric norm—Euphiletus has been manipulative. Besides keeping Eratosthenes from reaching the altar, he ties his hands behind his back, preventing him from making any gestures.

As we have noticed, merely verbal supplications do not necessarily fail, and some circumstances render them preferable or unavoidable. But there is no other case in which a supplicandus binds a suppliant. Euphiletus even admits to this unusual act, saying his binding Eratosthenes made it impossible for the suppliant to reach the hearth.[128] The reason for this admission is to rebut the charge that Eratosthenes was killed there, an act of sacrilege. But the effect is to suggest that the supplicandus forbade a supplication. To refuse to allow the procedure to take place differs from saying no, and again is unprecedented.

None of this proves that Euphiletus entrapped Eratosthenes. But it undermines his case, and it presents yet another commingling of supplication and the law.

122. Lys. 1.25–27.

123. ἠντεβόλει δὲ καὶ ἱκέτευε (Lys. 1.25).

124. Kill: Dem. 23.53. Abuse: Ar. *Nu.* 1083 with schol., *Pl.* 168 with schol. Ransom: Dem. 59.65. A summary view: Carey ad Lys. 1.25–26.

125. See 81–82 above.

126. Lys. 1.26.

127. Though Euphiletus denies this at 1.28, his arguments at 1.37–42 confirm it, as noted by Carey ad loc.; so also Dem. 59.67, in which a man accused of *moicheia* says that the female's guardian knew about the affair. The contrary view: Scafuro, *Forensic Stage*, 331–32.

128. Lys. 1.27.

Supplication requires that the supplicandus be honest. This requirement makes betrayal the worst of offenses. In the same spirit, the law of Athens requires that the avenger not entrap his victim.

Regulating Supplication: A Summary

Who is the supplicandus? According to tradition, he was some powerful person or group. Under the law of Athens, he is often the Assembly. The Assembly heard the monthly supplications referred by the Council, and it wrote laws regulating supplication in shrines. The magistrates carried out the Assembly's wishes, and the large panels of judges in classical Athens came from the citizen body, as did the Assembly.

How, though, would the Assembly wield its power? Other supplicandi adopted a personal approach; as Gylippus tell us, a collective supplicandus would do so no less than an individual. The Syracusans ask whether the Athenians have wronged them; Agamemnon claims that each and every Trojan has wronged him and his brother. But the Assembly did not adopt this approach. Instead it wrote and consulted statutes and resolutions. It judged suppliants who came before it by laws like those affecting the Naucratites; it required their supplications be *ennomos*; and it rewarded some suppliants by means of resolutions. It wrote rules for magistrates to follow; outside Athens, complex temple regulations have survived. The Assembly wrote the laws that the courts consulted and that suppliants and prosecutors both cited. Athenian supplication at altars, which was the province of the Assembly and magistrates, and Athenian courtroom supplication, which was the province of magistrates and mainly courts, formed part of Athenian legislative and judicial procedure. Some of the rules that governed the quasilegal practice have become statutes, and the supplicandus has become a public body or an official.

This change did not diminish the role of the gods or of prevailing standards of judgment. Tradition remained strong—strong enough, for example, to make punishing suppliants rare. But this change did bring a measure of uniformity to supplication at public altars. No longer need suppliants wonder whether they would receive one kind of justice at one place and another kind at another, or one kind from one priest or magistrate and another kind from the next. They would receive the same kind. The result would sometimes still depend on individuals, but not always; sometimes the law would dictate the result. When the law did dictate the result, it would incorporate and reinforce principles derived from long-established practice.

The Athenian network of regulation gave opportunities to metics, public slaves, and stateless persons, but it imposed restrictions on criminals. Within the pale of lawful conduct, solidarity was strong, so conditions for supplicating were propitious; beyond the pale, hostility replaced solidarity, and so conditions were unpropitious. Regulation drew boundaries that the unworthy could not cross.[129]

---

129. A contrary view of the position of slaves: Patterson, *Slavery and Social Death*, 4–5, holding that slaves were powerless, but without noticing supplication.

SUPPLICATION AND
INTERCOMMUNAL RELATIONS

So far, we have considered the effect of the written law on altar supplication in one community, Athens, and glanced at several other communities, especially Samos. The suppliant might be a citizen, like the Samian priest, or an immigrant, like Dioscurides, or a refugee, like the Plataeans. In any event, the suppliant submits to the laws of the community and to the judgment of the supplicandi, be they an assembly, magistrates, or judges.

But in some instances suppliants find themselves subject to treaties and resolutions to which several communities are parties. These agreements may impinge upon the independence of these communities and, in particular, on their power to deal with suppliants. A community like Athens had full powers: it not only could accept or reject but also could incorporate a suppliant by making him a citizen or resident.[130] Other communities found that treaties or resolutions left them with partial powers: they could accept or reject, but they could not incorporate. Nor could they protect unincorporated suppliants once these suppliants left a shrine. This liability might affect a suppliant in a shrine controlled either by a federation or by a dependent community. Shrines aside, partial powers might manifest themselves on the battlefield, where they would affect a suppliant's chances of being spared. Partial powers might be a matter of long-standing tradition or (some suppliants claim) they might clash with the norms of the practice. They could be either unproblematic or problematic.

The Greek term for a community with partial powers, *autonomos*, is liable to misunderstanding. As Bickerman showed, a classical Greek community of this kind received "autonomy" by a treaty or a grant. Besides setting forth the powers held by the community, this agreement would set forth some power or powers that the community would lack. Under the Peace of Nicias, for example, Delphi was autonomous but lacked the power to make alliances.[131] Just this kind of autonomy—not autonomy in the sense of "self-government"—applies to intercommunal supplication. At a federal shrine, suppliants would discover that their place of refuge was autonomous but that it lacked the power to protect them unless they stayed inside. Outside the shrine, town magistrates could seize them. At a dependent shrine, suppliants would discover that their place of refuge was not autonomous and could not protect them from another kind of magistrate, those from Sparta. These magistrates could seize them either inside the shrine or outside it.[132]

---

130. In Aristotle's terms, the political system or *politeia* was *kyrios* with regard to the shrines as at *Pol.* 3.1278b κυρίας πάντων with other instances cited by Hansen, *Polis and City-State*, 176 n. 340. "Sovereignty" in this sense need not be the same as the "sovereignty" of a modern state; it confines itself to autonomy in the management of a community's internal affairs, or what Hansen, *Polis and City-State*, 76, calls "independence."

131. Th. 5.18.2 with Bickerman, *"Autonomia,"* 327–30, giving other examples. Bibliography: Hansen, *Polis and City-State*, 178–79 n. 378. Ostwald, *Isonomia*, 20, holds that *autonomia* might allow for some outside control of shrines, but does not mention supplication.

132. A different view: Raaflaub, *Entdeckung*, 199–200, followed by Hansen, *Polis and City-State*, 80, inspired by ancient definitions of "autonomy" as "having one's own laws," as Cic. *Att.* 6.2.4. A similar view: Stengl, *"Asylon,"* 1882.

Few of the treaties or resolutions that gave shrines partial powers have survived, but sometimes a treaty dealing with a similar subject allows for reconstruction. So do examples of supplication at federal and other shrines. Parital powers on the battlefield inspire a debate in Thucydides that is the second-longest piece of ancient supplicatory literature and that—unlike the longest, the *Plataean Oration*—presents a problematic case.

Federal Shrines

If a public shrine in Attica had a single master, the Athenian Assembly, a federal shrine like that at Delphi had several—the communities belonging to the federation, or amphictyony. The amphictyonic Council would play much of the Assembly's role of passing regulations and supervising staff. If not in session, it would assign the task of evaluating a suppliant to priests or others. But an amphictyonic Council faced a difficulty that the assembly of a single community did not. A federal shrine would be vulnerable to the pretensions of any single member of the Council, especially any member or members located nearby. And so the Council faced the perpetual challenge of protecting the shrine from the two closest neighbors, the region of Phocis and the town of Delphi.[133] Though no historically attested suppliants came to Delphi and found that Phocis or Delphi interfered with them, a case from Euripides shows the shrine and the priestess taking charge of a suppliant despite the wishes of local magistrates. The story of Demosthenes, who supplicated at the federal shrine of Calauria, echoes Euripides. Here, too, the shrine resisted the pretensions of a member of the federation.

Three "sacred wars" turned on the issue of how much those who came to Delphi would depend on the favor shown to them by Phocis and the town of Delphi.[134] The Peace of Nicias marked another episode in this history, one that Thucydides thought showed that both Phocis and Delphi would give way to a "traditional arrangement" in which the shrine would be "autonomous."[135] Thucydides implies that a previous treaty must have established this "traditional arrangement." Resolutions passed by the amphicytony also contributed to this arrangement. One resolution proclaimed that those guilty of despoiling Delphi ought to be regarded as polluted persons to be expelled from shrines anywhere in any member community.[136] Another resolution showed that the amphictyony could give orders to the Delphic magistrates whom it told to post a regulation about sacred herds. In an emergency, the herald of the amphictyony ordered the Delphians to take up arms to defend the shrine. Most important, the amphictyony gave Delphi and Phocis no privileges with respect to consulting the oracle, even though Delphi

---

133. Though when and how Delphi acquired a vote distinct from one of the two Phocian votes is controversial; see Sanchez, *Amphictionie*, 118–120.

134. The three wars: Sanchez, *Amphictionie*, chaps. 3.2.3, 4.5.2, 6.5, with scepticism regarding many details, but not the theme of conflict between the amphictyony and neighboring communities.

135. Th. 5.18.2. "Traditional arrangement": κατὰ τὰ πάτρια.

136. D.S. 16.60.1–3. Polluted: ἐναγεῖς. To be expelled: ἀγωγίμους. A resolution to the same effect by a member of the amphictyony: *IG* ix² 1.171.5–7 (Aetolian League).

provided most of the temple staff.[137] The amphictyony would not and could not control everything, but they would vindicate the shrine's autonomy by giving orders to local magistrates and restricting local privileges.[138]

This situation—autonomous shrine and nearby town, amphictyonic resolutions and local magistrates—informs the supplication at the end of Euripides' *Ion*. Convicted of attempted murder by a court in the town of Delphi, Creusa goes to the shrine and takes refuge from pursuing elders who, like the elders in Sophocles, act as magistrates. With Creusa's intended victim, Ion, as their guide, they come as far as the edge of the temple—and stop.[139] Ion now complains that Apollo will not allow the elders to enter and expel Creusa: "It's terrible that the god did not establish the law well or wisely. It shouldn't be right for the unjust to sit at an altar. It should be right to expel them."[140] In response to Ion's complaint, the prevailing view has held that *Kontaktmagie* does indeed allow the "unjust to sit at an altar."[141] But neither Ion nor the prevailing view is right. As against Ion, the town elders have no jurisdiction over the shrine. As against the prevailing view, the temple staff do have jurisdiction so long as the Council is not on the scene. The Pythian priestess exercises this jurisdiction, but after a "pause" in which (as Wilamowitz says): "We do not know how things can work out—the right preparation for the Pythia's intervention."[142] During this "pause," Ion and the elders must wait for the Pythia to respond. She then reveals information that induces Ion to pardon the would-be murderer—a procedure that may have existed under the law of Athens.[143]

An amphictyony of seven cities, including Athens and Sparta, ran the federal shrine at Calauria where Demosthenes supplicated.[144] He arrived after being condemned to death in Athens, where he consequently could not supplicate successfully. In Calauria, in contrast, he could supplicate successfully. As a federal shrine, Calauria would protect him against magistrates from any one member— in this case, from his own community. Demosthenes feared only another state that was not a member—Macedon. The Macedonian regent Antipater wished to capture Demosthenes and had induced the Athenians to condemn him.[145] Would he expel Demosthenes from Calauria? As Polybius says, Antipater did not scruple

137. Inscription: *SIG* 636. Arms: Aeschin. 3.122. Lack of privileges: Dem. 9.32.

138. Similar view: Lefèvre, *L'amphictionie Pyléo-Delphique*, 51, "l'Amphictionie paraît plutôt dominer."

139. E. *Ion* 1255–1613.

140. E. *Ion* 1312–14.

141. Owen ad 1261–81, Mikalson, *Honor Thy Gods*, 75–76, and especially Burnett, "Human Resistance," 99, holding that the play's outcome vindicates the seemingly unjust *nomos*.

142. Wilamowtiz ad loc.: "So ensteht eine Pause, wir ahnen nicht, wie es weiter gehen kann: die rechte Vorbereitung für den Zwischentritt der Pythia."

143. I.e., supplication made by a would-be murderer to the person attacked. The source for the comparable practice of supplication by an *akousios* murderer, schol. Dem. 23.72, is subject to scholarly dispute; see chap. 2, n. 320.

144. The others: Hermione, Aegina, Epidaurus, Argos (on behalf of Nauplia), Orchomenus. The Spartans acted on behalf of Prasieis (Str. 8.6.14).

145. Condemned: Plut. *Dem.* 28.2, X *Orat. Vitae* 846e–f. A second possible instance of supplication by Demosthenes at Calauria: Paus. 1.8.2.

at expelling suppliants from other places. Two of these places, Hermione and Aegina, even belonged to the federation that controlled the shrine at Calauria.[146]

Antipater's course of action was both surprising and shrewd. He ostentatiously refused to expel Demosthenes. Instead, Antipater's lieutenant, Archias, negotiated with the orator, who proved uncooperative. To give the impression that he was about to be seized by the Macedonians, Demosthenes killed himself. But the Macedonians had no such wish. They even let the dying Demosthenes leave the shrine by himself. Thanks to their discretion, Demosthenes died without pollution and without any violation of the shrine.

The prevailing view would explain the Macdeonians' scruples by saying that a suppliant who made contact with the altar of a prestigious shrine received more protection than a suppliant who made contact with the altar of a less prestigious shrine. *Kontaktmagie* came in large or small doses, and Calauria administered a large dose.[147] But this view does not reckon with the choices made by Antipater and Demosthenes. Antipater spared a shrine controlled by seven communities as opposed to one: a political calculation. Whether or not a federal shrine was holier, he found it more prestigious. Demosthenes fled to a shrine controlled by seven communities as opposed to one: a legal calculation. The federal shrine, Demosthenes knew, would bar Attic magistrates, whereas the shrines in Attica would not. Antipater realized that Calauria was federal, and Demosthenes realized that it was autonomous.[148]

Calauria has left behind no written records. But the considerable record left by Delphi show how a federal shrine practiced an "autonomy" that Euripides retrojected to the Heroic Age. Autonomy began with a treaty, continued with several kinds of resolutions, and culminated in a division of responsibilities. Ion did not realize that his mother's case belonged to the Pythia rather than the elders. Antipater realized that Demosthenes' case belonged to Calauria.

Spartan Extraterritorial Rights

In Arcadia, a part of an alliance led by Sparta, and also in Taenarus, a dependent community in the Spartan homeland, more "autonomous" shrines provided refuge for suppliants. They derived their status from treaties like the Peace of Nicias. Though we cannot cite these treaties, we can reconstruct them from other treaties that have survived. We can also survey a half-dozen examples of the sort of supplication that these treaties allowed: in Arcadia, safe haven for Spartan refugees who stayed within the limits of a shrine; in Taenarus, a failure to provide safe haven.

Whenever and on whatever terms the Spartan Alliance began, by the start of the fifth century, when evidence for supplication in Arcadia appears, each mem-

---

146. Plb. 9.29.4. Demosthenes' supplication: Plut. *Dem.* 28.3–30.1.

147. Schumacher, "Sanctuaries of Poseidon," 76, though he does not cite Nilsson or Gould in explaining the incident. Caillemer, "*Asylia*," is perhaps the first scholar to draw this distinction, which appears in Paus. 3.5.6.

148. A sketchy incident at Paus. 7.24.6 may confirm the pattern: the people of the town of Helice apparently expel suppliants in 373 BCE only to suffer an earthquake caused by Poseidon. "Expel": ἀποστήσασιν ἐκ τοῦ ἱεροῦ, a term not used of expulsion elsewhere. Or the correct translation may be "betray" rather than "expel." The date: Str. 8.7.2.

ber of the alliance had made a treaty with Sparta. These treaties provided for "autonomy."[149] By the late fifth century, if not earlier, these treaties also provided that a member of the alliance could defy an alliance decision when "something to do with the gods or the heroes forbade it." This language would allow any member of the alliance to defy a decision that would threaten its shrines. Since the expulsion of suppliants by outsiders would be just such threat, this language implies that suppliants inside shrines would be safe.[150]

What about suppliants outside shrines? A treaty between Sparta and the Arcadian city of Tegea limited Tegea's freedom in dealing with Messenian fugitives who were evidently Helots. If these Helots fled to Tegea, Tegea was obliged to "expel the Messenians from the country and not make them citizens."[151] A treaty between Sparta and another community also dealt with fugitives, this time wrongdoers. Because the bronze plaque recording the treaty is fragmentary, we cannot identify this city, but the treaty does refer to "fugitives who have participated" in some act that has led to their taking flight, and it surely deals with refusing them help.[152] These two treaties suggest that a Spartan fugitive would not be safe in the territory of an ally. Taken together with the treaties already noticed, these treaties suggest that Spartan fugitives who supplicated would be safe in a shrine but not elsewhere.[153] These fugitive could gain protection as long as they had "something to do with the gods and heroes," in other words, as long as they stayed on holy ground, but like the Messenians of the Tegean treaty, they could not get other help. They could not, for example, become residents or citizens.

The treatment of suppliants at the shrine of Athena Alea at Tegea follows this pattern. Several prominent suppliants come here: Chrysis, a priestess of Hera at Argos, and the Spartan kings Leotychidas II and Pausanias.[154] The Argives held Chrysis responsible for the burning of the temple of Hera. The Spartans found Leotychidas guilty of accepting bribes; Herodotus says he was tried *in absentia* after he had fled Sparta, and another source, the author Pausanias, says that he was tried in person and fled once he was convicted.[155] The Spartan king Pausanias fled before trial on a capital charge. When all of these suppliants reached the shrine, they remained inside it. Chrysis and Leotychidas "sat" there, and King Pausanias remained within the *temenos*, or close. One statement shows that the

149. Th. 5.77.5, 79.1; Wickert, *Peloponnesische Bund*, 12.

150. Th. 5.30.1; similar is 5.30.3.

151. Arist. fr. 592 Rose = Plut. QG 292b (with QR 277b): Μεσσηνίους ἐκβαλεῖν ἐκ τῆς χώρας καὶ μὴ ἐξεῖναι χρηστούς ποιεῖν. "Citizens": Jacoby, "Chrestous Poiein." Date of the treaty: ca. 550 BCE, according to Wickert, *Peloponnesische Bund*, 12, with refs.

152. *Nomima* #1.55.13–14, dating from 500–475 BCE, according to Peek, "Staatsvertrag," but perhaps from as early as 550, according to Cartledge, *Sparta*, 178–79. The other signatory: perhaps the Erchadians mentioned at lines 17 and 22. Peek, "Staatsvertrag," 7–9, supplemented the relevant lines as follows: φεύγον[τας μὲ δεκέσθο] / ἄν κεκοιναvεκ[ότας ἄδικε---], "do not receive fugitives who have participated in (such?) crimes."

153. Another view: Cartledge, *Agesilaos*, 13, holding that the treaty provision that an alliance member "have the same friends and enemies as the Spartans" (as at *Nomima* #1.55.7–10 and X. HG 2.2.20) required alliance members to return fugitive Helots regardless of the circumstances in which the Helots entered a member's territory.

154. Chrysis: Paus. 3.5.6. Leotychidas: Paus. 3.7.10. King Pausanias: Paus. 3.5.6, Plut. *Lys.* 30.1.

155. Chrysis: Paus. 2.17.7. Leotychidas: Hdt. 6.72 vs. Paus. 3.7.10.

Spartans could have asked that the Tegeans surrender the two royal suppliants but knew that the Tegeans were not obliged to. The Spartans, it says, "did not even make a request" that the Tegeans surrender them.[156] Yet they could have made this request, and the Tegeans could have honored it. The Spartans chose not to make it because they reckoned that the Tegeans would not grant it. They knew Tegean past practice.

All this is familiar. Yet Tegea differs because the suppliants must stay in the *temenos* to be safe. Other suppliants, we should remember, were safe anywhere within the community that accepted them. Tragedy provides an example: in Sophocles, when Oedipus and his two daughters come to Colonus and Theseus accepts them, the Athenians protect them even when they leave the shrine. So, when Ismene leaves the shrine to fetch libations and Creon's men kidnap her, the Athenians come to her rescue. Nor is their response merely a courtesy to a guest. As Oedipus says to the chorus, they would betray their pledge if they did not rescue his daughter.[157] The Athenians have integrated Oedipus and his daughters into their community and must defend them.[158] This integration is the element missing in Tegea. The difference stems from one or more treaties. These treaties make Tegea dependent on Sparta. No such agreement ever made Athens dependent on Thebes.

The prevailing view would look at these three cases as instances of *Kontakt-magie*. Outside the shrine, the suppliant is at risk; inside, he or she is safe. But the Tegeans' freedom to reject and expel belies this view. They enjoy autonomy and, with it, a measure of power. Yet their autonomy does not let them incorporate a suppliant wanted by the Spartan authorities. As Bickerman observed, autonomy of this kind falls short of independence.[159]

Spartan kings did not always flee to Tegea. Another Arcadian community at Lycosura or Parrhasia (two adjacent places in the mountains to the west of Tegea) also received a Spartan ruler. Pausanias says that Lycosura and the shrine of Zeus at nearby Mt. Lycaon were founded at the same time and that Lycosura, the oldest settlement in Arcadia, was the first Arcadian capital; Homer, Pindar, and Thucydides mention Parrhasia and not Lycosura.[160] Parrhasia, Thucydides also says, enjoyed an "autonomy" granted to it by the Spartans.[161] Wherever this shrine was, it was modest—so modest that it lacked a temple though not a treasury. Yet

---

156. Paus. 3.5.6, speaking of the Spartans: καθεζομένους ἐνταῦθα ἱκέτας οὐδὲ ἀρχὴν ἐξαιτῆσαι θελήσαντες.

157. Ismene: S. *OC* 1171–88. Pledge: 822–23.

158. As at chap. 3 n. 89 above.

159. Cf. Hdt. 9.37, in which Hegisistratus flees from Sparta to Tegea because the two communities were not "friendly" at the time. As Wickert, *Peloponnesische Bund*, 54, notes, "friendly" or ἄρθμιος need not mean "allied," so the treaty between Sparta and Tegea might still be in effect. If so, this refugee wanted more than what the treaty provided, namely, to be safe throughout Tegea, and under the circumstances was able to satisfy his wish. Herodotus, at any rate, does not say that Hegesistratus went to the shrine, let alone that he confined himself to it.

160. Paus. 8.2.1 vs. *Il* 2.608, Pi. *Ol.* 9.95, Th. 5.33. Other passages in the same sense: Jost, *Arcadie*, 183–85, 267–68. Later Megalopolis controlled the shrine, as shown by *IG* v.2 444.12, a Megalopolitan inscription of the second century BCE. According to Sinn, "Sakrale Schutzzone," 85–89, the word *hiketeia* in this line refers to the boundary of the sanctuary of Zeus *Lykaios*.

161. Th. 5.33.3.

it fits the pattern of a tie to Sparta, a place of refuge, and "autonomy."[162] To this place came the Spartan king Plistoanax in 445 BCE. A Spartan court had tried and convicted him on a charge of taking bribes from Athens. Though no source calls him an *hiketês*, a remark of Thucydides, the main source, shows that his status did not differ from that of the kings who fled to Tegea. Out of "fear of the Spartans," he confined himself to the shrine.[163] For lack of a temple, he lived in a house that was half inside the shrine and half outside. One source, Ephorus, says that Plistoanax went to these lengths because the Spartans had fined him.[164] They more likely had condemned him to death.[165] Whatever the punishment, he timed his flight well. In 445 BCE, Parrhasia was a Spartan ally, so the shrine must have operated like the shrine of Athena Alea in Tegea. Sometime after the start of the Peloponnesian War in 434 BCE, the Arcadian city of Mantinea subdued Parrhasia and perhaps deprived it of autonomy. In 421 BCE the Spartans restored (or confirmed) this autonomy.[166]

In contrast, the port town of Taenarus could not stop Spartan magistrates at the shrine entrance. Unlike Tegea and Mt. Lycaon, it did not benefit from a relevant treaty. It was a polis, a community, and its citizens were free persons living in the vicinity of Sparta, *perioikoi*, but the Spartans did not recognize that it was autonomous in regard to suppliants.[167] So, although it received many more suppliants—from the Spartan king Cleombrotus to a henchman of the Spartan regent Pausanias to Spartan convicts and Helots—it did less to protect them.[168]

The defenselessness of Taenarus emerges from the treatment of a Spartan king, Cleombrotus. When he and his fellow king Agis failed to achieve their program of social reforms, they followed the examples of Leotychidas, Pausanias, and Plistoanax and supplicated. Agis went to the Brazen House, where his enemies blockaded him, and Cleombrotus to Taenarus.[169] Led by the ephor Leonidas, Cleombrotus's enemies pursued him and burst into the shrine. But for an act of supplication by Cleombrotus's wife to Leonidas, her father, they would have arrested him. Thanks to her intercession, Leonidas allowed Cleombrotus to go into exile by sea.[170] The Spartans treat Taenarus not as though it were Tegea but as though it were a shrine of their own.

162. No temple: Kourouniotis, *AEph* 21, 162–70. Treasury: schol. D.P. 415.
163. Th. 5.16.3. "Fear": φόβῳ τῶν Λακεδαιμονίων.
164. Ephor. 70 *FGrH* fr. 193.
165. Th. 5.16.3, also 2.21.1; and Plut. *Per*. 22.3. Death: de Ste. Croix, *Class Struggle*, 198.
166. Conquest by Mantineia: Th. 4.134, 5.33. The guarantee given before the Peloponnesian War: 5.31.5, where the Eleans refer to it as noticed by Busolt, *Griechische Geschichte*, 3.857 n. 2.
167. Taenarus as a polis: *h. Ap.* 410–13, Pherecyd. 3 *FGrH* fr. 39, Plut. *Ser. Num. Vind.* 560e. Adjacent Psamathus was also a polis (Str. 8.5.2). For the status of such poleis, see Cartledge, rev. of *Polis as An Urban Centre*, reviewing earlier literature but with no evidence to report on the control of shrines. Evidence for the position of the *perioikoi* in the Spartan legal system is scanty; MacDowell, *Spartan Law*, 10–11, discusses it without reference to shrines.
168. Cleombrotus: Plut. *Agis* 16.3. Henchman: Th. 1.133.1. Convicts: Paus. 4.24.5–6. Helots: Th. 1.128.1.
169. Presumably not at the shrine of Taenarian Poseidon in Sparta (Paus. 3.12.5). In the view of Caillemer, "*Asylia*," 510, supplication by a king at Taenarus is aberrant, as this sanctuary was mostly used by Helots.
170. Plut. *Agis* 17.1–18.2. Kahrstadt, *Staatsrecht*, 1.14 n. 1, notes the difference between the treatment given to suppliants at the Brazen House and the treatment given to those at Taenarus. Although located in Sparta, the Brazen House gave kings and regents protection against arrest by Spartan magistrates. No source explains why the Brazen House resembled shrines elsewhere, but the reason may be the position held by the suppliants.

The same holds true of an episode in which Spartan ephors do not burst in on the suppliant to arrest him. This episode involves a less well known stage in the career of Pausanias the regent, who supplicated unsuccessfully to Zeus *Phyxios* and later was starved out of the Brazen House. Suspecting him of treason, the ephors laid a trap for him at Taenarus. After gaining the help of Argilius, one of Pausanias's henchmen, they told this man to meet the regent in the shrine. There they made arrangements to eavesdrop:

> When this man went to Taenarus as a suppliant, he built a shelter divided in two by a partition and hid some of the ephors inside. When Pausanias came to him and asked him why he was taking refuge, the ephors clearly heard the whole conversation.

The "conversation" was that Pausanias had asked the man to take a message to the court of the Persian king. The man had agreed—evidence of treason on the part of Pausanias. Pausanias also persuaded the man to carry out this mission—more evidence of treason.[171] Just as the ephors can make arrests at Taenarus, they can also make investigations. The shrine is virtually theirs.

In two other cases at Taenarus, the Spartan magistrates err through abuse of power. In Thucydides, they make a promise to Helot suppliants sometime in the 460s BCE and betray them. We can now notice the special feature of this act of betrayal, which otherwise might seem unremarkable: it occurs in a shrine lacking autonomy.[172] The other case points to a feature of Taenarus that emerges from the treatment of Cleombrotus. Though overtaken, he was allowed to flee overseas. The chance to flee overseas was what made the otherwise defenseless shrine of Taenarus attractive to suppliants, among them some convicts. When Spartan magistrates burst in on them after they had escaped to Taenarus, they must have been waiting for a ship. The Spartans killed them and angered Poseidon, but for a reason different from that in the case of betrayal. This time the god punished them for interfering with suppliants who—far from expecting a promise—expected only the chance to keep running.[173] Taenarus, then, was not useless to a suppliant seeking protection. It was less useful than a shrine in a community protected by a treaty. Just as Tegea was less useful than a shrine in Attica, Taenarus was less useful than Tegea.[174]

Escape by sea points to a feature shared by Taenarus and Arcadian shrines: they are way stations. Arcadian shrines are way stations where an exiled king can wait on events. King Pausanias, for one, lived at Tegea for the rest of his life.

---

171. An adaptation of Hobbes's rendering of Th. 1.133.1. So also Aristodem. 104 *FGrH* fr. 1.8.1–3.

172. Th. 1.128.1. So also Nep. *Paus.* 4.5.

173. Paus. 4.24.5–6. Language of betrayal, e.g., *anistēmi*, is missing from this passage. The term for the expulsion: ἀποσπάσασα.

174. Doubting Taenarus's status as a place of refuge: Rigsby, *Asylia*, 93. Affirming it: Schumacher, "Sanctuaries of Poseidon," 74. Implicitly affirming it: Cartledge, *Sparta*, 178–79, suggesting that Laconian *perioikoi* made treaties with Sparta, though no such treaty is sure to have survived.

Plistoanax stayed at Mt. Lycaon for 19 years and then returned to the throne, turning his exile into a long term out of office. Both men needed to be out of Sparta yet near to it, independent yet protected by treaties. Taenarus was a way station of a different kind. As figure 4.1 shows, it juts out to sea like a dock.[175] Ships put in from both Italy and eastern points, and touched land only yards away from the temple.[176] A mile away was the large port of Psamathus, used by mercenaries.[177] Taenarus was for short stays, just as Arcadia was for long ones.

A way station need not be enormous. Plistoanax lived in a house. At 16 by 19 meters, the temple at Taenarus was probably even smaller.[178] The unyielding,

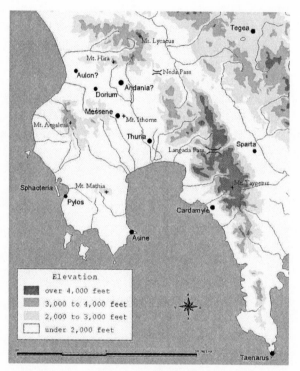

FIGURE 4.1   Southwestern Peloponnesus including shrines. Courtesy of Pusey Library, Harvard University.

175. Fig. 4.1 is a map drawn by Martin von Wyss, cartographer at the Pusey Library at Harvard. If Mt. Hira is Homeric Hire, as thought by Niese, *Geschichte*, 124 and Valmin, *Études*, 181, it should be located at MME #545, several miles to the north of the site indicated on this map. Aulon: as at MME #601. Andania: as at MME #607, but Valmin 55 thought it was eight miles east by northeast, at MME #609.

176. Cleomenes' mother leaves for Egypt via Taenarus (Plut. *Cl.* 22.5–7), and so do Harpalus (D.S. 17.108.4) and Mark Antony (Plut. *Ant.* 67.6)

177. Modern Porto Kayio: D.S. 17.108.7, 17.111.1, noted by Schumacher, "Sanctuaries of Poseidon," 72. References to thousands of mercenaries at Taenarus can only refer to this larger port.

178. Temple close to the beach, and only 16 by 19: Frazer ad 3.25.4, based on Bursian, "Taenaron," 778, and confirmed by Woodward, *ABSA* 13, 249–52, and Waterhouse and Simpson, *ABSA* 56, 123–24.

rocky cliffs nearby leave room for only a few other structures.[179] Nor need a way station be inviting. The larger part of the *temenos* at Mt. Lykaon was taboo,

> off-limits to human beings. If anyone ignores the law and enters, he must surely die within a year. And it is said that anything found within the shrine, whether man or beast, does not cast a shadow. So, when an animal takes refuge there, the hunter declines to pursue it. He remains outside.[180]

As for Taenarus, it was an entrance to the underworld, used by Heracles on his way to retrieve Cerberus.[181] But the grimness of these way stations was not merely picturesque. The local authorities would not want these way stations to be accessible to the Spartans, and neither would the suppliants. These wishes combined to yield remote, forbidding locales—prisons that protected the prisoner from outsiders.

Arcadia and Taenarus illustrate two degrees of dependency on Sparta, one established by a treaty and the other by force or tradition. Treaties gave jurisdiction mostly to the local community, spelling less dependency, and force or tradition gave jurisdiction mostly to Sparta, spelling more dependency. Jurisdiction, in turn, reflected political and military factors. Arcadia was a Spartan ally, Taenarus a part of the Spartan homeland. Change the political and military factors, eliminating Spartan dominance, and several communities would share jurisdiction, as at federal shrines. In any event, the issue of jurisdiction remained more complicated than in classical Athens. In Athens, jurisdiction belonged to the Assembly. In the Peloponnesus, it belonged to several parties, some of them distant. "Autonomy," a term covering most of these possibilities, varied from place to place.[182]

An Anomalous Shrine

The earthquake with which Poseidon punished the overzealous Spartan magistrates provided the Helots of Messenia and some Messenian *perioikoi* with a chance to revolt.[183] Fighting broke out sometime in the 460s BCE.[184] Within a few years, thousands of soldiers and their families took refuge at the shrine of Zeus

---

179. Houses cut from the rock: Bursian, "Taenaron," 778, again confirmed by Woodward, op. cit. and Waterhouse and Simpson, op. cit. Houses perhaps used by suppliants: Schumacher, "Sanctuaries of Poseidon," 73. Fortification since the time of the Homeric Hymns: *h. Ap.* 411, calling Taenarus a πτολίεθρον.

180. Paus. 8.38.6. For the loss of the shadow as a sign of imminent death, see Frazer ad 8.38.6. Confirming the taboo: Plut. *QG* 300c.

181. Heracles' descent: Paus. 3.25.5, Str. 8.5.1, and Mela 2.3.49.

182. A similar view: R. Parker, "Spartan Religion," showing local variation in Spartan territory.

183. *Perioikoi* among the rebels, and hence among the suppliants: Th. 1.101.2–3, mentioning Aethaea (location unknown, but see MME, 86 n. 41, and 94 n. 95) and Thuria (MME #534). Shipley, "The Other Lakedaimonians," 190, lists two more Messenian *poleis* that are attested in classical sources, may have been Perioecic, and may have participated in the supplication: Asine on the coast of the Gulf of Messenia (numerous sources, MME #512), and Aulon, perhaps near the border with Elis (X. *HG* 3.3.8, perhaps MME #601). Another Perioecic settlement, Cardamyle near the Laconian border (Hdt. 8.73.2, MME #147), may have been Messenian in the classical Period; later it was Laconian.

184. Starting point: sometime after 465 BCE according to D. Reece, "Date"; after 467, according to Gomme ad Th. 1.89–118.2; in 469–68 according to Badian, *From Plataea to Potidaea*, 100.

on Mount Ithome in central Messenia (figure 4.1).[185] They commenced the largest supplication in ancient history.

Unlike other armed suppliants, the Messenians did not go to a shrine after being
defeated, and so they did not appeal to the shrine for help.[186] Instead they went
to a shrine to defend themselves, and used it as a redoubt. In this situation, who
were the supplicandi? There would seem to be two answers: either the Spartans
who had come to suppress the rebellion or the people of Messenia. If the Spartans were in control, they would evaluate, condemn, and expel the rebels without
consulting people of Messenia. For their part, the people would have no standing. If the people were in control, they would protect the rebels without consulting the Spartans. This time the Spartans would have no standing. Spartan control
implied a subjugated Messenia, and Messenian control implied a free Messenia—
and the liberation of the Helots.[187] Yet different as these two answers are, they
suffer from the same drawback: they assume that the rebellion would end in complete victory for one side or the other. Either the Spartans would win and expel
the rebels, or the rebels would win and liberate the Messenians. In the event,
neither side won such a victory. Instead the Spartans consulted the Delphic oracle,
who mediated between the parties. Through the oracle, the suppliants obtained a
kind of autonomy.

This was not the first time Messenians had gathered at Ithome in large numbers: according to Pausanias, Messenians withdrew to Ithome during their first
war with Sparta, said to have occurred in the eighth century BCE; according to
Tyrtaeus as well as Pausanias, they made a stand near it in the second, said to
have occurred in the middle of the seventh.[188] The fighting lasted for years, each
winter witnessing a Spartan withdrawal to the east and each spring a new invasion.[189] Only when the Spartans found they could not defeat the rebellion did
they turn to the oracle. She told them what the Messenians may have told them
before: the Spartans were dealing with suppliants. The oracle advised the Spartans to "Release the suppliant of Zeus *Ithometes*."[190]

Taking "release" to mean "expel," the Spartans compelled the rebels to march
away under truce to Naupactus, outside Messenia.[191] Expulsion of the Messenians
established the Spartans as the supplicandi, and the truce marked a characteris-

---

185. Using Paus. 4.26.2, which is about the situation of the Messenians some 60 years later, and D.S. 14.32.2,
Kiechle, *Messenische Studien*, 85, estimated the number eventually evacuated at fifteen thousand to twenty thousand including women and children; how many more took refuge is impossible to estimate.

186. As at Hdt. 6.80, where Cleomenes burns supplicating Argive troops; and Th. 4.98–100, where defeated
Athenian troops supplicate as at 94 above. Similar to the Messenian situation: Polyaen. 5.5.1, where the suppliants are disarmed.

187. Liberation from "serfdom": Jones, *Sparta*, 10. From slavery: Paus. 3.20.6. From a position in between:
Lotze, *Metaxy eleytheron kai doylon*, 78, following Str. 8.5.4, Poll. 3.83. Bibliography: Cartledge, *OCD* s.v. *Helot.*

188. Ithome in the first war: Paus. 4.9.1–2, Tyrt. fr. 5 *IEG*. In the second war: Paus. 4.20.4. Dates: V. Parker,
"Dates." A retreat to another mountain, Hira, may be a doublet, as held by Kiechle, *Messenische Studien*, 65–66,
analyzing Paus. 4.17.10.

189. Ending five years after it started according to Lewis, "Ithome Again," 415; eight years after it started,
according to Gomme ad Th. 1.89–118.2; some 10 years after, according to Badian, *From Plataea to Potidaea*, 100.

190. Th. 1.103.2. Confirming the supplication: Paus. 4.24.5–7.

191. The same verb, *aphiēmi*, with the same sense: Paus. 7.1.8. Same verb and sense and a truce: Str. 6.3.2.

tic conclusion to the fourth step of the supplication. By inserting a clause that the Messenians would be enslaved if they returned to Messenia, the Spartans also reduced the chance of another rebellion. In return, the Messenians received the honor of taking the cult of Zeus with them. Transportating the cult was easy because it centered on a statue kept in the house of an annually elected priest.[192] Since there was a Perioecic settlement at the base of Mt. Ithome, the Messenians would have regarded the statue as theirs to dispose of.[193] The statue ended up in Naupactus.[194]

As for the Pythia, she did not need to resolve the contradiction between Spartan control of the shrine and Messenian transportation of the cult. The purpose of her advice was to prompt negotiations, and it was of a piece with earlier pronouncements that favored now one side and now the other.[195] In other ways, it was novel. Instead of an alliance with Sparta, there would be a truce; instead of a place of refuge, a place of egress; and instead of incorporation, a settlement outside Spartan territory. The oracle also gave new meaning to Ithome's location. As figure 4.1 shows, Ithome is the only high spot anywhere in the center of Messenia. To the west of Ithome is a valley and a spring where a city would later be built, and a few miles to the east are rivers and marshes that are difficult to cross on foot.[196] By calling for a "release," oracle converted this prominent place into a way station. The Spartans then put the way station into operation. In Naupactus, the suppliants laid claim to the result: a new community that soon came under the protection of Greece's other leading power, Athens.[197]

Autonomy on the Battlefield

We began this chapter with supplication and the laws of one community, Athens, turned to supplication and a treaty among several independent communities, and then to supplication and a treaty or grant affecting dependent communities. Last came supplication by a dependent community relying on an oracular response. First there were many shrines, but all under the same law; then several autonomous shrines; then a single, anomalous shrine. Now we come to supplication and two treaties that conflict with one another and to a battlefield where even the norms of supplication conflict with one another. We have also come to a new source, Thucydides. He has discovered (or partly contrived) a conundrum of the kind that regulations and orators overlook.

---

192. Paus. 4.33.2.

193. Perioecic Ithome: Themelis, *PAAH* 150, correcting Valmin's impression, *Études*, 69–71, that there had been no settlement at all. In the geometric period, there was a shrine at the spring at the foot of the mountain according to Touchais, *BCH* 113, 610, confirmed by Themelis, *PAAH* 148, 149, and 150.

194. Perhaps a statue made by Hageladas, as suggested by E. Pfuhl, *RE* 7.2.2189 s.v. *Hageladas*, dating the sculptor's career from the third quarter of the sixth century BCE to the second quarter of the fifth. Paus. 4.33.2 says that the statue was made by Hageladas in Naupactus, but not when.

195. Pronouncements: Morgan, *Athletes and Oracles*, 188. Negotiations: Th. 1.103.1–2, saying that the Spartans acted on the oracle some time after receiving it.

196. Spring: as in n. 193 above. Difficult to cross: Leake, *Travels*, 353.

197. A different view of way stations: de Polignac, *Naissance*, 42–49, describing shrines of this kind as occupying a "position limite" that makes them culturally different from urban shrines.

In Books 2 and 3, Thucydides devotes several dozen chapters to a diplomatic history that culminates in a supplication by the Plataeans, the same group that supplicates in Isocrates' oration. This history begins with an alliance between Athens and Plataea in 519 BCE. The treaty establishing this alliance it does not survive, but the Athenians interpret it as forbidding the Plataeans to be neutral in a war between Athens and a third party, and the Plataeans do not dispute this interpretation.[198] Forty years later, Sparta and Sparta's allies do most of the fighting at the battle of Plataea in 479 BCE, driving away the Persian army that had just sacked the city. The Spartans then take the lead in making a treaty that resembles the one that the Spartans would make with Parrhasia in 421 BCE. The Plataeans themselves describe this treaty to the Spartans:

> King Pausanias summoned all the allies and restored to the Plataeans their country and their community so that they might live there on terms of autonomy. No one ever was to make war on them unjustly or to enslave them.[199]

The Spartans and the Plataeans solemnized this grant by swearing oaths, the usual practice. On the one hand, the treaty says that the Plataeans must help Athens; on the other hand, they receive protection from Sparta.

At first glance, the treaty of 519 BCE and the grant of 479 BCE do not conflict with one another. The Spartans, however, interpret the grant as obliging the Plataeans to help those communities that fought against the Persian invasion. The Spartans hold that the grant of autonomy is conditional; in other words, that Plataean autonomy is limited, like the autonomy of other places. The Spartans state this condition when replying to the Plataeans:

> You are right. . . . But since Pausanias made you autonomous, act as an autonomous community. Free those who shared in the dangers of the Persian War and who also swore the oath and now are subject to the Athenians.[200]

According to this interpretation, the Plataean alliance with Athens and the Spartan (or Greek) grant of autonomy conflict with one another. Under the alliance, the Plataeans should fight alongside Athens. Under the Spartan grant, the Plataeans should fight alongside the victims of Athens.

The conflict lies dormant until the start of the Peloponnesian War. Then the Thebans, Sparta's ally, attack Plataea, the Plataeans turn to Athens for help, the Thebans respond by turning to the Spartans, and the Spartans ask that the Plataeans join the fight against Athens. Athens insists that the Plataeans honor their obligations

198. Th. 2.73. 3–74.1.
199. Th. 2.71.2. "Live on terms of autonomy": αὐτονόμους οἰκεῖν.
200. Th. 2.72.1, especially the first sentence: δίκαια λέγετε, . . . καθάπερ γὰρ Παυσανίας ὑμῖν παρέδωκεν, αὐτοί τε αὐτονομεῖσθε. . . .

under the treaty, and the Plataeans, caught between the treaty and the grant, try to negotiate. The Spartans give way and ask only that Plataea be neutral.[201] But the Plataeans refuse to be neutral, and join Athens. Now the Spartans attack after one of the strongest statements in defense of an act of war anywhere in Greek literature. The Spartan king asserts that the Plataeans are guilty of traducing the oaths made with Pausanias and calls upon the gods and heroes to bear witness to the violation of the grant.[202]

The yearlong Spartan attack and siege ends in a surrender that the Plataeans take pains to describe as an act of supplication that will entitle them to be protected by the Greek practice of sparing fellow Greeks who supplicate on the battlefield. But here another conflict arises. The Thebans, who wish to see the surrendering Plataeans treated harshly, point to an incident occurring when the Thebans attacked Plataea. The Thebans contend that they surrendered, supplicated, and received a promise of protection from the Plataeans, who then broke the promise, killing some of them. Denouncing this betrayal, the Thebans tell the Spartans to discount the practice of allowing Greeks to surrender peaceably and to reject the Plataean suppliants on the grounds that the Plataeans have been "violators of *nomoi*."[203] The Thebans in effect argue that the *nomos* of surrender does not protect a suppliant who is guilty of both betrayal and hypocrisy. Speaking in their own defense, the Plataeans point to the timing of the Theban onslaught. The Thebans attacked during a festival, proving themselves impious.

These charges and countercharges do not obscure the irony of the exchange between the Plataeans and the Thebans. Each side says that the *nomos* of surrender ought to give way before other criteria of rejection. They disagree only about what these criteria should be. The Thebans argue for rejecting surrender by treacherous hypocrites and the Plataeans admit that they rejected a surrender by impious aggressors. Neither side addresses the issue of whether the *nomos* of surrender ought to apply only to the deserving.[204] This issue stands alongside the issue of which agreement to honor as one of general importance and obvious difficulty. Besides a legal problem, there is a supplicatory one.

Thucydides bequeaths both problems to the Spartans. If they give weight to the grant of King Pausanias but not to the alliance with Athens, the suppliants stand condemned for violating the oath to which their forefathers committed later generations, and so the Spartans should reject them. Then, however, the Spartans must discount the *nomos* of surrender. If, on the other hand, the Spartans choose to give weight to the alliance with Athens and not to the grant, the Plataean suppliants still might be found guilty of betraying the Theban prisoners, and so the Spartans again might reject them. Or the Plataeans might be found justified in killing those who attacked on the day of a festival. No matter what, the Spar-

---

201. Th. 2.72.1.
202. Th. 2.74.2–3.
203. Th. 3.66.2. παρανομῆσαι: Th. 3.66.3.
204. A different view: Sheets, "Conceptualizing Law," 63–64, implying that no general issue would arise, the reason being the "horizontal" or self-contained character of each act of supplication.

tans find themselves in an imbroglio. Nor can they escape this imbroglio by investigating the competing claims. Thucydides has made sure that there is nothing to investigate. He lets the Plataeans describe the grant of Pausanias and then lets the Spartans interpret it differently than the Plataeans do, but he says nothing in his own person. He does report the deaths of the Thebans whom the Plataeans kill, but only the Thebans say that these Theban victims supplicated. Nor does Thucydides say whether the Plataeans themselves supplicated when they surrendered to the Spartans. Only the Plataeans say so.[205]

The Spartan response comes from a panel of judges who ask whether the Plataean prisoners have aided the Spartans in the course of the war. Panicking, the Plataeans ask to speak at length, and in response to this speech, the Thebans speak also, making the accusation of betrayal. But after these two speeches, the Spartan judges, unmoved, repeat their question.[206] It might seem that the legal and supplicatory problems have escaped the notice of the judges. But the Spartans have considered them. In their view, the fate of the suppliants ought to depend on whether the suppliants have honored the grant given by Pausanias:

> At other times the Spartans had thought it right for the Plataeans to be neutral in accordance with the grant given by Pausanias at the time of the Persian War. Afterwards, when they proposed to the Plataeans that the Plataeans abide by the grant and the Plataeans rejected them, they thought they were no longer bound by it, for their own goals had been just.[207]

To understand the Spartan attitude, we should remember Tegea and Mt. Lycaon. In those cases, an "autonomous" community owed Sparta rights of pursuit up to the gate of a sanctuary. In this case, the Plataeans owed Sparta military help or at least neutrality. If the Plataeans failed to honor their obligations, the Spartans would resort to a war on a treaty-breaking state, just as the Plataeans urged the Athenians to do in Isocrates. If the Spartans prevailed in the war, they would judge the suppliants according to a familiar standard, that of Gylippus at Syracuse, and so they would ask: were the suppliants aggressors? Since Spartans thought the Athenians were aggressors, they were effectively asking whether the Plataeans differed from the Athenians. Hence the judges' question whether any Plataeans had done some service to Sparta. A positive answer to this question would distinguish these Plataeans from the Athenians.

One obstacle stood in the way of this reasoning: the duty of a Greek who received the surrender of another Greek not to slay him. If this *nomos* was absolute, the Spartans could not reject the Plataeans.[208] But none of the parties to the

205. Death of Thebans: Th. 2.5 versus 3.66.2. Plataean surrender: 3.52 versus 3.58.2–3, 3.59.4.

206. Th. 3.52.4, 3.68.1–4.

207. Th. 3.68.1.

208. Absolute in the view of Sheets, "Conceptualizing Law," 57, for legal reasons; presumably absolute in the prevailing view by analogy to *Kontaktmagie*, but Gould, "*Hiketeia*," and Nilsson, *Griechische Religion*, do not discuss it.

dispute regarded this *nomos* in such a light. The Plataeans held that killing surrendering Thebans was acceptable; the Thebans held that killing surrendering Plataeans was acceptable. The Athenians make no comment, but in other situations they spared surrendering Greeks while reserving the right to try them later.[209] According to Diodorus, the Syracusans would receive surrendering Athenian suppliants and put them on trial in the very same way and then condemn them after listening to Gylippus. In these cases, the *nomos* was liable to be set aside after a trial. The Thebans of Thucydides make just this point: "The Plataeans will submit to what the law requires not as a result of extending their hands on the battlefield . . . but as a result of submitting to a judicial process."[210] Though the Spartans do not acknowledge this Theban argument, they implicitly accept it by regarding the Plataeans as defendants rather than (or as well as) suppliants. They proceed to condemn the Plataeans on two grounds, the violation of a grant and participation in Athenian aggression. Whatever the truth about this alleged aggression, the Spartans' decision is not unconsidered.[211] It is inadequate to a perplexing case.

After reporting the outcome, Thucydides says that the Spartans condemned the Plataeans in order to please the Thebans, who would prove more useful allies than the Plataeans. Some scholars endorse this view.[212] But this notion of Spartan *Machtpolitik* does not give credit to either the Spartans or the Plataeans and the Thebans. No party, we should remember, wanted the *nomos* protecting those who surrender to be absolute. Several parties, including Athens, wanted to make it possible for the supplicandus to set aside the *nomos*. A trial for those who surrender—for Byzantines, for example, and not just for Plataeans—was unusual but not unacceptable.

The Theban claim that a trial would decide a suppliant's fate—a banal claim in a court of law—is important for the future of supplication in other venues. In these venues, the Theban claim would reduce the suppliant to someone gaining access to a judicial proceeding. One of the Thebans' phrases, "what the law requires," epitomizes this shift. The Greek for these words is *ennoma*, the term found in the Attic inscriptions. In those documents, the suppliant who performed *ta ennoma* succeeded. Now *ta ennoma* is a matter for a judicial proceeding. *Machtpolitik* aside, the Plataean episode marks a further penetration of supplication by legal process.

---

209. D.S. 13.67.7, Th. 3.28.2.

210. Th. 3.67.5: ἔννομα γὰρ πείσονται καὶ οὐχὶ ἐκ μάχης χεῖρας προϊσχόμενοι, ὥσπερ φασίν, ἀλλ' ἀπὸ ξυμβάσεως ἐς δίκην σφᾶς αὐτοὺς παραδόντες.

211. As by Hornblower ad Th. 3.53–59 following MacLeod, "Plataian Debate," 242–43.

212. Gomme ad Th. 3.67.7, contrasting Athenian conduct on Mytilene with Spartan conduct at Plataea; de Romilly, *Thucydide et l'impérialisme*, 146–49, compares the same two episodes. But at Mytilene only the leaders supplicate (Th. 3.28.2), so the number who perish is presumably smaller.

OLD VERSUS NEW

The relation between supplication and legal systems varies from one act of supplication to the next. If someone pursues the suppliant and then the suppliant seeks refuge, and the pursuer appears and demands that the supplicandus surrender the suppliant, the suppliant acts as a defendant, the pursuer as a prosecutor, and the supplicandus as a judge. Thanks to this three-sided encounter, the act of supplication resembles a trial. This comparison explains the Greek term *feugôn*, "the one fleeing," which refers to both defendants and suppliants.[213] If the suppliant appears before the supplicandus but a pursuer is lacking, the act of supplication does not resemble a trial, but it may resemble a hearing. In this situation, the suppliant resembles the party presenting a request, and the supplicandus resembles the magistrate or deliberative body that responds to the request. In the first of these two situations, the act of supplication involves what Aristotle called corrective justice, and in the second, it involves what Aristotle calls distributive justice, the allotment of honor or help where honor or help are due.[214] Aside from these two situations, an act of supplication can occur during a trial, usually when a defendant pleads innocent and supplicates.

All these similarities are procedural, but other similarities are substantive. An act of supplication can depend on a plea of innocence, including a plea supported by *epeikeia*. It can depend on honoring treaties or grants or on complying with local laws. It can also depend on wrongs that the suppliant has done or on his legal status apart from any wrongs, such as his being a slave, and it can even depend on the place from which he has fled. For Messenians, the act of supplication can even depend on the status of the shrine to which the suppliant flees and thus on the political status of the suppliants and their neighbors.

Linking most of these situations is a supplication at a public altar and the regulation of this altar by an assembly, especially by the Assembly in Athens. If a suppliant came before the Athenian Assembly in search of help or honors, it regulated every step of the act of supplication. If the Assembly turned over some of its responsibilities to magistrates, they enforced the Assembly's regulations, and if supplication occurred in court, the Assembly wrote the laws that the court consulted. In every instance, arbitrary action became less likely. If the suppliant came before the Assembly, the first of these possibilities, the Assembly relied on *res iudicata*. If the Assembly turned the suppliant over to magistrates, the magistrates adhered to the law. If a suppliant appeared in court, the judicial oath discouraged the suppliant from departing from arguments in favor of his innocence. Sometimes the law dictated what must occur, as when the law barred slaves from the Acropolis. Sometimes it offered guidelines, as *Exodus* had to the Hebrew elders.

---

213. Other views of the three-sided acts: Kopperschmidt, *Hikesie als dramatische Form*, 48, and Burian, *Suppliant Drama*, 4–5, both seeing parallels with drama rather than law.

214. Arist. *NE* 5.1130b–31b. Of the two kinds of corrective justice, three-sided supplication deals with involuntary transactions, such as crimes (1130b–31a), and not with voluntary transactions, such as sale and purchase.

But even as the Assembly made supplication less arbitrary, it did not make supplication unfamiliar. It introduced no new kind of approach and no new words and gestures. It did introduce a new criterion of judgment, "legitimacy," but this criterion was a compound of familiar moral and social standards and a new standard of obedience to local laws. It did not so much change the practice as formalize it. The Assembly formalized another Greek practice, *xenia*, in the same way. Through laws and regulations it created a new form of *xenia*, *proxenia*, which provided help for visitors to Athens. *Proxenia* differed from *xenia* through formalities such as appointing a citizen to represent and assist visitors from a given place. Meanwhile *xenia* continued. Old and new coexisted, the same as unregulated and regulated supplication.

Supplicandi participating in intercommunal acts of supplication might also consult legal documents, notably treaties and resolutions. When considering the appeal of the Plataeans, the Athenians themselves did so. So might the members of Delphic amphictyony when evaluating suppliants who had committed *hierosulia*. In the Peloponnesus, a web of treaties and grants affected supplication in the communities belonging to the Spartan alliance. Communities that lacked recognition under these documents could not protect their suppliants, so those who came to Taenarus often left by sea, and those who went to Ithome left Messenia under truce. In contrast, communities and shrines that received recognition could protect suppliants against arbitrary action, the same as the Assembly in Athens. The Spartans respected the autonomy of the shrine at Mt. Lycaon for all of Plistoanax's 19 years there.

The gain in regularity did not benefit all suppliants alike. In Attica, slaves, metics, and citizens all supplicated at public altars, but our sources say that citizens supplicated there the most. In all of Attic drama and oratory—42 complete plays and some 150 complete speeches—only 10 citizens and other free persons perform acts that do not occur at public altars.[215] Moreover, only 3 of the 10 appear in oratory.[216] Since convicted murderers supplicated relatives of the deceased, this number is too low, but it shows all the better the character of acts at public altars. The new kind of supplication that the citizenry established affected citizens most of all.

If the law's safeguards against arbitrariness were to protect more suppliants, then the community would have to legislate and regulate more. Public officials might make themselves available to persons who would not or could not reach altars, such as the slave girl in Lysias 1. The community might encourage supplication by adopting more lenient standards of judgment, it might promulgate more regulations, and it might even make some kinds of supplication unnecessary. All these changes would occur not in Greece but in Rome, beginning with the early Republic.

---

215. S. *Ph.* 468–529 (Philoctetes to Neoptolemus), E. *Hec.* 1127–28 (Polymnestor to Agamemnon), *IA* 1153–56 (Agamemnon to Tyndareus), *Ph.* 923–59 (Creon to Tiresias); Ar. *Ach.* 414–34 (Dicaeopolis to Euripides), *Pax* 1113–21 (priest to Trygaeus), *Thes.* 179–205 (Euripides to Agathon); Aeschin. 1.61 (two citizens to a freedman), And. 1.19 (Andocides to father), Lys. 1.26–27 (Eratosthenes to Euphiletus). At E. *Hec.* 245–50 (Odysseus to Hecuba), the free adult male is disguised as a slave.

216. Aeschin. 1.61, And. 1.19, Lys. 1.26–27.

5

SUPPLICATION, REPUBLIC, AND PRINCIPATE

When Vercingetorix supplicated Caesar, he cited their friendship, but Caesar rejected this argument. The Gallic leader then made an appeal that we have not noticed, one common in supplication to Roman magistrates and especially common in the situation in which Vercingetorix found himself: surrender to Rome. As Dio Cassius explains, after the fall of Alesia to the Romans, Vercingetorix had been able to escape, . . . but he hoped that since he once had been Caesar's friend, he would find forgiveness."[1] The new appeal, one for forgiveness, rests on circumstances that Dio does not mention. Vercingetorix belonged to a tribe, the Arverni, that had yielded to Roman power long before. Vercingetorix had defied this power and now deserved chastisement.[2] To avoid it, he should ask for forgiveness, *suggnômê*. And Vercingetorix does. Friendship with Caesar does not exempt him from this task.

Now comes a piece of historical fiction: the sudden arrival of the armed Vercingetorix on horseback, a clatter of weapons no less suddenly discarded at Caesar's feet, the bent knees and extended hands of the Celtic rebel, a surprising moment when he keeps silent—thus attracting even more attention—and then his appeal to friendship. We have noticed the bent knees before, but this time we can explain this unusual gesture: suppliants bend the knee when approaching Roman magistrates in order to request forgiveness and sometimes (as in this scene) to surrender. From the perspective of the magistrate, the suppliant is appealing for a mercy that he may not deserve. And so the magistrate may prove difficult to persuade:

> The others felt grief at the memory of his previous good fortune and sympathy at the sight what he had become, but Caesar criticized Vercingetorix for the very thing that Vercingetorix thought would save him. Rebuking the appeal to friendship, Caesar contended that Vercingetorix's wrongdoing was thereby worse.[3]

According to Dio, Caesar now rejects Vercingetorix, taking him captive. Later he displays Vercingetorix in triumph. According to another source, Florus, Caesar

1. D.C. 40.41.1.
2. Since 121 BCE: Caes. *Gal.* 1.45.1–2.
3. D.C. 40.41.2–3. No such scene: Caes. *Gal.* 7.89.5.

accepts the surrender of Vercingetorix, a result that is not incompatible with the rest of Dio's account. Florus, as it happens, omits the two men's speeches but reports the same approach and gestures.[4]

Much about this scene lacks any Greek precedent. Some Greek magistrates serving as generals receive supplication from those who surrender. They send these suppliants to the assembly of their own community for trial.[5] As a Roman magistrate, however, Caesar need not consider any Roman assembly, or even the Roman Senate. His powers of command, his *imperium*, includes full powers to deal with suppliants. He can reject a friend, and he can reject him after an evaluation that concerns forgiveness for a suppliant who is in the wrong, as opposed to the Greek practice of acceptance for a suppliant who is in the right. The Latin term for this response is *clementia*, meaning not just forgiveness but mercy for those subject to punishment. Other Roman magistrates evaluate suppliants in this way, too, but Caesar adds his characteristic criterion for *clementia*: the suppliant must have opposed him once but not twice. In contrast, Greek supplicandi reject enemies the first and not the second time that they encounter them.[6] But the greatest difference between this act of supplication and any Greek one is Caesar's range of choices. They include captivity and death, as in Greece, but also a kind of surrender that Florus calls *deditio,* an agreement that obliged the suppliant to accept the terms set by Rome. *Deditio* often led to the suppliant's becoming a Roman subject. Like the *nomos* allowing Greeks to surrender on the battlefield, it conferred something like a right, and it conferred a better right than the *nomos* because it brought the suppliants under Roman rule.

These innovations—the *imperium* of the magistrate, mercy, and the provision of rights—give Roman supplication a distinct administrative, legal, and political character. Along with the regulations that the Roman Empire made necessary, these innovations constitute the chief topics of this chapter. For the most part, we will take them up in the order in which Vercingetorix experienced them—the magistrate and his power, the hope for mercy, the provision of rights—but pause to notice regulations before we pass on to rights. Along with rights, regulations formed the legal basis of Roman supplication.

MAGISTRATES

Everywhere in the ancient world, suppliants sought out the powerful. In classical Athens, they sought out the Assembly; in Rome, they once must have sought out the kings. But little evidence for supplication at this stage of Roman history survives, and much of that little is in Dionysius of Halicarnassus, who does not distinguish between Roman and Greek gestures of supplication.[7] For the early and

---

4. Flor. *Epit.* 1.45, specifying *deditio.*
5. D.S. 13.67.7, Th. 3.28.3. Or they summon judges: Th. 3.52.3.
6. *Il.* 10.454–56.
7. Greek gestures occur in all but nine of the acts at appendix 1b under his name.

early middle Republic, the evidence is not much better.[8] By the time of the Second Punic War, when the evidence improves, suppliants seek out magistrates and promagistrates with *imperium*: consuls and proconsuls, praetors and propraetors, and sometimes others, notably tribunes of the plebs who lacked *imperium* but possessed broad powers. The magistrates held *imperium* by virtue of their office, which they occupied for a year, and the promagistrates held it by virtue of prorogation, a legal fiction that allowed them to retain *imperium* after their term of office expired. *Imperium* itself is better defined as a capacity to act than as the possession of particular powers. It let the magistrate (or those comparable to him) act on behalf of the community in either war or peace. It was available to him both in Rome and elsewhere.[9]

By the middle Republic, some laws limited it, especially in Rome. Other limits resulted from magistrates' having colleagues who could impede one another and from the development of grades of *imperium*. But these limits mattered less for supplication than for other activities conducted by magistrates. Abroad, the suppliant often encountered a magistrate without a colleague. At home, the suppliant who found that one magistrate would not help him would turn to another, or to a tribune. So the suppliant did not need to consider the niceties of the legal position of the magistrate. He grasped what Vercingetorix did: the magistrate wielded power in the name of the Roman people.

The effects of these acts of supplication are familiar to students of Roman history. But save for several articles touching on the use of supplication by foreigners approaching magistrates outside Rome, the role of supplication in bringing about these effects has gone unnoticed.[10] If we notice the acts of supplication occurring when Vercingetorix surrenders, for example, or when Metellus Pius pleads on behalf of his father, several differences between Greek and Roman religion and law will emerge. First, because a Greek magistrate acted in the name of the assembly and not his own, he seldom evaluated suppliants. In contrast, Roman magistrates invariably do. Second, because the assembly's power extended throughout a Greek community, a Greek magistrate's location did not matter. In Roman supplication, however, the location of the magistrate is crucial. Abroad he mostly receives foreigners and soldiers; in Rome he mostly receives citizens.[11] Or magistrates and promagistrates act through a magistrates' council, the Senate, which receives far more suppliants than any comparable Greek body.

The chief difference between Greek and Roman supplication is that the Greek assembly made itself accessible to suppliants via public altars.[12] In contrast, the

---

8. Twenty-seven acts, or 15 in D.H. and 12 in Livy down to Cannae. Acts reported in Plutarch and other later writers, especially Dio, have the same principals and most of the same particulars.

9. A "capacity to act": as at *RSt.*, 1.22–24, 61–65 followed by Brennan, *Praetorship*, 15, with refs. at 12–15.

10. Hölkeskamp, "Deditio in fidem," 241–48, on foreigners; Freyburger, "Supplication grecque," drawing comparison with Greek practice.

11. Though it is not relevant to supplication that promagistrates lost their *imperium* when returning to the city in the late Republic, or that, as noted at *RSt.*, 1.66–71, the distinction between Rome and elsewhere is not always sharp.

12. On this score it resembled the authorities in Phoenicia if not Israel. We do not know, however, which Phoenician authorities: only magistrates are mentioned, and they are mentioned only as escorts in one act (D.S. 17.41.8).

imperium of the magistrate became accessible through the magistrate himself—through a person rather than a place. Had the Romans not devised the fiction of prorogation, this feature might have prevented suppliants from having the access that they needed. What prorogation did not provide, an increase in the number of magistrates did. Under the empire, the emergence of a single chief magistrate—the emperor—accompanied increased supplication to legates, lower ranking officials who also possessed *imperium*. Just as Greek supplication abounded in pubic altars, Roman supplication abounded in official supplicandi.

Most numerous among the magistrates acting as supplicandi are those dealing with foreigners. For such magistrates there are no comparable Greek figures. The reason is not that Greek supplicandi did not go abroad and make themselves powerful enough to be approached. They dealt with persons who went to altars when cities fell, and who then might be sent back to the home city. Or they went abroad in search of fugitives who would likewise go to altars and later be returned to the magistrate's home city. In the first role, magistrates were go-betweens; in the second, pursuers. Roman magistrates were neither. Instead they were supplicandi who appear in every period and in many provinces. The following more or less chronological list of places of supplication to Roman magistrates mirrors the growth of Roman power: peninsular Italy (three acts from the early Republic), Sicily (two acts at the end of the third century BCE), Africa other than Egypt (eight acts starting at the end of the third century BCE and continuing to the end of the second), Greece and Macedon (six acts from the early second to early first century BCE), Spain (four acts from the early and middle second century BCE), Egypt (two acts from the first century BCE), Asia Minor and Crete (one act apiece from the middle of the first century BCE), Armenia (four acts from the same time until the early second century CE), Gaul (nine acts from Caesar's proconsulate in the 50s BCE), Illyria (four acts mostly from the reign of Augustus), Judea (seven acts from the Jewish rebellion of 68–70 CE), and Germany (two acts from the first and one from the third centuries CE).[13] Supplication follows the standards of the Roman legions and establishes itself beside them, but sometimes departs soon after the legions arrive. If supplication persists in a province, the situation there is unsettled, as in Armenia. If supplication never appears, there may be a gap in the sources, as is perhaps true for Britain and Thrace.[14] If it seldom appears, magistrates may have found Rome's enemies less tractable, as is surely true for Germany. But if it ap-

13. Italy: D.H. 9.17.1–2, 9.36.2, 10.24.6–8, Liv. 8.20.6. Sicily: Liv. 25.6.1–7.1, Plut. *Marc.* 20.7. Africa: Plb. 1.35.4, Liv. 28.34.3–12, V. Max. 6.9. ext. 7, App. *Pun.* 130, Plb. 38.20.1–10, Sal. *Jug.* 38.1, 47.3, *B. Afr.* 92.4. Greece: Plut *Flam.* 15.5, Liv. 34.40.2–4, 36.28.1–8, 36.34.5–35.6, Plut. *Sull.* 14.5. Macedon: Liv. 45.4.2–6. Spain: V. Max. 3.2.16, App. *Hisp.* 43, 52, 61. Egypt: Cic. *Rab. Post.* 5, *B. Alex.* 32.3. Asia Minor: Plut. *Pomp.* 28.1. Crete: Plut. *Pomp.* 29.2. Armenia: Cic. *Sest.* 58, App. *Mith.* 104, Tac. *Ann.* 14.23.3, Fro. *Parth.* 16. Gaul: Caes. *Gal.* 1.20.1–5, 1.27.1–28.2, 1.31.1–33.1, 2.13.2–15.1, 2.28.2–3, 7.40.6, 7.78.3–5, Plut. *Caes.* 27.5, Caes. *Civ.* 2.11.4–13.3, Tac. *Hist.* 1.54, 1.66. Illyria: Liv. 44.31.13–15, App. *Ill.* 24, 28. Judea: J. *BJ* 1.139, 2.230–31, 2.314, 3.454–56, 4.553, 6.356–57, 6.378–79. Germany and environs: Tac. *Ann.* 2.22.3, D.C. 67.5.1, *Hist. Aug. Prob.* 14.2. Only the oldest source is given for each act and the acts for each province or region are listed in chronological order whenever possible.

14. Britain: Aug. *Anc.* 5.42.

pears more often, frequency depends as much on author as on circumstances. Josephus's Jews do not supplicate more magistrates because they are humbler than the subject peoples of other provinces. Josephus recounts their rebellion in greater detail than other authors dealing with comparable events, and so he reports more surrenders accompanied by supplications.

Because supplication follows the standards, it clusters around the most successful magistrates in the most demanding posts. The sources report that Julius Caesar is the most supplicated magistrate, followed by Flamininus and Pompey.[15] In this respect the Roman situation resembles situations in which supplicandi are often kings and commanders. But the *imperium* of magistrates makes itself felt in two particulars. These three magistrates served long periods of prorogation in important provinces. In these provinces they commanded large forces dealing with numerous suppliants, yet all the suppliants address themselves to these three men as opposed to their subordinates, even those who held *imperium* as legates. Only two supplicandi are subordinate to other commanders, and even in these cases the circumstances are unusual: a supplication at dinner and a supplication while the commander is absent.[16] Supplication is the prerogative of the commander with the highest *imperium*.

These commanders (and especially the leading three) receive supplications from numerous tribes; several cities, notably Syracuse and Massilia; and several kings, notably King Jugurtha of Numidia, who supplicated twice before becoming (as a coin would have it) another suppliant's stock in trade.[17] Many suppliants wish to surrender and be spared or given good terms; others, such as Jugurtha, wish to make treaties or truces.[18] A few wish to become clients of the magistrate.[19] Whoever the suppliant and whatever the request, nearly all acts concern the magistrate in his official capacity or (with clients) his future capacity as a senator. Rarely does the magistrate act in a private capacity.[20]

The magistrate's *imperium* met with two obstacles: higher ranking magistrates and subject peoples who challenged the highest authority of all, the government in Rome. Both obstacles appear only in Josephus, a circumstance that may make them seem rarer than they were. The first obstacle appears when some Jews dissatisfied with the procurator governing Judea, Gessius Florus, supplicated his

15. Caesar: Gaul as immediately above, D.C. 42.43.4, *B. Alex.* 32.3, 67.1–68. Flamininus: Greece as immediately above. Pompey: Plut. *Pomp.* 28.1, 29.2, Cic. *Sest.* 58, App. *Mith.* 104.

16. Dinner: L. Quinctius Flamininus, cos. 192 when acting as supplicandus at Liv. 39.42.10–12. Absence: A. Postumius Albinus, legate pro praetore for Sp. Postumius Albinus, cos. 110 when acting as supplicandus at Sal. *Jug.* 38.1.

17. Syracuse: Liv. 25.7.1. Massilia: Caes. *Civ.* 2.11.4–13.3. Tiberias: J. *BJ* 3.454. Capharabis: J. *BJ* 4.553. Jugurtha: Sal. *Jug.* 38.1, 47.3. Others: Syphax (Val. Max. 6.9 ext. 7), Perseus (Liv. 45.4.2–6), Tigranes II (Cic. *Sest.* 58), Deiotaurus (*B. Alex.* 67.1–8, differing from the supplication at a hearing found at Cic. *Deiot.* 40), Ptolemy XII (Cic. *Rab. Post.* 5).

18. Surrender: see the treatment of *deditio in fidem* at below. Treaties, etc.: Liv. 34.40.2–4, 36.34.5–35.6, Sal. *Jug.* 38.1, 47.3 (truce), Caes. *Civ.* 2.11.4–13.3 (recognition of neutrality).

19. Antony (J. *BJ* 1.393–94), L. Flamininus (Liv. 39.42.10–12). Other help: land grant (App. *Hisp.* 61), compact (D.C. 72.16.1), military aid (D.H. 9.17.1–2), financial aid (Cic. *Rab. Post.* 5), diplomatic recognition (Fro. *Parth.* 16).

20. Liv. 39.42.10–12, where the action is criminal.

superior, the governor of Syria, Cestius Gallus. But Florus remained uncooperative. Even in regard to issues of Jewish religious law, he rejected Jewish requests.[21]
As a result of similar complaints, the Emperor Claudius banished another magistrate, Ventidius Cumanus, but Florus remained in office even though he rejected
suppliants as part of a plan to goad them into revolt.[22] These examples show that
the higher ranking magistrate did not impede the activity of the lower ranking
unless the higher ranking magistrate was the emperor.

The united Jewish people proved a more difficult obstacle, as magistrates serving
Tiberius and Caligula discovered when they set about bringing imperial images
into Jerusalem. Tiberius's prefect, Pontius Pilate, introduced imperial standards
into the city, and in response to this violation of their laws, the Jews supplicated
outside his house, lying prostrate for five days. Pilate replied by holding a hearing
about the standards. Once the suppliants arrived at the hearing, Pilate tricked
them, ordering his troops to surround them and to threaten to kill them unless
they accepted the introduction of the standards. The suppliants responded by
prostrating themselves again and exposing their necks to the Romans' swords.
Pilate gave up, withdrawing the standards. His trick had failed to overcome the
suppliants' argument that their religious laws were of supreme importance—of
greater importance than their own lives.[23] The trick failed because the Jews had
challenged Rome to provide the troops needed to kill or intimidate the population, and Rome had declined.

The next prefect, Petronius, did not trick the Jews, but he fared no better than
Pilate had. One reason was that he faced an even harder task: introducing imperial statues into the Temple. Another reason was his own good conduct. Unlike Pilate, he announced his plans, and when the Jews once again supplicated,
this time on a plain outside Jerusalem, he responded with a hearing unmarred by
trickery. At this gathering, the Jews pleaded the holiness of their religious laws;
Petronius countered by citing Rome's laws. As before, the Jews declared that they
were willing to die for their laws. As before, an impasse resulted. But in this case
the Jews persisted for seven weeks, not five days. Going on a sort of strike, they
refused to sow the fields. And so this honorable *supplicandus* capitulated just as
his dishonorable predecessor had done.

Honorable as he was, he did not leave the matter there. Instead he announced
that he would go to the emperor, Caligula, to defend his decision to grant the
suppliants' request.[24] Told about this plan by letter, Caligula vowed to execute
Petronius unless the statues were installed in the temple. Unlike the dishonorable
supplicandus, the honorable one would pay for his conduct—a prospect that so
disturbed Josephus that he tells his readers that Yahweh had taken note of Caligula's
impious order. The Lord of the Hebrews even caused Caligula to die before the

21. Complaints about Florus to Gallus, legatus pro praetore: J. *BJ* 2.280–81. Rejection by Florus: 2.292, 2.314.
22. Rejection by Cumanus: J. *BJ* 2.233. Revolt: 2.282.
23. J. *BJ* 2.171–74.
24. J. *BJ* 2.192–201.

emperor has a chance to execute Petronius. But the contrast between Pilate and Petronius teaches a lesson not about the Lord's watchfulness but about the perils of the magistrate. No matter how he acted, he could not accommodate both the edict of Rome and the wishes of the suppliants. If the magistrate had no need to fear a superior (and usually he did not), this problem would not arise. But if the suppliants proved intransigent and numerous, Rome was sure to hear of their demands, and then the *imperium* of the magistrate would no longer suffice.

In nearly a dozen cases, Roman magistrates receive suppliants in their role as military commanders. Either soldiers or officers may approach.[25] These offenders have attacked when not ordered to, refused to fight when ordered to, or engaged in other misconduct.[26] A few have even begged an unwilling general to fight.[27] Here, too, there are no comparable Greek supplicandi, and once again the reason cannot be that the Greek commander did not place himself in a situation in which an entire class of suppliants would not find it worthwhile to make requests. In Athens, at least, the reason was that the highest ranking commanders of the late classical period, the ten *stratêgoi*, had no right to punish any soldier, only the right to take him into custody and to dismiss him from service.[28] Violations of military discipline led to lawsuits at which the general presided and the defendant's fellow soldiers served as judges. If the defendant supplicated, he would supplicate these judges in the same way that other defendants supplicated other judges.[29] The one exception to these arrangements was summary punishment inflicted by generals seeking to maintain order.[30]

In contrast, a magistrate's *imperium* comprehended full powers over his soldiers, who swore an oath to obey orders.[31] Polybius says that some misconduct merited the death penalty and that commanders punished infractions committed outside of camp.[32] The Porcian Laws of the late Republic forbade commanders from executing soldiers who were citizens, but as Mommsen noticed, these laws went into abeyance during the Principate.[33] The evidence for supplication by soldiers to commanders either antedates this law or comes from the Principate, so it belongs to the period in which the commander's power was greatest. The consequence was inevitable: soldiers supplicated the sole judge of their misconduct.[34]

25. One soldier: Plut. *Caes.* 16.4. Groups of soldiers: Liv. 25.37.9–11, Tac. *Ann.* 1.29.1–2, 1.44.1, J. *BJ* 5.127–8. One officer: Liv. 8.35.3–8. Group of officers on behalf of troops: App. *BC* 2.7.47.

26. Attacked: J. *BJ* 5.127–28, Liv. 8.35.3–8. Refused: Tac. *Ann.* 1.29.1–2, 1.44.1, Liv. 25.37.9–11. Other misconduct: Plut. *Caes.* 16.4.

27. Luc. 7.68–127, Tac. *Hist.* 2.46–47.

28. Arist. *Ath.* 61.2.

29. The various charges: Harrison, *Procedure*, 32. A prosecutor's speech on such a charge hints at supplication by the defendant (Lys. 14.40).

30. Summary punishment: Hamel, *Athenian Generals*, 59–63. Harrison, *Procedure*, 31, notes that at an earlier time, including the fifth and early fourth centuries, the generals could impose the death penalty, as at X. *HG* 1.1.15, Lys. 13.67.

31. Plb. 6.21.1–3, 10.16.7. A loyalty oath of Hellenistic origin supplanted (and eventually complemented) it from Julius Caesar onward, as in Beare, "Imperial Oath."

32. Plb. 6.37–8.

33. *RStr.*, 31.

34. The only exception: Plut. *Caes.* 16.4. The general might delegate his jurisdiction to an inferior (*RStr.*, 33), but this would not make it any less necessary for the soldier to supplicate an individual.

Like any supplicandus, the commander would win popularity by granting some requests and would maintain authority by denying others. In the four most important cases, all involving groups of soldiers who disobeyed orders, two supplicandi executed soldiers and two supplicandi did not.[35] Both of those who did execute soldiers responded to the supplication favorably by reducing the number killed. Caesar executed only 12 soldiers after threatening to decimate a legion, and Drusus also executed only a portion of those whom he originally threatened. Each commander spared the less guilty, a version of the *clementia* denied to Vercingetorix, but also a way of reinforcing loyalty among those who survived. In that sense, all these supplications succeeded. They ran parallel to the great majority of supplications by foreigners, for these succeeded, too.[36] These supplications inspired loyalty, whereas military supplications confirmed this same emotion.

Because supplication abroad included both provincials and Romans, subjecting the former to treaties and acts of surrender and the latter to military law, it encompassed several pairs of opposites: province and city, soldiers and civilians, Romans and foreigners. It was a versatile tool.

Magistrates in Rome

In Rome, the *imperium* of the magistrate combined with the weakness of the several Roman assemblies to give him an important role in framing legislation. Another feature of Roman magistracies, collegiality, made the magistrate useful as an intercessor with his colleagues or with other high officials. A third feature, the *auctoritas* or prestige of magistrates as opposed to their *imperium* or other powers, manifested itself in the Senate, which influenced domestic and dominated foreign policy. All these aspects of the magistrate's position attracted suppliants. If no one of these aspects attracted as much supplication as foreign service by legates and promagistrates, the sum is comparable and the acts of supplication are more diverse.

In regard to some of these aspects, classical Athens offers contrasts. An Athenian citizen wishing to affect legislation needed only attend the Assembly; he did not need to supplicate. Others who wished to affect legislation did have to supplicate, as at Rome, but they addressed the Council, not magistrates. Former magistrates comprised the Areopagus, but save for the murder trials conducted before it, the Areopagus received only a few suppliants, such as the king archon who asked to have a fine remitted.[37] For the most part, those who would have supplicated the Senate in Rome would have supplicated the Assembly in Athens. Power that in Greece went mostly to the assembly went to one or more magistrates in Rome. In Rome, only magistrates could convene assemblies, introduce bills, and speak, and only the Senate had great influence over bills, so magistrates

---

35. Executions: Caesar (App. *BC* 2.7.47), Drusus (Tac. *Ann.* 1.29.1–2). No executions: J. *BJ* 5.127–8, Tac. *Ann.* 1.44.1.

36. The only rejections: J. *BJ* 2.292, 6.433–34, Cic. *Verr.* 2.5.21, Liv. 36.34.5–6, 39.42.10–12, 45.4.2–6. Sal. *Jug.* 47.3–4, Vell. 2.109.2.

37. Council as at 174–76 above; Areopagus as at 191–92 above.

individually and collectively accounted for all legislation. The one exception, legislation by the tribunes, was nominal: these officials, who differed from magistrates by representing the plebs rather than the people as a whole, introduced legislation in much the same way. Nor did magistrates deal with suppliants at one stage rather than at another. Suppliants approached them during two stages of the process, consideration by the Senate and consideration by an assembly. During the Second Punic War, two consuls and one proconsul entertained requests to put matters on the agenda of the Senate.[38] At the time of the passage of the law that compelled Cicero to go into exile, his prospective son-in-law supplicated the consul Piso, presumably asking him to oppose the law at an assembly. Piso refused the request. Later, when Cicero had gone into exile, Roman knights who wished to help Cicero approached the consul Gabinius, asking him to speak in favor of Cicero's return at another assembly, but he, too, refused.[39]

Besides introducing bills and speaking for or against them, a magistrate could influence his colleagues or other magistrates. In a pause in the civil wars, a special board of three magistrates, the triumvirs, had secured a bill allowing them to seize land and distribute it to their troops. Widespread confiscation followed, and the victims approached various Roman leaders. All but one, the consul L. Antonius, rejected the suppliants.[40] Antonius negotiated with the triumvirs on behalf of the victims and reached an agreement with them, only to see the agreement broken.[41] Another power possessed by magistrates was introducing suppliants to the Senate. Because they presided over the Senate, this power fell to consuls. Only one instance survives, the introduction of suppliants from Locri, but there must have been many others. Livy mentions this one because when the Locrians approach the consuls, they carry boughs, a gesture appropriate for approaching an altar. Herodotus's Aristagoras makes the same mistake.[42] The Locrians, however, make this mistake for a different reason. As Greeks, they expect to approach a deliberative body by going to an altar, and so they approach magistrates the same way. They do not grasp that the consul's *imperium* and other powers have replaced the altar—that an elected official has replaced holy ground.

The reason that consuls do not bulk large among *supplicandi* who deal with legislation and deliberative bodies is the business transacted by the college of tribunes. As officials of the plebs, the tribunes may have seemed more accessible to the humble, but the humble are not those that the sources record as using tribunes as legislative intermediaries.[43] The archetypal Roman suppliant, Metellus Pius, supplicated a tribune in 98 BCE; friends of Cicero imitated him. More prized than supplication of either consuls or tribunes was supplication of

---

38. To a consul requesting a matter go before the Senate: Liv. 29.16.6–7. To a proconsul: 25.7.1.
39. Cic. *Sest.* 54.
40. App. *BC* 5.3.19. Antonius alone "received them," ὑπεδέχετο. For this usage, see appendix 5.
41. App. *BC* 5.3.20–21.
42. Liv. 29.16.6–7.
43. The view that they could be approached as a group at the temple of Ceres, and that this temple was also a sanctuary: Spaeth, *Ceres*, 84–85, with refs. For C. Gracchus taking "sanctuary" here, see Beness and Hillard, "Theatricality," 135. But no act of supplication is ever reported here, nor any consecration.

the Senate, which included both. The Locrians, who asked the consuls to help them approach the Senate, reveal the puzzle that this Roman body presented to any Greek (or Hebrew). Here were the Roman elders, so to speak, comparable to the elders at the gate in *Joshua*. Where was the gate or altar—the fixed, perhaps sacred place? The Senate met in several locations, not just the Senate house. And where was the king who joined with a council of chieftains to receive Homeric suppliants?[44] The Senate was an idiosyncratic council that for suppliants often replaced an assembly yet in principle was neither a council nor an assembly, only a group of promagistrates—nominally powerless persons whom a suppliant would not seek out. The Senate made nonsense out of the rule of seeking out the powerful, yet it also confirmed this rule. It wielded power of a new kind: extralegal power in a legal system. The legal system of classical Athens had lacked any such counterweight.[45]

Supplication to the Senate is correspondingly more sophisticated. The tribune Clodius, defeated in his attempts to keep Cicero out of Rome, asked the Senate to recommend that the assembly not establish a new court in which Clodius would likely be assailed by Cicero and his other enemies.[46] The friends of Mark Antony, whom we noticed on the streets of Rome, supplicating, singled out senators to ask them to influence an assembly vote on a resolution to have Antony declared a public enemy.[47]

But suppliants did not confine themselves to asking favors for individuals. Along with family, the Roman prisoners spared after the great defeat at Cannae supplicated the Senate, asking it to endorse the prisoners' return to Rome. But too many Romans had died at Cannae for the Senate to be willing to help the survivors. After a long debate, the Senate refused.[48] Tax farmers supplicated the Senate when they could not make their payments to the state. They chose the Senate partly because of its power to superintend public finance.[49] The exiled Cicero also dispatched some of his supplicating friends to the Senate.[50] Some of Cicero's suppliants were senators themselves. Other senators supplicated the Senate on matters relating to Senate membership. One senator might supplicate the whole Senate on behalf of a member who had lost the Senate's confidence. Or senators might supplicate in order to retain their office.[51]

But the most important supplications addressed by Romans to the Senate came from the mass of the population. Accounts of some of these acts are exaggerated, like the supplication that "the Fatherland" made to the Senate to save it from Catiline.[52] Some are fictions created by sources wishing to heighten the Senate's

44. *Od.* 7.139–71.

45. I discount the power wielded by the Areopagus, as no acts of supplication were involved in any episode discussed by Wallace, *Areopagus Council.*

46. Cic. *Att.* 1.14.5.

47. App. *BC* 3.8.51.

48. Liv. 22.60.1–61.3.

49. Serv. *G.* 2.161.

50. Cic. *Sest.* 130, where all Italy supplicates the Senate.

51. V. Max. 5.5.1, D.C. 54.14.2–3.

52. Cic. *Cat.* 4.18.

fame as a place of supplication.[53] The most grandiose of all is a likely fiction that shows that supplicating the Senate is better than either ignoring it or approaching it without supplication. When Rome's debt bondmen, the *nexi*, first appear in Book 2 of Livy, a bondman being led to a creditor's private jail does much of what a suppliant might: he displays scars from a creditor's whippings, tears his clothes, and cites his military record. He does not supplicate, however, and other *nexi* burst into the forum and "call upon their fellow citizens' good faith," language that does not befit the gestures or attitude of a suppliant.[54] So far, the *nexi* have failed to supplicate any one, let alone the Senate. They are relying on their mutual solidarity. And Livy is pointing to the consequence of this self-reliance: the *nexi* do not succeed in freeing themselves from their burdens.

Next the debtors ask for help from the Senate but fail to supplicate. Livy describes the debtors with some sympathy, but adds that they speak "much more in menace than in supplication."[55] Some of the senators are for leniency, but others are for retribution, and debt bondage continues.[56] Then, some books later, the *nexi* do supplicate the Senate. They begin well, by rallying to a bondman who is the victim not only of imprisonment but also of sexual assault. When they address the senators, they again do well, not only by going to the Senate house but by presenting proof that the bondman was punished for defending himself: "And when the consuls, compelled by the sudden tumult, convened the Senate, they fell at the feet of each senator as he entered the curia, and showed him the boy's wounded back." This proof of the worthiness of the victim comes where it should, at the third step. Livy now turns to the fourth step, at which the Senate recommends abolishing debt bondage, and the assembly votes accordingly. In Livy's words, "the chains of credit," *magnum uinculum fidei*, fall victim to the injury suffered by a powerless individual, or—to give supplication to the Senate its due—fall victim to the magnification of this injury through supplication to the most powerful of Roman Republican *supplicandi*.[57] Like the supplication by the Messenians on Mt. Ithome, this act ranks as an occasion when supplication betters the lives of a group.

Even more impressive than this case was the sum of cases in which foreign leaders supplicated the Senate. According to Dionysius, the first case came after the battle of Lake Regillus in 496 BCE, when the defeated Latins approached the Senate. After that, every single century furnishes a more reliable example: in the fourth century, the Campanians who seek Roman protection supplicate the Senate; in the third century, Sicilians supplicate the Senate after suffering mistreatment at the hands of Roman magistrates; in the second, Carthaginians supplicate

53. E.g., D.H. 6.51.2. Fame of the Senate: Calp. *Decl.* 18.

54. Liv. 2.23.3–24.1. "Implorant Quiritium fidem": 2.23.8.

55. "Multo minaciter magis quam suppliciter": Liv. 2.23.11. Senators: 2.23.15.

56. As do the protests, which resume at Liv. 2.27.1. Another such scene: 6.14.3–8, but without supplication. Refs. at Oakley ad 8.28.1–9 do not address the topic of supplication.

57. Liv. 8.28.7. Other sources do not mention supplication, but include the suffering youth (D.H. 16.5.1–3, V. Max. 6.1.9).

and obtain a hearing in which they may accuse their neighbors before a Roman panel; in the first, at a time before all Italians have received Roman citizenship, large numbers of them supplicate the Senate on Cicero's behalf. Only under the Principate does a gap appear, and as late as 103 CE the envoys of the Dacian King Decebalus supplicate when surrendering to the Senate.[58] Only magistrates stationed abroad attract so many suppliants from so many places over so long a time.

Most of these suppliants want a treaty or truce or some other formal relation with Rome.[59] Others want to preserve ties.[60] But several want a hearing or trial, like the Carthaginians.[61] These suppliants go to the Senate for the reason that Jews go to higher ranking magistrates. Denied justice by a lower power, they appeal to a higher one. But the Senate differs from higher ranking magistrates in that it does not always respond by making a decision of its own. Instead it assigns the task to a panel, as it does in Spain when people in that province complain of ill treatment. The motive for this shift emerges from some cases in which the Senate debates whether or not to grant a suppliant's request.[62] The Senate finds itself divided, and so it assigns the issue to a hearing. Or it grants part of the request but not all. One nice answer greets the Rhodians who have been Rome's allies but have offended Rome by recently siding against her. The Senate informs the suppliants that it will treat them as neither allies nor enemies.[63]

Only rarely does the Senate grant a suppliant's request, make a recommendation to an assembly, and then learn that the assembly has declined to adopt the recommendation. In foreign policy, this happens only once, when the Samnites ask the Senate to renew a treaty signed before the long and bitter war that including the disaster that the Sabines inflicted on the Romans at the Caudine Forks. The Senate is ready to forget this defeat in the light of later Roman victories, but an assembly is not, and it prevents the renewal of the treaty. But even here the suppliants obtain a truce.[64]

So far, we have noticed magistrates, especially consuls and tribunes, and the Senate. Greek precedent would now lead us to the assembly. That was the sequence described by Aristotle and followed by suppliants such as the metic Dioscurides: first altar, then council, then assembly.[65] But the power of the magistrates and the influence of the Senate leave the assemblies few suppliants. Tusculan suppliants approach an assembly after learning that a magistrate will introduce a proposal to punish them for inciting rebellion, but in this instance they may have assumed that the Senate is hostile.[66] Supplication of assemblies is rare, but least

58. Liv. 7.31.5–9, Zonar. 9.6, Liv. 42.23.5–24.10, Cic. *Sest.* 130, D.C. 68.10.1.

59. Treaty or truce: D.C. 68.10.1, D.H. 17/18.1.3–4, Zonar. 9.26. Other arrangement: Justin 38.3.4, Liv. 7.31.5–9, 42.23.5–24.10, 43.2.2–3, 44.19.7–14, Zonar. 9.26.

60. Liv. 9.20.2; 45.20.9–25.4 is also described at D.S. 31.5.3.

61. Spain: Liv. 43.2.2–3. Sicily: Zonar. 9.6.

62. Liv. 45.20.9–25.4, Zonar. 9.26.

63. Liv. 45.25.4. Other such answers: Liv. 42.24.6–10.

64. Liv. 9.20.2–3.

65. Arist. *Ath.* 43.2 and *IG* ii² 218, both discussed at 173–76 above.

66. V. Max. 9.10.1.

rare is when an assembly serves as a court or—if it is to repeal a law so as to help an individual—where it serves as a virtual court of appeal.[67] Nothing says more about the importance of *imperium* and of the Senate than this paucity of supplications to the bodies that corresponded to the chief *supplicandus* in classical Athens. If supplication as a whole centered on the one—the king, master, or husband—and Athenian supplication centered on the many, meaning the Assembly, Roman supplication centered on the few: the magistrates and their club, the Senate.[68]

Since this oligopoly intimidated suppliants, some of them used an intercessor, a practice as common among the Romans as the Greeks. Cicero used notables to intercede on his behalf with gatherings of voters.[69] He also used relatives of a magistrate to intercede with a magistrate.[70] An associate of the *supplicandus* would also serve: Ovid wished to use the aristocrat Paullus Fabius Maximus to intercede for him with Augustus.[71] And family would serve: Metellus Pius again is the model.[72] Unlike their Greek counterparts, Roman intercessors are often prestigious. One leader intercedes with another, even if the intercessor approaches in a private capacity, as Paullus Fabius Maximus would have. This practice confirms the centrality of magistrates.

Supplicatory Electioneering

Imperium and related powers, senatorial influence and foreign-policy leadership: after insisting that these things make Roman supplication unique, we should admit that we have departed from what Polybius and other ancient sources say or suppose, which is that the Roman government rested on the consent of the citizenry. We have done so because supplication does not give Rome's assemblies much scope. Now we come to the rejoinder Polybius perhaps would make: one kind of supplication, by far the most common of all, gives power to the assemblies, not the magistrates, and even reduces the magistrates' power. The assemblies act as *supplicandi*, not the magistrates, and the magistrates act only as suppliants. This is not an Athenian kind of supplication in which the Assembly evaluates suppliants. It is a distinctly Roman kind in which would-be magistrates beg assembly members for votes. He who wields *imperium* for a year or more must spend days or weeks begging for the votes of those whom he will command in the field, assist by introducing a bill, or intercede for with another magistrate. He has his perdurable power, they their temporary power.

---

67. Court: D.S. 36.15.2–3. Virtual court of appeal: D.S. 36.16, Plut. *Ant.* 59.1 and the numerous instances involving Cicero's exile, discussed at 270–72 below.

68. Assuming that the consuls are reckoned as elected officials and hence as strengthening the oligarchic (or alternatively the aristocratic) element as defined at Arist. *Pol.* 3.1279a, 4.1293b. Polybius thought of the consuls as elective kings (6.12), thus weakening the oligarchic element.

69. Pompey: Cic. *Pis.* 80, *Red. Sen.* 31, *Sest.* 107. His brother: *Red. Sen.* 37.

70. Cic. *Sest.* 54, 74.

71. Ov. *Pont.* 4.6.10–12. Others: J. *BJ* 1.566 (Livia to Herod the Great rather than Augustus), Cic. *Fam.* 4.4.3.

72. Aside from Metellus Pius and also Livia, App. *BC* 3.8.51, D.C. 47.8.5, Cic. *Fam.* 4.4.3, *Planc.* 24.

The few sources for supplicatory electioneering are unanimous about the frequency and importance of this practice. Sallust can report the Roman leader Marius as claiming that all candidates for office supplicated the people.[73] Cicero, a man without consular ancestors, supplicated for votes; so did the other leading self-made man of his day, Octavian; and so did Rome's archetypal suppliant, the plebeian aristocrat Metellus Pius, who supplicated on behalf of a tribune running for higher office.[74] The practice appears in an informal election manual, and Horace alludes to it.[75] According to Dionysius of Halicarnassus, Servius Tullius, a captive's son, originated the practice.[76] Only one Roman, Scaevola Augur, is known to have objected to it.[77]

Supplicatory electioneering involved approaching the voters, "begging" for their votes, and proving oneself worthy. Cicero explains the several proofs of worth, beginning with good birth. He is speaking to another plebeian aristocrat, Marcus Juventius Laterensis, who has just lost an election:

> Suppose you had thought that it suited your position to do what other nobles have often done when they realized that they were weaker at the polls than expected, and postponed the vote in order to supplicate the people with a humble and broken heart? I don't doubt that the entire populace would have rallied to your cause.

The phrase "other nobles" refers to high birth as a standard of worth. Elsewhere in this passage, Cicero calls this quality *nobilitas*. Since this nobilitas is *integra . . . atque innocens*, it consorts with a second proof of worth, innocence. Next comes a third proof, victimization. As Cicero explains, Laterensis has suffered a loss of what Cicero calls *dignitas* and *magnitudo animi*, influence and assertiveness. All these proofs support the request to be elected. As for the first two steps in the supplication, Cicero takes them for granted. The candidate makes his approach and performs such gestures as allow Cicero to say that he supplicates with a "humble and broken heart." Worth, innocence, victimization, and humble request: the supplicandus cannot say no, and so he votes for the suppliant. Cicero insists on this result, mentioning it not only in the passage quoted but also later in the same speech.[78]

Once we allow candidates to supplicate, we must reckon with their supporters supplicating, too. Like supplication directed to a panel of judges numbering 75—as in the case of Aemilius Scaurus—supplication directed to an electorate of many thousands would require specialization and orchestration. Numerous acts

---

73. Sal. *Jug.* 85.1.
74. Cicero: *Planc.* 24. Octavian: App. *BC* 3.4.28 (44–43 BCE), though while appealing for loyalty and not while running for office. Metellus Pius on behalf of Q. Calidius, a candidate for the praetorship: V. Max. 5.2.7. The same practice under the empire, when only the Senate voted: Plin. *Pan.* 69.2.
75. [Cic.] *Commentar. Petitionis* 8, Hor. *Ep.* 2.2.103.
76. D.H. 4.10.6, with the twist that the candidate asks only that the people express their opinion. Then his partisans, stationed in the crowd, call for him to be chosen.
77. V. Max. 4.5.4.
78. Cic. *Planc.* 50.

or ostensible acts would accompany appeals falling short of acts. But allowing for this similarity between supplicatory electioneering and Roman supplication of the usual kind, as at a trial, should not lead us to overlook how much the two kinds of supplication differ from one another. In electioneering, the suppliant, who in principle was a single person, approached a body that in principle numbered thousands or even millions. In other supplication, the contrast in numbers was far less. In electioneering, there was only one request, and it was always the same. In other supplication, there might be several requests, and requests were diverse. In electioneering, the supplicandi did not need to answer on the spot. In other supplication, they did.

The chief difference lay at the fourth step, and this difference prompted complaint by Sallust. This author does not reject electioneering altogether. Unlike the bribing of voters, electioneering is not a crime. Instead Sallust complains that magistrates would supplicate, win office, and then, when supplicated by others, would fail to help them. Once again Sallust speaks through Marius: "Many do not seek high office from you in the same fashion as they exercise it. . . . At first they are assiduous, supplicant, moderate. Then they lead lives of idle arrogance."[79] Did Sallust write these words in light of Marius's later life, including his saving himself by supplicating boatmen and a ditch digger?[80] If so, Sallust was giving Marius the ironic consolation of denouncing supplicatory electioneering before having to supplicate in another way. But whether or not Sallust had this consolation in mind, Marius is a good spokesman for this complaint. He was the most successful candidate for office in Roman Republican history. Had he seemed to have betrayed the voters, he could not say what he does. His is a good magistrate's protest against evil colleagues.

Supplicatory electioneering also suffered from another drawback at the fourth step. Unlike other supplication, it did not lead to a tie between supplicandus and suppliant. It did not, for example, lead to the candidate turned suppliant becoming the client of the voters. Supplicatory electioneering was an inversion in which the party that ought to do the supplicating, the socially inferior party, was the supplicandus, and the party that ought to entertain the supplication, the superior party, was taking the inferior's place.[81] Only in novels do Greek suppliants and supplicandi participate in such inversions; typical is a freeborn heroine supplicating to preserve her chastity now that she has become a slave.[82] The Roman inversion contributes to a different fiction: the duty of the magistrate to serve the Roman people. Every election featured this fiction, every magistrate acceded to it, and every magistrate to some degree—we cannot and need not say to what degree—let the fiction affect his tenure of office. The cynicism of Sallust's Marius points to other supplications that were sincere if belied.

79. Sal. *Jug.* 85.1.
80. Plut. *Mar.* 37.2–4, 5–6.
81. A similar view of the importance of bribery and of the unimportance of patron-client ties: Mouritsen, *Plebs and Politics*, chap. 5. Clients no doubt often supplicated in private life, as at Ter. *Eu.* 886–9, a passage in which the client makes no gestures but does use the word *obsecro*, making the act resemble supplication.
82. X. Eph. 2.9.4, 3.5.5.

The Emperor as Supplicandus

Since suppliants seek out the powerful, they sought out the emperor. In principle, the emperor wielded the powers of a provincial governor when abroad and of a tribune if not a consul when in Rome; he also possessed original and appellate jurisdiction and served as head of state. All these powers proved attractive to suppliants, but some more than others.[83] The emperor seldom replaced the provincial governor by receiving defeated suppliants, but during his modestly successful campaigns in Illyria, Augustus received two groups of such suppliants. One group surrendered, and he chastised the other for rebelling.[84] Marcus Aurelius and Probus received suppliants in the field, too. Both were German, showing the interest of the sources in reporting supplication by the most prestigious enemies.[85] The column of Trajan adds another example, Dacian suppliants conquered by this emperor.[86] Yet the sum of evidence is meager. The emperor did better when replacing the provincial governor in an administrative capacity. Suggestive evidence comes from Horace, who briefly describes a special situation, an imperial journey to Egypt, the only province regarded as the emperor's personal property. He administered it through a prefect, but when he visited Egypt he could assume the position of a successor to the pharaohs. Here if anywhere the emperor would have the power to grant requests, and so Horace imagines the people of Alexandria supplicating him as they greet him on his approach to the city.[87] This greeting, the ritual of *aduentio*, would accommodate supplication whenever those who greet also ask, and so the blend of the two practices may have been common. In Alexandria, where the emperor ranked as a god, the blend would have resembled worship. An absolute ruler, in turn, would inspire a unique request: to remain on the throne from which he provided benefits to his supporters. Tacitus reports this request, made by the Emperor Otho's troops to Otho during a civil war.[88] Like Horace, Tacitus grasps that the emperor replaces others yet stands apart. Besides monopolizing powers, he changes the character of power.

Did the emperor make old supplicatory methods obsolete? When Augustus sent Ovid into exile, and Ovid wanted an associate of the emperor, Paullus Fabius Maximus, to intercede, Ovid might have told Fabius to ask the emperor to use the tribunician power. Two prototypes of supplication—the supplication of a tribune by Metellus Pius and the supplication of another tribune by a friend of the exiled Cicero—involved this power.[89] But Augustus, unlike a tribune, did not have to propose a law before an assembly or give way to the objections of a colleague.

83. A similar view: Millar, *Emperor*, 17. A contrary view: Syme, *Aristocracy*, 42–43, stressing the tribunician power over "civil government," the sphere in which most acts of supplication occur. Omitted from this survey: acts in which the emperor is a supplicandus by virtue of owning slaves (Tac. *Ann.* 11.30.1–2), being married (14.61.3–62.1), or being addressed by a friend's slave (D.C. 54.23.3).

84. Punishment: App. *Ill.* 24. Surrender: 28.

85. Marcus: D.C. 72.16.1. Probus: *Hist. Aug. Prob.* 14.2.

86. The Column: as at 32 above. The tradition: Barden, *Development of Clementia*, chap. 4.

87. Hor. *Carm.* 4.14.34–6; J. *BJ* 2.336–41, by Jerusalemites to Agrippa II.

88. Tac. *Hist.* 2.46–47.

89. Ov. *Pont.* 4.6.10–12 versus acts discussed at 4–6 above and 270–72 below.

Supplicating him was substantially different from supplicating one of them. For this reason, Ovid does not mention this power. But another example, this one involving Tiberius, showed that old methods might be used for a new reason—to give an impression of modesty. When this emperor came to power he possessed the tribunician power, the same as Augustus, but he did not happen to possess a position as emperor. The Senate wished to correct this anomaly, and so it decided to acknowledge him as emperor by means of a resolution. But would Tiberius veto the resolution by virtue of his tribunician power? The Senate decided to forestall a veto by supplicating Tiberius. Their maneuver had two purposes. Formally speaking, they were supplicating an official with the tribunician power not to veto a resolution. Such a supplication had several Republican precedents, especially that of Metellus Pius. But in substance they were asking Tiberius to assume the throne. They resorted to the formality in order to allow Tiberius to assume the throne passively. If a passive supplicandus is an oxymoron, the author need not be so blatant as to say so, especially if the author is Tacitus.[90]

The emperor's power to hold hearings and conduct trials either privately or in the Senate also had two purposes. On the one hand, the suppliant asked to be granted a hearing, as did his counterparts in classical Athens. Just as they went to the Athenian Council, he went to the head of state. But the Roman suppliant was also appealing to the party that would decide the case. By asking the emperor to grant a hearing, he was inviting the emperor to take his side. So, when the Emperor Vitellius's brother begs Vitellius to hear evidence incriminating a third party, Vitellius agrees to hear the evidence and then acts against the person accused.[91] The emperor was also the cynosure of any hearing in which the Senate joined him. Then the suppliant would ignore the Senate and supplicate the emperor. After Caligula made the Senate listen to a long speech of his against Domitius Afer, a senator who had offended him, Afer not only did not supplicate the senators, he did not speak to the emperor. Although a famous orator, he refused to say a word in his own defense, and instead supplicated Caligula by means of gestures. Gratified to discover that a good speaker would not dare argue against him, Caligula spared Afer.[92] If the emperor found the defendant supplicating the Senate and not himself, he could cut short the proceeding. After Nero convenes the Senate and lets a senator accuse Junius Gallio, Seneca's brother, other senators object, Gallio supplicates the Senate, and the nonplussed Nero halts the trial.[93]

As before, Tiberius proves a more challenging supplicandus. When the defendant Libo addresses himself to Tiberius in the course of a trial conducted by Tiberius and the Senate, Tiberius rejects Libo's supplication. This rejection spells Libo's conviction, and Libo commits suicide shortly afterward. After his death,

---

90. Resolution and failure to use veto: Tac. *Ann.* 1.13.5. Supplication: Tac. *Ann.* 1.11.3, 1.12.1, and Suet. *Tib.* 24.1.

91. Tac. *Hist.* 3.38. An emperor who allows supplication, then rejects the suppliant: D.C. 65.16.2.

92. D.C. 59.19.5–6.

93. Tac. *Ann.* 15.73.4.

Tiberius makes the tardy complaint that he would not have allowed the Senate's conviction of Libo to stand. Instead he would have pardoned Libo. Why, then, did Tiberius not accept this suppliant? The emperor valued the formality of a Senate verdict, just as he valued the formality of a Senate resolution.[94]

Foreign legates had no illusions about the emperor's position. As they once went to the Senate, they now went to him. Augustus receives such suppliants, and emperors down through Septimius Severus follow his example.[95] The emperor's success in replacing a body numbering hundreds underscores the concentration of power in his hands and the consequent replacement of a class of supplicandi with a single supplicandus. This change, in turn, lead to a change in the act of supplication. Foreign legates and rulers did obeisance to the emperor. The best-reported instance is Tiridates II, the king of Armenia, doing obeisance to Nero when coming to Rome to request aid. This practice had the same advantage as combining *aduentio* and supplication: suppliants acknowledged the emperor's power even as they asked the emperor to use it. Similarly, Diodorus Siculus recommended obeisance to benefactors.[96]

Easy to describe with regard to its purpose, obeisance is not easy to describe with regard to gestures. In the ancient world, these gestures differed according to obvious variables like country and era but also by three variables that affect supplication: author, genre, and medium. Disagreement arises even concerning the distant model for obeisance to the Roman emperor: obeisance to the kings of Achaemenid Persia, a ritual known as *proskynêsis*. In the lower right-hand corner of figure 5.1, there appears one possibility: prostration or genuflection.[97] Another gesture consists of bowing and putting one's hand to one's lips to send a kiss. Supporting this possibility is a passage in Aelian, where a man fakes *proskynêsis* by bowing and touching the ground with his fingers.[98] The cardinal point is that these gestures more or less resemble those of supplication.[99] (So do other gestures appearing in figure 5.1, but not so much.)

Nor is obeisance easy to describe in its implications. For the Persians, it did not imply that the suppliant worshipped the king. For the Romans and the Greeks, however, it did. As a consequence, *proskynêsis* toward a person implied obsequiousness on the part of those performing this act. Themistocles, for example, was thought to have behaved obsequiously when he supplicated and

94. Tac. *Ann.* 2.29, including supplication at 2.29.2.

95. Augustus: Aug. *Anc.* 5.54–6.38. Nero: Suet. *Nero* 13.2, [Sen.] *Oct.* 627–8. Domitian: D.C. 67.5.1. Hadrian: *Hist. Aug. Had.* 21.14. Trajan: Fro. *Parth.* 16. Septimius Severus: Hrd. 3.9.2. Going to the emperor and the Senate both, but chiefly to the emperor: Clinton, "Maroneia," a decree from Maroneia recording this practice during the reign of Claudius.

96. D.S. 1.90.3.

97. Fig. 5.1: red-figure volute crater of ca. 300 BCE, Naples 3253 = Trendall-Webster 112 III.5.6 s.v. *Persai*, which presents a scene from a lost play.

98. Ael. *VH* 1.21, where a reluctant Ismenias fakes the gesture in order to obtain an audience. The same fakery: Plut. *Art.* 22.4. Expressing doubt about the interpretation of the passage: Briant, *Empire perse*, 235.

99. Weighing the two possibilities, the first of which appears in Persian visual art: Briant, *Empire perse*, 234–36. A collection of literary and older visual sources: Delatte, *Baiser*, chap. 1.

FIGURE 5.1   *Proskynesis* and other gestures. Singer 71.454, courtesy of the
Deutsches Archäologisches Institut Rom.

performed *proskynêsis* when going into exile in Persia.[100] Had the Greeks known
of other Near Eastern examples of the same double practice, they would have
condemned them as well.[101]

An example of objectionable *proskynêsis* appears in *Oedipus the King*. As the
play begins, the chorus prays to the gods and supplicates Oedipus, suggesting some
confusion of religious practices. This scene does not go so far as to include *proskynêsis*. Then, soon afterward, another supplication occurs, and this time *proskynêsis* is indeed mentioned, if not performed. The person addressed is the prophet
Tiresias, not Oedipus, who is now among the suppliants. He says to Tiresias, "In
god's name, don't turn away if you know who killed Laius. We are here as suppli-

100. Plut. *Them*. 28.1–29.2. Greek fear of impiety and Persianness: Hall, *Inventing the Barbarian*, 96–98,
with refs, esp. to Plut. *Super*. 166a.

101. As at 2 *Ki*. 14.4–5, *Es*. 8.3, Curt. 5.10.13–15. In these instances, the act of *proskynêsis* comes first, the
request second. Similar are the supplications at chap. 3, n. 17.

ants, doing obeisance to you (προσκυνοῦμεν)."[102] What Oedipus and the others are doing, or what he says they are doing, is a matter of dispute—either of the two possibilities would serve.[103] This cardinal point once again is that the gestures resemble those of supplication. These gestures let Oedipus and the people do— or say they are doing—two or even three things. They are making a request of Tiresias; they are performing obeisance to him; and they are apparently worshipping him. Such a people and such a king are not handling their religious duties circumspectly. The confusion of the opening scenes recurs, but ominously, and Oedipus's relations with Tiresias begin poorly.

The action of Oedipus and the Thebans is unique: in extant literature describing events before (or supposedly before) Alexander the Great, no other Greek performs a gesture of obeisance to a Greek.[104] But several other scenes in tragedy show Barbarians and slaves performing the gesture while supplicating, the pair of actions found in Sophocles. In *Orestes*, a Trojan slave supplicates as he performs a gesture that he describes as προσκυνῶ σε. Similarly, a slave in Euripides' *Trojan Women* supplicates her master's brother in a scene where she says others perform *proskynêsis*.[105] These scenes confirm the obsequiousness of supplicating and doing obeisance at the same time.

Over time, hostility toward this double practice began to diminish. Some Greeks who supplicated and did obeisance were met with mockery rather than an accusation of impiety. Plutarch reports that when a follower of Epicurus supplicated and did obeisance to him, the philosopher made jokes.[106] Or mockery was tempered by sympathy, as in Lucian, where the poor use the double practice in order to beg from the rich.[107] Since the supplication of Themistocles is reported late, in Plutarch, who sympathizes with Themistocles, the same is true of this act. First, Plutarch says, the suppliant performs the gestures of *proskynêsis*, rises, and states his name. Then he declares that he is a suppliant and makes the usual arguments: promises of aid for the supplicandus, and divine portents in his favor. Since the grand vizier told him only to perform *proskynêsis* and then rise, Themistocles displays cleverness in the second part of this scene, just as he displays obsequiousness in the first part.[108] Nor does Diodorus, a contemporary of Augustus,

---

102. S. *OT* 326–7. This is only occurrence of the word in this play, and one of only two in Sophocles. In the other, *OC* 1654, the context is worship and not obeisance, and the gesture is the familiar one reported at Plb. 15.1.6, where a Roman says that all mankind "salute the gods and venerate the earth" (ἀσπάσαιντο τοὺς θεοὺς καὶ προσκυνήσαιεν τὴν γῆν).

103. Actual *proskynêsis*: Jebb in his translation, though he makes no comment ad loc. No gesture: Kamerbeek ad loc. A different view: Hall, *Inventing the Barbarian*, 96 n. 188, saying that it is fitting for Tiresias to receive *proskynêsis* as Apollo's intermediary.

104. I.e., performs *proskynêsis* in this sense. *Proskyneô* has several unrelated meanings as at *LSJ* s.v., but the meaning "to respect" is not post-classical, as *LSJ* implies: see Aeschin. 2.150. *Vita Alex.* 1.46a retrojects an instance of *proskynêsis* and supplication to the siege of Thebes by Alexander.

105. E. *Or.* 1506–7; E. *Tro.* 1021 (*proskynêsis* desired by Paris) and 1042–59 (supplication made to Menelaus).

106. Plut. *Adv. Colotem* 1117b.

107. Lucianus *Tim.* 5.4, where Timon complains of no longer receiving obeisance now that he has ceased disbursing monies.

108. *Proskynêsis*: Plut. *Them.* 28.1. Self-declared suppliant: 28.3. Another Persian case, but in exceptional circumstances: Plut. *Art.* 29.6–7.

find anything remarkable about the defeated Milesians performing obeisance to Alexander the Great while supplicating him.[109]

But the biggest step came when Roman magistrates found themselves in the lands that had once belonged to the Persian Empire. In this case, a Greek or a Roman would not perform the double practice to an emperor. Instead Easterners would perform it toward a Roman magistrate. A forerunner is Scipio Africanus, venerated and supplicated by the Carthaginians according to Livy and Polybius.[110] An early example is Pompey, venerated and supplicated by Tigranes, who even gave up his crown, recovering it after Pompey made him rise.[111] The source, Dio, does not mention *proskynêsis*, but since Tigranes was Armenian, he may have performed it.[112] But what is the first instance of the double practice directed to one Roman by another Roman? Dio and Cicero say that Antony supplicated Caesar while putting a crown on Caesar's head, but not even Cicero says that Antony performed *proskynêsis*, though he does say that he threw himself at Caesar's feet.[113] Antony might have defended himself by saying that he was masquerading as a slave, a role that he played as part of the Lupercalia. The slave would properly perform this humiliating gesture.

Last come sources from the early Principate. By now the double practice is occurring to the distress of the sources as opposed to the participants. The first such report is Seneca's that a man pardoned by Caligula thanked the emperor by prostrating himself and kissing his foot. Here there is no supplication, for there is no request, but Dio says that the courtier Juventius supplicated Domitian while performing what Dio expressly says is *proskynêsis*, or obeisance in the Persian manner.[114] Herodian says that *proskynêsis* was customary by the time of Septimius Severus, so we may guess that even before the end of the Principate, there must have been many suppliants like Juventius.[115] Several suppliants whom the sources do not describe as performing *proskynêsis* prostrate themselves before the emperor, a similar if not identical act.[116] The double practice thus became suitable when supplicating an emperor. No longer exotic, it had become customary.[117]

So, by a path beginning with the tyrant Oedipus and perhaps ending with the tyrant Caesar, the blend of supplication and obeisance became a way of approaching Caesar's successors. They had already absorbed the duties of lesser magistrates and turned Rome into something like an additional province, and now they

---

109. D.S. 17.22.4.

110. Liv. 30.16.4, "more adulantium"; Plb. 10.17.8. But Scipio himself is too modest to mention veneration as well as supplication (Plb. 15.8.12). No information: Zonar. 9.11.

111. D.C. 36.52.3; similar is V. Max. 5.1.9. No such gestures occur at Vell. 2.37.4, who emphasizes that Tigranes did not use intermediaries.

112. No *proskynêsis* mentioned: Flor. *Epit.* 1.40, Vell. 2.37.4. Perhaps implied: "supplicem abiectum," Cic. *Sest.* 58. Dio probably retrojects when saying that Prusias of Bithynia performed *proskynêsis* to the Senate (9.24).

113. D.C. 45.32.3–4; Cic. *Phil.* 2.86.

114. Sen. *Ben.* 2.12.1–2, D.C. 67.13.3–4.

115. Hrd. 3.11.8. Ovid's expressions at *Pont.* 2.9.21–2, 4.8.21–4, and elsewhere are omitted, since they do not form part of acts of supplication. Ovid's use of supplication in his exilic writings: appendix 6.

116. D.C. 59.19.5–6, Flor. *Epit.* 2.21.

117. A similar view of the gradual introduction and reconfiguration of *proskynêsis* alone: Kolb, *Herrscheride-ologie*, 39–40, with refs.

acquired still more power. But their power lay largely in their *imperium*, and in that sense they resembled Caesar's Republican predecessors. In this respect, they differed from earlier supplicandi. Kings and others had personal power, and the magistrates of classical Athens had powers assigned by the Assembly. *Imperium* differed from these powers. It gave the supplicandus more scope to help the suppliant, and it gave the suppliant more ways to seek help. In the Republic, when *imperium* belonged to elected magistrates, the suppliants also enjoyed some apparent and even some genuine recompense for the power that the supplicandus wielded: supplicatory electioneering. In this respect, Roman supplication was superior to Greek. The same superiority marked the balance between supplicandi with power, including magistrates and promagistrates, and a supplicandus with influence, the Senate. And it marked the double practice of supplication and obeisance, which let the suppliant give support to the power on which he relied.

These advantages were procedural or structural: more effective supplicandi, supplicandi doubling as suppliants, supplicandi of two types, twofold supplication. More important was another advantage, one affecting the substance rather than the procedure of supplication. The Greeks judged suppliants as either worthy or unworthy. The Romans would add a third category.

MERCY

Most Roman suppliants claimed to be innocent or otherwise deserving, and many asked for pity, the same as Greek suppliants. To cite but one: Seneca's Medea (but not Euripides') says that Creon should accept her supplication because she speaks on behalf of her innocent children and not of herself.[118] By the same token, Roman suppliants would make excuses like involuntary wrongdoing, the same as Greeks.[119] The Romans were also aware of *epieikeia* as analyzed by Aristotle. Like some Greeks, some Romans argued that if the judges considered some principle such as the lawgiver's intention, the suppliant would deserve acquittal.[120]

The Romans differed from the Greeks in allowing a suppliant to admit his own guilt and ask for mercy. A new pair of ideas—guilt and mercy—would stand alongside the long-standing pair of innocence and pity.[121] As a result, suppliants could make either of two kinds of pleas, and supplicandi could answer with either of two kinds of reasons to say "yes." The background for this change lay in the Latin language and in Roman ethics and law, and the results—several dozen cases in which suppliants beg for mercy and succeed—appeared in many genres over several centuries.

---

118. Sen. *Med.* 282–83.
119. D.H. 1.58.3, Serv. *G.* 2.161. In court: *Rhet. Her.* 2.23.
120. *Rhet. Her.* 2.20, translating *epieikes* as *aequum*; Bonner, *Declamation*, 46–47, 57, 122–24.
121. Two ideas, and not one, as Statius misleadingly implies when he describes the Athenian "altar of pity" as an altar of *clementia* (*Theb.* 12.481–82). The "altar of pity" was itself a literary convention as shown by Wycherley, "*Eleos.*"

The fundamental Roman supplicatory term, *supplico*, derives from a root meaning either "to appease" or "to bend (the knee)."[122] The fundamental Greek supplicatory term, *hiketeuô*, derives from a root meaning "to approach."[123] It differs from the Latin term in two ways: it refers to the first step rather than to the second or third, and it refers to the suppliant's movements rather than to his purpose or to an expressive gesture. If *supplico* refers to bending the knee, Latin differs in yet another way: it is vertical in its orientation, whereas Greek is both vertical and horizontal.[124] Other Greek and Roman terms confirm these contrasts. The Greek poetic term *prostropaios* derives from roots meaning "to turn toward," and vernacular Greek terms for sitting at an altar often include a prepositional prefix meaning "down" or "at."[125] Yet Latin translations of Greek terms sometimes refer only to the suppliant's words or to his purpose or demeanor.[126] *Supplico* and other Latin terms also differ from those in modern languages. The German verbs *bittflehen* and *schutzflehen* specify a request and imply desperation, whereas English "beg" specifies not a request but an act. All three words have more to say than Latin does about supplication as a whole. Once again Latin stands apart, but this time for being psychological.

If we derive *supplico* from "bending the knee," Latin differs from other languages in yet another way. It implies that the suppliant debases himself, like a worshipper, and that the supplicandus rises superior to him, like a god. The Latin word *supplex* confirms these comparisons, for it refers to both suppliants and worshippers, and so does the Latin word *supplicatio*, which refers to worship alone. Besides being far removed from modern languages, these words are somewhat removed from Greek, in which one common word, *hiketês*, refers to supplication but not worship, and two others, *hiketeia* and *hikesia*, refer to supplication as well as worship.[127] A passage in Virtruvius broadens this distinction by adducing several particulars about the performance of *supplicatio*. In this passage, those performing the ritual are matrons who enter a temple on their knees and crawl in single file, embracing the plinths and columns as they go. There are so many worshippers and so little space that they may block one another's view of the doors to the sanctum and of the image inside it, or prevent others from entering.[128] Once they enter, Polybius adds, they sweep the floor with their hair.[129] "Suppliants" of

122. Freyburger, "Supplication grecque," 502–4, and Benveniste, *Vocabulaire*, 2.252–54.

123. Benveniste, *Vocabulaire*, 2.252–54, but also found in Chantraine, *Dictionnaire* and *GrEW*, s.v. *hiketês* or *hikô*. Letoublon, "Le vocabulaire de la supplication," 329–30, holds that it means to touch the knees of the supplicandus, but even he implies an approach.

124. Vertical vs. horizontal orientation: Lakoff and Johnson, *Philosophy*, 51, 53.

125. *Prostropaios* as "turning towards god for protection": A. *Eu.* 178, 237, S. *Ph.* 930, E. *Heracl.* 1015. As "turning towards god for vengeance": A. *Ch.* 287; so also *prostropos hiketês* in S. *Ph.* 773, *OT* 41. For discussion, see R. Parker, *Miasma*, 108. For the common terms καθίζομαι and ἐφέστιος, see *LSJ* ss. vv.

126. See chap. 1, n. 75. *Gounoumai* as *progeniculo*: *Hermeneumata* s.v. γουνοῦμαι, a mistranslation in which the suppliant's approaching and clasping a knee is mistaken for his bending his own knee without necessarily approaching.

127. Some examples from just one author, Livy: 8.33.20, 30.21.10, 37.47.5, 41.28.1 (thanksgiving, or *gratulationes*); 32.1.9, 32.37.3, 32.40.2, 42.2.7, 42.20.3, 43.13.8, 45.16.6 (expiatory sacrifices); 22.9.10, 36.1.2 (offerings at *lectisternia*); 45.2.8 (at *puluinaria*).

128. The substance of Vitr. 3.3.3, describing two styles of temple, the *pycnostylos* and *systylos*.

129. Plb. 9.6.3.

this sort are not approaching but adoring. By the same token, they give thanks or express remorse but they do not assert their own worth.

Another cognate of *supplico*, the noun *supplicium*, means "punishment." Several acts of Roman supplication feature both these words, or feature *supplicium* and some other cognate of *supplico*, including an act in Fronto in which a Parthian king supplicates Trajan. After reporting that Trajan killed the king, Fronto says it would have been better for Rome's reputation for the suppliant to live and *luere supplicium*, "pay a price."[130] In contrast, the Greek language does not link supplication and punishment. Neither *hiketeuô* nor *lissomai* nor two common gestural terms, *gounazomai* and *kathizomai*, have any cognates denoting punishment. The same contrast applies to Roman and Greek gestures, but somewhat less so. In both societies, a person about to punished might assume the same posture as a suppliant, but Roman sources describe such persons more often than Greek ones do.[131] Besides being psychological and worshipful, Latin terms connote guilt.

All these traits would incline the supplicandus toward mercy. The stress on demeanor would draw attention to the suppliant's repentance, debasement would give the supplicandus a sense of power and corresponding responsibility, and guilt would give the supplicandus a moral advantage. But the supplicandus would also need a rationale for granting mercy, and here ethical and legal ideas entered in. A suppliant might do wrong, but under mitigating circumstances that would entitle the supplicandus to accept him. These mitigating circumstances differed from involuntary wrongdoing, a long-established plea, because they did not absolve the suppliant of responsibility. The suppliant had committed a crime, but a forgivable one. In response, the supplicandus might give a reprieve, issue a reprimand, or acknowledge the suppliant's repentance. As Seneca says, the suppliant might be good enough to respond to correction but not bad enough to require deterrence or expulsion from society.[132]

Which crimes were forgivable and which were not? *Culpa*, a "fault," was forgivable, but *maleficium* and *iniuria*, two kinds of grievous wrongdoing, were not.[133] Cicero uses the career of Catiline to explain the difference. Before this adventurer undertook the conspiracy that made him a public enemy, he was "vicious . . . and reckless, but a friend," and so he was able to supplicate successfully when asking for legal representation following an indictment for extortion. The advocate whom Catiline approached agreed to defend him even while admitting his client's vices. This advocate said that the Catiline of those days before the conspiracy had committed minor offenses or been guilty of *culpa*, carelessness or poor judgment.[134] The Catiline who led a conspiracy was indefensible. In this contrast, Cicero omits only

---

130. Fro. *Parth.* 16, using *supplex* and *supplicium*. Other passages using this pair of words: Curt. 3.2.17, Petr. 107.4 with 108.1, Sen. *Phaed.* 667–68 with 706, V. Max. 9.2 ext. 2.

131. Cic. *Verr.* 2.5.140, *Clu.* 38, *Flac.* 68, Liv. 23.10.5.

132. Sen. *Cl.* 1.22.1. Similarly, Taurus apud Gell. 7.14.2.

133. Gell. 7.2.13 disapproves of figurative supplication by those guilty of both *culpa* and *maleficium*, whereas Tac. *Ann.* 3.24.3 approves of *clementia* toward likely suppliants guilty of the *culpa* of adultery.

134. Catiline: *Sul.* 81. *Culpa* as at *OLD* s. v. *culpa* 3c–d, 4a.

one important feature: the suppliant who asks for forgiveness must acknowledge that the supplicandus is in the right and that he is in the wrong.[135]

In reply, the supplicandus would offer to grant *uenia*, "pardon," or to forgive, *ignoscere*, or to spare, *parcere*.[136] If the suppliant was a military opponent, the supplicandus spoke somewhat differently, perhaps because the suppliant was guilty not of carelessness but of a more serious fault, waging unjust war or committing treason. The term for mercy, *clementia*, appears in these military cases, which form a more prominent if not more important group. *Clementia*, however, does not differ from *uenia* in its effect, which is to pardon the suppliant.[137] *Clementia* has, moreover, another aspect that is relevant to all these cases. It is an attitude. Any supplicandus might feel it, just as any supplicandus might feel pity. The difference between *clementia* and pity is ethical. *Clementia* is for the pardonable suppliant, pity for the deserving one. By the same token, *clementia* toward a suppliant differs from kindliness, Greek *philanthropia* and Latin *humanitas*. A suppliant might feel kindly, but he would not pardon a suppliant for this reason alone.[138] Emotion and reasoning form a whole, as they do for the Athenian judge.

It bears repeating that this new way of accepting a suppliant does not supplant or even challenge the old. In particular, it does not affect the need for suppliant defendants to assert their innocence. As Quintilian says, *clementia* is to be invoked in speeches made before deliberative bodies rather than in court.[139] If *clementia* is invoked in court, the suppliant defendant is admitting guilt and asking for a lesser punishment.[140] At most, such a defendant will hint that the judge might set his guilt aside.[141] The defendant will not presume to say that *clementia* should prevail over the demands of justice. In Attic terms, *clementia* might be invoked at the second stage of a proceeding, when the court imposes a punishment, but not (or not plainly) at the first stage, when it renders a verdict.[142] Cicero asks for *clementia* for not a single suppliant defendant.[143]

---

135. A condition noted by Brunt, *"Laus Imperii,"* 314–16, but without regard to supplication in particular.

136. *Venia* for a suppliant addressing a Roman supplicandus: *B. Afr.* 92.4, Cic. *Lig.* 2, Liv. 8.35.7, Tac. *Ann.* 2.22.3. Similarly, *ignosco, parco,* or cognates used of the response to a suppliant: *B. Alex.* 67.1, Cic. *Deiot.* 12, Luc. 4.343, Tac. *Ann.* 1.44.1, 3.61.2. The Greek equivalents are *apoluô* (App. *BC* 5.1.4, 1.7), *suggignôskô,* and *suggnômê* (App. *Mith.* 104, Paus 4.4.7, Plut. *Caes.* 16.4, *Pomp.* 24.7, Zonar. 9.6, and the Greek original inspiring Curt. 8.10.35).

137. So at *B. Afr.* 92.4 the suppliants hope for *clementia* and receive *uenia*. General statement to this effect: Sen. *Cl.* 1.2.2, combining *clementia* and *ignosco.*

138. *Philanthropia* and *humanitas* versus *clementia*: H. Bell, *"Philanthropia,"* though he does not deal with cases of supplication. No Latin suppliant or supplicandus refers to *humanitas,* but doubtless many supplicandi felt it. Like pity, it emerges from the situation and especially the suppliant's arguments, and not merely from a request.

139. Quint. *Inst.* 5.13.6. So also 7.4.18, where it is for the *princeps* or a deliberative body and again not for a court. *Rhet. Her.* 1.24, 2.26 also rule out courtroom appeals for mercy (i.e., *ignosci postulare*).

140. [Quint.] *Decl.* 14.2, 17.1. Since these defendants are not said to supplicate, there may be no appeal to *clementia* by the courtroom suppliant even in these cases.

141. Quint. *Inst.* 9.2.90. "Hint": *suspicionem.*

142. *Clementia* thus differs from *epieikeia* or *aequitas,* which is relevant to the first stage. But not all ancient sources respect this distinction: Plutarch (*Caes.* 57.3) calls the altar of *clementia* of Tiberius the altar of *epieikeia.* Agreeing with Plutarch: Barden, *Development of Clementia,* 111, citing him and linking *clementia* and *epieikeia.*

143. And Cicero speaks of *clementia* toward only one courtroom defendant of any kind (*S. Rosc.* 85).

We begin with cases where the term *clementia* is missing but not some other, such as *uenia*. One suppliant who finds mercy is a slave who drops a costly goblet in the house of Vedius Pollio, an epicure who is then entertaining Augustus. Pollio orders that the slave be eaten alive by predatory fish, and so the slave falls at the emperor's feet, humbling himself. In Greek practice, Augustus would either raise the slave or refuse to do so, perhaps by turning away. If he chose to raise him, the emperor might say or imply that the slave had done no wrong. But Augustus chooses to do something altogether different. First he asks Pollio not to punish the slave. When that fails, he tries to show Pollio that there is a mitigating circumstance:

> When Pollio refused, Augustus said, "Come then, bring all the other similar cups that you have bought and any other expensive ones, so that I may use them." And when they were brought, he ordered them all to be smashed.[144]

Augustus has not asserted the suppliant's innocence. He has done something like the opposite and asserted his own guilt. Will Pollio dare to punish him for it? If not, the emperor implies, Pollio should not punish a slave for a lesser offense. As a slave says in a similar case in Petronius, "My sin is a small one."[145]

Augustus is also implying a second reason to spare the suppliant. His own conduct was deliberate. The suppliant's was negligent, and so it should be all the less culpable. This same notion of negligence appears in a case of mitigating circumstances in military service. A centurion of Julius Caesar's loses his shield, a mishap that is commonly seen as evidence of cowardice and thus is not a venial offense. He lost it, however, while fighting bravely, and so his misdeed is careless but not disgraceful. When he supplicates Caesar, the commander recognizes this mitigating circumstance and gives a reprieve, as Pollio should.[146]

Another military case introduces a third mitigating circumstance, poor judgment on the part of the suppliant. This suppliant is a high-ranking officer, Q. Fabius Rullianus, who has disobeyed orders but helped win a Roman victory over Italian neighbors in the late fourth century BCE. Like the centurion, he has fought bravely, but unlike the centurion he cannot say he has committed a venial offense. He cannot, moreover, say that he has acted carelessly rather than deliberately. Instead, the notion of *culpa* must shift so as to mean poor judgment. This shift allows Rullianus to plead for mercy, like the centurion—and when his own pleas prove insufficient, it allows him to enlist his own father, another high-ranking officer, to plead for him. When mercy is granted, it comes with a reprimand for the violation of military law. Poor judgment is harder for the *supplicandus* to accept than

---

144. D.C. 54.23.3. Similar: Sen. *Dial.*3.40.2–5; *Cl.* 1.18.2 lacks supplication. A similar incident including supplication: Petr. 30.7–11. Pollio the epicure: Syme, "Vedius Pollio," 29.

145. Petr. 30.7, where a supplicating house slave says, "nec magnum esse peccatum suum." A different view of such scenes, ignoring supplication: W. Fitzgerald, *Slavery and the Roman Literary Imagination*, 55–56.

146. Plut. *Caes.* 16.4.

carelessness, but it remains a mitigating circumstance that a suppliant may cite.[147] Other military suppliants fall into this category, too: disobedient, brave, and foolish. Like Rullianus, they are spared and reprimanded.[148]

Just as the centurion forms a bridge between the careless slave and the imprudent Rullianus, Rullianus forms a bridge between military suppliants who have disobeyed orders and the more numerous military suppliants who have fought against the supplicandus. As aggressors and traitors, they are the most difficult to pardon, and it is just in these cases, where *clementia* is hardest to give, that the term most frequently appears.[149] The rationale would seem to be that the enemy is in the wrong but subject to another mitigating circumstance—willingness to recognize his mistake and change sides. Unlike Rullianus, who showed poor judgment and won, these suppliants show poor judgment and lose. They must repent.

Clementia of this kind comes from conquerors.[150] A reliable early report concerns Marcellus, the first Roman to capture a great city, Syracuse. He received conquered Syracusan suppliants *clementer*, "mercifully," after they testified against him in a lawsuit brought by his political opponents. This testimony, charging him with misconduct after capturing their city, was the mainstay of the case, and no wonder: according to another source, Diodorus, they had supplicated him before, extracted a promise that he would not kill them, and then went hungry after he seized their property. But the prosecution failed. Only then did the Syracusans approach him and ask to become his clients. In response, he viewed them as foes who had repented their opposition to him, and he accepted their supplication.[151]

A century and a half later, Marcellus influences the famed *clementia Caesaris*. Caesar himself, curiously, does not refer to *clementia* or *uenia* in dealing with suppliants.[152] But other sources report that Numidians and several kings obtain these two things from him, the suppliant Gaul Divitiacus begs for *clementia*, and Cicero makes a general statement to this effect.[153] They also report Caesar's practice of sparing the first time but killing the second.[154] This practice is partly the same as that of Marcellus: spare those who have compensated for poor judgment by changing sides. But Caesar extends the practice by not allowing a second offense. His unstated reasoning must have been that the change in allegiance must be permanent.

---

147. Liv. 8.35.3–8 (325 BCE). Another comic parody: Pl. *Cas.* 1000–9, where an errant husband admits his poor judgment to his wife.

148. J. *BJ* 5.127–28.

149. Military and political cases: *B. Afr.* 92.4, Caes. *Gal.* 7.15.6, Cic. *Lig.* 2 (all *uenia*); *B. Alex.* 67.1, Cic. *Deiot.* 12, Luc. 4.343 (all *ignosco* or *parco*); App. *BC* 5.1.4, 5.1.7, *Mith.* 104, Zonar. 9.6 (Greek terms). General statement: Val. Max. 5.1 pr.

150. Hölscher, *Victoria Romana*, 106–7. *Clementia* as a virtue of the high-ranking: Cic. *Inv.* 2.164.

151. V. Max. 4.1.7, Plut. *Marc.* 23.6; D.S. 26.20.1–2.

152. I.e., no mention at *Gal.* 1.20.1–5, 1.27.1–28.2, 1.31.1–33.1, 2.13.2–15.1, 2.28.2–3, 7.40.6, although the Helvetii (1.27.1–28.2) and Haedui (7.40.6) are aggressors, and the latter are violators of pledges.

153. Numidians: *B. Afr.* 92.4. Ariobazarnes of Armenia: *B. Alex.* 67.1. Diuitiacus: Caes *Gal.* 2.14.5. Deiotarus, king of the Galatians: Cic. *Deiot.* 43.

154. Spared after the first capture: Suet. *Jul.* 75.1, a general statement. A case where the captive is sure to have supplicated: Luc. 4.337–64, where Caesar spares Afranius.

These are all cases that Caesar heard in the field, but he could render similar judgments when acting as a one-man tribunal. When Caesar's erstwhile opponent Q. Ligarius came before Caesar in such a venue, Cicero pleaded for Ligarius and persuaded Caesar to grant *uenia*.[155] The principle of sparing the first time and killing the second was thus both military and judicial, a circumstance that helped make it familiar. When Julius Caesar rejects and kills a distant relation, Lucius Caesar, even though Lucius is supplicating for the first time, Dio stresses that Lucius resembles those who have been spared. Lucius is not a captive and has supplicated "voluntarily."[156] Lucius's anomalous punishment thus stands exposed.

Perhaps because imperial *clementia* gives more power to the *supplicandus*, he sometimes does what other *supplicandi* do not, and takes the initiative away from the suppliant. On one occasion, Drusus advises rebellious troops that he will be forgiving if they supplicate, and so they do.[157] On another, troops do not supplicate after Germanicus tells them to, but they confess their wrongdoing after he makes it clear that this is what he wishes. They then supplicate. During this act, the troops ask him to spare those who "slipped," *lapsis*, but to condemn the "guilty," *noxios*—a distinction not between the deserving and the undeserving, but between those who deserve forgiveness for "slipping" and those who deserve rejection for grievous wrongdoing. But Germanicus retains the initiative, ordering them to select those who are "guilty" and vote for either life or death.[158] The suppliants end up condemning some that are not among their number but also some who are. To that degree, Germanicus turns their act of supplication against them. Nero does the same. When one group of suppliants asks for forgiveness, the emperor rejects their request but allows them to choose the manner of their death.[159]

Unlike other sorts of mercy, *clementia* for enemies meets with an obvious criticism: those who supplicated this way were guilty not of poor judgment but of bad luck. They chose the right side but met with the wrong result, defeat. After Lucius Domitius Ahenobarbus receives Caesar's forgiveness, Lucan makes him complain: "For a free man it is the ultimate punishment for him to be *forgiven* for following the camp of his country, of Pompey the Great, and of the whole Senate."[160] Ahenobarbus states the objection in political terms, but Greek supplication allows us to state it in general terms. If a suppliant is accepted because of mitigating circumstances, the suppliant is guilty, not worthy, and so he suffers a loss of stand-

---

155. *Veniam*: Cic. *Lig.* 2. Supplication: 36.

156. D.C. 43.12.3 (46 BCE). "Voluntarily": ἐθελούσιον. The considerable scholarship on Caesar's *clementia* does not consider supplication as a distinct factor, e.g., Weinstock, *Divus Julius*, 45–47, comparing Caes. *Civ.* 3.98, Suet. *Jul.* 20.4, and Plut. *Cat. Mi.* 66.1, none of which are acts of supplication, with Cic. *Fam.* 6.14.2, which is.

157. Tac. *Ann.* 1.29.1–2 (14 CE).

158. Not quite supplicating: "orant obsistunt" (Tac. *Ann.* 1.41.4). Confessing afterward: "supplices ad haec et vera exprobari fatentes" (1.44.1). Slippage and guilt: 1.44.1–4.

159. Pardon denied by Nero: *Ann.* 13.25.2–3. Cf. Suet. *Tib.* 53.2, where Tiberius shows *clementia* to Agrippina, who may have supplicated, by letting her starve to death rather than having her strangled and thrown downstairs. Here again, the considerable scholarship on the topic does not consider supplication as a distinct factor, e.g., Adam, *Clementia*, which does not mention supplication; so also the other works listed at Barden, *Development of Clementia*, 20 n. 31. Assyrian parallels (chap. 1, n. 89) have also escaped notice.

160. Luc. 2.519–21.

ing. He is debased, a result implicit in the very language of Roman supplication. Hence Caesar's *clementia*, intended as a means of reconciliation, alienated Republicans.[161] They rejected Caesar's condescension.

The Roman notion that the suppliant could be guilty yet acceptable had an evil twin, the notion that he could be acceptable yet treacherous. The trouble was not that the suppliant had performed poorly in previous acts of supplication, and thus was a hypocrite to supplicate again, or even that he was performing poorly at present, as Odysseus does when supplicating the Cyclops. The trouble was that he set out to entrap the supplicandus. First he would gain acceptance, then he would exploit the supplicandus or attack him. No twist in Parthenius, no horror in Thucydides, or blunder in Herodotus departed so far from the norms of the practice.[162]

It would have suited the Romans to regard treachery as a foreign flaw. Kings are treacherous; so are Greeks; the Massilians had the nerve to betray Caesar.[163] Treachery occurs several times in a Greek genre, the novel.[164] (Yet Petronius's Latin novel is the most outrageous: only here do fictive suppliants approach an individual and then attack him.)[165] The Greek expert on stratagems, Polyaenus, regarded a treacherous suppliant as a military asset.[166] Then there are the numerous Greeks and other foreigners who merely lie to the supplicandus.[167] When Sextus Tarquinius uses supplication to trick the people of Gabii, Livy can say that he acts *minime arte Romana*, "hardly in a Roman fashion," an allusion to Sextus's Greek and Etruscan origin. And the record supports the Romans. The Republican period, at least, knows of only one treacherous Roman suppliant, or to be exact, of one treacherous group.

This group, however, killed Julius Caesar:

> Then the others stood milling around Caesar, for in those circumstances he was approachable and talkative. Some chatted him up, and some, ironically, supplicated him, so that he would not be at all suspicious. And when the time came, someone approached him as if to express gratitude and yanked the cloak from his shoulder, signaling his fellow conspirators. And then men fell upon him from all sides.[168]

161. Including Cicero, as noticed by Dyer, "*Rhetoric and Intention*," 23–26, where *clementia* is described as a virtue that only a tyrant has occasion to exercise.

162. Parth. 17.5: a son supplicates his mother, refuses to accept her refusal to grant his request, and in so doing causes her death. Another treacherous suppliant: J. *BJ* 1.139–40.

163. Tac. *Hist.* 3.48 (69 CE); Ov. *Met.* 5.210–35; Caes. *Civ.* 2.11.4–13.3 (49 BCE). Spaniards, too: App. *Hisp.* 61.

164. Longus 2.19.1–3, X. Eph. 2.5.6–6.1, 2.6.5.

165. Petr. 107–8. Attack from a distance: Act. Tat. 4.13.1. A parody: Petr. 97.9–98.6, where the supplicandus says he would not kill a suppliant (97.10), then learns that the suppliant has lied to him and changes his mind (98.5–6).

166. Polyaen. 5.17.2, 8.55.1, developing E. *Hec.* 245–50. Similar is the deceit practiced by a diplomatic suppliant on Alexander the Great (Paus. 6.18.3–4.). Deceitful and successful in Hdt.: 4.165–67.1 versus 4.200–5.

167. Curt. 5.10.14 (330 BCE), when traitors both supplicate and betray Darius, a sequence found in no other Alexander historian; 6.7.3–15 (also 330), where the suppliant draws a sword, like Telephus; Ov. *Met.* 11.274–88, where Peleus lies to his supplicandus; Longus 4.16.1. To Romans: App. *Hisp.* 43.

168. D.C. 44.19.3.

The report that the assassins supplicated Caesar finds support in Cicero, who says that three years earlier the consul Gaius Marcellus supplicated Caesar in the Senate and that the whole Senate joined him, if not by prostrating themselves, like Marcellus, then by crowding round.[169] To be sure, most sources for Caesar's death do not go so far as to say that any of the assassins supplicated. They refer to some other way of making a request, and they also omit the suppliants' expression of gratitude.[170] Perhaps the source just quoted, Dio, wanted the greatest supplicandus of them all to perish in an act of supplication. Exaggeration, bias, irony—supplication is rich in these, and an historian may evince a taste for them, just as Euripides did.

But the same thing almost happened again a century later, when Piso and his coconspirators assigned Plautius Lateranus the task of supplicating Nero:

> They had made arrangements for their plot: as though asking for help in a money matter, Lateranus was to fall pleading at the knees of the emperor and lay him low when he was unawares and pin him, for Lateranus was a man of good courage and great size. As the emperor lay there, stuck, the tribunes and the centurions and any of the others that had the nerve could run up and stab him.[171]

The wrestling match between suppliant and supplicandus is a comic touch, but practical, too, since the supplicandus may not be satisfied to turn his head or wave his hand, as Julius Caesar had. He may struggle with the suppliant. For this reason, Tacitus changes the use of a common supplicatory term, *prosterno*, usually found in the passive and meaning that the suppliant is prostrate. Here it appears in the active and means that the suppliant has "laid low" the supplicandus.

Later, the emperors responded with preemptive supplications addressed to those who might kill them or their favorites. Nero intended to beg for his life, and Didius Julianus, a far-sighted emperor, begged for his life by offering to abdicate.[172] Gordion begged on behalf of an imperiled favorite.[173] A candidate for the purple, like Claudius, could beg to be spared by those seeking to eliminate him in favor of some other choice.[174] But as Herodian says, the emperor was not supposed to humiliate himself, not even if he was a good emperor like Pertinax.[175] And it is true that on occasions of mortal peril, a supplicating emperor would likely be rejected. Nero would have been rejected, and Didius

169. Cic. *Fam.* 4.3.3.

170. Plut. *Caes.* 66.3–4, Suet. *Jul.* 82.1, and App. *BC* 2.16.117 all refer to requests, whereas Cicero (*Div.* 2.23, *Phil.* 2.88–9) lacks details. Nic. Dam. 90 *FGrH* fr. 130.88 agrees with Dio: ἐν προσχήματι . . . τοῦ ἀντιβολεῖν.

171. *Ann.* 15.53.2–3. Furneaux ad loc. notes the similarity to the attack on Julius Caesar.

172. Suet. *Nero* 47.2, seeking *uenia*; Hrd. 2.12.5–6.

173. Hdn. 7.5.4–7 (238 CE), an act that Townsend, "Revolution of 238," says may be insincere. A different view of such "play-acting": Gunderson, "Discovering the Body," who regards it as an integral part of symbouleutic and other oratory.

174. Suet. *Cl.* 10.2.

175. Hrd. 2.5.5, where Pertinax earns praise for not supplicating the Praetorians. A disgraceful supplication by Sardanapalus: D.C. 80.19.3.

Julianus was. The only persons likely to accept a supplicating emperor were foreign rulers, and Roman sources refuse to countenance this possibility. (For this reason, we cannot know whether the emperor Valens supplicated the Persians after being captured by them.)[176]

Like the role of magistrates, the acceptance of the guilty takes us far from any Greek practice of the classical period. Athenian supplication said "no" to the guilty suppliant and either barred, killed, or ignored him. But in the period for which evidence about supplication comes, Athens was largely at peace. Only one act of Athenian supplication occurred during a war in which an Athenian who had fought on the losing side needed to supplicate an Athenian or foreign victor. This act, occurring near Syracuse, was large and important, but it cannot be altogether misleading that it is the only reported act of its kind.[177] For the period with Roman evidence, however, many Romans who fought on the losing side needed to supplicate a Roman victor, and many foreigners needed to do likewise. Rome required a criterion of evaluation that would let a magistrate spare these persons, whether traitors or aggressors. Otherwise Rome faced the threat of wars waged to avenge rejected suppliants.[178] *Clementia* met this threat.

Along with the Roman fear of the treacherous suppliant, *clementia* changed the ambience of supplication. In the usual practice, the suppliant was on his best behavior. In the regulated practice of classical Greece, the suppliant would avoid staying too long in a shrine. Now, the suppliant was sometimes suspect, and so the supplicandus was wary. The shift appears most clearly in acts of supplication in which Roman writers or late Greek writers introduce this new ambience into acts of supplication that otherwise would lack it. The historians of Alexander the Great provide several examples. When suppliants from conquered cities present themselves to him, they bring boughs, but Alexander does not accept them in the Greek way. He spares them in the Roman way. Diodorus says that he "releases them" as though they were prisoners.[179] Arrian, in contrast, avoids this language.[180]

But the play of old and new kinds of supplication did not confine itself to anachronisms in late authors. This play was a matter of different laws and institutions: on the one hand, Greek laws and public altars, and on the other hand, the attitude of Roman magistrates and the assemblies and emperors whom they served. Since the Romans ruled the cities in which these altars stood, Roman notions and the means of making them felt were sure to impinge on the Greeks. This is our next topic.

---

176. Valens's supplication to Shapur I: the Sassanian rock reliefs at Naqs-I-rustam. But the accompanying inscription, reproduced in Mariqc, "Res Gestae," does not go quite so far, nor do other sources (Eus. 7.13, Lac. 5, Eut. 9.7).

177. As at 144–45 above.

178. Sen. *Cl.* 1.8.7.

179. D.S. 17.91.4, 17.96.5, 17.102.7, 17.103.8. "Release": ἀπέλυσε.

180. Arr. *An.* 5.1.4–2.4. But Arrian reports an unsuccessful request for pardon at 1.8.8, with the complication that the soldiers kill the rejected suppliants without any order from Alexander.

REGULATION

The Romans regulated supplication more than even the Athenians had done. The effect of these regulations was to strengthen the position of the Roman magistrate, be he the emperor or the provincial governor. First the Romans eliminated rivals to the magistrate. Next they found a way to provide virtual access to the emperor and—at about the same time—they regulated supplication in Greek shrines that they had long since begun to interfere with. The leitmotif of all these regulations was the Roman preference for supplication to an official as opposed to supplication of other kinds, particularly supplication on holy ground.[181]

As scholars have long remarked, there are so few reports of suppliants taking refuge in Roman shrines that even if the reports are true, the practice is rare and unimportant.[182] The inviolability of a Roman shrine, or of any shrine, would have to rest on an act of consecration by the Roman assemblies, or, in later times, on an imperial edict, and we know of only one consecrated shrine, the temple of Divus Julius.[183] Even here, we know of no act of supplication; Mommsen and other scholars thought that the provision was nullified.[184] Nor are any acts of supplication reported at the altars of the *clementia Caesaris* or of the *clementia* of Tiberius.[185] The way to obtain the *clementia* of Caesar or Tiberius was to go to the men themselves.

The *asylum* of Romulus, as Livy calls it, represents not an exception to this norm but an illustration of the Roman habit, already noticed in Cicero, of using the language of Greek temple refuge. Cicero wants his clients to come to the altar of justice, not, as we would say, to the bar.[186] Livy wants his slaves and shepherds to go to an asylum, as in Greece, and not to a hideout.[187] Tellingly, Livy says nothing of any god, altar, or shrine. If not careless, he is ironic—more likely the latter, since Romulus will shortly appoint patricians from among a population consisting of runaways.[188] In Juvenal's words, "To trace your name and unroll the scroll

181. Reports of supplication to priests as opposed to magistrates: Freyburger, "Droit d'asile," 149–50, but without any examples. Gel. 10.15.8 reports that a suppliant to the Flamen Dialis received a temporary reprieve from corporal punishment inflicted as a penalty for crime.

182. Thus Rigsby, *Asylia*, 574–75, preceded by Bellen, *Sklavenflucht*, 65–66, in a tradition beginning with RStr., 458–62. An asylum at Tarracina in Latium: Altheim, *Roman Religion*, 255–58, based on Serv. A. 7.799. At a few Greek temples, but no Roman ones: Wissowa, *Religion und Kultus*, 474 n. 3. At the temple of Diana on the Aventine, linked to the inviolability of the tribunes: 251 below. Perhaps at the temple of Veiovis: Freyburger, "Droit d'asile," 148, but without examples.

183. Even this temple was an asylum in name only: D.C. 47.19.3. Act of consecration needed for an asylum: Serv. A. 2.761. Consecration only on authority of the Roman people: Cic. *Dom.* 127–28 (for Italy), Gaius *Inst.* 2.7 (elsewhere). On authority of emperor: Ulp. *dig.* 1.8.9.1.

184. RStr.: 461 n. 1, cited by Rigsby, *Asylia*, loc. cit., whose brief discussion I follow, except with respect to the importance of consecration.

185. *Caesaris*: Plut. *Caes.* 57.3. *Tiberi*: Tac. *Ann.* 4.74.

186. Cic. *Verr.* 2.2.8; so also 2.5.126, *Caec.* 100, *Red. Sen.* 11. Dumont, *Servus*, 139, and Gamauf, *Ad statuam licet confugere*, 195–96, are less sceptical of such statements.

187. Though the story is much older than Livy 1.8.5; see Bruggisser, *Romulus*, 163–83, for the numerous sources, including Sil. It. 15.89–92. Serv. A. 8.342 misleadingly traces Romulus's act to Attic precedents. Rigsby, *Asylia*, 576, observes that Augustan and early imperial writers were the first to call Romulus's place of refuge an *asylum*. A verse illustrating Cicero's habit: V. A. 1.666, where Venus says "confugio."

188. Liv. 1.8.7: "Centum creauit senatores, siue quia is numerus satis erat, siue quia solum centum erat qui creari patres possent." Plut. *Rom.* 9.3 speaks of a θεοῦ ἀσυλαίου and Serv. A. 2.761 refers to Lycoreus, two dubious divinities rejected by Caillemer, "Asylia," 510.

a long ways, you must derive your family from an asylum of ill fame."[189] In a less censorious spirit, we should not distort the few other reports of Romans taking asylum or refuge. Gaius Gracchus died in the grove of Diana and Scaevola Pontifex before the image of Vesta, but neither used the language or gestures of a suppliant. They thought they would be safer on holy ground, and with reason, for the Romans, like the Greeks, preferred shrines to remain undisturbed. But they did not think that they would be untouchable according to some custom, as in Sparta's Brazen House, or untouchable until given a hearing, as in Athens and elsewhere. No such practice applied to them.[190] They were acting less like suppliants than like those who took refuge in *loca sacra*, "sacred places" set aside as safe havens during fires.[191] If those in a shrine took up arms, the authorities assaulted them without any of the compunction sometimes shown by Greeks.[192] And, of course, private shrines gave no defense against assault, as the young Caesar learned when hauled from the *lares*, or family images, at the hearth of cottage in which he had taken refuge during the Sullan terror.[193] By the same token, those who took refuge in *collegia*, semipublic gathering places for professional and trade groups, could be ejected.[194] As a senator in Tacitus says, no one flees to any Roman shrine to escape the consequences of his acts.

Behind this observation lies an assumption as much Greek as Roman: the gods favor only the righteous.[195] But the consequences of the assumption differ. For the Greeks, and perhaps for some Italians, the suppliant must go to a shrine and prove himself.[196] For the Romans, proving oneself meant going to a magistrate and supplicating, as we have seen so far, or going to court and defending oneself, as we saw in chapters 2 and 3. The first of these two kinds of supplication was distinctly Roman, and the second was not, but neither kind required a suppliant to go to a shrine. If a suppliant did go to a shrine, he or she would find no place (or hardly any place) that could help him.

As long as magistrates and courts were accessible to suppliants, this situation did not need to change. It changed only when power began to concentrate in the hands of a single magistrate, the emperor. In a society of tens of millions of persons, reaching this individual proved difficult. In the *Res Gestae*, Augustus does not once refer to himself as a *supplicandus*; for his part, Tiberius refers to himself

---

189. Juv. 8.272–5.

190. Gracchus: Plut. *CG* 17.2–3 in 122 BCE. Scaevola Pontifex: Cic. *de Orat.* 3.10 and D.S. 38/39.17 (82 BCE), the latter saying that he died just before reaching the altar and thus introducing irrelevant Greek concepts of sanctuary. Koch, "Vesta," 1727, notes that the shrine of Vesta was not a *templum*. Cf. L. Calpurnius Piso Frugi Licinianus, who is expelled and then killed, the proper procedure, though Tacitus does not fail to supply the ironic detail "in foribus templi" (*Hist.* 1.43). Expulsion without fatal violence: Cic. *de Orat.* 2.197.

191. Serv. *A.* 2.512, perhaps also Cic. *Agr.* 2.36, referring to "sacella . . . periculi perfugia," noticed by Bellen, *Sklavenflucht*, 65 n. 463.

192. E.g., the attack on Saturninus and his supporters, Cic. *Rab. Perd.* 21, 31, where Marius's letting others attack is a political maneuver, not an expression of religious scruple. Similarly, Tac. *Hist.* 3.69–72 (69 CE).

193. V. Max. 5.3.3, referring to the *lares* that should have made the *supplicandus* ashamed of himself.

194. Cic. *Q. fr.* 2.6.2 in spite of personal supplication by the victim.

195. Tac. *Ann.* 3.36.2–3.

196. Italians (but not Romans) supplicate in the Greek manner at Liv. 30.20.6, where deserters take refuge in the temple of Juno Lacinia in 203 BCE.

only once in this role. He expressed embarrassment for almost executing a suppliant mistakenly thought to have caused him to fall.[197] Instead Tiberius relied on Livia as an intercessor; some three centuries later, the empress Eusebia served as one.[198] Among later emperors, only Nero, Vespasian, and Commodus were reportedly supplicated more than once, and they had no Livias.[199] Other would-be suppliants could not circumvent the Praetorian guard.[200]

With regard to this matter of access, an emperor's reputation made no difference. A good emperor, Trajan, disliked being supplicated. But so did a bad one, Caracalla. Only in the arena could suppliants reach him. There, Dio says, a defeated gladiator implored him. Caracalla declined. "When he was beaten and begged to be saved, Caracalla said, 'Go and ask your opponent. I can't spare you.'"[201] Since gladiators were slaves, the emperor named a slave as an intercessor, a generous departure from custom. He also let the intercessor tell him what to do and not merely make a request, another generous departure. But to no avail:

> And so the wretch perished, though he might have been saved had those words not been spoken. For the intercessor did not dare spare him, lest he appear to be more humane than the emperor.

On the one hand, the emperor was inaccessible; on the other hand, no one dared to speak in his place.

How to reach this unreachable supplicandus? The answer came from Ptolemaic Egypt, where as early as the late third century BCE a Capuan, apparently unable to reach either the pharaoh or any adequate substitute, went to a statue of Ptolemy IV. In 30 BCE, Marc Antony's son went to a statue of Caesar in the same place, Alexandria, but without obtaining the protection he sought.[202] By the time of Tiberius, if not before, the practice had spread to Rome, where suppliants went to the statue of the ruling emperor.[203] The emperors accepted the practice. But what were the rules for it to be? Like Greek temple regulations, they emerged piecemeal. The fundamentals—a four-step supplication of approach to the statue, contact, statement of request to some representative of the emperor, perhaps at the statue, perhaps elsewhere, and then a decision by this representative—

---

197. Augustus does report Parthian supplication to the Roman people (Aug. *Anc.* 5.42) and refuge taken in Rome by kings (5.54–6.38). Fig. 3.2 says otherwise, reporting that CAESAR AVGVSTVS SIGN RECE, "Augustus received the (captured) standards," and thus acted as supplicandus. Tiberius: Tac. *Ann.* 1.13.

198. Jul. *Caes.* 275c.

199. Nero: Tac. *Ann.* 14.61.3–62.1, Suet. *Nero* 13.2 (Lateranus being omitted from this list). Vespasian: Tac. *Hist.* 4.81, D.C. 65.16.2. Commodus: Hdn. 1.16.4.

200. Hdn. 1.2.4.

201. D.C. 78.19.3–4. The amphitheater as the one place with easy access to the emperor: Coleman, "Fatal Charades," 72, with refs. at n. 237.

202. Liv. 23.10.11, Suet. *Aug.* 17.5.

203. Under Tiberius: Tac. *Ann.* 3.36.3–4 (21 CE). Under Trajan: Plin. *Ep.* 10.74, dating from 109–11 CE, according to Sherwin-White, *Letters of Pliny*, 81. Undateable: Philostrat. *VA* 1.15. The best proof that the practice was common: its presence in Sen. *Con.* 10.2.10, another reference to it at Sen. *Cl.* 1.18.2, and Agrippina's possibly supplicating at a statue (Tac. *Ann.* 4.67.6, Suet. *Tib.* 53.2, both 27 CE). Bauman, *Impietas*, 86–87, thinks that the wording of Tac. *Ann.* 3.36.3–4 (21 CE) shows that the practice began under Augustus.

followed tradition. So did optional features like a pursuer or an intercessor. But there were legal elements, too, and they crop up one by one in the two known imperial examples of this type of supplication, one in Tacitus and one in Pliny, and in passages in the jurists. Some of these elements are procedural, and some are substantive.

One legal element concerned the first step in this type of supplication: the approach to an image of the emperor. At first suppliants may have been able to go to a statue of the emperor, leave it, and remain safe provided that they had an image of the emperor on their persons. They may have been immune not only to pursuers but also to magistrates. In Tacitus the suppliant Annia Rufilla went to a statue of Tiberius and then left the statue and came to the Senate, all without being pursued or even arrested, a string of events that make this explanation plausible. Suetonius says that other suppliants did the same thing.[204] In any event, the state sooner or later responded to this stratagem, decreeing that only consecrated images would provide immunity.[205] As we have seen, consecration was a public act, and so it provided a means of curtailing the use of portable images.[206]

Pliny reports another development. In Bithynia circa 110 CE, a runaway slave named Callidromus represented himself as a free man in order to make a labor contract. When the two contractors learned his true status, they detained him until he escaped and fled to a statue of the emperor. A local Roman magistrate then ordered that Callidromus be brought, *perductum*, to a hearing. Pliny does not tell us what the magistrate decided to do with him. But the fundamentals are clear: approach to the statue, contact, a statement at a hearing, and then a decision by the emperor's representative. If he wished, the representative could consult his superiors, as happened in this case. The legal element that this case reveals is the transportation of the suppliant from the statue to the magistrate. This element did not appear in the traditional procedure. In that procedure, the authorities came to the suppliants.[207] Now the suppliants came to them—for they had no choice. Transporting them had the effect of a summons. It therefore differed from expelling them. This innovation perhaps sprang from a change in procedure in civil cases. In the Republic, a civil case began when the plaintiff brought the defendant before the magistrate. Under the empire, the magistrate sometimes took the initiative and brought the defendant to court or, if the defendant lived elsewhere, wrote a letter that the plaintiff could take to the authorities there.[208]

Another development may have facilitated this new procedure. To transport the suppliant, the authorities needed the right to take him from the statue. The

204. Tac. *Ann.* 3.36.3, Suet. *Tib.* 58.3–4.

205. Ven. *dig.* 48.4.5.2 (middle of first century CE) with 48.4.6 (a rescript of Antoninus Pius), both cited by Gamauf, *Ad statuam licet confugere*, 35–36; similarly, Bauman, *Impietas*, 87–92, but envisioning a more complicated process.

206. A contrary view: Bauman, *Impietas*, 89, envisioning a ban in 29 CE. The same view: Gamauf, *Ad statuam licet confugere*, 36–38, though he does not see the power of expulsion as crucial.

207. Plin. *Ep.* 10.74. Brought: "perductumque ad magistratus indicasse <se> seruisse." Sherwin-White ad loc. notes that "perductum" implies that police escorted the suppliant.

208. Jolowitcz, *Roman Law*, 459–60.

lex Julia de maiestate, which forbade desecration of imperial images, may have denied the authorities this right. If it did, the Romans must have changed the law before the incident in Bithynia.[209]

Approaching a statue and being transported were not the Romans' only concerns. Tacitus says that when Annia Rufilla went to the statue she denounced the senator Gaius Cestius, who had accused her of fraud. One of the consuls for the year, Drusus, the emperor's son, ordered her to be tried. Presumably this trial would require her to leave the statue, in other words, to be transported, as the runaway slave had been. But the interest of this episode lies in her denunciation of Cestius. This denunciation constitutes the offense of *iniuria*, a term that in this instance means a criminal affront to dignity. Anticipating the outcome of the trial, Drusus provided in advance for Annia's expulsion from the altar and for her arrest.[210] Drusus assumed that a suppliant who inflicted *iniuria* would be rejected and charged with a crime. The difference between *iniuria* and the Athenian restrictions on supplication, such as prohibiting murderers from supplicating, is that *iniuria* is the occasion for a charge as well as for the rejection of the suppliant.[211]

Several juristic texts confirm that acts of *iniuria*, *atrox iniuria*, or *inuidia* ("insult") give ground for rejecting suppliants; of these three, the first two are grounds for criminal charges also. The earliest such text is Labeo, from the late Republican period, so Drusus did not need to create a new standard for rejection or a new reason for accusing a suppliant He needed only to take up Labeo's standard and apply it to supplicating at the statue of the emperor.[212] But neither Labeo nor the other sources discuss individual cases. Of these there are only two that are reliable, the case of Annia Rufilla and Pliny's, and there is only one other, found in the *Life of Apollonius of Tyana*. In this instance, a magistrate finds himself pursued by a mob, and so he goes to the statue as a suppliant instead of having a suppliant transported from there to his tribunal. Then the hero, the philosopher Apollonius, arrives to pacify the crowd and give the magistrate a chance to prove his innocence. In effect, Apollonius replaces the magistrate.[213] Taken together, the juristic texts and the three examples show that this kind of supplication did allow for criminal charges against a suppliant and did occur often enough for a

209. For the interpretation that this law may have forbidden removing a suppliant, see Suet. *Tib.* 58.3–4, where offenses against a statue or image of the emperor included beating a slave in the vicinity of either—perhaps an exaggeration, but one that suggests that expulsion without the emperor's permission was unlawful. Thus *RStr.*, 585, followed by Gamauf, *Ad statuam licet confugere*, 35.

210. Action by Drusus: "donec accitam conuictamque attineri public custodia iussit" (3.36.3–4). Convicted as a matter of course: Woodman and Martin ad 3.36.4. For this common translation of *iniuria*, see Watson, *Lawmaking*, 187.

211. Which is not to say that *iniuria* was the only ground for rejection: *RStr.*, 760 n. 1, holding that the emperor and his representatives could reject any suppliant, including those who did not commit *iniuria*. Other views: Rogers, *Criminal Trials*, 58–59; Bauman, *Impietas*, 88–90; Talbert, *Senate*, 468; and Gamauf, *Ad statuam licet confugere*, 144. None compare *iniuria* to Greek criteria for expulsion.

212. *Iniuria* or *atrox iniuria* by suppliants: Labeo *dig.* 47.10.7.8 (before 22 CE), Call. *dig.* 48.19.28.7 (second to third centuries CE). *Inuidia*: 48.19.28.7, Scaev. *dig.* 48.10.38 pr (second half of the second century CE). Gamauf, *Ad statuam licet confugere*, 146–50, says that jurists' fear of *iniuria* increased in the second and third centuries CE. A different view: Balzarini, *Iniuria*, 133–34, seeing no link to Greek supplication.

213. Philostr. *VA* 1.15. Discounted: Tac. *Ann.* 12.17.3, a diplomatic case.

celebrity such as Apollonius, a subject of legend as much as of biography, to toy with the procedure.[214]

So far, we are dealing with a standard of judgment applicable to any suppliant. But the Romans also established a standard exclusively for slaves who came to an imperial statue. Under the Republic, when there were no statues to flee to, runaway slaves who failed to escape either returned to their masters or were sold.[215] Later, as Seneca makes plain, some official heard slaves' complaints, perhaps after they took refuge at a statue, but we do not know who or how. We learn more only later, from Antoninus Pius, the first emperor known to have established a rule about supplication of this kind.[216] Gaius reports: "Regarding slaves who flee to the shrines of the gods or the statues of the emperors, he issued this ruling: if the inhumanity of the masters seems unbearable, the masters should be compelled to sell their slaves."[217] "Inhumanity" included physical abuse, sexual abuse, and starvation.[218] If, on the other hand, the inhumanity was "bearable," the slave would be returned to master, as Antoninus makes clear elsewhere: "The power of masters over their own slaves must be unimpaired, nor should any man's right be denied him."[219] "Inhumanity" and other misconduct form an exception. The emperor says it "is in the master's interest that those who justly protest not be denied help in dealing with brutality, hunger, or unbearable abuse." By the same token, it is in the slave's interest that the protest be "just." As the jurist Ulpian says, quoting Callistratus, another authority, it is not in the slave's interest to flee to the statue for the purpose of insulting others, a version of the rule about *iniuria*.[220]

For slaves, then, going to the statue led to the same sequence of events, presumably including the summons and the test of *iniuria*. The standard of judgment differed but not greatly. In contrast, the results did differ greatly. The security of slave property depended on the Romans preventing many slaves from supplicating

214. For different views of supplication at statues by free persons like Annia Rufilla, see *RStr.*, 460–61, and Woess, *Asylwesen Ägyptens*, 209–10, holding that such supplication was rare until the fourth century; and Bauman, *Impietas*, 89, holding that it was forbidden in 29 CE, the same as supplicating with a portable image. As for Mommsen's view, there is no way of knowing how rare it was, except by comparison with similar supplication by slaves, a type for which there is only one example, Pliny's. As for Bauman's view, it rests on the fact that Annia Rufilla supplicated before 29, and that Pliny's suppliant is a runaway.

215. In the Republic, the *tresviri capitales* captured runaways (*RSt.*, 594–96), and under the Principate the task passed to other magistrates, among them the *praefectus urbi* (1059), but without any bearing on supplication until slaves began going to statues. I follow *RStr.*, 24 n.1, in dismissing D.H. 20.13.2, according to which mistreated slaves could appeal to, and presumably supplicate, the censors.

216. Sen. *Ben.* 3.22.3. The official was perhaps the *praefectus urbi*, as supposed by Bellen, *Sklavenflucht*, 66 with refs. Speculation about development of the slave's right to take refuge: Gamauf, *Ad statuam licet confugere*, 54 n. 40. Tac *Ann.* 3.36 would seem to imply that the right developed under Tiberius or Augustus.

217. Gaius *Inst.* 1.53 (around 161 CE).

218. Physical abuse: "saeuitia" (Ulp. *dig.* 1.12.1.8); "intolerabilius saeuitia" (Gaius *Inst.* 1.53); "intolerabilis iniuria" (Ulp. *dig.* 1.6.2, where this noun refers to physical and not verbal abuse); "duritia" (*dig.* 1.12.1.8); "maior asperitas" (Gaius, loc. cit.). Sexual abuse, "obscenitas," and hunger: *dig.* 1.12.1.8. Gamauf, *Ad statuam licet confugere*, 84–88, provides these and other particulars, and examples including Vedius Pollio; a briefer account appears in Bellen, *Sklavenflucht*, 66–67.

219. Ulp. *dig.* 1.6.2. Similarly, Ulp. *dig.* 47.11.5 and Sen. *Cl.* 1.18.2. Examples of "inhumanity": Hopkins, "Evidence for Roman Slavery," 7–10.

220. Call. *dig.* 48.19.28.7. Nor was the slave to make general accusations (Ulp. *dig.* 47.11.5), as noted by Buckland, *Law of Slavery*, 38–39.

successfully. If the juristic sources do not acknowledge this difference with respect to results, the failure to do so underscores the obvious drawback to these sources, one that justifies describing supplication at statues by way of examples as well as rules: the juristic sources confine themselves to one or more essentials. They nonetheless can provide confirmation. With regard to slaves, they confirm the double standard found in other supplication, just as they confirm Tacitus with regard to *iniuria*.[221]

Whether for slave or free, the statue is not a Roman version of a shrine. At a shrine, the suppliant may submit to a priest or, eventually, to an assembly; at a statue, neither priests nor assemblies participate. At a shrine, suppliants are judged by local rules; at a statue, they are judged by imperial rules. At a shrine, suppliants may be rejected, but at a statue they could be both rejected and arrested for *iniuria*. At a shrine, suppliants are inviolable until a decision is rendered; at a statue, they are subject to transportation. Above all, regulation of a shrine is optional. A shrine offers protection in the same manner as any other altar, and an altar does not have to be regulated. As regards supplication, private altars are never regulated. Regulation of supplication at an imperial statue is essential. Without it, magistrates will not know how to act on behalf of the *supplicandus* whom they represent. These differences militate against the view that supplication at statues derived from shrine supplication and support the view that it was a kind of supplication to magistrates.[222]

Rome and Greek Shrines

Meanwhile, what of supplication at Greek shrines? The Roman response to this kind of supplication varies by period. Under the Republic, magistrates found themselves pursuing foreign or domestic enemies who took refuge in famous shrines such as the one in Samothrace. These shrines were in allied states or in provinces. The magistrates had to decide how much to impinge on the local authorities. Often the magistrates were ambivalent about their task. Under the Principate, the same problem—pursuing wanted men—led to the regulation of numerous Greek shrines by the emperor and Senate. At this point, ambivalence ceased.

The pursuit of wanted men interested the Romans for the same reason that the "autonomy" of shrines interested the members of Greek amphictyonies and of the Spartan Alliance. Romans and Greeks wanted to settle an issue of jurisdiction: which outsiders had the right to expel a suppliant from a shrine? In an amphictyony, the answer was a council of members; in the Spartan Alliance, the answer was Sparta, provided that the suppliant left holy ground and the Spartans

---

221. Double standard: Bellen, *Sklavenflucht*, 69. Essentials: Kehoe, *Investment*, 11–12. Scepticism regarding essentials: Watson, *Law of Obligations*.

222. Other theories of origins: from the power of officials to sell runaways, according to Bellen, *Sklavenflucht*, 71, and Gamauf, *Ad statuam licet confugere*, 62; from Greek precedents, according to *RStr.*, 461 n. 3, and to Latte, *Heiliges Recht*, 107 n. 18; and from a Republican precedent for complaints by slaves to magistrates, according to Westermann, *Slave Systems*, 82. Hopkins, *Conquerors*, 201, notes that statues were venerated during the Republic, but he does not cite instances of supplication.

captured him. For the Romans, the answer was less simple. At first the Romans would pressure the local authorities to expel the suppliant, but unlike the Greeks, they would not bring this pressure to bear by means of arson or blockade. Instead they would use diplomacy and the threat of force. Later the Roman magistrate would expel and also arrest the suppliant. And under the Principate, the Romans would regularize expulsion and arrest by means of regulations.

As it happens, the Romans recognized the privileges of shrines from the second century onward.[223] But none of these acts of recognition (now collected by Rigsby) told the Greeks how to treat suppliants. The closest we come is a letter, supposedly from Mithridates VI, allowing a shrine in Nysa to preserve practices concerning *hiketeia* as opposed to *asylia*.[224] This slender evidence will not tell us how suppliants fared at Nysa and still less how they fared elsewhere.[225] Rather than describe privileges given to one or more shrines, we must seek instances when the Roman magistrates pursuing wanted men choose to interfere with an act of supplication.

In 168 BCE, the Romans defeated the Macedonian king Perseus, who fled to the sanctuary of the Great Gods on the island of Samothrace. Perseus was an enemy, Samothrace a Greek ally of Rome. No doubt the Romans would have preferred that this enemy avoid any shrine belonging to an ally and instead supplicate a Roman magistrate. Perhaps the magistrate would have offered him *clementia*—before this episode is over, a magistrate will do just that. But Perseus's flight to a shrine postpones the inevitable.

The Romans begin by dispatching a fleet to the island. For a time, they wait upon events. Then Perseus hands them an advantage. He is traveling with one Evander, known to have assaulted King Eumenes II at Delphi. Whereas Perseus is arguably a worthy suppliant, Evander is not. To deprive Perseus of his companion, the Romans demand that the community expel Evander from the shrine. We have already noticed how the community reacts, by telling Evander to leave, but now we need to notice that the community speaks to him because the Romans have asked them to expel him. The Romans wish to isolate Perseus without violating the autonomy of the shrine. Perseus now grants them their wish. Fearing lest Evander leave the sanctuary and give information to the Romans, he kills his confederate.[226] Now Perseus has become no better than Evander. Perseus's entourage deserts him. Utterly isolated, Perseus surrenders to the Romans. Diplomacy (and the navy) have prevailed.

One of the sources for this event, Diodorus, confines himself to an explanation that is unusual enough to have been noticed as an example of rejection on

223. Teos in 193 BCE as in Rigsby, *Asylia* #153, and Colophon ca. 190 BCE (#173).

224. Rigsby, *Asylia* #186.11 = *CIG* 2943. Dionysus of Nysa: Rigsby, *Asylia* #185.5 = Welles, *Royal Correspondence* #64. Several grants set dimensions for the refuge, including Caesar's grant to Aphrodisias, *OGI* 454 = Rigsby, *Asylia* #212, and Caesar's act of March 4, 44 BCE (*SEG* XXXIX 290) affecting the Artemisium at Sardes.

225. In the terms of Wenger, "Asylrecht," 837, these decrees involve official rather than supplicatory asylum; Rigsby, *Asylia* 9–11, implicitly accepts this distinction also, while Dignas, *Economy of the Sacred*, 290, notes that the proper term for a place of refuge in a temple, i.e., for Wenger's supplicatory asylum, was not *asylon* but *phyximon*.

226. Liv. 45.5.2–4, 9–12.

moral grounds. Perseus, he says, performed a supplication that was "invalid."[227] This is a Greek explanation, founded on the criterion of the suppliant's worth. The episode also furnishes a Roman explanation for Perseus's fate: without conceding any rights to the suppliant or the shrine, the Romans have allowed the shrine some control over its own affairs. The Greek *nomos* coexists with Roman power.

That same year, the Romans show less forbearance when pursuing another defeated enemy, Polyaratus, a pro-Macedonian Rhodian who has fled to Egypt after the Romans defeated Perseus. The Romans order King Ptolemy to send him to Rome. "Out of regard for Egypt and for Polyaratus," the king refuses and sends Polyaratus back to Rhodes.[228] Rhodes, however, fears Romans. Recognizing that sending Polyaratus to Rhodes is risky, Ptolemy dispatches one of his trusted advisers, Demetrius, as Polyaratus's escort.

Polyaratus never reaches Rhodes. According to Polybius, Polyaratus panics, and when the ship stops at Phaselis, a Rhodian foundation on the coast of Lycia, he takes refuge there.[229] From the Roman perspective, Phaselis is no less subject to Roman rule than Rhodes itself, and in this regard the Phaselitans agree with the Romans. Once Polyaratus takes refuge in Phaselis, the community asks the Rhodians to send a ship to Phaselis and take him away. They seem to be dismissing the suppliant just as the Chians once dismissed Pactyes. But the Rhodian response belies this parallel. For although the Rhodians comply with the request to send a ship, they insist that Polyaratus not board the vessel. Instead the suppliant will sail in his own vessel, and they will accompany him—to Rome. The game is up. Demetrius, Ptolemy's agent, attempts to persuade Polyaratus to leave sanctuary and make the voyage. Polyaratus agrees, but only because he has no choice. The community wants him out.[230]

So far, the Romans have made it impossible for the Phaselitans to send Polyaratus to Rhodes, and they have forced Polyaratus to make a "voluntary" departure from Phaselis. But now they make further inroads. After Polyaratus boards ship, he goes ashore again, this time at Caunus. On the grounds that they are subject to Rhodes, the Caunians refuse to accept him—and refuse to let him supplicate. Polyaratus ends up in Rome, where he may well have been executed.[231]

Once again the Romans have avoided expelling a suppliant. But they have interfered far more than in the case of Perseus. In that case, the suppliant surrendered. In this case, several communities that may have offered him sanctuary refuse to do so or force him to leave. The Romans had deprived them of several options available to them under the long-standing Greek practice: dismissing a suppliant (not possible at Phaselis), expelling a suppliant according to local rules

---

227. As at 141 above. The other Greek source, Plutarch, avoids the issue by omitting Evander and having Perseus try to escape from Samothrace (*Aem.* 26.2–5).

228. ἐντρεπόμενος τὴν πατρίδα καὶ τὸν Πολυάρατον (Plb. 30.9.2).

229. διανοηθεὶς ἄττα δή ποτ᾽ οὖν (Plb. 30.9.4).

230. Raising the suppliant: κελεύοντος ἀνίστασθαι (Plb. 30.9.10). Popular support for Demetrius's attempt to make Polyaratus leave sanctuary: συνεπισχυόντων αὐτῷ.

231. Thus Walbank ad Plb. 30.9.19.

and wishes (not possible at Phaselis), and even receiving a suppliant (not possible at Caunus). In the case of Pactyes, the Persians accomplished some of this through bribery. The Romans accomplish it without even dispatching a fleet such as the one that went to Samothrace. Less blatant than the Persians, the Romans are more successful. Power and diplomacy work better than power and money.

How often during the middle and late Republic did Roman pursuers impinge on Greek supplicandi? Rarely, if their only reason to do so was to dispose of foreign enemies such as Polyaratus. Often, if they wished to deal with domestic enemies like the foes of the late Julius Caesar, who took refuge at Ephesus in the Roman province of Asia. When Mark Antony arrived in order to pass judgment on them, the local authorities had nothing to do with the business. Antony did not even allow them to gain his favor by expelling the suppliants themselves.[232] If Antony would act this way at Ephesus, the most famous place of refuge in Asia Minor, what would he do elsewhere? He ordered suppliants expelled from shrines in Tyre and Aradia, and at Miletus he did Cleopatra's bidding by slaying suppliants.[233] All these supplications had occurred amid the disturbances following the assassination of Caesar and Antony's decision to make Cleopatra his coruler in the Roman East. Antony regarded them as part of Roman politics. He would not let any local authorities decide the fate of Rome's—or Cleopatra's—enemies. With him, Roman pursuit becomes Roman intrusion.[234]

All the sources dwell on Antony's impiety, but another incident shows that other magistrates of Antony's time acted as he did. When one Marcus Aurelius Scaurus (not the Scaurus who supplicated in court) was quaestor in Asia in the seventies BCE, he found that he could not expel a slave of his who had taken refuge in the Artemisium at Ephesus. He cannot have been happy to match wits with his slave, as the procedure at Ephesus provided. When he resorted to force, a local notable, Pericles, resisted him. According to our only source, Cicero, Scaurus asked the Senate to intervene. It hailed Pericles to Rome for questioning and surely for punishment.[235]

The implications of this incident go even deeper than those of the actions taken by Antony. Scaurus was acting in circumstances that from now on would be typical. Ephesus was probably a free city, not a power like Rhodes or an ally like Samothrace. The magistrate was lower ranking, and the person pursued, a fugitive slave, belonged to a much larger class than the public enemies sentenced by Antony or pursued by Roman navies in the previous century. The fame of the

232. Antony sits in judgment: App. *BC* 5.1.4. "Pardon": ἀπέλυε. He applies the same standards in dealing with personal suppliants (5.1.7).

233. Tyre and Aradia: App. *BC* 5.1.9. Cleopatra's bidding: App. *BC* 5.1.9, J. *AJ* 15.89–90. Or the scene of the supplication was Ephesus, and there was no murder, as at D.C. 48.24.2.

234. More impiety: Vell. 2.79.5, where Antony has a suppliant strangled. Interference by one of Antony's subordinates: D.C. 49.20.4–5 (38 BCE), where Vetidius demands that Antiochus I of Commagene surrender suppliants and makes war when refused.

235. Cic. *Verr.* 2.1.85. "High-ranking": *homo nobilissimus*. A different view of this passage: Dreher, "Rom und Asyle," suggesting that Pericles did not act qua magistratus but as leader of a faction.

shrine made no difference and neither did precedents provided by Alexander the Great and Mithridates, neither of whom had interfered with supplications at Ephesus.[236] This trivial incident, as Cicero called it, was thus not trivial for the Greeks. How often would Roman magistrates intrude and to what effect? As we have seen, recognition of privileges did not answer this question, for it omitted *hiketeia*. If we judge the Romans by their conduct, we have nearly exhausted the particulars. The proconsul Servilius Isauricus ruled in favor of the shrine of Pergamine Asclepius against an unknown Roman citizen, but we cannot be sure that this ruling is about supplication.[237] Even if it is, and we conclude that Servilius was preventing a Roman citizen from removing a suppliant from a shrine, we should avoid the general conclusion that the shrine of Pergamine Asclepius could resist any and every Roman seeking to expel a suppliant. A generation earlier, the commander Fimbria, a suppliant of no mean standing, took refuge in the same temple. But Sulla was closing in, and Fimbria committed suicide rather than wait for execution, expulsion, or both.[238] We might also wonder whether Servilius was a typical magistrate.[239]

Did the Romans want to wield jurisdiction over Greek shrines? In the second century BCE, they had not wanted it; at Samothrace they were scrupulous, yet they enjoyed the chief advantage of wielding jurisdiction, which was to capture wanted men who took refuge. In the first century, Antony wielded jurisdiction, but not in any and every case. He limited himself to Rome's and his own and Cleopatra's enemies, a group resembling the wanted men of the century before. Only Scaurus took an action that showed a Roman magistrate wielding jurisdiction in something like ordinary circumstances, and Scaurus met with resistance. And even Scaurus did not interfere to repossess some other man's slave; he sought to repossess his own. His conduct does not imply that the Romans wished to handle every case of slaves taking refuge in the great shrine. Intrusion combines with reluctance. The Romans give the impression that supplication at shrines is uncongenial to them— that matters of supplication should be personal and official but not local. But the question of jurisdiction remained, and under Tiberius the Romans attempted to answer it.

Imperial Regulation

We now come to what might seem to be the climax of the relation between Rome and the practice of taking refuge at Greek temples: the regulations promulgated by Tiberius in 23 CE. The main source, Tacitus, says that these regulations resulted from a Greek request.[240] Though we do not know what the Greeks asked for, we do know that the Roman Senate, and Tacitus himself, responded with

---

236. Arr. *Ann.* 1.17.12 (334 BCE); App. *Mith.* 23 (88 BCE).

237. Rigsby, *Asylia* #181.12–18.

238. App. *Mith.* 60 (84 BCE), also Vell. 2.24.1 but without supplication.

239. Atypical: Magie, *Roman Rule*, 417, citing instances in which this magistrate may have acknowledged local *nomoi*, presumably including *nomoi* of supplication.

240. "Postulata prouinciarum ad disquisitionem patrum" (Tac. *Ann.* 3.60.1).

scepticism. Perhaps the Senate went so far as to make the Greeks plead for some regulation of supplication. Certainly the Greeks made supplicatory arguments: "the good offices performed by our ancestors, agreements with allies, and even the decrees of kings who had ruled before the Roman era, and the religious duties due to the gods themselves."[241] For their part, the Romans judged some shrines worthy and some unworthy. The former received recognition, and the latter did not. Only the former would have any privileges that might prevail against a Roman magistrate. In this respect, the Romans expanded on earlier acts of recognition going back to the late Republic. Before they acted in detail, and now they acted in general.

The centerpiece of the regulations was a rule concerning when and how and why Roman magistrates might intrude. Tacitus does not expressly state the purpose of this rule, but he hints at a purpose in the following words that describe the Senate's opinion about conditions in the shrines to be regulated:

> There was not sufficiently powerful authority to check the sedition of populations protecting human vices as though they were divine ceremonies.[242]

Tacitus also reports the Senate's response to the "sedition":

> Resolutions were passed by which . . . a *limit* was nevertheless prescribed. The Greeks were ordered to post in the temples bronze signs serving as sacred memorials. This way they would not slip into fractiousness on the pretext of religious duty.[243]

The meaning of these words, and especially of "a limit," has prompted much speculation, but we do not need to speculate about the background. It is striking and unmistakable: for the first time, regulation aims not at suppliants, their "receivers," or officials, but at the community in charge of the shrine. The use of bronze signs makes this shift all the more noticeable, for signs of this same kind served as ways of expressing the gratitude of a successful suppliant or of recording the acts of the shrine.[244] In Rome as at Athens, they also served to ban slaves from certain shrines.[245] Now the same bronze signs, posted at Rome's order, set a *modus* or limit—in other words, they would describe people, conditions, or acts that Rome prohibited. These prohibited acts, in turn, would be subject to corrective action by Roman magistrates. The *modus* told the Greeks what would bring the Roman authorities to the scene.

---

241. Tac. *Ann.* 3.60.3.
242. Tac. *Ann.* 3.60.1.
243. Tac. *Ann.* 3.63.4.
244. Gratitude: *SEG* XXVI 449 for refuge. Gratitude for cures, as at chap. 3, n. 31 above. Action of the shrine: *IG* iv 492, for which see appendix 4a.
245. "A seruo non tangi," as at Furneaux ad Tac. *Ann.* 3.36. How common these inscriptions were is impossible to say; meanwhile, emperors were instructing prefects to give hearings to supplicating slaves (Severus: Ulp. *dig.* 1.12.1.1).

What limit, then, did these bronze signs announce? In previous cases, Roman magistrates had changed the size of sanctuaries, so *modus* might mean a limit on size. Size would affect the number of persons taking refuge, and so the Romans might well reduce it.[246] But the *seditiones* feared by Tacitus did not result from the number of suppliants on the scene. They resulted from resistance by notables like Pericles. Similarly, *modus* is not likely to refer to an absolute limit on the number of shrines offering asylum, or if it does, it is of little value, for it excludes Egypt, where clauses in contracts from the first century CE refer to taking refuge.[247] If this idea were right, Tacitus might list the shrines that the Romans forbade suppliants from using, but he does not do so. Still less does Tacitus go so far as Suetonius, who mistakenly said that Tiberius abolished temple refuge.[248]

The most likely meaning of *modus* emerges from the history of Roman intrusion: no enemy of Rome and no runaway Roman slave was to be protected. If local magistrates did not seize these persons, the Romans would. Perhaps the *modus* also provided for the expulsion of those convicted of capital crimes in local courts. But the more numerous the suppliants affected by the rule, the less likely they are to concern Roman rather than local magistrates and the less likely the Romans are to bother to ban them. For if the Romans ban a group, they must be prepared to expel them if the local magistrates will not.[249] Whatever the *modus* was, it imposed a burden on the Romans.

As for the question of jurisdiction, it is only partially answered. The Romans have asserted some measure of jurisdiction, but what? We cannot say, and if we turn from the regulations to acts of supplication, we find very few after the reign of Tiberius. This absence of evidence suggests that the question of jurisdiction lost importance. Many suppliants were no longer going to shrines. Instead, they went to the emperor's statue. As always, suppliants were following power. The statue also had a second advantage over the shrine. At the statue there was no need to guess what the Roman authorities would do, no *modus*, no Roman rules for local magistrates.[250] To judge from the case in Pliny, which occurs in Nicomedia, a Greek city that must have had a shrine, suppliants came to prefer an

---

246. Thus Dreher, "Rom und Asyle," citing the precedents described above and following *RStr.*, 460.1. Stengl, "Asylon," anticipates this view, saying that supplication would only be practicable in a large shrine, but see the dimensions of the shrine at Taenarus at 209–10 above. Caesar's act of March 4, 44 BCE (as at n. 224 above) enlarged rather than reduced the size of a shrine.

247. Limit: Rigsby, *Asylia*, 29. Egypt: *POxy.* 1258 (ca. 45 CE); 1471 (81 CE); and *Oxy. descrip.* 785 (first century CE), all of which appear in Woess, *Asylwesen Ägyptens*, 93–94. *POxy.* 1258.6–7 refers to an individual who is to remain outside of an asylum: ὄντα ἐκτ[ὸ]ς ἱεροῦ βω[μοῦ τε]μένους παντὸς ἀσοίλου τόπου [σκέπης] πάσης. The documents in 1471 contain only the word ἀγώγιμος, but as Woess explains (97), it refers to expulsion from sanctuaries. *Oxy. descrip.* 785 resembles 1258.

248. Suet. *Tib.* 37.3. Mommsen believed him (*RStr.*, 460 n. 1), as does Bauman, *Impietas*, 89, but other scholars beginning with Barth, *Asylis*, 3–4, have not, relying on Tacitus instead. Epigraphic evidence for at least nominal asylum in Aphrodisias: Rigsby, *Asylia* #212. On Samos: Rigsby, *Asylia* #184.

249. A similar view: Dignas, *Economy of the Sacred*, 293, noting that the Senate does not close any refuges on the grounds that they harbor criminals. A different view: Bowersock, "Mechanics of Subversion," 306, agreeing with Tacitus that criminal suppliants were a grave problem.

250. The contrast: Stengl, "Asylon," 1885; Wenger, "Asylrecht," 839–40; and others listed by Gamauf, *Ad statuam licet confugere*, 26 n. 93. But these authors do not suppose that the one came to replace the other, only that they were equivalent.

appeal to the statue. Callidromus is a Greek name, and one of the two men from whom he has fled has a Greek name, too. Even so, the suppliant prefers the statue.[251]

Like *imperium* and like *clementia*, Roman regulation had no Greek counterpart. Athenian (and Greek) regulation controlled suppliants and guided supplicandi. Magistrates were subordinate to local assemblies, and shrines were more important than magistrates. Roman regulation controlled communities, including supplicandi. Magistrates were superior to local assemblies, and shrines became less important than imperial statues that gave access to magistrates. But the Romans also undermined supplication at shrines in another way. Far more than the Greeks, they devised rights that made supplication at shrines unnecessary.

RIGHTS

If a supplicandus consulted the law, the procedure developed in Athens (and implied by *Exodus*), he might find the results unsatisfactory for two reasons. First, he might prefer that supplication be unnecessary. In that case, he would want to bestow on the suppliant a right that would keep the suppliant from needing to make a request. Second, he might want to change the law. In this case, he might set aside what some court or magistrate had done in the law's name, or he might correct a defect in a law. Rather than become unnecessary, the act of supplication proves useful as a way to correct some misinterpretation or difficulty. Common to both cases is the link between supplication and rights. In the first case, a right replaces supplication. In the second case supplication provides a right of appeal.

The first of these changes, replacing supplication with rights, did have one Greek precedent. After the heroic period, Greeks do not supplicate when requesting their opponents to let them bury those who have fallen in battle. Instead, opponents grant this request as a matter of course. According to Plutarch, Theseus set the precedent for this practice.[252] The Romans, however, provided several such rights. *Prouocatio* was available to citizens, but only in Rome, and *intercessio*, though available to others, was practically limited to Rome.[253] *Deditio*, on the other hand, extended to foreigners.

Prouocatio concerned arrests and trials. In Athens, a suppliant might go to an altar to avoid one or obtain the other. In Rome, he need only protest to a magistrate, using the right of *prouocatio*, by which he would both prevent an arrest and

---

251. A similar conclusion: Gamauf, *Ad statuam licet confugere*, 174–75, and Rigsby, *Asylia*, 29, pointing out that there are no reports of taking refuge in temples under the Principate. Even in Egypt, there are no reports of taking refuge as opposed to contracts governing refuge, leading *RStr.* to conclude that the practice had ceased (460).

252. Plut. *Thes.* 29.4–5. Supplication being unneeded in some situations, such as presenting requests to the kings of Macedon, is a different matter; see Adams, "Macedonian Kingship."

253. *Intercessio* for foreigners in Rome provided by the praetor peregrinus: Plut. *CG* 12.1–2 with Greenidge, *Procedure*, 291, though he notes that *intercessio* must be obtained in person, hence was limited to where magistrates could be found.

obtain a trial. In Athens, a suppliant wishing to avoid being victimized by a law or a magistrate would again go to an altar. In Rome, he would turn to the tribune, who would protect him by means of *intercessio*, a power of estoppel. By the same token, a tribune might refuse to give any help, but then the Roman might go to another tribune. He would not supplicate anyone. When Cicero spoke of the *ara tribunatus*, "the altar of the tribunate," he was indulging in a mixed metaphor.[254] Appeal to a tribune is not *supplicatio*, and it does not occur at an altar.[255] Similar to the rights provided by *prouocatio* and *intercessio* were laws that deprived persons of the occasion to supplicate. Some took the form of treaties that made it unnecessary for Romans going into exile to supplicate when they arrived, the norm found, inter alia, in the Sacred Law of Cyrene.[256] To be spared or admitted into a community were among the most serious requests, but a similar but less serious one—to receive honors, particularly citizenship—eventually disappeared from the suppliant's repertoire, thanks to the *Constitutio Antoniana*, which granted Roman citizenship to almost all free persons.

These were published laws—deliberate, public attempts to make supplication needless, and thus different from the unwritten practice supposedly established by Theseus. They are all the more striking in the light of the Roman habit of supplicating a magistrate when the request is not to avoid arrest or avoid victimization, but to present a bill to an assembly. In that situation, supplication is still needful, as it was in Greece, or as it was in the Near East.

More complicated was the situation in which a foreign community surrendering to the Romans enjoyed the unwritten right to *deditio in fidem*, a procedure by which the community surrendered unconditionally and in return was spared and allowed to become a Roman dependency. Sometimes a community would add supplication to this procedure, and sometimes it would not. Supplication accompanied *deditio* because it could help the defeated obtain better terms. It did not make so much difference that it could prevent the defeated from being slain rather than spared. *Deditio* was an imperfect right that supplication ameliorated.

We do not need to describe *deditio*, a considerable subject in its own right, but in order to understand the relation between *deditio* and supplication, we do need to pinpoint several similarities and a crucial difference.[257] The similarities are an approach to the victor, an entreaty, a grant of protection, and a new relation.[258]

---

254. Cic. *Red. Sen.* 11. At Sen. *Con.* 3.9 and *RLM* 96.20–22, a slave seeks help from a tribune but without supplicating. A different view: Dumont, *Servus*, 147.

255. *Prouocatio* in a situation in which supplication would be suitable: Liv. 2.55.5 (by Volero). Similar but no express *prouocatio*: 4.14.4 (by Spurius Maelius).

256. A treaty recognizing the right of a foreign state to receive Roman exiles: Plb. 6.14.8, with refs. by Wallbank ad loc. A case of exile without supplication: C. Maenius Gemellus (Cic. *Fam.* 13.19.2).

257. A brief introduction to the legal issues: Dahlheim, *Struktur und Entwicklung*, 20–31, and Timpe, "Rechtsformen," 280–87. For the use of some of the same gestures in both, see Hölkeskamp, "Deditio in fidem," taking a ritualistic approach. Like Dahlheim, *Struktur und Entwicklung*, 23, and Timpe, "Rechtsformen," 281, and against Heuss, *Völkerrechtlichen Grundlagen*, 60–61, I assume that *deditio* should not be defined so strictly as to create doubts about the validity or genuineness of many acts.

258. A similar view of the similarities: Hölkeskamp, "Deditio in fidem," 241–48. Timpe, "Herrschaftsidee," 357–58, observes that *deditio* is both legal and moral, another broad similarity with supplication. Gestures are

These features let the two practices appear together. At this point, following acceptance, the difference emerges: *deditio* was far less generous to the defeated than supplication was. In Livy's portrayal of *deditio* in an idealized past, this comparison holds good:

> If a nation was not bound in friendship to the Romans by virtue of a treaty or obligations couched in equal terms, *the old custom of the Romans was not to hold sway over them until they surrendered everything human and divine*, hostages had been received, arms confiscated, and garrisons posted in their cities.[259]

Suppliants did not "surrender everything human and divine"; on the contrary, they asserted their merits, especially the gods' support. They might surrender, as described in Livy, but if they did they might negotiate. Most important, they might not submit to the sway of the supplicandus. According to both Virgil and Dionysius, Roman history began with Aeneas's supplication of an Italian leader, and friendship between equals resulted.[260] Under *deditio*, however, suppliants surrendered, did not negotiate, and—the most important point—submitted to the sway of the supplicandus. Like a guilty party, they could make no claims on their own behalf and, instead, relied on the magnanimity of the conqueror.

Here, then, are two similar but distinct practices, one more favorable to those surrendering than the other. Which did these communities use? Supplication would seem more likely, but communities preferred to use *deditio* or occasionally to combine *deditio* and supplication. *Deditio* was what the Romans expected. If those who were surrendering resisted it, the Romans forced it upon them. As some Greek suppliants learned, not even an attempt to supplicate would prevent the Romans from forcing *deditio* on those who surrendered. When the Aetolians speak to Valerius Flaccus, a Roman legate in Greece, and ask him how to supplicate Flamininus and the Senate, they wonder at the terms of acceptance that he recommends, and they even remonstrate, saying that their act of supplication is not concluding as they would wish:

> Even as the Roman was speaking, the Greek interrupted him and said, "We entrusted ourselves to you, we did not enslave ourselves, and I'm sure that you are getting carried way. . . . You are giving us orders that do not suit Greek custom."[261]

Flaccus answers,

> By heaven! Right now I don't especially care what the Aetolians think has been done according to the Greek custom—not as long as I am commanding

---

omitted from the list of similarities, for although *deditio* often includes a right hand used to make a pledge, this gesture is optional and in some cases impossible, as noted by Nörr, *Aspekte*, 36–38.

259. Liv. 28.34.7, especially "non prius imperio in eum tamquam pacatum uti quam omnia diuina humanaque dedidisset."

260. V. A. 8.115–174, with Evander; D.H. 1.58.2–59.1, with Latinus leading to a treaty.

261. Liv. 36.28.4–6.

according to the Roman custom over those who according to their own declaration have just surrendered and have been previously defeated in battle.

Flaccus means that the act of supplication will terminate in *deditio*, and he proceeds to enchain them. As Livy says, they must surrender everything.[262]

The action of Flaccus should not be taken to mean that Roman commanders
were inflexible.[263] Flaccus is, in fact, more generous than Livy requires, for he
takes no hostages and posts no garrisons. When dealing with a defeated African
king, Scipio Africanus is more generous, too.[264] Some early Roman commanders
are also more generous, at least if we credit the source, Dionysius of Halicarnassus.[265] In spite of Livy's ideal, the terms of subjection vary. Prestigious subjects,
like Greeks, fare well, and so do those who deal with early, weaker Rome, rather
than the Rome of the middle Republic.[266]

But Livy's example does show that the victor could impose *deditio*. Livy also
shows why the defeated sometimes resort to supplication: it invites the victor to
be less harsh. If we think of *deditio* as a right, supplication becomes a way to try
to influence the supplicandus's response to this right. If we then ask how successful it was, we must turn to the one supplicandus who receives numerous
communities who supplicate while surrendering: Caesar. In this author and those
writing on his behalf, supplication appears alongside *deditio* seven times: surrender by five tribes in the *Bellum Gallicum* and by Egyptian soldiers and another
tribe, the Isseni, in the *Bellum Alexandrinum*. Before performing the double act
of *deditio* and supplication, four tribes suffer defeat. Caesar accepts them all but
imposes harsh terms.[267] The Egyptian soldiers are in similar trouble, for their
comrades have been defeated, even though they have not, and Caesar again accepts them, but without information about the terms.[268] The Isseni are not similar, since they surrender without being defeated, but they form an exception
because the supplicandus is Vatinius rather than Caesar.[269] So far, the pattern is
defeat, supplication, and harsh terms. Caesar is not one of the more generous
Roman conquerors, but he does allow those who supplicate to obtain *deditio*, in
short, to survive as Roman subjects.

---

262. Plb. 20.9–10 excludes supplication, and so the difference of opinion does not concern supplication as
opposed to *deditio in fidem*, but the Greeks' notion of "entrusting themselves" by way of *pistis* as opposed to Roman *deditio*. Gruen, "Πίστις and *Fides*," objects to Polybius's version, but does not consider the supplication found
in Livy. The same treatment for a surrendering individual: App. *Ill.* 9, where the suppliant is raised and then put
in chains.

263. Similarly, Dahlheim, *Struktur und Entwicklung*, 20–22, and Ziegler, "Völkerrecht," 96, both point out
that *deditio* is not a contract; so also Timpe, "Rechtsformen," 288.

264. Liv. 28.34.3–12, where Scipio takes no hostages from and imposes no garrisons on Mandonius. The
other extreme: Liv. 44.31.13–15, where an Illyrian king expects *deditio* and instead is taken into custody.

265. D.H. 3.50.1, 6.25.2, 8.19.4, 10.24.6–8.

266. Early and weak: Liv. 7.31.5–9 (Campanians, 345–43 BCE), 28.34.3–12 (Spanish tribes, 206 BCE).

267. Helvetii: Caes. *Gal.* 1.27.1–28.2, some being unforgiven and all disarmed. Bellovaci: 2.13.2–15.1, hostages taken and all disarmed. Nervii: 2.28.2–3, hostages taken. Haedui: 7.40.6, voluntarily disarmed.

268. *B. Alex.* 32.3.

269. *B. Alex.* 47.4.

These are six cases; there remains one more, the tribe of the Mandubii. Like the Isseni and just a few other suppliants in other sources, they supplicate and surrender without being defeated. Since they are starving, they beg for food. But they are not dealing with a supplicandus who will think of the undefeated as worthy or of the starving as pitiable. They are dealing with Caesar. His preferred course of events—defeat, supplication, and harsh terms—is missing, so he acts differently than before. Rather than accept the suppliants, he rejects them.[270] Here the term *deditio* does not appear, but Caesar's failure to use it does not becloud the situation: the Mandubii supplicated and surrendered, expecting *deditio*, and Caesar rejects them, even denying them food. Eventually he defeats and slaughters them. Now we find one instance of another possible pattern: avoidance of defeat, unsuccessful supplication, and death. Just as other authors shows the soft side of the blend of *deditio* and supplication, Caesar reveals the hard side. Just as he is harsh toward those who have been defeated in battle, he is harsh toward those who have not been defeated—so harsh that he rejects them. Not to have been defeated is an implicit crime committed against him by the suppliants, a crime that he punishes with rejection. The use of supplication to mollify *deditio* proves to depend on the suppliants' meeting a condition. They must not threaten the Romans—or at least not threaten Caesar.

So far, we have discussed supplication and surrender by peoples, but Caesar and other magistrates also entertained supplication and surrender on the part of individuals. This practice goes back at least as far as Aemilius Paullus, who spared Perseus after the Roman fleet overtook this fleeing Macedonian king in Samothrace.[271] Dio, Florus, and Plutarch say that Julius Caesar entertained such a supplication from Vercingetorix.[272] But all these supplicandi, even Caesar, accepted the suppliants. Only one Roman leader, Trajan, is known to have broken the pattern and killed a defeated person who surrendered and supplicated, Parthamasiris. As we have noticed, Fronto criticizes Trajan. Other sources for this encounter report no such aberrant result.[273]

With persons, then, the Romans almost always accept supplicatory surrenders; with peoples, they usually do. Terms vary, but supplication and *deditio* form a pair in which acceptance is normal, just as it was normal for Greeks surrendering to Greeks. But this comparison to Greek surrender should not obscure the fundamental difference between the Greek and the Roman practices. The Greek who surrendered to a Greek had the right to survive. The foreigner surrendering to a

270. Caes. *Gal.* 7.78.3–5. In Dio, Caesar treats the Egyptians the same way: no defeat, no acceptance (42.43.4). A third instance of this kind of rejection: Sal. *Jug.* 47.4. Variation: Sal. *Cat.* 34.1, where the rebels decline an offer to go to Rome as *supplices* in accordance with the notion that the wicked do not supplicate.

271. Paullus and Perseus: Amp. 16.4, Vell. 1.9.4. Sulla: App. *BC* 1.9.80 (83 BCE). L. Licinius Lucullus: App. *Hisp.* 52. Pompey: Vell. 2.37.4, mentioning *dicio*, a synonym for *deditio*; also Cic. *Sest.* 58 but without mention of *dicio*. Augustus: App. *Ill.* 28 (35, 33 BCE). Probus: *Hist. Aug. Prob.* 14.2 (277 CE). In the background: Alexander (Curt. 5.1.17, and also 8.13.1, but without language of supplication).

272. Flor. *Epit.* 1.45, Plut. *Caes.* 27.5.

273. Parthamasiris killed by Trajan: Fro. *Parth.* 2.16. No death reported: *Hist. Aug. Had.* 5.4, D.C. 68.30.3 (all ca. 116 CE).

Roman had the right to survive as a dependent of Rome provided that he did not threaten Rome. This right might seem less generous, but it was available to larger numbers. Again unlike the Greek right, it was for foreigners.

So far, we have noticed appealing to rights as an alternative or complement to supplicating. Now we come to the second of our two cases—supplication to set aside a decision or rectify a law. The Romans allowed *appellatio*, "appeal," of imperial decisions, but recognized that an appeal would not always be possible or adequate. In these circumstances, the appellant might supplicate. This is not to say that appeal and supplication were the same. According to the jurists, appeal allowed a remedy for the bias or inexperience of judges, a concern not relevant to supplication, where the word of the supplicandus was final.[274] Appeal also allowed the appellant to make errors yet pursue his efforts, another contrast with supplication.[275] A third contrast was subject matter. In the main, decisions by the most powerful persons, including the emperor and the Senate, did not admit appeal; neither did decisions made in accordance with the judicial authority embodied by the Praetorian edict.[276] Supplication, though, could be a response to any decision.

Most important, appeal was a written procedure, whereas supplication as we have defined it was an oral procedure. In this respect, appeal resembled not supplication but any written request that someone might make of a Roman official, especially the written requests to emperors that scholars call "petitions," or earlier similar written requests to the Ptolemaic pharaohs of Egypt. As against these ways of presenting requests, supplication was personal and informal. Nor did the supplication often overlap with them. A petitioner might present his written request in person and might even supplicate when doing so (as in just one surviving example), but in such a case he would remain a petitioner. The act of supplication would be a grace note.[277]

But *appellatio* also resembled supplication, and so we can understand how they came to complement the other. An appellant must, like a suppliant, have a personal interest. For this reason, intercession on behalf of an appellant occurs only when a family tie justifies it or when the subject of the appeal makes pity important.[278] The special status of slaves reappears under appeal also. They may not appeal unless a severe sentence has been passed against them, and their masters do not appeal on their behalf. This exception hearks back to Roman notions of excessive abuse of a slave who supplicates.[279] Another similarity concerns the person to whom an appeal may be made. The rule, which is to appeal to the judge who has decided against the appellant, allows for an exception, which is to appeal in public if the judge is hostile. The link to supplication is that the person making the request wishes to avoid appealing to an enemy.[280]

274. Ulp. *dig*. 49.1.1.
275. Ulp. *dig*. 49.1.3.
276. Ulp. *dig*. 49.2.1, Paul. *dig*. 49.5.7.
277. For petitions and the like, including Ptolemaic *enteuxeis*, see appendix 6.
278. Ulp. *dig*. 49.5.1.1. Pity in capital cases: 49.1.6.
279. Marcel. *dig*. 49.1.15.
280. Marcian *dig*. 49.1.7.

These similarities should not be exaggerated. Appeal is a legal procedure, and supplication is a quasilegal practice. But they show why the jurists turned to supplication as a way of ensuring that all who had the right to appeal might do so. Supplication is an attention getter, a way of bringing pressure to bear. Not that it should be needed, Ulpian says:

> If someone's appeal is not accepted, it suffices for him to say that it was not. Let his appeal be taken under consideration, whatever reason he gives for this situation.[281]

But he adds,

> If his appeal is not accepted, and he must appeal to the emperor, he should *supplicate* the emperor; if he was appealing to someone else, he should go to that person.

The italicized word shows that supplication is for the case in which getting attention and bringing pressure are hardest—for emergencies. In Ulpian's words, *supplicare* is for extraordinary appeals, whereas *appellationes* are ordinary appeals.

This distinction was new. Greek law knew of appeals, and someone who made an appeal might happen to supplicate while making it, as happens in Demosthenes, where the appellant is complaining of a decision by a local court that has deprived him of his citizenship.[282] But no Greek supplicated in order to make his appeal possible. In Athens, *res iudicata* forbade such a supplication.

So much for the innovation accepted by the jurists. Examples of this innovation are so few and so sketchy that they amount to a postscript. To illustrate "extraordinary" appeals, Ulpian cites an address to the emperor after a previous address to the wrong party, who had not responded.[283] This emergency arose because of a procedural error, and so it confirms the opinion that errors should not lead to the rejection of appeals, even as it shows that supplication, as Ulpian says, lets an appellant address the emperor. Another instance appears in Paulus, where a woman thought to be dead regains her inheritance by supplicating the emperor. Here we cannot tell why a lower court did not hear the case, but the emergency is obvious.[284] The remaining case presents a general, not personal, emergency. It was when damage to lakes near Puteoli made it impossible for tax farmers to meet their quotas that they supplicated for relief.[285] Did the response of the Senate reflect or anticipate any principle set forth by the jurists—for example,

281. Ulp. *dig*. 49.5.5. A possible Republican precedent: appeal via supplication to overturn illegal land seizures, an episode in which L. Antonius helped some suppliants (App. *BC* 5.3.19). But Antonius is not known to have acted in an official capacity.
282. Dem. 57, with supplication at 57.1.
283. Ulp. *dig*. 49.5.5.3.
284. Paul. *dig*. 28.5.93.
285. Serv. *G*. 2.161.

a principle of fairness like the one expounded by Aristotle? We do not know of any. Supplication lets appeals work better, but it does not introduce a new principle of judgment.

Now to the other possibility afforded by the second case: supplication meant not to correct a mistaken decision but to correct a defect in the law. This sort of supplication may seem to resemble supplication by defendants, for they, too, find the legal process wanting. But no defendant ever supplicates to correct a defect. Even those who appeal to fairness supplicate to be acquitted. The difference is one of purpose, but also one of timing: those who supplicate to correct defects do so after the law has wronged them, whereas those who supplicate to be acquitted do so before the verdict, just as those who supplicate for mercy do so before sentencing, as in today's courts. The only exceptions are a few suppliants described by Tacitus. They supplicate not in response to defects, but in anticipation of them—a satirical variation.

A handful of examples cluster around Cicero's response to his exile. This episode began in 59 BCE, at the start of a triple alliance among Caesar, Crassus, and Pompey. For his part, Cicero sought friends among other politicians, including P. Clodius Pulcher, who would become tribune the next year. But Cicero had testified against Clodius in a lawsuit two years before, and when Clodius took office, he attacked Cicero, who was vulnerable because he had put several of the Catilinarians to death, a proceeding in which he failed to let them to use *prouocatio* and thus obtain a trial. To defend himself, Cicero would need to interpret a relevant law, the *Lex Sempronia*, in his own favor. Although this law said that magistrates might not kill citizens, it apparently did not say whether citizens regarded as enemies were included, and Cicero held that they were not.[286] Once he won this point, he could show that the Catilinarians were regarded as enemies and thus might be killed. But the origin of this law made Cicero's task difficult. It sprang from public outrage at an earlier incident in which citizens were unjustly regarded as enemies and then killed. It could hardly serve Cicero's purpose.[287]

Cicero, then, was in no strong position. His political foes needed only to wait for the right moment to strike. It came as soon as Clodius became tribune. With no objections from the triple alliance, Clodius won passage of a bill reaffirming the law against killing citizens without trial. The penalty was exile; the target was Cicero. Cicero responded by arguing that Clodius's patrician origin made it unlawful for him to be tribune. He also deemed the bill invalid on the grounds that it was directed against an individual, him, and thus was a *priuilegium*, comparable to a bill of attainder under Anglo-American law. Several prominent jurists agreed with Cicero.[288] Nor did Cicero confine himself to legal arguments. Like others before him, he staged supplications in his own cause. Pompey decided to

---

287. I.e., the Gracchans slain in 131 BCE. C. Gracchus, the brother of the chief victim, proposed the *lex Sempronia*.

286. The *lex Sempronia*: Plut. CG 4.1–2 with other sources cited by Greenidge, *Procedure*, 324. Cicero's view: *Catil.* 4.10.

288. Clodius's origin: Cic. *Dom.* 35. *Priuilegium*: *Sest.* 65, *Dom.* 43.

participate. Like many others, he supplicated at public meetings discussing Clodius's bill and begged voters to reject it.[289] The supplication failed, as did supplications to the consuls Piso and Gabinius, who were asked to join the supporters. Piso rejected his own son-in-law, and Gabinius ordered one of the suppliants to stay 200 miles from Rome—an unprecedented and, Cicero thought, unlawful, punishment.[290] At this point, Cicero had supplicated against an unlawful bill, failed, and then encountered an arguably unlawful restriction on the activities of suppliants.

So far, supplication can not compensate for the arguable misuse of the law. Now comes a second episode. Once Clodius won passage of his bill, Cicero fled, and Clodius introduced another bill, this one to exile Cicero. Cicero's supporters now raised more objections, saying that the new bill was illegal because it exiled him without trial and had not issued from the appropriate assembly.[291] The first objection rested on differences between this instance of punishment by exile and earlier instances, which all may have occurred after a trial, or at least after setting a date for a trial and not earlier. The second objection rested on a peculiar feature of exile. Exile could mean death if the exiled person returned, and so, like any sentence of death, it was the province of just one of Rome's assemblies, the cumbersome and antiquated *comitia centuriata*, and Clodius had not presented his bill to this assembly. As a tribune, he had no right to.

More supplications were sure to follow, and they did. What made them different from other acts of supplication on behalf of exiles, like the act that earned Metellus Pius his cognomen, was yet another complication. Clodius tried to discourage efforts to repeal his bills. As provided by the second bill, he posted the following decree on the door of the Senate house: "No one shall introduce, vote on, debate, discuss, support, or help draft a repeal."[292] This gag forbade not just legislation but discussion. And it worked. Some magistrates refused to help Cicero, and others who did help him introduced a bill that was to be regarded as void if it conflicted with Clodius's decree.[293]

In response, Cicero's supporters supplicated in defiance of the decree. Pompey led the way in importuning the assembly. When a tribune sought to delay the assembly's action, the tribune's own father-in-law did the supplicating.[294] Provincials even supplicated the Senate, presumably in plain view of the decree that they were defying.[295] Not all these suppliants succeeded, but the number and size of these acts shows that supplication strengthened the campaign against Clodius's gag. Cicero's supporters could also defy the decree and speak in forbidden venues without supplicating. Some did just that. But supplication gave Cicero's side

289. Cic. *Pis.* 80.
290. Piso: Cic. *Sest.* 54. Gabinius: *Sest.* 26, 29, *Red. Sen.* 12. Unprecedented: *Fam.* 11.16.2.
291. Cic. *Sest.* 73–4, *Dom.* 26. Assessment largely hostile to Cicero: Greenidge, *Procedure*, 328–30, 61–66, discussing other objections as well.
292. Cic. *Red. Sen.* 8; similar is *Att* 3.12.1.
293. Cic. *Pis.* 29. The cowardly bill: *Att.* 3.23.2–3.
294. Cic. *Red. Sen.* 31, 37. To the tribune: *Sest.* 74.
295. Cic. *Sest.* 130.

a moral advantage. Cicero's victory, in the form of a bill allowing his return, followed this supplicatory campaign.

Some in Cicero's camp deprecated this last bill, arguing that it conferred legality on the two bills of Clodius. In this view, all the supplication should have been needless. But this criticism did not reckon with Cicero's need to flatter Pompey while rallying other elements. The participants in this supplicatory campaign—Pompey in the van, then Cicero's relatives, the Senate, provincials, and knights—accomplished these two purposes and also allowed Cicero to try to revive his *concordia ordinum*, the coalition of well-to-do Romans and provincials that he thought ought to predominate. We do not need to declare this attempt successful to grasp its meaning. Using supplication to change laws was a partisan as well as a legislative maneuver. Just as the hybrid of supplication and *appellatio* was judicial, the hybrid of supplication and legislation was political. Both brought supplication and the legal system closer together than in Athens, where *res iudicata* forbade the first hybrid and where the absence of powerful magistrates made it unnecessary for citizens to supplicate magistrates in order to change laws.

Like some changes occurring in classical Athens, the Roman blend of supplication and the law made supplication less arbitrary. The magistrate in charge of an imperial statue had more powers than his counterpart in Athens but exercised these powers according to regulations. The new standard of judgment—mercy—had the same double effect. This standard gave magistrates greater freedom, but it also gave help to suppliants, and thus made it harder for magistrates to reject them. In Rome, moreover, new institutional barriers surrounded the supplicandus who ignored the law. The magistrate who rejected a suppliant abroad would have to reckon with the suppliant applying to the magistrate's superior. The magistrate who rejected a suppliant at home would have to reckon with the suppliant applying to the magistrate's colleagues. The judges who rejected a suppliant and found him guilty would have to reckon with a suppliant making an extraordinary appeal. Most important, rights like *prouocatio* took away the supplicandus's right to refuse by making supplication unnecessary.

The magistrate's response to *prouocatio* or *appellatio* might seem simple: he must do as the law required. But in the main the magistrate found his task harder, not easier, than before. He no longer merely followed the Greek (and Hebrew) precedent of saying "yes" or "no" in the light of the law. He sometimes said "yes, change the law" or said "yes" for either pity's sake or mercy's sake. And, of course, he had more power than his predecessors. The Jews who supplicate in Josephus, the dispossessed Italians who appeal to the consul L. Antonius, the supplication of not just Vercingetorix but countless Gauls to Julius Caesar: these acts alone dwarf all known acts of supplication in Attica. These acts also lend urgency to a question that is not legal but psychological: what emotional and intellectual equipment did the magistrate need? Just as this chapter began with an act of supplication that had new, Roman legal features—a magistrate, an appeal for pardon, and a surrender—it will end with one that asks a novel, Roman question about the supplicandus.

Judgment and Restraint

The more demanding the tasks faced by the supplicandus, the greater the need for the supplicandus to be dispassionate. Otherwise he could not use his judicial and legislative acumen or make the ethical distinctions required by the alternatives of mercy and pity. But to be dispassionate was difficult. A supplicandus had a duty to reject the unworthy or unjust—and in Rome, he had a duty to punish the suppliant who committed *inuria*. This duty could tempt the supplicandus to feel righteous anger. To resist this temptation, he would need to restrain himself.

The need for restraint appears first in Homer, where Phoenix, one of the ambassadors sent to Achilles in *Iliad* 9, reproaches Achilles for being angry toward Agamemnon. First, he praises restraint:

> Achilles, control your great anger; you should not have a pitiless heart. The gods, too, can be swayed, even though their worth, honor, and power are superior to ours.[296]

Next, he claims that those who depend on the restraint of the supplicandus are like worshippers who depend on the compunction shown by the gods:

> Whenever a man transgresses and makes a mistake, people supplicate (λισσόμενοι) and turn aside the gods' wrath with sacrifices and gentle prayers, offerings that are poured and burnt.

Since the gods are the persons addressed, Phoenix should say "pray" (*euchomenoi*), not λισσόμενοι.[297] He should mention supplication only if he showed that the worshipper was approaching a statue. But he makes no such showing. He wishes to turn Achilles' anger toward Agamemnon into a failure to follow Zeus's example. So he conflates prayer and supplication.

But if we overlook this sleight of hand, we can trace the problem down to the Romans. Elsewhere in Homer, two angry supplicandi, Agamemnon and the Achilles of *Iliad* 20, draw criticism from the narrator of the *Iliad*.[298] Some sources associate angry supplicandi with madness: the infuriated Heracles rejected the supplications of his own children, and the infuriated Lycurgus did likewise.[299] A

---

296. *Il.* 9.496–501.

297. As noted by Hainsworth ad *Il.* 12.502–12 and Aubriot-Sévin, *Prière*, 405–6, 444–54, where she summarizes the differences between this term and *lissomai*, commonly used in supplication. The speech of Phoenix is also peculiar on other grounds, as noted by Hainsworth ad 9.524, with refs. Only D. Wilson, *Ransom*, 81, has noted that it is unusual for Agamemnon, denounced by the authoritative Nestor as a wrongdoer at 9.106–13, to supplicate the man whom he has wronged. A recent expression of the contrary view: Zanker, "Beyond Reciprocity," 83.

298. Agamemnon: *Il.* 11.137 (ἀμείλικτον . . . ὄπ'). Achilles: *Il.* 20.467 (οὐ . . . γλυκύθυμος . . . οὐδ' ἀγανόφρων). Parodic condemnation of Achilles: Lucianus *D mar.* 1.

299. Lycurgus rejecting his supplicating son: an Attic red-figure hydria, Cracow 11.1225 = *ARV²* 1121.17 = Trendall-Webster 3.1.13; another Attic red-figure hydria, Rome Villa Giulia = *ARV²* 1343a = *LIMC* 6.2 s.v. *Lykourgos I*, 12 (A. Farnoux). Extant literary sources do not report this supplication, which presumably derives from a lost play.

maddened Alexander the Great killed one of his companions, Clitus, when others were supplicating on Clitus's behalf, and felt such shame that he wanted to kill himself.[300] Mindful of such examples, Seneca warned that an angry supplicandus could not tell the guilty from the innocent.

The answer was not to ban anger. Anger, Seneca reasoned, could be good; Aristotle says so; but for a supplicandus or other authorities it could be harmful.[301] The answer was to control anger by tempering it with *clementia*, mercy. *Clementia*, Seneca says, is rational, more rational than pity; pity is for women, and old women at that.[302] *Clementia* respects limits: "One must have neither a promiscuous and commonplace *clementia* nor one that is cut short. It is as cruel to pardon all as it is to pardon none."[303] With these views, a new need arises. Besides showing restraint, as urged by Phoenix, the supplicandus should make sure that his mercy is proportionate. He must examine himself. As Seneca says, *clementia* is an exercise in reasoning.[304]

Seneca addressed this remark to Nero. But the chief weakness of his argument that the supplicandus should examine himself was not that it rested on the unstated assumption that the supplicandus was equal to the task—an assumption that Nero would prove false by his response to several supplications.[305] Instead the chief weakness was that, no matter the supplicandus, supplication was an affective as well as cognitive procedure. Even *aidôs*, which Seneca translates as *pudor*, is an *affectus*, a strong emotion. And strong emotion was sure to make self-examination difficult.[306]

The most famous of Roman supplications, occurring at the end of the *Aeneid*, happens to anticipate Seneca. Earlier, Aeneas had supplicated a Greek emigrant, seeking an alliance with him, and succeeded.[307] Others had supplicated, too, but not always successfully.[308] Later, Aeneas and his band had defeated an alliance of Italian natives. Two native warriors had supplicated Aeneas, who had rejected them both.[309] Now comes the last act of supplication in the epic, one that will outrank the rest if only because it invites comparison with the supplications that come last in Homer—Odysseus's acceptance of Phemius and Medon, and, no less important, his rejection of Leodes; and, in the *Iliad*, the rejection of Hector, the last suppliant on the battlefield at Troy, and the acceptance of Priam, the last suppliant of any kind. This time the suppliant will be the leader of the natives, bested by Aeneas in single combat, a circumstance that points to Hector but also to Leodes, one of the suitors. The themes of restraint and self-examination also

300. Curt. 8.1.48–9.

301. Seneca on Aristotle: Sen. *Dial*. 3.9.2, 3.17.1.

302. Sen. *Cl*. 2.5.1, so also Konstan, *Pity Transformed*, 102.

303. Sen. *Cl*. 1.2.2. Same warning not needed by Trajan: Plin. *Pan*. 80.1.

304. Sen. *Cl*. 2.5.1.

305. Tac. *Ann*. 14.61.3–62.1, 15.73.4.

306. *Pudor* as affectus: Sen. *Dial*. 5.1.2–3. Affectus essential: Quint. *Decl*. 349.

307. V. A. 8.115–74.

308. Successful other than Aeneas with Evander: V. A. 3.590–667, 6.42–155. Unsuccessful: 1.487, 2.515–25, 2.533–53.

309. V. A. 10.522–36, 10.594–601.

point to both these precedents. Achilles is an impetuous supplicandus, and Odysseus loses his temper when rejecting Leodes.

The considerable literature about this supplication has not dealt with these themes. Instead it has asked whether Aeneas's response, which is to reject Turnus, is justifiable.[310] To ask this question is to summon up Greek precedents, including not only Odysseus and Achilles but also Agamemnon.[311] Yet Aeneas differs from these Greek supplicandi. Even loyalty to a friend, his motive for rejecting Turnus, has inflections different from that of Achilles' loyalty to Patroclus. There is also a seldom-noticed Roman aspect to this supplication: Turnus's language resembles that of *deditio in fidem*, a resemblance heightened by his performing both a supplication and a surrender, as do other suppliants who resort to *deditio*: "Clearly I deserve this (*merui*), and I do not beg to avoid the consequences. Make use of your good luck."[312] These words echo Livy's formula, and the violation of a treaty by Turnus's allies in the same book complicates the echo. The choice before Aeneas is difficult: spare Turnus as a suppliant seeking *deditio*, or slay him as the leader of treaty breakers.[313]

This issue points away from justification—even justification by a Roman, legal standard—toward the supplicandus's need to weigh alternatives. Aeneas is the first supplicandus to change his mind without receiving advice from a third party. He is also the first supplicandus to hesitate without a third party's influence. Fitzgerald's translation, using the idiom "bring him round," turns these features into a process:

> Fierce under arms, Aeneas
> Looked to and fro, and towered, and stayed his hand
> Upon the sword-hilt. Moment by moment now
> What Turnus said began to bring him round
> From indecision.[314]

"Moment by moment": this, too, appears for the first time, not because Greek plays and other works do not show these moments when a supplicandus responds, but because they do not report the supplicandus's thoughts and feelings as opposed to the speech that he delivers once he has made up his mind. Virgil has isolated the moment at which the supplicandus checks his anger and pauses, the moment for restraint and self-examination.

---

310. For which see Horsfall, *A Companion to Virgil*, 192–216 and Clausen, *Virgil's Aeneid*, ch. 6, both citing the Homeric parallels. A selection of other views: *EV* s.v. *Turno* (A. Traina). Horsfall's view: justifiable and unambiguous. Clausen's view: justifiable yet ambiguous. Unjustifiable yet ambiguous: R. F. Thomas, *Augustan Reception* 295–96. Unjustifiable: Perret, "Optimisme et tragédie," 352.

311. Achilles: Aeneas's rejections of suppliants at V. A. 10.522–36, 594–601. Agamemnon: "Agamemnon . . . immolauit (Aeneas's word at 12.949) . . . Iphigeniam" (Cic. *Off.* 3.95.). In the background lie Greek rejections at Troy (V. A. 2.515–25, 2.533–53).

312. V. A. 12.931–32. *Deditio*: Hölkeskamp, "Deditio in fidem," 241, citing Liv 7.31.5, 30.12.17, 44.42.4; Traina ad V. A. 12.935–36, citing Liv. 42.47.8.

313. Slay as treaty breaker: Galinsky, "Anger of Aeneas," 324. Spare: Traina as immediately above.

314. V. A. 12.938–41.

Many supplicandi, to be sure, listen to the suppliant. The Menelaus of *Iliad* 6 not only listens but also changes his mind, and so do two others. A guilty Neoptolemus changes his mind after rejecting Philoctetes in the play of the same name, and Theseus changes his mind in the *Suppliants* of Euripides. Tacitus responded to these models by letting Tiberius only pretend to change his mind.[315] But these supplicandi do not experience Aeneas's moment. They are not introspective. Nor are collective supplicandi who debate a suppliant's fate.

Another feature of this act confirms this distinction. Nowhere else in Greek or Latin literature does a supplicandus lay eyes on a work of art representing or alluding to any aspect of an act of supplication. Aeneas, though, notices the buckle on Turnus's belt. It portrays the Danaids, famously unworthy suppliants who were famously, but foolishly, accepted.[316] Aeneas does not respond to this image and perhaps does not realize its significance, but Virgil has seen to it that the reader will, and thus invites the reader to ask whether Aeneas might have, too. Does good conduct include responding to works of art? It did when Aeneas came to Carthage, and he had to decide how to act as a guest, though not as a supplicandus. Then a painting of the fall of Troy reminded him of the humanity that he shared with the Carthaginians.

Image or no, Aeneas pauses, he thinks. He is on the verge of deliberating, as Seneca would wish him to. Then Aeneas notices the belt and remembers its owner, Pallas, a friend's son. Turnus killed Pallas, and so Aeneas kills Turnus in Pallas's name. Rather than examine himself, he abjures responsibility for his acts. To adapt the phrase of Gylippus, he no longer wishes to have the name of supplicandus.[317]

So far, this book has quoted fifty-odd ancient writers. Only Seneca and a few others link legal and psychological changes and even they do not balance decisions with doubts. Yet no fateful decision excludes doubts. The task is not to think of the gods alone. The task is to think of oneself.[318]

A Christian Epilogue

Supplication in early Christendom resembles ancient supplication. The four steps, a criterion of judgment, acceptance alternating with rejection—all appear in Gregory's history of sixth-century Gaul, the text with the most numerous instances. So does the coexistence of supplication at altars and supplication addressed to per-

---

315. *Il.* 6.45–65; S. *Ph.* 927–35, preceding 1261; E. *Supp.* 1–361. Tacitus: *Ann.* 1.11.1–13.5. So also Suet. *Tib.* 24.1.

316. Foolishly not only because acceptance led to war, but because it led to murder, both part of lost plays in the Aeschylean trilogy analyzed by Winnington-Ingram, *Aeschylus*.

317. Among other supplicandi, only the Orestes of Aeschylus does likewise: σύ τοι σεαυτήν, οὐκ ἐγώ, κατακτενεῖς (A. *Ch.* 923). A different view: Dyson, *The King of the Wood*, chap. 5, equating Aeneas's failings with those of Turnus, but without reference to supplication.

318. First poet known to imitate Virgil: St. *Theb.* 10.589–98 and 11.375–89, with the twist that the supplicandus is prevented from accomplishing his purpose once he changes his mind. Parody: Apul. *Met.* 9.19, as a servile supplicandus offered a bribe briefly struggles with his conscience.

sons.[319] Supplication at altars resembles Greek temple refuge. Gregory and the other supplicandi, however, resemble Roman magistrates. They have great if not absolute power over the acts of supplication that occur before them. They administer a Greek or even Semitic kind of supplication in a Roman way. Their legal position is also ambidextrous. Since they act in substantial agreement with Gratian's *Decretal*, a later law code, they resemble Greek supplicandi. Since the *Decretal* is a universal and not local code, they resemble Roman supplicandi.

In most acts of supplication in Gregory, the suppliant goes to an altar and lays hold of it. Once there, he or she speaks to the priest or bishop in charge of the church. If a pursuer appears, the priest interviews him as well. The legitimate suppliant receives protection from the priest; the illegitimate does not, and either leaves voluntarily or is expelled, again at the behest of the priest.[320] Sometimes the priest avoids expulsion by inducing the suppliant and the supplicandus to bargain and strike an agreement; in one case, a legal procedure supervenes.[321] The cardinal point is that no outsider may interfere: no community, no ruler, and no pursuer. Even if there is bargaining, the priest presides. All this will appear in the *Decretal*, too, even though it lies several centuries in the future.[322]

If these steps seem Greek or even Hebrew, the priest resembles a Roman magistrate on two counts. First, he seeks to enforce uniform rules. So, in one case, a murderer in Gregory's Gaul went from shrine to shrine throughout the country looking for refuge, but no place accepted him.[323] This murderer differs from ancient murderers such as Heracles and Orestes, who find acceptance in one place after meeting with rejection in others, or from Homeric or classical murderers who found acceptance provided that they went to some community other than their own.[324] In Greek supplication, acceptance may be a function of distance. Not so in Gregory's Gaul.

Second, the priest acts independently, in this instance surpassing even the Roman magistrate. Whereas the magistrate consulted imperial edicts, and priests in the later Middle Ages consulted canon law, Gregory cites no laws. Yet no one expels a suppliant from his church without his approval. Only one person even presumes to do so, and he is the king of the Franks speaking in a dream. Gregory does report that when a defeated Duke's wife took refuge in a church, she was forced out, the priest of the church apparently doing nothing. Yet she soon finds

---

319. Personal suppliant accepted: *Hist. F.* 4.49. Accepted, but conditionally: 6.32, 9.8. Rejected: 6.32. A different view of the similarity: Wenger, "Asylrecht," 839–43, Bellen, *Sklavenflucht*, 1.6, and Dreher, "Asyl von seinen Ursprüngen," 94–95, all centered on late antique legal texts such as the *Codex Theodosianus* rather than on the narration of examples as in Gregory.

320. Evaluation: *Hist. F.* 5.4, where a charge of murder does not lead Gregory to reject a suppliant. Voluntary departure: 7.21–22, discussed below.

321. Agreement including oath: *Hist. F.* 5.2. Including pledge: 5.3.

322. Gratian confirms priests' power to remove: c. 17; q. 4; 35. Confirms bargaining, even between pursuers and criminals: c. 17; q. 4; 9, "legitime [supplex] componat quod inique fecit." C. 17. q. 4; 33, 35 explain the mechanics of the process, including *satisfactio* offered by suppliant to pursuers and *securitas* given in return.

323. *Hist. F.* 5.5.

324. As Orestes says (A. *Eu*. 280).

another church.[325] For the most part, the clergy do their duty. In principle, nothing can stop them. As for a priest's superiors, they go largely unmentioned. Gregory never mentions them in connection with supplication. Elsewhere in this period, St. Augustine does rebukes one bishop for giving refuge to a perjurer and another bishop for excommunicating a pursuer who had done nothing except ask the bishop to take action against a fugitive.[326] But Augustine, like the queen of the Franks, is responding to unusual errors in judgment.

Priestly power sometimes manifests itself in a miracle. If a suppliant is starving because of a blockade, the priest uses a miracle to provide wine to drink; the grateful suppliant becomes a priest himself, Gregory's version of a *hierodoulos*. If a priest is perplexed, God may send him a dream. After this happens to Gregory, he admonishes a suppliant to leave in accordance with the meaning of the dream; the suppliant duly departs.[327] Still, the circumstances attending the dream are not reassuring. One Eberulf, a royal chamberlain accused of murder, has just fled to Gregory's church. The pursuer is a Frankish king, Gunthram, whom Gregory imagines bursting into church:

> I thought . . . I was celebrating mass . . . when I suddenly saw king Gunthram entering. In a loud voice he said, "Drag away the enemy of my family, pull the murderer from God's sacred altar." And when I heard him I turned to you, Eberulf, and said, "Wretch, take hold of the altar cloth . . . lest you be removed from here." And although you laid hold of it you held it with a loose hand and not forcefully.[328]

This suppliant is not said to be unworthy because he is a murderer or for any other reason, and so Gregory prevents the king from expelling him. Yet the loose hand is ominous. Mistakenly concluding that Gregory will fail to defend him, the suppliant leaves the sanctuary. Without ever telling the suppliant to leave, Gregory has virtually expelled him.

Virtual expulsion was nothing new. In Greek sources, pursuers used arson and starvation to achieve this purpose. The Romans used intimidation. But the priest will not allow himself these or other devices. They are all secular, and, as Gregory says, expulsion by secular authorities had not occurred "since ancient times."[329] Gratian agrees, saying that if laymen removed suppliants from churches they were to be excommunicated.[330] Nor will the priest expel the suppliant. He may fear yielding to the king. But he may fear defying the king, too—hence the dream, which offered a *via media* between unwelcome alternatives. The dream let the participants accomplish what they otherwise could not.

325. *Hist. F.* 6.12.
326. August. letter *1, *CSEL*; letter 250a ed. Goldbacher.
327. Starving: as immediately above. Dream sent to Gregory: *Hist. F.* 7.22. Yet no advice for a pursuer: 5.14.
328. *Hist. F.* 7.22.
329. *Hist. F.* 5.4, 5.14. Secular attempts foiled: 4.18, 5.14.
330. Gratian c. 17; q. 4; 6.

Similar to virtual expulsion was declining to exercise one's powers as a media-tor. When hostile relatives seized the queen dowager's property and insulted her family, she went to a sanctuary and turned it into a base for intrigues. Joining her was a minister who committed the wrong of taxing the Franks and feared for his life. When the king ordered the queen to leave sanctuary and retire to her villa, the priest did nothing. No negotiations took place and, on the other hand, no forcible expulsion. After a time, the queen complied with the king's order. It would seem that she had too much to lose.[331]

The problem that we are describing does not affect any and every kind of sup-plication. Gregory reports a number of cases of supplication addressed to indi-viduals, and they closely resemble ancient and especially Roman instances. One man approached a bishop after being found guilty in a Frankish court. The bishop was not in church, so the miscreant took him hostage. Leave and supplicate those who found you guilty, the bishop advised, and ask for mercy. He refused and was promptly captured and killed.[332] Another contretemps begins when a noble who fears the queen supplicates the king, who promises to intercede with her. But the noble does not trust the king, and so he goes to the queen himself and suppli-cates her in church on the Sabbath, throwing himself at her feet. He has miscal-culated, for she rejects him. The interest here lies in the failure to make use of intercession.[333]

But the problem does affect all supplication at altars. Though imperfect, the priest's monopoly of power makes expulsion difficult and thus strengthens sup-pliants. As a result, the suppliants are effectively claiming a right to asylum as opposed to a right to ask for help. This right, or this shadow of a right, is not yet universal: only Christians may exercise it. But because it is available to millions of people throughout much of Europe, it resembles a human right more than *prouocatio* does. It anticipates the human rights that have replaced supplication in modern times.

331. *Hist. F.* 7.4, 7.19.
332. *Hist. F.* 9.10.
333. *Hist. F.* 6.32.

6

CEREMONY AND MORALS

Supplication falls into two parts: a ceremony and an act of judgment sometimes followed by a pledge. The ceremony comprises the first three steps—approach, gesture, and request—and the judgment and possible pledge comprise the two aspects of the fourth. Without the ceremony the parties to the act of judgment could not present themselves and play their parts. Without the judgment the ceremony would be pointless, and without the pledge a favorable judgment would be insecure. The book has tried to reckon with every element—to accommodate both ceremony and morals. Most scholars, however, have concentrated on the ceremony. In the view of Gould, the fourth step was the occasion for automatic success provided that the suppliant performed the ceremony properly. In the view of some literary critics, the fourth step was the occasion either for automatic success or for exceptional failure due to poetic license. In Burkert's view, the fourth step was not predictable but remained less important than the ceremony, which was a biological imperative leading to an act of judgment that was to be understood in scientific and not moral or legal terms. Legal scholars did not overlook these moral and legal terms, but they did not consider the ceremony that occurred outside of court as part of their subject matter, and so they divorced ceremony and morals, too, but to the neglect of ceremony.

Chapters 2 and 3 have shown the drawbacks of this division. Studies of supplication as a ceremony have sometimes overlooked the moral and legal claims that suppliants make and the criteria of evaluation that supplicandi use, and they have almost always overlooked the many cases of justifiable rejection and expulsion: in sum, they have overlooked the features of supplication that make it a quasilegal practice. Gould and Burkert prefer to call supplication a "ritual," a term susceptible to many meanings, but in their work a term drawing attention to gestures—to the second step as opposed to the fourth. The notion of automatic success sprang from this fixation on the second step. The countervailing notion presented in this book—the alternation of success and failure, yes and no—springs from attention to the fourth step. A quasilegal practice climaxes at this step. Second in importance are the arguments made at the preceding step. These arguments form a bridge between the ceremony and the act of judgment.

Aside from these weaknesses, the treatment of ceremony has been inflexible. Many scholars noticed the knee clasp, but few noticed other important gestures such as prostration and the use of mourning clothes. Early, Greek genres and media like tragedy and vase painting received more attention than later, often Roman genres and media like biography and coins. Nor did scholars ask how Roman supplication could resemble Greek in spite of the lack of a cult comparable to Zeus *Hikesios*. With this neglect of cultural differences came neglect of political differences. In Gould's view, fourth-century Athenian democracy deprived supplication of its essence and destroyed it.[1] But a practice consisting of a series of steps need not cease to exist when assemblies regulate those steps. The steps and the sequence remain. By the same token, a practice does not cease to exist when the identity of the chief supplicandus changes. The king, the Athenian Assembly, the Roman magistrate, or the emperor: all can be the chief supplicandus. At the same time, the father, master, or husband remain important supplicandi at home rather than in public. Again, the practice does not cease to exist because of changes in political procedure or diplomacy. Athenian evaluation by two supplicandi—the Assembly and Council—remains a kind of evaluation. In the same vein, the argument that the suppliant is a fellow Greek remains an argument about kinship. It marks an extension of the argument found in Homer, just as dual evaluation marks a duplication of the practice described by Homer. For the study of supplication, the important feature of this change in the argument is that it makes the suppliant harder to reject.

Gould's (and Ostwald's) notion of a decline in supplication in the classical period points to a tendency to assign ceremonies to one period or place. But the ceremonial part of supplication is perdurable. At the altars of the churches of Gregory the Great it differs little from what it was at the altars of Greece or even Israel. Change occurs mostly at the fourth step, where the evaluator and the criteria of evaluation differ. Gregory's evaluator is a priest, and Gregory's criteria include being Christian.

The two elements of ceremony and judgment do not appear only in supplication. They appear in other ancient religious practices, too. Prayers end in a request to a god who, like a supplicandus, responds either favorably or not. In the *Iliad*, Athena rejects a prayer made by the Trojan women on behalf of their city. The women ask that Diomedes perish in battle, and Athena not only rejects the request but continues to aid the Greeks. She signals her rejection of the request by raising her chin in a gesture of denial—the same gesture Zeus used in *Odyssey* 9 and the reverse of the gesture Zeus used when granting the supplication made to him by Thetis.[2] In Book 16, when Achilles prays for Patroclus's success in battle and for Patroclus's safe return, Zeus grants only the first part of the prayer. He, too, raises his chin in denial. But the crux of rejection is not a gesture. The Sun god makes no gesture when he rejects the prayer of Odysseus's crew after they

---

1. Gould, "*Hiketeia*," 102–3; similar is Ostwald, *Nomos* cited at 171 above. Also similar: Traulsen, *Das sakrale Asyl*, confining supplication to early Greece and Israel.

2. *Il.* 6.311 vs. 1.528. Aristarchus athetized 6.311 (A/Ar ad loc.), objecting to the gesture, but even if the verse were athetized, the request remains rejected.

steal his cattle.[3] Offerings, too, meet with acceptance or rejection. We have already encountered a rejected offering. After escaping from the Cyclops, Odysseus sacrifices a ram to Zeus, who refuses to accept it.[4]

These rejections confirm that offerings and prayers, like supplications, culminate in an act of judgment. They also confirm that these practices include similar criteria of evaluation. Athena rejects the Trojans' request on the unspoken grounds of her enmity toward the Trojans; Zeus rejects Odysseus's sacrifice partly on the grounds of the hero's misconduct toward the Cyclops. The Sun rejects the prayer of those who steal his cattle for reasons of misconduct alone. Zeus grants only part of Achilles' prayer on the grounds that Achilles must eventually return to battle, his honor restored, as Zeus swore to Thetis. This range of reasons—enmity, wrongdoing, and honoring oaths—runs parallel to supplication. A god (or goddess) receiving a request from a worshipper uses as many criteria of judgment as a mortal receiving a request from a suppliant. By the same token, a god would not use identical criteria. He would not consult written laws; instead he might consult unwritten laws of his own creation. Every judge is idiosyncratic, the divine judge no less than the human one.[5]

Offerings and prayers, in turn, form part of most religious activity—of libations, festivals, acts of divination, or sacrifice. The alternatives of acceptance and rejection are ubiquitous, and the questions we may ask about these alternatives are correspondingly important. Yet scholarship on ancient religion has paid little attention to these questions. Prayers and offerings—especially animal sacrifice—have been studied from the perspective of myth as opposed to ritual, from the perspective of one ritual or place as opposed to another, and from the perspectives of the social or natural sciences.[6] But all these perspectives are extrinsic—in other words, they are not perspectives adopted by the worshippers.[7] The perspective of an act of judgment preceded by requests and arguments is intrinsic. Odysseus, for example, wants a favorable judgment from Zeus, just as he wanted a favorable response from the Cyclops.

Asking whether and why Odysseus obtains this favor are not always relevant questions. They will not elucidate instances in which prayers and the like do not end in an act of judgment. But this same caveat applies to supplication. Some acts of what the Greeks call *hiketeia* do not end in an act of judgment. Nor, for that matter, do these acts end in a pledge once the supplicandus grants a request.

---

3. Libation: *Il.* 16.231–32. Nod: 16.249–50. Sun god *Od.* 12.353–65.

4. *Od.* 9.533–35. Other rejected offerings: *Od.* 3.159–61, *Il.* 8.550–52.

5. Similarly, Scullion, "Olympian and Chthonian," 76–77, with refs., comments on the tendency for those stressing ceremony to minimize the role of the gods, or, in the language of this book, the role of the divine judge.

6. Examples from the study of supplication: G. Murray apud J. Harrison, *Themis*, on myth and ritual; Herman, *Ritualised Friendship*, on supplication as opposed to *xenia*; Pulleyn, *Prayer*, on supplication as opposed to prayer; Sinn, "Greek Sanctuaries," on supplication in a particular place; Gould, "*Hiketeia*," for social science; and Burkert, *Creation of the Sacred*, for natural science. Among studies of Greek religion, Nilsson, *Griechische Religion*, and Burkert, *Greek Religion*, do not discuss the acceptance or rejection of prayers and the like.

7. Extrinsic and psychological approach: the essays by several hands in Baumgarten, *Sacrifice in Religious Experience*. Extrinsic and socioeconomic: Bloch, *Prey into Hunter*. Extrinsic and political: Lincoln, *Death, War, and Sacrifice*.

But many acts of *hiketeia* do. For these acts, the judgment (and sometimes the pledge) is indispensable.

The modern tendency to neglect the act of judgment in favor of the ceremony does not lack for an ancient precedent. According to diverse ancient sources, misguided worshippers might evince the same tendency. They would perform a ceremony—in particular, they would bring the gods gifts—but would forget that the gods would evaluate them and might require more of them than a gift. When Phoenix advised Achilles to forgo his anger, he made this mistake, for he implied that gifts to the gods ought to be enough to gain their favor. In response, Socrates says that a good man and a god do not accept gifts from the wicked—thus rejecting many, if not most, offerings to the gods. The notion that the wicked may give gifts to appease the gods meets with rejection, too, for other passages show that gifts are no more acceptable for this purpose than for any other.[8] In the same vein, Isocrates says that rites would help a good man win the gods' favor more than they would help a bad man. Aristotle says that rites alone would never satisfy the gods; a worshipper needed to be deserving.[9] Even Homer may support this view, albeit subtly: Phoenix thinks of gifts and pleas to the gods as being crooked, whereas Homeric justice is straight.[10]

This same view passed into Roman literature partly through Plautus, who says that Jupiter looks with disfavor on sacrifices made by the guilty.[11] Plautus also applies this view to supplication. In a conversation about a supplicatory letter that makes a request for money, a character who hears the letter being read aloud exclaims, "This man who is in the wrong is ready to supplicate everybody!" Like Euripides' Ion, this speaker is complaining about the abuse of supplication, but unlike Ion he is not blaming a god. He is blaming the suppliant, who ought to be worthy as well as importunate.[12]

This same view also accommodates itself to the Roman practice of *clementia*. In this case, the suppliant may be guilty yet deserving. For his part, the supplicandus would remember that he, too, might someday be an imperfect suppliant, and would benefit by setting a standard of generosity. As Cicero says, reporting the views of those he calls Academics: "For a wise man, gratitude sometimes has value; a good man's place is to feel pity; . . . a firm man finds occasions for forgiveness; . . . the same man pleads and is placated."[13] Cicero speaks about emotions, not practices like supplication, but supplication informs his words "pleads and is placated." He envisions the same man as both suppliant and supplicandus.

---

8. Pl. *Lg.* 4.716d–717a; *Lg.* 10.885b, *Rep.* 2.364b–e.

9. Isoc. 2.20, Arist. *NE* 8.1163b; similarly, Plut. *Is. et Os.* 351c, observing that sensible men pray for what is good.

10. A distinction noticed by Aubriot-Sévin, "*Litai*," 14–15. A somewhat different interpretation of the contending views: R. Parker, "Spartan Religion," 79–80, seeing the criticism of gifts as characteristic of the fourth century BCE and characterizing it as "Protestant."

11. Jupiter: Pl. *Rud.* 22–24, rejecting the guilty altogether, although 25–26 say only that the innocent have an advantage.

12. Pl. *Bac.* 1024. Another balanced view, but inclining toward morals: Cic. *Cael.* 79, where the defendant appeals to the judges as a "supplicem abiectum non tam ad pedes quam ad mores."

13. Cic. *Mur.* 63.

None of these sources object to supplication as such. They object to supplication by the undeserving—to the performance of a ceremony when moral requirements have gone unmet. They want ceremony and morals to conform to one another.

But just as the modern view of supplication meets with rebuke in some ancient sources, it meets with support in others. These sources—once again beginning with Socrates—divorce the ceremony from moral concerns, but they do not approve of the divorced or isolated ceremony. Nor do they anticipate later writers by explaining the ceremony from the perspective of natural or social science or literary convention. What modern writers explain according to one or another of these extrinsic standards these ancient sources decline to explain. Rather than explain ceremony of this kind, they condemn it. The modern object of study is an ancient occasion for obloquy.

Socrates leads by example. Speaking in his own defense, he refuses to supplicate. Instead he says that his arguments on his own behalf should suffice. Far from putting his wife beside him on the stand, he asks his friends to keep her out of sight.[14] Other exemplars followed. Rutilius Rufus, the man Cicero called an imitator of Socrates, found himself on trial for extortion in spite of an exemplary record as a provincial governor. He, too, refused to supplicate, a decision Cicero approved:

> That man was a model of innocence. There was no one more honorable or righteous in the community, and he refused not only to supplicate the judges, but also to let his case be put more elaborately or freely than plain, truthful reasoning required.[15]

As Valerius Maximus reported, Rufus refused to wear mourning dress and forbade his advocates to supplicate on his behalf.[16] A second Roman Socrates, Cato the Younger, rejected an act of supplication by the women in his family, who asked him to flee Caesar. Cato later fought Caesar, who eventually retaliated by causing Cato's death, just as the jury put an end to Rufus's career.[17] Rhetoricians praised Cato's defiance, which became a commonplace.[18]

Less influential were Cynic reasons to reject supplication and similar practices. According to Cynic doctrine, religious ceremonies were nugatory, and if they were not, those that resembled supplication would fail at the fourth step, when the supplicandus would make an evaluation according to a standard of worth. No human, the Cynics maintained, could make such an evaluation properly.[19] The Pythagoreans agreed with the Cynics' conclusion but reasoned differently. *Philia,*

---

14. Pl. *Ap.* 35c–d, *Phd.* 60a. The one pre-Socratic defendant who refuses to supplicate, Palamedes, is a retrojection (Philostrat. *Her.* 715). Post-Socratic: Isoc. 15.321, a suppositious defense.
15. Cic. *de Orat.* 1.229.
16. Cic. *de Orat.* 1.229, V. Max. 6.4.4.
17. Plut. *Cat. Mi.* 32.4.
18. Sen. *Suas.* 6.2.
19. Cynics: D.L. 6.42. Pythagoreans: D.S. 10.8.2.

they held, dictated that a friend or associate be protected regardless of who they were or what they had done. The evaluation and judgment of the suppliant thus became superfluous. This reasoning would seem to resemble that of modern scholars who also believe in a norm of acceptance, but the Pythagoreans did not tie acceptance to gestures. Kindliness, not any gesture, compelled the supplicandus. Like the Cynic view, this one cannot have been influential. It nonetheless confirmed the Socratic notion that traditional supplication was inappropriate.

Plutarch introduced the Socratic view into his Greek *Lives*. In a total of 24 biographies of Greek statesmen, he reports only five supplications of one adult male Greek or Macedonian by another, as opposed to seven such acts lacking an introductory word or gesture.[20] Nor are the five incidents random. In two cases, Alexander's men beg to be readmitted to his favor and gather at his door; in another, Timoleon and his associates gather around the tyrant of Corinth, Timoleon's brother, and plead with him to abdicate; in the fourth, messengers from Syracuse weep and fall at the feet of Dion, the liberator of Sicily. Each time, Greek men supplicate the great or the notorious, before whom a man may go to extremes.[21] The fifth case, the supplication of Nicias to Gylippus after the defeat of Nicias's army at Syracuse, is an embarrassment for Nicias. In general, Greek men do not supplicate one another. Similarly, Greek men rarely supplicate Romans and Persians.[22] Greek women supplicate more often.[23]

Plutarch rescues Greek men from impropriety and perhaps effeminacy by omitting words and gestures, but other authors rescue them from the same fate by omitting acts. In the *Iliad*, the only Greek who supplicates in battle is Nestor.[24] The same difference between victor and vanquished obtains in Virgil. On the battlefields of the *Aeneid*, Trojans do not supplicate.[25] These writers show how the philosophers' strictures penetrated some imaginative literature, even at an early time when these strictures must have come from didactic poetry and other wisdom literature.

Ancient condemnations of ceremonies without morals cannot have influenced modern writers on supplication and sacrifice, none of whom cite them. But these ancient condemnations did influence the church fathers. They, too, objected to pagan ceremonies, and for the same reason: pagan ceremonies were morally inadequate. With regard to the first three steps, these ceremonies were licentious and with re-

20. Plut. *Dio* 42.3–43.6, *Alex*. 62.3, 71.4–5, *Timol*. 4.5–6, *Nic*. 27.4–28.4. No word or gesture: *Ages*. 3.2, 25.2, *Pelop*. 26.2, *Dio* 31.2, *Eumen*. 17.2, *Phoc*. 16.3, *Per*. 32.3.

21. As they may in temples: Plut. *Dem*. 29.1, *Per*. 31.2. An act at a temple but with Timoleon present, making the situation more like a personal supplication: *Timol*. 16.5–8, where the introductory word or gesture is missing.

22. Romans: Plut. *Sull*. 14.5. Persians: *Them*. 28.1–29.2.

23. Words derived from the *hik-* root for female suppliants, Plut. *Dio* 31.2, *Rom*. 19.7; similarly, δεομένη προσεύχεται, *Thes*. 8.2; gestures at *Agis* 20.2–5, *Arat*. 42.1, *Cat. Mi*. 32.4, *Cor*. 36.3.

24. Homer's bias in reporting casualties: Hyg. *Fab*. 114–15. Nestor: *Il*. 15.659–66. Whitfield, *Restored Relation*, 22–23, notices the difference.

25. V. A. 10.522–36, 10.594–601, as well as 12.930–52, all instances of Italians supplicating Aeneas. Instances off the battlefield do show Trojans and their protectrix, Venus, supplicating in varied circumstances: 1.666 (Venus to Cupid), 2.515–53 (Trojans at altar), 8.115–74 (Aeneas to Evander), 8.382 (Venus to Vulcan).

gard to the fourth step, they were defective, for there was no true god to evaluate the request made by the performer of the rite. To cite but one of the Fathers, St. Augustine says that worshippers of pagan gods show no concern for good conduct. Accordingly the worshippers show no concern for the true God. Since only this god can help them, their ceremonies prove nugatory.[26] St. Augustine praises Plato for describing the gods as unfailingly good, and goes on to observe that a good god would never approve of ceremonies that lacked moral character—in particular, stage plays that Augustine calls rites performed in honor of the gods.[27]

Among nineteenth-century writers who noticed the Christian rejection of pagan rituals, Nietzsche is the most apposite, but not because he was a classical scholar. More than any other writer, he valued pagan rituals; he even valued them because Christian writers did not. The vice that Socrates and Augustine complained of was no longer a vice, but a virtue. Writers of a temper different from Nietzsche's now found that these same rituals served purposes revealed by the application of social science. For supplication, Durkheim's solidarity was the most important of these newfound purposes. Scholars held that the fourth step in an act of supplication led to solidarity between the suppliant and the group or community that accepted him. In some acts of supplication, such solidarity is indeed the result.

The modern stress on ceremony has several parts: an inversion of Plato and the church fathers, an endorsement of Nietzsche, an adaptation of social science to the classical curriculum. But none of these parts includes any comparison between Greek and Near Eastern practices, and the endorsement of Nietzsche militates against such comparisons. Yet as *Exodus* and other passages show, Greek and Hebrew supplication resemble one another. A feature of supplication that might seem distinctively Greek—the punishment of those who betray suppliants—appears in a bicultural text, *Second Maccabees*. Comparable similarities link Greek and Hebrew sacrifice, especially Greek sacrifice to the Olympians and Hebrew sacrifice to Yahweh.[28] Early divines had studied such similarities; Robertson Smith studied them, too. But later scholars of Greek and Roman religion did not.[29] With regard to supplication, the loss is small, for Near Eastern examples are few. But with regard to sacrifice and other topics, too, like prayer, the loss is great. Compensating for this loss depends on describing these practices in a way that keeps the link between Greece and Rome from being exclusive. Supplicatory gestures, for example, show that the Romans can resemble the Hebrews or even the Persians more than they do the Greeks.

Besides elucidating the study of supplication, the balance between ceremony and morals can elucidate the study of other practices and of societies other than Greece and Rome. As we shall now see, it can also elucidate the study of ancient law.

26. August. *C.D.* 6, especially 6.12.
27. August. *C.D.* 8.14.
28. Scullion, "Olympian and Chthonian," 101–2, with refs.
29. Wenger, "Asylrecht"; Freyburger, "Supplication grecque"; Dreher, "Asyl von seinen Ursprüngen."

SUPPLICATION AND ANCIENT LAW

Just as scholars of ancient religion have concentrated on ceremony as opposed to morals, scholars of ancient law have concentrated on procedure as opposed to substance. But supplication points to the importance of substance—of descriptions of wrongdoing and subsequent punishments. Assertions of innocence and countervailing assertions of guilt dominate supplication. In Athens, regulations make supplication at altars impossible for persons guilty of several crimes. In Rome, *clementia* creates a third category midway between guilt and innocence. No other topic attracts so much attention. The Trojans of Homer, the Plataeans of Thucydides, the clients of Cicero—all are occasions for tortured arguments about guilt and innocence. Supplication is less a chapter in the history of ancient regulations than a chapter in the history of ancient legal reasoning, especially as it pertains to murder.[30]

In the prevailing view, which saw regulation as inimical to supplication, this reasoning ought to have led to conflict between the practice of supplication and legal imperatives. Not so: regulations mostly formalized long-standing practices. Some Athenian regulations changed supplication so as to bring it into conformity with the political system. Other regulations compensated for a weakness in the system—the exclusion of metics and slaves from public life. Nor did supplication and lawmaking clash in international affairs, where the laws took the form of treaties providing autonomy to federal shrines or shrines in the territory of allies or dependent states. These shrines could protect suppliants but could not incorporate them into the community. Instead a suppliant who left a shrine made himself vulnerable to the magistrates of one of the signatories of the treaty—in the Peloponnesus, to Sparta.

Unlike their Greek counterparts, scholars of Roman supplication have acknowledged the importance of regulated supplication, especially under the Principate. But comparison with Athenian practice reveals two distinctively Roman elements: the *imperium* of the supplicandus who was a high-ranking magistrate and the development of mercy as a second ground for accepting a suppliant. The first of these elements shows that supplication is once again adapting itself to the political system. In Athens, we should remember, the relation between the two deliberative bodies influenced supplication so as to bring about a dual evaluation of the suppliant, first by the Council and second by the Assembly. In Rome, the power of the magistrates influenced supplication so as to eliminate any evaluation by a deliberative body. Rather than let the deliberative body evaluate him, the suppliant let the magistrate evaluate him and then let the magistrate speak on his behalf at an assembly meeting. The one exception to this practice, evaluation of the suppliant by the Senate, was not truly an exception: the Senate was a deliberative

---

30. Stressing procedure as opposed to substance: Sealey, *Justice*, 59–60; Gagarin, *Early Greek Law*, 12–17; Todd, *Athenian Law*, 64–66; and Cohen, *Violence and Community*, 190; this view originates with Maine, *Dissertation on Early Law and Custom*, 389. A balanced view: Carey, "Shape of Athenian Laws." Stressing substance: Harris, "*Epieikeia.*"

body composed of present and former magistrates. It made recommendations to the assemblies just as individual magistrates did. The second element, mercy, introduced a legal and moral refinement affecting the third and fourth steps in any act. The chief drawback of supplication in Athens or elsewhere had been rigid criteria of judgment. If suppliants were not innocent without reservation, they were innocent by virtue of extenuating circumstances such as involuntary wrongdoing. They could not be in any way guilty. Mercy enabled suppliants to acknowledge guilt.

Still more far-reaching was another Roman departure from Greek practice: the development of rights that made supplication unnecessary, and the countervailing use of supplication when the legal system failed. In Athens, the relation between supplication and the law had been complementary. In Rome, it was complementary and also reciprocal. The law replaced supplication with rights, and thus improved the suppliant's position in one way, and supplication provided an appeal against unjust decisions or laws, and thus improved the suppliant's position in another way.

These changes did have precedents. In Greece, requests for purification were so likely to end in acceptance that they had the character of a right, one that assemblies feared that suppliants would abuse. But practices such as *prouocatio* went much further in the same direction. A suppliant—say, a murderer—need no longer go to an altar to secure a trial. Instead, the practice of *prouocatio* would guarantee a trial. The same was true for appeals by suppliants. Any suppliant appearing before the Athenian Assembly could beg them to pass a law or decree. But the principle of *res iudicata* made it impossible for the suppliant to ask for a decree that would relieve him of the consequences of being found guilty in court. In Rome, however, suppliants could appeal for a decision that would relieve them of the consequences of a guilty verdict. Under the Republic, they could also supplicate for the repeal of the law under which they had been convicted.

Roman innovations did not supplant all Greek regulations any more than Greek regulations supplanted the unregulated practice. The slave girl who did not wish to be sent to the mill illustrates this survival of old forms. She could have made her supplication at any time in antiquity and in any place. If her master rejected her, she might have fled to a local shrine and supplicated there. This, too, could have happened anywhere and at any time, even under Roman rule. If the shrine had won the right to receive suppliants under the imperial regulations of 22 CE, it could have not only received her but also gained Roman recognition for any decision that it took. It would, of course, act under regulations passed by the local assembly or other deliberative body. So much for the local shrine, but if she fled her master during the Principate, she might have a third choice: going to a statue of the Roman emperor. Now the imperial authorities would appear and would bring her before a magistrate. Once transported to his tribunal, she would once again make her case, but the magistrate would follow written rules that jurists have more or less preserved. Roman law would also make itself felt in another way: if she calumniated her master, the magistrate would arrest her for the crime of *iniuria*. If found guilty of *iniuria* she could not appeal, but her owner might appeal on her behalf. If the owner supplicated while making his appeal, her decision to run away would lead to yet another kind of supplication.

We cannot name a slave who did all this. But enumerating the possibilities that might have existed for a runaway slave in late antiquity reveals the effect of centuries of development. It also reveals that the unregulated act with which she begins and the regulated acts to which she may later turn do not fundamentally differ. The unregulated act includes principles of fairness and perhaps innocence and culminates in an act of judgment. The regulated acts include the same four steps as the unregulated act and the same or similar principles. The act at the local shrine adds local regulations and the act before the imperial statue adds Roman regulations. The act of appeal adds a new legal principle. Along with layers of regulation, these three acts add layers of power and organization running from small to large.

At the top stood the emperor, whom few appellants would reach. But the emperor was also a supplicandus of another, familiar kind—the head of the household. Messalina, for example, wished to approach Emperor Claudius as a husband who might forgive her for her infidelity and not as an emperor who would not forgive this insult to his position. Yet Claudius might and did refuse to act as her husband, choosing to act as emperor instead.[31] Unlike other heads of household— say, Odysseus during the supplications with which this book begins—the emperor was both a traditional and a legal figure. He epitomizes the ever more numerous ties between supplication and the legal system.

Because these ties are reciprocal, neither supplication nor the legal system should be thought dependent or inferior. To say, for example, that the legal system or part of it grew out of supplication is unfounded.[32] This statement misrepresents the history of supplication and fails to acknowledge the autonomy of the legal system. Suppliants in court must plead innocent; outside of court, Roman suppliants must accept the consequences of their guilt when asking for mercy. Yet merely to reply that legal systems are autonomous underestimates the importance of these ties—the pervasiveness of legal reasoning, the parallels for legal proceedings, the prestige of the paradigm of plea and judgment.[33] Nor do these ties weaken legal systems. On the contrary: quasilegal practices relieve pressure on legal institutions, reinforce legal principles, and fill gaps. If we return to the slave girl in Lysias 1, she will be able to plead a case before her master, thus relieving Athenian magistrates of any responsibility. She will plead involuntary wrongdoing, thus reinforcing a legal principle. And she will be able to do so even though

---

31. Tac. *Ann.* 11.37.

32. As thought by Murray and others at 16 above. The contrary view: Schömann, *Alterthümer*, 2.24, saying that in Greece there was never a time of "gänzliche Rechtslosigkeit."

33. Autonomy of legal systems in respect to supplication: Gamauf, *Ad statuam licet confugere*, with bibliography. Dependence on political factors: Dreher, "Asyl von seinen Ursprüngen." On political and religious factors: Auffarth, "Protecting Strangers."

she is a slave, thus filling a gap in the Athenian system, one that did not allow slaves to defend themselves against their masters in court.[34]

So much is true of the quasilegal practice as such. Once regulated, the quasi-legal practice serves to extend the legal system. In Athens, the laws keeping felons out of shrines kept felonious suppliants out of shrines, too, and so these laws reached into a previously untouched sphere of activity. In Rome, the law of Tiberius regulating Greek shrines established a *modus* where presumably none existed. These regulations show that in most cases, the law does not replace supplication. That occurs in some instances, but in more instances the law and the quasilegal practice remain complementary and reciprocal, like Siamese twins.

Centuries later, the law would seem to have discarded its twin brother, supplication. Whereas the Romans provided a right to a trial to those who otherwise would have to beg for it, treaties and conventions of the twentieth century provide numerous rights that might appear to make supplication unnecessary. The soldier has a right to surrender and not be killed; the refugee has the right to asylum; the beggar has the right to food, clothing, shelter, and means of earning a livelihood.[35] If a soldier or some other erstwhile suppliant is denied his rights, an international court may come to his aid or even punish those who fail to respect the law.[36] But the substitution of rights for requests is not the whole story. The Geneva Conventions do not provide for sanctions against those who deny rights to others. As a consequence, the correction of abuses usually results not from a trial but from some political action taken in response to public protest. And as Hannah Arendt observed only years after the conventions were ratified, this protest does not arise as a matter of course. It depends on publicity or, as Arendt said in an essay on refugees, on "fame":

> Only fame will eventually answer the repeated complaint of refugees of all social strata that "nobody here knows who I am"; and it is true that the chances of the famous refugee are improved just as a dog with a name has a better chance to survive than a stray dog who is just a dog in general.[37]

---

34. MacDowell, *Law in Athens*, 80–81. The interdependency of the law and "extralegal rules" among which supplication is not mentioned: H. L. A. Hart, *The Concept of Law*, 170–73, noting that laws and "extralegal rules" may have much the same content.

35. Surrender: The Geneva Convention Relative to the Treatment of Prisoners of War Adopted on 12 August 1949, article 3.1. Refuge: The Geneva Convention Relating to the Status of Refugees Adopted on 28 July 1951, article 1(a)2. Food, clothing, and shelter: Universal Declaration of Human Rights ratified by the United Nations General Assembly on December 10, 1948, article 25.1. The right to food is also secured by the International Covenant on Economic, Social, and Cultural Rights, article 11.2, but this document, unlike the Universal Declaration, has not yet been ratified. Employment: Universal Declaration of Human Rights, 23.1.

36. Forsythe, *Human Rights*, 13–14. The prospect for more such cases via strengthened international courts: G. Robertson, *Crimes against Humanity*, 325–42, listing some crimes that might be prosecuted in such courts, including some that constitute violations of the Geneva Conventions governing refugees and surrendering soldiers. Utopian alternatives to international courts: Derrida, *Cosmopolitanism*, 4–5, and Payot, *Des villes-refuges*. Both propose that some European cities declare themselves asylums.

37. Arendt, "Decline," 287, quoted by Derrida, *Cosmopolitanism*, 15.

Arendt did not foresee, however, that too much publicity might be as harmful for refugees and other erstwhile suppliants as too little. Each report of violated rights makes a demand on the public's conscience, time, and energy.[38] Too many reports, and the public will suffer from fatigue. Meanwhile, what of the erstwhile suppliants who discover that they are only Arendt's "dogs in general"? Will they make demands on the authorities? No—they will supplicate.

The development of rights does not render supplication obsolete. Some who lack rights supplicate instead and the public sometimes intercedes on their behalf. Nor does this happen only because rights are violated. The public that is to intercede on the victim's behalf may be happy that the victim supplicates, and may even prefer that he does. Like Siamese twins, supplication and the legal system remain joined.

HOMER AND HUMAN RIGHTS

The government of Afghanistan in 2001 did not consider itself bound by the Geneva Convention protecting surrendering soldiers. But in an incident reported by the *New York Times*, Afghan government troops did not bear the responsibility of accepting a surrender made by others. Instead, a single government soldier surrendered to troops of the Northern Alliance, a rebel group financed and guided by the United States:

> Near an abandoned Taliban bunker, Northern Alliance soldiers dragged a wounded Taliban soldier out of a ditch today. As the terrified man begged . . . , the Alliance soldiers pulled him to his feet.[39]

Two *Times* photos, figures 6.1 and 6.2, record the scene. In 6.1, the captors drag the Taliban soldier along a road after taking him from the ditch. In 6.2, they have come to a halt, and he has a chance to beg for his life. As he squats on the ground, a captor holds him by one arm. Perhaps he has extended this arm in supplication. His other arm is hidden, but he is surely using supplicatory words. In this case, as in so many others, his choice of gesture or word is less important than communicating his intent to supplicate. He is also making his request to be spared. Soon will come his arguments. The *Times* does not say how long he has to make them, but perhaps long enough to cite or at least allude to the prohibition in the Koran against killing a Muslim captive.[40] This prohibition corresponds to the Greek *nomos* against killing a fellow Greek and to the Roman practice of showing mercy to those defeated in civil wars. Perhaps the Taliban soldier makes other arguments; per-

---

38. A more pessimistic formulation: Enzensburger, *Bürgerkrieg*, 59, complaining of the way in which television, "the most corrupt medium of all," invites those who see images of refugees and war victims to become "more like god" (58).

39. "Executions and Looting as Alliance Nears Kabul," *New York Times*, Nov. 13, 2001, A1. Accompanied by the three photos taken by Tyler Hicks.

40. Muslim prisoners: Koran 4.92.

haps he is a fellow tribesman.[41] He surely does not cite or allude to the Geneva Convention protecting prisoners of war.

Our captive has now come to the fourth and last step. The supplicandi, the Northern Alliance soldiers, respond:

> They searched him and emptied his pockets. Then, one soldier fired two bursts from his rifle into the man's chest. A second soldier beat the lifeless body with his rifle butt.

Figure 6.3 shows the scene a moment later.

Like some ancient sources, the *Times* condemns the decision of the supplicandi. The reason is not that the supplicandi rejected the suppliant, or even that they rejected and killed him. The supplicandi violated the Geneva Convention. A *Times* editorial accompanying the story not only makes this reason clear but also demands that the paymaster of the Northern Alliance, the U.S. government, compel Alliance soldiers to respect the Convention. For the *Times*, this story is one of the failure of the law to make supplication unnecessary. Not that the law is wrong: it is unenforced.

Suppose the law were enforced. Do we want the suppliant to approach these soldiers, hands and also head held high, and to do no more than recite his name and rank, as the convention requires? Have we no use for the Koran or the appeal to a fellow tribesman? Or do we prefer that this soldier supplicate and be spared? We might not go so far as to demand that the prisoner beg for his life, for if we did, we would be impugning his right to be treated as a prisoner of war, but we might want to go some ways in that direction. We might want the law enforced but supplication encouraged; we might want both.

Then there are the Alliance troops. Should they have no chance to hear the prisoner beg? If so, we face another question, which is how to prevent them from acting as supplicandi. For if they do act as supplicandi, they will be able to reject the prisoner. The convention has one answer, rights; the supplicandus has two, yes and no.

So far we have only observed the scene. But are we observers? The point of view of the photographer suggests otherwise. He is standing behind the soldiers because they are assuring his safety. First the soldiers, then the photographer, then us—witnesses by degrees. We are intercessors after the fact, primed to demand that the U.S. government heed the *Times* editorial demanding enforcement of the convention. Or do we overemphasize this matter of principle? Suppose otherwise: suppose we feel pity, as the Taliban soldier would wish. Suppose we feel anger, as the Alliance soldiers might prefer. Now we step into the photo and do the captors' work, becoming virtual supplicandi. Or suppose we check our anger

---

41. Protection for suppliants who are fellow tribesmen but not foreigners in another, more southerly region of Afghanistan: "In the Hiding Zone," *New Yorker*, July 26, 2004, 40.

FIGURE 6.1   Capturing the suppliant. Courtesy of Getty Images.

FIGURE 6.2   Listening to the suppliant. Courtesy of Getty Images.

FIGURE 6.3   Rejecting the suppliant. Courtesy of Getty Images.

and, like Seneca's Nero, feel mercy. We become virtual supplicandi and judges, too, obliged to consider the limits of clemency.[42]

We can, if we like, escape these questions. Save the suppliant—never mind who armed the supplicandi or took the photo or where the suppliant looked for succor. But this resort to the Geneva Convention is only the beginning. What of protection, food, clothing, shelter, and perhaps a trial? Saving the suppliant turns us into guardians. We may as well have granted a request to establish the rule of law all over the world. Then we find that we cannot honor this request. Meant to arouse indignation, the pictures of the soldier's death arouse despair.

Like Siamese twins, supplication and the law come to the same end. But perhaps the next captured soldier to come to our attention will find that supplication can help the law come to a different end. Every act of supplication is new, every suppliant starts afresh. Supplication varies as much as rights should not.

42. Recently discussed in the official American context by K. Moore, *Pardons*, part 1.

Appendix 1

ACTS OF SUPPLICATION

This appendix provides a catalogue of the acts of ancient supplication cited in this work or found in the same authors or sources. It includes supposititious and interrupted acts and supplications addressed to statues, including statues of gods, but excludes most other supplications addressed to gods and heroes. It also excludes planned but unattempted acts, descriptions of types of supplications, acts of intercession in which the interceder does not supplicate himself, petitions and other epistolary requests described in appendix 6, supplicatory electioneering and, most notably, courtroom supplications other than in Cicero. Courtroom supplications in Cicero appear in two additional lists under this author, one list for defendants and one for plaintiffs.

The following entry is typical. It comes from the *Ilias Latina*, one of many minor works that report the same acts of supplication as major works:

SUPPLIANT/SUPPLICANDUS	GESTURE/WORD	RESPONSE	PAGES(S)
Ilias 1026–45 Priam/Achilles	effusus genibus	alleuat	

The citation begins with the source, here abbreviated as *Ilias*. Next comes the verse or section in which the suppliant makes his approach, followed by the verse or section in which the response of the supplicandus is complete. Here the relevant verses are 1026–45. Last come the names of the suppliant and the supplicandus, here Priam and Achilles. If the place of supplication is a statue, shrine, or altar, and the name of the god or goddess is known, he or she appears as the supplicandus, and the location of the altar or the like is given also; sometimes the name of the shrine is given. If the name of the divinity is not known, the name of those in charge of the place of supplication appears instead. If the suppliant is an intercessor, the name of the person for whom he intercedes appears in parentheses. If the intercessor is a diplomat, the names of those for whom he intercedes are usually omitted. If the suppliant or supplicandus is a prominent Roman other than a king or emperor, a reference to a biographical entry in *RE* appears in a footnote. If the suppliant or supplicandus is a prominent Carthaginian, a reference to a biographical entry in Geus appears.

The second column contains the gesture or words with which the suppliant communicates his intent. Here the gesture is *effusus genibus*. If *supplex, hiketês,* or cognate words appear in the source, or if the suppliant uses a gesture, as here, verbs of speaking such as *hiketeuô* and *oro* are usually omitted.

The third column contains the supplicandus's response. Here it is *alleuat*, "[the suppliant] rises." This response implies that the request was granted, and a pledge given. When no gesture or other quotable word or phrase conveys this information, this column includes a very brief report, as in the case of Thetis, another suppliant found in the *Ilias Latina*:

Ilias 87–96 Thetis/ Jupiter	genibus . . . affusa	request
[on behalf of Achilles]		granted

The contrary to this response is "request denied." "Accepted" means "granted protection"; sometimes "spared" appears instead. "Rejected" means "denied protection"; sometimes "slain" appears. "Removed" means expelled by the authorities or repossessed by a slavemaster entitled to take his property from the shrine. "Voluntary departure" appears only when the suppliant leaves after the supplicandi at a shrine have failed to reply to the suppliant's request. These words do not appear when the suppliant leaves after the supplicandi have rejected the suppliant's request. In such a case, the suppliant's voluntary departure is taken for granted.

The fourth and last column refers to the pages at which the act is cited or discussed. Numbers following periods are footnote numbers or numbers of items in a table.

Appendix 1a contains individual Greek authors. These authors appear in alphabetical order, but Homer is divided into two lists, one for the *Iliad* and the other for the *Odyssey*; Hesiod, the Homeric Hymns, the Epic Cycle, and Alcaeus form one list, as do Dio, Zonaras, and Xiphilinus; the canonical orators all appear in one list bearing that title; and authors reporting fewer than five acts appear together alphabetically under "Other Authors." The list for Apollodorus includes several acts occurring in lost plays of Euripides and Sophocles, but otherwise no citation appears twice. In each list, complete works appear first, in the order found in *LSJ*. They are followed by lost works and fragments. Philo Judaeus, Josephus, and the evangelists are omitted, but all acts in Heliodorus are included.

Appendix 1b contains individual Latin authors. These authors appear in alphabetical order, including a list for anonymous authors arranged alphabetically by title; works appear in the order found in *OLD*. Terence appears with Plautus. As noted, Cicero includes acts performed in court. Aug. *Anc.* appears under "Other Authors."

Appendix 1c contains a list of acts recorded in other Greek and Roman sources, mainly epigraphical, as well as several Greek regulations of supplication. Acts in this appendix are listed by type, date, and location, the oldest of each type appearing first.

Appendix 1d contains acts found in Hebrew, Akkadian, and some Assyrian sources and also Hebrew regulations of supplication. Although it excludes acts in the Septuagint and Philo Judaeus, it includes acts in Josephus and the evangelists.

Appendix 1e contains Greek and Latin acts of supplication with foreign principals, that is, acts lacking either a Greek or Roman suppliant or supplicandus. It excludes such acts in Near Eastern sources, in epic poetry, and in Heliodorus and Josephus.

As explained in chapter 1, the *terminus ante quem* for all acts in Appendices 1a–c is the end of the Principate. Most sources also date from before that time, but not the *Historia Apollonii Regis Tyri*, Justin, Orosius, the Alexander Romance, and Tzetzes.

I have not compiled an appendix listing acts known from visual sources. For some acts occurring in Greek tragedy and preserved on vases, see *LIMC* and Trendall-Webster; for acts occurring in both Greek and Roman tragedy but preserved on vases alone, see Schmidt, *De partibus scaenicis*, chap. 2; for acts occurring at the fall of Troy and preserved in several media, see M. Hart, *Athens and Troy*. For some acts occurring on Roman imperial coins, see the indices to *RIC* V.2; the indices to Cr. and *BMCI* lack relevant entries. For pictures of acts addressed to herms, see Siebert, "Pilier hermaïque," and Vorberg, *Ars erotica*; for Roman sculpture, see Schneider, *Bunte Barbaren*, as at chapter 1, n. 78..

Appendix 1a

ACTS OF SUPPLICATION IN GREEK AUTHORS

Achilles Tatius

SUPPLIANT/SUPPLICANDUS	GESTURE/WORD	RESPONSE	PAGES(S)
3.10.2–6 *Clitophon/Egyptians*	ἱκετεύειν . . . νεύμασι	*not stated*[1]	24.96
4.13.1–6 Elderly bandits/soldiers	ἐπιθέντες ἱκετηρίας ῥάβδους	trick successful	56.143
5.9.3 Clinias/ship	χεῖρας ἀνασχών	rescued	43.83
5.17.3–5 Lacaena/Melite[2]	προσπίπτει	ἀνάστηθι γόνασιν	72.239, 98.403, 102.430, 109, 110
7.13.3–8.19.2 Leucippe/Artemis	ἔχεται τοῦ νεώ	test of virginity	93, 119.90, 149
8.2.2–19.2 Clitophon/Artemis	ἱκέτης γενόμενος	hearing held	93, 180, 383.1
8.17.3–4 Callisthenes/Calligone	προσπεσών . . . γόνασι	marriage proposal eventually accepted	

1. Suppositious act.
2. In fact, Leucippe to Melite.

Aeschylus

SUPPLIANT/SUPPLICANDUS	GESTURE/WORD	RESPONSE	PAGES(S)
Ag. 231–47 Iphigenia/Agamemnon	suppressed	rejected	35.34, 45.92, 86.343, 163.11
Ch. 315–380[1] *Children/ Agamemnon*	ἱκέτας δέδεκται καὶ φυγάδας	*prayer granted*[2]	
Ch. 896–930 Clytemnestra/ Orestes	τόνδε αἴδεσαι . . . μάστον	rejected	45.92, 80.298, 85.338, 134.180, 141.217, 163.12, 276.317
Eu. 1–93 Orestes/Apollo	ἕδραν ἔχοντα προστρόπαιον	dismissed	37.41, 92.372, 159.301, 168.40
Eu. 276–488 Orestes/Athena *Polias*	βρέτας ἧσαι	ὅρκον περῶντας	7.18, 36.38, 108.16
Supp. 1–519 Danaids/gods	ἱκετῶν . . . κλάδοισιν	referred to assembly	36.37, 40.67, 41.68, 43.82, 56.144, 68.222, 71.237, 84–86, 92.274, 108.14, 113.52, 114.60, 134.178, 383.3
Supp. 520–624 Danaus/Argives	κλάδους ἐν ἀγκάλαις λαβών	ἔδοξεν Ἀργείοσιν	113.52, 177.21
Th. 109–80 *Chorus/gods*	παρθένων ἱκέσιον λόχον	*prayer not granted*	
Ixion Ixion/Zeus[3]	unstated	unstated	10

1. Excluding the lines spoken by the chorus.
2. Supplicatory prayers are italicized.
3. A. *Eu.* 441, 717.

Apollodorus

Suppliant/Supplicandus	Gesture/Word	Response	Pages(s)
1.8.3 Calydonians/Meleager	μεθ' ἱκετηρίας	rejected	56.140, 164.36
1.9.8 Sidero/Hera	τὸ τῆς Ἥρας τέμενος κατέφυγε	slain	37.41, 157.298
1.9.24 Jason and Medea/Circe	ἱκέται	καθαίρονται	141.219, 383.1
1.9.28 Medea's children/Hera	ἱκέτας	ἀναστήσαντες κατετραυμάτισαν	37.41, 110.35, 125
2.4.3 Danaë and Dictys/altars	προσπεφευγυῖαν τοῖς βωμοῖς	rescued	
2.8.1 Heraclidae/Altar of Pity	καθεσθέντες	accepted	
3.5.9 Oedipus/Furies	ἱκέτης	προσδεχθεὶς	383.3
3.7.1 Adrastus/Altar of Pity	ἱκετηρίαν θεὶς	request granted	
Epit. 2.13 Sons of Thyestes/Zeus	ἱκέτας	slain	36.41, 157.298
Epit. 6.10 Meda and Clisithyra/ unnamed temple	ἐν τῷ ναῷ καταφυγοῦσαν	slain	157.298

Apollonius of Rhodes

Suppliant/Supplicandus	Gesture/Word	Response	Pages(s)
2.202–62 Phineas/Argonauts	Ἱκεσίου πρὸς Ζηνος . . . λίσσομαι	request granted	114
2.1121–36 Argus/Jason	γουναζόμεθ'	request granted	98.403
3.701–39 Chalciope/Medea	περίσχετο γούνατα χερσίν	ὑπόσχεσιν	45.91, 36
3.967–1014 Jason/Medea	γουνούμενος[1]	request granted	70.226
4.82–100 Medea/sons of Phrixus	τούσγε γούνων . . . περισχομένη	παρασχεδὸν ἤραρε χειρί δεξιτερήν[2]	45.91, 83.324
4.693–748 Medea and Jason/Circe	ἐφ' ἑστίῃ ἀίξαντε ἵζανον	ἔρχεο	114, 141
4.1011–57 Medea/Arete and Argonauts	χερσίν . . . γούνων . . . θίγεν	accepted[3]	45.91, 111
4.1759–61 Lemnians/Sparta	ἐφέστιοι	request granted	40.164, 118–89

1. Figurative, since Jason and Medea are both standing (967).
2. By Jason, not the supplicandi.
3. By the Argonauts. Arete reports the request to her husband, Aeetes, but without supplicating, and he agrees to grant it on the condition that she marry Jason (1106–9).

Appian

Suppliant/Supplicandus	Gesture/Word	Response	Pages(s)
BC 1.3.26 M. Fulvius Flaccus[1]/ friend's workshop	καταφυγόντος	ὑποδεξάμενος	383.3
BC 1.4.33 Q. Caecilius Metellus Pius[2]/P. Furius[3] (on behalf of father)	ποσὶ προσπίπτοντος	request denied	5.10, 50.118
BC 1.9.80 P. Cornelius Cethegus[4]/ L. Cornelius Sulla Felix[5]	ἱκέτης	ἑαυτὸν ὑπηρέτην . . . παρέχων	267.271
BC 2.7.47 Officers/C. Julius Caesar[6]	προσπεσόντες	mitigated punishment	225.25, 226.35
BC 3.2.15 M. *Junios Brutus*[7] and *C. Cassius Longinus*[8]/Capitol	ὡς ἐς ἱερὸν ἁμαρτόντες ἱκέται		
BC 3.4.28 Octavian/people	ἱκέτευεν	request granted	231.72
BC 3.8.51 Family of M. Antonius[9]/ senators	ῥιπτούμενοί τε πρὸ ποδῶν . . . μελαίνη στολῆ	ἐκάμπτοντο	50.118, 60.171, 228.47, 231.72
BC 4.9.67–70 Archelaus/ Cassius	τῆς δεξιᾶς λαβόμενος	ὑφελόντα	87.347, 96.397, 162.314, 130.150, 130.151
BC 5.1.4 Sundry/Artemis of Ephesus	ἱκέτας	ἀπέλυε[10]	36.41, 142.224, 243.136, 245.149, 259.232
BC 5.1.7 L. Cassius Longinus[11] and others/Antony	ἱκέται	ἀπέλυε[12]	142.224, 243.136, 245.149
BC 5.1.9 Arsinoe/Artemis of Miletus	ἱκέτιν	slain	36.41, 157.298, 259.233
BC 5.1.9 Serapion/Tyrians	ἱκέτην	removed[13]	23.93, 259.233
BC 5.1.9 Unnamed/Aradians	ἱκέτην	removed[14]	149.251, 259.233
BC 5.1.9 Ephesians/Antony	ἱκετευσάντων	request granted	
BC 5.3.19 Farmers/L. Antonius[15]	ἱκέτας	ὑπεδέχετο	112.43, 227.40, 269.281, 383.1
Hisp. 43 Complegans/ T. Sempronius Gracchus[17]	σὺν ἱκετηρίαις	interrupted[16]	222.13, 247.167
Hisp. 52 Caucaean elders/ L. Licinius Lucullus[18]	στεφανωσάμενοί . . . φέροντες ἱκετηρίας	betrayed	32.16, 57.155, 75.267, 125.129, 222.13, 267.271
Hisp. 61 Spaniards/C. Vetilius[20]	σὺν ἱκετηρίαις	γῆν . . . ὑπισχνεῖτο[19]	19.74, 112.43, 222.13, 223.19, 247.163
Ill. 9 Genthius/Cn. Anicius[21]	γονυπετὴς	ἀνίστη	50.119, 109.20, 266.262
Ill. 24 Segestans/Augustus	ἱκετεύειν	χρήμασιν ἐζημίωσε	222.13, 234.84
Ill. 28 Dalmatians/Augustus	σὺν ἱκετηρίᾳ	σφᾶς παρέδοσαν	19.74, 222.13, 234.84, 267.271
Mith. 23 Romans/Artemis of Ephesus et al.[22]	συμπλεκομένους τοις ἀγάλμασιν	ἐξέλκοντες ἔκτεινον	36.41, 121.107, 149.251, 260.236
Mith. 53 Ilians/Athena	ἐς τὸν νεών καταφυγόντων	burned	155.285

(continued)

Appian (*continued*)

Suppliant/Supplicandus	Gesture/Word	Response	Pages(s)
Mith. 73 Cyzician prisoners/ Pisistratus	χεῖρας . . . ὀρέγοντες	rejected	51.123
Mith. 104 Tigranes V/Cn. Pompeius Magnus[23]	κατέφευγεν ἱκέτης	συνεγίνωσκε	222.13, 223.15, 243.136, 245.149
Pun. 83–90 Carthaginian legates/ L. Marcius Censorinus[24] and P. Cornelius Scipio Africanus Aemilianus[25]	ἱκεσία	ἄπιτε	78.288, 96.397, 132.169
Pun. 130 Byrsans/Aemilianus	ἱκετηρίας λαβόντες	spared[26]	222.13

1. *RE* 58.
2. *RE* 98.
3. *RE* 22.
4. *RE* 97.
5. *RE* 392.
6. *RE* 131.
7. *RE* 53. Suppositious act is italicized.
8. *RE* 59, hereafter "Cassius."
9. *RE* 30, hereafter "Antony."
10. By Antony, who did not spare Petronius, privy to the murder of Caesar, and a centurion who betrayed Dolabella. They may have been removed.
11. *RE* 65.
12. By Antony, who did not spare those privy to the murder of Caesar.
13. Assuming that he came to an altar.
14. Same.
15. *RE* 23.
16. By an attack by the suppliants, who were defeated and conquered.
17. *RE* 53.
18. *RE* 104.
19. Later repudiated by the suppliants.
20. *RE* 1.
21. *RE* 3.
22. Pergamine Asclepius, the statue of Hestia in the Caunian Council chamber, and the temple of Concord in Tralles, but without removing before killing as at Ephesus.
23. *RE* 31.
24. *RE* 46.
25. *RE* 335, hereafter "Aemilianus."
26. Except for Roman deserters, who were burned in the temple of Asclepius.

Aristophanes

Suppliant/Supplicandus	Gesture/Word	Response	Pages(s)
Ach. 414–34 Dicaeopolis/Euripides	πρὸς τῶν γονάτων	request granted	70.226
Lys. 1139–40 Periclides/Athens	ἱκέτης καθίζετο	request granted	
Pax 1113–21 Priest/Trygaeus	πρὸς τῶν γονάτων	request denied	63.190, 70.228, 163.26, 218.215
Pl. 382–85 *unnamed/Athens*	ἐπὶ τοῦ βωμοῦ καθεδούμενον ἱκετηρίαν λαβὼν	*unstated*[1]	100
Thes. 179–208 Euripides/Agathon	ἱκέτης ἀφῖγμαι	rejected	132.168, 163.25, 218.215
Thes. 689–946 Mnesilochus/altar of Demeter	flight	δῆσον αὐτὸν εἰσαγών	37.41, 47.107, 100.416, 153, 168.25, 178

1. Ostensible act.

Canonical Orators

Suppliant/Supplicandus[1]	Gesture/Word	Response	Page(s)
Aeschin. 1.60 Pittalicus/Mother of the Gods	καθίζει ἐπὶ τὸν βωμὸν	πείθουσιν ἀναστῆναι	127.136, 177.23
Aeschin. 1.61 Two citizens/ Pittalicus	same	same	109.23, 130.150, 218.216
Aeschin. 1.99.1 Mother/Timarchus	ἱκετευούσης	request denied	35.33, 163.27
Aeschin. 1.104 Pauper/council	ἱκετηρίαν θέντος	request denied	76.271, 163.28, 177.23, 180.42, 192.94
Aeschin. 2.15 Relatives of captives/council	ἱκετηρίαν θέντες	request granted	
And. 1.19 Andocides/father	λαμβανόμενος τῶν γονάτων	request granted	35.34, 218.215
And 1.44 Two councillors/ council altar	ἐπὶ τὴν ἑστίαν ἐκαθέζοντο	request granted	75.262, 131.164
And. 1.50–53 Charmides/Andocides	ἱκετεύοντος	request granted	
And. 1.110 Unknown/council altar	ἱκετηρίας, ὡς καταθείην	request denied	36.37, 56.144, 131.164, 174.12, 177.23
And. 2.15 Andocides/council altar	προσπηδῶ πρὸς τὴν ἑστίαν	spared[2]	149.251, 168.3 184.60
Dem. 24.12 Naucratite shipowners/ council	ἔθεσαν τὴν ἱκετηρίαν	request denied	131.164, 163.31 177.26, 180.43
Dem. 24.49–52 Timocrates/ Council	*τὸ δεῖσθαι καὶ μετὰ συμφορᾶς ἱκετεύειν*	*request denied*	179.37
Dem. 50.5 Allies/Assembly	ἱκετεύον	request granted	57.156
Dem. 59.81–83 Theogenes/ Areopagus	ἐδεῖτο ἱκετεύων	pardoned	33.23, 191.89
Din. 1.18–19 Thebans/Arcadians	herald's wand	request denied	56.14
Is. 8.22 Widow/grandson	ἱκετευούσης	request granted	35.33, 59.160, 74.252
Isoc. 6.23 Cresphontidae/Spartans	ἱκέται κατέστησαν	accepted	108.12
Isoc. 6.75 same	ἱκετεύοντας	same	
Isoc. 14 Plataeans/Athens	ἱκετεύουντες	request denied	134.179, 163.33, 177.26, 181–182
Lycurg. *in Leocr*. 93 Callistratus/Twelve gods	ἐπὶ τὸν Βωμὸν τῶν δώδεκα θεῶν καταφύγοντα	voluntary departure	149.251, 174.13, 196.111
Lycurg. *in Leocr*. 128 Pausanias/ Athena of the Brazen House	καταφυγὼν εἰς τὸ τῆς Χαλκιοίκου ἱερόν	starved	153.279
Lys. 1.19–20 Slave/Euphiletus	πρὸς τὰ γόνατα πεσοῦσα	πίστιν λαβοῦσα	35.30, 74.256
Lys. 1.25–27 Eratosthenes/ Euphiletus	ἱκέτευε	rejected	74.258, 163.34, 199–200, 218.216
Lys. 13.23–29 Agoratus/Artemis of Munichia	καθίζουσιν ἐπι τὸν βωμόν	removed[3]	36.41, 38.49, 149.251, 192–193
Lys. 32.10–11 Widow/speaker	ἱκέτευε	request granted	

1. Supplication of jurors excluded, as are cases of supplication reported in Homer and tragedy. Suppositious act is italicized.
2. But removed and imprisoned.
3. Or voluntarily departed. 13.28 gives both outcomes.

Chariton

Suppliant/Supplicandus	Gesture/Word	Response	Page(s)
2.7.2–3 Plangon/Callirhoe	λαβομένη . . . γονάτων	request granted	46.102, 80.303
2.10.2–11.6 Callirhoe/Plangon	προσπεσοῦσα γόνασι	request taken under advisement	46.102, 63.187 113.210
3.2.1 *Dionysus/Callirhoe*	*γόνασι προσπεσεῖν*	*not performed*[1]	46.102
3.5.5–6 Mother/Chareas	γονάτων . . . λαβομένη	no reply	46.102, 80.302
4.3.9–4.2 Chareas/Mithridates	γόνασι προσπεσῶν	request granted[2]	46.102
5.10.4 Son/Callirhoe (on behalf offather)	ἱκέτευσον	prevented	46.72, 46.102, 86.343

1. Suppositious act.
2. This is the second request, to make a trip. The first request, to be put to death, is denied.

Dio Cassius, Zonaras, and Xiphilinus

Suppliant/Supplicandus[1]	Gesture/Word	Response	Page(s)
1.5.5–7 Sabine women/soldiers	τὰ ἱμάτια καταρρηξ- άμεναι, τούς τε μαστοὺς καὶ τὰς γαστέρας γυμνώσασαι	comitium formed[1]	83.325, 97.402
28.95.1 Q. Caecilius Metellus Pius[2]/public	ἱκέτευεν	unstated	
36.52.3–4 Tigranes II/Cn. Pompeius Magnus[3]	ἐς τὴν γῆν πεσόντα	ἐξανέστησε	109.20, 239.111
40.41.2–3 Vercingetorix/ C. Julius Caesar[4]	πεσὼν δὲ ἐς γόνυ τώ τε χεῖρε πιέσας	slain	219.1, 219.3
42.43.4 Egyptians/Caesar	ἱκετείαν	οὐκ ἐδέξατο	223.15, 383.3
42.49.2 Family of Pompey/ Heracles Melkarth	ἔφυγον	ὑπεδέξαντο	23.93, 383.3
43.12.3 L. Julius Caesar[5]/Caesar	ἱκετεύσαντα	slain	246.156
44.19.3 Unnamed/Caesar	ἱκέτευον	supplicandus slain	247.168
45.32.3–4 M. Antonius[6]/Caesar	ἱκέτευες	no reply	73.251, 239.113
47.8.5 Julia[7]/Antony (on behalf of L. Julius Caesar)	ἱκετευσάσης	spared	35.33, 42.77
48.24.2 Cleopatra's brothers/ Ephesus Artemis	none stated	ἀποσπάσας	36.41, 156.290, 168.32, 259.233
48.31.6 Octavian/mob	τήν τε ἐσθῆτα περιερρήξατο καὶ πρὸς ἱκετείαν	spared	60.176
49.12.4 M. Aemilius Lepidus[8]/ Octavian	ἐν ἐσθῆτι φαιᾷ ἱκέτης	relegated	59.161
49.20.4 Syrians/Antiochus I of Commagene	κατέφυγον	accepted	259.234
54.14.2–3 Licinius Regulus[9] and Articuleius Paetus[11]/Senate	τήν τε ἐσθῆτα ... κατερρήξατο, καὶ τὸ σῶμα γυμνώσας	unstated[10]	60.176, 73.248, 81.310, 228.51
54.23.3 Slave/Augustus	προσπεσόντος οἱ	accepted	31.8, 234.83, 244.144
59.19.5–6 Cn. Domitius Afer[12]/ Caligula	ἔς τε τὴν γῆν κατέ- πεσε ... χαμαὶ κείμενος ἱκέτευσεν	spared	31.10, 50.118, 235.92, 239.116
64.14.4 Soldiers of Vitellius/ soldiers of Vespasian	χεῖράς ... προετείνοντο	ὁμολογίαν[13]	51.122, 112.43
65.16.2 Imposter's wife/Vespasian	τὰ παιδία ... προβαλοῦσα	slain	31.10, 55.135, 99.412, 235.91, 252.199
67.5.1 Chariomerus/Domitian	ἱκέτευσε	request denied	31.10, 222.13, 236.95
67.13.3–4 P. Juventius Celsus[14]/ Domitian	προσκυνήσας	ἀφεθεὶς	239.114, 381.4
68.10.1 Ambassadors of of Decebalus/Senate	συνῆψαν τὰς χεῖρας ἐν αἰχμαλώτων σχήματι	treaty	59.163, 60.176, 230.59
72.16.1 Zanticus/Marcus Aurelius	ἱκετεύσαντος	ἐς ὁμολογίαν ἦλθον	31.10, 112.43, 234.85
77.9.3 Pollenius Sebennus[15]/ Noricans	ἐπί ... τῆς γῆς κείμενον ... ἱκετεύοντα	spared	50.118, 74.258

Dio Cassius, Zonaras, and Xiphilinus (*continued*)

Suppliant/Supplicandus[1]	Gesture/Word	Response	Page(s)
78.19.3–4 Gladiator/Caracalla	ἱκετεύοντος	rejected	31.10, 252.201
80.19.3 Sardanapalus/soldiers (on behalf of Hierocles)	ἱκετεύσαντα	spared	41.72, 83.322, 248.175

1. ἐς λόγους αὐτοῦ, ὥσπερ εἶχον, ἐν τῷ κομιτίῳ δι’ αὐτὸ τοῦτο κληθέντι συνελθεῖν.
2. *RE* 98.
3. *RE* 31, hereafter "Pompey."
4. *RE* 131, hereafter "Caesar."
5. *RE* 144.
6. *RE* 30, hereafter "Antony."
7. *RE* 543.
8. *RE* 73.
9. *RE* 149.
10. Since D.C. does not say whether these men obtained their requests, though he does say that Augustus made a new revision of the Senate roll. His previous revision led to the acts of supplication.
11. *RE* 2.
12. *RE* 14.
13. I.e., surrender.
14. *RE* 13.
15. *RE* 5.

Zonaras

8.4 Tarantines/Pyrrhus	ἱκετεύοντας	request granted	
9.6 Syracusans/Senate	εἰς ἱκετείαν	συγγνώμης τυχεῖν	230.58, 243.136, 245.149
9.24 Cretans/Romans	ἱκετείαις	σύμμαχοι καλεῖσθαι	119.95
9.24 Prusias II/Senate	τὸν οὐδὸν φιλήσας ... προσκυνήσας	same	50.118, 119.95
9.26 Carthaginian ambassadors/ Senate	ἱκετείαν	σπονδὰς	41.72, 119.95, 230.62
9.30 Hasdrubal[1]/P. Cornelius Scipio Africanus Aemilianus[2]	ἱκετηρίαν ἔχων	spared	

1. Geus, "Hasdrubal," 14.
2. *RE* 335.

Xiphilinus

77.8 Cleopatra/ Octavian	ἱκέτευεν	κατανεύσαντος 70	

Diodorus Siculus

Suppliant/Supplicandus[1]	Gesture/Word	Response	Page(s)
10.16.4 Lydians/Polycrates	ἱκέται	betrayed	45.93, 46.98, 126.134
11.45.4–5 Courier/Poseidon at Taenurus	καθεζόμενος ἐν τῷ ... ἱερῷ	silence purchased	
11.45.5–9 Pausanias/Athena of the Brazen House	κατέφυγεν	removed	153.279, 154.280
11.56.1–4 Themistocles/Admetus	πρὸς ... ἑστίαν	dismissed	31.7, 38.54, 45.93, 46.99
Themistocles/Lysithides	ἱκέτης κατέφυγεν	dismissed	383.1
11.92.1–4 Ducetius/marketplace altars of Syracusans	ἱκέτης	dismissed	159.302, 168.42, 383.1
12.9.2–4 Sybarites/altars at Croton	καταφυγόντων ἐπὶ τοὺς ... βωμοὺς	accepted	177.22
12.57.3–4 Corcyrans/altars	ἱκέται	dismissed[1]	169.47
13.19.2–33.1 Athenians/ Syracusans	ἱκέται	slain or enslaved	32.18, 45.93, 51.122, 87.350, 112.44, 113.54, 127.139, 144–145, 164.43, 383.1
13.57.3–4 Selinuntians/temples	εἰς τὰ ἱερὰ καταπεφευγότας	enslaved[2]	121.105, 151.265, 168.14
13.62.4 Himerans/temples	καταφυγόντας ἱκέτας	ἀποσπάσας	121.105, 151.265, 168.15
13.67.7 Byzantines/altars	ἱκέτας ὄντας	trial promised	114.66, 220.5
13.90.1–2 Acragantines/temples	ἐν τοῖς ναοῖς καταπεφευγότας	ἀποσπῶντες ἀνῆρουν	121.105, 151.265, 168.16
13.108.6 Geloan women/altars in marketplace	καταφυγουσῶν	request granted	
14.4.6–5.4 Theramenes/council altar	ἀνεπήδησε ... πρὸς ... Ἑστίαν	ἀποσπάσαντες	
14.53.1–4 Motyans/shrines	εἰς τὰ ἱερὰ φυγεῖν	enslaved	121.105, 151.265, 168.13
17.13.6 Thebans/altars	εἰς τὰ ἱερὰ καταπεφευγότες	enslaved[3]	121.105, 151.261, 168.12
17.22.4 Milesians/Alexander	μεθ' ἱκετηριῶν προσπίπτοντες	φιλανθρώπως προσηνέχθη	32.13, 45.93, 56.140, 230.109
17.35.5 Persian women/ Macedonians	προσπίπτουσαι γόνασι	enslaved	19.74, 45.93, 46.96
17.91.4 Indians/Alexander	μεθ' ἱκετηριῶν	ἀπέλυσε	19.74, 32.113, 45.93, 249.179
17.96.5 Agalasseis/Alexander	μεθ' ἱκετηριῶν	ἀπέλυσε	32.13, 45.93, 249.179
17.102.7 Brahmins/Alexander	μεθ' ἱκετηριῶν	ἀπέλυσε	32.13, 45.93, 249.179
17.103.8 Harmatelians/Alexander	μεθ' ἱκετηριῶν	ἀπέλυσε	32.13, 45.93, 249.179
17.108.6–7 Harpalus/Athenians	ἱκέτης	dismissed	45.93, 159.302, 168.41 177.26
18.66 Phocion/Alexander, son of Polyperchon	κατέφυγον	dismissed under guard	159.303, 169.44
19.7.2–4 Syracusans/shrines	εἰς τὰ τεμένη κσταφυγοῦσιν	slain or enslaved	157.298
19.63.5 Friends of Alexander, son of Polyperchon/Artemis of Orchomenus	καταφυγόντων	βιαίως ἀναστήσαντες	36.41, 110.35, 149.251, 151.263, 168.8
24.12.1–2 Carthaginian prisoner/ widow of M. Atilius Regulus[4]	ἱκεσίας	request denied	
26.20.1–2 Syracusans/ M. Claudius Marcellus[5]	μεθ' ἱκετηρίας	eventual enslavement	45.93, 121.105, 245.151
29.25 Perseus/Samothrace	ἱκεσίαν	ἄκυρον	131.163, 141.216, 164

Diodorus Siculus (*continued*)

Suppliant/Supplicandus[1]	Gesture/Word	Response	Page(s)
31.5.3 Rhodians/Senate	πένθιμον ἀναλαβεῖν ἐσθῆτα	request partially granted	45.93, 60.177, 230.60
32.6.3–4 Carthaginians/Romans	ῥιψάντων ἑαυτοὺς ἐπὶ τὴν γῆν	rejected	19.74, 41.72, 45.93, 50.118
32.23 Hasdrubal[6]/P. Cornelius Scipio Africanus Aemilianus[7]	προσπεσὼν γόνασι	accepted	45.93, 46.96, 56.143
34/35.28 Q. Antyllius[8]/ C. Sempronius Gracchus[9]	προσέπεσε γόνασιν	slain	45.93, 46.96, 50.116
36.15.2–3 L. Appuleius Saturninus[10]/plebs	πρὸς τὰ γόνατα πίπτων ... ταῖς χερσίν ἐπιφυόμενος	acquitted	45.93, 46.97, 50.116, 59.162, 231.67
36.16 Q. Caecilius Metellus Pius[11]/people	προσπίπτων ... γόνασι	request denied	45.93, 46.97, 50.116, 231.67
37.19.5–20 Children of Pinna/ fathers	none stated	request denied	35.32, 55.135, 99.413

1. I.e., sent into exile, ἐκ τῆς πόλεως .. ἐξέπεμψαν.
2. 13.58.2, in reference to women and children. Perhaps the men were removed and killed.
3. 17.14.3–4.
4. *RE* s.v. "Marcius," 112.
5. *RE* 220.
6. Geus, "Hasdrubal," 6.
7. *RE* 335.
8. *RE* s.v. "Antullius," 1.
9. *RE* 47.
10. *RE* s.v. "Apuleius," 29.
11. *RE* 98.

Dionysius of Halicarnassus[1]

Suppliant/Supplicandus[1]	Gesture/Word	Response	Page(s)
1.20.1 Pelasgians/Aborigines	ἱκετηρίας	λαβεῖν συμμαχίαν	19.74, 57.157, 119.95
1.58.2–59.1 Aeneas/Latinus	ἱκέται	συνθῆκαι	95.387, 112.47, 119.95, 240.119, 26.260
1.79.2 Amulius's daughter/Amulius (on behalf of Ilia)	ἱκετευούσης	spared	42.77
3.41.5 Volscians/Ancus Marcius	σὺν ἱκετηρίαις	εἰρήνην καὶ φιλίαν συντίθεται	57.157, 119.95
3.50.1 Nomentans/Tarquinius Priscus	ἱκετηρίας ἀναλαβόντες	παρέδοσαν ἑαυτούς	266.265
4.10.6–12.3 Servius Tullius/people	ἐσθῆτα πιναρὰν περιβεβλημένος	request granted	81.309, 87.347, 232.76
4.27.4–6 Etruscans/ServiusTullius	σὺν ἱκετηρίαις	forgiven[2]	19.74
4.66.1–67.1 Lucretia[3]/Sp. Lucretius Tricipitinus[4]	γονάτων αὐτοῦ λαβομένη	ἀνιστάντος	35.32, 50.116, 60.177, 95, 109.20, 110.31
5.3 Tarquinus Superbus/ Tarquinians	ἱκέτου	accepted	81.309, 96.398
5.59.5 *Fidenates/Latins*	ἱκετηρίας φέροντας	*overtaken by events[5]*	
6.18.1–21.2 Delgates of Latins/ Senate	τῶν γονάτων ἁπτό- μενοι . . . τὰς ἱκετηρίας παρὰ συμμαχίαν τοῖς ποσὶ . . . τιθέντες	τὴν ἀρχαίαν φιλίαν καὶ καὶ τοὺς ὅρκους	41.72, 50.116, 57.157, 144.232
6.25.2 Volscians/P. Servilius Priscus[6]	ἱκετηρίας ἀναλαβόντες	deditio	266.265
6.51.2 Plebeians/senators	ἐν ἐσθῆσιν ἐλεειναῖς καὶ σχήμασι πενθίμοις	unstated	59.163, 60.177, 229.53
7.5.1–2 Legates of Aricini/ Cumaeans	σὺν ἱκετηρίαις	request granted	32.19, 41.72
8.1.5–2.1 Cn. Marcius Coriolanus[7]/ Attius Tullus	καθεζόμενος ἐπὶ τῆς ἑστίας	ἐμβαλὼν τὴν δεξιάν	38.52
8.17.6 Tolerienses/Coriolanus	ἱκεσίας	spared	51.124
8.19.4 Labicani/Coriolanus	προτείνοντες ἱκετηρίαις	deditio	266.265
8.40.1–43.2 Women/Veturia[8]	γονάτων ἁπτόμεναι	request granted	42.77, 50.116
8.45.1–54.1 Veturia/Coriolanus (on behalf of Romans)	ἔρριψεν ἑαυτὴν χαμαὶ	request granted	42.77, 50.118, 60.117, 99.412
8.67.8 Volscians/Romans	ἱκεσίας	spared	51.124
9.17.1–2 Veians/L. Aemilius Mamercus[9]	ἱκετηρίας φέροντες	request granted	119.95, 222.13, 223.19
9.36.2 Veians/A. Manlius Vulso[10]	ἱκετηρίας φέροντες	συγγνώμης τυχεῖν	119.95, 222.13
9.47.1 *Claudii/Rome*	ἱδρύθησαν ἱκέται	*accepted[11]*	
9.60.5 Antiates/Aequi	ἱκέτας	accepted	
10.24.6–8 Aequi/L. Quinctius Cincinnatus[12]	ἱκετηρίας ἀναλαβόντες	deditio	142.224, 222.13, 266.265
17/18.1.3–4 Delegates of Lucani/ Senate	ἱκέτας	φιλίαν . . . συνάψαι	41.72, 119.95, 230.59
Comp. 12.18 Persian/Alexander	γόνατα συγκαμφθεὶς	slain	50.119

1. Suppositious or interrupted acts are italicized. Except for the last act, all acts occur in the *Antiquitates Romanae*.
2. Save for three cities, Caere, Tarquinii, and Veii.
3. *RE* 38.
4. *RE* 30.
5. Capture of Fidenae by the Romans, against whom the Fidenates sought aid.
6. *RE* 76.
7. *RE* 51 in Suppl. 5, hereafter "Coriolanus."
8. *RE* 24.
9. *RE* 96.
10. *RE* 89.
11. Suppositious since no supplication reported at 5.40.3–5.
12. *RE* 27.

Euripides

Suppliant/Supplicandus[1]	Gesture/Word	Response	Page(s)
Alc. 400–3 Child/Alcestis	καλοῦμαι ὁ σὸς ποτὶ σοῖσι πίτνων στόμασιν	none	35.35
And. 1–412 Andromache/Thetis	at altar	betrayed	37.43, 71.237, 75.262, 127–8, 155.288, 168.28, 184.61
And. 537–40 Molossus/Menelaus	προσπίτνεις	rejected	45.92, 99.411, 146.240, 163.19
And. 539–717 Andromache/Peleus	πίτνουσα γονάτων	ἔπαιρε σαυτὴν	45.92, 92.374
And. 859 Hermione/gods	ἄγαλμα θεῶν ὁρμαθῶ	presumably rejected	
And. 860 Hermione/Andromache	γόνασι προσπέσω;	same	
And. 894–984 Hermione/Orestes	προστίθημι γόνασιν ὠλένας	ἄξω σ᾽ ἐς οἴκους	45.92, 86.343
Cyc. 285–327 Odysseus/Cyclops	ἱκετεύομεν	request denied	97.399, 165.a
El. 1206–15 Clytemnestra/ Orestes	ἔδειξε μάστον πρὸς γένυν τιθεῖσα χεῖρα	rejected	35.33, 55.136, 80.298, 85.338
HF 1–327 Family/Zeus Sôtêr	interrupted		36.41, 71.237, 92.374, 155.288, 168.29, 177.22, 188.79
HF 327–32 Megara/Lycus	ἱκνοῦμαι	request granted	
HF 715–16 Megara/Hestia	ἱκέτιν θάσσειν	prayer granted	
HF 986–95 Children/Heracles	πρὸς γένειον χεῖρα καὶ δέρην	slain	35.34, 45.92, 55.136, 163.16
Hec. 245–50 Odysseus/Hecuba	ἤψω γονάτων;	accepted	45.92, 247.166
Hec. 286–305 Hecuba/Odysseus	φίλον γένειον ... οἴκτιρον	request denied	45.92, 134.180, 163.21
Hec. 342–45 Polyxena/Odysseus	μή σου προσθίγω γενείαδος	κρύπτοντα χεῖρα καὶ πρόσωπον στρέφοντα	45.92, 47.111, 130.52, 163.22
Hec. 752–856 Hecuba/Agamemnon	τῶνδε γουνάτων καὶ σοῦ γενείου δεξιᾶς τ᾽	request granted	45.92, 81.306, 95.391
Hec. 1127–28 Polymnestor/ Agamemnon	πρὸς θεῶν ... λίσσομαι	request granted	86.340, 218.215
Hel. 1–556 Helen/Proteus	τόνδ᾽ ἐς οἶκον Πρώτεως ἱδρύσατο	accepted	37.43, 71.237
Hel. 894–1004 Helen/Theonoë	ἱκέτις ... πίτνω γόνυ	accepted	42.79, 45.92, 84.331, 85.334
Heracl. 1–308 Iolaus and Heraclidae/Zeus Agoraios	καθεζόμεσθα βώμιοι	accepted then rejected[2]	69.224, 86.343, 103.432, 108.15, 113.52, 134.178, 156.293, 168.34, 177.21, 381.3
Hipp. 325–35 Nurse/Phaedra	χειρὸς ἐξαρτωμένη	σεβάς χειρός	35.30, 45.92, 47.109
Hipp. 605–11 Nurse/Hippolytus	πρὸς τῆσδε δεξιᾶς	οὐ μὴ προσοίσεις χεῖρα	45.92, 69.224, 131.160, 163.17
IA 900–36 Clytemnestra/ Achilles (on behalf of Iphigenia)	προσπεσεῖν τὸν σὸν γόνυ	accepted	45.92, 69.224, 110.35
IA 1153–56 Agamemnon/Tyndareus	ἱκέτην γενόμενον	accepted	218.215, 383.1

(continued)

Euripides (*continued*)

Suppliant/Supplicandus[1]	Gesture/Word	Response	Page(s)
IA 1214–75 Iphigenia/Agamemnon	ἱκετηρίαν δὲ γόνασιν ἐξάπτω	rejected	45.92, 53–55, 86.343, 131.159, 165.b
IA. 1245–48 Orestes/Agamemnon	none stated	unstated	53–55
IT 1068–78 Iphigenia/Chorus	πρός σε δεξιᾶς ἱκνοῦμαι	request granted	45.92, 110.33
Ion 1255–1613 Creusa/Apollo	ἵζε νῦν πυρᾶς ἔπι	accepted	37.41, 71.237, 203.139
Med. 324–51 Medea/Creon	πρὸς γονάτων	request granted	45.92, 70.227, 135.188
Med. 709–53 Medea/Aegeus	τῆσδε πρὸς γενειάδος γονάτων τε τῶν σῶν	ὄμνυμι	45.92, 47.110, 69.224, 83.324
Med. 853–55 Chorus/Medea	πρὸς γονάτων	unstated	
Med. 856–65 *Children/Medea*	*unstated*	*unstated*	35.35
Or. 380–721 Orestes/Menelaus	γονάτων ... θιγγάνω	aversion	45.92, 80.301, 81.306, 107.6, 163.20
Or. 1506–27 Phrygian/Orestes	προσκυνῶ σ'	accepted	238.105
Ph. 923–59 Creon/Tiresias	πρὸς γονάτων καὶ γεραισίμου τριχός	aversion	45.92, 74.253, 131.160, 140.211, 163.24, 218.215
Ph. 1567–69 Jocasta/sons	μάστον ἔφερεν ... ἱκέτιν	request denied[3]	35.33, 45.92, 80.296, 163.23
Supp. 1–361 Argives/Demeter	ἱκτῆρι θαλλῶι προσπίτνουσ' ἐμὸν γόνυ	προσάψας φίλην χεῖρα[4]	37.41, 41.71, 51.120, 68.222, 74.252, 107.11, 108.15, 109.22, 132–133, 177.21, 276.315, 387–388
Tro. 1042–57 Helen/Menelaus	πρὸς ... γονάτων	rejected[5]	35.31, 100.422, 131.160, 163.18, 238.105
Tro. 1042–57 Hecuba/Menelaus	λίσσομαι	request granted	75.260, 95.391
Alexander Paris/Zeus	in aram Iouis insiluit	spared[6]	71.237
Dictys Danaë and Dictys/altars		rescued[7]	71.231, 156.294
Phaethon fr. 781.72–75 *TGF* *Clymena/Oceanus*	πρόσπεσε γόνυ	*unstated*	
Telephus Telephus/altar[8]	unstated		100.416
Fr. 937, 38 *TGF* Unknown	μὴ κτεῖνε· τὸν ἱκέτην οὐ γάρ θέμις κτανεῖν	unstated	
Fr. 1049 *TGF* Unknown	βωμὸν προσίζει	unstated	

1. No line numbers for acts coextensive with the entire play. Suppositious acts are italicized.
2. Rejection of the supplicandus's offer of protection: 344–52. The offer is effectively rescinded by the suggestion that one of the suppliants be sacrificed: 420–22.
3. 1428–35 offers another version of the same events, but excludes supplication.
4. Theseus taking the hand of Aethra, who has interceded on behalf of the Argives, who also supplicate him personally 277–85. Temporary rejection: 248–49.
5. Temporary. He later spares Helen, but the play does not indicate when. Another version of the same act: *Or.* 526–28.
6. Hyg. *Fab.* 91.
7. Apollod. 2.4.
8. Ar. *Thes.* 694–95; for other sources, see Handley and Rhea, *Telephos*, 8–20.

Heliodorus

Suppliant/Supplicandus[1]	Gesture/Word	Response	Page(s)
1.12.3 Aristippus/Cnemon	προσπίπτει ... γόνασι	spared	46.103
2.13.4–14.1 Thermouthis/ Theagenes	ὑποπεσὼν ... ἱκέτευε	ἀνέστησε	24.96, 87.345, 109.21, 110.35
4.18.1–3 Theagenes and Chariclea/Calasiris	γόνασιν ... προσπεσόντες	ἀνίστων	46.103, 62.184, 110.35
5.25.1–2 Phoenicians/pirates	προσπεσόντες ἱκέτευον	spared	34.27, 71.234, 112.48
5.26.2–4 Chariclea/Trachinus	γόνασι προσέπιπτεν	ἀναστήσας	46.103, 62.184, 109.21, 110.35
7.23.7 Cybele/Arsace	προσπεσοῦσα τοῖς γόνασιν	request granted	46.103
9.6.1–3 Synaeans/Ethiopians	white flag	surrender accepted	46.103, 56.142
9.11.4–13.1 Synaeans/ Ethiopians	κλάδους εἰς ἱκετηρίαν ... ἔδη τῶν θεῶν προβεβλημένοι γονυπετοῦντες ... τὰ νεογνὰ ... ἐπὶ γῆς προκαταβάλλοντες	tentative agreement[1]	46.103, 50.116, 56.142, 57.153, 68.222, 92.374, 98.403, 99.413
10.10.1–2 Chariclea/ Sismithres	προσπίπτει ... γόνασι	trial granted	46.103, 75.262
10.38.1–2 *Chariclea/Charicles*	γόνασι ... προσπεσοῦσα	*response forestalled*[2]	46.103

1. I.e., no further hostilities, but the Ethiopians do not enter the city in force, as the suppliants request, and make unspecified promises (9.13.1).
2. Interrupted act.

Herodian

SUPPLIANT/SUPPLICANDUS[1]	GESTURE/WORD	RESPONSE	PAGE(S)
1.11.4–5 Vestal/populus	ἱκετεύει	appeal granted[1]	75.262
1.16.4–5 Marcia[2]/Commodus	προσπίπτουσα	request denied	31.10, 132
1.16.5–17.1 Q. Aemilius Laetus[3] and Eclectus/Commodus	ἱκέτευον	same	
2.12.5–6 Didius Julianus/Senate	ἱκετεύεοντος	request denied	248
3.9.2 King of Armenia/Septimius Severus	ἱκετεύων	request ignored	31.10, 119.95, 236
7.5.4–7 Gordion/troops	ῥίψας . . . ἐς γῆν ἑαυτὸν	spared[4]	50.118, 248.173
7.8.8 *Italians/Maximinus*	ἱκετηρίους· θαλλοὺς καὶ τέκνα προτείναντες	*unstated*[5]	

1. I.e., her appeal to let the goddess try the case against the Vestal, who was accused of unchastity; the goddess immediately works a miracle on her behalf.
2. *RE* 118.
3. *RE* 57.
4. On condition that he accept the throne. In the view of Townsend (1955), Gordion's initial reluctance to accept this condition is insincere.
5. Supposititious act.

Herodotus

SUPPLIANT/SUPPLICANDUS[1]	GESTURE/WORD	RESPONSE	PAGE(S)
1.157–59 Pactyes/Cymaeans	ἱκέτης … φεύγων	accepted and dismissed	71.238, 82.317, 108.13, 124.124, 159.304, 169.45
1.160 Pactyes/Chians	not stated	ἐξ ἱροῦ … ἀποσπασθείς	124.124, 149.251, 169.45
2.113 Slaves/Heracleum	ἱκέται ἱζόμενοι	accepted	19.74, 24.95
3.48 Corcyran youths/ Artemisium	ἱροῦ ἅψασθαι	accepted	36.41, 71.238, 92.374, 154.283, 168.22
3.147 Samians/shrines	flight implied	slain by Persians	157.298
4.145.4–47.1 Minyae/Spartans	ἥκειν ἐς τοὺς πατέρας lighting cultic fire	accepted	118.88, 247.166
4.165.2–67.1 Pheretima/satrap	ἱκέτις ἕζετο	accepted	31.7, 38.52, 46.99, 75.261
5.46 Euryleon/Zeus *Agoraios*	καταφύγοντα	slain by people	36.41, 157.299
5.51 Aristagoras/Cleomenes	λαβὼν ἱκετηρίαν	request denied	45.93, 46.99, 82.317, 144.233, 164.37
5.71 Cylonians/Athena *Polias*	ἱκέτης ἵζετο	ἀνιστᾶσι and betrayal	36.41, 71.238, 109.20, 110.35, 125.127, 194.101
5.119.2 Carians/Zeus of Labraunda	διαφυγόντες αὐτῶν κατειλήθησαν ἐς … ἱρόν	voluntary departure	56.145, 132.171
6.68 Demaratus/mother	κατικέτευε	ambiguous	45.93, 46.98, 64.195, 74.253
6.78–80 Argives/sacred wood	καταφυγόντας	ἄποινα and betrayal	56.145, 125.128, 155.285, 211.186
6.91.2 Argive/Demeter	καταφεύγει	door locked	37.47
6.108.4 Plataeans/Athenians	ἱκέται ἱζόμενοι	accepted	57.156, 174.13
7.141 Athenians/Apollo of Delphi	ἱκετηρίας λαβοῦσι	rejected, then accepted	30.3, 37.41, 74.253, 84.331, 85.336
7.233 Thebans/Persians	χεῖράς τε προέτεινον	τοὺς δὲ πλεῦνας ἔστιξαν στίγματα βασιλήια	51.123, 95.387, 120.104
8.53.2 Athenians/Athena *Polias*	κατέφευγον	ἱκέτας ἐφόνευον	157.298
9.76.2–3 Concubine/Pausanias	λαβομένη γούνων	request granted	32.12, 45.94, 72.239, 95.387

Hesiod, the Homeric Hymns, the Epic Cycle, and Alcaeus

Suppliant/Supplicandus[1]	Gesture/Word	Response	Page(s)
Hesiod			
Sc. 83–85 Amphitryon/ Creon and Eniocha	ἵκετο[1]	ἠσπάζοντο	
Fr. 257 M–W Hyettus/ Orchomenus	φεῦγ' ... ἷξεν	δέξατο[2]	31.6, 142.223, 383.3
The Homeric Hymns			
h. Ven. 130–54 Aphrodite/ Anchises	γουνάζομαι	λάβε χεῖρα	63–64, 110.33
h. Ven. 181–95 Anchises/ Aphrodite	γουνάζομαι	φίλος ἐσσὶ θεοῖσι	64
The Epic Cycle			
Procl. *Chr.* 107 Priam/ Zeus *Herkeios*	ἐπὶ ... βωμὸν καταφύγοντα	slain[3]	36.41
Procl. *Chr.* 108 Cassandra/ Athena *Ilias*	ἀποσπῶν συνεφέλκεται[4]		36.44, 151.265, 152.271, 168.19
Procl. *Chr.* 108 Ajax/ Athena *Ilias*	καταφεύγει καὶ διασῷζεται[5]		36.41
Alcaeus			
130.31–35 *PLG* Alcaeus/ Hera of Lesbos	ἐς τέμενος θεῶν ... οἴκημι		71

1. Confirmed by the words ἦ δίκη ἔσθ' ἱκέτῃσι.
2. Paus. 9.36.6–7.
3. *EGF* p. 62.
4. ibid.
5. ibid.

Homer's *Iliad*[1]

Suppliant/Supplicandus[1]	Gesture/Word	Response	Page(s)
1.12–34 Chryses/Greeks	στέμματ' ἔχων ἐν σκήπτρῳ λίσσετο	ἐπευφήμησαν and rejected by Agamemnon	19.73, 56, 81.311, 103.431, 114.60, 132.169, 134.180
1.495–530 Thetis/Zeus	λάβε γούνων ὑπ' ἀνθερεῶνος ἑλοῦσα λισσομένη	νεῦσε Κρονίων	11.36, 45.88, 49.112, 63.186, 111.40, 123.113, 175.116
2.653–57 Tlepolemus/?	φεύγων . . . ἷξεν	none stated	45.90, 71.236, 111.36
6.45–65 Adrastus/Menelaus	λαβὼν . . . γούνων ἐλίσσετο	ἀπὸ ἔθεν ὦσατο χειρί	45.89, 70.231, 81.311, 107.11, 120.99, 130.151, 131.158, 143.227, 143.228, 163.7, 276.315
9.451–53 Mother/Phoenix	λισσέσκετο γούνων	τῇ πιθόμην	35.33, 45.88, 70.227, 111.36
9.478–83 Phoenix/Peleus	φεῦγον . . . ἐξικόμην	ὑπέδεκτο	45.90, 71.236, 117.81, 383.3
9.581–96 Colydonians/ Meleager	λιτάνευε . . . ἐλίσσονθ' . . . λίσσετ' . . .	τοῦ δ' ὠρίνετο θυμός	35.31, 111.36, 165.d
10.454–56 Dolon/Diomedes	ἔμελλε γενείου χειρὶ . . . ἁψάμενος λίσσεσθαι	slain	70.231, 131.158, 136.192, 163.5, 220.6
11.130–47 Pisander and Hippolochus/Agamemnon	ἐκ δίφρου γουναζέσθην (figurative)	Πεισάνδρον . . . ἀφ' ἵππων ὦσε χαμάζε and slain	34.26, 62.182, 70.231, 81.311, 120.99, 141.218, 163.4, 273
13.694–97 Medon/unnamed	flight implied	evidently accepted[2]	45.90, 111.36
14.258–61 Sleep/Night	*ἱκόμην φεύγων*	*accepted[3]*	45.9
15.431–32 Lycophron/Ajax and Teucer	flight implied	ἶσα φίλοισι . . . ἐτίομεν[4]	31.6, 45.90, 111.36
15.660–7 Nestor/Greeks	λίσσσεθ' γουνούμενος (figurative)	ὄτρυνε . . . θυμὸν ἑκάστου	62.182
16.570–74 Epigeus/Peleus	ἱκέτευσε	accepted	31.6, 45.90, 64.194, 71.236, 111.36
18.421–67 Thetis/ Hephaestus	τά σά γούναθ' ἱκάνω (figurative)	vow	63.186, 111.36
20.463–69 Tros/Achilles	ἥπτετο . . . γούνων ἱέμενος λίσσεσθ'	slain	34.26, 45.89, 70.231, 131.158, 163.1, 273.298
21.64–119 Lycaon/Achilles	ἑλὼν ἐλίσσετο γούνων	slain	34.26, 45.89, 70.231, 86, 120.99, 132.167, 134.180
22.37–78 Priam/Hector	ἐλεεινά προσηύδα χεῖρας ὀρεγνύς	οὐδ' . . . ἔπειθε	163.3
22.79–91 Hecuba/Hector	*exposure of breasts λισσομένω with husband*	οὐδ' ἔπειθον	80.297, 134.178
22.337–60 Hector/Achilles	λίσσομ' ὑπὲρ . . . γούνων	ὑπόδρα ἰδὼν	34.26, 62.181, 70.231, 86.339, 163.3
23.85–90 Patroclus/Peleus	flight implied	δεξάμενος	31.6, 45.90, 71.236, 95.389, 117.81, 140.213, 383.3
24.477–570 Priam/Achilles	λάβε γούνατα καὶ κύσε χεῖρας λισσόμενος	χειρὸς ἀνίστη	19.73, 47.104, 50.117, 74.252, 99.410, 108.18

1. "Figurative" designates figurative use of γουνάζομαι/γουνοῦμαι. Except in the Meleager story, all entries refer to acts as opposed to reports of acts.
2. Italicized acts are missing from the lists given at 18 above.
3. Also 15.333–36.
4. 15.439.

Homer's *Odyssey*

Suppliant/Supplicandus[1]	Gesture/Word	Response	Page(s)
3.92–108 Telemachus/Nestor	τά σά γούναθ' ἱκάνω (figurative)	request granted	31.6, 35.29, 63.188, 73.244, 111.36
4.322–50 Telemachus/ Menelaus	same	request granted	31.6, 35.29, 63.188, 73.244, 111.36
5.444–50 Odysseus/River God	same	prayer granted	63.192
6.141–94 Odysseus/Nausicaa	γουνοῦμαί (figurative)	accepted	39, 63.189, 111.36
7.139–71 Odysseus/Arete and Alcinous	βάλε γούνασι χεῖρας . . . σόν τε πόσιν σά τε γούναθ' Ἱκάνω	χειρὸς ἑλὼν . . . ὦρσεν	39, 108.18, 139.204, 228.44
9.250–80 Odysseus/Cyclops	τὰ σὰ γοῦνα ἱκόμεθ' (figurative)	rejected	62.182, 73.245, 86.340, 97.399, 139.203, 163.9
10.62–76 Odysseus/Aeolus	τὸδ' ἱκάνεις	*request denied[1]*	35.29, 132, 135.185, 163.8
10.264–73 Eurylochus/ Odysseus	λαβὼν ἑλίσσετο γούνων	request granted	111.36
10.323–47 Circe/Odysseus	λάβε γούνων	accepted after oath by suppliant	111.36, 114.62
10.480–95 Odysseus/Circe	γούνων ἐλιτάνευσα	request granted	45.88, 63.192, 111.36
10.521–55 Odysseus/ghosts	πολλά . . . γουνοῦσθαι *(figurative)*	*prayer granted*	
11.66–80 Elpenor/Odysseus	γουνάζομαι (figurative)	request granted	74.252, 86.339, 98.408, 111.36
11.530–32 Neoptolemus/ Odysseus	πόλλ' ἱκέτευσε	*unstated*	
13.226–49 Odysseus/Athena as herdsman	γούναθ' ἱκάνω (figurative)	request granted	63.192, 111.36
13.324–51 Odysseus/Athena as goddess	γουνάζομαι (figurative)	request granted	63.192, 111.36
14.29–54 Odysseus/Eumaeus	ἱκέτην[2]	request granted	37.46, 111.36
14.276–80 Odysseus/Pharaoh	κύσα γούναθ' ἑλὼν	ἐς δίφρον . . . μ' ἕσας	45.89
15.256–84 Theoclymenus/ Telemachus	ἱκέτευσα	request granted	71.236, 111.36, 115–116
16.424–30 Antinous's father/ Odysseus	ἵκετο φεύγων	accepted	31.6, 45.90, 71.236, 111.36
20.222–23 Philoetius/ Unnamed king	ἐξικόμην φεύγων	*none stated*	19.73, 45.90
22.310–29 Leodes/Odysseus	λάβε γούνων	ὑπόδρα ἰδών	3.5, 4.6, 4.7, 4.8, 34.26, 81.305, 97.401, 130.153, 131.158, 134.180, 163.10
22.330–56 Phemius/Odysseus	same	accepted	3–4, 34.26, 97.401
22.361–77 Medon/Telemachus	same	same	

1. Italicized acts are missing from the recent lists given at 18 above; one of these acts, 20.222–23, is supposititious. Quotation marks enclose words spoken by the suppliant or supplicandus, and "figurative" designates figurative use of γουνάζομαι/γουνοῦμαι. Except for the wanderings of Odysseus and the supplication of Antinous's father, all references are to acts and not reports of acts.
2. 14.511.

Longus

Suppliant/Supplicandus[1]	Gesture/Word	Response	Page(s)
2.14.4 Daphnis/Damon and Dryas	ἱκέτευε	informal hearing	
2.19.1–3 Youths/ Methymnians	ἱκετηρίας θέντες	declaration of war	95.391, 247.164
2.20.3 Chloe/Nymphs	καταφεύγει . . . ἱκέτις	removed	71.238, 151–152, 168.11
2.37.1 Pan/Syrinx[1]	*ἱκέτευε*	*request denied*	78.286
3.18.1 Daphnis/Lycaenium	καταπεσὼν πρὸ τῶν ποδῶν . . . ἱκέτευεν	request granted	70, 78.286
4.10.1–2 Lamon/Astylus	πρὸ τῶν ποδῶν καταπεσὼν . . . ἱκέτευεν	request granted	
4.16.1–17.1 Gnatho/Astylus	πόδας καὶ χεῖρας κατεφίλει	request granted	78.286, 86.341, 247.167
4.25.2 Gnatho/Dionysus	*ὥσπερ ἱκέτης*	*needless refuge*	

1. I.e., Daphnis/Chloe. Suppositious acts are italicized.

Lucian

Suppliant/Supplicandus[1]	Gesture/Word	Response	Page(s)
Cat. 4 King/Hermes	ἱκέτευε	request denied	165.a
D deor. 9.2 Ixion/Hera	ὑβριστικά ἱκετεύοντος	request denied	78.286, 165.a
D mar. 1 Xanthus/Achilles	ἱκετεύσας	ignored	
Lex. 12 *Damasias and wife/Artemis*	προσπεσόντες . . . *ἱκέτευεν*	*ἐπένευσε*[1]	98.403, 111.41
Nec. 21 Menippus/Tiresias	ἱκέτευον	request denied	165.a
Par. 46 Hector/Achilles	προσπίπτων	unstated	62.181
Pisc. 1–10 Lucian/philosophers	ἱκετεύω	trial granted	75.262, 86.341
Symp. 22 Pammenes/Lycinus	ἱκετεύοντι	οὐκ ἐπένευσα	111.41, 165
Tox. 35 Demetrius/Egyptian Magistrate	ἱκετεύων	acquitted	24.95
VH 1.19–20 Endymion/Moonites	ἱκέτευε	treaty made	119.95
VH 2.21 Empedocles//Elysium	πολλά ἱκετεύων	οὐ . . . παρεδέχθη	383.3
VH 2.27 Lucian/Rhadamanthys	πολλά ἱκέτευον	request denied	165.a

1. Supplicatory prayer is italicized.

Appendix 1a: Acts of Supplication in Other Authors

Suppliant/Supplicandus[1]	Gesture/Word	Response	Page(s)
Ael. *VH* 3.26 Ephesians/Croesus	ἱκετηρίαν	spared	56.139, 57
Ael *VH* 6.7 Helots/Poseidon of Taenarus	ἱκέτας	παρασπονδήσαντες	119.95
Aristodem. 104 *FGrH* fr. 1.8.1–3 Argilius/Poseidon at Taenarus	ἱκέτυεν	unstated	
Aristodem. 104 *FGrH* fr. 1.8.3–4 Pausanias/Athena of the Brazen House	ἱκέτυεν	removed	153.279
Aristodem. 104 *FGrH* fr. 1.10.2 Themistocles/King of Molossians	ἐπὶ τῆς ἑστίας ἱκετεύοντα	dismissed	
Aristodem. 104 *FGrH* fr. ap 2 Cylon/Athena *Polias*	ἱκέτης	betrayed	194.102
Arr. *An.* 1.8.8 Thebans/shrines	πρὸς ἱεροῖς ἱκετεύοντας	slain	
Arr. *An.* 1.17.12 Syrphax and sons/Artemis of Ephesus	ἐκ τοῦ ἱεροῦ ἐξαγαγόντες		36.41, 168.1
Arr. *An.* 5.1.4–2.4 Nysaeans/ Alexander	πεσόντας εἰς γῆν	ἐξανέστησέ	32.13
Arr. *An.* 7.11.4–7 Soldiers/ Alexander	ἱκετηρίαν	ἐφίλησε	37.45
Ath. *Deip.* 13.590e–f Phryne/jury	via Hyperides	acquitted	33.22, 102.428
Ath. *Deip.* 13.593a–b Ptolemy "the son"/Artemis of Ephesus	καταφυγόντος εἰς τὸ τῆς Ἀρτέμιδος ἱερὸν	slain	38.41, 157.298
Batto of Sinope 268 *FGrH* fr. 3 Girls/temple	καταφυγούσας	starved	154.284, 168.23
Chrysermus 287 *FGrH* fr. 4 Pausanias/Athena of the Brazen House	unstated	starved	153.279, 154.280
Ctes. 688 *FGrH* fr. 9 Croesus/ Apollo of Sardis	καταφεύγει	πεδηθείς[1]	37.41
Ephor. 70 *FGrH* fr. 186 Greek ambassadors/Gelon	ἱκετεύοντας	request denied	57.156, 75.267
Him. *Or.* 6.169–75 Persian ambassadors/Spartans	ἱκετηρία	request denied[2]	57.156, 75.267
Men. *Per.* 1–?[3] Davus/altar	διαφυγών	unstated	153.276
Parth. 5.2 Son/mother	καθικέτευε	request granted	35.32, 78.286, 84.331
Parth. 9.3 Polycrita/Diognetus	καθικετεύει	καθωμολογήσατο	112.43
Parth. 17.5 Periander/Mother	ἐξικετεῦσαι	request denied	35.32, 78.286, 164.50, 247
Parth. 18.4 Neaera/Naxians	ἱκέτις προσκαθίζετο	accepted	
Schol. *Dem.* 1.41 Unnamed/ shrine of Amyntas at Pydna	ἔφυγον ἐπὶ τὸ Ἀμύντιον ἱερὸν	betrayed	37.43, 128.145
Str. 6.1.14 Heracleans/Athena	ἀποσπωμένων τῶν ἱκετῶν	ὑπὸ Ἰώνων	36.41, 168.9, 381.3
Str. 6.3.2 *Partheniae*/Spartans	ἱκέτευον	φυλακῇ παρέδοσαν	108.12, 211.191, 381.4
Str. 8.6.14 Demosthenes and others/Poseidon of Calauria	ἱκέτας	accepted	36.41, 203.144
Str. 14.2.17 Ada/Alexander	ἱκετεύει	request granted	73.248
Suid. s.v. Ἔφορος Theopompus/ Artemis of Ephesus	ἱκετης	unstated	36.41, 383.1

(*continued*)

Appendix 1a: Acts of Supplication in Other Authors (*continued*)

Suppliant/Supplicandus[1]	Gesture/Word	Response	Page(s)
Tryph. 258–287 Sinon/Priam	ἥψατο γούνων	φίλος ἔσσεαι	45.91, 117.83
Tryph. 634–39 Priam/Zeus Herkeios	παρ' Ἑρκείῳ ... βωμῷ	slain	
Tryph. 647–48 Cassandra/ Athena of Ilium	ὑπὸ γοῦνα πεσοῦσαν	removed	45.91
Tz. H. 1.456–62 Thyestes/Hera	βωμῷ φυγόντες	ὁρκώσαντες	37.41, 112.47, 114.61
Tz. H. 12.472-82 Pausanias/ Athena of the Brazen House	τῷ ἱερῷ προσέδραμε	starved	153.279
Tz. ad Lyc. 307 Troilus/ Thymbraean Apollo	προσφεύγει εἰ̂ς τὸν του Θυμβραίου Ἀπόλλωνος νεών	slain	157.298
Vita. Alex. 1.46a Theban/ Alexander[4]	ἱκετεύευειν ... παρὰ τοὺς πόδας	spared	238.104
PBerol. 11771.12–22 Unknown/ Demeter	Δήμητερ, ἀνατίθημί σοι ἐμαυτόν	unstated	37.41, 178.32

1. But released by Apollo.
2. And legates slain.
3. As in Gomme and Sandbach.
4. Included by way of an example of supplication in one version of the Alexander Romance. Other, more fanciful examples are not cited.

Pausanias

Suppliant/Supplicandus[1]	Gesture/Word	Response	Page(s)
1.10.4 Lysandra/Seleucus I	καταφεύγουσι	preempted	75.261
1.12.1 Tarentines/Pyrrhus	ἱκέτας	request granted	
1.20.7 Aristion/Athena *Polias*	καταφυγόντα ἐς τὸ τῆς Ἀθηνᾶς ἱερὸν	ἀποσπάσας	36.38, 36.41, 151.265, 168.17
1.32.6 Heraclidae/Theseus	ἱκέται	accepted	142.222, 169.c
1.36.6 Cephisodorus/Romans	ἱκέτευεν	alliance	
1.39.2 Adrastus/Theseus	ἱκετεύσαντος	request granted	
2.6.2 Nyctaeus/Lycus	ἱκέτευσε	preempted	74.259
2.20.2 Maiden/Argives	κατέφυγεν ἱκέτις	accepted	82.32
3.4.1 Argives/Argus	καταφεύγουσιν	burned	56.145
3.5.6 King Pausanias/Athena *Alea*	ἱκέτην	ἐδέξαντο	36.40, 36.41, 204.147, 205.154, 206.156, 383.3
3.5.6 Chrysis/same	same	same	36.40, 204, 205
3.7.10 Leotychidas II/same	ἱκέτευε	accepted	36.40, 205–206
3.9.13 Boeotians/ Athena *Itonia*	ἱκέτας	accepted	36.41
3.17.9 Pausanias/Zeus of Byzantium	ἱκεσίας δεξαμένῳ Διὸς Φυξίου	rejected	36.41, 142.220
4.4.7 Euaephnus/Polychares	ἱκέτευε νεῖμαί οἱ συγγνώμην	request granted	
4.5.9 Messenians/altars	καθημένους ἱκέτας	slain	157.298
4.8.3 Dryopes/Spartans	ἱκέται	ὑπηκόους ... συνακολουθοῦντας	119.92
4.23.8–9 Zancleans/altars	πρὸς τὰ ἱερὰ καταφεύγουσιν	ἀνίστασαν ... ὅρκους δόντες	112.47
4.24.5–6 Convicts/Posidon of Taenarus	ἱκέται καταφεύγουσιν	ἀποσπάσασα	36.41, 157.296, 168.38, 207.168, 208.173
4.24.7 Helots/Zeus of Ithome	ἐς τοῦ Διὸς τοῦ Ἰθωμάτα τὸν ἱκέτην	ὑπόσπονδοι	211.19
4.34.10 Dryopes/Eurystheus	ἱκέται	accepted	118.88
5.5.1 Aristodemus/Zeus *Sôtêr*	ἐπὶ Διὸς Σωτῆρος βωμὸν καταφυγόντα	slain	36.41
5.22.2 Thetis and Day/Zeus	ἱκετεύουσαι	unstated	
6.9.6–8 Cleomedes/Athena of Astypalaea	κατέφυγεν ἐς ... ἱερόν	vanished	36.41
6.18.3–4 Anaximenes/ Alexander	ἱκετεύειν	request mistakenly granted	112.47, 247.166
7.1.8 Ionians/Poseidon of Helice	καταπεφευγότας ἐς Ἑλίκην	ἀφιᾶσιν ἀπελθεῖν ὑποσπόνδους	36.40, 36.41, 119.95, 211.191, 381.4
7.2.7 Thermodonian women/ Artemis of Ephesus	ἱκέτιδες	accepted	36.41, 72.239, 119.90
7.24.6 Unnamed/Poseidon of Helice	ἱκέτας	ἀποστήσασιν ἐκ τοῦ ἱεροῦ	36.41, 204.148
7.25.1–2 Spartans/Areopagus	καταφεύγουσιν ἐς τὸν Ἄρειον πάγον	accepted	134.179
7.25.3 Cylonians/Athena *Polias*	ἱκέτας	slain	194.102
8.11.11 Hannibal the Great[1]/ Prusias II	ἀφικόμενος ... ἱκέτης	ἀπωσθεὶς	130.15

(continued)

Pausanias (*continued*)

Suppliant/Supplicandus	Gesture/Word	Response	Page(s)
8.23.3 Caphyans/Cepheus	ἱκέτας	ἐς Ἀρκαδίαν οἰκῆσαι	118.88, 383.1, 384.7
8.27.6 Lycorsurans/Demeter of Lycorsura	ἐλθοῦσιν ⟨ἐς⟩ τὸ ἱερόν	spared	37.41
9.5.1 Aonians/Cadmus	ἱκέτας	καταμεῖναι ... ἀναμιχθῆναι τοῖς Φοίνιξιν	118.88, 383.1, 384.7
10.19.7 Ptolemy "the Thunderbolt"/Seleucus II	καταπεφευγὼς ... ἱκέτης ὡς αὐτόν	accepted	38.52
10.35.3 Phocians/Athena of Abae	ἐκπεφευγότας	burned	36.41, 155.285

1. Geus, "Hannibal," 9.

Philostratus

Suppliant/Supplicandus	Gesture/Word	Response	Page(s)
VA 1.10 Rich Cilician/ Asclepius of Pergamum	ἱκετεύσας	request denied	72.242, 132, 146.244
VA 1.15 Magistrate of Aspendus/emperor	προσκείμενον τοῖς βασιλείοις ἀνδριᾶσιν	spared	252.203, 254
VA 1.23 *Fish out of water/ Dolphin*	ἱκέτευον	*unstated*[1]	
VA 4.10 Demon/mob in Ephesus	ἱκέτευε	slain	76.276, 134, 146.244
VA 4.11 Pilgrims/Asclepius of Pergamum	ἱκετεύουσι	many cured	72.242
VA 4.16 Trojans/Achilles	ἱκετηρίαν	rejected	146.244
VA 7.35 *Apollonius/ Domitian*	*ἱκέτην γίγνεσθαι*	*unstated*	
VA 8.7.12 *Arcadian/ Apollonius*	*ἱκετεύοντά*	*slain*	
Her. 703 Neoptolemus and Diomedes/Philoctetes	ἱκετεύσαντες	request granted	
Her. 706–7 Cassandra/ Athena/*Ilias*	ἱκετεύουσαν	ἀποσπάσαι	152.271
Her. 746 Thetis/Poseidon (on behalf of Achilles)	ἱκετεύει	request granted	70.227

1. Alleged acts are italicized.

Plutarch[1]

Suppliant/Supplicandus	Gesture/Word	Response	Page(s)
Aem. 23.11 Perseus/Dioscuri of Samothrace	ἱκέτευεν	voluntary departure[2]	132.171
Aem. 26.7–27.1 Perseus/ L. Aemilius Paullus[3]	προβαλὼν ἑαυτὸν ἐπὶ στόμα	ἀναστήσας … δεξιωσάμενος	50.118, 109.20
Ages. 19.1 Boeotians/Athena *Itonia*	flight	release by Agesilaus	36.41
Agis 11.5–12.1 Leonidas II/Athena of the Brazen House	ἱκέτης	ἀνέστησαν	36.41, 154.281, 168.20
Agis 16.3 Agis IV/Athena of the Brazen House	κατέφυγεν	voluntary departure and arrest[4]	36.41
Agis 16.3 Cleombrotus/Poseidon of Taenarus	ἱκέτευε	see next entry	36.41, 207.168
Agis 17.1–18.2 Chilonis/Leonidas II (on behalf of Cleombrotus)	ἱκέτις	Κλεόμβροτον ἀναστάντα φεύγειν	42.77, 207.170
Agis 20.2–4 Agesistrata/Amphares (on behalf of Agis)	προσπεσοῦσαν	betrayed	128.143, 286.23
Alex. 42.1 Slave/Artemis of Ephesus	ἱερῷ καθεζομένου	unstated	36,41
Alex. 62.3 Troops/Alexander	seated at door	request granted	30.4
Alex. 71.4–5 same	same	same	30.4, 37.45
Ant. 18.3 Troops of M. Aemilius Lepidus[5]/M. Antonius[6]	χεῖρας ὀρέγοντας	surrender	51.122
Ant. 59.1 Friends/people (on behalf of Antony)	ἱκέτευον	unstated	73.250, 231.67
Arat. 42.1 Women of Aegium/ Aratus	ἐξήρτηντο … αὐτοῦ περιεχόμενοι καὶ δακρύοντες	request granted	286.23
Caes. 16.4 Soldier/C. Julius Caesar[7]	προσέπεσε	unstated	34.28, 75.263, 225.25, 243.136, 244.146
Caes. 27.5 Vercingetorix/Caesar	καθίσας ὑπὸ πόδας	taken captive	222.13, 267.272
Cam. 8.5 Liparian vessels/Romans	προϊσχομένων χεῖρας	enslaved	43.83, 120.102
Cat. Mi. 32.4 Women/M. Porcius Cato "Uticensis"[8]	καθικέτευον	request granted	285.17, 286.23
Cic. 30.4 M. Tullius Cicero[9]/ Roman people	ἐσθῆτα τε μετήλλαξε καὶ κόμης ἀνάπλεως	interrupted	60
Cic. 31.1 Knights/Roman people (on behalf of Cicero)	as above	request denied	
Cleom. 8.2 Agylaeus/temple of fear	συνεισενεγκὼν ἑαυτὸν ἀπέκλεισε τὸ θύριον	accepted	36.39
Cor. 23.1–5 Cn. Marcius Coriolanus[10]/Attius Tullus	ἑστίας ἱκέτης	δεξίαν ἐμβαλὼν	95.392, 110.31
Cor. 36.3–4 Veturia[11]/Coriolanus (on behalf of Romans)	προσπίπτει ποσί	ἐξανίστησι	42.77, 109.20, 286.23
Dem. 28.2–30.1 Exiles/sanctuaries	ἱκέτην	removed by soldiers[12]	203–204, 286.21
Dio 42.3–43.6 Messengers/Dion	προσπίποντες	reference to assembly	286.2
Flam. 15.5 Aetolians/T. Quinctius Flamininus[13]	χεῖρας ὀρεγόντων	seemingly rejected	51.123

Plutarch[1] (*continued*)

Suppliant/Supplicandus	Gesture/Word	Response	Page(s)
Lyc. 5.5 Charillus/Athena of the Brazen House	κατέφυγε πρὸς τὴν Χαλκίοικον	oaths and ἀνέστη[14]	109.23, 112.47
Lyc. 11.1 Lycurgus/unnamed shrine	εἰς ἱερὸν καταφυγὼν	overtaken	36.39
Lys. 30.1 King Pausanias/Athena *Alea*	ἱκέτης	accepted	36.41, 205.154
Mar. 37.2–4 C. Marius[15]/boatmen	ἱκετεύοντος	betrayed	233.8
Mar. 37.5–6 Marius/ditchdigger	περιπεσὼν ἱκέτευεσε	request granted	233.8
Marc. 20.7 Nicias/M. Claudius Marcellus[16]	χειρῶν καὶ γονάτων ἁπτόμενος	spared	222.13
Marc. 23.6 Syracusans/Marcellus	προσπίπτουσιν	pardoned	245.151
Nic. 27.4–8.4 Nicias/Gylippus	προσπεσὼν	ἀναλαβών[17]	286.2
Per. 31.2–3 Phidias's servant/ Twelve gods	ἱκέτην	accepted[18]	74.254, 102.427, 174.13, 286.20, 286.21, 383.3
Pomp. 3.3 Cn. Pompeius Magnus[19]/troops	ῥίψας ἑαυτὸν ἐπὶ στόμα	request granted	50.118
Pomp. 24.7 Cilician pirates/Romans	προσέπιπτον	forgiven	120.103, 243.136
Pomp. 28.1 Cilicians/Pompey	ἱκετηρίας	surrender	222.13, 223.15
Pomp. 29.2 Cretan pirates/Pompey	ἱκετηρίαν	surrender	120.103, 222.13, 223.15
Pomp. 55.6 P. Plautius Hypsaeus[20]/ Pompey	γονάτων λαβόμενος	request denied	32.16, 130.157
Pop. 16.1 Tarquinius Superbus/ Lars Porsenna	ἱκέτευσε	ὑπέσχετο	30.4, 73.248
Rom. 19.1–6 Sabine women/soldiers	ἱκετεύομεν	σπονδὰς	83.325
Sol. 12.1 Cylonians/Athena *Polias*	ἱκετεύοντας	betrayed	125.127, 194–195
Sol. 12.2 Cylonians/wives of magistrates	ἱκετεύσαντες	accepted	42.77, 194.103
Sull. 13.3 Athenian councillors/ Ariston	ἱκετεύοντας	assaulted	107.9
Sull. 14.5 Medias and Calliphon/ L. Cornelius Sulla Felix[21]	προκουλινδουμένων	forgiven	222.13, 286.22
Them. 24.1–3 Themistocles/ Admetus	flight	accepted	31.7, 38–39, 159.303
Them. 28.1–29.2 Themistocles/ Artaxerxes[22]	ἱκέτην	accepted	18.71, 237.100, 238.108, 286.22
Thes. 8.1 Perigune/shrubs	ἱκέτευσε	πίστιν	112.44
Timol. 4.5–6 Timoleon/brother	καθικέτευον	request denied	73.251, 146.240, 157.299, 164.45
Timol. 16.5–8 Assassin/altar	βωμοῦ λαβόμενος	accepted by Timoleon[23]	74.254, 286.21
Mul Virt. 247c Tyrrhenean women/ Spartan jailers	ἱκεσίαις	request granted	
Mul.Virt. 251a–c Micca/Philodemus	περιπλεκομένη καὶ καθικετεύουσα	interrupted	35.34, 72.239
Mul. Virt. 262e Miners' wives/ Mine owner	ἱκετηρίαν	request granted	42.77
QG 298d Nauplius/Chalcidians	ἱκετεῦσαι	accepted	
QG 299d Poemander/Tanagrans	ἐφέστιον καὶ ἱκέτην ξένον	ἐκβεβληκότων	40.64, 108.12, 141.215, 164.46, 383.1

(*continued*)

Plutarch[1] (*continued*)

Suppliant/Supplicandus	Gesture/Word	Response	Page(s)
Gen. Socrat. 599c Prisoners/ escapees	ὀρέγουσι χεῖρας	unstated	51.123
Amat. Narr. 774f Callirrhoe/ Athena *Itonia*	ἱκέτις καθέζεται	accepted	72.239
Unius in Rep. 825b Friends of Orsilaus/Athena *Pronaia*	ἱκετεύοντας	slain	157.298

1. For supplicatory letters, see appendix 6. *Lives* listed in alphabetical order, followed by *Moralia* listed by section number.
2. 26.1–3.
3. *RE* 114 dubitanter.
4. 19.1, where he leaves to bathe and is ambushed on his way back to the temple.
5. *RE* 73.
6. *RE* 30, hereafter "Antony."
7. *RE* 131, hereafter "Caesar."
8. *RE* 20.
9. *RE* 29.
10. *RE* 51 in Supp. 5, hereafter "Coriolanus."
11. *RE* 24.
12. Same events at *X Orat. Vitae* 846e–f.
13. *RE* 45.
14. Same event at *Cleom.* 10.4.
15. *RE* 14 in Supp. 6, hereafter "Marius."
16. *RE* 220, hereafter "Marcellus."
17. i.e., ἀναστήσας but pending trial.
18. On condition of giving information.
19. *RE* 31, hereafter "Pompey."
20. *RE* 23.
21. *RE* 392.
22. Xerxes according to Ephorus and others cited by Plut. *Them.* 27.1.
23. On condition of giving information.

Polyaenus

Suppliant/Supplicandus	Gesture/Word	Response	Page(s)
2.36 Heraeans/Dioetas	ἱκετεύοντες	parley	119.95
4.3.30 Indians/Alexander	μετὰ ἱκετηριῶν	surrender	32.13
5.5.1–2 Megarans/altars	ἐπὶ τοὺς βωμοὺς ἱκέται καταφυγόντες	ἐξέβαλε[1]	149.251, 168.7
5.17.2 Heraclides/altar	βωμῷ προσέφυγεν ἱκετηρίας λαβὼν	unstated	96, 247
5.17.2 Heraclides/Rhodians	ἱκέτης	accepted	90, 247.166
8.25.3 Women/Cn. Marcius Coriolanus[2]	προσπεσοῦσαι ἱκετηρίας προΐσχουσι	request granted	42.77
8.46.1 Themisto/Poseidon of Helice	προσέφυγεν ἱκέτις	removed	157.296
8.47.1 Pheritima/King of Cyprus	ἱκέτευσεν	request denied	73.248, 164.47
8.47.1 Pheritima/Satrap of Egypt	καταφυγοῦσα	request granted	73.248
8.50.1 Berenice "the Syrian"/mob	ἱκέτις	request denied	146, 164.48
8.51.1 Pausanias/Athena of the Brazen House	ἱκέτης	starved	153
8.55.1 Hecataeus and Satyrus/Tirgatao	ἱκετηρίας	συνθέμενοι τοὺς ὅρκους	30.4, 112, 247.166
8.55.1 Sons of Satyrus/Tirgatao	ἱκέτας	accepted	30.4

1. By Theocles, who made sure that they were disarmed before doing so.
2. *RE* 51 in Supp. 5.

Polybius

Suppliant/Supplicandus	Gesture/Word	Response	Page(s)
1.35.4 Carthaginians/ M. Atilius Regulus[1]	πταίουσιν παρὰ πόδας	rejected	41.72, 50.118
2.6.1 Epirots/Aetolians and Achaeans	μεθ' ἱκετηρίας	accepted	
4.80.13 Elean towns/Philip V	μεθ' ἱκετηρίας	accepted	
5.76.9–10 Selgians/Achaeus and Garsyeris	μεθ' ἱκετηριῶν	σπονδὰς ποιησάμενοι	114, 119.95
9.9.11 Tarentines/Bomilcar[2]	μεθ' ἱκετηρίας	request granted	
9.29.4 Enemies of Macedon/ Athens and elsewhere	ἐκ τῶν ἱερῶν ἀγόμενοι μετὰ βίας ... ἀπὸ τῶν βωμῶν ἀποσπώμενοι		155–56, 168.31, 204
10.18 Captive woman/ P. Cornelius Scipio Africanus[3]	προσπεσούσης	λαβόμενος τῆς δεξιᾶς	75, 110
15.8.12 Carthaginians/ Romans	μεθ' ἱκετηρίας	συνθήκας	41.72, 119.95, 334
15.29.7–33.8 Oenanthe/ Demeter of Alexandria	καθίσασα	ἀποσπάσαντες[4]	151.265, 168.10
15.31.12–13 Agathocles and Agathoclea/mob	πορτείναντες τὰς χεῖρας ... καὶ τοὺς μασθοὺς	slain[5]	80.302
18.26.9–12 Macedonians/ Romans	ἀνασχόντων τὰς σαρίσας	attacked	51.122
30.9.1–11 Polyaratus/ Phaselitans	λαβὼν θαλλοὺς κατέφυγεν ἐπὶ τὴν κοινίαν ἑστίαν	removed[6]	40.64, 149.252, 168.2, 258–9
30.9.12–13 Polyaratus/ Caunians	κατέφυγφε	rejected	131, 164.42, 259
38.20.1–10 Hasdrubal[7]/P. Cornelius Scipio Africanus Aemilianus[8]	ἱκέτου ... τοῖς ... γόνασι	accepted	383.1

1. *RE* 51.
2. Geus, "Bomilcar," 2.
3. *RE* 336.
4. 15.33.8; then slain with Agathocles and Agathoclea.
5. 15.33.8.
6. When an emissary from the king of Egypt bids him leave and the Phaselitans agree with the emissary, συνεπισχυόντων αὐτῷ.
7. Geus, "Hasdrubal," 14.
8. *RE* 335.

Sophocles

Suppliant/Supplicandus	Gesture/Word	Response	Page(s)
Aj. 587–90 Tecmessa/Ajax	ἱκνοῦμαι	request denied	45.92, 86.343, 99.410, 163.13
Aj. 1171–1373 Eurysaces/ Ajax	ἱκέτης ἔφαψαι πατρός	request granted	37.43
OC 44–641 Oedipus/ Furies of Colonus	θάκησιν εἴ τινα βλέπεις ... πρὸς ἄλσεσιν θεῶν, στῆσόν με κἀξίδρυσον	rejected, then accepted[2]	71.237, 94.383, 108.15, 113.55, 118.89, 184.59, 383.3
OC 1156–1205 Polynices/ Poseidon of Colonus	βωμῷ καθῆσθαι	request granted	36.41, 206.157
OC 1267–1396 Polynices/ Oedipus	'Αιδὼς ... πρὸς σοί.... παρασταθήτω	μή μ' ἀποστραφῇς	35.34, 73.248, 83.323, 86.343, 103.432, 130.149, 163.14
OT 1–77 People/Oedipus	ἕδρας ... θοάζετε ἱκτηρίοις κλάδοισιν ἐξεστεμμένοι	accepted	177.22, 237
OT 19–21 People/gods	ἐξεστεμμένον ἀγοραῖσι θακεῖ	*prayer not granted*	237
OT 326–29 People/Tiresias	προσκυνοῦμεν οἵδ' ἱκετήριοι	rejected and later aversion (447)	45.92, 74.254, 163.15, 238.102
Ph. 468–529 Philoctetes/ Neoptolemus	ἱκέτης ἱκνοῦμαι	betrayed[3]	45.92, 62.181, 86.340, 97.402, 99.409, 111.41, 218.215
Ph.. 927–35 Philoctetes/ Neoptolemus	ἱκνοῦμαι σ' ... ἱκετεύω	ὧδ' ὁρᾷ πάλιν reversed (1261)	45.92, 97, 124.121, 130.149, 276.315
Chryses Iphigenia, Orestes/ Chryses	flight implied	accepted[4]	156.294
Tyro Sidero/Hera	εἰς τὸ ... τέμενος κατέφυγε	*slain*[5]	71.237

1. No line numbers for acts coextensive with the entire play. Incomplete plays at end. Supplicatory prayers italicized.
2. Rejection 226, 254–58. Acceptance: 555–59.
3. A nod sought, 484; not given, 525–29.
4. Hyg. *Fab.* 120, 21.
5. Apollod. 1.9.8.

Thucydides

Suppliant/Supplicandus	Gesture/Word	Response	Page(s)
1.24.6–7 Epidamnians/ Corcyrans	ἱκέται καθεζόμενοι	οὐκ ἐδέξαντο	87.353, 132.171, 164.38, 384.6
1.101.2–103 Messenians/ Zeus of Ithome	τὸν ἱκέτην τοῦ Διός	σπονδαί	36.40, 119.95, 154.284, 168.24, 210.183, 211.190, 212.195, 381.4, 384.7
1.126.3–1.127 Cylonians/ Athena *Polias*	καθίζουσιν ἱκέται	ἀναστήσαντες and betrayed	109.20, 125.127, 135.189, 194.102
1.128.1 Helots/Poseidon of Taenarus	τῶν Εἱλώτων ἱκέτας	same	36.41, 207, 208.172
1.133 Pausanias's lover/same	τοῦ ἀνθρώπου ἱκέτου	ἀναστάσεως πίστιν	112.44, 207–8
1.134.1 Pausanias/Athena of the Brazen House	προκαταφυγεῖν	ἀπῳκοδόμησαν	36.41
1.136.2–37.1 Themistocles/ Admetus	ἱκέτης γενόμενος καθέζεσθαι ἐπὶ τήν ἑστίαν	accepted	31.7, 38.53, 45.93, 98, 383.1
3.8–14 *Mytileneans/ Spartans*	ἴσα καὶ ἱκέταις	request granted[1]	
3.28.2 Mytileneans/altars	ἐπὶ τοὺς βωμοὺς καθίζουσιν	ἀναστήσας	109.20, 216.209
3.58.2–3 *Plataeans/ Spartans*[2]	τῆς ὑμετέρας πίστεως ἱκέται	rejected	45, 46.95, 64.195, 87.350, 164.40, 214–16
3.66.2 *Thebans/Plataeans*	χεῖρας προϊσχομένους	betrayed[3]	51.122
3.67.3 *Theban elders/ Spartans*	ἱκετείαν ποιοῦνται	unstated	
3.70.5–6 Corcyrans/shrines	ἱκέτων καθεζομένων	request denied	70.229, 132, 164.39
3.75.3–5 Corcyrans/ Dioscuri	καθεζεμένων ἐς ἱερόν	ἀνίστησί	109.2
3.81.2–4 Corcyrans/Hera	ἐς τὸ Ἥραιον ἐλθόντες	δίκην ὑποσχεῖν ἔπεισαν and betrayal	37.41, 127.138
4.38.1 Spartans/Athenians	χεῖρας ἀνέσεισαν	ξυνῆλθον ἐς λόγους	45.93, 46.95, 51.124, 114.67, 119.95
4.98–100 Athenians/Apollo of Delium	καταφυγὴν εἶναι τοὺς βωμοὺς	assaulted	94.385, 151.264, 176.19, 211.186
5.16.3 Plistoanax/Zeus *Lykaios*	καταφυγόντα	accepted[4]	207.163, 207.165
5.60.6 Thrasyllus/altar	same	spared	67.211, 75.266
6.19.1 Egestan and Leontine fugitives/ Athenians	ἱκέτευον	request granted	96.397
8.84.3 Astyochus/altar	same	spared	75.266

1. Italicized acts are suppositious or alleged.
2. Also 3.59.4.
3. Occurrence of supplication at 3.58.2–3 expressly denied by Thebans 3.67.5; occurrence of supplication at 3.66.2 implicitly denied by Plataeans at 3.56.2.
4. So also 2.21.1.

Xenophon

Suppliant/Supplicandus	Gesture/Word	Response	Page(s)
An. 1.6.7 Orontas/Artemis of Ephesus	ἐλθὼν ἐπὶ τὸν βωμὸν	πιστὰ	36.41, 112.44
An. 7.1.21–22 Soldiers/ Xenophon	προσπίπτουσι	request granted	73.249
An. 7.4.22–24 Thynians/ Seuthes	ἱκέτευον	προσωμολόγουν	112.44
HG 2.3.52–55 Theramenes/ council altar	ἀνεπήδησεν ἐπὶ τὴν ἑστίαν	εἷλκε ... ἀπὸ τοῦ βωμοῦ	40.64, 149.251, 150–51, 168.4
HG 4.3.20 Thebans/Athena of Helicon	ὑπὸ τῷ νεῷ εἰσι	spared	36.41, 137
HG 4.4.3–5 Corinthian oligarchs/public shrines	πρὸς τὰ ἀγάλματα τῶν ἐν τῇ ἀγορᾷ θεῶν, οἱ δ' ἐπὶ τοὺς βωμούς	slain	137–38, 157
HG 4.5.5–6 Corinthians/ Hera	εἰς ... τὸ Ἡραιον κατέφυγον	voluntary departure	37.41, 132.171
HG 6.3.1 Plataeans and Thespians/Athenians	καταπεφευγότας ... ἱκετεύοντας	unstated	182.50
HG 6.5.9 Tegean minority/ Artemis of Pallanteum	εἰς τὸν τῆς Ἀρτέμιδος νεὼν καταφυγόντες, καὶ ἐγκλεισάμενοι	siege and departure	36.41, 154.281, 168.21

Xenophon of Ephesus

Suppliant/Supplicandus	Gesture/Word	Response	Page(s)
1.13.6–14.1 Habrocomes and Anthia/Corymbus	λαβόμενοι τῶν γονάτων	spared and enslaved	34.27, 120.102
2.3.4–5 Manto/Rhoda	πρὸς τὰ πατρῷα ἱερὰ ... ἱκέτευε	request granted under threat	40.65, 63.187, 85.337
2.5.6–6.1 Manto/Apsyrtus	προσπεσοῦσα πρὸς τὰ γόνατα	request granted	46.102, 60.175, 247.164
2.6.5 Anthia/Apsyrtus (on behalf of Habrocomes)	προσπίπτει ... γόνασι	request denied	42.77, 46.102, 131.161, 146.243 164.54, 247.164
2.9.4 Anthia/Lampon	προσπίπτει ... γόνασιν	oath sworn	46.102, 112.47, 233.82
2.10.2 Habrocomes/ Apsyrtus	προσπίπτει ... γόνασι	ἀνίστησι	35.30, 46.102, 109.21
3.2.3 Hippothous/ Hyperanthes	ἱκέτευω	πάντα ὑπισχνεῖται	78.286, 112.43
3.5.5 Anthia/Eudoxus	προσπίπτει ... γόνασιν	oath sworn[1]	46.102, 112.47, 233.82
3.8.4–5 Anthia/brigands	τῶν ποδῶν προκυλιομένη	request denied	34.27, 51.125, 131.161, 146.243, 164.55
5.4.6–8 Anthia/Isis and Apis	ἱκέτις γενομένη	oath sworn by pursuer	383.1
5.5.6 Anthia/Clytus	προσπεσοῦσα γόνασι	request denied	46.102, 131.161, 146.243, 164.56

1. But the supplicandus refuses a later request that he poison her (3.5.8).

Appendix 1b

ACTS OF SUPPLICATION IN LATIN AUTHORS

Anonymous

SUPPLIANT/SUPPLICANDUS	GESTURE/WORD	RESPONSE	PAGE(S)
Hist. Apoll. 12 Apollonius/ fisherman	prosternens ad pedes	erigit eum	50.118
B. Afr. 89.4 L. Julius Caesar[1]/ C Julius Caesar[3]	ad genua proiecit	accepted[2]	32.14
B. Afr. 92.4 Numidians/Caesar	supplicibus	uenia data	19.74, 32.14, 222.13, 243.136, 245.149
B. Alex. 32.3 Egyptian soldiers/ Caesar	ueste . . . sumpta . . . deprecari	in fidem receptos	32.14, 59.161, 60.169, 222.13, 223.15, 266.268, 384.10
B. Alex. 47.4 Issani/P. Vatinius[4]	supplices	se . . . dederunt	266.269
B. Alex. 67.1–68 Diotarus/Caesar	habitu . . . supplex	ignoscere	32.14, 113.53, 223.15, 243.136, 245.153
[*Quint.*] *Decl.* 5.10 father/pirates	*genua tenui*	*unstated[5]*	
[*Quint.*] *Decl.* 17.6 son/father	*genua teneo*	*unstated*	47.108, 60.176, 96.394
[*Sal.*] *Rep.* 1.4.1 Marian leaders/ Cn. Pompeius Magnus[6]	supplices	slain	32.16, 166.23
[*Sen.*] *Her. O.* 925–37 Nurse/ Deianira	supplex . . . obsecro	request denied	
[*Sen.*] *Her. O.* 1316–36 Hercules/ Juno	*supplices . . . manus*	*prayer denied*	
[*Sen.*] *Oct.* 627–28 Parthians/ Nero	supplices dextram petant	unstated	19.74, 236.95

1. *RE* 144.
2. Later slain (D.C. 42.12.3, Suet. *Caes.* 75.3)
3. *RE* 131, hereafter "Caesar."
4. *RE* 3.
5. Prayers and suppositious acts are italicized.
6. I.e., Cn. Domitius Ahenobarbus (*RE* 22), Cn. Papirius Carbo (*RE* 38), and M. Junius Brutus (*RE* 52) to Cn. Pompeius Magnus (*RE* 31).

C. Julius Caesar[1]

Suppliant/Supplicandus	Gesture/Word	Response	Page(s)
Civ. 1.22–23 P. Cornelius Lentulus Spinther[2]/Caesar	orat atque obsecrat	potestate facta	44.85
Civ. 2.11.4–13.3 Massilians/Caesar	cum infulis . . . supplices manus	accepted[3]	32.14, 114.66, 222.13, 223.17, 247.163
Civ. 3.98 Pompeians/Caesar	proiecti ad terram	consurgere iussit	50.118, 246.156
Gal. 1.20.1–5 Diviciacus/Caesar	complexus obsecrare	dextram prendit	32.14, 110.33, 222.13, 245.152
Gal. 1.27.1–28.2 Helvetii/Caesar	ad pedes proiecissent	in deditionem accepit[4]	32.14, 50.118, 71.232, 222.13, 245.152, 266.267, 384.10
Gal. 1.31.1–33.1 Gauls/Caesar	ad pedes proiecerunt	pollicitus	32.14, 50.118, 222.13, 245.152
Gal. 2.13.2–15.1 Bellovaci/Caesar	manus . . . tendere	in fidem recepturum	32.14, 71.232, 222.13, 245.152
Gal. 2.28.2–3 Nervii/Caesar	supplices usus	accepted	71.232, 98.404, 222.13, 245.152, 266.267
Gal. 7.40.6 Haedui/Caesar	manus tendere et deditionem significare		32.14, 71.232, 222.13, 245.152, 266.267
Gal. 7.47.5 Gallic women/Romans	passis manibus obtestabantur	spared	19.74
Gal. 7.78.3–5 Mandubii/Caesar	precibus orabunt ut se in seruitutem receptos	rejected	71.232, 166.13, 222.13, 267.270

1. *RE* 131, hereafter "Caesar."
2. *RE* 238.
3. But the suppliants proceed to betray the supplicandi by renewing hostilities, 2.14.
4. Excluding absent runaways.

Cicero

Suppliant/Supplicandus	Gesture/Word	Response	Page(s)
Att. 1.14.5 P. Clodius Pulcher[2]/ senators	ad pedes accidente	request denied	50.118, 66.210, 147.245, 166.11 228.46
Brut. 90 Serv. Sulpicius Galba[3]/ Quirites	propter pueros misericordia	vindicated[4]	66.21
Cat. 4.18 Patria/Senate	*supplex manus tendit*	*accepted*	51.123, 67.214, 228.52
Fam. 4.4.3 C. Claudius Marcellus[5]/ C. Julius Caesar[6] (on behalf of M. Marcellus)	se ad pedes . . . abiecisset	request granted	50.118, 231.72, 248.169
Fam. 4.4.3 Cunctus senator/ Caesar (on behalf of M. Marcellus)	ad Caesarem supplex accederet	same	50.118, 248.169
Fam. 6.14.2 Cicero et al./Caesar (on behalf of Q. Ligarius)	supplicare	request granted	246.156
Inv. 2.153 Shipwrecked man/ship	manus ad se tendentem	rescued	
Man. 21 Mithridates VI/various	supplicem	unstated	38.52
Q. fr. 2.6.2 M. Furius Flaccus[7]/ priests of Mercury	praesentem ad pedes	eiecerunt	50.118, 133.174, 251.194
Phil. 2.45–46 C. Scribonius Curio[8]/ Cicero	ad pedes . . . prosternens	request granted	50.118
Phil. 2.86 M. Antonius[9]/Caesar	supplex . . . ad pedes	ut seruires	50.118, 121.107, 239.113
Pis. 80 Cn. Pompeius Magnus[10]/ populace (on behalf of Cicero)	supplicem	unstated	67.210, 231.69, 271.289
Planc. 24 Cn. Plancius[11]/populace (on behalf of his son)[12]	supplicabat	elected	67.210, 231.72
Planc. 69–70 Q. Caecilius Metellus Pius[13]/T. Calidius	supplicauisse	unstated	5.1
Quinct. 96 P. Quinctius/S. Naeuius	ad pedes iacuit	unstated	50.118
Rab. Post. 5 Ptolemy XII/ C. Rabirius Postumus[14]	supplex	unstated	222.13, 223.19
Red. Pop. 12 Cn. Oppius Cornicinus[15]/Clodius (on behalf of Cicero)	ad pedes flens	request denied	5.10, 50.118, 147.245, 166.9
13 Senate and equites/populus	mutata ueste . . . supplicare	unstated	60.173, 66.210
20 C. Marius[16]/Africans	supplex	accepted	
Red. Sen. 12 Multitudo/ A. Gabinius[17] (on behalf of Cicero)	supplex . . . sordidata	request denied	60.169, 67.214, 166.6, 271.290
31 Pompey/populus (on behalf of Cicero)	supplex obsecrasset	request granted[18]	66.210, 67.214, 231.69, 271.294
37 Q. Tullius Cicero[19]/populus (on behalf of Cicero)	frater . . . squalore	request granted	60.176, 67.214, 231.69, 271.294
37 Multitudo/unstated (on behalf of P. Popilius)	deprecata	request granted[20]	66.21
37 Metellus Pius/unstated (on behalf of father)	deprecatus	request granted[21]	5.1
Scaur. 35 All Asia/C. Claudius Pulcher[22]	*retentus . . . supplice*	*request granted*	
Sest. 26 Equites/A. Gabinius (on behalf of Cicero)	ueste mutata . . . ad pedes proiecistis	request denied	50.118, 60.176, 147.245, 166.6, 271.290

(*continued*)

Cicero (*continued*)

Suppliant/Supplicandus[1]	Gesture/Word	Response	Page(s)
Sest. 54 C. Calpurnius Piso Frugi[23]/ L. Calpurnius Piso Caesoninus[24] (on behalf of Cicero)	pedibus supplex	reiiciebatur	50.118, 166.7, 227.39, 231.70, 271.290
Sest. 58 Tigranes II/Pompey	supplicem abiectum	erexit	112.45, 222.13, 223.15, 239.112, 267.271
Sest. 74 Oppius/Sex. Atilius Serranus Gavianus[25]	ad pedes abiectus	request denied	166.8, 231.70, 271.294
Sest. 107 Pompey/populace (on behalf of Cicero)	supplicem	unstated	231.69
Sest. 130 Italians/Senate (on behalf of Cicero)	supplicarent	unstated	228.50, 230.58, 271.295
Sul. 81 L. Sergius Catalina[26]/ L. Manlius Torquatus[27]	supplex	request granted	119.94
Verr. 2.1.85 slave of M. Aurelius Scaurus[28]/Artemis of Ephesus	in . . . asylum confugisset	unstated	259.235
Verr. 2.5.21 Senate of Panhormus/C. Verres[29]	supplicem. . . obsecrantem	request denied	166.5, 226.36
Verr. 2.5.129 Sicilian woman/ Cicero	ad pedes . . . iacuit	request granted	50.118
Verr. 2.5.153 Sertorians/Pompey	supplicanti	dextera . . . fidem porrexit	47.107

Acts of Supplication by Defendants, Supporters, and Advocates in Cicero

Citation	Gesture/word[30]	Charge	Page(s)
Arch. 31:	petimus . . . ut eum . . . in uestram accipiatis fidem	Lex Papia	91.367
Cael. 79:	*supplicem abiectum non tam ad pedes quam ad mores*	*Lex Plautia*	284.12
Clu. 200:	*leuate . . . supplicem*	*veneficium*	33.24, 74.258
Deiot. 40	*miericordia . . . occurrere solet supplicibus*	*unstated*	223.17
Flac. 3:	*perfugia*	*repetundae*	
4:	*confugere*		
24:	*supplicem*		
106:	*puero . . . supplici*		
Font. 35:	amici ac propinqui supplicent	repetundae	98.405
48:	tendit Vestalis manus supplices (soror)		
Lig. 36:	supplex (frater ad Caesarem)	*non pertinet*	67.213, 246.155
37:	obsecro (Cic. ad Caesarem)		34.25, 67.213
Mil. 100:	me plurimis . . . supplicem abieci (Cic.)	parricidium	34.25, 44.85, 67.213, 74.258
103:	oro obtestorque (Cic.)		34.25, 44.85, 67.213
Mur. 6:	*partes misericordiae (ad Cic.)*	*ambitus*	
86:	obsecro (Cic.)		34.25, 98.405
86–87:	squalore et sordibus confectus . . . obsecrat		34.24, 60.176, 67.213, 91.368
Planc. 21:	(Atinatum) multitudinem supplicem sodalicium	ambitus	60.169
102:	deprecor . . . deprecamur (Cic. et pater)		34.25, 67.213, 91.368
104:	obtestor (Cic. ad praetorem) . . . lacrimae . . . uestraeque . . . meae		34.25, 67.213
Rab. Perd. 5:	obsecro (Cic. ad populum)	perduellio	34.25, 67.213, 74.258, 92.371
36–37:	hasce . . . cicatrices		81.31
37:	obsecrat		33.24, 67.213, 74.258

Acts of Supplication by Defendants, Supporters, and Advocates in Cicero (*continued*)

Citation	Gesture/word[30]	Charge	Page(s)
Rab. Post. 48:	obsecro (Cic.)	repetundae	34.25
Sest. 144:	P. Lentulum . . . in squalore et sordibus . . . deprecantem	ambitus	60.176, 91.368
147:	obtestor et obsecro (Cic.)		34.25
S. Rosc. 9:	oro atque obsecro (Cic.)	parricidium	
Sul. 18:	Autronius supplex (ad Cic.)	unstated	
20:	supplicem (ad Cic.)	Lex Plautia	67.215, 119.94
88:	supplex confugit		67.215, 98.405
89:	orat paruus (filius)		67.215
Verr. 2.5.2:	Hortensius . . . deprecabitur (supplicem) constituitque in conspectu omnium tunicamque eius a pectore abscidit	repetundae	

Acts of Supplication by Plaintiffs to Jurors in Cicero

Citation	Gesture/word	Charge[31]	Page(s)
Quinct. 10:	*misericordiam confugerit*	*praeiudicalis*	68.217
99:	obsecrat		

1. Acts by defendants, supporters, and defendants' supporters excluded unless occurring out of court. Acts on behalf of Cicero in *Red. Sen.* and *Red. Pop.* are listed only once. Populace: i.e., in contionibus. *Populus*: comitia tributa. *Quirites*: comitia centuriata.
2. *RE* 48, hereafter "Clodius."
3. *RE* 58.
4. By securing the defeat of a bill that alluded to his alleged misconduct as a promgistrate.
5. *RE* 216.
6. *RE* 131, hereafter "Caesar."
7. *RE* 58.
8. *RE* 11.
9. *RE* 30.
10. *RE* 31, hereafter "Pompey."
11. *RE* 3.
12. *RE* 4.
13. *RE* 98. Hereafter "Metellus Pius."
14. *RE* 6.
15. *RE* 28, hereafter "Oppius."
16. *RE* 14 in Supp. 6.
17. *RE* 11.
18. Others as well as Pompey: *Red. Pop.* 13, 18.
19. *RE* 31.
20. So also *Red. Pop.* 9, 11.
21. So also *Red. Pop.* 6, 9, 11.
22. *RE* 303. Suppositious acts are italicized.
23. *RE* 93.
24. *RE* 90.
25. *RE* 70.
26. *RE* 23.
27. *RE* 79.
28. *RE* 215.
29. *RE* 1.
30. Defendant to jurors except where indicated. Cic.: by Cicero as advocate. *Ad Cic.*: to Cicero as advocate by defendant. *Ad Caesarem*: to C. Julius Caesar. *Ad praetorem*: to presiding judge. Unnamed persons are supporters of the defendant. At *de Orat.* 1.53, Serv. Sulpicius Galba supplicates as advocate but the particulars are not divulged.
31. *Praeiudicalis*: at a preliminary hearing, not a trial.

Curtius Rufus

Suppliant/Supplicandus[1]	Gesture/Word	Response	Page(s)
3.2.17 *Charidemus/Darius III*[1]	*supplicem*	*rejected*[2]	
3.12.10–12 Persian women/ Leonnatus	prouolutae ad pedes	alleuari	110.33
3.12.17 Sisigambis/Alexander	aduoluta . . . pedibus	alleuans	32.13, 110.33, 242.130
4.4.12–13 Tyrians/temples	supplices in templa	spared	
4.6.15–16 Arab/Alexander	genibus . . . aduoluitur	assurgere	19.74, 32.13
5.1.17–19 Mazaeus/Alexander	supplex	urbem seque dedens	32.13, 55.135, 78.288
5.3.12–15 Persians/Sisigambis	supplicum precibus	abnuens[3]	388.16
6.7.3–15 Dymnus/Nicomachus	supplex	request granted[4]	83.323, 110.28, 126.135, 247.167
6.7.33–35 Philotas/Alexander	complexus	dextram pignus[5]	47.107, 110.32
7.3.17 Parapanisadae/Alexander	orantes . . . iacentes	erigens	32.13
7.5.33 Didymaeans/Alexander	supplicum uelamentis	slain	32.13, 134.183, 135.187
8.1.48–49 Ptolemy and Perdiccas/Alexander	genibus aduoluti	request denied	274.3
8.10.34–35 Cleophis/Alexander	genibus regis	ueniam	32.13, 55.135, 102.430, 243.136
10.9.21 Meleager/unnamed Babylonian temple	confugit in templum	slain	24.98, 157.298

1. Supposititious act.
2. The suppliant's words and gestures are incompatible with *supplicem*.
3. The request, to help them supplicate Alexander, is shortly granted.
4. But the supplicandus is lying, and he betrays the suppliant.
5. Possibly betrayed, but the author will not commit himself.

Florus's *Epitome*

Suppliant/Supplicandus[1]	Gesture/Word	Response	Page(s)
1.1 Fugitives/Romans	asylum facit	accepted	
1.17 Romans/ Gauls	supplices	[Camillus] uindicauit	
1.28 Philip V/Great Gods of Samothrace	supplex	unstated	
1.40 Tigranes II/Cn. Pompeius Magnus[1]	supplicem	accepted	19.74, 239.116
1.41 Cilician pirates/Romans	abiectis . . . telis remisque	spared	51.124
1.45 Vercingetorix/C. Julius Caesar[2]	ecum et phaleras et sua arma ante . . . genua proiecit	in deditionem redigit	32.14, 220.4, 267.272
2.21 Cleopatra/Octavian	ad pedes . . . prouoluta	rejected	62.185, 166.14, 239.116

1. *RE* 31.
2. *RE* 131.

Justin

Suppliant/Supplicandus[1]	Gesture/Word	Response	Page(s)
4.4.2–3 Catanian legates/ Athenians	sordida ueste	request granted	60.176
11.9.14–16 Persian women/ Alexander	prouolutae genibus	request granted	97.402
11.10.6–9 Syrian kings/Alexander	obuios cum infulis	alios in societatem recepit, aliis regnum ademit	96.395, 142.224
18.1.1 Tarentine legates/Pyrrhus of Epirus	supplicum precibus	polliceretur	32.16
20.2.11–12 Locrians/Spartans	supplices	rejected	7.19
27.1.4–7 Berenice "the Syrian"/ Apollo and Artemis of Daphne	Daphnae se claudit	removed dolo circumuenta	23.93, 36.41, 125.131, 128.145
35.1–2 DemetriusPoliorcetes/ Orophernes	supplicem	recepit	96.398
38.3.4 Nicomedes/Senate	supplex	decernitur	230.59
39.1.8 Demetrius II/Heracles Melkarth	religione templi se defensurus	overtaken and slain	23.93

Livy

Suppliant/Supplicandus[1]	Gesture/Word	Response	Page(s)
1.13.1–5 Sabine women/soldiers	scissa ueste . . . orantes	request granted[1]	60.175, 83.325, 93–94, 99.412
1.53.4–10 Sextus Tarquinius/ Gabii	supplicibus	benigne excipitur	32.19, 96.396
2.6.2–4 Tarquinius Superbus/ Veians and Tarquinians	supplex	accepted	87.353, 95.392
2.39.12 Priests/ Cn. Marcius Coriolanus[2]	suis insignibus uelatos	request denied	57.150, 166.16
2.49.12 Veians/Romans	supplices	accepted[3]	32.19
3.50.5 L. Verginius[4]/mob	tendens manus . . . appellans	aid pledged	51.123, 71.238, 95.392
3.58.1–6 C. Claudius Sabinus Inregillensis[5] and gens/people (on behalf Ap. Claudius)	sordidatus . . . prensabat orabatque	interrupted	41.72, 59.162, 60.169, 65.198
6.3.4 People/M. Furius Camillus[6]	turba ad pedes	request granted	68.222
6.3.9 Etruscans/Camillus	iactare . . . arma inermes . . . se hosti offerre	accepted	
7.31.5–9 Campanians/Senate	manus tendentes . . . procubuerunt	deditos	32.20, 230.59, 266.266, 275.312
8.20.6 Priuernati/C. Plautius[7]	caduceam praeferentes	se in deditionem . . . permississe	32.19, 222.13
8.28.5–9 Nexi/Senate	procumbentes ad . . . pedes	request granted	32.20, 71.238, 96.395, 229.56
8.35.3–8 M. Fabius Ambustus[8] and Q. Fabius Maximus Rullianus[9]/L. Papirius Cursor[10]	procumbere ad genua	ueniam dedisset	34.28, 50.115, 225.25, 243.136, 245.147
8.37.9–10 Tusculans/Romans	genibus se aduoluens	accepted	32.19, 50.115, 60.176
9.20.1 Samnites/Senate	humi strati	mouissent[11]	32.20, 119.95
22.60.1–61.3 Relatives/Senate (on behalf of captives)	manus . . . tendebant	request denied	32.20, 41.72, 42.77, 83.326, 166.17, 228.48
23.10.11 Decius Magius/statue of Ptolemy IV	confugisset	deportatus ad Ptolemaeum	8.22, 252.202
25.6.1–7.1 Sicilians/M. Claudius Marcellus[12]	ad genua . . . procubuerant	request denied	50.115, 223.17 227.38
25.37.9–11 Soldiers/commanders	strati humi . . . implorare	interrupted	225.25
26.49.11–15 Wife of Mandonius/ P. Cornelius Scipio Africanus[13]	ad pedes	accepted	75.268
28.34.3–12 Mandonius/Scipio	aduolutus genibus	spared	50.115, 222.13 266.264
29.16.6–7 Locrians/consuls[14]	ramos oleae porgentes	request granted	41.72, 56.141, 59.163, 60.176, 227.38
30.20.6 Italians/Juno Lacinia	concesserant in . . . delubrum	slain	251.196
30.23.4 Carthaginians/Scipio	supplices	not stated	
34.40.2–4 Diplomat/T. Quinctius Flamininus[15]	aduolutum . . . genibus	indutiae	50.115, 75.267, 119.95, 222.13, 223.18
36.28.1–8 Aetolians/Flamininus[16]	supplices	se in fidem permitterent Romanorum	33.21, 222.13 265.261

(continued)

Livy (*continued*)

Suppliant/Supplicandus[1]	Gesture/Word	Response	Page(s)
36.34.5–35.6 Naupactians/ Flamininus	manus . . . tendentes	request granted[18]	51.123, 130.149, 166.18, 222.13, 223.18, 226.36
39.13.1–14.3 Fecenia Hispala/ Sulpicia[17]	ad pedes . . . procidit	attollere	109.2
39.42.10–12 Boian/L. Quinctius Flamininus[20]	transfugam[19]	interrupted	107.10, 223.20, 226.36
42.23.5–24.10 Carthaginians/ Senate	strati . . . humi	request partially granted	32.20, 114.63, 230.58
43.2.2–3 Spaniards/Senate	nixi genibus	accepted	32.20, 50.119, 230.61
43.16.14–16 Senate leaders/Plebs	uestem mutarunt	acquitted	59.164, 60.176
44.19.7–14 Egyptians/Senate	ramis oleae . . . procubuerunt	accepted	32.20, 59.163, 60.176, 230.59
44.31.13–15 Gentius/L. Anicius Gallus[21]	genibus . . . accidens	arrested	95.390, 222.13, 266.264
44.42.4 Macedonians/Roman sailors	manus . . . tendentes	slain	166.20, 275.312
45.4.2–6 Perseus/L. Aemilius Paullus[22]	legatos . . . flentes ac sordidatos	rejected	59.163, 166.21, 222.13, 223.17, 226.36
45.5.1–6.10 Perseus/Samothrace	supplex	voluntary departure	71.238, 165
45.5.6–12 Evander/Samothrace	supplex	voluntary departure[23]	160.305, 169.46
45.20.9–25.4 Rhodians/Senate	prostrauerunt[24]	accepted[25]	32.20, 41.72, 59.163, 60.176, 95.390, 144.232, 230.60 & 63

1. But with complication that the nominal request is not for peace, but to be attacked.
2. *RE* 51 in Supp. 5.
3. They proceed to betray the supplicandi *ab insita animis leuitate*.
4. *RE* 7.
5. *RE* 322.
6. *RE* 44, hereafter "Camillus."
7. *RE* 18.
8. *RE* 44.
9. *RE* 114.
10. *RE* 52.
11. Then rejected by the people, presumably after another act of supplication.
12. *RE* 220.
13. *RE* 336, hereafter "Scipio."
14. I.e., M. Cornelius Cethegus (*RE* 92) and P. Sempronius Tuditanus (*RE* 96).
15. *RE* 45.
16. Also 36.35.3.
17. *RE* 108.
18. After initial rejection (36.34.6)
19. A lictor held a sword over the suppliant's head, showing that he had bowed or kneeled.
20. *RE* 43.
21. *RE* 15.
22. *RE* 114 dubitanter.
23. Prevented by his being assassinated.
24. 45.20.9. Ueste sordida: 45.20.10.
25. But with a reservation: ut nec hosties fierent nec socii permanerent (45.25.4).

Lucan

Suppliant/Supplicandus[1]	Gesture/Word	Response	Page(s)
3.303–72 Massilians/ C. Julius Caesar[1]	praelata fronde Mineruae	rejected	147.246
4.337–64 L. Afranius[2]/ Caesar	supplex stetit ante pedes	ignoscere	32.14, 83.326, 243.136, 245.154
7.68–127 Pompeians/Cn. Pompeius Magnus[3]	cum supplice mundo adfusi	request granted	225.27
7.369–84 Romans/ Pompeians	crinibus effusis . . . pedibus prosternere . . . adferre preces	unstated[4]	68.222
8.287–88 P. Attius Varus[5]/ Juba	supplice	request granted	30.4

1. *RE* 131, hereafter "Caesar."
2. *RE* 6.
3. *RE* 31.
4. Suppositious act.
5. *RE* 2.

Other Authors

Suppliant/Supplicandus[1]	Gesture/Word	Response	Page(s)
Amp. 14.7 Pausanias/Athena of the Brazen House	in asylum . . . confugit	fame confectus	153.278
Amp. 16.4 Philip V/Great Gods Samothrace	Samothracam confugit	data fide	267.271
Apul. *Met.* 4.12 Widow/Alcimus	genibus . . . profusa	request granted[2]	
Apul. *Met.* 6.2 Psyche/Ceres	pedes . . . aduoluta	request denied	50.118, 78.286
Apul. *Met.* 6.22 Cupid/Jupiter	supplicat	consauiat[3]	
Apul. *Met.* 9.18–19 Philesitherus/ Myrmex	supplex	bribe taken	276.318
Asc. *Sc.* Various/judges	ad genua iudicum	acquitted	60.176, 65.199, 65.200, 66.202
Aug. *Anc.* 5.41–43 Parthians/ Quirites	supplices	accepted	222.14, 252.197
Aug. *Anc.* 5.54–6.38 kings/ Augustus[4]	confugerunt	accepted	19.74, 31.8, 236.95, 252.197
Fro. *Parth.* 16 Parthamasiris[5]/ Trajan	supplex	interfectus	31.10, 166.15, 267.273
Gran. *Ann.* 35.8 C. Marius[6]/troops	deformis habitu et cultu . . . supplicem	accepted	
Hist. Aug. Had. 21.14 Bactrian legates/Hadrian	supplices	unstated	19.74, 31.10, 57.156, 236.95
Hist. Aug. Heliog. 2.3 Heliogabalus/god of same name	in templum . . . confugisse	accepted	
Hist. Aug. Max. 9.3 Balbinus/ rioters	manus . . . [te]ten[d]it	request denied	166.24
Hist. Aug. Prob. 14.2[7] German kings/Probus	stratique iacerunt	virtual deditio	19.74, 222.13, 234, 267.271
Hor. *Carm.* 4.14.35 Alexandrians/ Augustus	supplex	unstated	31.8, 234.87
Hyg. *Astr.* 2.6.3 Thamyris/Muses	ad genua iacentem	excaecatum	
Ilias 17–27 Chryses/Agamemnon	genibus affusus	negat	
Ilias 87–96 Thetis/Jupiter	genibus . . . affusa	request granted	298
Ilias 1026–45 Priam/Achilles	effusus genibus	alleuat	297
Nep. *Ag.* 4.6–8 Athenians et al./ Athena	in templum coniecissent	spared	137.197
Nep. *Paus.* 4.5 Argilius/Poseidon of Taenarus	confugisse	unstated	
Nep. *Paus.* 5.2–5 Pausanias/ Athena of the Brazen House	in aedem . . . confugit	removed	153.278
Nep. *Them.* 8.4–5 Themistocles/ King of Molossians	supplicem	dismissed	31.7
Orosius 4.12.3 Carthaginians/Rome	supplicantibus	request granted	119.95
Plin. *Ep.* 1.18.3 *Mother-in-law/ Pliny*	*aduoluta genibus*	*request denied[8]*	
Plin. *Ep.* 10.74 Callidromus/ Statue of Trajan	confugisse	perductum	8.22, 252.203, 253.207
Sal. *Jug.* 38.1 Legates of Jugurtha/ A. Postumius Albinus[9]	supplicantis	unstated	83.321, 222.13, 223.17

Other Authors (*continued*)

Suppliant/Supplicandus[1]	Gesture/Word	Response	Page(s)
Sal. *Jug.* 47.3–4 Legates of Jugurtha/Q. Caecilius Metellus Numidicus[10]	supplices	rejected	75.267, 83.321, 166.22, 222.13, 226.36, 267.270
Serv. *A.* 3.73 Leto/Jupiter (on behalf of Asterie)	supplicante	request granted	42.77
Serv. *G.* 2.161 Redemptores/ Senate	supplicauerunt	request granted	70.229, 95.388

1. Acts reported in Hyg. *Fab.* are excluded, and listed instead under the poet presumed to be the source.
2. But to the disadvantage off the supplicandus, who is defenestrated.
3. Followed by conditional grant of request.
4. reges Parthorum Tirida[tes et postea] Phrat[es] regis Phrati[s filius];   Medorum [Artavasdes, Adiabenorum A]rtaxares, Britann[o]rum Dumnobellau[nus] et Tin[commius, Sugambr]orum Maelo, Mar[c]omanorum Sueborum [. . . rus]
5. I.e., Parthamaspates.
6. *RE* 14 in Supp. 6.
7. Also 15.2.
8. Supposititious act.
9. *RE* 32; 33, according to *MRR*.
10. *RE* 97.

Ovid

Suppliant/Supplicandus[1]	Gesture/Word	Response	Page(s)
Am. 1.7.61–68 Speaker/mistress	procumbere supplex	unstated	78.285
Am. 2.5.49–52 Speaker/mistress	supplex	request granted	77.283
Fast. 4.317–27 Claudia/Cybele	summisso . . . genu	prayer granted	
Met. 2.394–400 Heavenly bodies/ Sun	supplice uoce	request granted	
Met. 4.238–55 Leucothoë/Sun	tendentem . . . manus	tardily rescued	51.125
Met. 5.210–35 Phineus/Perseus	supplex. . . manus tendens	spared[1]	247.164
Met. 5.514–32 Ceres/Jupiter	supplex	request granted[2]	35.32, 114.61
Met. 6.348–62 Leto/Lycians	supplex . . . bracchia tendunt	request denied	
Met. 6.494–508 Pandion/Tereus	supplex	pignus dextras. . . poposcit	110.28 & 32
Met. 6.639–42 Procne/Itys	tendentem. . . manus	slain	
Met. 7.298–300 Medea/Pelias	ad limina supplex	excipiunt	37.44, 384.10
Met. 7.852–58 Procris/Cephalus	supplex	no reply	86.341
Met. 8.260–62 Daedalus/Cocalus	pro supplice	mitis	
Met. 9.413–17 Callirhoe/Jupiter	supplex	request granted	35.32
Met. 10.414–30 Nurse/Myrrha	antes pedes procumbit	information disclosed	50.118, 74.253
Met. 11.39–43 Orpheus/unnamed	tendentem. . . manus	slain	
Met. 11.274–88 Peleus/Trachinius	uelamenta manu praetendens supplice	accepted	247.167
Met. 11.400–01 Thetis/Psamathe (on behalf of Peleus)	supplex	accepit ueniam	274.309
Met. 13.584–619 Aurora/Jupiter	genibus procumbere	adnuerat	111.4
Met. 13.854–56 Polyphemus/ Galatea	preces . . . supplicis	request denied	77.284, 98.404
Met. 14.372–85 Circe/Picus	supplex	request denied	35.32, 77.284
Met. 14.701–42 Iphis/Anaxarete[3]	supplex ad limina	request denied	37.44, 77.284
Pont. 4.6.10–12 *Paullus Fabius Maximus*[4]*/Augustus (on behalf of Ovid)*	*supplice uoce*	*forestalled*	41.72, 231.71, 234.89

1. Then slain by a trick.
2. According to a *lege certa*, i.e., that Persephone not eat before she returns.
3. Via servants.
4. *RE* 102.

Petronius

Suppliant/Supplicandus[1]	Gesture/Word	Response	Page(s)
17.9–18.4 Servant/Encolpius	protendo . . . ad genua . . . supinas manus	pollicitationem	75.263, 112.43
30.7–11 House slave/guests	procubuit ad pedes	pardoned	75.263, 244.145
97.9–10 Eumolpus/Ascyltus	genua . . . procubui	spared	247.165
101.2–3 Ascyltus/Eumolpus	comprehendi genua	interrupted	
107 Eumolpus/Lichas and Tryphaena	supplices iacent	interrupted	50.118, 93.380, 242.130

Plautus and Terence

Suppliant/Supplicandus	Gesture/Word	Response	Page(s)
Plautus			
Amph. 256–9 Teleboans/ Amphitryo	uelatis manibus orant	dedunt se	
Cist. 566–84 Syra/ Gymnasium	amplexa . . . genua	request granted	114.64
Most. 1094–1180 Tranio/ public altar	aram . . . occupabo	abi inpune	114.64, 155.287, 168.27, 375.1
Rud. 274–80 Palaestra and Ampelisca/Ptolemocratia	amplectimur genua	exsurgite	109.21, 376.5
Rud. 559–680 Same/statue of Venus at Cyrene	signum . . . amplexae	ab signo . . . ui deripuit	37.43, 134.180, 157.395, 168.36, 193.99, 376.5 & 6
Rud. 615–56 Trachalio/ Daemones	per genua	interrupted	92.374
Rud. 688–869 Same/altar of Venus at Cyrene	adsidite . . . in ara	removal of remover	37.43, 168.26, 376.9, 377.11
Terence			
And. 315–32 Charinus/ Pamphilus	supplicabo[1]	request granted	
Hec. 378–402 Myrrina/ Pamphilus	ad genua accidit	pollicitus sum	112.49

1. 312.

Younger and Elder Seneca

Suppliant/Supplicandus	Gesture/Word	Response	Page(s)
Seneca the Younger			
Dial. 3.40.2–5 Slave/ Augustus	confugit ad . . . pedes	accepted	50.118, 244.144
Her. F. 202–523 Heraclidae/ Zeus	iuxta praesides adstat deos	rescued	155.288
Her. F. 1002–7; 1015, 1022–23 Heraclidae/ Hercules	manus ad genua tendens . . . tendat manus	slain	
Her. F. 1192–93 Hercules/ Amphitryon	supplices . . . manus	preempted	98.405
Med. 247–48 Medea/Creon	genua attigi . . . fidem . . . dextra peti	accepted	112.49
Med. 282–95 Medea/Creon	supplex . . . precor	request partially granted	114.63, 240.118
Phaed. 246–52 Nurse/ Phaedra	supplex	request granted	134.18
Phaed. 622–24 Phaedra/ Hippolytus	sinu receptam supplicem . . . tege[1]	request denied	78.286
Phaed. 666–706 same	adlapsa genibus	request denied	78.286
Thy. 517–29 Thyestes/ Atreus	supplicem . . . vides	a genibus manum aufer	112.46
Tro. 691–704 Andromache/ Ulysses	accido genua	see immediately below	
Tro. 705–38 Astyanax/ Ulysses	supplice dextra stratus	rejected	55.136
Seneca the Elder			
Con. 1.5.3 Rapist/victim	supplices summisit manus	accepted	
Con. 10.1.1 Poor man/rich man	ad tua genua . . . uenissem	request denied	
Con. 10.2.10 Son/father	deprecatus . . . ad templa iturum . . . ad statuas . . . confugiam	unstated	74.253, 252.203

1. Cf. 666–67: supplex iacet adlapsa genibus.

Silius Italicus

Suppliant/Supplicandus	Gesture/Word	Response	Page(s)
2.412–13 Aeneas/Dido	dextra precantem	unstated	55.137
4.408–9 *Rome/troops*	*tendere palmas*	*unstated*[1]	51.123
8.59–60 Anna/Battus	supplice	dextram . . . tetendit	110.32
8.71–75 Anna/Iulus and Aeneas	allapsam genibus	attolit	45.91
12.589–90 Romans/troops	tendentum palmas	request granted	
14.161–77 Beryas/Asilus	supplex	attolit	110.35
15.89–92 Fugitives/Romans	asylo	dextris	250.187
15.317–19 Philip V/Romans	supplex	foedera sanxit	112.47, 119.95
16.243–74 P. Cornelius Scipio Africanus[2]/Syphax	supplex	foedera	112.47, 119.95, 119.96 & 97

1. Suppositious act is italicized.
2. *RE* 336.

Statius

Suppliant/Supplicandus	Gesture/Word	Response	Page(s)
Ach. 1.48–51 Thetis/Neptune	supplex	repulsa	42.77
Theb. 10.422–34 Dymas/Amphion	supplex	request granted	
Theb. 10.589–98 Troops/Tiresias	supplice coetu	request granted	85.336
Theb. 624–27 Creon/Tiresias	genua amplectens	request denied	
Theb. 11.375–89 Jocasta/Eteocles	gemitu . . . supplice	repulsa	276.318
Theb. 11.739–40 Antigone/Creon	humi . . . voluitur	non . . . omnia supplicis . . . indulget	
Theb. 12.581–95 Argive women/ Theseus	tenduntque precantis manus	request granted	

Suetonius

SUPPLIANT/SUPPLICANDUS	GESTURE/WORD	RESPONSE	PAGE(S)
Jul. 63 L. Cassius Longinus[1]/ C. Julius Caesar[2]	supplicem	ad deditionem hortatus	
Aug. 16.4 M. Aemilius Lepidus[3]/Augustus	supplicem	relegauit	
Aug. 17.5 M. Antonius Antyllus[4]/ statue of the deified Caesar	confugerat	abreptum interemit	252.202
Tib. 24.1 Senate/Tiberius	procumbentem sibi ad genua	interrupted	31.9, 235.90
Cl. 10.2 Claudius/guard	ad genua sibi accidentem	imperatorem salutauit	248.174
Nero 13.2 Tiridates/Nero	subeuntem ad genua	adleuatum	31.10, 110.35, 112.45, 236.95, 252.199

1. *RE* 65.
2. *RE* 131, hereafter "Caesar."
3. *RE* 73.
4. *RE* 32.

Tacitus

Suppliant/Supplicandus	Gesture/Word	Response	Page(s)
Ann. 1.11.1–13 Senate/ Tiberius	ad genua . . . manus tendere	unstated	234–5
Ann. 1.13.7 Q. Haterius[1]/ Tiberius	genua . . . aduolueretur	prope interfectum	31.9, 50.116, 252.197
Ann. 1.29.1–2 Troops/Nero Claudius Drusus[2]	supplices . . . orantibus	mercy denied	147.247, 167.27, 225.26, 226.35, 246.157
Ann. 1.39.7 L. Munatius Plancus[3]/soldiers	signa et aquilam amplexus	religione sese tutebatur	
Ann. 1.44.1 Troops/ Germanicus Julius Caesar[4]	supplices	ignoscere	225.25, 226.35, 243.136
Ann. 2.22.3 Angrivarii/ L. Stertinius[5]	supplices	ueniam accepere	222.13, 243.136
Ann. 2.29.1 M. Scribonius Libo Drusus[6]/wife's relatives	ueste mutata . . . orare adfines	abnuentibus	60.176, 147.247, 167.28
Ann. 2.29.2 Libo/Tiberius	manus . . . ad Tiberium tendens	immoto . . . uultu	31.9, 130.155, 147.247, 167.29
Ann. 3.36.3 Annia Rufilla[7]/ statue of emperor	ob effigiem imperatoris oppositam	removed	8.22, 252.203, 253.204
Ann. 3.61.2 *Amazons/Bacchus*	*supplicibus . . . quae aram insiderant*	*ignouisse*[8]	243.136
Ann. 4.14.3 Romans/ Asclepius of Cos	Romanos templo induxerant	slain	
Ann. 11.30.1–2 Calpurnia[9]/ Claudius	genibus . . . prouoluta	unstated	31.10, 50.116, 234.83
Ann. 12.17.3 Zorsines/effigy of emperor	procubuit	accepted	254.213
Ann. 14.23.3 Armenians/ C. Domitius Corbulo[10]	misericordia aduersum supplices		222.13
Ann. 14.61.3–62.1 Poppaea Sabina[11]/Nero	prouoluta genibus	unstated	50.116, 83.324, 93.379, 96.396, 234.83, 252.199, 274.305
Ann. 15.53.2–3 Plautius Lateranus[12]/Nero	genibus . . . accidens	assassination foiled	
Ann. 15.73.4 L. Junius Gallio Annaeanus[13]/Senate or Nero	supplicem	charges dropped	235.93, 274.305
Hist. 1.54 Lingones/troops	in squalorem . . . compositi	no reply	60.176, 222.13
Hist. 1.66 Viennenses/troops	uelamenta et infula praeferentes	accepted	56.140, 222.13
Hist. 2.46–47 Troops/Otho	tendere manus . . . prensare genua	request denied	147.247, 166.25, 225.27, 234.88
Hist. 3.10 L. Tampius Flavianus[14]/troops	supplicis manus	slain	147.247, 166.26
Hist. 3.31 Beseiged Vitellians/ Othonians	velamenta et infulas ostentant	accepted	56.14

(*continued*)

Tacitus (*continued*)

Suppliant/Supplicandus	Gesture/Word	Response	Page(s)
Hist. 3.38 L. Vitellius[15]/ Emperor Vitellius	filium . . . complexus . . . genibus accidens	information acknowledged	50.116, 74.255, 115.71, 235.91
Hist. 4.81 Blind and crippled/Vespasian	genua . . . aduoluitur	request granted	50.116, 252.199

1. *RE* 3a in Supp. 3.
2. *RE* 139.
3. *RE* 30.
4. *RE* 138.
5. *RE* 7.
6. *RE* 23, hereafter "Libo."
7. *RE* 126.
8. Alleged act.
9. *RE* 128.
10. *RE* 50.
11. *RE* 4.
12. *RE* 42.
13. *RE* 12 s.v. *Annaeus.*
14. Omitted from *RE*; see *PIR* T5.
15. *RE* 7d in Supp. 9.

Valerius Flaccus

Suppliant/Supplicandus	Gesture/Word	Response	Page(s)
3.637–91 Telamon/ Argonauts	prensat . . . uiros . . . supplex	request denied	
4.60–79 Apollo/Jove (on behalf of Prometheus)	supplex	request granted	41.72
4.535–49 Jason/Phineus	supplex	request granted	74.253
4.647–55 Jason/Argonauts	manus intendit	request granted	
6.74–75 Perses/Syenes	supplex	unstated	
6.458–76 Juno/Venus	supplex	adnue	111.41
7.410–60 Jason/Medea	supplicis ora	request granted	111.37
7.475–87 Medea/Jason	arripit dextra ac summisa	see next	111.37
7.490–510 Jason/Medea	precor, adnue, coniunx	iuro	44.85, 111.37, 111.41, 112.47

Valerius Maximus

Suppliant/Supplicandus	Gesture/Word	Response	Page(s)
2.7.8 Q. Fabius Maximus Rullianus[1]/tribunes (on behalf of son)	supplex	request granted	41.73
2.9.3 Philip V/unstated	supplices manus	unstated	
3.2.16 Spaniards/M. Porcius Cato "Censorius"[2]	supplices . . . uenerunt	surrender	119.93, 222.13
3.8 ext. 4 Demochares/Ephialtes (on behalf of father)	genibus . . . aduolutum	operto capite	130.156
4.1.7 Sicilians/M. Claudius Marcellus[3]	supplices	in clientelam reciperentur excepit	119.93, 384.10
4.6 ext. 3 Minyae/Spartans	ramis	accepted	118.88 & 89
5.1.8 Persian/L. Aemilius Paullus[4]	ad genua procumbere	adleuauit	110.35
5.1.9 Tigranes II/Cn. Pompeius Magnus[5]	iacere supplicem	accepted	32.16, 73.248, 119.93
5.2.7 Q. Caecilius Metellus Pius[6]/people (on behalf of Q. Calidius)	supplicare	elected	232.74
5.3.3 C. Julius Caesar[7]/Sextilius[8]	genibus adnixum	rejected	50.116, 147.245, 167.30
5.4.1 Priests/Cn. Marcius Coriolanus[9]	supplicare	rejected	
5.5.1 P. Cornelius Scipio Africanus[10]/Senate (on behalf of his brother)	supplex	request granted[11]	114.68, 228.51
6.8.4 C. Cassius Longinus[12]/Pindarus	se . . . genibus summitteret	spared	50.116
6.9 ext. 7 Syphax/Scipio	genibus supplex	accepted	222.13, 223.17
8.1.6 L. Calpurnius Piso Caesoninus[13]/judges	prostratus . . . pedes . . . oscularetur	acquitted	67.21
9.2 ext. 2 Hannibal the Great[14]/Prusias II	supplicem factum	slain[15]	167.31
9.5.3 P. Plautius Hypsaeus[16]/Pompey	prostratum	request denied	167.32
9.10.1 Tusculans/Quirites[17]	squalore obsiti	enslaved	59.163, 60.176, 121.108, 230.66

1. *RE* 114.
2. *RE* 9.
3. *RE* 220.
4. *RE* 114 dubitanter.
5. *RE* 31, hereafter "Pompey."
6. *RE* 98.
7. *RE* 131.
8. *RE* 1.
9. *RE* 51 in Supp. 5.
10. *RE* 336, hereafter "Scipio."
11. On the condition that Scipio serve as legate to his brother.
12. *RE* 59.
13. *RE* 90.
14. Geus, "Hannibal," 9.
15. By order of the Senate.
16. *RE* 23.
17. I.e., comitia centuriata.

Velleius Paterculus

Suppliant/Supplicandus	Gesture/Word	Response	Page(s)
1.8.5 Fugitives/Rome	asylo facto	accepted	
1.9.4 Perseus/Great Gods of Samothrace	templique se religioni supplicem credidit	accepted[1]	267.271
2.37.4 Tigranes II/Cn. Pompeius Magnus[2]	supplex	dicioni eius	239.111, 267.271
2.79.5 Sextus Pompeius Magnus[3]/M. Antonius[4]	inter ducem et supplicem . . . uitam precatur	iugulatus	259.234
2.80.4 M. Aemilius Lepidus[5]/Octavian	genibus . . . aduolutus	spared	110.33
2.109.2 Legates of Maroboduus/Caesars	interdum ut supplicem . . . interdum ut pro pari	request denied	41.72, 226.36

1. Ad eum Cn. Octauius praetor . . . ratione magis quam ui persuasit ut se Romanorum fidei committeret.
2. *RE* 31.
3. *RE* 33.
4. *RE* 30.
5. *RE* 73.

Virgil's *Aeneid*

Suppliant/Supplicandus	Gesture/Word	Response	Page(s)
1.64–80 Juno/Aeolus	supplex	request granted	
1.487 Priam/Achilles	tendentem . . . manus . . . inermis	unstated	274.308
1.666 Venus/Cupid	*confugio . . . supplex*	*request granted*[1]	78.286, 250.187
2.515–25 Trojan women at altars and penates	circum altaria . . . sedebant	unstated	274.208, 275.311, 286.25
2.533–53 Priam at altar	supplicis ad altaria trementem	slain	274.308, 275.311
3.590–667 Achaemenides/ Trojans	genua amplexus	recepto supplice	45.91, 274.308, 384.10
6.42–155 Aeneas/Sybil	supplex . . . arasque tenebat	request granted	274.308
8.115–174 Aeneas/Evander	ramum praetendit oliuae	accepted	265.260, 274.307, 286.25
8.382 Venus/Vulcan	supplex	request granted	63.186, 70.226, 286.25
10.522–36 Magus/Aeneas	genua amplectens	slain	45.91, 147.245–6, 166.1, 274.309, 275.311, 286.25
10.594–601 Liger/Aeneas	tendebat . . . palmas	slain	147.246, 166.2, 274.309, 275.311, 286.25
11.336–82 Drances/Turnus	*en supplex uenio*	*request denied*	
12.930–52 Turnus/Aeneas	supplex dextram . . . protendens	slain	55.136, 147.246, 166.3, 275.312, 275.314, 286.25

1. Suppositious acts are italicized.

Appendix 1c

ACTS AND REGULATIONS OF SUPPLICATION IN NON–LITERARY SOURCES

Page references are placed at the end of the entries.

Decrees:

IG i³ 14 (Athens, 434–31 BCE): 177.23, 384
ii² 192 (Athens, fourth century BCE): 177.23
   211: 73.246, 177.23
   218: 73.244, 73.246, 134.179, 173–77 passim, 186.69, 188.78
   276: 73.246, 81, 175–77 passim, 188.78
   336: 70.229, 73.248, 81, 118.89, 175–77 passim
   337: 175–77 passim, 186.69
   404: 57.404, 119.98, 175–77 passim, 181
   502: 175–77 passim
LSCG #123 = Michel #371 (Samos, third century BCE) : 78.288, 174, 384
   Habicht, "Hellenistische Inschriften," #9: 188–91, 383.5
   Habicht, "Samische Volksbeschlüsse," #59: 93.375, 373
SEG XXXIX 729 (Lindos, third century BCE): 73, 186, 187, 383,
Servais, "Suppliants" (Cyrene, 331–23 BCE): 73, 185, 383
IG v.1 1390 = *SIG* 7340 (Andania, 91 BCE): 150
Clinton, "Maroneia," decree C (Maroneia, 41–54 CE): 236

Dedications and other objects:

M–L #21, an ostrakon (Athens, 483–82 BCE): 381
SEG XXVI 449 (Epidaurus, 475–450 BCE): 380
SEG XXXIII 244d, a dedicatory graffito on an aryballos (Athens, fifth century BCE): 380.8
SEG XLIV 524 (Chalastra, 400–350 BCE): 77
IG iv² 1.125 (Epidaurus, third century BCE), 1.126 (ibid., ca. 160 CE), 1.516 (ibid., Roman period), 1.537 (ibid., first to fourth centuries CE): 72
IC 1.xvii 17–18 (Lebena, first century BCE): 72
Gerasa 5–7 (Gerasa, 69–70 CE): 380
SEG XXXIII 1100 (a plaque, Paphlagonia, 195–96 CE): 380

Defixiones:

IG iii Ap. 100 (Athens, fourth-third centuries BCE): 8.23
SEG XLIII 434 (Macedon, 380–350 BCE): 8.23
IG xii 7, p. 1 (Amorgos, second century BCE): 8.23

Notices:

IG iv 492 (Mycenae, 500–480 BCE): 261.44, 379–80
IG i³ 45 (Athens, fifth century BCE): 184
IG iv² 1.121–22 (Epidaurus, mid-fourth century BCE): 72, 112.51
IC 1.xvii 9 (Lebena, second century BCE): 72
LT (Rome, late first century BCE): 42

Papyri:

PCair. Zenon 4.59620 = *CPS* #1.79 (third century BCE)
PAthens 8 (second century BCE): 151.263
UPZ 1.3, 1.4 = *CPS* #1.83 (164 BCE): 119.91
UPZ 1.121 = *CPS* #1.81 (156 BCE): 148.250, 374.10
Chr. W. 330 (114 BCE): 114.68
BGU 8.1797 (80–51 BCE): 148.250

Appendix 1d

ACTS AND REGULATIONS OF SUPPLICATION IN NEAR EASTERN SOURCES

SUPPLIANT/SUPPLICANDUS	GESTURE/WORD	RESPONSE	PAGE(S)
SB 5.144–265 Humbaba/ Gilgamesh	?	slain[1]	21, 42
1 Ki. 25.23–35 Abigail/David (on behalf of Nabal)	וַתִּפֹּל לְאַפֵּי דָוִד עַל־אַפֶּנֶיהָ	spared	51.120
2 Ki. 14.4–24 Woman/David	וַתִּפֹּל עַל־אַפֶּיהָ אַרְצָה	request granted	30.5, 43, 51.120
3 Ki. 1.50–53 Adonijah/ tabernacle	וַיַּחֲזֵק בְּקַרְנוֹת הַמִּזְבֵּחַ	spared	115
3 Ki. 2.28–34 Joab/tabernacle	וַיַּחֲזֵק בְּקַרְנוֹת הַמִּזְבֵּחַ	slain[2]	20, 21
3 Ki. 20.32–34 Ben–Hadad/ Ahab	וַיַּחְגְּרוּ שַׂקִּים בְּמָתְנֵיהֶם וַחֲבָלִים בְּרָאשֵׁיהֶם	וַיַּעֲלֵהוּ עַל־הַמֶּרְכָּבָה	30.5, 59–60, 108, 112.46
Es. 7.7–10 Haman/Esther	נֹפֵל עַל־הַמִּטָּה אֲשֶׁר אֶסְתֵּר עָלֶיהָ	slain	61
Es. 8.3–8 Esther/Asahuerus	וַתִּפֹּל לִפְנֵי רַגְלָיו	וַתָּקָם אֶסְתֵּר	20, 51
2 Macc. 4.33–38 Onias/Apollo and Artemis at Daphne	ἀποκεχωρηκὼς εἰς ἄσυλον	δοὺς δεξιάν[3]	36.41, 125–26
Ev. Marc. 5.22–24 Jairus/Jesus	πίπτει πρὸς τοὺς πόδας	request granted	31.11
Ev. Marc. 7.25 Tyrian mother/ Jesus (on behalf of daughter)	προσέπεσεν πρὸς τοὺς πόδας	request granted	31.11
Ev. Luc. 5.12–16 Leper/Jesus	πεσὼν ἐπὶ πρόσωπον	request granted	31.11, 51.121
Ev. Luc. 8.41–42 Jairus/Jesus	πίπτει πρὸς τοὺς πόδας	request granted	31.11
Ev. Matt. 8.2–4 Leper/Jesus	προσεκύνει	request granted	31.11, 51.121
Ev. Matt. 9.18–19 Ruler/Jesus	προσεκύνει	request granted	31.11, 51.121
Ev. Matt. 15.22–8 Mother/Jesus (on behalf of daughter)	προσεκύνει	request granted	31.11, 51.121

Hebrew Regulations

Ex 21.14, Nu. 35.9–34, De. 4.41–43, Jo. 20.1–7			21, 30, 149

Assyrian Inscriptions

Esar. 68.2.1.3–35 king of Shubria/Esarhaddon	ka-mi-is e-li dûr	rejected	22.87, 23.89
Esar. 68.2.2.18–41 king of Uppume/Esarhaddon	ša-lam [. . . u]-še-piš-ma u-ḫal-li-pa ba-ša-a-mu . . . ki-a-am iq-bu-nim	rejected	23.89
Sg. 8.55–61 Ullusunu/Sargon II	u-ṣal-lu-ni	aq-bi-šu-nu-aḫulap	22.87
Sg. 8.69–73 Chiefs of Gizilbundl/ Sargon II	u-nu-aš-ši-qu GIR[II]-ia	accepted	22.87

(continued)

(*continued*)

SUPPLIANT/SUPPLICANDUS	GESTURE/WORD	RESPONSE	PAGE(S)
Acts of Supplication in Josephus			
AJ 1.337–38 Sychemmes/ Emmorus	ἱκέτευε	request granted	
AJ 7.182–84 Woman/David	ἱκέτευσεν	request granted	43.81, 100
AJ 7.204 David/Chusis	παρακαλεῖ καὶ τέλος ἱκέτευσεν	request granted	
AJ 7.361–62 Adonijah/tabernacle	ἱκέτης γίνεται τοῦ θεοῦ καὶ τῶν τοῦ θυσιαστηρίου κεράτων . . . ἐλλαβόμενος	spared	
AJ 8.385–87 Ben-Hadad/Ahab	σάκκους ἐνδυσάμενοι καὶ σχοινία ταῖς κεφαλαῖς περιθέμενοι	ἐπιδοὺς αὐτῷ τὴν δεξιὰν	60.167
AJ 8.13–15 Joab/tabernacle	καταφεύγει μὲν ἐπὶ τὸ θυσιαστήριον	slain	89.356
AJ 15.89–90 Arsinoe/Artemis at Ephesus	ἱκετεύουσαν	slain	151.298, 259
AJ 19.234–36 Tribunes/Claudius (on behalf of Senate)	τοῖς γόνασιν αὐτοῦ προσπεσόντες	request granted	50.116
AJ 20.54–59 Artabanus/Izates	ἱκέτην . . . παρεστῶτα	σύμμαχον	68, 73.248
BJ 1.32 sons of Tobias/ Antiochus IV of Commagene	καταφυγόντες . . . ἱκέτευσαν	request granted	75.266
BJ 1.58 Mother/John Hyrcanus	χεῖρας ὤρεγε	alternately accepted and rejected[4]	51.123
BJ 1.124–26 John Hyrcanus/ Aretas	προσφυγόντα	accepted[5]	
BJ 1.139 Aristobulus/ Cn. Pompeius Magnus[6]	ἱκέτης	accepted	115, 222.13
BJ 1.238 Brother of Malichus/ Herod the Great	ἱκέτην	ἀφῆκεν	164.57
BJ 1.281–84 Herod the Great/ M. Antonius[7]	ἱκέτης	Senate resolution	73.248, 104
BJ 1.353 Antigonus/C. Sosius[8]	προσπίπτει . . . ποσὶν	imprisoned	51.120
BJ 1.393–94 Alexas/Antony	ἱκέτην γενόμενον	rejected	164.58, 223.19, 383.2
BJ 1.506–10 Pheroras/Herod the Great	μελαίνη τε ἐσθῆτι . . . προσπίπτει . . . ποσὶν	pardoned	51.120, 60.177, 92, 95
BJ 1.561–55 Antipater/Herod the Great	ἱκετεύειν ἄντικρυς	request denied	164.59
BJ 1.566 Livia[9]/Herod the Great (on behalf of Salome)	ἱκετεύουσαν	request denied	41.72, 164.60, 231.71
BJ 1.621–40 Antipater/Herod the Great	πεσὼν πρηνὴς πρὸ τῶν ποδῶν	imprisoned	51.120, 92, 164.61
BJ 1.663 Antipater/jailers	ἱκέτευεν	rejected	82, 164.62
BJ 2.171–74 Jews/Pontius Pilatus[10]	πρηνεῖς καταπεσόντες	request granted	51.120, 84, 224
BJ 2.192–201 Jews/P. Petronius[11]	καθικέτευον	request granted	70.228, 84.330, 224
BJ 2.230–31 Jews/Ventidius Cumanus[12]	ἱκετεύοντες	request granted[13]	95, 222.13

(*continued*)

Suppliant/Supplicandus	Gesture/Word	Response	Page(s)
BJ 2.233 Galilaeans/Cumanus	ἱκέτας	ἀπέπεμψεν	70.228, 164.63, 224
BJ 2.237–38 Magistrates/Jews	σάκκους ἀμπεχόμενοι καὶ τέφραν τῶν κεφαλῶν	request granted	60.168
BJ 2.280–81 Jews/Cestius Gallus[14]	ἱκέτευον	δοὺς ἔμφασιν	112.43, 224
BJ 2.292 Jews/Gessius Florus[15]	ἱκέτευον	jailed	148.242, 164.64, 224, 226.35
BJ 2.314 Berenice/Florus	ἱκέτευε	rejected	71.235, 164.65, 222.13, 224
BJ 2.322–25 Priests/Jews	καταμωμένους μὲν τὴν κεφαλὴν κόνει, γυμνοὺς δὲ τὰ στέρνα τῶν ἐσθήτων διερρηγμένων	request granted	60.168, 70
BJ 2.336–41 Jews/Agrippa II	ἱκέτευεν	request taken under advisement	115, 234.87
BJ 2.497–98 Alexandrian Jews/ Romans	πρὸς ἱκετηρίας ἐτράποντο	spared	56.140, 71.238
BJ 2.601–610 Josephus/rebels	περιρρηξάμενος μὲν τὴν ἐσθῆτα, καταπασάμενος δὲ τῆς κεφαλῆς κόνιν	spared[16]	60.168, 73
BJ 2.637–641 Josephus/rebels	κατασείοντες ἱκετηρίας	spared	56.140
BJ 2.643–44 Clitus/Josephus	ἱκέτευεν	request granted	75, 115
BJ 3.202–4 Jews/Josephus	τοῖς ποσὶν ἐμπλεκόμενοι	request granted	51.120
BJ 3.334–35 Jew/centurion	ἱκετεύει	ὤρεγε τὴν χεῖρα[17]	110.33
BJ 3.454–56 Elders of Tiberias/ Vespasian	προσπίπτουσιν ἱκέται	λαβόντων δεξιὰς	222.13, 223.17
BJ 4.77 Jews/Romans	χεῖρας προΐσχοντας	interrupted[18]	51.122
BJ 4.311 Temple guards/ Idumaeans	ἱκετεύεουσι	slain	71.233, 87.352, 146, 164.66
BJ 4.360 Niger/Zealots	ἱκέτευεν	slain	71.233, 146.240, 165.67
BJ 4.553 People of Capharabis/ Sex. Cerealius Vetilianus[19]	μεθ' ἱκετηριῶν	spared	56.140, 71.233, 135, 222.13, 223.17
BJ 4.640 Tribunes/soldiers (on behalf of Caecina)	προσπίπτοντες	request granted	
BJ 5.109–19 Jews/Romans	δεξιὰν ᾐτοῦντο	interrupted	
BJ 5.127–28 Soldiers/Vespasian (on behalf of comrades)	ἱκέτευε	request granted	225.26, 226.35, 245.148
BJ 5.317–330 Castor/Titus	προτείνας . . . τὰς χεῖρας ὡς ἱκετεύων	interrupted	51.123, 93
BJ 5.548–52 Jewish deserters/ Romans	ἱκέτας	accepted[20]	71.235
BJ 6.118–21 Jews/Zealots	ἱκέτευον	request denied	146.240, 165.68
BJ 6.271 Jews/Romans	ἱκετεύοντας	slain	165.69
BJ 6.319–21 Boy/Romans	ἱκέτευε	δόντων δεξιὰς[21]	70.227

(*continued*)

(*continued*)

Suppliant/Supplicandus	Gesture/Word	Response	Page(s)
BJ 6.356–57 Izatidae/Titus	ἱκέτευσαν	δέχεται δοῦναι δεξιὰν	71.238, 222.13, 383.3
BJ 6.378–79 Idumaeans/Titus	ἱκέτευον	κατανεύει δοῦναι δεξιὰν	71.233, 111.41, 222.13
BJ 6.433–34 John of Gischala/ Romans	δεξιὰν λαβεῖν ἱκέτευσε	request denied	74.256, 165.66, 226.36
BJ 7.202–6 Eleazar/Zealots	ἱκέτευεν	δεξαμένων	71.233
Vit. 210–12 Galilaeans/ Josephus	ἐπὶ στόμα ῥίψαντες ἑαυτοὺς	request granted	51.120
Vit. 328–29 People of Tiberias/Josephus	ῥίπτουσιν τὰ ὅπλα	spared	51.124, 71.233

1. Text fragmentary; see figs. 1.1–3. Another version: *Bilgames*, 158–79, where the introductory gesture follows a preceding plea.
2. Whether removed or not.
3. Betrayed.
4. So also *AJ* 13.232–34. All acts in *AJ* that also occur in *BJ* appear in the notes.
5. So also at *AJ* 14.15–16, with πίστεις.
6. *RE* 31.
7. *RE* 30, hereafter "Antony."
8. *RE* 2.
9. *RE* 37.
10. *RE* s.v "Pilatus, Pontius."
11. *RE* 24.
12. *RE* 7, hereafter "Cumanus."
13. So also *AJ* 20.116.
14. *RE* 9.
15. *RE* 5, hereafter "Florus."
16. Temporarily; some supplicandi remain hostile.
17. Slain by suppliant.
18. By suicide of the suppliants.
19. *RE* s.v. "Carialis," 11.
20. Only to be slain unknown to the supplicandi.
21. After which the supplicandi are deceived. They nevertheless supplicate their commander on his behalf (322).

Appendix 1e

ACTS OF SUPPLICATION WITH FOREIGN PRINCIPALS

SUPPLIANT/SUPPLICANDUS[1]	GESTURE/WORD	RESPONSE	PAGE(S)
App. Hisp. 94 Rhetogenes/Areraci	σὺν ἱκετηρίας	audience denied	
Arr. *An.* 2.24.5 Tyrians/Heracles Melkarth	ἐς τὸ ἱερὸν ... καταφυγοῦσιν	spared	19.74, 23.93
Caes. *Gal.*			
7.15.3–6 Bituriges/Gauls	procumbunt ad pedes	uenia data	25, 245.149
7.26.3–4 Gallic women/men	proiectae ad pedes suorum	rejected	25
7.48.3 Gallic women/men	manus tendebat ... liberosque in conspectum proferre	unstated	25
Curt.			
5.10.14 Traitors/Darius III	preces ... suppliciter	forgiven	237.101, 247.167
6.6.34 Rebels/Darius III	supplicibus semet dedentibus	parceret	
D.S.			
11.57.3 Mandana/Darius III	πενθίμην ἐσθῆτα λαβοῦσα ... ἱκέτευε	request denied	75.261
16.45.2–3 Sidonians/Artaxerxes III	μεθ' ἱκετηριῶν	slain	75.267, 107, 114.66
17.36.4 Satraps' wives/royal family	προσπιπτούσαις	none stated	
17.41.7–8 Youth/Melkarth Heracles	καταφυγὼν εἰς τὸ ἱερὸν	accepted	23.93
24.10.2 Elders of Hecatompylus/ Hamilcar[3]	μεθ' ἱκετηριῶν	request granted	
33.5.1–4 Marathenes/Aradians	ἱκετηρίαν κομίζοντας	slain	23.93, 45, 87
34/35.31 Adherbal[2]/Jugurtha	μεθ' ἱκετηρίας	slain	83.321
Hdt.			
1.35 Adrastus/Croesus	ἐφέστιος	accepted	38.52, 46.99
1.112 Wife/shepherd husband	λαβομένη τῶν γουνάτων	request granted	19.74, 45, 115
1.73.3 Scythians/Cyaxares	**flight** ὡς ἱκέτας	accepted	
1.73.6 Scythians/Alyattes	ἱκέται ἐγένοντο	accepted	383.1
Liv.			
29.30.2 Masinissa/Baga	supplex infimis precibus	request granted	
30.12.11–18 Sophoniba/Masinissa	genibus aduoluta	data dextra	30, 50.115, 110.32

(*continued*)

(*continued*)

Suppliant/Supplicandus[1]	Gesture/Word	Response	Page(s)
Lucianus			
Tox. 40, 42 *Dandamis/Sarmatians*	ἱκέτευε	*ransom accepted*[4]	39.58
Tox. 55 Enemies/Scythians	ἱκέται	φιλίαν ποιεῖσαι	19.74, 119.95
Plut.			
Alex. 30.5–7 Tirius/Darius III	καταβαλὼν ἐπὶ τοὺς πόδας ... ἑαυτὸν	none stated	51.120
Art. 2.2 Artaxerxes II/mother	ἱκέτης	request granted	86.343
Art. 29.6–7 Darius III/Artaxerxes II	ἐπὶ στόμα πεσόντα ... ἱκετεύειν	slain	51.120
Luc. 14.7 *Mithridates VI/Tigranes II*	ἱκέτην	*accepted*	38.52
Polyaen. 7.48.1 Salnataeons/ Hannibal the Great[5]	ἱκετεύουσιν	betrayed	128.145
Tac.			
Ann. 12.18.3–19.1 Mithridates "The Bosporan"/Eunones	genibus ... prouolutus	adleuat	110.35, 112.45
Hist. 3.48 Anicetus /king of Sedochezi	supplicem	betrayed	81.312, 112, 128, 247.163
X.			
An. 7.2.33 Seuthes/Medocus	ἐκαθεζόμην ἱκέτης	request granted	74.259
Cyr. 3.3.67 Assyrian women/ Assyrian soldiers	καταρρηγνύμεναί τε πέπλους ... ἱκετεύουσαι	not stated	19.74
Cyr. 4.6.1–10 Gorbyas/Cyrus	προσπίπτω	δέχομαί τε ἱκέτην σε καὶ ... ὑπισχνοῦμαι.	74.259, 114, 383.3

1. For Heliodorus and Josephus, who are excluded, see appendices 1a and 1d, respectively.
2. Geus, "Adherbal," 3.
3. Geus, "Hamilcar," 9.
4. Putative on supposititious acts are italicized.
5. Geus, "Hannibal," 9.

Appendix 2

Expulsion of Slaves by Temple Personnel

The most informative source for the expulsion of slaves by temple personnel and the like is a late-third-century letter by the king of Egypt, Ptolemy Euergetes.[1] In this letter, Ptolemy expresses concern about the treatment of fugitive slaves in the Heraeum on Samos, then an Egyptian dependency. The minister who received the letter from Ptolemy forwarded it to the Samians, who responded by passing a decree. Lines 1–5 of this decree, which is where the letter survives, quote either the minister or Ptolemy.

As supplemented by Habicht, lines 1–5 explain how the Samians expel some of the slaves: "concerning that part . . . is administered in Alexandria . . . to turn them over . . . whenever they have appeared at a hearing before the temple officials and clearly have a better case. Farewell."[2] "Turn them over" refers to runaways, and Habicht's supplement reads, "turn them over [to their masters]," resulting in a situation in which temple officials may perform expulsion, the same as at Andania. The phrase "a better case" indicates the standard used to judge the suppliants.[3] Lines 9–10 describe the slaves as καταφυγόντων εἰς τὸ [ἱερὸν, confirming that they have fled to the shrine.

A second source for the possible expulsion of slaves is Aristophanes, who says that an Athenian slave seeking refuge there would sit at the altar of the Theseum and announce, "I request a sale (πρᾶσιν αἰτῶ)" to a new master.[4] A priest may then have conducted a hearing, as at Andania.[5] As a result, the slave would either

---

1. Habicht, "Hellenistische Inschriften," #59.
2. Ibid., 1-5:

> [-----ca. 20--------] ΑΙ . . Υ [-------ca. 22----]
> [-----ca. 19------] περὶ τοῦ μέρους τούτου ΑΥ[. . . . .]
> [-----ca. 15----ἐν ’Α]λεξανδρείαι διοικεῖται, παραδιδόνα[ι]
> [δὲ τοῖς κυρίοις αὐτ]ῶν, ὅταν ἐπὶ τῶν νεωποιῶν δικαιολογ[η-]
> [θέντες φανεροὶ ὦσ]ιν εὐγνωμονέστερα λέγοντες· ἔρρωσθε.

2: or AC. 4: Habicht. 5: Klaffenbach.

"Hearing" to indicate that the temple officials may have only made a preliminary finding and that another body made the final decision: Thür and Taeuber, "Prozessrechtlicher Kommentar," 221. The final decision made by the temple officials: Habicht, "Hellenistische Inschriften," ad loc.

3. Habicht, "Hellenistische Inschriften," ad loc., cites a letter of T. Flamininus (SIG. 593.15-16) in which εὐγνώμονα λέγοντες refers to pleading before a magistrate.

4. A. Eq. 1311-12 with schol., PCG 577, Eupolis PCG 229.

5. Reconstructions of the hearing: Lipsius, Attische Recht, 2.643; Harrison, Procedure, 172, 180; and Klees, Herren und Sklaven, 41–42.

obtain a new master or be repossessed—and thus expelled—by his old one. Or he might argue that he was not a slave, and should be freed by means of a procedure known as *aphairesis ep' eleuthêrian*. Then the priest would refer him to a court of law. Alternatively, the slave might have the right to remain at the Theseum indefinitely, causing a standoff. However, evidence for a standoff here or elsewhere is lacking.[6] Aristophanes says nothing about a standoff or about the management of the shrine, and neither do later sources.[7]

Evidence from other locations is scantier. In Sicily, a slave refuge located amid craters near Mt. Etna allowed masters to give pledges in order to repossess their dissatisfied slaves, but Diodorus says nothing about dealings between the two sides. Nor does he mention any priests who would conduct a hearing as at Andania and Samos.[8] In Gortyn, a fifth-century law code has received a cautious interpretation by Koerner, who follows the lead of Lipsius and others by suggesting that after a year's stay, a runaway slave would be sold to a new master.[9] At Alexandria in Egypt, runaways probably had to present themselves to priests or officials, and Woess concluded that they might be sold to a new master, as at Gortyn.[10] At Phliasa in Argos, slaves enjoyed some kind of "freedom from fear," but the source does not describe this fear.[11]

At Taenarus and elsewhere, evidence for supplication by free persons combines with evidence for manumission of slaves to suggest that the slaves sought refuge as at Samos and at the Theseum, and obtained freedom as a result.[12] But manumission records do not make this plain, let alone rule out the possibility of expulsion.

The expulsion of slaves, then, was a Greek practice founded on the right of any *supplicandus* to reject those who appealed to him. The particulars of the procedure are mostly unknown, and so are the results. Yet expulsion must have been an ever-present possibility, as above and also as in a passage in Plautus's *The Rope*. Because the party expelling the slave is not a member of temple staff, discussion of this passage appears in appendix 3.

6. Suggested by Christensen, "Theseion" 24–25, the idea of a standoff runs against the juridicial character of temple supplications, including not only Andania but also Ptolemaic Egypt as in Woess, *Asylwesen Ägyptens*, 165–66, and the Ephesus of Achilles Tatius (7.13).

7. D.S. 4.62.4, schol. Aeschin 3.13, and Hsch. and Phot. s.v. Θησεῖον.

8. D.S. 11.89.6-8.

9. *I. Cret.* iv 41 col. 4.6-10 with Koerner #128.

10. *UPZ* 1.121 = *CPS* #181. Priests: Rigsby, *Asylia*, 542–43. New master: Woess, *Asylwesen Ägyptens*, 176–78.

11. ἄδεια at Phliasa: Paus. 2.13.4. Caillemer, "Asylia," 507, thought that the slaves were unexpellable.

12. *GDI* 4588–92, dedications to Poseidon including names of witnesses and a temple official, the *ephoros*. Freedom as a result: Sokolowski, "Sacral Manumission." Westermann, "*Paramone*," 9–13, describes a related practice, *paramonê*, so as to rule out supplication.

Appendix 3

Plautine Altar Supplication

Scenes of altar supplication in this author merit a separate appendix because of the unique question that they raise: Do they present a Greek procedure, a Roman procedure, a parody, or a hybrid?

In the first scene, from *Ghosts*, a slave owner learns of the part played by his slave, Tranio, in the confusion of his estate, and questions him. The setting is a street in front of a house, and the slave decides to go to an altar there. He excuses himself by saying that if he occupies the altar, it will be impossible for others to do so, including other slaves whom his master wishes to interrogate.[1] This is doubly nonsensical: one person on an altar would not keep others from using it, and no altar would protect a slave against interrogation. So far, the scene presents a parody of Greek supplication.

Unable to coax Tranio into leaving, the master now threatens to burn him. As we have seen, pursuers might burn a suppliant in order to discern the attitude of the god of the altar, but in any situation in which the *polis* provided a hearing for a suppliant, burning was unnecessary and improper. Once again, the scene parodies Greek supplication. Whether the parody derives from Plautus's Greek models is impossible to say.

Next a friend of the slave appears, and the slave suggests that this friend serve as a mediator, or *disceptator*. In regard to mediators or evaluators, Greek procedure differed from place to place, but it never allowed for a mediator chosen by the suppliant as opposed to the pursuer and the community.[2] Evidence from Andania, Ephesus, and Samos all suggests that the suppliant would go before a priest or official who would differ from a mediator by virtue of the being chosen by the *polis* and empowered to bind the parties.[3] This question aside, all the mediators and judges found in Greek supplication operate within shrines, and do not deal with refuge at an altar in a street in front of a house. We do not know how or even whether they would respond to such a situation. We do not have

---

1. Pl. *Most.* 1095.

2. A *disceptator* or mediator, that is, a person chosen by the parties and apparently unable to bind them: Cic. *Fam.* 13.26.2. For Roman mediation or, as Scafuro calls it, "arbitration," including *arbitrium ex compromiso*, see Scafuro, *Forensic Stage*, 150, and Ziegler, "Völkerrecht," 16–23.

3. Mediators: Christensen, "Theseion," who assumes that they would be chosen by the *polis* but lack the power to make a binding decision. Judges: Lipsius, *Attische Recht*, and others, as at 149–50 above.

even a single example of a slave in a Greek source taking refuge at an altar in front of a house.[4] For these reasons, we cannot characterize this part of the scene.

In the second scene, from *The Rope*, the situation is altogether different. While en route to Cyrene to be sold, two female slaves are shipwrecked. Escaping from the pimp who is their master, the girls supplicate in Cyrene's temple of Venus. Welcomed by the priestess of the temple, they go to work as servants, like Euipides' Ion, only to be overtaken by the pimp, who enters the temple and seizes them.[5] In the course of resisting him, they make two arguments: first, their being in the shrine, and second, their being freeborn and hence not the property of the pimp. The priestess intervenes to no avail.[6] So far, Plautus has reported a typical Greek procedure of slave refuge followed by priestly evaluation, and capped it with an unusual, but certainly not unprecedented, act of improper expulsion. The *nomos* at Cyrene may even have been as the play reports.[7]

After the pimp repossesses the girls, a complication arises. A citizen arrives and defends them, undoing the expulsion. Then comes another complication: the citizen turns on the pimp and expels the erstwhile repossessor.[8] Nor is Plautus through, for at this point, the stories of the girls split. One has been purchased by the citizen, who has paid earnest money for her; she happens to be freeborn. He takes the pimp to court, and in an offstage scene, the court compels the pimp to surrender her to him—yet another complication. Meanwhile, the pimp retains ownership of the other girl. No earnest money has been paid for her, and there is no proof that she is freeborn. Eventually he sells her.[9] Into what categories do these complications fall?

The first of these complications, undoing the repossession of the girls, is common practice. The pimp is acting impiously and illegally, and so a citizen takes notice and defends the suppliants, as in Greek tragedy. The next complication, the expulsion of the pimp, is common practice, too. The citizen is performing a procedure known in Athens as *apagôgê*. As for the last complication, the trial, it affirms the justice of the citizen's action. The expulsion of the wrongdoer was deemed lawful—yet another common practice. In all, these complications adhere to Greek norms, the same as the act of taking refuge in the temple of Venus.[10] Unlike the scene in *Ghosts*, the scene in the *Rope* is not a parody.

In interpreting with the *Rope*, legal scholars have concentrated on the citizen's reasons for expelling the pimp. As it happens, the citizen gives or suggests three reasons for his act. The first is legal. As the citizen says to Labrax, "Didn't you

---

4. For comment on *disceptator*, found at Cic. *Leg.* 3.3.8 in reference to the praetor, see Scafuro, *Forensic Stage*, 150; at 182, she assumes that Attic practice included mediators as opposed to judges.

5. Supplication by slaves: Pl. *Rud.* 274. Raised by priestess: 280. Temple tasks: 331–411. To the statue of the goddess to escape the advancing pimp: 559–63. Removal: 664–73. Cf. Scafuro, *Forensic Stage*, appendix 4.

6. The two arguments: Pl. *Rud.* 647-49.

7. And it may have differed from Athens, as noted by Fredershausen, *Jure Plautino*, 22.

8. *Apagôgê*, or in the victim's words: "rapior optorto collo" (868).

9. Earnest money: Pl. *Rud.* 860–63. The court's decision: 1281–83. Sale: 1408–10. Pringsheim, *Law of Sale*, 423, dismisses the possibility that the court was responding to information about her status.

10. Which is not to say that every detail has an Attic parallel. Plautus's term for judges, *recuperatores*, has no such parallel, as noted by Marx ad 1282.

receive earnest money from me on account of this girl?"[11] By this question, the citizen means that after the payment of the earnest money, the pimp had a legal obligation to surrender the girl and failed to meet this obligation. To explain this obligation, Pringsheim referred to the Greek law of sale; others have referred to Roman law. Watson referred to Roman law, but unlike Pringsheim and the others did not stress the payment of the earnest money.[12] But there are two other reasons besides this legal one. The citizen points to one of them when he says to the pimp, "Didn't you take her away?" The pimp, he is saying, has performed an improper expulsion. In addition, the pimp has violated an oath that he swore to the citizen, the remaining reason for the citizen's act, but one that the citizen does not mention. These reasons are complementary. The pimp has broken the law, offended the goddess, and committed perjury, offending the gods in general. Though he is not a kidnapper like Mnesilochus in *Women of the Thesmophoria*, he is holding a free person in captivity, the same as Mnesilochus. He is a candidate for expulsion. Resting as it does on Greek law, Roman law, and religious commonplaces, the case against him is a hybrid.[13]

What of the other girl, for whom no one had paid, and who cannot prove that she is freeborn? She went to the altar and was saved by the citizen but remained the property of the pimp. Taking refuge thus did not change her status. Contemptible though he was, the pimp was a slave owner, with an owner's right to reclaim his property. The act of taking refuge did not overthrow this right. Only refuge in conjunction with earnest money and free birth sufficed to overthrow it. For slaves, successful supplication was difficult—a truism applicable to Greece and Rome both.

---

11. Pl. *Rud.* 862–3.

12. Pringsheim, *Law of Sale*, 422–23, MacCormack, "*Arra*," 364, Watson, *Law of Obligations*, 40-41.

13. Hueffner, *de Plauti exemplis*, 27 n. 113, thought that the Greek original did not include these particulars.

Appendix 4a

IG IV 492

Phrahiaridas from Mycenae became a suppliant at the behest of Athena, [going] out of the city. In the term of office of Antias and Pyrhias, Antias, Cithius and Aeschro dismissed him.[1]

Found at the site of the sanctuary of Athena Polias at Mycenae, this plaque was thought to have been dedicated by the suppliant, Phrahiaridas.[2] The last sentence was originally translated, "Let Antias, Cithius, and Aeschro be the judges (or purifiers)." The Greek for "let . . . be the judges (or purifiers)" was EIEN, presenting several difficulties. One is syntactical: there is no predicate. Another is contextual: the optative of wish requires someone to make the wish, and the only candidate proposed was an oracle.[3] A full translation would thus be, "And the oracle says, 'Let Antias etc.'" But several collections of oracles show that oracular wishes reported in nonliterary sources are not in the optative but instead in the infinitive of indirect statement.[4] A third difficulty is typological: if the suppliant had received an oracle, he ought to have acknowledged it by making a dedication. Instead, magistrates take action regarding the suppliant. In response to these difficulties, Jeffery emended EIEN to I-IEN or ἷεν, a dialectal form of εἷσαν.[5] This requires supplying *spiritus asper*, but the inscriber omitted it when he wrote

---

1. Spelling regularized as in *IG* iv 492:
Φραιαρίδας Μυ-
κανέαθεν παρ' 'Α-
θανίας ἐς πόλιος
ἱκέτας ἔγεντο
ἐπ' Αντία καὶ Πυρ-
Fία. Εἶεν δὲ 'Αντί-
ας καὶ Κίθιος καἶσ-
χρων

2. The shrine: Boethius, *ABSA* 25.

3. By Koehler, ad loc., saying that the oracle was at Argos and that Phrahiaridas became a suppliant there, not at Mycenae. Criticism: Levi, "Gleanings," 301–2, observing that Athena is not oracular except at Alea.

4. As shown by all the Delphic oracles classified as "historical" (meaning from nonliterary sources) by Fontenrose, *The Delphic Oracle*, 244–67, and found in Parke and Wormell, *Delphic Oracle*, 2 passim. Although I have not surveyed oracles in literary sources, indirect statement is typical, e.g., the Laius oracles (S. *OC* 969-70, *OT* 713–14, A. *Th* 747–56, E. *Oedipus* fr. 59 *TGF*).

5. Jeffery, *Local Scripts*, 172, 174 n. 2. The dialectal iota instead of the diphthong epsilon-iota: Bechtel, *Dialekte*, 440. The ending εν instead of εσαν: Buck, *Greek Dialects*, 112, and Thumb, Kiecher and Scherer, *Handbuch*, 122.

ΙΚΕΤΑΣ, a few words before, and may have omitted it twice. The translation then became: "Antias, Cithius, and Aeschro dismissed him."

This translation does not mean that the magistrates provided refuge to Phrahiaridas. Had they provided refuge, the record kept of Phrahiaridas's supplication would have resembled the record of another act of supplication, this one at the temple of Apollo Maleatas in nearby Epidaurus at about the same time: "Along with his household, the Argive leader Callipus, the son of Eucles, was a suppliant of the Epidaurians at the behest of Pythian Apollo."[6] This text is a part of a dedication, not a notice, and it comes from the suppliant, Callipus, not any magistrates. If Callipus is described as a "landowner" accompanied by "slaves" rather than as a "leader" accompanied by his "household," these distinctions hold good.[7]

On this view, the inscription from Mycenae is in one sense ordinary: the suppliant is dismissed, like Pactyes. In another sense it is extraordinary: no other inscription announces this result.[8] *IG* iv 492 is a duly commemorated dismissal of a suppliant, a public record made by magistrates who could not decide to say either "yes" or "no."[9]

6. *SEG* XXVI 449, dated to 475–450 BCE.

7. "Landowner": Klees, *Herren und Sklaven,* 176–77. Background: Orlandos, "Epidauros," 104–5. "Household" and "slaves," the two translations of ϝοικιᾶται, are both unsatisfactory. For an exiled citizen to mention his household is unusual, but if "slaves" are to be significantly different from "household members," Argive history must be adduced, as by Lambrinoudakis, "Refugié argien," who links this inscription to the battle of Sepeia.

8. In contrast, several thank offerings by successful suppliants survive: *SEG* XXXIII 244d, an aryballos dedicated to Zeus *Hikesios* found on Mt. Parnes in Attica (fifth century BCE); *SEG* XXXIII 1100, a plaque dedicated to Demeter and Kore found in Paphlagonia (195–96 CE); and *Gerasa* 5–7 (Gerosa, 69–70 CE).

9. For bibliography, see Lambrinoudakis, "Refugié argien"; for comment, Marcadé's response to Lambrinoudakis, holding that the magistrates rejected the suppliant. Practically speaking, rejection of this suppliant would mean expulsion, an unusual course of action. Nothing in this inscription that shows that it occurred.

Appendix 4b

M-L #21

. . . the son of . . . achus who . . . suppliants.

Just as the crux of the previous document is the meaning of a form of *hiêmi*, the crux of this document, an early-fifth-century BCE *ostrakon*, is a lacuna for which Raubitschek proposed a form of *aphiêmi*.[1] He reads, "Aristides the son of Lysimachus, who released suppliants."[2] I read ". . . who expelled suppliants," that is, "dragged them away from the altar," using a form of *apospaô*.[3]

Whether or not Aristides is the offender named in this *ostrakon*, the offense cannot be "releasing" a suppliant, for this action is one in which the suppliant fares comparatively well. As shown by three instances in which this word appears, but especially by a passage in Thucydides, in which the Delphic oracle uses this word, the supplicandus performs this action after he has defeated the suppliants in battle and has chosen to let them go, usually under a truce.[4] Nor (for reasons given in chapter 3) can the offense be one of rejecting a suppliant. Instead the offense must be improper expulsion. Such expulsion compares with Medism, the only other offense mentioned in the *ostraka* reviewed by Meiggs and Lewis.[5]

---

1. As supplemented by Raubitschek, "Datislied": [Ἀριστείδες | ὁ Λυσιμ]άχο | [ὃς τὸ]ς ἱκέτας | [ἀπέοσ]εν.

2. Aristides since he was archon in 498–97 BCE. He might have drawn criticism for his treatment of the Aeginetans who fled to Athens and were settled at Sunium at about this time (Hdt. 6.90 but without reference to supplication). Further speculation: Welter, "Aeginetica," 30–31.

3. I.e. [ἀπέσπασ]εν, as at Str 6.1.14 and E. *Heracl.* 249 with the sense of ἀποβιάζεσθαι, the term used at Rigsby, *Asylia* #223.28, a Ptolemaic grant of asylum dated 57 BCE.

4. Th. 1.103.3, Paus. 7.1.8, Str. 6.3.2. Similar: Plut. *Ages.* 19.1 and D.C. 67.13.4, where a suppliant is "released" conditionally.

5. *M-L #21* introduction, describing about a thousand Kerameikos *ostraka*.

Appendix 5

GIGNOMAI AND *DECHOMAI* AS VERBS OF SUPPLICATION

Unnoticed in scholarship on supplication, the verbs *gignomai* and *dechomai* deserve notice not only because they are commonly used but also because they draw attention to the fourth and last step in an act of supplication, and in particular to the acceptance of a suppliant. *Gignomai hiketês*, meaning "to become a suppliant" denotes acceptance from the suppliant's perspective. *Dechomai hiketên*, "to receive a suppliant," denotes it from the perspective of the supplicandus.

The first instance of *gignomai hiketês*, "to become a suppliant," is in Herodotus; the last instance in a major author is in Clement of Alexandria.[1] This phrase refers to successful supplication in all but three instances. In Josephus, the negative *ou* is added, so the rejected party is said not to have become a suppliant. In Isocrates, this negative word is not added, and so Eurystheus is said to have "become a suppliant" only to be rejected. The same happens in Plutarch, except that the suppliant is expelled from a hearth.[2] These two instances of "becoming" and rejection must thus be considered aberrant. In both these instances and all others, the tense of the verb is aorist or perfect and the voice is middle.

Nearly as common is the phrase *dechomai hiketên* and its compounds. In the first known uses, in Homer, Hesiod, and Aeschylus, this phrase refers to the action of both divine and human supplicandi; in Sophocles, to divine supplicandi; in prose authors, to human supplicandi.[3] In two inscriptions, one from Lindos and one from Cyrene, it refers to the use of supplication as a preliminary procedure.[4] All these are instances of successful supplication, but in a third inscription the same phrase refers to unsuccessful supplication. As before, *ou* is added.[5] It also refers to unsuccessful supplication in another passage in which *apopempein*

---

1. In approximate chronological order: Hdt. 1.73.6; Th. 1.136.3; E. *IA* 1156; Isoc. 4.59, 4.63, 12.169, 12.194; Dem. *Ex.* 24.3; D.S. 11.56.1, 11.92.1, 13.24.1; J. *BJ* 1.393–94; Plut. *QG* 299d; Paus. 8.23.3, 9.5.1; App. *BC* 5.3.19; Ach. Tat. 8.2.2; Apollod. 1.9.24; Xen. Eph. 5.4.6; Plb. 38.20.1 and Clem. *Strom.* 6.3.28, with *paragignomai*; and Suid., s.v. Ἔφορος, and Eust. ad *Il.* 14.260. Two where the suppliant is dismissed: D.S. 11.56.1, 11.92.1. Successful only temporarily: D.S. 13.24.1.

2. J. *BJ* 1.393–94, Isoc. 12.169, 12.194 (both Eurystheus); Plut. *QG* 299d.

3. In approximate chronological order: *Il.* 9.480, 23.89, Hes. fr. 257, M-W A. *Supp.* 27; S. *OC* 44; Isoc. 4.63; Xen. *Cyr.* 4.6.8; schol. ad *Il.* 1.23; Plut. *Per.* 31.3; App. *BC* 1.3.26, 5.3.19; J. *BJ* 6.356–57, Apollod. 3.5.9; D.C. 42.43.4, 42.49.2, Paus. 3.5.6; Lucianus *VH* 2.21, Apollon. *Lex.* 15.3. ὡς ἱκέτην: Hld. 2.21.7.

4. Lindos: *SEG* XXXIX 729.6. Cyrene: line 55 at Servais, "Suppliants," 117–18.

5. Habicht, "Hellenistische Inschriften" #9, l. 21. Also negative: D.C. 42.43.4.

accompanies *dechomai*.[6] Once again the tense of the verb is always aorist or perfect, and the voice is always middle.

In two instances, a form of *dechomai* may refer to supplication even when *hiketês* or a similar word is missing. One such instance is Thucydides' statement that the Athenians "received" the Messenians who left Ithome. The Messenians may have supplicated the Athenians, as two groups of resettled exiles do in Pausanias.[7] Another is the Athenian treaty with Erythrae in 453–52 BCE. According to the provisions of this treaty, councilors at Erythrae were forbidden to "receive" Erythraeans who had Medized, left the city, and now sought to return. This prohibition appears in the italicized lines of the bouleutic oath imposed by Athens:

> I shall serve in the council on behalf of the majority of Erythrae and Athens and behalf of the alliance and do so as well and as justly as I can, I shall not revolt against the Athenian majority nor against their allies, whether by own accord or when persuaded by others, nor shall I desert, whether by own accord or when persuaded by others. *Without the consent of the Athenian council and people I shall not receive any of those who have fled to the Persians, whether by own accord or when persuaded by others.* And without the consent of the Athenian council and people I shall not exile anyone that remains in Erythrae."[8]

Two particulars make it likely that the italicized words refer to suppliants. First is the council's role, in Athens and elsewhere, as a body that made a preliminary evaluation of suppliants. Second is the public character of the prohibition. This, too, suits supplication at the altar of a council. In adducing these particulars, we must assume that the procedure was the same at Erythrae as at Athens, but we know it was the same at Samos as Athens.[9]

Besides drawing attention to the fourth step in supplication, the phrases "to become a suppliant" and "to receive a suppliant" signal awareness of a process. In this respect, these phrases differ from *hiketeuô* and related words, which show awareness of an act. If only because it lacks a middle voice, Latin lacks comparable phrases. Instead, a suppliant in a Latin source performs a gesture or expresses an attitude, *supplico*, and a supplicandus "receives" a suppliant in the active, *accipio*.[10] The awareness of process is Greek.

---

6. Th. 1.24.7.

7. Th. 1.103.3; Paus. 8.23.3, 9.5.1.

8. *IG* i³ 14.21–29 = M-L #40.21–29 and Tod #1.29.21–29, especially the italicized words; the spelling is regularized as in Tod.

[-----] τῶν φ[υγά]δων [κατ]αδέχσομαι οὐδ[ὲ] ἕνα οὔτ[--------------------]
[ἄλλω]ι πείσο[μ]α[ι τῶν ἐς] Μήδους φε[υ]γό[ντω]ν ἄνευ τῆ[ς] βου[λῆς τῆς]
['Αθη]ναίων καὶ [τοῦ] δήμου οὐδὲ τῶν μενόντων ἐχσελῶ [ἄ]ν[ευ] τῆς β[ου]-
[λῆς] τῆς 'Αθηναίων καὶ [τοῦ] δήμου·

As explained by Highby, *Erythrae Decree*, 24 n. 3, the words "those who have fled" are repeated.

9. As shown by *LSCG* #123 = Michel #371, where a suppliant is deemed legitimate by the Samian Council.

10. *Accipio* vel sim. including instances in which the verb is passive and the supplicandus is the agent: *B. Alex.* 32.3, Caes. *Gal.* 1.28.2, Ov. *Met.* 7.300, V. Max. 4.1.7, V. A. 3.666.

Appendix 6

Epistolary Supplication

Rather than approach in person, someone making a request may send a message such as a letter or petition. The distinction between a personal approach and a message informs a scene in Plutarch. As they flee from rebels, the attendants of the infant Pyrrhus, the future king of Epirus, encounter an impassable stream:

> Rain had made the stream rise and become violent and the darkness of the night added to the horror. They decided not to carry over the child and the women attendants on their own and when they saw some of local people on the other side, they asked them for help in crossing. Displaying Pyrrhus, they called aloud and begged (ἱκετεύοντες).

But this attempt to make an approach fails: "The country people," Plutarch explains, "could not hear for the noise and roaring of the water." So the refugees hurl a missile:

> Then one of the party stripped off a piece of bark from an oak and wrote on it with the tongue of a buckle. He explained what they needed and the situation of the child and then wrapped the bark around a stone and threw it over to the other side. . . . When the men on the other bank read the message and realized time was short, they cut down some trees, lashed them together, and crossed over.[1]

Another expedient would have been to hurl the child instead of the missile. Improbable as this is, it happens in the *Aeneid*, in which Metabus hurls his daughter, Camilla, over an impassable stream. Since he is alone, Metabus addresses a god; rather than supplicate, he prays. Like the attendants to Pyrrhus, he obtains his request.[2]

We have, then, examples of three kinds of responses: a shout that fails, a letter that succeeds, and a fulfilled prayer. The shout marks an approach, and thus is

---

1. Plut. *Pyrr.* 2.4–6. Plut. *Dio* 31.2 is similar, as is the supplication accomplished by wrapping letters around stones at Hld. 9.5.2–4.

2. Cf. V. A. 11.544–66. *Supplex:* 559. The only comparable later passage: Ov. *Ep.* 10.145–46, where Ariadne's supplicatory hands reach across the sea to the letter's recipient, Theseus.

part of an act of supplication. The letter is a substitute for an approach, and is an epistolary supplication. The prayer is neither. Having drawn this distinction, we should note the ensemble of child, escort, river, and spear, so singular that it seems to derive from a myth about the wanderings of a holy infant. This ensemble points to two features of epistolary supplication in both Plutarch and other sources beginning with Sophocles. Epistolary supplication tends to evoke actual supplication, and to archaize.[3]

In other respects, epistolary supplication may differ from the case of the infant Pyrrhus. Making a written appeal may be a matter of convenience. The supplicandus may be busy or far away; often he is a monarch atop a bureaucracy. Rather than visit him, the suppliant writes him. Sometimes the suppliant may be forced to make a written appeal because he has gone into exile. Like Pyrrhus, he finds himself on the wrong side of a divide, but not by accident. The supplicandus has put the exile in this position, and so the exile makes a written appeal to him to reverse the decision.

We now turn to two examples, one of each kind. In the first example, the suppliants could have chosen to travel to Rome to see their master, the Roman emperor, but as he is busy and far away, they decided to send a letter. Although petitions to the emperor were very common, this one, coming from Thrace in the third century CE, happens to be the only one that survives in its entirety. Addressed to the Emperor Gordion III, this petition comes from the village of Skaptopara. It begins:

> You have often written in your rescripts that in your very happy and everlasting reign villages should be inhabited and flourish rather than lie abandoned, for this wish tends towards the salvation of mankind and the profit of the sacred treasury. For that very reason we have sent *a proper and lawful supplication* to your worship, praying that you graciously nod in assent as we ask in this way.[4]

The words for "proper and lawful supplication," ἔννομον ἱκεσίαν, recollect the phrases ἔννομα and ἔννομος ἱκετεύειν, used in Attic and Samian supplications of the classical period. The emperor has replaced the assembly, and a village has replaced an individual or group, but the standard that the suppliant must meet has remained the same. The reaction expected from the supplicandus has remained the same, too, for after describing their sufferings, they ask him to take pity on them. Then they ask him to issue a ruling that will constitute the solemn pledge that concludes a supplication, and, like Attic or Samian suppliants, they ask that it be recorded on a stele.[5] The emperor's nod is one more archaism, but Homeric and not classical.[6] Since petitions were numerous, perhaps some of them were

3. S. *Ph.* 495–96.
4. Hauken, *Petition and Response*, #5.11–21, especially . . . ἔννομον ἱκεσίαν.
5. Pity: Hauken, *Petition and Response*, #5.94–99. Stele: 99–107.
6. Homeric and other nods: 111 above.

read aloud to one of the emperor's subordinates and he and not the emperor nodded in reply.[7] This use of a substitute for the supplicandus does not affect the archaism of the appeal.

Among petitions addressed to persons besides the emperor, some describe the act as the figurative presentation of a supplicatory bough, or as a way of taking refuge. Others use the language of the Greek courtroom, δέομαι καὶ ἱκετεύω, or combine supplication with *proskynêsis*.[8] The language is no less archaic if the petitioner goes to Rome and presents his petition in person to the emperor's representative or even to the emperor. In this situation, the language of democratic Athens is incongruous.[9]

An example of the second kind of epistolary supplication, a plea from an exile, takes the form of a verse letter. The author, Ovid, wrote this letter at Tomi by the Black Sea. Augustus had relegated him to this location, farther from Rome than even Skaptopara, as a punishment for offenses including writing love poetry. Realizing that Augustus (or his successor, Tiberius) would be hostile, Ovid addressed this letter and others to friends who might help him win clemency. He set himself no easy task. From Homer onward, exiles were among those who supplicated and met with rejection, and they were in no position to make further appeals. Those who dared to try did so through others: the son of Metellus Numidicus and the brother of Cicero supplicated on behalf of these two exiles, but the father himself said and did nothing, and neither did Cicero. Even the triumvir Lepidus, exiled by Augustus, did not presume to beg to return.[10]

Undeterred, Ovid wrote four books of *Epistulae Ex Ponto*. The second letter in Book 2 is the one that resembles Plutarch or the Thracian petition. First Ovid uses the language of Greek temple refuge. Granted that Ovid is a wrongdoer, he is not the worst of wrongdoers, a "violator of a temple":

> From time to time a violator of a temple flees to an altar, and does not fear to ask for help from the offended god.[11]

The poet acknowledges an obvious objection to his appeal: "Someone may say that this action is not safe. I admit it." Ovid now turns to Euripides, the best-known poet of supplication. Euripides launched the fashion of comparing suppliants to animals. The title characters in *The Suppliant Women* say,

7. Speculation on this point: Millar, "Empereur comme décideur," 217.

8. Boughs: *PStrassb.* 4.285.18, *PTeb.* 2.326.3, *POxy.* 1.71.3, *PSI* 13.337.18, all third century CE and later. Two literary examples: Jul. *Caes.* 275c, *Alex. Rom.* 26.107–9. Refuge: *PEnteux.* 82.8 from 221 BCE, *PLond.* 7.2045.4 from the third century CE. δέομαι καὶ ἱκετεύω: *PCair. Zenon* 4.59421.1, 4.59520.8, *PCol.* 3.6.7, all Ptolemaic; *PMich.* 1.87.5 from the third century CE; and *PSI* 4.402.7, sixth century CE. Proskynêsis: *P. Oxy.* 14.3366.2 from 266 CE. Mere supplication: *IG* ii² 2.1.1094.3, 211–22 CE; *OGI* 519, 244–47 CE.

9. I follow Wilcken, "Kaiserreskripten," 2–6, in distinguishing between *epistulae*, of which the letter to Gordion provides an example, and *subscriptiones* that were petitions presented by individuals, not communities. The latter are more likely to accompany an act of supplication by the party making the request.

10. Suet. *Aug.* 16.4 describes this exile, which was internal, like Ovid's, as "relegatio."

11. Ov. *Pont.* 2.2.27–29.

> An animal finds refuge beside a rock, a slave beside the altars of the gods, and a storm-beaten city cowers beside a city.[12]

Later writers went further and compared suppliants to grasshoppers, fish, sparrows, cockerels, doves, rabbits, kids, deer, boars, elephants, and lions, many in temples.[13] But these writers were usually Greek poets. Roman writers avoided this trope, which was inappropriate for suppliants modeling themselves on Metellus Pius. Ovid had compared suppliants and animals in the *Metamorphoses*, but in order to observe that supplicating animals lack hands and voices.[14] In his letter, though, Ovid speaks as the suppliant women did: "Fearing a hawk, an exhausted bird with trembling wings dares to approach a human being's lap."[15] Ovid's two comparisons are vivid and immediate. The temple violator must be forgiven or punished, and the bird must be taken in or put out. Ovid is creating a sense of urgency meant to annihilate the distance between himself and his supplicandus. Where earlier petitioners hurled spears, he hurls a missive that he hopes will fly with a bird's swiftness.

We should remember that Ovid's archaic appeals and those of the Thracians both fall short of an act of supplication. The individual or community presenting the request does not usually appear in person, so at most we might speak of an act of intercession. The supplicandus may not appear in person, either, and then the procedure becomes entirely literary. For petitioners like the Thracians, a literary procedure may be prestigious. For Ovid and his readers, it is poignant, a *tour de force* and yet a failure.

Most written requests no doubt lacked archaisms. Several requests in Ovid lack archaisms, and so do requests in Tacitus.[16] When comparing his own requests to those made on behalf of supplicating Dacian captives, Martial eschews archaic diction, too.[17] Archaism was perhaps more common in the late-antique, bureaucratic documents like the petition from Thrace. Here it expresses a twofold nostalgia. First, it evokes a world small enough for a suppliant to reach and touch a supplicandus. Second, it defers to precedent. Eyes trained on the past, the writers of these documents move backward toward their goal. They anticipate suppliants in today's world of rights.

---

12. E. *Supp.* 268–70.
13. Grasshoppers: Longus 1.26.3. Fish: Philostrat. *VA* 1.23. Sparrow: D.L. 4.10. Cockerels: Iamb. *VP* 48 [= 58 C 5 D-K]. Kid: Longus 1.6.1. Deer: V. A. 7.500–502, Phaed. 2.8.8, Mart. *Sp.* 29.4. Rabbit in temple: St. Byz., s.v. Ἑκατήσια. Boar in temple: Ps.-Plut. *Fluv.* 21. Elephants: Ael. *NA* 4.10, Plin. *NH* 8.21. Lions: 8.57.
14. Hence Io can do nothing more than low when supplicating Argus (*Met.* 1.633–36). Callisto and Actaeon suffer in the same way (2.477–84, 3.237–41).
15. Ov. *Pont.* 2.35–36.
16. Ov. *Pont.* 2.8.44, 2.9.5; Tac. *Ann.* 2.63.1 and 15.30. So also Gran. *Ann.* 33.6 and Curt. 5.3.14–15, *Alex. Rom.* 26.107–9. A supplicatory book: Mart. *Ep.* pr. 8. Others' supplicatory *libelli*: 8.31.3.
17. Mart. 6.10.5–8.

Bibliography

Adam, T. *Clementia Principis; Der Einfluss hellenistischer Fürstenspiegel auf den Versuch einer rechtlichen Fundierung des Principats durch Seneca* (Stuttgart 1970).

Adams, W. L. "Macedonian Kingship and the Right of Petition," in *Ancient Macedonia* 4. *Institute for Balkan Studies* 204 (Thessalonica 1986) 43–52.

Ahl, F., and H. Roisman. *The* Odyssey *Reformed* (Ithaca, N.Y. 1996).

Aleshire, S. *The Athenian Asclepieion: The People, Their Dedications, and the Inventories* (Amsterdam 1989).

Alexander, M. L. *Trials in the Late Roman Republic* (Toronto 1990).

Altheim, F. *A History of Roman Religion*, tr. H. Mattingly (New York 1938).

Arend, W. *Die typischen Scenen bei Homer* (Berlin 1933).

Arendt, H. "The Decline of the Nation-State and the End of the Rights of Man," in *The Origins of Totalitarianism* (London 1967) 267–302.

Asad, T. *Genealogies of Religion: Discipline and Reasons of Power in Christianity and Islam* (Baltimore 1993).

Aubriot-Sévin, D. "Les *litai* d'Homère et la *diké* d'Hésiode," *REG* 97 (1984) 1–25.

———. *Prière et conceptions religieuses en Grèce ancienne jusqu' à la fin du Ve siècle avant J.-C.* (Lyon 1992).

Auffarth, C. "Protecting Strangers: Establishing a Fundamental Value in the Religions of the Ancient Near East and Greece," *Numen* 39 (1992) 194–210.

Austin, J. L. *How to Do Things with Words* (Cambridge, Mass. 1975[2]).

Badian, E. *From Plataea to Potidaea: Studies in the History and Historiography of the Pentecontaetia* (Baltimore 1993).

———. "The Road to Prominence," in *Demosthenes, Statesman and Orator*, ed. I. Worthington (London 2000) 9–35.

Balzarini, M. *De iniuria extra ordinem statui: contributo allo studio del diritto penale romano dell' età classica* (Padua 1983).

Barden, M. *The Development of* Clementia *during the Roman Principate* (diss. Columbia University 1995).

Barkun, M. *Law without Sanctions: Order in Primitive Societies and the World Community* (New Haven, Conn. 1968).

Barmash, P. *Homicide in the Biblical World* (Cambridge 2005).

Barnes, J. *A Cambridge Companion to Aristotle* (Cambridge 1995).

Barth, B. *De Graecorum asylis* (Strasbourg 1888).

Bauman, R. *Impietas in principem: A Study of Treason against the Roman Emperor with Special Reference to the First Century A.D. Münchener Beiträge zur Papyrusforschung und antiken Rechtsgeschichte* 67 (Munich 1974).

Baumgarten, A. I. *Sacrifice in Religious Experience* (Boston 2002).

Beare, R. "The Imperial Oath Under Julius Caesar," *Latomus* 38 (1979) 469–73.

Bearzot, C. *Lisia e la tradzione su Teramene: commento storico alle orazioni xii et xiii del corpus lysiacum* (Milan 1997).

Beaujon, E. *Le dieu des suppliants* (Neuchâtel 1960).

Bechtel, F. *Die griechischen Dialekte* (Berlin 1921–24).

Bell, C. *Ritual: Perspectives and Dimensions* (Oxford 1997).

Bell, H. "*Philanthropia* in the Papyri of the Roman Period," in *Hommage à Joseph Bidez et à Franz Cumont* (Brussels 1940) 31–37.

Bellen, H. *Studien zur Sklavenflucht im römischen Kaiserreich. Forschungen zur antiken Sklaverei* 4 (Wiesbaden 1971).

Beness, J., and T. Hillard. "The Theatricality of the Deaths of C. Gracchus and Friends," *CQ* 51 (2001) 135–40.

Benveniste, E. *Le vocabulaire des institutions indo-européennes* (Paris 1969).

Bers, V. "Dicastic *Thorubos*," in *Crux: Essays Presented to G. E. M. de Ste Croix on his 75th Birthday,* ed. P. A. Cartledge and F. D. Harvey (London 1985) 1–15.

Bickerman, E. J. "*Autonomia*: sur un passage de Thucydide (I,144,2)," *RIDA* 5 (1958) 313–44.

Birdwhistell, R. *Kinesics and Context: Essays on Body Motion Communication* (Philadelphia 1970).

Blech, M. *Studien zum Kranz bei den Griechen* (Berlin 1982).

Bloch, M. "Symbols, Song, Dance, and Features of Articulation," *Archives européennes de sociologie* 15 (1974) 55–81.

———. "Property and the End of Affinity," in *Marxist Analyses and Social Anthropology,* ed. M. Bloch (New York 1975) 203–29.

———. *Prey into Hunter: The Politics of Religious Experience* (Cambridge 1992).

Blundell, M. W. *Helping Friends and Harming Enemies: A Study in Sophocles and Greek Ethics* (Cambridge 1989).

Boegehold, A. *When a Gesture Was Expected* (Princeton, N.J. 1999).

Boethius, C. "Hellenistic Mycenae," *ABSA* 25 (1921–23) 408–29.

Bonner, S. F. *Roman Declamation in the Late Republic and Early Empire* (Berkeley, Calif. 1949).

Bourdieu, P. *Language and Symbolic Power,* tr. J. Thompson (Cambridge 1991).

Bowersock, G. W. "The Mechanics of Subversion in the Roman Provinces," in *Opposition et résistances à l'empire d'Auguste à Trajan. Entretiens Hardt* 23, ed. A. Giovannini (Geneva 1987) 291–320.

Bradley, K. *Slavery and Society at Rome* (Cambridge 1994).

Bravo, B. "*Sulân*: Représailles et justice privée contre les étrangers dans les cités grecques. Étude du vocabulaire et des institutions," *Annali della scuola normale superiore de Pisa, classe di lettere e filosofia* (ser. 3) 10 (Pisa 1980) 675–989.

Bremmer, J. N. "Gelon's Wife and the Carthaginian Ambassadors," *Mnemosyne* 33 (1980) 366–68.

———. "Walking, Standing, and Sitting in Ancient Greek Culture," in *A Cultural History of Gesture: From Antiquity to the Present Day,* ed. J. N. Bremmer and H. Rodenburg (Cambridge 1991) 16–33.

———. "Religion, Ritual and the Opposition 'Sacred vs. Profane': Notes towards a Terminological 'Genealogy'," in *Ansichten griechischer Rituale,* ed. F. Graf (Stuttgart 1998) 9–33.

Brennan, C. *The Praetorship in the Roman Republic* (Oxford 2000).

Briant, P. *Histoire de l'empire perse de Cyrus à Alexandre* (Paris 1996).

Brilliant, R. *Gesture and Rank in Roman Art: The Use of Gestures to Denote Status in Roman Sculpture and Coinage. Memoirs of the Connecticut Academy of Arts and Sciences* 14 (New Haven, Conn. 1963).

Bruggisser, P. *Romulus Servianus: la légende de Romulus dans les commentaires à Virgile de Servius* (Bonn 1987).

Brunt, P. A. "*Laus Imperii*," in *Roman Imperial Themes* (Oxford 1990) 288–323.

Buck, C. D. *The Greek Dialects* (Chicago 1968⁴).

Buckland, W. *The Roman Law of Slavery* (Cambridge 1908).

Bulmerincq, A. *Das Asylrecht in seiner geschichtlichen Entwickelung beurtheilt vom Standpunkte des Rechts und dessen völkerrechtliche Bedeutung für die Auslieferung flüchtiger Verbrecher: eine Abhandlung aus dem Gebiete der universellen Rechtsgeschichte und des positiven Völkerrechts* (Dorpat 1853).

Burchfiel, K. "The Myth of Prelaw," in *Symposion 1993*, ed. G. Thür (Cologne 1994) 79–105.

Burian, P. *Suppliant Drama: Studies in the Form and Interpretation of Five Greek Tragedies* (diss. Princeton University 1971).

———. "Supplication and Hero Cult in Sophocles' *Ajax*," *GRBS* 13 (1972) 151–56.

Burkert, W. *Zum altgriechischen Mitleidsbegriff* (diss. University of Würzburg 1955).

———. *Structure and History in Greek Mythology and Ritual* (Berkeley, Calif. 1979).

———. *Homo Necans*, tr. P. Bing (Berkeley, Calif. 1983).

———. *Greek Religion*, tr. J. Raffan (Cambridge, Mass. 1985).

———. *The Creation of the Sacred: Tracks of Biology in Early Religions* (Cambridge, Mass. 1996).

Burnett, A. "Human Resistance and Divine Persuasion in Euripides' *Ion*," *CP* 57 (1962) 89–104.

Bursian, C. "Über das Vorgebirg Taenaron," *ABAW, philosophisch-philologische Klasse* 7 (1855) 771–95.

Busolt, G. *Griechische Geschichte bis zur Schlacht bei Chaeroneia* (Gotha 1893–1904, reprinted Hildesheim 1967).

Caillemer, E. "Asylia," D-S 1.505–10.

Cairns, D. *Aidos:The Psychology and Ethics of Honour and Shame in Ancient Greek Literature* (Oxford 1993).

———. "Representations of Remorse and Reparation in Classical Greece," in *Remorse and Reparation*, ed. M. Cox (London 1999) 171–79.

Calmeyer, P. *Reliefbronzen in babylonischem Stil. ABAW, philosophisch-historische Klasse* (new ser.) 73 (Munich 1973).

Cantarella, E. *Norma e sanzione in Omero: contributo alla protostoria del diritto greco* (Milan 1979).

Carey, C. *Lysias: Selected Speeches* (Cambridge 1989).

———. "*Nomos* in Athenian Rhetoric and Oratory," *JHS* 116 (1996) 33–46.

———. "The Shape of Athenian Laws," *CQ* 48 (1998) 93–109.

Carlholm, G. *Tractatus de asylis* (Uppsala 1682).

Cartledge, P. A. *Agesilaos and the Crisis of Sparta* (London 1987).

———. Rev. of *The Polis as an Urban Centre and as a Political Community*, ed. M. Hansen, in *CR* 49 (1999) 465–69.

———. *Sparta and Lakonia: A Regional History, 1300–362 B.C.* (London 2002²).

Chaniotis, A. "Asylon," in *Der neue Pauly. Enzyklopädie der Antike*, ed. H. Cancik and H. Schneider (Stuttgart 1996) 2.143–44.

———. "Conflicting Authorities: *Asylia* between Secular and Divine Law in the Classical and Hellenistic Poleis," *Kernos* 9 (1996) 65–86.

———. "Justifying Territorial Claims in Classical and Hellenistic Greece: The Beginnings of International Law," in *The Law and the Courts in Ancient Greece*, ed. E. Harris and L. Rubenstein (London 2004) 185–229.

Chantraine, P. *Dictionnaire étymologique de la langue grecque* (Paris 1999²).

Christensen, K. "The Theseion: A Slave Refuge at Athens," *AJAH* 9 (1984) [1990] 23–33.

Clark, M. "Chryses' Supplication: Speech Act and Mythological Allusion," *CA* 17 (1998) 5–24.

Clausen, W. *Virgil's Aeneid and the Tradition of Hellenistic Poetry* (Berkeley, Calif. 1987).

Clinton, K. "Maroneia and Rome: Two Decrees of Maroneia from Samothrace," *Chiron* 33 (2003) 379–417.

Cohen, D. "Prosecution of Impiety in Athenian Law," *ZRG* 105 (1988) 695–701.

———. *Law, Violence, and Community in Classical Athens* (Cambridge 1995).

Coleman, K. "Fatal Charades: Roman Executions Staged as Mythological Enactments," *JRS* 80 (1990) 44–74.

Collmann, W. *De Diodori Siculi fontibus commentationis criticae capita quattuor* (Marburg 1869).

Cook, A. B. *Zeus: A Study in Ancient Religion* (Cambridge 1914–40).

Cooper, C. "Hyperides and the Trial of Phryne," *Phoenix* 49 (1995) 303–18.

Cooper, J. *Reason and Emotion: Essays on Ancient Moral Psychology and Ethical Theory* (Princeton, N.J. 1999).

Crotty, K. *The Poetics of Supplication: Homer's* Iliad *and* Odyssey (Ithaca, N.Y. 1994).

———. *Law's Interior: Legal and Literary Constructions of the Self* (Ithaca, N.Y. 2001).

Crusius, G. C. *Ilias*. Hanover (1852–64³).

Dahlheim, W. *Struktur und Entwicklung des römischen Völkerrechts im dritten und zweiten Jahrhundert v. Chr. Vestigia* 8 (Munich 1968).

David, M. "Die Bestimmungen über die Asylstädte in Josua XX," *OTS* 9 (1951) 30–48.

de Jong, J. *De iure iurando apud Aeschylum, Sophoclem, Euripidem observationes* (Rotterdam 1910).

de Morgan, J., et al. *Recherches archéologiques. Première série. Fouilles à Suse en 1897–1898 et 1898–1899* (Paris 1900).

de Polignac, F. *La naissance de la cité grecque: cultes, espace et société VIIIe-VIIe siècles avant J.-C.* (Paris 1984).

de Romilly, J. *Thucydide et l'impérialisme athénien* (Paris 1947).

———. *La loi dans la pensée grecque: des origines à Aristote* (Paris 1971).

———. "L'assemblée du peuple dans l'*Oreste* d'Euripide," in *Studi classici in onore di Quintino Cataudella* (Catania 1972) 1.237–51.

de Ste. Croix, G. E. M. *The Class Struggle in the Ancient Greek World* (London 1973).

Debord, P. "L'esclavage sacré: état de la question," in *Actes du colloque 1971 sur l'esclavage. Annales littéraires de l'Université de Besançon* 140 (Paris 1972) 135–50.

Delatte, A. *Le baiser, l'agenouillement et le prosternement de l'adoration: proskynesis chez les Grecs. Academie royale de Belgique, bulletin de la classe des lettres et des sciences morales et politiques* 37 (Brussels 1951).

Deonna, W. "Le genou, siège de la force et de vie et sa protection magique," *RA* 6 (1939) 224–35.

Derlien, J. *Asyl: Die religiöse und rechtliche Begründung der Flucht zu sakralen Orten in der griechisch-römishen Antike* (Marburg 2003).

Derrida, J. *On Cosmopolitanism and Forgiveness*, tr. M. Dooley and M. Hughes (London 2001).

Dignas, B. *The Economy of the Sacred in Hellenistic and Roman Asia Minor* (Oxford 2002).

Dillon, M. *Pilgrims and Pilgrimage in Ancient Greece* (London 1997).

Doederlein, L. *Ilias* (Leipzig 1863).

Donlan, W. "Reciprocities in Homer," *CW* 75 (1982) 137–75.

Donnelly, J. *Universal Human Rights in Theory and Practice* (Ithaca, N.Y. 1989).

Douglas, M. *Natural Symbols* (New York 1973).

Dover, K. J. *Greek Popular Morality in the Time of Plato and Aristotle* (Oxford 1974).

Dreher, M. "Zu *IG* ii² 404, dem athenischen Volksbeschluss über die Eigenstaatlichkeit der keischen Poleis," in *Symposion* 1985, ed. G. Thür (Cologne 1989) 263–81.

———. "Das Asyl von seinen griechischen Ursprüngen bis zur christlichen Spätantike," *Tyche* 11 (1996) 79–96.

———. "Rom und die griechischen Asyle," forthcoming in *Symposion* 2001, ed. G. Thür.

Ducrey, P. *Le traitement des prisonniers de guerre dans la Grèce antique des origines à la conquête romaine* (Paris 1968).

Dumont, J. C. *Servus: Rome et l'esclavage sous la république* (Paris 1987).

Durkheim, E. *Les formes élémentaires de la vie religieuse: le système totémique en Australie* (Paris 1925²).

Dyer, R. R. "Rhetoric and Intention in Cicero's *Pro Marcello*," *JRS* 80 (1990) 17–30.

Dyson, J. *The King of the Wood: The Sacrificial Victor in Virgil's* Aeneid (Norman, Okla. 2001).

Edelstein, L., and E. Edelstein. *Asclepius* (Baltimore 1945).

Eilers, C. *Roman Patrons of Greek Cities* (Oxford 2002).

England, W. *The Laws of Plato* (Manchester 1921).

Enzensburger, H. *Aussichten auf den Bürgerkrieg* (Frankfurt am Main 1993).

Ernout, A., and A. Meillet. *Dictionnaire étymologique de la langue latine* (Paris 1979⁴).

Fauth, W. "Asylon," in *Der kleine Pauly. Lexikon der Antike*, ed. K. Ziegler and W. Sontheimer (Stuttgart 1974) 1.670–71.

Fenik, B. *Studies in the* Odyssey (Wiesbaden 1974).

———. *Homer and the* Nibelungenlied (Cambridge, Mass. 1986).

Ferrari, G. "Figures of Speech: The Picture of *Aidos*," *Métis* 5 (1990) 185–204.

———. "Figures in the Text: Metaphors and Riddles in the *Agamemnon*," *CP* 92 (1997) 1–45.

Finley, M. I. *The Ancient Greeks* (London 1963).

Fitzgerald, R. *The Aeneid* (Garden City, N.Y. 1974).

Fitzgerald, W. *Slavery and the Roman Literary Imagination: Roman Literature and Its Contexts* (Cambridge 2000).

Fontenrose, J. *The Delphic Oracle: Its Responses and Operations* (Berkeley, Calif. 1978).

Forsythe, D. P. *Human Rights in International Relations* (Cambridge 2000).

Fowler, R. "Greek Magic, Greek Religion," in *Oxford Readings in Greek Religion*, ed. R. Buxton (Oxford 2000) 317–44.

Frazer, J. G. *Pausanias's Description of Greece* (London 1898).

Fredershausen, O. *De jure Plautino et Terentiano* (diss. University of Göttingen 1906).

Freyburger, G. "Supplication grecque et supplication romaine," *Latomus* 47 (1988) 501–25.

———. "Le droit d'asile à Rome," *LEC* 60 (1992) 139–51.

Furneaux, H. *The Annals of Tacitus* (Oxford 1896²).

Gagarin, M. *Drakon and Early Athenian Homicide Law* (New Haven, Conn. 1981).

———. *Early Greek Law* (Berkeley 1986).

Galinsky, K. "The Anger of Aeneas," *AJP* 109 (1988) 321–48.

Gamauf, R. *Ad statuam licet confugere: Untersuchungen zum Asylrecht im römischen Prinzipat* (Frankfurt am Main 1999).

Garlan, Y. "War, Piracy, and Slavery in the Greek World," in *Classical Slavery*, ed. M. I. Finley (London 1987) 7–21.

Garvie, A. F. *Aeschylus' Supplices: Play and Trilogy* (Cambridge 1969).

Gauthier, P. *Symbola: Les étrangers et la justice dans les cités grecques* (Nancy 1972).

———. *Les cités grecques et leur bienfaiteurs. BCH Supp.* 12 (Paris 1985).

Gernet, L. "Quelques rapports entre la pénalité et la réligion dans la Grèce ancienne," *AC* 5 (1936) 325–39, reprinted in *Anthropologie de la Grèce antique* (Paris 1968) 288–301.

―――. "Droit et prédroit en Grèce ancienne," *L'année sociologique* 3 (1948–49) 21–119, reprinted in *Anthropologie de la Grèce antique* (Paris 1968) 175–260.

Giordano, M. *La supplica: Rituale, istituzione sociale e tema epico in Omero. Annali dell' istituto universitario orientale* 3 (Naples 1999).

Gödde, S. "Hikesie," in the *Der neue Pauly. Enzyklopädie der Antike,* ed. H. Cancik and H. Schneider (Stuttgart 1998) 3.554–55.

―――. *Das Drama der Hikesie: Ritual und Rhetorik in Aischylos'* Hiketiden. *Orbis Antiquus* 35 (Münster 2000).

Goldhill, S. "Supplication and Authorial Comment in the *Iliad: Iliad* Z 61–2," *Hermes* (1990) 118: 373–77.

Gomme, A. W., et al. *A Historical Commentary on Thucydides* (Oxford 1945–81).

Gomme, A. W., and F. Sandbach. *Menander: A Commentary* (Oxford 1973).

Gould, J. *"Hiketeia," JHS* 93 (1973) 74–103.

Greenidge, A. H. J. *The Legal Procedure of Cicero's Time* (Oxford 1901).

Gruber, M. *Aspects of Nonverbal Communication in the Ancient Near East* (Rome 1980).

Gruen, E. "Greek πίστις and Roman *fides*," *Athenaeum* 70 (1982) 50–68.

Gunderson, E. "Discovering the Body in Roman Oratory," in *Parchments of Gender: Deciphering the Bodies of Antiquity,* ed. M. Wyke (Oxford 1998) 169–89.

Habicht, C. "Samische Volksbeschlüsse der hellenistischen Zeit," *MDAI(A)* 72 (1957) 224–31 [= #59].

―――. *Die Inschriften des Asklepieions. Altertümer von Pergamon* 8.3 (Berlin 1969).

―――. "Hellenistische Inschriften aus dem Heraion von Samos," *MDAI(A)* 87 (1972) 210–12 [= #9].

Hainsworth, B. *The Iliad: A Commentary, Volume 3* (Cambridge 1993).

Hall, E. *Inventing the Barbarian: Greek Self-Definition through Tragedy* (Oxford 1989).

Halliwell, S. "The Uses of Laughter in Greek Culture," *CQ* 41 (1991) 279–96.

Halm, K. *Über einige controverse Stellen in der Germania des Tacitus* (Munich 1864).

Hamel, D. *The Athenian Generals: Military Authority in the Classical Period. Mnemosyne Supp.* 182 (Leiden 1998).

Hammond, N. L. G. *Epirus: The Geography, the Ancient Remains, the History and the Topography of Epirus and Adjacent Areas* (Oxford 1967).

Hamp, E. "Φίλος," *BSL* 77 (1982) 251–62.

Handley, E., and J. Rea. *The Telephos of Euripides. BICS Supp.* 5 (London 1957).

Hands, A. R. *Charities and Social Aid in Greece and Rome* (Ithaca, N.Y. 1968).

Hansen, M. *Apagoge, Endeixis, and Ephegesis against Kakurgoi, Atimoi, and Pheugontes* (Copenhagen 1976).

―――. *"Procheirotonia* in the Athenian *Ecclesia,"* in *The Athenian Ecclesia* (Copenhagen 1983) 123–30.

―――. *Polis and City-State: An Ancient Concept and Its Modern Equivalent. Acts of the Copenhagen Polis Centre* 5 (Copenhagen 1998).

Harding, J., and R. Ireland. *Punishment: Rhetoric, Rule, and Practice* (London 1989).

Harris, E. *Aeschines* (Oxford 1994).

―――. "Antigone the Lawyer," in *The Law and the Courts in Ancient Greece,* ed. E. Harris and L. Rubenstein (London 2004) 19–57.

―――. "Le rôle de l'*epieikeia* dans les tribunaux athéniens," in *Revue historique du droit français et étranger* 82 (2004) 1–13.

Harris, W. *Restraining Rage: The Ideology of Anger Control in Classical Antiquity* (Cambridge, Mass. 2001).

Harrison, A. R. W. *The Law of Athens, II: The Procedure* (Oxford 1971).

Harrison, J. *Themis: A Study of the Social Origins of Greek Religion* (Cambridge 1912).

Hart, H. L. A. *The Concept of Law* (Oxford 1961).

Hart, M. *Athens and Troy: The Narrative Treatment of the* Iliou Persis *in Archaic Athenian Vase-Painting* (diss. UCLA 1992).

Hauken, T. *Petition and Response: An Epigraphic Study of Petitions to Roman Emperors, 181–249* (Bergen 1998).

Havelock, E. A. *The Liberal Temper in Greek Politics* (New Haven, Conn. 1957).

Hegel, G. *Phenomenology of Spirit,* tr. A. Miller (Oxford 1977).

Hellwig, A. *Das Asylrecht der Naturvölker. Juristische Beiträge* 1 (Berlin 1903).

Henrichs, A. "The Tomb of Aias and the Prospect of Hero Cult in Sophokles," *CA* 12 (1993) 165–80.

———. "'Why Should I Dance': Choral Self-Referentiality in Greek Tragedy," *Arion* (ser. 3) 3 (1994–95) 56–111.

Henssler, O. *Formen des Asylrechts und ihre Verbreitung bei den Germanen.* (Frankfurt am Main 1954).

Herman, G. *Ritualised Friendship and the Greek City* (Cambridge 1987).

Hermann, G. *Sophoclis tragoediae* (Leipzig 1830³).

Heubeck, A., and A. Hoekstra. *A Commentary on Homer's Odyssey, Volume 2* (Oxford 1989).

Heuss, A. *Die völkerrechtlichen Grundlagen der römischen Aussenpolitik in republikanischer Zeit. Klio Beiheft* 31 (Leipzig 1933).

Higbie, C. *Heroes' Names, Homeric Identities* (Oxford 1995).

Highby, R. *The Erythrae Decree. Klio Beiheft* 36 (Berlin 1936).

Hirzel, R. *Agraphos Nomos* (Leipzig 1900).

———. *Der Eid: Ein Beitrag zu seiner Geschichte* (Leipzig 1902, reprinted Aalen 1966).

Hölkeskamp, K.-J. "Fides—deditio in fidem—dextra data et accepta: Recht, Religion, und Ritual in Rom," in *The Roman Middle Republic: Politics, Religion, and Historiography c. 400–133 B.C.,* ed. C. Bruun (Rome 2000) 223–50.

Hölscher, T. *Victoria Romana: Archäologische Untersuchungen zur Geschichte und Wesensart der römischen Siegesgöttin von den Anfängen bis zum Ende des 3. Jhrs. n. Chr.* (Mainz 1967).

Holman, S. R. *The Hungry Are Dying: Beggars and Bishops in Roman Cappadocia* (Oxford 2001).

Holoka, J. "Looking Darkly, ὑπόδρα ἰδών: Reflections on Status and Decorum in Homer," *TAPA* 113 (1983) 1–16.

Homolle, T. "Inscriptions d'Amorgos," *BCH* 25 (1901) 412–30.

Hopkins, K. *Conquerors and Slaves* (Cambridge 1978).

———. "Novel Evidence for Roman Slavery," *Past and Present* 138 (1993) 3–27.

Hornblower, S. *A Commentary on Thucydides* (Oxford 1991–).

Horsfall, N. *A Companion to the Study of Virgil. Mnemosyne Supp.* 151 (Leiden 1995).

Howald, E. "Meleager und Achill," *RhM* 73 (1924) 402–25.

Hueffner, F. *De Plauti comoediarum exemplis atticis quaestiones maxime chronologicae* (Göttingen 1894).

Hunter, V. *Policing Athens: Social Control in the Attic Lawsuits, 420–320 B.C.* (Princeton, N.J. 1994).

Jacoby, F. "*Chrestous Poiein,*" *CQ* 38 (1944) 15–16.

Jebb, R. C. *Sophocles: The Plays and Fragments* (Cambridge 1890–1924).

Jeffery, L. *The Local Scripts of Archaic Greece* (Oxford 1990²).

Jessen, H. "*Hikesios, Hikesia,*" *RE* (1st ser.) 8.2.1592–93.

Johnstone, S. *Disputes and Democracy: The Consequences of Litigation in Ancient Athens* (Austin, Tex. 1999).

Jolowitcz, H. F. *Historical Introduction to the Study of Roman Law* (Cambridge 1967²).

Jones, A. M. H. *Sparta* (Cambridge, Mass. 1967).

Jost, M. *Sanctuaires et cultes d'Arcadie. Études péloponnésiennes* 9 (Paris 1985).

Kahrshtadt, U. *Griechisches Staatsrecht* (Göttingen 1922).

Kaimio, M. *Physical Contact in Greek Tragedy: A Study of Stage Conventions. Annales Academiae Scientarum Fennicae* 244 (Helsinki 1988).

Kakridis, J. T. *Homeric Researches* (Lund 1949).

Kamerbeek, J. C. *The Plays of Sophocles* (Leiden 1953–84).

Kearney, J. "*Alitemon: Il.* 24.157," *Glotta* 59 (1981) 67–69.

Kehoe, D. P. *Investment, Profit, and Tenancy: The Jurists and the Roman Agrarian Economy* (Ann Arbor, Mich. 1997).

Kendon, A. "Introduction: Current Issues in the Study of Nonverbal Communication," in *Noverbal Communication, Interaction, and Gesture: Selections from "Semiotica,"* ed. A. Kendon (The Hague 1981) 1–57.

Kiechle, F. *Messenische Studien: Untersuchungen zur Geschichte der Messenischen Kriege und der Auswanderung der Messenier* (Kallmünz 1959).

Klees, H. *Herren und Sklaven: d. Sklaverei im oikonom. u. polit. Schrifttum d. Griechen in klass. Zeit. Forschungen zur antiken Sklaverei* 6 (Wiesbaden 1975).

Knippschild, S. "*Drum Bietet zum Bunde die Hände": rechtssymbolische Acte in zwischenstaatlichen Beziehungen im orientalischen und griechisch-römischen Altertum* (Stuttgart 2002).

Koch, C. "Vesta," *RE* (2nd ser.) 8.1718–75.

Kolb, F. *Agora und Theater: Volks- und Festversammlung* (Berlin 1981).

———. *Herrscherideologie in der Spätantike* (Berlin 2001).

Konstan, D. *Pity Transformed* (London 2001).

Kontorini, V. *Anekdotes epigraphes Rodou II* (Athens 1989).

Kopperschmidt, J. *Die Hikesie als dramatische Form: Zur motivischen Interpretation des griechischen Dramas* (diss. University of Tübingen 1967).

Koschaker, P. *Über einige griechische Rechtsurkunden aus den östlichen Randgebieten des Hellenismus. Abhandlungen der sächsischen Akademie der Wissenschaften zu Leipzig, philologisch-historische Klasse* 42.1 (Leipzig 1931).

Kourouniotis, K. "Ανασκαφαὶ Λυκαίου," *AEph* 21 (1905) 153–21.

Kuettler, O. *Precationes quomodo oratores veteres usurpaverunt in orationibus* (diss. University of Jena 1909).

Kullmann, W. "Gods and Men in the *Iliad* and the *Odyssey*," *HSCP* 89 (1985) 1–23, reprinted in *Homerische Motive: Beiträge zur Eigenart, und Wirkung von Ilias und Odyssee* (Stuttgart 1992) 243–63.

Lacey, W. K. *The Family in Classical Greece* (London 1968).

Lakoff, G., and M. Johnson. *Philosophy in the Flesh* (New York 1999).

Lambrinoudakis, B. "Un réfugié argien à Épidaure au Ve siècle avant J.-C.," *CRAI* (1990) 174–85.

Lane Fox, R. *Pagans and Christians* (New York 1986).

Lang, A. *Myth, Ritual, and Religion* (London 1887).

Lateiner, D. *Sardonic Smile: Nonverbal Behavior in Homeric Epic* (Ann Arbor, Mich. 1995).

Latte, K. *Heiliges Recht* (Tübingen 1920).

———. "Ein sakrales Gesetz aus Kyrene," *Archiv für Religionswissenschaft* 26 (1928) 41–51, reprinted in *Kleine Schriften zu Religion, Recht, Literatur und Sprache der Griechen und Römer* (Munich 1968) 112–22.

Lattimore, R. *The Iliad* (Chicago 1951).

Lattimore, S. *The Peloponnesian War* (Indianapolis 1998).

Lavency, M. *Aspects de la logographie judiciaire attique* (Louvain 1964).

Leaf, W. *The Iliad* (London 1900–2²).

Leake, R. *Travels in the Morea* (London 1830).

Lefèvre, F. *L'amphictionie pyléo-delphique: Histoire et institutions* (Paris 1998).

Letoublon, F. "Le vocabulaire de la supplication en grec. Performatif et dérivation délocu-tive," *Lingua* 52 (1980) 325–36.

Levi, D. "Gleanings from Crete," *AJA* 49 (1945) 270–329.

Levine, B. *Numbers 21–36. The Anchor Bible* (New York 2000).

Lewis, D. M. "Ithome Again," *Historia* 2 (1953–4) 412–18.

Lézine, A. *Carthage, Utique, études d'architecture et d'urbanisme* (Paris 1968).

Lincoln, B. *Death, War, and Sacrifice: Studies in Ideology and Practice* (Chicago 1991).

Lipsius, J. H. *Das attische Recht und Rechtsverfahren* (Leipzig 1905–15).

Lloyd-Jones, H. "The Cologne Fragment of Alcaeus," *GRBS* 9 (1968) 125–39, reprinted in *Greek Epic, Lyric, and Tragedy: Academic Papers of Sir Hugh Lloyd-Jones* (Oxford 1990) 38–54.

———. *The Justice of Zeus* (Berkeley, Calif. 1971).

———. *Sophocles. Loeb Classical Library* 20–21 (Cambridge, Mass. 1994–96).

———. "Ritual and Tragedy," in *Ansichten griechischer Rituale*, ed. F. Graf (Stuttgart 1998) 271–96.

Löhr, M. *Das Asylwesen im Alten Testament. Schriften der Königsberger gelehrten Gesel-lschaft, geisteswissenschaftliche Klasse* 7.3 (Halle 1930) 177–217.

Loomis, W. *Wages, Welfare Costs, and Inflation in Classical Athens* (Ann Arbor, Mich. 1998).

Lotze, D. *Metaxy eleytheron kai doylon: Studien zur Rechtsstellung unfreier Landbevöl-kerungen in Griechenland bis zum 4. Jahrhundert v. Chr.* (Berlin 1959).

Lynn George, M. *Epos: Word, Narrative, and the* Iliad (London 1988).

MacCormack, G. "A note on *arra* in Plautus," *The Irish Jurist* 6 (1971) 360–66.

MacDowell, D. M. *Andokides. On the Mysteries* (Oxford 1962).

———. *The Law in Classical Athens* (Ithaca, N.Y. 1978).

———. *Spartan Law* (Edinburgh 1986).

———. "Law and Procedure, Athenian," in *OCD* (1996) 825–27.

MacLeod, C. W. "Thucydides' Plataian Debate," *GRBS* 18 (1977) 227–47, reprinted in *Collected Essays* (Oxford 1983) 103–23.

———. *Homer. Iliad XXIV* (Cambridge 1982).

Magie, D. *Roman Rule in Asia Minor to the End of the Third Century after Christ* (Princeton, N.J. 1950).

Maine, H. S. *Dissertations on Early Law and Custom* (London 1883).

Mannzmann, A. "*Asylia*," in *Der kleine Pauly. Lexikon der Antike*, ed. K. Ziegler and W. Sontheimer (Stuttgart 1974) 1.670.

Mariqc, A. "Res Gestae Diui Saporis," *Syria* 35 (1958) 295–360.

Marshall, B. *A Historical Commentary on Asconius* (Columbia, Mo. 1985).

Marx, F. *Rudens* (Amsterdam 1959).

Mastronarde, D. "The Optimistic Rationalist in Euripides: Theseus, Jocasta, Tireisias," in *Greek Tragedy and Its Legacy: Essays Presented to D. J. Conacher*, ed. M. Cropp, E. Fantham, and S. Sunley (Calgary 1979) 201–11.

Mathieu, G. and É. Brémond. *Isocrate. Collection des universités de France* (Paris 1956–62²).

McNiven, T. *Gestures in Attic Vase Painting: Use and Meaning, 550–450 B.C.* (diss. University of Michigan 1982).

Mercier, C. Rev. of Crotty, *Poetics* in *CP* 93 (1998) 192–96.

Meuli, K. "Griechische Opferbräuche," in *Phyllobolia, für P. von der Mühll zum 60. Geburtstag am 1. August 1945* (Basel 1946) 185–288, reprinted in *Gesammelte Schriften* (Basel 1975) 2.907–1021.

Meyer-Laurin, H. *Gesetz und Billigkeit im attischen Prozess* (Weimar 1965).

Mikalson, J. *Honor Thy Gods: Popular Religion in Greek Tragedy* (Chapel Hill, N.C. 1991).

Millar, F. *The Emperor in the Roman World* (Ithaca, N.Y. 1977).

————. "L'empereur romain comme décideur," in *Du pouvoir dans l'antiquité: mots et réalités*, ed. C. Nicolet (Geneva 1990) 207–20.

Moore, J., et al. *Moore's Manual: Federal Practice and Procedure* (New York 1997).

Moore, K. *Pardons: Justice, Mercy, and the Public Interest* (Oxford 1989).

Morgan, C. *Athletes and Oracles: The Transformation of Olympia and Delphi in the Eighth Century BC* (Cambridge 1990).

Morris, I. "Poetics of Power: The Interpretation of Ritual Actions in Archaic Greece," in *Cultural Poetics in Archaic Greece: Cult, Performance, Politics*, ed. C. Dougherty and L. Kurke (Cambridge 1993) 15–46.

Mosley, D. *Envoys and Diplomacy in Ancient Greece* (Wiesbaden 1973).

Mouritsen, H. *Plebs and Politics in the Late Republican Rome* (Cambridge 2001).

Much, R. *Die Germania des Tacitus* (Heidelberg 1967³).

Naiden, F. S. "Supplication on Roman Coins," *AJN* 15 (2003) 41–52.

————. "Supplication and the Law," in *The Law and the Courts in Ancient Greece*, ed. E. Harris and L. Rubenstein (London 2004) 71–91.

————. "*Hiketai* and *Theoroi* at Epidaurus," in *Pilgrimage in Greco-Roman and Early Christian Antiquity*, ed. J. Elsner and I. C. Rutherford (Oxford 2005) 73–97.

Nehrbass, R. *Sprache und Stil der Iamata von Epidauros: Eine sprachwissenschaftliche Untersuchung. Philologus Supp.* 27.4 (Leipzig 1935).

Neumann, G. *Gesten und Gebärden in der griechischen Kunst* (Berlin 1965).

Newton, R. "The Rebirth of Odysseus," *GRBS* 25 (1984) 5–20.

Niese, B. *Geschichte der griechischen und makedonischen Staaten* (Gotha 1903).

Nilsson, M. P. *Geschichte der griechischen Religion* (Munich 1967–74³).

Nörr, D. *Aspekte des römischen Völkerrechts: Die Bronzetafel von Alcántara. ABAW, philosophisch-historische Klasse* (new ser.) 101 (Munich 1989).

Noveck, M. *The Mark of Ancient Man: Ancient Near Eastern Stamp Seals and Cylinder Seals. Brooklyn Museum Catalogue for the Gorelick Collection* (New York 1975).

Oakley, S. P. *A Commentary on Livy, Books 6–10* (Oxford 1997).

Onians, R. B. *The Origins of European Thought about the Body, the Soul, the World, Time, and Fate; New Interpretations of Greek, Roman, and Kindred Evidence, Also of Some Basic Jewish and Christian Beliefs.* (Cambridge 1954).

Orlandos, A. K. "Ἐπίδαυρος. Ἱερὸ Ἀπόλλονος Μαλεάτα," *Ergon tes Archaiologikes Hetaireias* (1977) 98–105.

Osiander, J. A. *De asylis hebraeorum, gentilium, christianorum* (Tübingen 1673).

Ostwald, M. *Nomos and the Beginnings of Athenian Democracy* (Oxford 1969).

————. *Autonomia, its Genesis and History* (Chico, Calif. 1982).

————. *From Popular Sovereignty to the Sovereignty of Law: Law, Society, and Politcs in Fifth-Century Athens* (Berkeley, Calif. 1986).

Owen, A. S. *Ion* (Oxford 1939, reprinted Bristol 1986).

Page, D. L. *History and the Homeric* Iliad (Berkeley, Calif. 1959).

————. *Aeschyli septem quae supersunt tragoediae* (Oxford 1972).

Papachatzes, N. D. *Pausaniou Hellados Periegesis* (Athens 1974–81).

Parke, H. W., and D. E. W. Wormell. *The Delphic Oracle* (Oxford 1956).

Parker, R. *Miasma: Pollution and Purification in Early Greek Religion* (Oxford 1983).

————. "Spartan Religion," in *Classical Sparta*, ed. A. Powell (London 1989) 142–72.

————. *Athenian Religion: A History* (Oxford 1996).

————. "What Are Sacred Laws?" in *The Law and the Courts in Ancient Greece*, ed. E. Harris and L. Rubenstein (London 2004) 57–91.

Parker, V. "The Dates of the Messenian Wars," *Chiron* 21 (1991) 25–47.

Patterson, O. *Slavery and Social Death: A Comparative Study* (Cambridge, Mass. 1982).

Payot, D. *Des villes-refuges: Témoinage et espacement* (Paris 1992).

Pedrick, V. "Supplication in the *Iliad* and the *Odyssey*," *TAPA* 112 (1982) 125–40.

Peek, W. *Ein neuer spartanischer Staatsvertrag. Abhandlungen der Sächsischen Akademie der Wissenschaften zu Leipzig, philologisch-historische Klasse* 65.3 (Berlin 1974).

Perret, J. "Optimisme et tragédie dans l'*Énéide*," *REL* 45 (1967) 342–62.

Pley, J. *De lanae in antiquorum ritibus usu* (Giessen 1911).

Pospisil, L. *Anthropology of Law: A Comparative Theory* (New York 1971).

Pötscher, W. "Die Hikesie des letzten Ilias-Gesanges," *Würzburger Jahrbücher für die Altertumswissenschaft* (new ser.) 18 (1992) 5–16.

———. "Die Strukturen der Hikesie," *WS* 107 (1994) 51–75.

Poyatos, F. *Paralanguage: A Linguistic and Interdisciplinary Approach to Interactive Speech and Sound* (Amsterdam 1993).

Pringsheim, F. *The Greek Law of Sale* (Weimar 1950).

Propp, V. *Las raíces históricas del cuento,* tr. J. M. Arancibia (Caracas 1979²).

Pulleyn, S. *Prayer in Greek Religion* (Oxford 1997).

Raaflaub, K. *Die Entdeckung der Freiheit* (Munich 1985).

Raubitschek, A. "Das Datislied," in *Charites: Studien zur Altertumswissenschaft,* ed. K. Schauenburg (Bonn 1957) 234–48, reprinted in *The School of Hellas: Essays on Greek History, Archaeology, and Literature* (Oxford 1991) 146–55.

Reece, D. "The Date of the Fall of Ithome," *JHS* 82 (1962) 11–20.

Reece, S. *The Stranger's Welcome* (Ann Arbor, Mich. 1993).

Rehm, R. *Marriage to Death: The Conflation of Wedding and Funeral Rituals in Greek Tragedy* (Princeton, N.J. 1994).

Reinhardt, K. *Von Werken und Formen. Vorträge und Aufsätze* (Godesberg 1948).

Remotti, F. "L'essenzialità dello straniero," in *Lo Straniero ovvero l'identità culturale a confronto,* ed. M. Bettini (Siena 1992) 19–35.

Remus, H. 1996, "Voluntary Association and Networks: Aelius Aristides at the Asclepieion in Pergamon," in *Voluntary Associations in the Greco-Roman World,* ed. J. S. Kloppenborg and S. G. Wilson (London 1996) 146–75.

Rhodes, P. J. *The Athenian Boule* (Oxford 1972).

———. "A Graeco-Roman Perspective," in *Human Rights: Problems, Perspectives, and Texts,* ed. F. E. Dowrick (Westmead, Eng. 1979) 62–78.

———. "Keeping to the Point," in *The Law and the Courts in Ancient Greece,* ed. E. Harris and L. Rubenstein (London 2004) 137–59.

Rhodes, P. J., and D. M. Lewis. *The Decrees of the Greek States* (Oxford 1997).

Richardson, N. J. *The* Iliad: *A Commentary, Volume 6* (Cambridge 1993).

Rigsby, K. J. *Asylia: Territorial Inviolability in the Hellenistic World* (Berkeley, Calif. 1996).

Robert, L. "Eulaios, histoire et onomastique," *Epistemonike epeteris tes Philosophikes Scholes tou Panepistemiou Athenon* (Athens 1962–63) 519–29, reprinted in *Opera minora selecta: épigraphie et antiquités grecques* (Amsterdam 1969–90) 2.977–89.

Robertson, G. *Crimes against Humanity: The Struggle for Global Justice* (London 1999).

Robertson Smith, W. *Lectures on the Religion of the Semites* (London 1927²).

Rofé, A. "*Joshua* 20: Historico-Literary Criticism Illuminated," in *Empirical Models for Biblical Criticism,* ed. J. H. Tigay (Philiadelphia 1985) 131–49.

Rogers, R. S. *Criminal Trials and Criminal Legislation under Tiberius* (Middletown, Conn. 1935).

Rose, P. W. "Sophocles' Philoctetes and the Teachings of the Sophists," *HSCP* 80 (1976) 49–107.

Roth, C. C. *Suetoni Tranquilli quae supersunt omnia* (Leipzig 1902).

Rudhardt, J. "La définition du délit d'impiété d'après la législation attique," *MH* 17 (1960) 87–105.

Ruschenbusch, E. *Untersuchungen zur Geschichte des athenischen Strafrechts* (Cologne 1968).

Rütte, K. "ἄποινα," *Lexikon des frühgriechischen Epos*, ed. B. Snell (Göttingen 1955–)
    1092–94.

Said, S. "Les crimes des prétendants, la maison d'Ulysse, et les festins de l'Odyssée," *Études
    de littérature ancienne* 1 (1979) 7–50.

Sanchez, P. *L'amphictionie des Pyles et de Delphes: recherches sur son rôle historique, des
    origines au IIe siècle de notre ère. Historia Einzelschriften* 148 (Stuttgart 2001).

Scafuro, A. *The Forensic Stage: Settling Disputes in Graeco-Roman New Comedy* (Cam-
    bridge 1997).

Schlesinger, E. *Die griechische Asylie* (diss. University of Giessen 1933).

Schlunk, R. "The Theme of the Suppliant-Exile in the *Iliad*," *AJP* 97 (1976) 199–209.

Schlüsner, J. *Nouus thesaurus philologico-criticus* (London 1829²).

Schmid, R. "Miqlat," *ThWAT* 4 (1984) 1132–37.

Schmidt, F. *De supplicum ad aram confugientium partibus scaenicis* (diss. University of
    Königsberg 1911).

Schmitt, C. *Begriff des Politischen. Text von 1932 mit einem Vorwort und drei Corollarie*
    (Berlin 1963).

Schneider, R. M. *Bunte Barbaren: Orientalenstatuen aus farbigem Marmor in der römischen
    Repräsentationskunst* (Worms 1986).

Schömann, G. *Griechische Alterthümer* (Berlin 1855–59).

Schumacher, R. "Three Related Sanctuaries of Poseidon; Geraistos, Kalaureia, and Tainaron,"
    in *Greek Sanctuaries: New Approaches*, ed. N. Marinatos and R. Hägg (New York
    1993) 62–88.

Scodel, R. Rev. of Giordano, *Supplica* in *CR* 50 (2000) 395–97.

Scullard, H. *From the Gracchi to Nero: A History of Rome from 133 B.C. to A.D. 68* (Lon-
    don 1982⁵).

Scullion, S. "Olympian and Chthonian," *CA* 13 (1994) 75–119.

Seaford, R "The Tragic Wedding," *JHS* 107 (1985) 106–30.

———. *Ritual and Reciprocity: Homer and Tragedy in the Developing City-State* (Oxford
    1994).

Sealey, R. *The Justice of the Greeks* (Ann Arbor, Mich. 1974).

———. *Demosthenes and His Time: A Study in Defeat* (Oxford 1993).

Segal, C. P. *Interpreting Greek Tragedy: Myth, Poetry, Text* (Ithaca, N.Y. 1986).

———. *Singers, Heroes, and Gods in the* Odyssey (Ithaca, N.Y. 1994).

Segre, M. "Sull'asilia dell'Asclepieio di Pergamo," *MC* 3 (1933) 485–88.

Servais, J. "Les suppliants dans la 'Loi Sacrée' de Cyrène," *BCH* 84 (1960) 112–47.

———. "Στέμματ' ἔχων ἐν χερσίν," *AC* 36 (1967) 415–56.

Settis, S., et al. *La Colonna Traiana* (Turin 1988).

Sheets, G. "Conceptualizing International Law in Thucydides," *AJP* 115 (1994) 51–73.

Sherwin-White, A. N. *The Letters of Pliny: A Historical and Social Commentary* (Oxford
    1966).

Shipley, G. "The Other Lakedaimonians: The Dependent Perioikic Poleis of Laconia and
    Messenia," in *The Polis as an Urban Centre and as a Political Community. Acts of the
    Copenhagen Polis Centre* 4, ed. M. Hansen (Copenhagen 1997) 189–282.

Sidwell, K. "Purification and Pollution in Aeschylus' *Eumenides*," *CQ* 46 (1996) 44–57.

Siebert, G. "Une image dans l'image: le pilier hermaïque dans la peinture de vases grecques,"
    in *L'image et la production du sacré. Actes du colloque de Strasbourg 20–21 janvier
    1988*, ed. F. Dunand, J.-M. Spieser, and J. Wirth (Paris 1991) 103–21.

Sinn, U. "Das Heraion von Perachora. Eine sakrale Schutzzone in der korinthischen
    Peraia," *MDAI(A)* 105 (1990) 53–116.

———. "Greek Sanctuaries as Places of Refuge," in *Greek Sanctuaries: New Approaches*,
    ed. N. Marinatos and R. Hägg (London 1993) 88–109.

Sittl, C. *Die Gebärden der Griechen und Römer* (Leipzig 1890).

Slater, N. "The Vase as Ventriloquist: *Kalos* Inscriptions and the Culture of Fame," in *Signs of Orality: The Oral Tradition and Its Influence in the Greek and Roman World. Mnemosyne Supp.* 188, ed. E. Mackay (Leiden 1999) 143–63.

Smith, J. Z. *To Take Place: Towards Theory in Ritual* (Chicago 1987).

Sokolowski, F. "The Meaning of Sacral Manumission," *HThR* 47 (1954) 173–81.

Sommerstein, A. "Notes on the *Oresteia*," *BICS* 27 (1980) 63–75.

Spaeth, B. *The Roman Goddess Ceres* (Austin, Tex. 1996).

Stengl, W. "*Asylon*," *RE* (1st ser.) 2.2.1881–86.

Stevens, E. "Some Attic Commonplaces of Pity," *AJP* 65 (1944) 1–25.

Stevens, P. T. *Andromache* (Oxford 1971).

Sullivan, F. A. "Tendere manus: Gestures in the *Aeneid*," *CJ* 63 (1967) 358–62.

Syme, R. "Who Was Vedius Pollio?" *JRS* 51 (1961) 23–30, reprinted in *Roman Papers* (Oxford 1979) 2.518–29.

———. *The Augustan Aristocracy* (Oxford 1986).

Talbert, R. *The Senate of Imperial Rome* (Princeton, N.J. 1984).

Taplin, O. *Greek Tragedy in Action* (Berkeley, Calif. 1978).

Taubenschlag, R. *The Law of Greco-Roman Egypt in the Light of the Papyri, 332 B.C.–A.D. 640* (New York 1944–48)

Themelis, P. "Ἀνασκαφὴ Μεσσήνης," Parts 1–3, *PAAH* 148 (1993) 57–59; 149 (1994) 86–88; 150 (1995) 60–63.

Thomas, R. *Oral Tradition and Written Record in Classical Athens* (Cambridge 1989).

Thomas, R. F. *Virgil and the Augustan Reception* (Cambridge 2001).

Thornton, A. *Homer's* Iliad: *Its Composition and the Motif of Supplication. Hypomnemata* 81 (Göttingen 1984).

Thumb, A., E. Kieckers, and A. Scherer. *Handbuch der griechischen Dialekte* (Heidelberg 1932–59²).

Thür, G. and H. Taeuber. "Prozessrechtlicher Kommentar zur 'Krämerinschrift' aus Samos," *AAWW* 115 (1978) 205–25.

Timpe, D. "Herrschaftsidee und Klientelstaatenpolitik in Sallusts *Bellum Jugurthinum*," *Hermes* 90 (1962) 334–75.

———. "Rechtsformen der römischen Aussenpolitik bei Caesar," *Chiron* 2 (1972) 277–95.

Tiverios, M. "Ἀρχαιολογικὴ ερευνὰ στὴ διπλὴ τράπεζα, κοντὰ στὴ σημερινὴ Ἀγχίαλο καὶ Σίνδο. 1990–92: Ο αρχαίος οικισμός," *Egnatia* 3 (1991–2) 209–34.

Todd, S. *The Shape of Athenian Law* (Oxford 1993).

Touchais, G. "Chronique des fouilles et découvertes archéologiques en Grèce en 1988," *BCH* 113 (1989) 581–694.

Townsend, P. W. "The Revolution of A.D. 238: The Leaders and Their Aims," *YCS* 14 (1955) 49–105.

Traina, A. "Il libro xii dell' Eneide," *Poeti latini (e neolatini): Note e saggi filologici* 4 (Bologna 1994) 59–89.

Traulsen, C. *Das sakrale Asyl in der antiken Welt. Jus ecclesiasticum* 72 (Tübingen 2004).

Turner, C. "Perverted Supplication and Other Inversions in Aeschylus' Danaid Trilogy," *CJ* 97 (2001) 27–51.

Usener, H. *Götternamen: Versuch einer Lehre von der religiösen Begriffsbildung* (Bonn 1896).

Valmin, M. *Études topographiques sur la Messénie ancienne* (Lund 1930).

van Gennep, A. *Les rites de passage. Étude systématique des rites de la porte et du seuil, de l'hospitalité, de l'adoption, de la grossesse et de l'accouchement, de la naissance, de l'enfance, de la puberté, de l'initiation, de l'ordination, du couronnement, des fiançailles et du mariage, des funérailles, des saisons, etc.* (Paris 1909).

van Wees, H. *Status Warriors: War, Violence, and Society in Homer and History* (Amsterdam 1992).

Vernant, J.-P. *Mythe et pensée chez les Grecs: Études de psychologie historique* (Paris 1965).

Versnel, H. "The Appeal to Justice in Supplicatory Prayers," in *Magika Hiera: Ancient Greek Magic and Religion*, ed. C. Faraone and D. Obbink (Oxford 1991) 60–107.

Veyne, P. *Did the Greeks Believe in Their Myths?*, tr. P. Wissing (Chicago 1988).

Volonaki, E. *A Commentary on Lysias's Speeches 13 and 30* (diss. Univesity of London 1998).

von Wilamowitz-Moellendorff, U. *Aristoteles und Athen* (Berlin 1893).

———. *Euripides Herakles* (Berlin 1895²).

———. *Euripides Ion* (Berlin 1926).

———. "Heilige Gesetze, eine Urkunde aus Kyrene," *SPAW* (1927) 155–201.

von Woess, F. *Das Asylwesen Ägyptens in der Ptolemäerzeit und die spätere Entwicklung. Münchener Beiträge zur Papyrusforschung und antiken Rechtsgeschichte* 5 (Munich 1923).

Vorberg, G. *Ars erotica veterum: Das Geschlechtsleben im Altertum* (Hanau 1968).

Voutiras, E. *Dionysophôntos Gamoi: Marital Life and Magic in Fourth-Century Pella* (Amsterdam 1998).

Wächter, T. *Reinheitsvorschriften im griechischen Kult* (Giessen 1910).

Walbank, F. *A Historical Commentary on Polybius* (Oxford 1957–79).

Wallace, R. *The Areopagus Council to 307 B.C.* (Oxford 1989).

Waterhouse, H., and R. H. Simpson. "Prehistoric Laconia: Part II," *ABSA* 56 (1961) 114–75.

Watson, A. *The Law of Obligations in the Later Roman Republic* (Oxford 1965).

———. *Lawmaking in the Later Roman Republic* (Oxford 1974).

Weinreich, O. *Antike Heilungswunder: Untersuchungen zum Wunderglauben der Griechen und Römer.Religionsgeschichtliche Versuche und Vorarbeiten* 8.1 (Giessen 1909).

Weinstock, S. *Divus Julius* (Oxford 1971).

Welcker, F. G. *Griechische Götterlehre* (Göttingen 1857–63).

Welles, C. B. *Royal Correspondence in the Hellenistic Period: A Study in Greek Epigraphy* (New Haven, Conn. 1934).

Welter, G. "Aeginetica," *AA* (1954) 28–48.

Wenger, L. "Asylrecht," *Reallexikon für Antike und Christentum*, ed. T. Klauser (Stuttgart, 1950) 1.836–43.

West, M. L. *Hesiod. Works and Days* (Oxford 1978).

———. *The East Face of Helicon: West Asiatic Elements in Greek Poetry and Myth* (Oxford 1997).

Westermann, W. "The *Paramone* as a General Service Contract," *JJP* 2 (1948) 9–44.

———. *The Slave Systems of Greek and Roman Antiquity* (New York 1955).

Whitehead, D. *The Ideology of the Athenian Metic: Cambridge Philological Society Supp.* 4 (Cambridge 1977).

Whitfield, G. *The Restored Relation: The Suppliant Theme in the* Iliad (diss. Columbia University 1967).

Wickert, K. *Der peloponnesische Bund von seiner Entstehung bis zum Ende des archidamischen Krieges* (diss. University of Nuremburg 1961).

Wickert-Micknat, G. *Studien zur Kriegsgefangenschaft und zur Sklaverei in der griechischen Geschichte. Abhandlungen der Akademie der Wissenschaften und der Literatur, Geistes- und Sozialwissenschaftliche Klasse* 11 (Mainz 1955).

Widengren, G. *Die Religionen Irans* (Stuttgart 1965).

Wilcken, U. "Zu den Kaiserreskripten," *Hermes* 55 (1920) 1–41.

Wilhelm, A. *Beiträge zur griechischen Inschriftenkunde mit einem Anhange über die öffentliche Aufzeichung von Urkunden* (Vienna 1909).

Williams, B. *Shame and Necessity* (Berkeley 1993).

Wilson, D. *Ransom, Revenge, and Heroic Identity in the* Iliad (Cambridge 2002).

Wilson, J. *The Hero and the City: An Interpretation of Sophocles' Oedipus at Colonus* (Ann Arbor, Mich. 1997).

Wilson, N. G. *Aelian: Historical Miscellany. Loeb Classical Library* 486 (Cambridge, Mass. 1997).

Wilutzky, P. *Vorgeschichte des Rechts: prähistorisches Recht* (Breslau 1903).

Winnington-Ingram, R. P. *Studies in Aeschylus* (Cambridge 1983).

Wissowa, G. *Religion und Kultus der Römer. Handbuch der Altertumswissenschaft* 4.5. (Munich 1912², reprinted 1971).

Wolff, H. J. "The Origin of Judicial Litigation among the Greeks," *Traditio* 4 (1946) 31–87.

———. *Das Recht der griechischen Papyri Ägyptens in der Zeit der Ptolemaeer und Prinzipats. Handbuch der Altertumswissenschaft* 10.5 (Munich 2002).

Woodman, L., and R. Martin. *The Annals of Tacitus, Book* 3 (Cambridge 1996).

Woodward, A. M. "Laconia. Topography. Taenarus," *ABSA* 13 (1907) 238–67.

Wycherley, R. "The Altar of *Eleos*," *CQ* (new ser.) 4 (1954) 143–50.

Zanker, G. "Beyond Reciprocity: The Akhilleus-Priam Scene in *Iliad* 24," in *Reciprocity in Ancient Greece*, ed. C. Gill, N. Postlethwaite, and R. Seaford (Oxford 1998) 73–93.

Zeitlin, F. *The Ritual World of Greek Tragedy* (diss. Columbia University 1970).

Zelnick-Abramovitz, R. "Supplication and Request: Application by Foreigners to the Athenian Polis," *Mnemosyne* 51 (2001) 554–73.

Ziegler, K.-H. "Das Völkerrecht der römischen Republik," *ANRW* 1.2 (1972) 68–114.

Zuntz, G. *Political Plays of Euripides* (Manchester 1955).

———. *Persephone: Three Essays on Religion and Thought in Magna Graecia* (Oxford 1971).

Index of Sources

For acts of supplication, see appendix 1.

INDEX OF SUPPLIANTS

Unnamed individuals are excluded, but groups are included.

Greek and Macedonian Suppliants

All suppliants in Homer, the Homeric hymns, the epic cycle, and tragedy, among them suppliants who also appear in Latin and later Greek sources, are included, as are some Greek-speaking suppliants of partly foreign descent. Excluded from this list are all supplicating defendants and prosecutors and all individuals named in IG iv² 121–22, 125–26, and IC 1.xvii 9, 17–18, for which see Edelstein, *Asclepius*.

ROMAN SUPPLIANTS

Italians under the Principate, persons in Plautus and Terence, persons in Seneca the Younger other than in his tragedies, and putative ancestors in Virgil and Silius Italicus are included. Excluded are all supplicating defendants and advocates. For Petronius, Statius, and Valerius Flaccus, see "Greek and Macedonian Suppliants."

OTHER SUPPLIANTS

Index of Supplicandi

For the classification of supplicandi, see the Index of Suppliants. Altars are identified by the controlling party, and where possible gods are identified by city. The ethnic or local name, such as "Athenians," designates the assembly of the area. The name of a polis, such as "Athens," appears where the Assembly was not the supplicandus or the source does not indicate who was.

GREEK AND MACEDONIAN SUPPLICANDI

Abae, Athena of, 328
Achaeans, 131, 334
Achaeus, 114, 334
Achilles, 34, 46–47, 58, 62,
   98, 99, 107, 108, 120,
   130, 131, 136, 163,
   164, 272, 274, 315,
   321, 324, 329, 350,
   364
Acragas, 312
Admetus. King of Molossia,
   312, 325, 331, 336
Aegeus, 315
Aeolus, 132, 135, 163, 322,
   364
Aetolians, 334
Agamemnon, 34, 53, 55, 86,
   95, 131, 141, 146,
   163, 272, 302, 315,
   321, 350
Agathon, 163, 307
Ajax, son of Oileus, 49, 152
Ajaz, son of Telamon, 86
   n. 343, 163, 321, 335
Alcestis, 315
Alcinous, 111 n. 39, 322
Alexander the Great, 30, 32, 37
   n. 45, 55, 121 n. 105,
   134, 142 n. 224, 239,
   249, 274, 286, 312,
   314, 325, 327, 330,
   333, 344, 346
Alexandria, Demeter of, 168,
   334

Alexandria, mob in, 334
Amorgos, Demeter of, 365
   (IG xii 7, p. 1, a
   defixio)
Amphares, 330
Amphion, 357
Amphitryon, 157, 355
Anaxarete, 352
Anchises, 63, 320
Andania, Demeter of, 36, 365
   (IG v.1 1390, a
   decree)
Andania, priest of Demeter
   of, 149–50, 374
Andocides, 308
Andocides, father of, 308
Antiochus I of Commagene,
   310
Antiochus IV of Commagene,
   368
Aphrodite (also Venus in V.
   Fl.), 63, 111 n. 41,
   320, 361
Apollo, 37 n. 41, 315
Apollo Maleatas, 380
Apollo, Thymbraean, 325
Aratus, 330
Arcadians, 57, 163, 308
Areopagus, 191–92, 308,
   327
Arete, 131, 303, 322
Argives, 40, 124, 302, 327
Argonauts, 303, 361
Argos, gods of, 302

Argos, king of, 108, 124
Argus, 125, 327
Aristides, 365 (M-L #21, a
   supplicatory object),
   381
Ariston, 107, 331
Artemis, 36 n. 41, 111 n. 41,
   301, 324
Ascyltus, 247 n. 165, 353
Astylus, 323
Astypalaea, Athena of, 327
Athena, 7, 36 n. 41, 63
   n. 192, 92, 98 n. 408,
   108, 322
Athena Alea, 36 n. 40, 38,
   205–7
Athena Itonia, 327, 330, 332
Athena Polias, 36, 38, 205–7,
   302, 319, 327, 331,
   336, 350, 366 (IG i³
   45, a notice)
Athenians, 57 n. 156, 81,
   114, 118, 138, 159,
   162, 163, 176–83,
   217, 312, 319, 336,
   346, 365 (IG ii² 192,
   211, 218, 276, 336,
   337, 404, 502, all
   decrees)
Athens, 307
Athens, council of, 36, 149,
   150–51, 163, 174–76,
   180 n. 42, 192 n. 94,
   308, 337

ROMAN SUPPLICANDI

OTHER SUPPLICANDI

Index of Topics